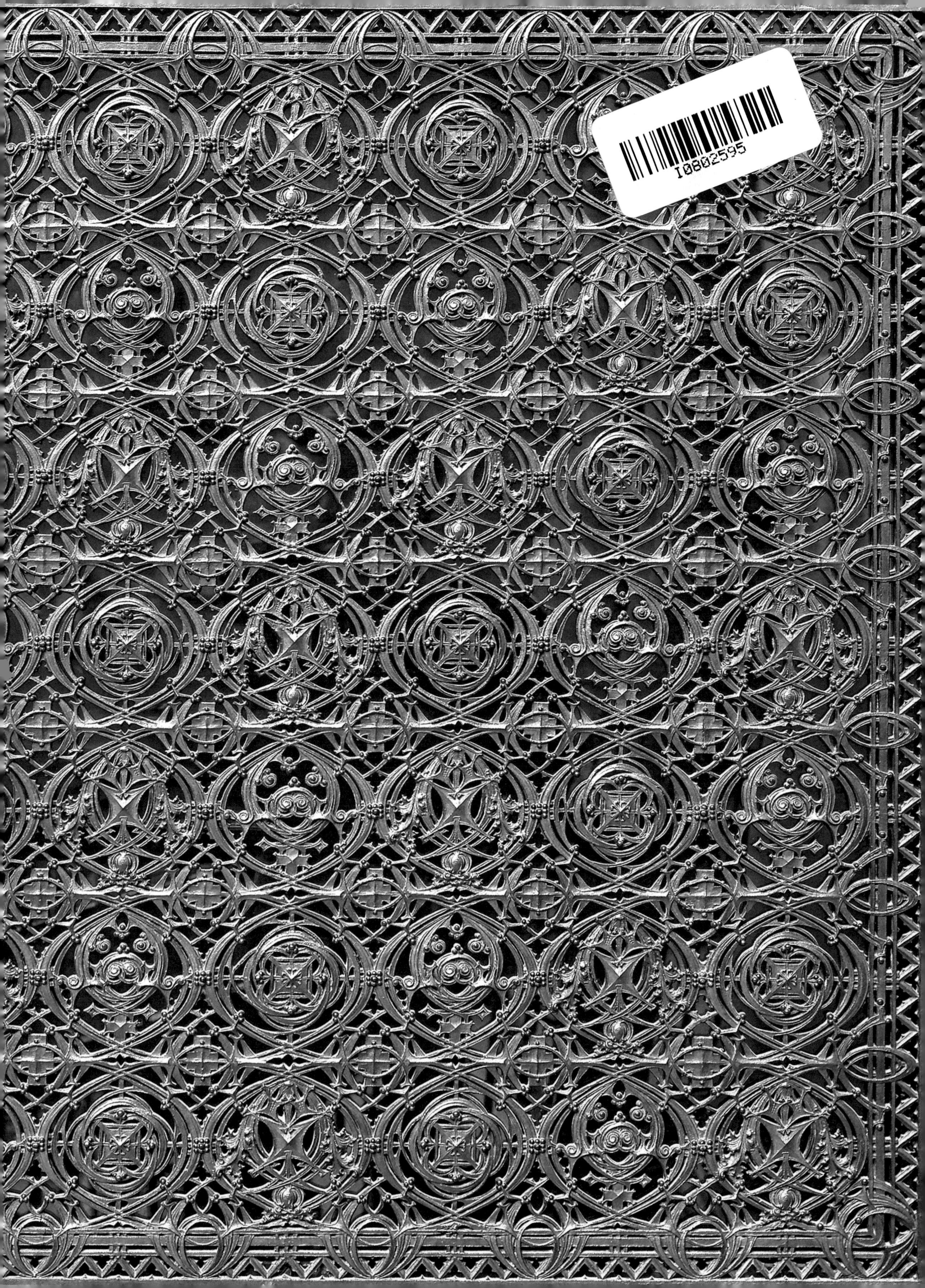

LOUIS SULLIVAN
AN AMERICAN ARCHITECT

PATRICK F. CANNON

photographs by
JAMES CAULFIELD

GLESSNER HOUSE
PRAIRIE AVENUE | CHICAGO

ISBN 978-1-517-91885-9

A Cataloging-in-Publication record for this book
is available from the Library of Congress.

First Edition Revised
Includes bibliographical references.

Published by
Glessner House
1800 South Prairie Avenue
Chicago, Illinois 60616
www.glessnerhouse.org
312 326 1480
info@glessnerhouse.org

Distributed by
the University of Minnesota Press
111 Third Avenue South, Suite 290
Minneapolis, Minnesota 55401
www.upress.umn.edu

Front cover: The Guaranty (Prudential) Building
in Buffalo, New York designed by Louis Sullivan & Dankmar Adler
and completed in 1896.

Rear cover: A cartouche from the south facade
of the first of Louis Sullivan's "jewel box" bank designs,
the National Farmer's Bank of Owatonna, Minnesota, built in 1908.

This book was made possible
by a generous grant from
the Richard H. Driehaus Foundation
www.driehausfoundation.org

CONTENTS

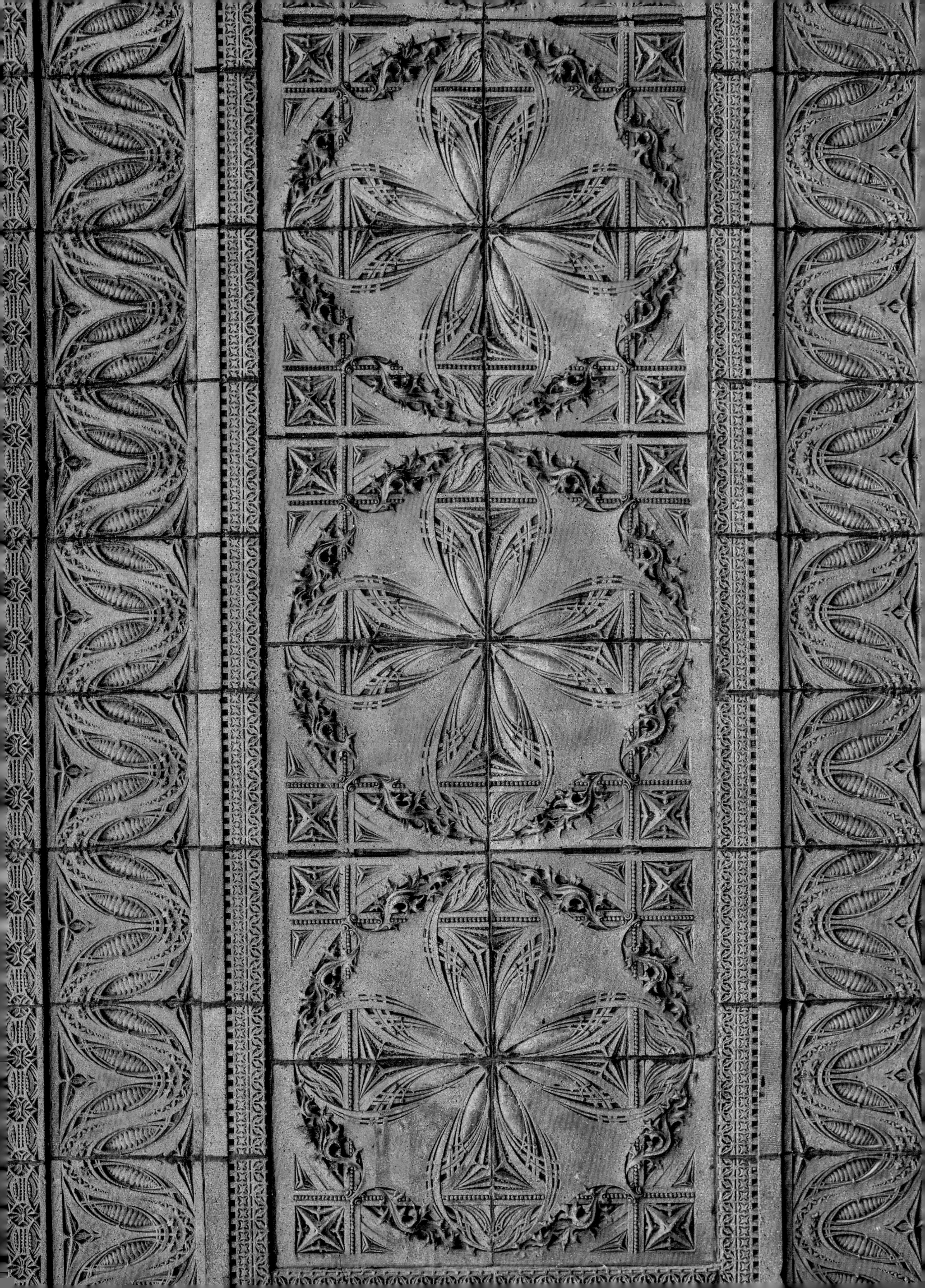

DEDICATED TO THE MEMORY OF RICHARD NICKEL,
WHO LIT THE TORCH; AND TIM SAMUELSON,
WHO KEEPS IT BURNING, AND CONTRIBUTED
SO GENEROUSLY TO THIS BOOK.

AUTHOR'S NOTE

Louis Sullivan's forty surviving structures are treated differently than the far greater number of those that have been lost. Each survivor has at least two pages devoted to it (some have many more). The heading will identify the name of the structure and the date of its construction. It can be assumed that structures built until 1895 are by Adler & Sullivan and, afterward, by Sullivan alone. However, in most cases before 1909, Sullivan's assistant George Grant Elmslie would have made many contributions. All the main images of the forty structures are contemporary, taken for this book by my partner, collaborator, and friend, James Caulfield.

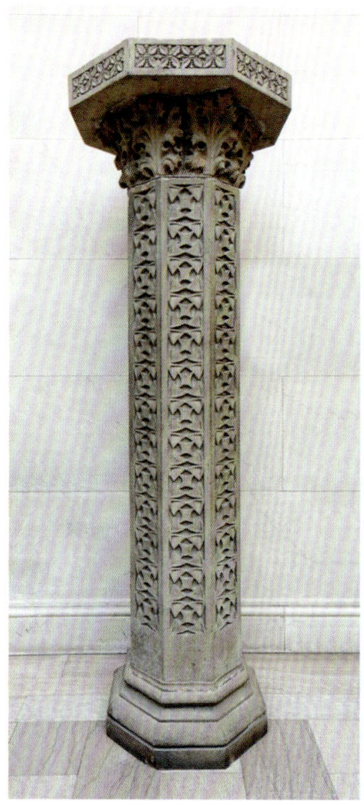

As is usual for historic buildings, in some cases, different sources show different dates. Because several of the dates are associated with contemporary sources, e.g., building permits and publication accounts, I have used the dates from what is really the catalog raisonné of Adler & Sullivan's (and exclusively Sullivan's, after the partnership ended) work, *The Complete Architecture of Adler & Sullivan* (see Bibliography).

Although I have used footnotes and endnotes quite often for research papers, I chose not to use them for this and my other books, which are largely based on secondary sources. The sources are listed in the Bibliography. If I quoted directly from a source, I provided attribution in the text. I tried diligently to get everything right in this book, but if you think I've erred, please feel free to contact me through the publisher.

What is terra cotta?

Because you'll see the term throughout this book, I thought it might be helpful to define what is meant by "terra cotta," also spelled "terracotta" as one word. In Latin, it means "cooked earth." Perhaps its most common use is in the gardener's pot, that orangish-brown vehicle for plants and flowers. Terra cotta is also used extensively for drain tiles and was once used to fireproof building frames. But because it can be molded into almost any shape, terra cotta came to be used for both sculpture and building ornament. After being glazed and fired, terra cotta becomes impervious to moisture and resistant to soot and other contaminants. It can also, within reason, be made in any color.

It's impossible to imagine any Sullivan design without terra cotta. Indeed, as you will see, some of the buildings in this book—the Guaranty and Bayard-Condict, for example—are largely clad in terra cotta. Other buildings depend on terra cotta for most of the decorative elements. Sullivan worked primarily with two companies: Northwestern Terra Cotta Company and American Terra Cotta Company. In many cases and for both companies, sculptor Kristian Schneider was one of the artists responsible for taking two-dimensional drawings from Sullivan (and his assistant Elmslie) and making three-dimensional models in clay.

Both architects would work very closely with the sculptor throughout the process. When all were satisfied, a mold was made. Large pieces might have required several molds, which were jointed together, usually on site. Some of the designs were one of a kind—a large cartouche on one of the banks, for example—but many were repetitive, like the designs that make up the facade of the Guaranty Building in Buffalo. Eventually, terra cotta ornament—or ornament of any kind, actually—went out of style. Fortunately, there are still companies that can replicate terra cotta ornament required for restoration, although most terra cotta in modern architecture are relatively plain panels used for curtainwalls, roofing, and other exterior purposes.

Luxfer Prisms

Luxfer prisms were small glass panels designed to amplify exterior light into a building's interior. The Luxfer Prism Company was founded in 1896 as the Radiating Light Company and, in 1920, was bought out by a competitor, American 3-Way Luxfer Prism Company. Since the 1930s, Luxfer prisms have been replaced by the hollow glass block, which can also have structural properties, unlike the prisms.

The typical prism was approximately 4 × 4 inches. The flat exterior would have a design, usually geometric, while the

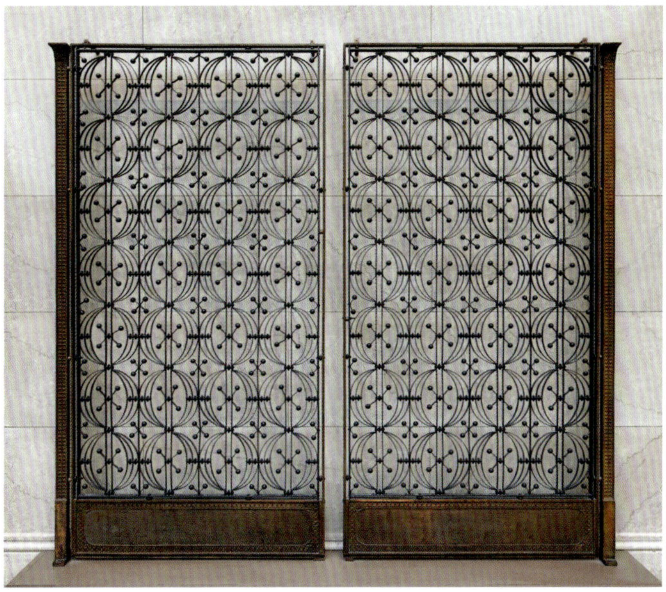

interior had ridges to amplify and direct the light. The prisms were typically set in metal frames above the main display windows in retail stores. In some cases, they were set in canopies above the windows. Interestingly, Frank Lloyd Wright was commissioned to design several prisms as well as an office building that used them. Although the office was never built, the prisms that Wright designed have become collectors' items.

Collaborators

You will find several mentions of **Healy & Millet** in this book, which refer to the partnership of artists George L. Healy and Louis Millet. Sullivan had met them in Paris, where they were also students at the École des Beaux-Arts. After Healy and Millet settled in Chicago and formed a partnership, Sullivan relied on the diverse talents of both artists to help decorate a building like the Auditorium, where they not only executed art glass, mosaics, and stenciling but also helped to select other artists as needed, including muralists Albert Fleury and Oliver D. Glover. Aside from the work that Healy and Millet completed for Sullivan, they worked with many other architects, including Daniel Burnham and Shepley, Rutan and Coolidge, for whom they executed the Tiffany-designed dome that is such a feature of the Grand Army of the Republic rooms at the Chicago Cultural Center. Three of Sullivan's assistants deserve special mention.

Frank Lloyd Wright, who would unquestionably become America's most famous architect, was twenty years old when he joined Adler & Sullivan in 1887, when the firm was gearing up to prepare the drawings for the Auditorium Building. Wright would eventually become the firm's chief draftsman and "the pencil in the master's hand," as he later claimed. It's not far-fetched to say that in the nearly five years spent with the firm, Wright learned his profession from Sullivan. Although Sullivan fired Wright in 1893 for taking work outside the firm, which was a violation of his contract, the two would eventually reconcile.

George Grant Elmslie was born in Scotland in 1871, later immigrating to Chicago in 1884. He began his career as a draftsman for William LeBaron Jenney and then joined Wright and George Maher in the office of Joseph Lyman Silsbee. At Wright's recommendation, Elmslie joined Adler & Sullivan in 1889 and became Sullivan's chief assistant after Wright left. Elmslie remained loyal to Sullivan until 1909, when lack of regular income forced him to leave. He became adept at working out Sullivan's decorative designs and often made significant contributions to the buildings himself.

Parker N. Berry became Sullivan's assistant after Elmslie left. Born in 1888 in Nebraska, Berry grew up in Princeton, Illinois. He studied architecture at the University of Illinois but left before graduating. He joined Sullivan as a draftsman in 1909. In 1912, Berry passed the Illinois architect's registration test with the first perfect score ever attained. Berry left Sullivan in 1917 to start his own practice but died in 1918 at only thirty years old during the global flu pandemic

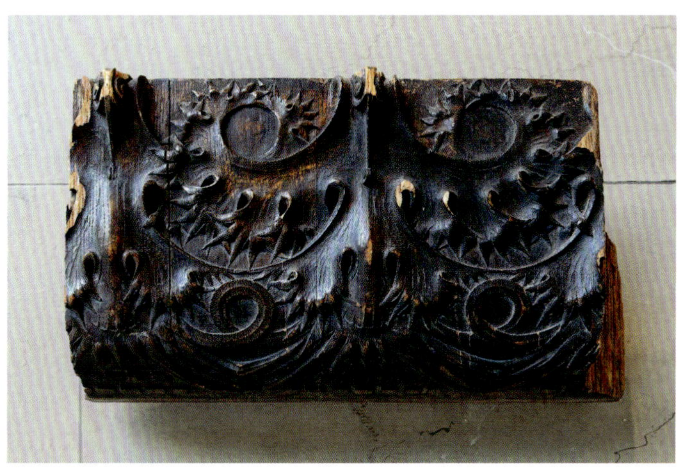

INTRODUCTION

A hundred years after the death of Louis Sullivan, we are tempted to think of his life story as tragic. After all, when he died on April 14, 1924, at age sixty-seven, Sullivan was broke and living in a cheap Chicago hotel. He was without architectural work and had finished his last commission in 1922, a façade only for a modest neighborhood music store in Chicago. From 1908 on, he had averaged only one built commission per year, mostly small-town banks. After Sullivan died in 1924, his debts and funeral expenses were covered by still-loyal friends, who also paid for the modest but heartfelt monument that marks his grave site at Chicago's Graceland Cemetery.

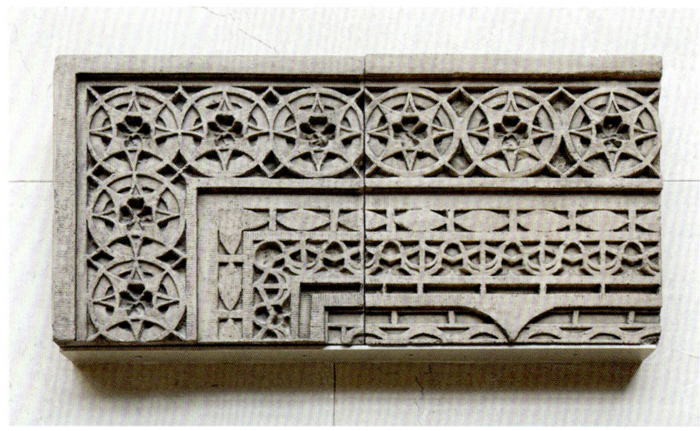

Despite the unfortunate circumstances surrounding his later years, Sullivan never stopped thinking and working. In his last year, he completed both his autobiography and a major portfolio that demonstrated his architectural ornament philosophy, which, thanks to his friends, he was able to see in print before he died. His autobiography, consciously titled *The Autobiography of an Idea*, was not a life story in the conventional sense but rather the story of how a young man became an artist. It ends in 1893, when Sullivan felt his education reached fruition. The most lyrical passages describe the years that Sullivan spent on his grandfather's farm. His love of the natural world—its trees, plants, and flowers and how they had developed from tiny seeds—provided the basis for much that would follow.

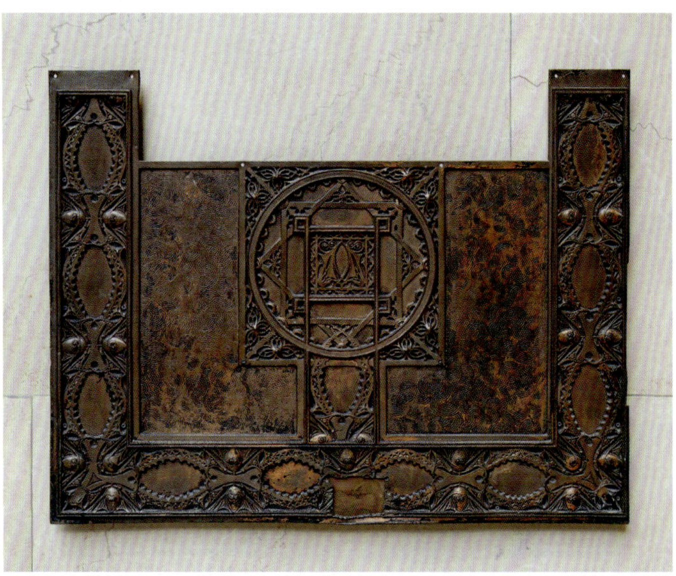

Curiously written in the third person, the book tells the story of a young man and his eventual emergence as an architect. It mainly focuses on Sullivan's education and those who most influenced the development of the budding architect, including his time in Paris at the École des Beaux Arts. But it was a visit to Rome and the Sistine Chapel that most inspired him. He was in awe of Michelangelo's great frescoes and saw the artist as his hero, one he would attempt to emulate.

This excerpt from his autobiography can, I think, be described as an epiphany and is worth quoting at length: "Louis spent three days in Rome—two of them in the Sistine—alone there, almost all the time. Here he communed in silence with a Super-Man. Here he saw and felt a great Free Spirit. Here he was filled with the awe that stills. Here he came face to face with the first great Adventurer. The first mighty man of Courage. The first man with a Great Voice ... The first to cry YEA in thunder tones. The first mighty craftsman. The man, the man of super power, the glorified man, of whom he had dreamed in his childhood ..."

Sullivan was in his sixties when he wrote this. When he returned to Chicago from Paris in 1873, astonishingly still only eighteen years old, he believed he had almost all the technical education he would ever need. But he was after something more. Technique alone can give us a polished craftsman like Norman Rockwell; technique plus genius can give us a Michelangelo.

When Michelangelo painted the Sistine Chapel, Sullivan's hero was thirty-three years old. Sullivan was the same age when his first great building, Chicago's Auditorium, was completed. It was almost as if a light had come on in his creative being. According to Robert Twombly in his excellent biography (see Bibliography), "Before the Auditorium, houses constituted well over 40 percent of their output, but during and afterward, only 18 percent . . . by the time the Auditorium was completed, Adler & Sullivan received larger, more substantial . . . and costlier work."

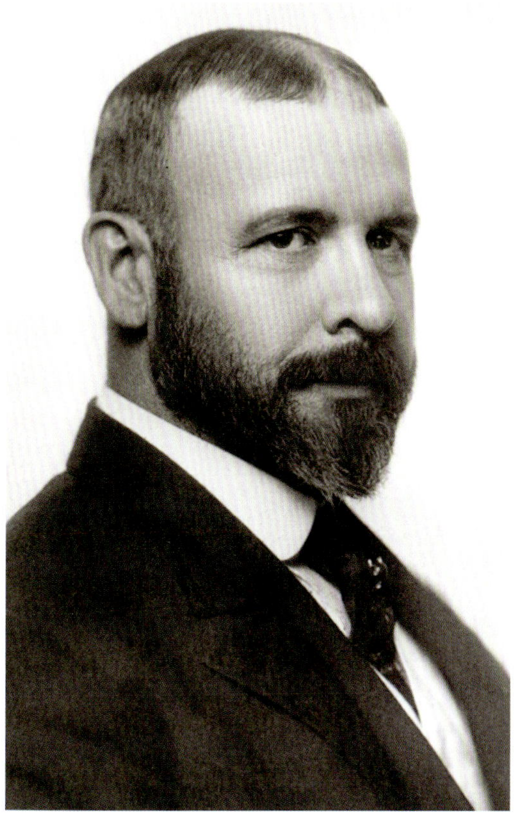

Sullivan in his early forties. Courtesy Ryerson and Burnham Librairies, Art Institute of Chicago.

In the coming years, Sullivan would transform American architecture with groundbreaking tall buildings like the Wainwright in St. Louis, the Schiller and Stock Exchange in Chicago, the Guaranty in Buffalo, and the Bayard-Condict in Manhattan. He is widely credited as the "father" of the skyscraper. Although not technically a skyscraper, Sullivan's last major work, the Schlesinger & Mayer department store in Chicago of 1904 (later Carson, Pirie Scott, now the Sullivan Center, in honor of its architect), is a building that many believe to be the finest of its type ever built.

In addition to Twombly's work, there have been at least two other biographies of Sullivan. All authors had access to Sullivan's voluminous writings; indeed, few architects wrote as much while revealing so little about their personal relationships. For example, Sullivan lived and socialized with his older brother Albert—who rose high in the Illinois Central Railroad—for many years, but when Albert married, and his wife asked Louis to move out of the family home, which was actually owned by Albert, it caused Louis to become estranged from his brother, who is never mentioned in the autobiography!

When Sullivan mentions people at all, they are usually ones who had some influence on his artistic or professional development—John Edelmann; John Wellborn Root; and, of course, Dankmar Adler all come to mind. Two young architects who worked for and with Sullivan most closely—Frank Lloyd Wright and George Grant Elmslie—he mentions not at all. Wright went out on his own in 1893 after an acrimonious separation, but Elmslie stayed loyal to Sullivan until 1909, when he was finally forced to leave for family and financial considerations.

Who were his friends? His drinking buddies? Did he have any relationships with women that predated his marriage to Margaret in 1899? What plays did he see? What concerts did he attend? He didn't tell us, although we know he belonged to men's clubs like the Chicago and Union League—then and now bastions of the establishment—and the Cliff Dwellers, which catered to artists and writers. He was also quite active in architectural groups, both local and national. He belonged to committees; he was an active speaker at conventions and meetings.

Much of what Sullivan wrote and said involved his philosophy of architectural design. He continuously sought out opportunities to influence younger architects. His *Kindergarten Chats* is only one example. While these efforts consumed much of his time and perhaps hundreds of thousands of words, their essence is relatively simple. The most important principle he learned at the École in Paris was this: every project must start with its distinct program.

What is the purpose of the building? Let's say it's a bank. How does a bank operate? How many and what kinds of people will work there? What are the needs of its clients and customers? How can the space be organized to provide the most efficient layout for both? These factors and more must be fully considered before the architect's pen touches paper. Frank Lloyd Wright tells the story of Sullivan emphatically placing his initial sketch of the Wainwright Building on his drafting board. Wright's point is that the sketch showed that Sullivan had solved the "problem" of how to express a building's essence, in this case, its height.

But another important point is that the final building did not vary much from the sketch created by Sullivan, because that sketch came only after he had thought deeply about it. When he famously said that "form ever follows function," that is what he meant. He railed against perpetuating European styles, not because they had not been valid for their time and place but

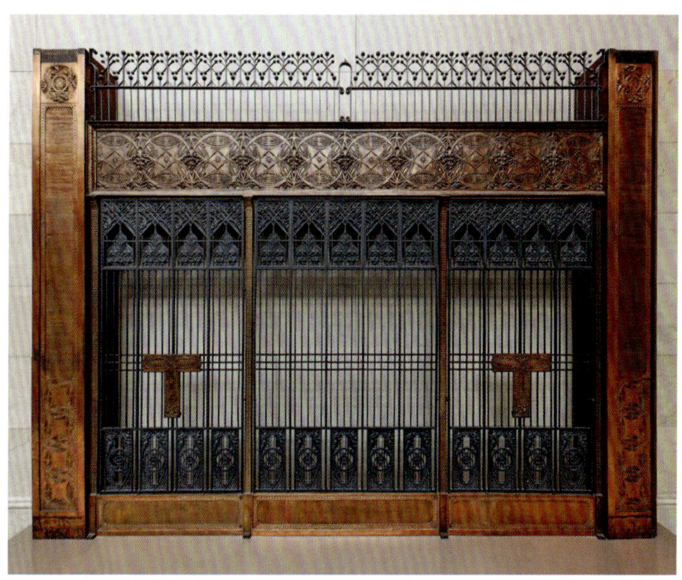

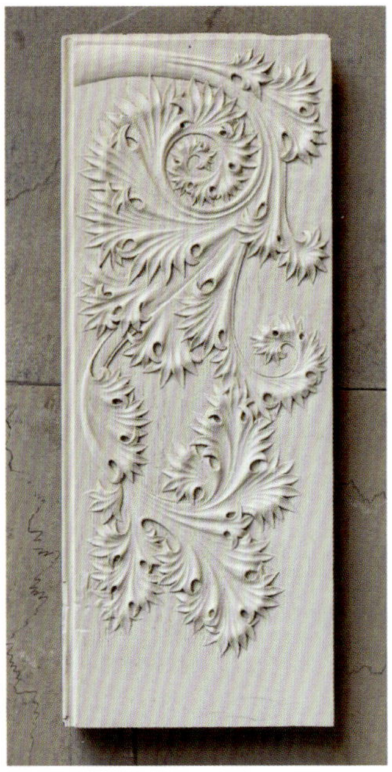

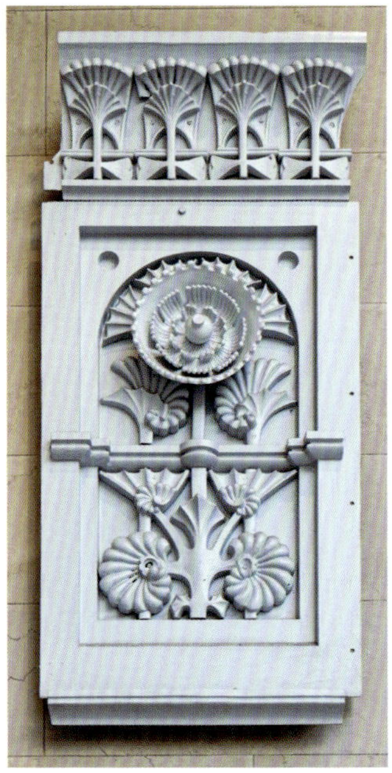

because America was not that time and place. Architects who worked in those idioms were doing the opposite of what they should be doing: they were falsely trying to make function fit into existing forms.

Sullivan never believed that his way of enhancing a building through decoration was the only or best way. If you were faithful in expressing the function of a building, then the creativity of expressing its form should be yours alone. For example, Sullivan wrote a long and appreciative article about Wright's Imperial Hotel in Tokyo and later supported Eliel Saarinen's entry in the 1922 competition for the Chicago Tribune Tower, even though its simple art deco form was about as far from Sullivan's own aesthetic as it could be. But to Sullivan, it was that architect's most authentic and personal response to the program that mattered.

We think Sullivan had an unforgiving nature, not only in defense of his architectural philosophy but in his personal relationships. How else can we explain his unwillingness to resume his partnership with Adler, who had departed from Sullivan in 1895 after a deep recession left the firm with no commissions? Unlike Sullivan, his partner had a family to support, so he took a job with an elevator company. When business conditions improved, Adler suggested they resume the partnership, but Sullivan refused.

Although most Chicago architects who practiced in the late nineteenth and early twentieth centuries would have seen some of their once famous works fall to later development, Sullivan's buildings suffered more than most. Of Sullivan's nearly 190 built designs—both with Adler and alone—only forty survive today, and one of them is just a shell. Major losses in Chicago include the Chicago Stock Exchange, the Schiller (later Garrick) Building, the Victoria Hotel (Chicago Heights), and the Walker Warehouse.

In other parts of the country—for in their heyday, Adler & Sullivan had a national practice—losses included the New Orleans Union Station, Pueblo Colorado Opera House, the St. Nicholas Hotel (St. Louis), and even Sullivan's own beloved vacation home in Ocean Springs, Mississippi, destroyed in 2005 by Hurricane Katrina. (One of Adler & Sullivan's greatest achievements, the Transportation Building at the 1893 Columbian Exposition, with its glorious "Golden Door," was never meant to be permanent.)

I was in the Army when the Schiller was demolished in 1962. In 1967, I took a course called Chicago Building at Northwestern University, taught by faculty member Dr. Carl W. Condit (1914–1997). Although his doctorate was in English, which was a subject that he taught for several years, he became increasingly interested in the history of building technology and, by 1967, was a professor in the art department. The course textbook was his own *The Chicago School of Architecture* (see Bibliography). I still have it, as well as his follow-on, *Chicago, 1910–29*.

He was a stimulating lecturer, but the highlights of the course were the field trips we made around the city to see the actual buildings. The Chicago Stock Exchange building was still standing, its once colorful exterior covered with decades of Chicago coal soot. We were also given access to the newly restored Auditorium Theater. I have been in the theater many times since, but the thrill of seeing it for the first time is still with me.

When the Stock Exchange was demolished in 1972—despite the heroic efforts of preservationists, including Richard Nickel, who lost his life trying to save fragments of Sullivan's genius—I was working across the street at City Hall. Day by day, I saw a landmark of American architecture destroyed, to be replaced by yet another steel and glass box.

In this book, photographer James Caulfield and I have attempted to pay reverent homage to the man who we think was, in fact, the first genuine American architect, hence the title of this book. By the time Sullivan died, his obsession with ornament had been rejected in favor of yet another invasion of European style, one that now rejected ornament altogether. It was only when great Sullivan buildings like the Schiller and Chicago Stock Exchange began to fall that architects and scholars began to realize that an important aspect of the nation's artistic legacy was disappearing. While it was too late for too many, what's left is more than sufficient to prove our point.

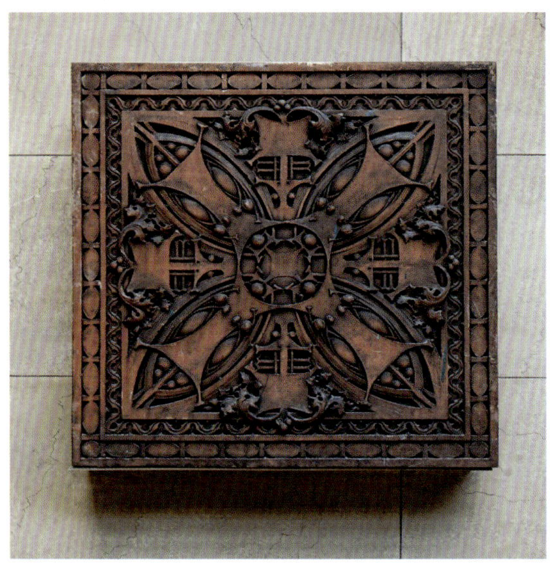

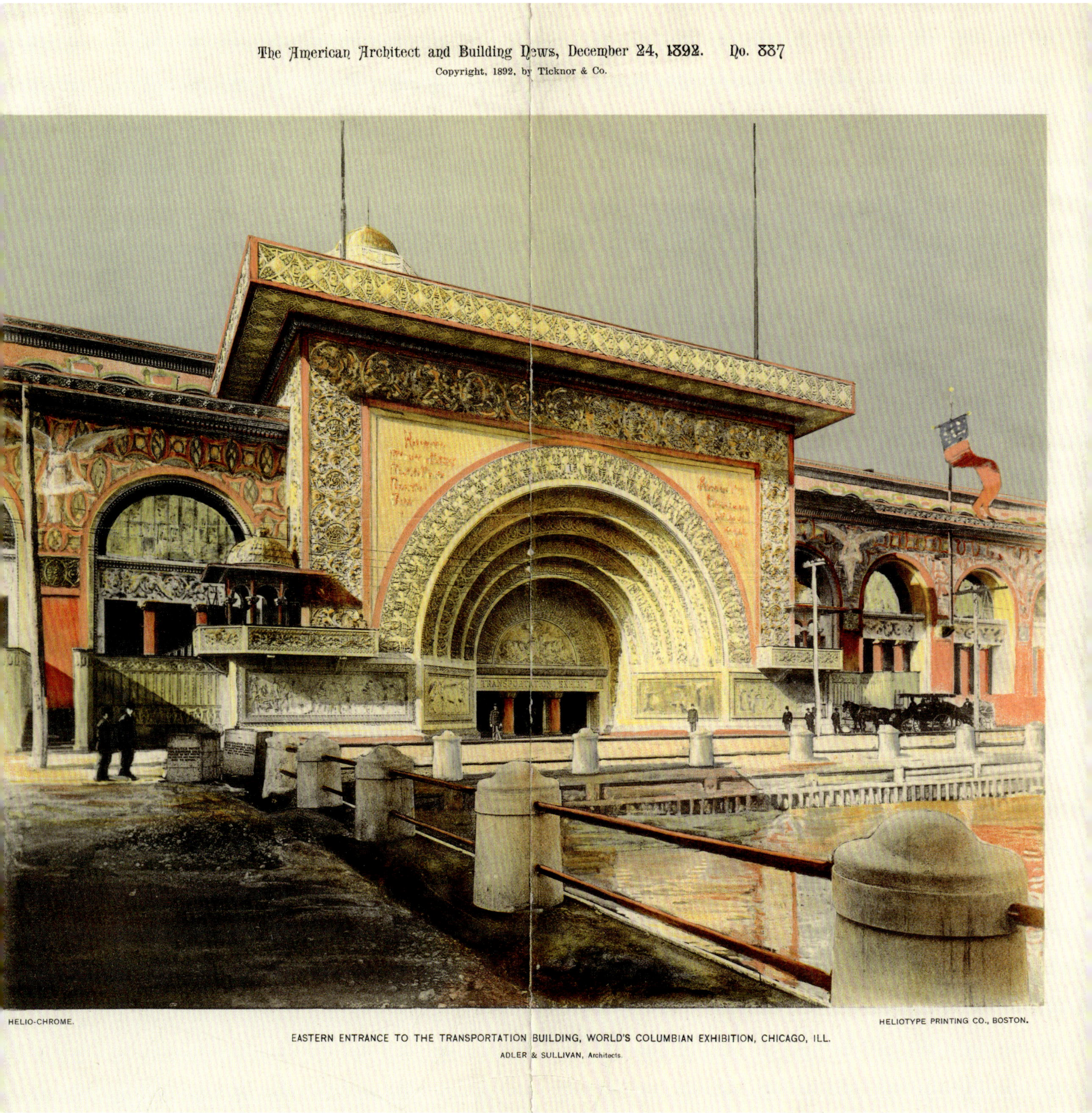

Sullivan typically went his own way when he designed the Transportation Building at the 1893 Columbian Exposition in Chicago. With its famous "Golden Door," it thumbed its nose at the dominant classicism of the rest of the fair buildings.

A LIFE IN ARCHITECTURE

"... about the age of twelve ... this ... boy, to his own surprise, became aware that he had become interested in buildings: and over one building in particular ... It stood at the northeast corner of Tremont and Boylston Streets. It was a Masonic Temple built of brown granite, light gray in tone and joyous of aspect."
LOUIS SULLIVAN, The Autobiography of an Idea

Louis Henry Sullivan was born on September 3, 1856, in Boston to Patrick and Andrienne List Sullivan. In his curious autobiography (which ended in 1893, although it was written shortly before he died on April 3, 1924), Louis was strangely dismissive of his father, ascribing little merit to him other than the undoubted fact that he had been a self-made man. And though he grew up with his older brother, Albert, and even lived with him for several years in Chicago, because of an estrangement, Louis makes not a single mention of him in his autobiography.

His father was born in Ireland, but apparently had learned and practiced his trade as a dancing master in London before immigrating to Boston in 1847. His son tells a possibly fanciful story of Patrick being separated from his father at a fair in Ireland at the age of twelve, not being able to find him again, and wandering Ireland as an itinerant violinist thereafter. According to his son, Patrick learned his adult trade in London and perfected it in Paris at the feet of the leading French masters.

Unlike the majority of Irish immigrants in 1847, Patrick traveled to Boston not to escape the effects of the potato blight and famine but to advance in his trade in a country where his "Irishness" might be slightly less of a hindrance than it might have been in class-conscious England, where the Irish were considered barely human by many.

Something should be said to clarify what a "dance master" was at that time. It wasn't like a teacher at today's Arthur Murray or a similar studio, who essentially teaches adults how not to embarrass themselves at weddings and dinner dances. While there would have been some of that, what dancing masters mostly did was teach the young the dancing and social skills they would need in a far busier formal social scene than exists today. The privileged classes would routinely attend debuts, balls, and cotillions and would be expected to do their share of the dancing.

Louis's mother, Andrienne List, was born in Geneva, Switzerland, in 1835. Her father, Henri, was German; her mother, Anna, was Swiss-French. After business reverses in Geneva, the Lists, whose family was reasonably prosperous, were given sufficient funds to reestablish themselves in America. They arrived in Boston in 1850. How Patrick and Andrienne met is not known, but Patrick was attracted to her musical ability—she was an accomplished pianist—and the couple was married on August 14, 1852. Patrick was then thirty-four; Andrienne was only seventeen.

They had two sons. Albert Walter was born on September 17, 1854. Louis Henry—his middle name a tribute to his grandfather—was born two years later. The unhappiness that Louis felt for his father may have been related to the endless search that Patrick undertook for a better place to practice his profession. Over the years, the family moved to New York City; back to Boston; then to Newburyport, Massachusetts; and even out of the country to Halifax, Nova Scotia, before finally moving to Chicago in 1868. Between these various excursions, the Sullivans often stayed with the Lists at their small farm in South Reading, Massachusetts. Although Louis was still only twelve, it was decided that he would stay with his grandparents and finish his schooling in Boston before joining the family in Chicago.

Both Patrick and Andrienne could draw competently and enjoyed sketching during family outings in the countryside, so artistic abilities came naturally for Louis. Although most of his surviving drawings are of architectural ornament, those of people and landscapes suggest that he might well have succeeded as a painter had he not chosen architecture. He later wrote that his love of nature was heightened by the years spent wandering around his grandparents' farm and the surrounding countryside.

The pages devoted to his time there are among the most lyrical he ever wrote. He became fascinated by the transformation of plants and flowers from simple seeds to complex organisms. This fascination informed his later obsession with architectural ornament—almost unique among American architects—and persisted until the end of his life. Indeed, his last work was *A System of Architectural Ornament According with a Philosophy of Man's Powers* (1922). His fascination also explains his love for the vacation cottage that he built for himself in Ocean Springs, Mississippi, where he was able to have the gardens that were denied him in Chicago.

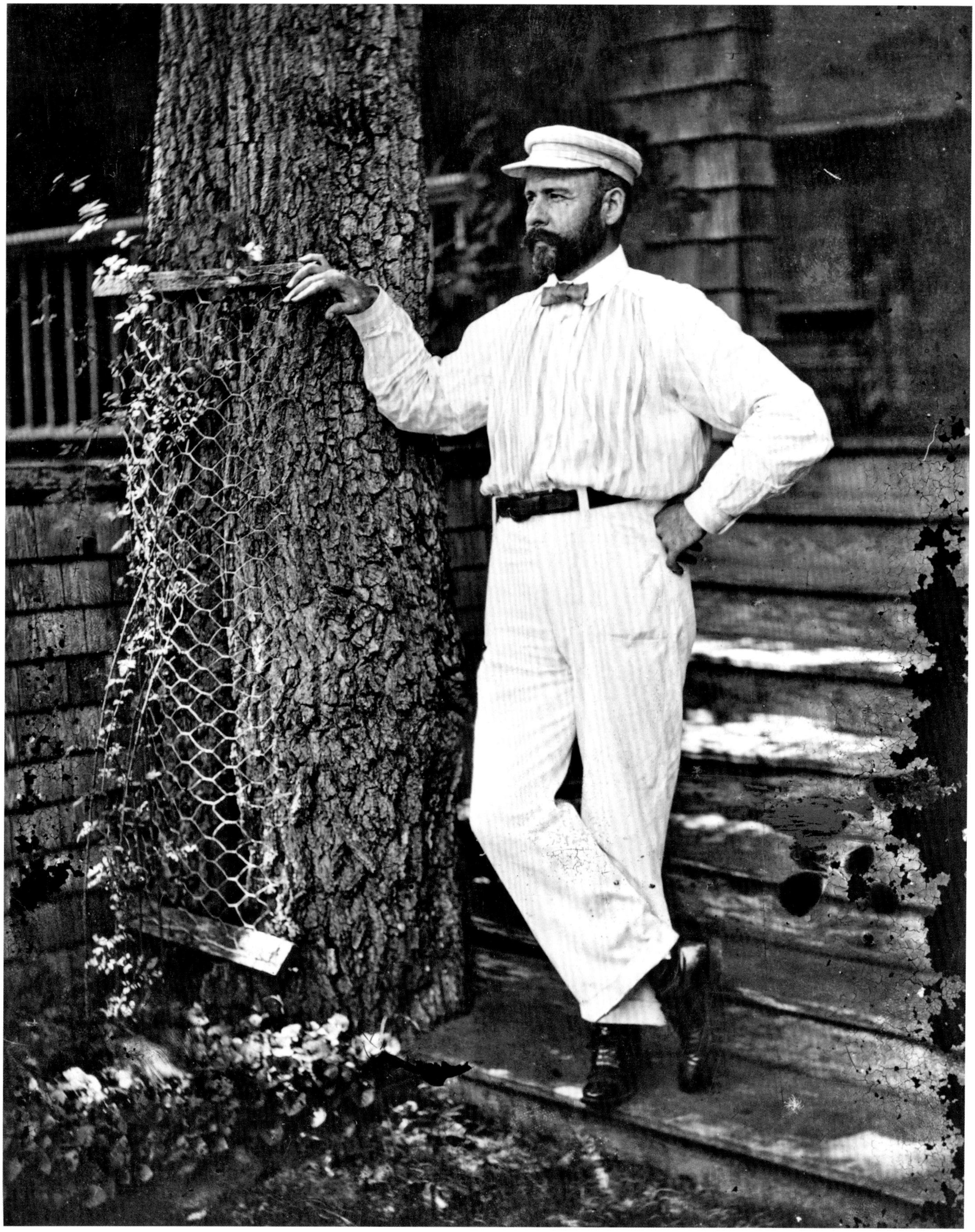

Sullivan on the steps of the cottage, c. 1900. Courtesy Ryerson and Burnham Librairies, Art Institute of Chicago.

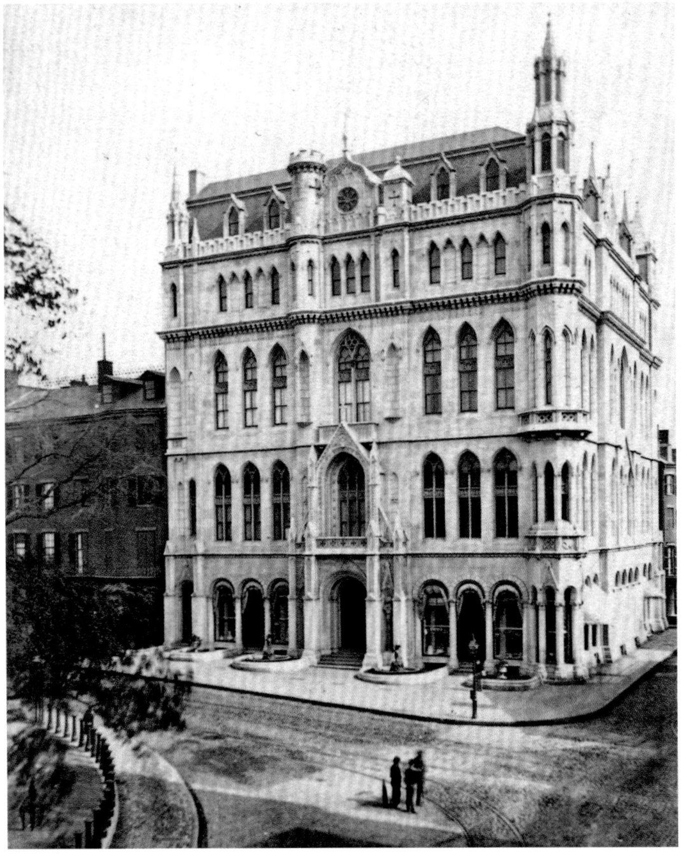

As a young boy, Sullivan liked to walk the streets of Boston, studying its impressive buildings. One he particularly admired was Merrill G. Wheelock's Masonic Temple of 1867. Its eclectic Gothic Revival design appealed to him more than did the very common Classical Revival structures then in fashion. Courtesy Bostonian Society, Old State House Museum.

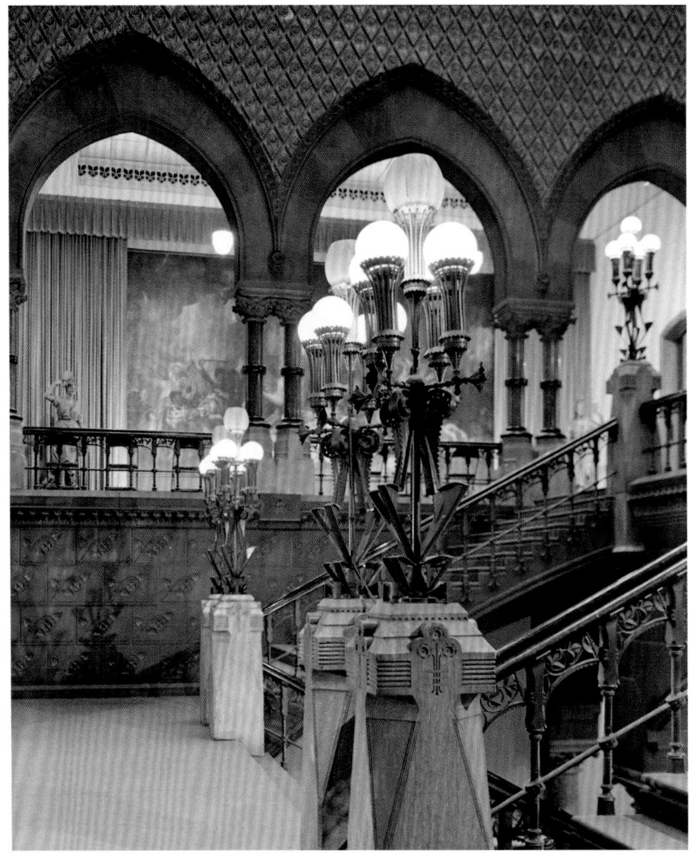

Main Hall at the Pennsylvania Academy of the Fine Arts. Like Furness, Sullivan would use his considerable talent to lavishly decorate the interiors of his buildings. Courtesy Historic American Buildings Survey.

In his autobiography, Louis also tells of walking the streets of Boston, admiring its impressive buildings, and how he dreamed of becoming an architect. One building he particularly admired was Merrill G. Wheelock's Masonic Temple, a neo-Gothic building whose exuberance appealed to Louis's young imagination. And it turned out that Louis was in a great hurry to make his dream come true.

It would be hard to imagine a more driven young man than Louis Sullivan. While he managed to graduate from grammar school (Rice, Boston, 1870), it would be the last time he graduated from anything. He attended Boston English High School, founded in 1821, which, although not as famous as the adjacent Boston Latin (founded in 1635!), did have a more rigorous curriculum than most high schools have today.

According to Sullivan, it was there that he had his first positive educational experience, due primarily to his charismatic teacher, Moses Woolson, "whose appearance suggested ... a farmer of the hardy, spare, weather-beaten ... successful type—apparently a man of forty or under." Woolson told his young charges, "You are here as wards in my charge; I accept that charge as sacred ... I will give you all that I have, you shall give me all that you have ..." For the young Sullivan, "A veil was parted, as if by magic, and behold! There stood not alone a man, but a TEACHER of the young!"

The subjects mentioned by Sullivan are Algebra, Geometry, English Literature, Botany, Mineralogy (!), and French. But always a young man in a hurry—and firmly settled on architecture as a career—after two years at Boston English, still only sixteen, he was accepted as a special third-year student at the Massachusetts Institute of Technology (MIT).

Founded in 1861, MIT soon gained a reputation for excellence in engineering and the sciences. In 1868, a school of architecture was added, the first in the United States. Its initial four students had grown to twenty-seven by the time Sullivan arrived in 1872. The school was led by William R. Ware, a Harvard graduate who had trained as an architect at a Boston firm before moving to New York to work for William Morris Hunt, the first American to attend the École des Beaux-Arts in Paris.

Hunt, whose legacy includes George Vanderbilt's Biltmore estate in Ashville, North Carolina, America's largest private home, was then the acknowledged leader of the profession. Like Hunt, Ware was an exponent of French architectural ideas, so the curriculum was also based on the École model.

In 1873, after only one year, Sullivan decided he had learned all he needed at MIT, so he went to New York to visit Hunt—perhaps with an introduction from Ware—to seek his advice or (more hopefully) a job. This was not possible, but Hunt suggested that the young man go to Philadelphia to seek employment with Furness and Hewitt. Frank Furness had been one of the young architects who had worked in Hunt's office. Adding to the city's attractiveness, Louis also had his grandfather and an uncle there, who offered a place to stay. They had moved to Philadelphia after Louis's grandmother died.

It turned out that Frank Furness was just the kind of architect who would appeal to young Louis, still only seventeen years old. His eclectic and exuberant designs—which matched his own larger than life personality—were as far from the classicism taught at MIT as they could be. While the Panic of 1873 and the attendant loss of business cut short Sullivan's tenure at Furness and Hewitt and forced the young man to join his family in Chicago, he learned a great deal about the practical workings of an architectural practice during his time there. While it can't be known what commissions Sullivan might have worked on, Furness' colorful and unique Philadelphia Academy of Arts would have been one possibility.

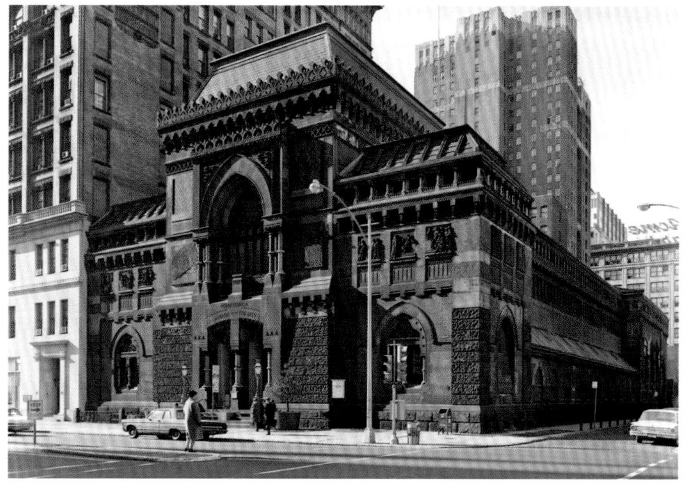

Frank Furness was Sullivan's first architectural employer. The colorful and flamboyant Pennsylvania Academy of the Fine Arts in Philadelphia reflected his personality. Courtesy Historic American Buildings Survey.

Chicago—At Long Last (But Not for Long)

***"The train neared the city; it broke into the city; it plowed its way through miles of shanties disheartening and dirty gray. It reached its terminal at an open shed. Louis tramped the platform, stopped, looked toward the city, ruins around him; looked at the sky; and as one alone, stamped his foot, raised his hand and cried in full voice:* This is the place for me!"**

Louis Sullivan, The Autobiography of an Idea

Written when Sullivan was in his sixties, this description may well have been his reaction when he first saw a city still rebuilding and reinventing itself after the famous 1871 fire had largely destroyed its center. He arrived the day before Thanksgiving. After enjoying Thanksgiving dinner with his parents and brother Albert—now working as a machinist for the Illinois Central Railroad, whose Chicago to New Orleans division he would one day head—Louis spent some time exploring the city before looking for work. What he saw must have astounded him, for not only was Chicago rebuilding, but it was also in the midst of raising its grade so proper sewers could help alleviate chronic outbreaks of waterborne disease.

Unlike Philadelphia, Chicago offered an abundance of opportunities for young architects. Louis later wrote that he walked the city to find a building he admired and then looked up its architect. The building he admired was the Portland Black; its architect was Major William LeBaron Jenney (1832–1907). A product of Phillips Exeter Academy and the Lawrence Scientific School (like Louis's MIT teacher William Ware), Jenney completed his engineering education at the École Centrale des Arts et Manufactures in Paris in 1856. After service in the Civil War, he eventually made his way to Chicago and opened an architectural practice in 1869.

His young employee later commented that Jenney "was not an architect except by courtesy of terms. His true profession was that of engineer." He is known today primarily for developing the steel framing techniques that led to the skyscraper, of which his Home Insurance Company of 1885 is considered by many scholars to be the first. In addition to Sullivan, many of the young architects who would later be associated with the Chicago School passed through Jenney's office, including William A. Holabird, Martin Roche (he and Holabird would become partners), Irving K. Pond, Howard Van Doren Shaw, and John Edelmann.

It was Edelmann who became a close friend and a mentor to Louis and sponsored his membership in the Lotus Club, a group of amateur athletes who met weekly at a site on the Calumet River, some fifteen miles south of the city. His brother Albert also became a member, and both Louis and Albert competed against each other in swimming, running, rowing, and other sports, and also competed as a team with similar clubs.

It isn't known what buildings Sullivan worked on in Jenney's office, but it's likely he continued to develop his drafting and tracing skills. He wrote little about his work there, but his *Autobiography* makes clear his enjoyment of the physical exercise and camaraderie of the Lotus Club.

His membership was, however, to be interrupted, for after less than eight months in Chicago, Sullivan left for New York in July 1874 to take ship for England, with Paris and the École des Beaux Arts as his intended destination.

European Interlude

Louis had thought about Paris for some time. His father had lived there as a young man. His mother's family was French-speaking and had extolled the virtues of Paris to Louis. At MIT, the architectural program was based upon École principals, and Parisian Eugene Letang had been William Ware's closest associate at the university. Before he boarded the *Britannic* for the ten-day passage to Liverpool, Sullivan visited Hunt's office and talked to Sidney Stratton, who offered valuable advice on what Sullivan would need to do in Paris. Upon arrival in Liverpool, he took a train and spent approximately two weeks in London, enjoying its

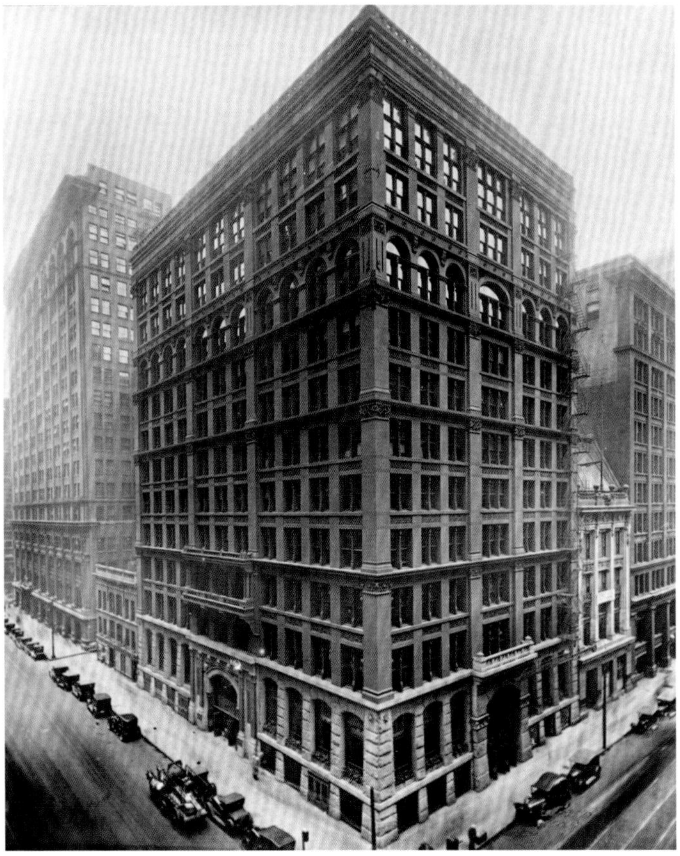

William Le Baron Jenney's Home Insurance Building (Chicago, 1885) is considered by some to be the first skyscraper. Sullivan didn't consider his employer to be a true architect, but his innovations in steel framing would enable Adler & Sullivan to create some of the most notable early tall buildings. Courtesy Ryerson and Burnham Libraries, Art Institute of Chicago.

architectural sights while being somewhat repelled by its pockets of poverty and the coldness of shopkeepers and others he met.

Early in August, Sullivan set out for Paris. Along the way, he saw Rouen cathedral, with which he was suitably impressed. He eventually found lodgings at 17 Rue Racine in the Latin Quarter, conveniently located near the École.

Since there were then only thirty places available for incoming architectural students, entrance was determined by competitive exam. Sullivan would have to improve his French and prepare in other subjects, but he would also need a sponsor and letters of recommendation, for which his MIT and Hunt connections were likely critical. He found a sponsor in Emile Vaudremer, who had been Eugene Letang's instructor; Sullivan may have had letters of introduction from Hunt and Stratton.

In addition to mathematics and other related subjects, the test included preparing a plan, a section, and an elevation for an assigned building. This had to be done in twelve hours, with the results judged the next day. Many aspirants failed the test once or never passed. Unlike Henry Hobson Richardson, who failed on his first try, Sullivan passed. He was still just eighteen years old but was obviously a young man in a hurry.

Sullivan spent only ten months in Europe. In addition to his lectures and studio work at the École, he traveled to Rome, which was then a place of pilgrimage for architectural students and budding artists. While he enjoyed the usual monuments, he was particularly impressed by the work of Michelangelo, seeing his Sistine Chapel as the work of "a great free spirit" and "first mighty man of Courage." Michelangelo's example of melding painting, sculpture, and architecture to create a coherent and powerful visual whole would inform Sullivan's own vision to the end of his life. Sullivan would, in his own way, seek to emulate his hero's unwavering commitment to his art.

And although he left the École before completing its entire course, Sullivan did return to Chicago having learned the creative techniques he would retain for the rest of his life. Every project on which he worked at the École started with an "esquisse," or preliminary sketch, done freehand but based on considerable thought about the building's intent. This initial creative inspiration would be referred to as the plan and was developed and finally rendered as working drawings. Sullivan would adhere to these techniques for the rest of his life.

Chicago Again—And Forever

With an architectural education that had stressed classicism, Sullivan—astonishingly still only eighteen, an age when most are just beginning their higher education—returned to Chicago to begin a career that would lead him to create a more purely American architecture.

He moved in with his parents and brother and reestablished his relationship with the Lotus Club and his friend John Edelmann, who not only gave Sullivan work but became his intellectual mentor and companion. He began to read more widely, not only the art histories of Hippolyte Taine and other Europeans but also the works of more purely and proudly Americans such as Bret Harte, Mark Twain, and James Russell Lowell.

For Edelmann's firm, Johnson & Edelmann, Sullivan participated in two commissions. In 1876, he executed interior frescoes of the famous evangelist Dwight Moody for the Chicago Avenue Church and did similar work for the Sinai Synagogue. On the latter, Burling & Adler had acted as associate architects, beginning a relationship that would last for nearly twenty years. Although accounts of Sullivan's work in the local papers were highly complementary, no photos or illustrations are known to exist.

Edelmann left Chicago later in 1876 to seek the commission for a large cathedral in Cleveland. Although Edelmann later returned after trying his hand at horse farming, his close relationship with Sullivan had largely ended.

It appears that Sullivan began working with Dankmar Adler on a freelance basis in the late 1870s, after the former had set up shop as "Louis Sullivan, Designer." He became an employee of Adler & Company in the spring of 1880, given a partial financial stake in the spring of 1882, and became a full partner in the new Adler & Sullivan on May 1, 1883. Until the partnership was dissolved in 1895, Adler & Sullivan received approximately 180 commissions. Of these, sixty were residences, thirty-three were commercial or office buildings, twenty-seven were manufacturing facilities, seventeen were theatres of various kinds, and eleven were warehouses. The rest were a mix that included hotels, railroad stations, synagogues, churches, and even tombs. By any measure, Adler and Sullivan were among the leaders of the profession in Chicago.

Dankmar Adler was twelve years Sullivan's senior. He was born in 1844 in Stadt Lengsfeld in the German principality of Saxe-Weimar. His father was a rabbi and a cantor, who, in 1854, moved his family to Detroit to become chief rabbi of Temple Beth El. It was there that his son developed his interest in architecture, serving an apprenticeship in the office of E. Willard Smith. In 1861, Adler's father accepted a position in Chicago with the Kehilath Anshe Ma'ariv synagogue. Young Adler found work with the architect and engineer Augustus Bauer, but the Civil War intervened, and Adler enlisted on his birthday in 1862.

Adler saw a great deal of action and was wounded. The last nine months of his service were spent with the Topographical Engineers Office, which substantially broadened his professional knowledge. When the war was over, he returned to Bauer's office. After working there and in other offices, he formed his own firm with Edward Burling in 1871. Burling was later charged with malpractice involving a government project. He was acquitted, but when the promoters of the Central Music Hall were uneasy about him and offered the commission to Adler alone in 1879, he dissolved the partnership.

The widely held assumption that Adler wasn't an architect at all but essentially a talented engineer and acoustician is wrong. Prior to Sullivan joining the firm and probably even for some time after, Adler would have been largely responsible for designing the buildings credited to both Adler & Burling and Adler & Company. While not works of genius, the designs were competent and compared favorably to the work of other Chicago firms of the time.

Adler soon recognized Sullivan's developing genius for design. Therefore, Adler eventually and very sensibly left design to Sullivan while concentrating on the increasingly complex engineering demands of the firm's ever larger and more complex commissions.

While Sullivan was certainly not anti-social, Adler seems to have been mostly responsible for getting clients and keeping them happy. Although he didn't have many close friends, Sullivan was widely acquainted and belonged to several clubs, including the prestigious Chicago Club. But he could be quite opinionated, particularly about his work. This was not a major issue so long as Sullivan had Adler as a buffer, but it became much more of a problem when the partnership dissolved.

Adler's Jewish background was also a major advantage for the firm. The client list shows dozens of Jewish names; many were members of the congregation led by Adler's father. The firm also got commissions for synagogues and the Jewish Standard Club.

The firm's prosperity in the 1880s and early 1890s not only permitted club memberships for its principals but also a new vacation home for Sullivan, who otherwise seemed content to live in apartment hotels. He was first exposed to Ocean Springs, Mississippi, on the Gulf Coast a few miles from Biloxi, by his Chicago friends Helen and James Charnley, for whom the firm would design their now famous Chicago house. By the winter of 1890–91, Sullivan had built a cottage on the eleven acres of land he purchased. He fell in love with his retreat and spent as much time during the winter there as he could for the next twenty years, constantly expanding his beloved gardens. The house was destroyed by Hurricane Katrina in 2005.

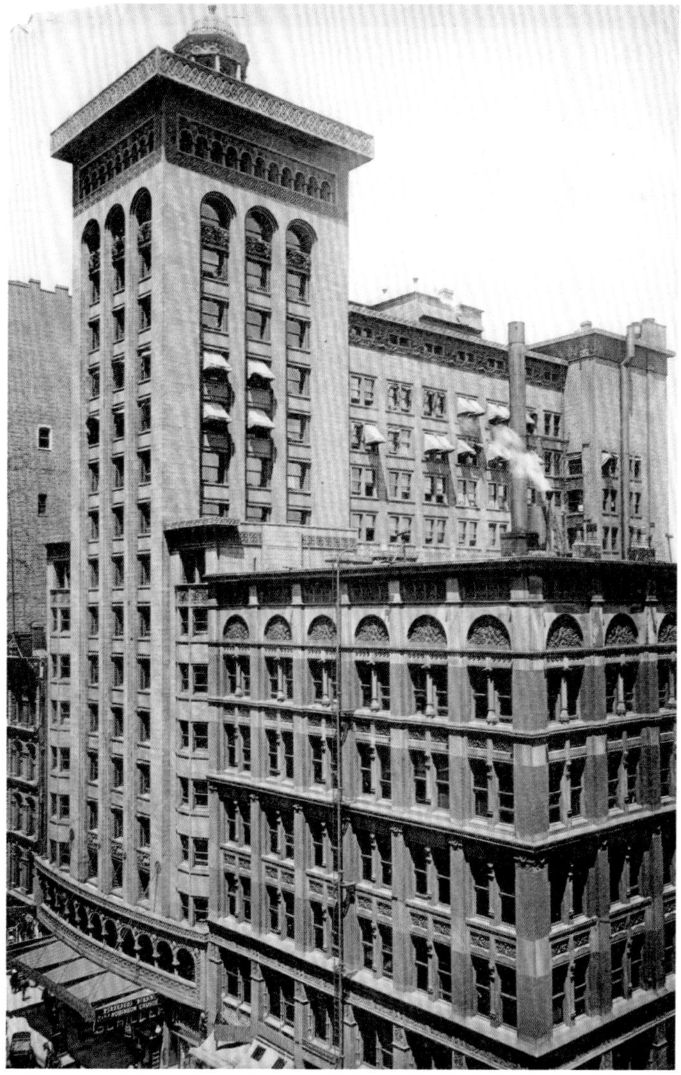

The Borden Block (foreground; Chicago, 1880) was designed by Adler & Company after Sullivan joined the firm but prior to his being made a partner. Looming behind it is Adler & Sullivan's Schiller Building, designed just ten years later. Courtesy Ryerson and Burnham Libraries, Art Institute of Chicago.

His brother Albert also purchased land in the area but never built a cottage, being content to park his private railroad car on a nearby spur. By then, he was general superintendent for the division of the Illinois Central that ran from Chicago to New Orleans. The brothers' relationship seems to have remained close until Albert married Mary Spellman in 1893. Louis was living with the couple in a house he designed, but he was apparently asked to leave when Mary had a daughter in 1896. While the actual details of the incident are not known, it may have been related to Mary's discovery that Louis was carrying on an affair with the wife of a University of Chicago faculty member. Whatever the cause, Louis took it hard and became estranged from his brother, an estrangement that would last for the rest of their lives.

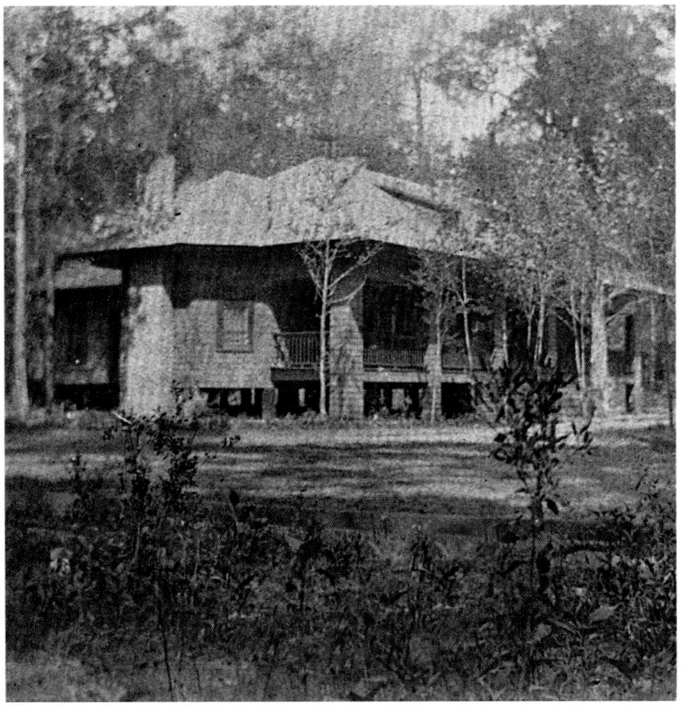

Sullivan's cottage at Ocean Springs, Mississippi, provided both a refuge from Chicago's harsh winters and an opportunity to enjoy the natural world he loved so much. Courtesy Ryerson and Burnham Libraries, Art Institute of Chicago.

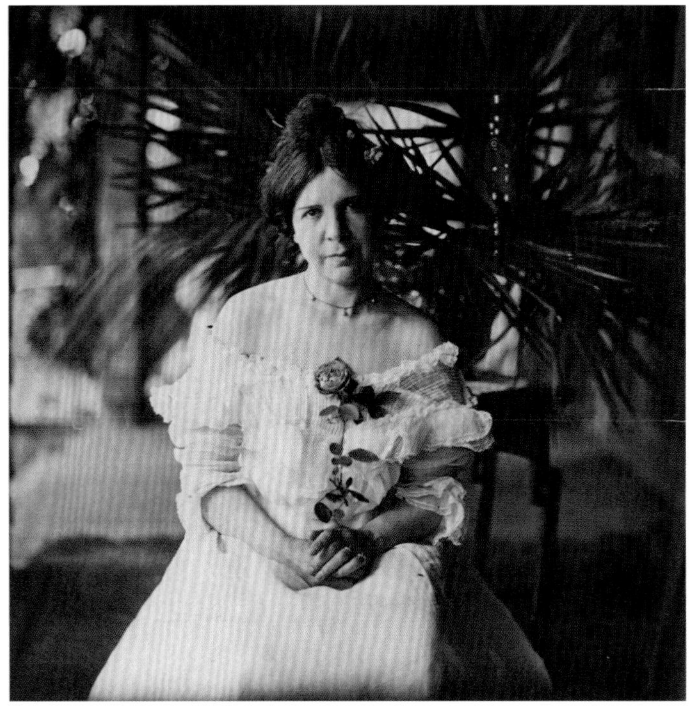

Margaret Sullivan at the time of her marriage to Louis. Courtesy Ryerson and Burnham Libraries, Art Institute of Chicago.

The year before (1895), Sullivan also lost his partner. Business had dried up after the Panic of 1893, and Adler felt he had to take a job to support his family. Sullivan, who had no family to support, took this personally and would refuse to reform the partnership when conditions later improved.

Another loss came in 1893, when an argument over a loan and Wright's moonlighting led to Frank Lloyd Wright's departure. The loan had been personally made by Sullivan to Wright in 1889, enabling him to build his home in Oak Park. The $5,000 loan having been repaid, Wright asked for the deed, which Sullivan apparently refused to provide. They argued, and either Wright quit (his version) or was fired. Not open to question is that Wright was Sullivan's most talented assistant.

Fortunately, Sullivan's dwindling staff after 1895 included George Grant Elmslie, who remained faithfully with Sullivan until leaving in 1909 due to the lack of commissions. Elmslie then formed a partnership with William Gray Purcell; their firm would go on to produce Prairie style buildings whose numbers were second only to Wright.

After 1895, Sullivan's most important client was the Schlesinger & Mayer department store (later Carson Pirie Scott). Between 1896, when Sullivan did alterations to existing buildings on State Street, and 1903, when he did the same on Wabash Avenue, his work for the company was almost continuous. Included was the flagship store at State and Madison, one of the icons of retail design and one of the architect's masterpieces.

The reasonable income of those years permitted Sullivan to marry in 1899. His sexual orientation has been questioned by some biographers, perhaps because of his participation in the Lotus Club and other men's clubs and because of his long bachelorhood (he was forty-two when he married). There is absolutely no evidence to support this. Indeed, private clubs were generally segregated by sex until late in the twentieth century. What is certain is that he married Margaret (born Mary Azona Hattabaugh on May 29, 1858, on a farm in California's Santa Clara Valley) on July 1.

Little was known about Margaret until research on her background was published in a 2002 journal article by architectural historian Paul Sprague (see Bibliography). In the 1900 Federal Census, the birth date listed for Margaret is May 29, 1873, which would have made her twenty-seven rather than forty-one (her actual age) at the time of her wedding. Whether or not Sullivan was aware of Margaret's true age is unknown. The document also lists a son, Lester, born in April 1900. Since the same document shows that Margaret had no children, it may be that the child had a different mother.

Birth records are unavailable for that period, so the identity of the mother can't be determined. Sprague did find records for a Lester Sullivan, as the adopted son of David and Margaret Pigott, in the 1910 and 1920 Censuses. While suggestive, the surviving information makes it impossible to determine for certain whether this Lester was indeed Sullivan's son. Neither Elmslie nor any of Sullivan's other friends mentioned the existence of any child.

The marriage seemed to have been successful, at least for a time. The couple spent a good deal of time at the Ocean Springs

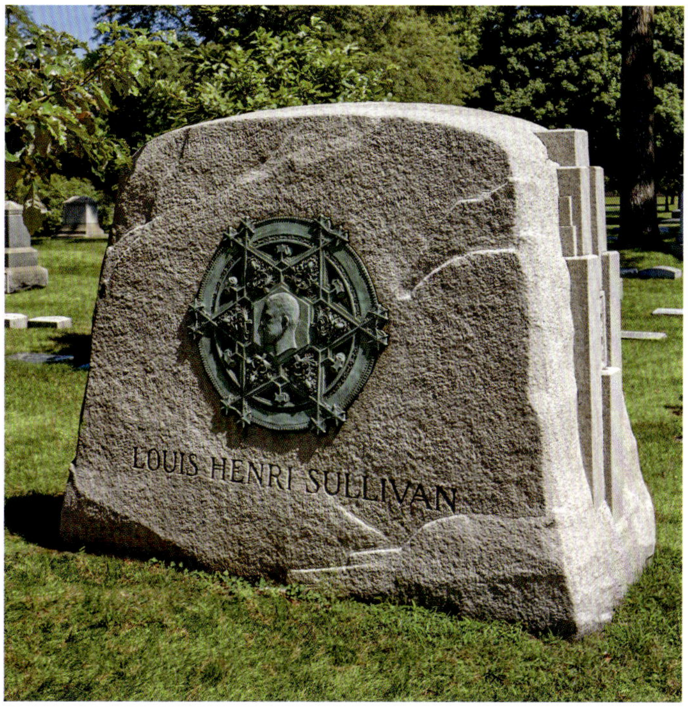

Sullivan's friends took up a collection to pay for his headstone at Chicago's Graceland Cemetery, where Sullivan's parents are also buried and where the tombs he designed for Martin Ryerson and Carrie Eliza Getty draw thousands of visitors every year. The spelling of Sullivan's middle name used here ("Henri") is a common mistake.

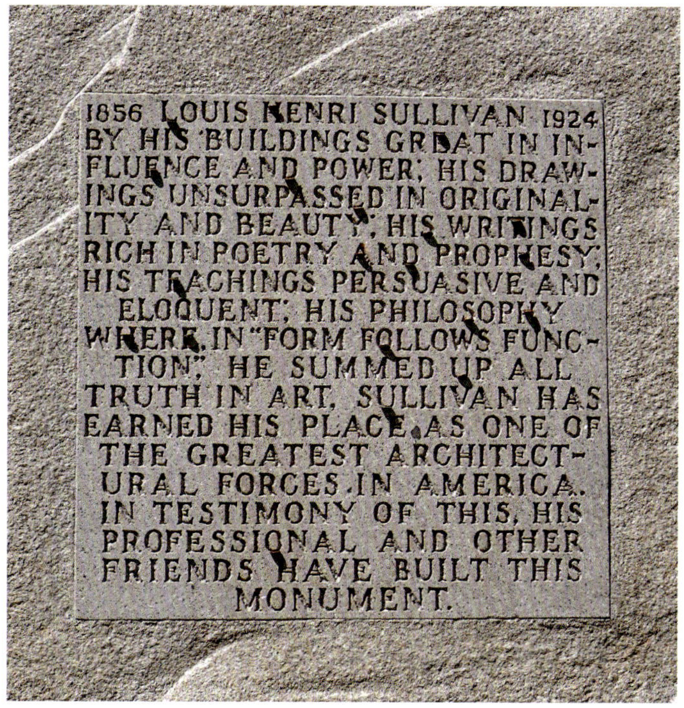

The rear of the headstone contains a heartfelt tribute from Sullivan's friends and fellow architects.

home, and in letters to friends, Sullivan mentioned missing Margaret when he needed to be in Chicago, and she remained in Mississippi. The eventual decline of their marriage mirrored the decline in Sullivan's fortunes. Between 1903 and 1909, Sullivan completed only five buildings. Not only was Sullivan increasingly depressed, he seemed to have been drinking heavily, a fault that, according to some, had plagued him for most of his life. These and other factors—including the fact that Sullivan moved to cheaper and cheaper apartments as his fortunes declined—couldn't have been pleasant for Margaret.

According to Sprague, Sullivan borrowed $5,000 against the Ocean Springs property in 1905 from Gustav Hottinger of the Northwestern Terra Cotta Company. By 1909, Sullivan was forced to sell most of his personal possessions—books, pictures, rugs, and furniture—at an auction that failed to realize what he had hoped it would. Finally, he sold his beloved summer home, for which he realized $8,500. This enabled him to repay Hottinger and provide funds to Margaret for a move to New York to pursue a career as a novelist. That effectively ended the marriage, although their divorce didn't become final until 1917.

Ironically, the few commissions that Sullivan received after 1909—mostly small-town banks—have come to be widely admired. They were not enough to support him, even supplemented with his continued writing. He came to depend increasingly on the generosity of his friends, including Frank Lloyd Wright, with whom Sullivan had reconciled, and Adler's son Sidney. The written pleas from Sullivan to these friends and others make painful reading, coming as they did from a man who had been recognized as one of America's greatest architects.

Sullivan spent his last years working to finish his autobiography (*The Autobiography of an Idea*) and *A System of Architectural Ornament*, both published by the press of the American Institute of Architects. At the urging of his friends, copies were rushed to Sullivan, arriving on April 11, 1924, three days before he died at the age of sixty-seven. He died penniless. His debts and funeral expenses were paid by his friends, who also paid for the headstone that marks his grave and expresses their respect for him.

HOUSING A GROWING CHICAGO

Frank Lloyd Wright gave the impression in his *Autobiography* that Louis Sullivan turned over residential commissions to Wright because Sullivan wasn't interested in them. Like much of what Wright wrote about his early career, it was typically self-serving and misleading. While Wright may (the word is used advisedly) have indeed been given wide latitude to design residences like the famous Charnley House, the reason was more because Sullivan was busy with major commissions and simply couldn't do all the work himself.

In fact, prior to when Wright joined the firm, Adler & Sullivan designed more houses and other residential buildings (nearly sixty) than any other type. With the success of the Auditorium Building, the firm did not seek residential commissions as aggressively, since Adler and Sullivan correctly felt that more important work could be had.

In a list included in Professor Robert Twombly's biography, his first such design was for a residence for John Borden in 1880. As we shall see, these designs along with the majority of the architect's residences were subsequently demolished. Indeed, of the slightly more than sixty single-family and multiple-unit residences that Sullivan designed, fewer than ten remain standing today, including his last built residence, the 1909 Harold Bradley House in Madison, Wisconsin.

The location of the residences is one simple reason so many of them have been lost. Many of Adler & Sullivan's clients in the 1880s were part of Chicago's South Side German-Jewish community whom Adler knew through his religious and social relationships. These neighborhoods experienced complex changes in demographics and economic resources during the 20th century, with the majority demolished for construction of the Illinois Institute of Technology campus or destroyed as part of mid-century urban renewal projects.

With a few exceptions, most of Adler & Sullivan's residences were what would now be called town or row houses and were separated from their next-door neighbors by little more than a party wall or narrow gangway, so Sullivan had to design only the front and rear façades. While his designs were mostly tasteful and even pleasing, they did not often stand out from the work of other architects who did similar housing. Their ornamental exuberance, however, often stood out in the streetscape.

The Charnley House of 1891, which will be shown in some detail, was a departure from what came before, just as the Wainwright Building in St. Louis signaled a new and higher level of accomplishment in office building design for Adler & Sullivan. It is a pity, then, that in the last thirty years of his career, Sullivan was able to construct only two more residences: the 1908 Babson House in Riverside, Illinois, which was later demolished, and the surviving 1909 Bradley House in Madison, Wisconsin, both of which are shown with his later work in the book's final section.

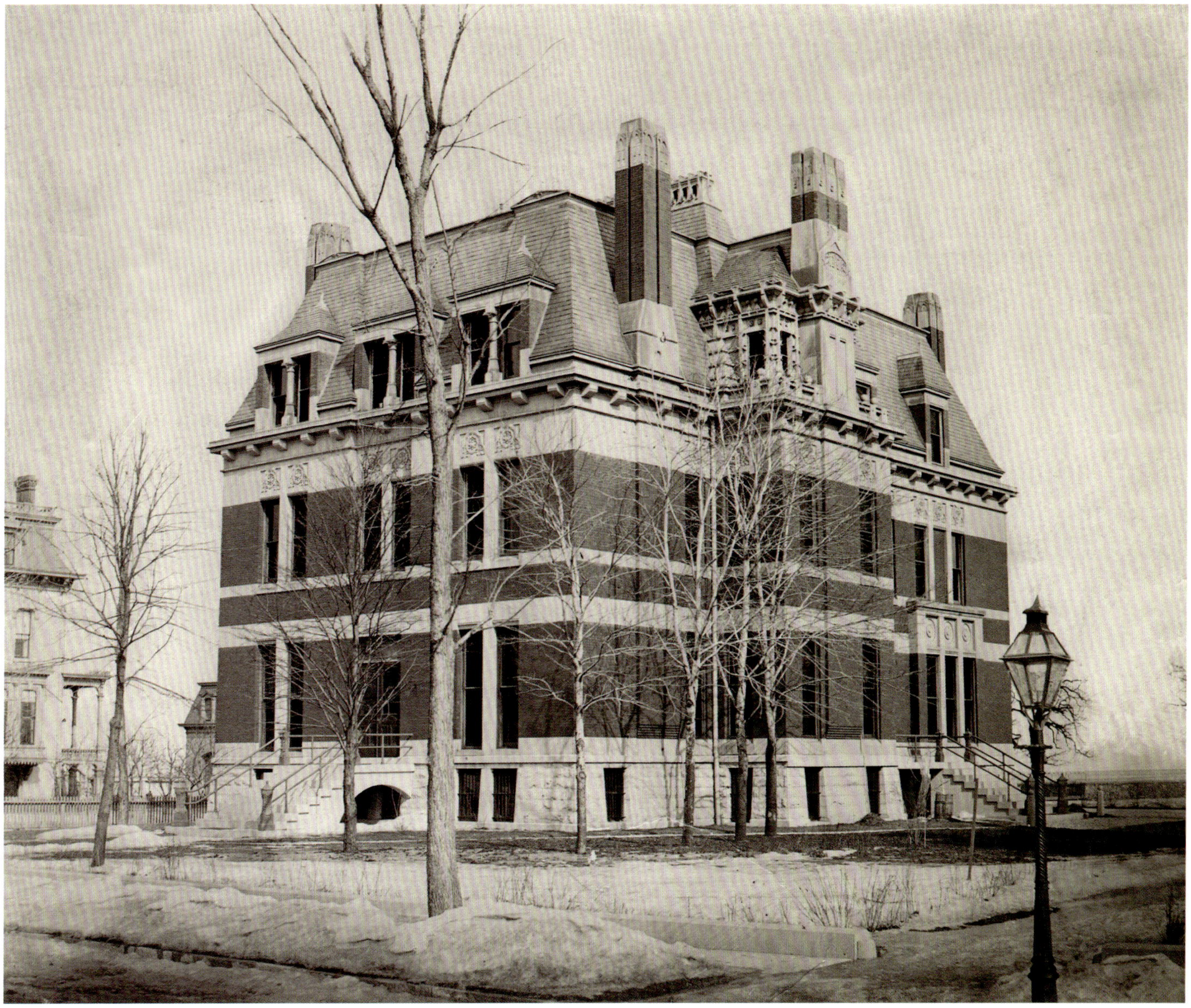

The John Borden House (Chicago, 1880) was one of Dankmar Adler, Architect's largest residential commissions for which Sullivan, not yet a partner, acted as designer. It later led to a commission for the downtown Borden Block. Photograph courtesy Chicago History Museum.

ANN HALSTED HOUSE

1883, CHICAGO

The Ann Halsted House, which is Adler & Sullivan's only remaining free-standing house in Chicago, occupies a generous lot in the Lincoln Park neighborhood. The client was the widow of a major Great Lakes ship owner, and she made it clear that she didn't want too much ornamentation. Thus, on the symmetrical façade, with its arched windows and entrance, exterior decoration is restrained, limited to the cornice and roof dormer, whose fan finial is repeated in the living room fireplace.

The project began while the firm was still Dankmar Adler & Company; by the time work was finished, the firm had become Adler & Sullivan. Halsted lived in the house for nearly fifty years until she died in 1931. In 1973, the house was added to the National Register of Historic Places.

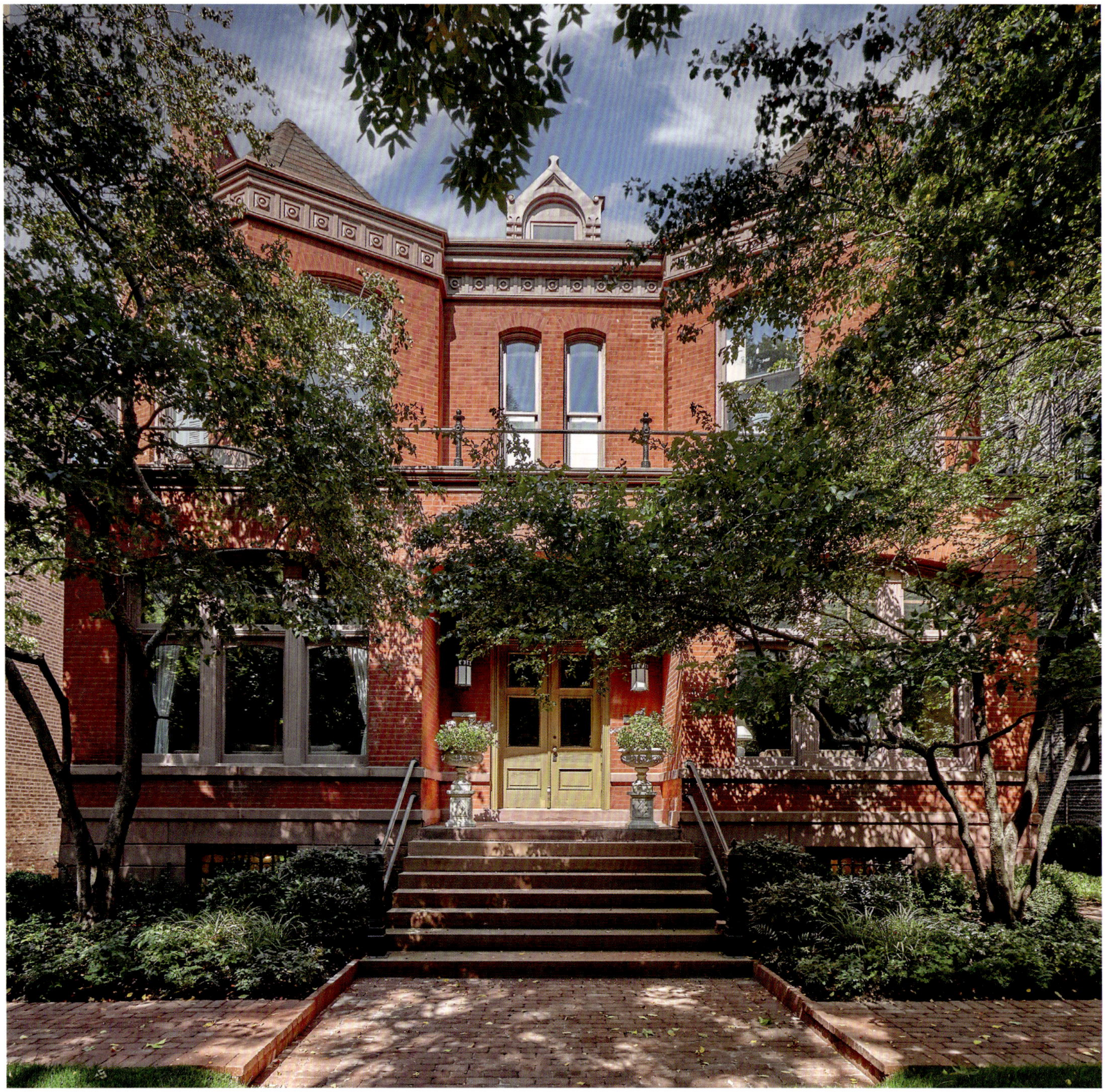

OPPOSITE: *This view from the living room to the front hall shows the original art glass panes on the inside doors, as well as the pocket doors, which still function with very little effort.*

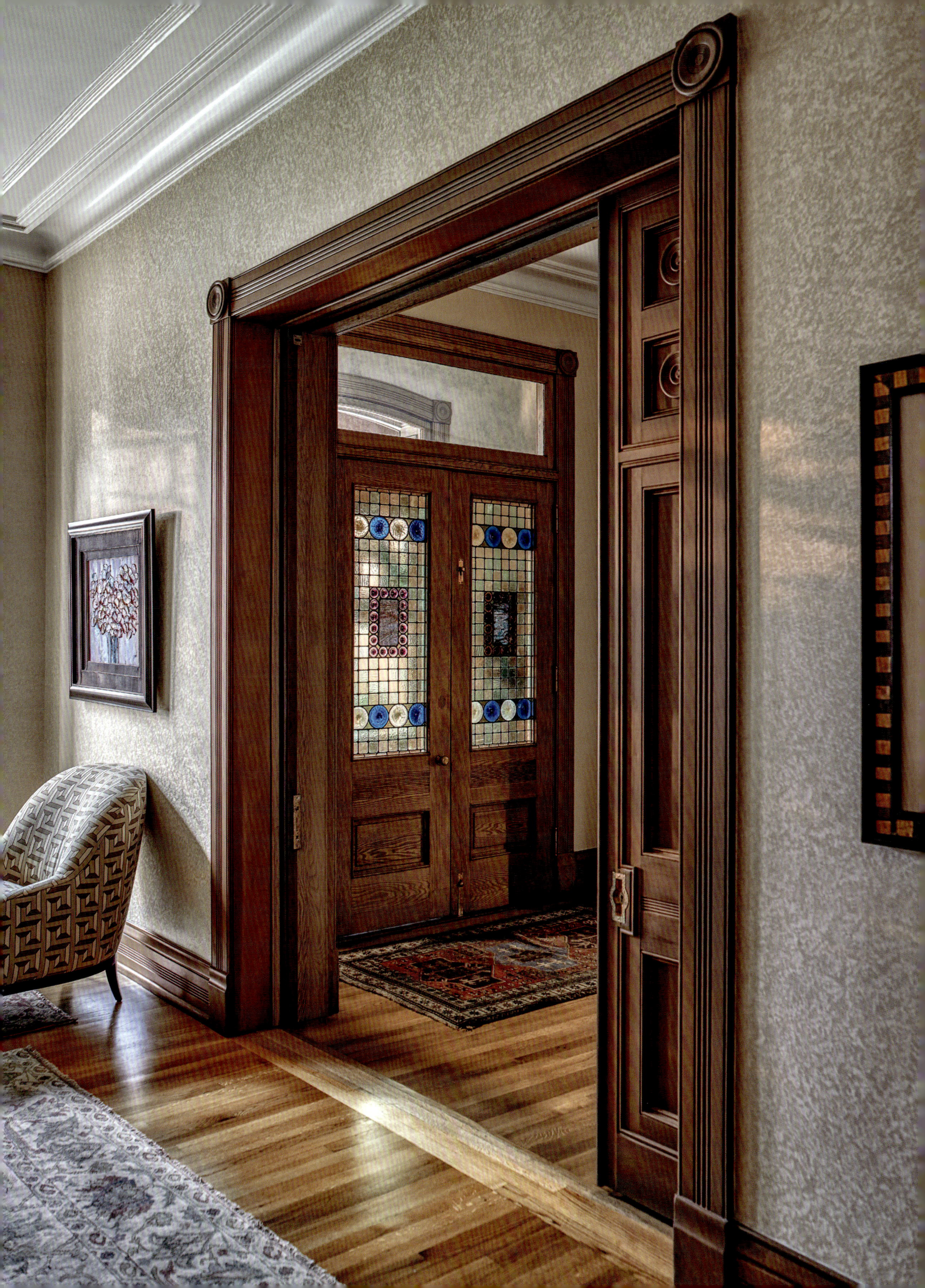

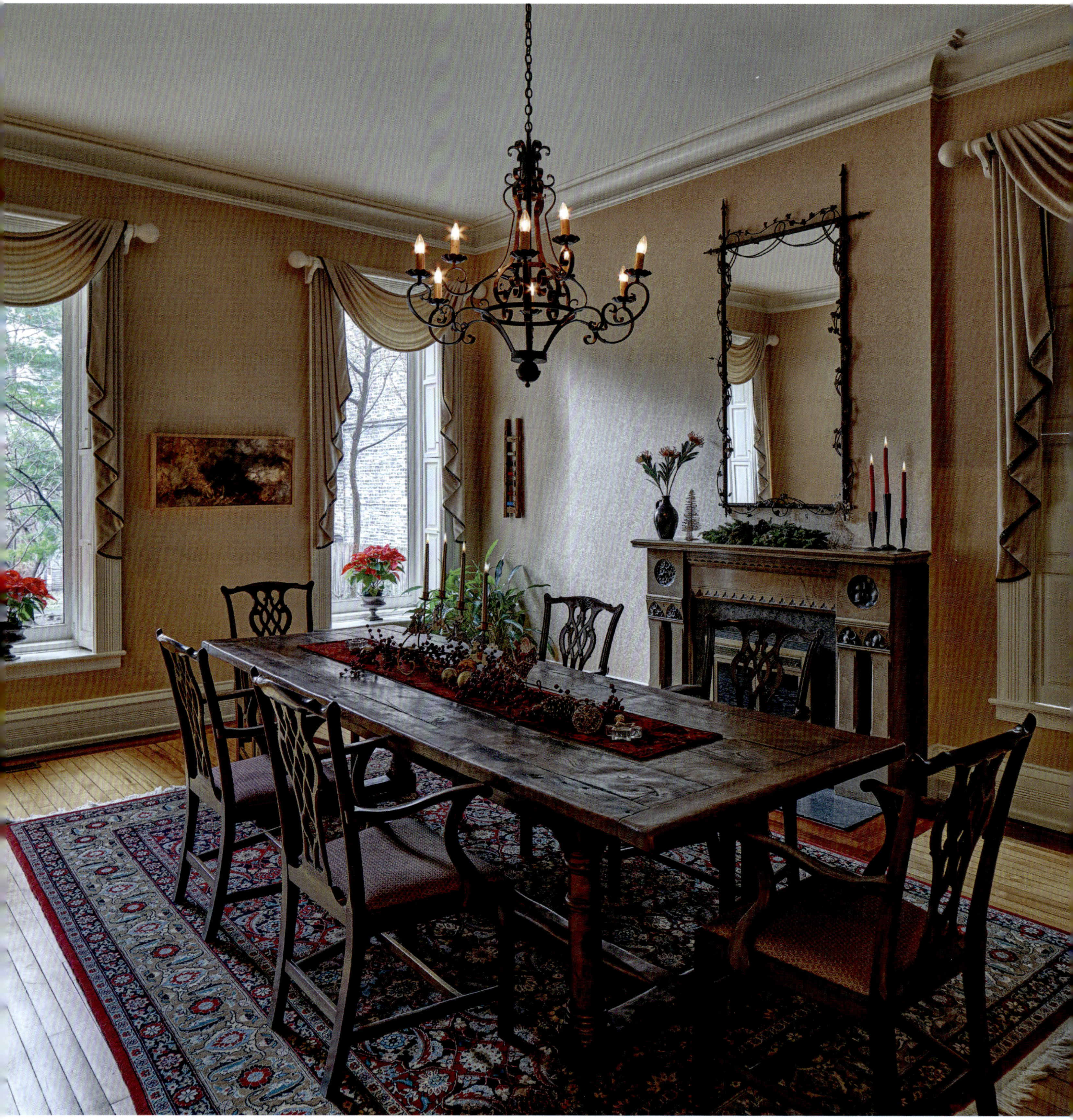

The Halsted dining room retains its original carved marble fireplace, ceiling and window trim, and floor.

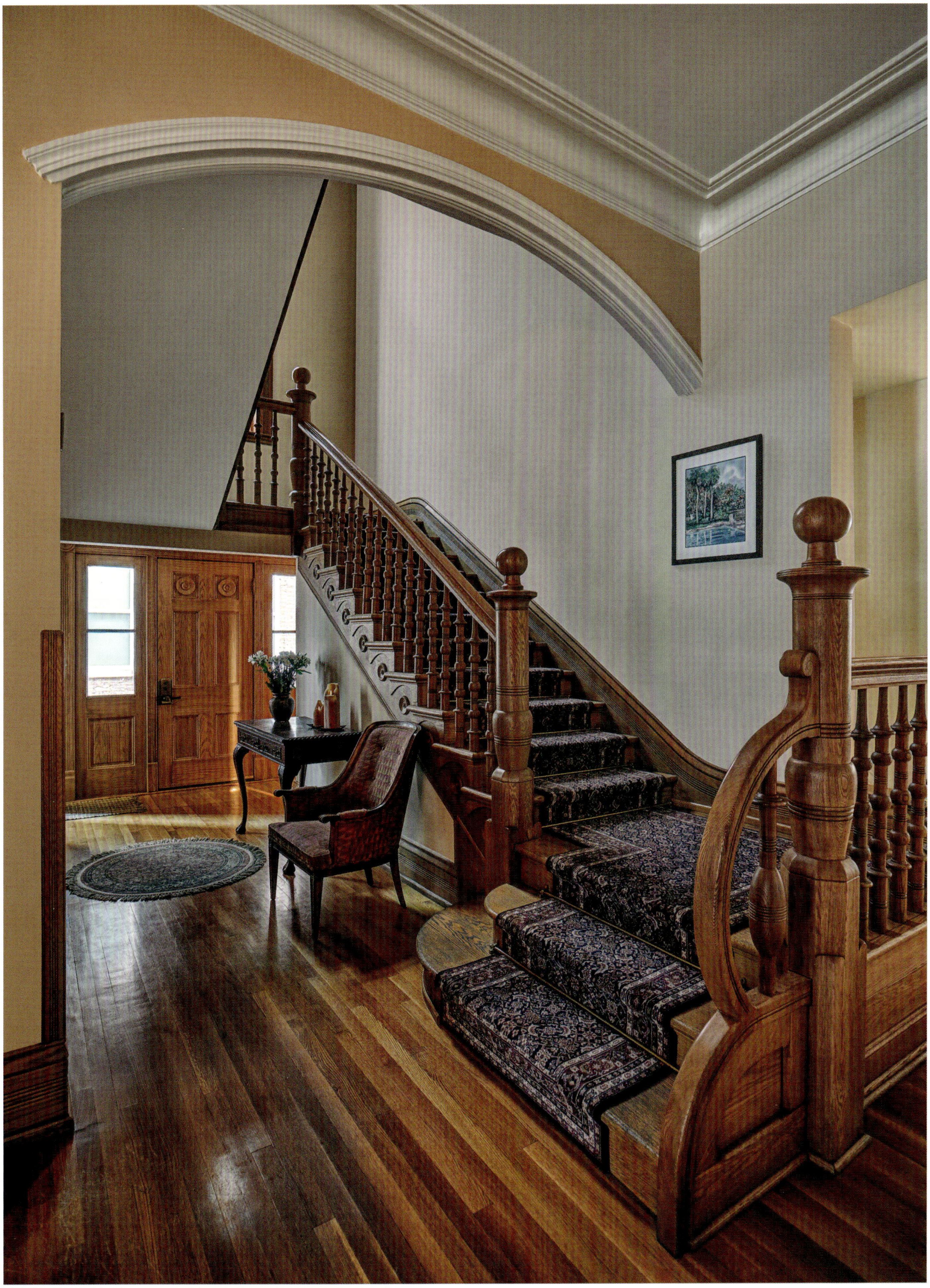

A view of the main staircase, hall, and side door.

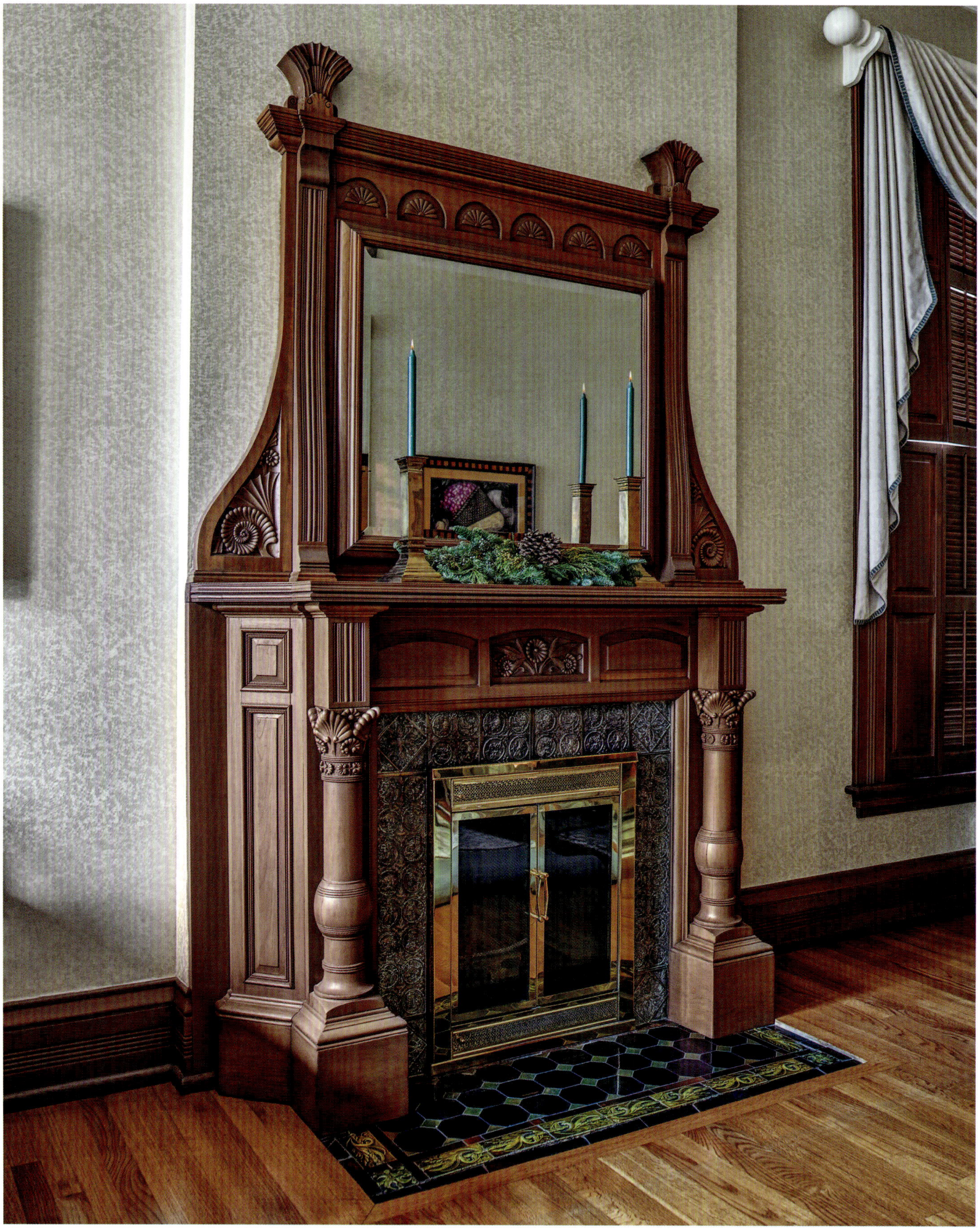

The living room fireplace includes leaf, shell, and fan motifs that are more traditional than Sullivan's later, more inventive decorations. Notice the fan finials, which are used on the exteriors on some of Sullivan's early designs.

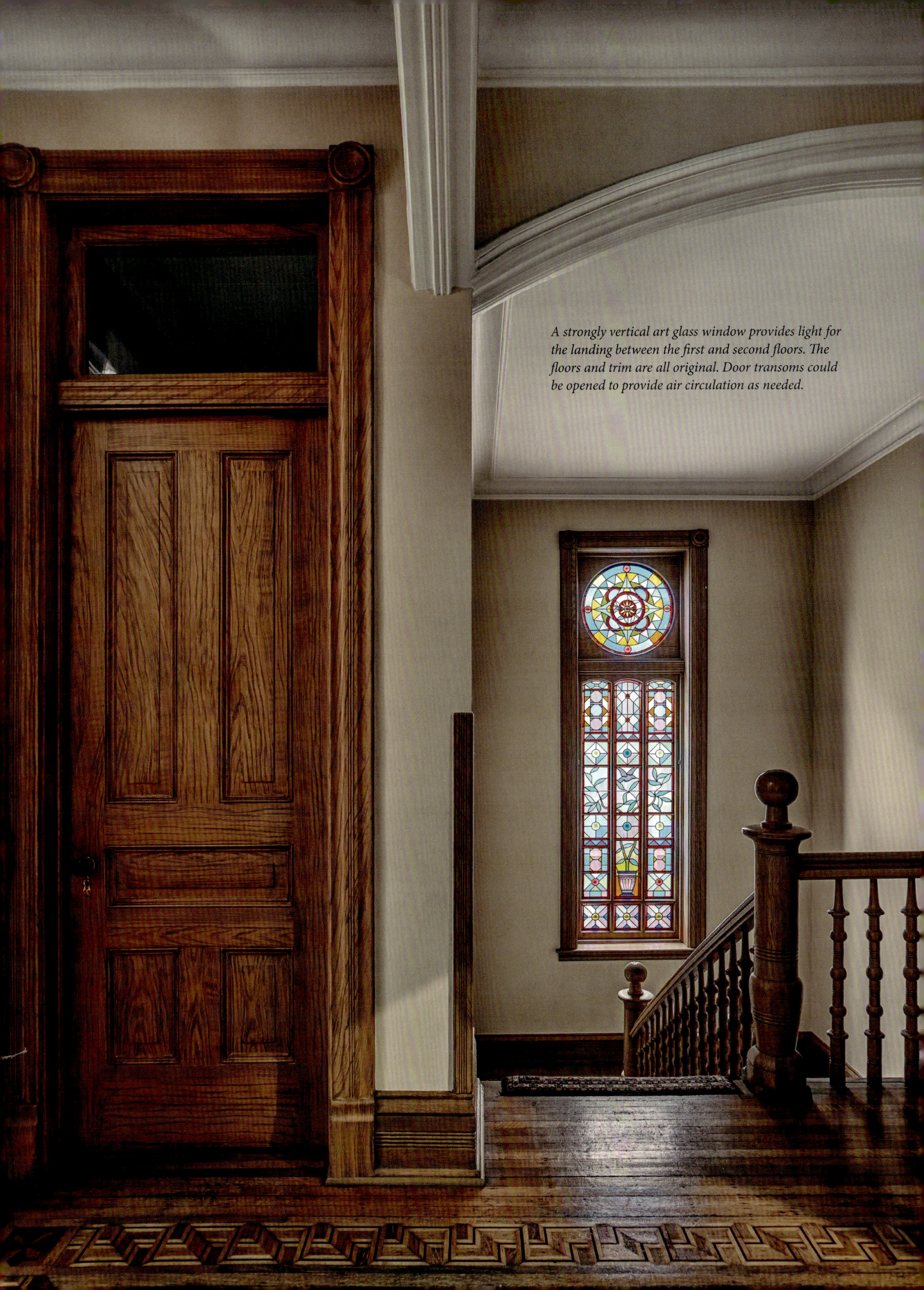

A strongly vertical art glass window provides light for the landing between the first and second floors. The floors and trim are all original. Door transoms could be opened to provide air circulation as needed.

HALSTED ROW HOUSES

1884–85, CHICAGO

Near her former home on Lincoln Park West, Halsted had Adler & Sullivan design three row houses as income properties. In contrast to the simplicity of her own home, the three had more decorative facades, expressed in brick, terra cotta, leaded glass, and decorative sheet metal.

In 1885, using the lot of her former home, she had two additional units added. They are two feet narrower than the original, although they share similar design elements. It has been assumed that they are by Adler & Sullivan, but no records exist to confirm this. Over the units' long life, interior remodelings—which included combining two units—have been made, although many original details remain, including custom-designed woodwork and cabinetry.

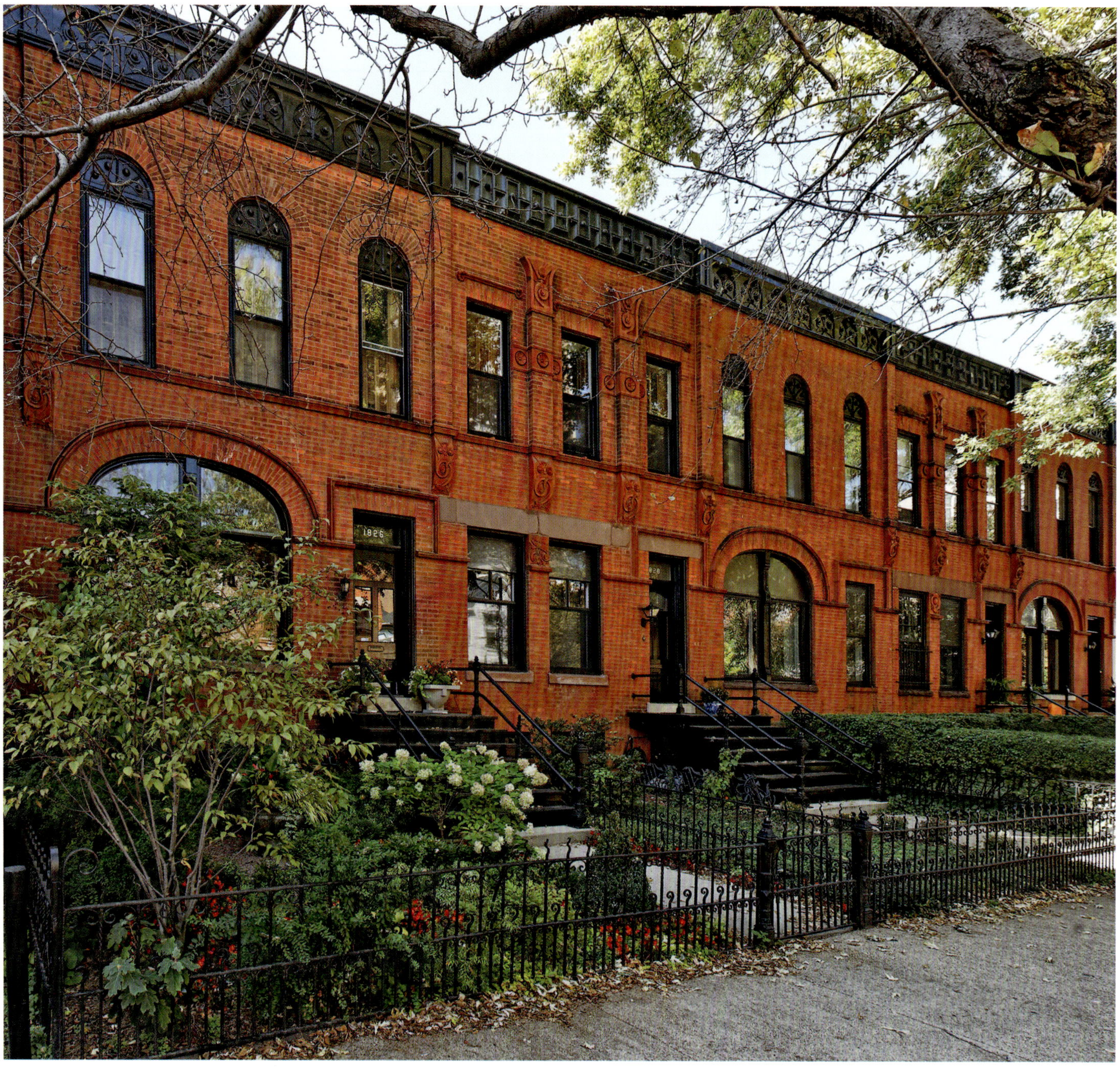

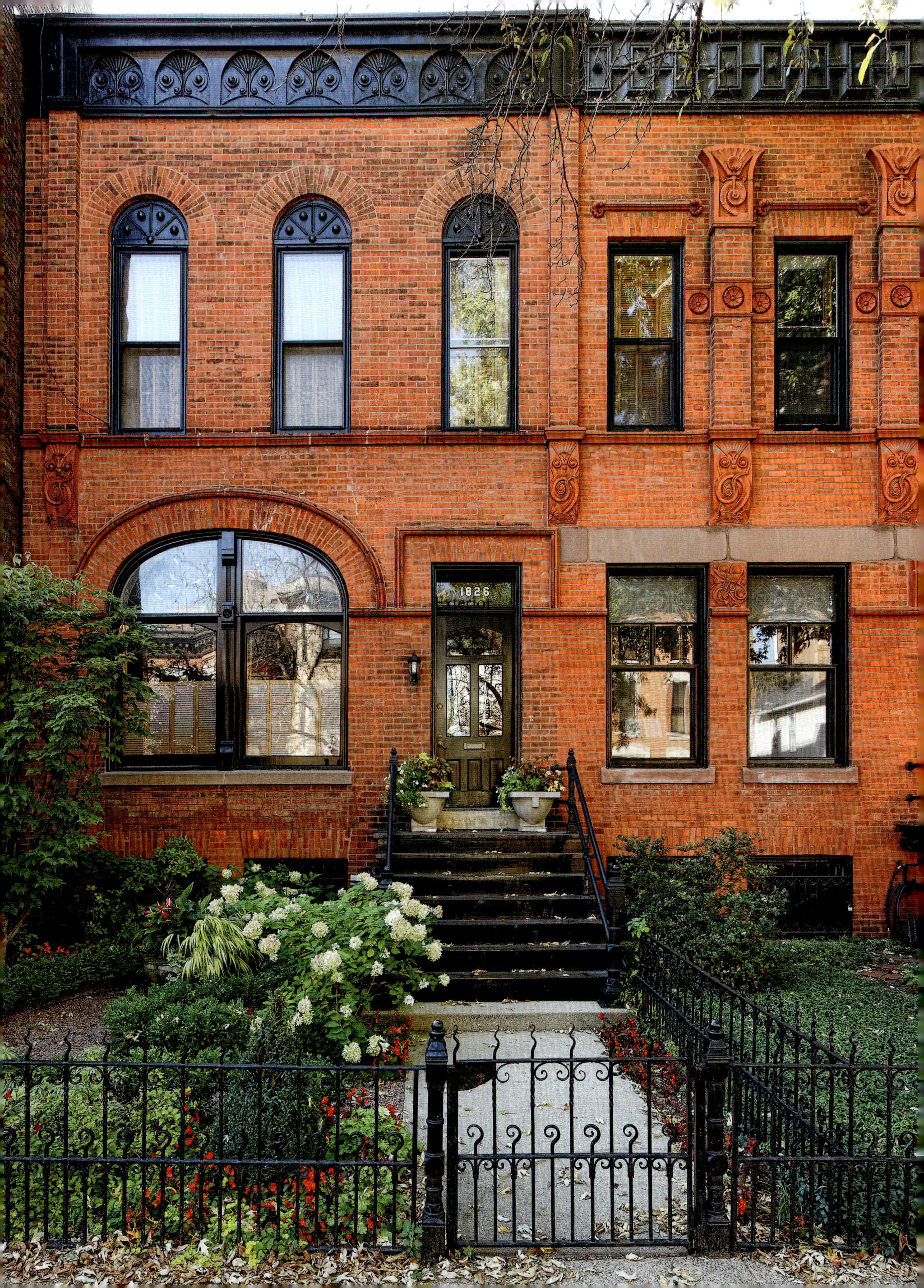
1826

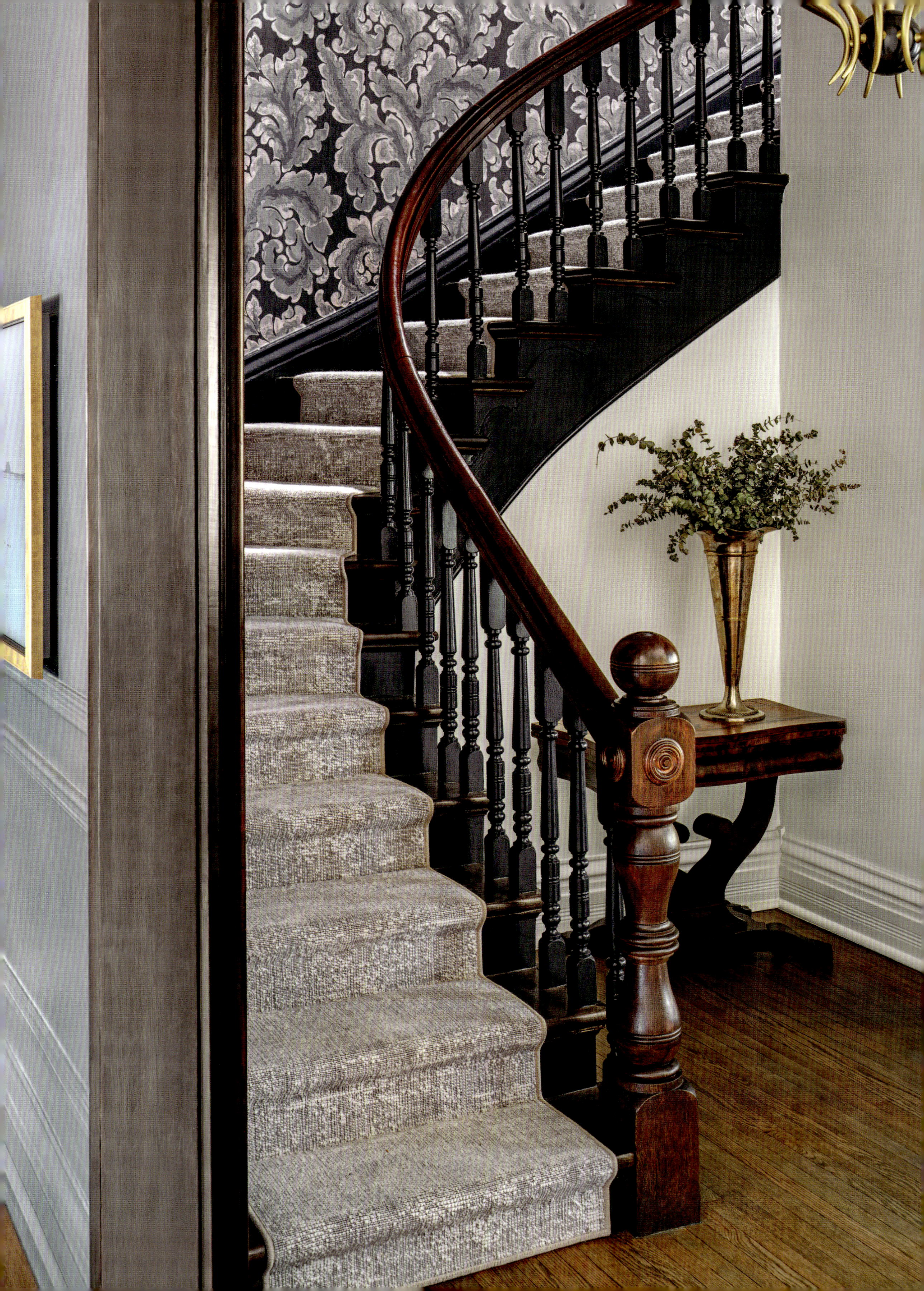

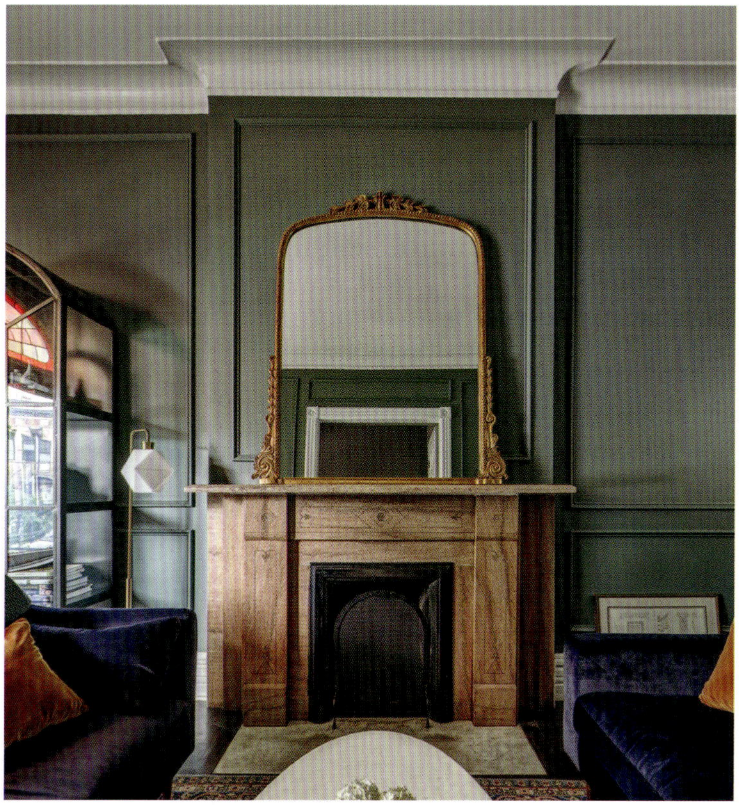

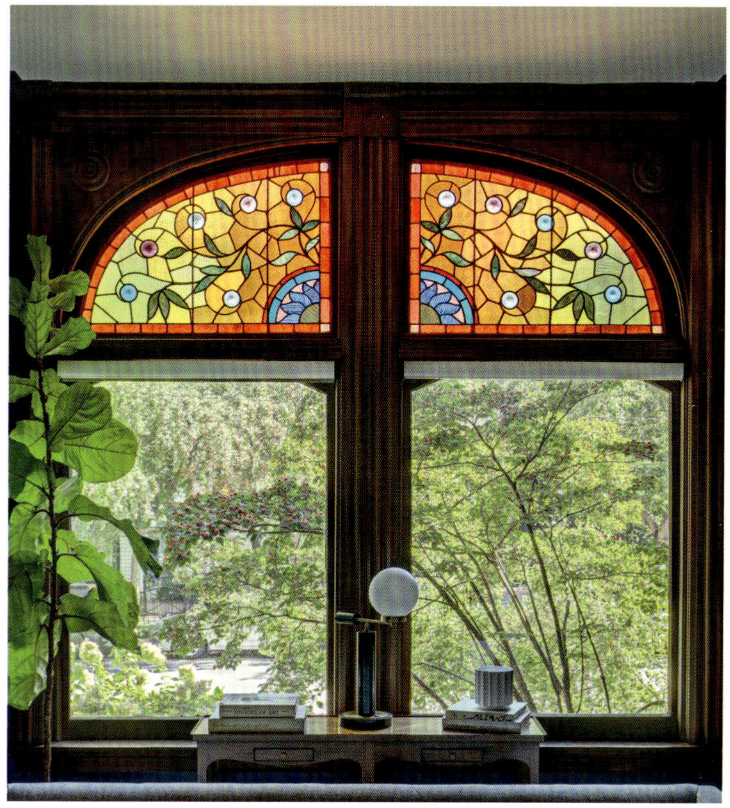

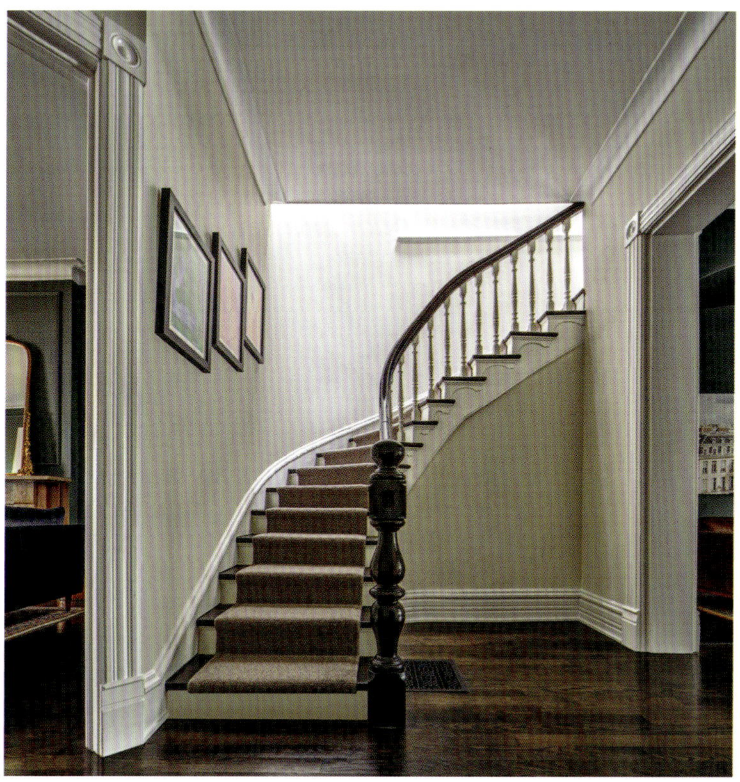

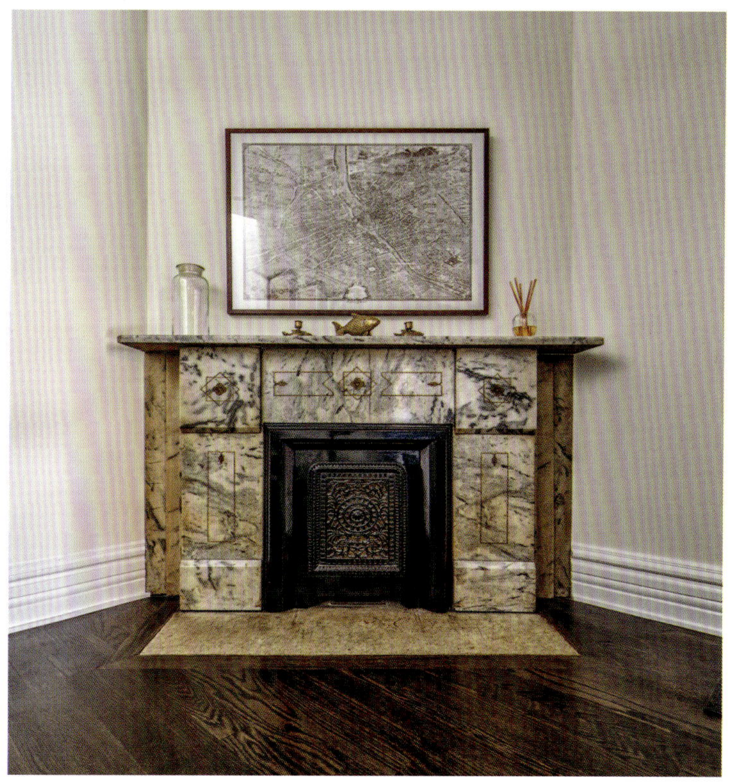

Several of the row houses retain original elements, including fireplace surrounds, art glass and the main staircase.

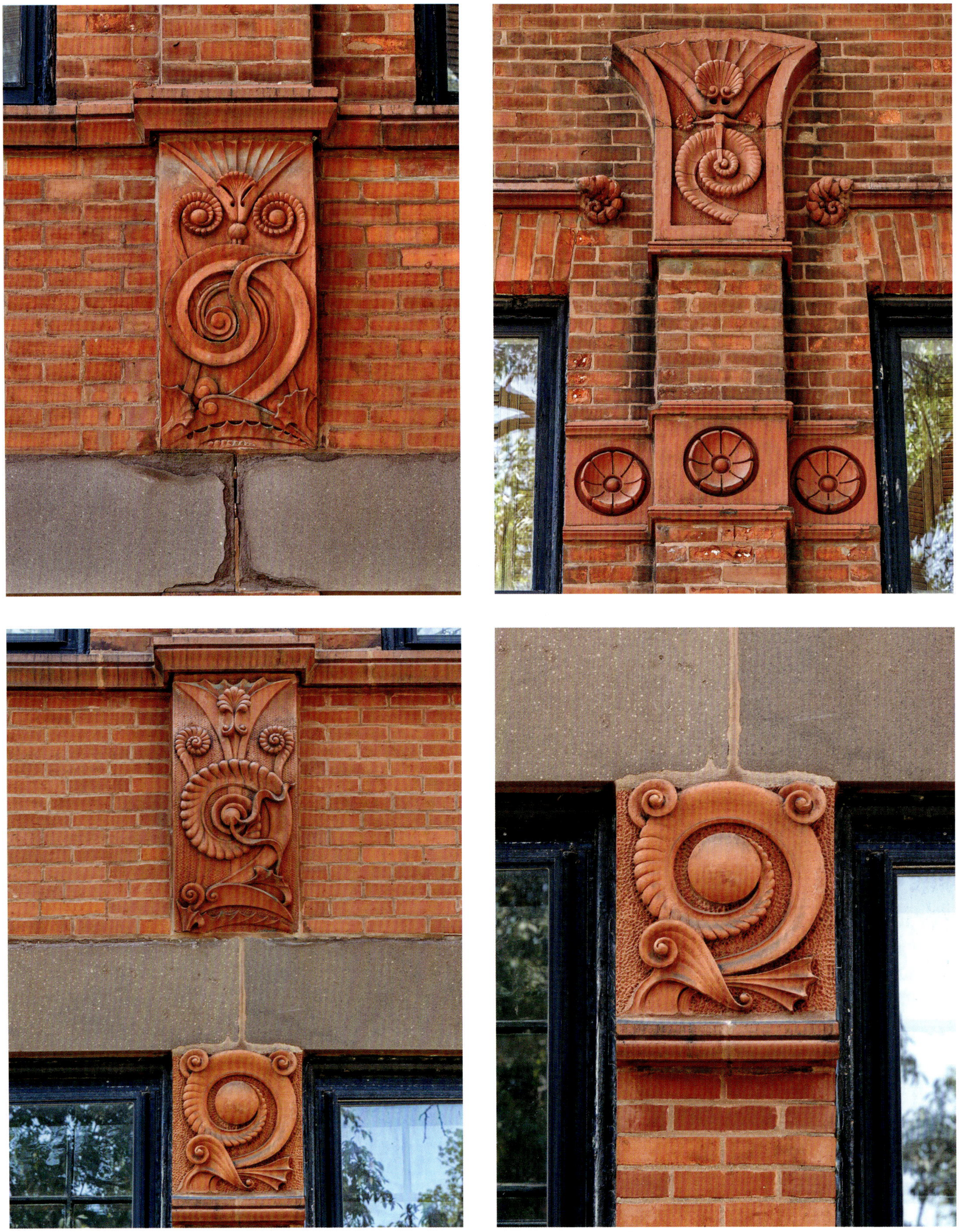

Exterior decorative elements, typical of Sullivan during this period.

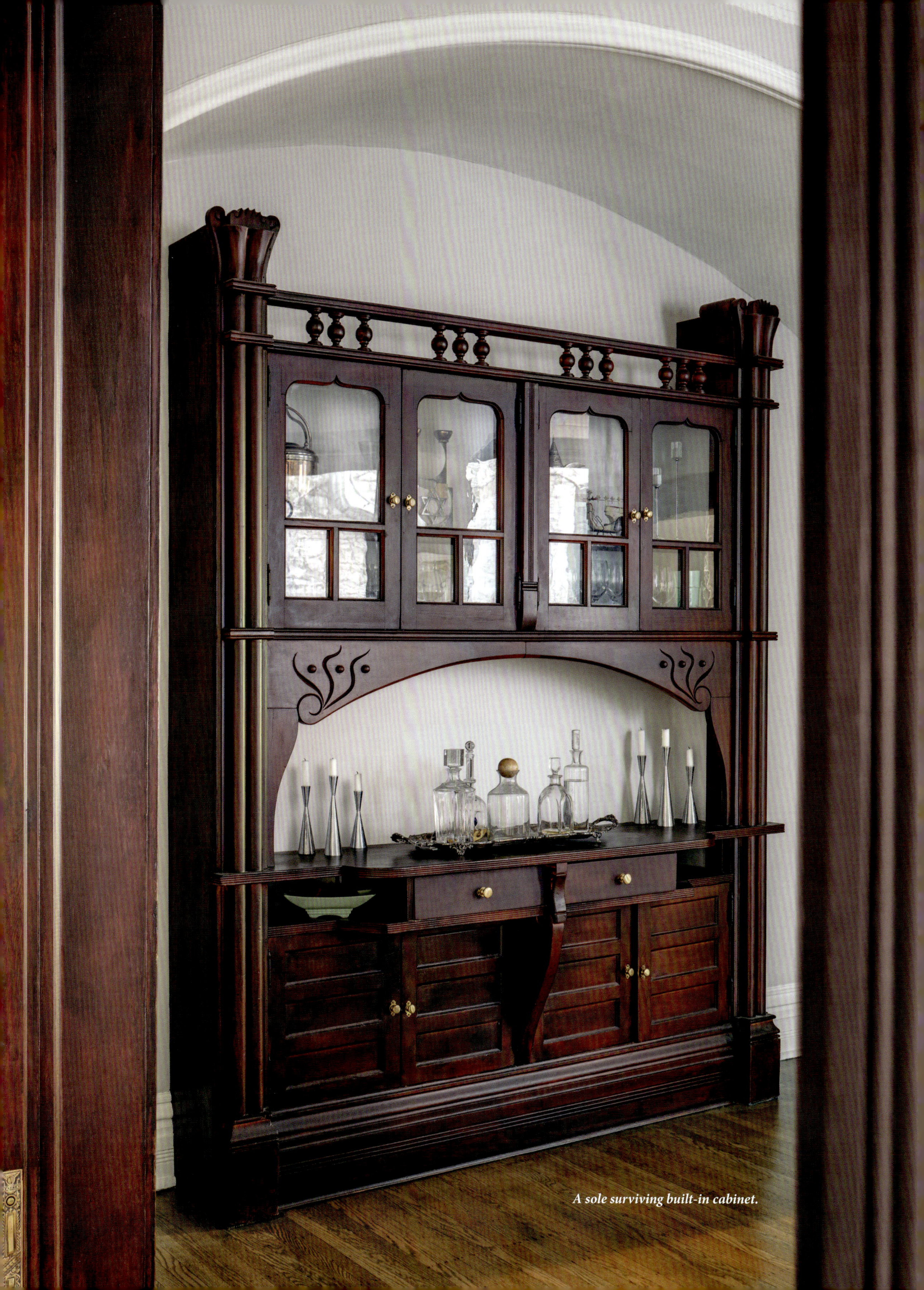

A sole surviving built-in cabinet.

LEON AND ROSE MANNHEIMER HOUSE

1884, CHICAGO

The client was a shoe merchant and an accountant whose brother-in-law, real estate developer Adolph Loeb, was a long-time client of Adler & Sullivan. The Mannheimer House has a large bay window that would have helped bring more natural light into an interior that originally would not have had electric lighting.

During this period, Sullivan was apparently smitten with fan finials. While it's impossible to know for certain some 140 years after the construction of the house, many interior details—staircase, wood trim, living room fireplace, and others—appear to be original.

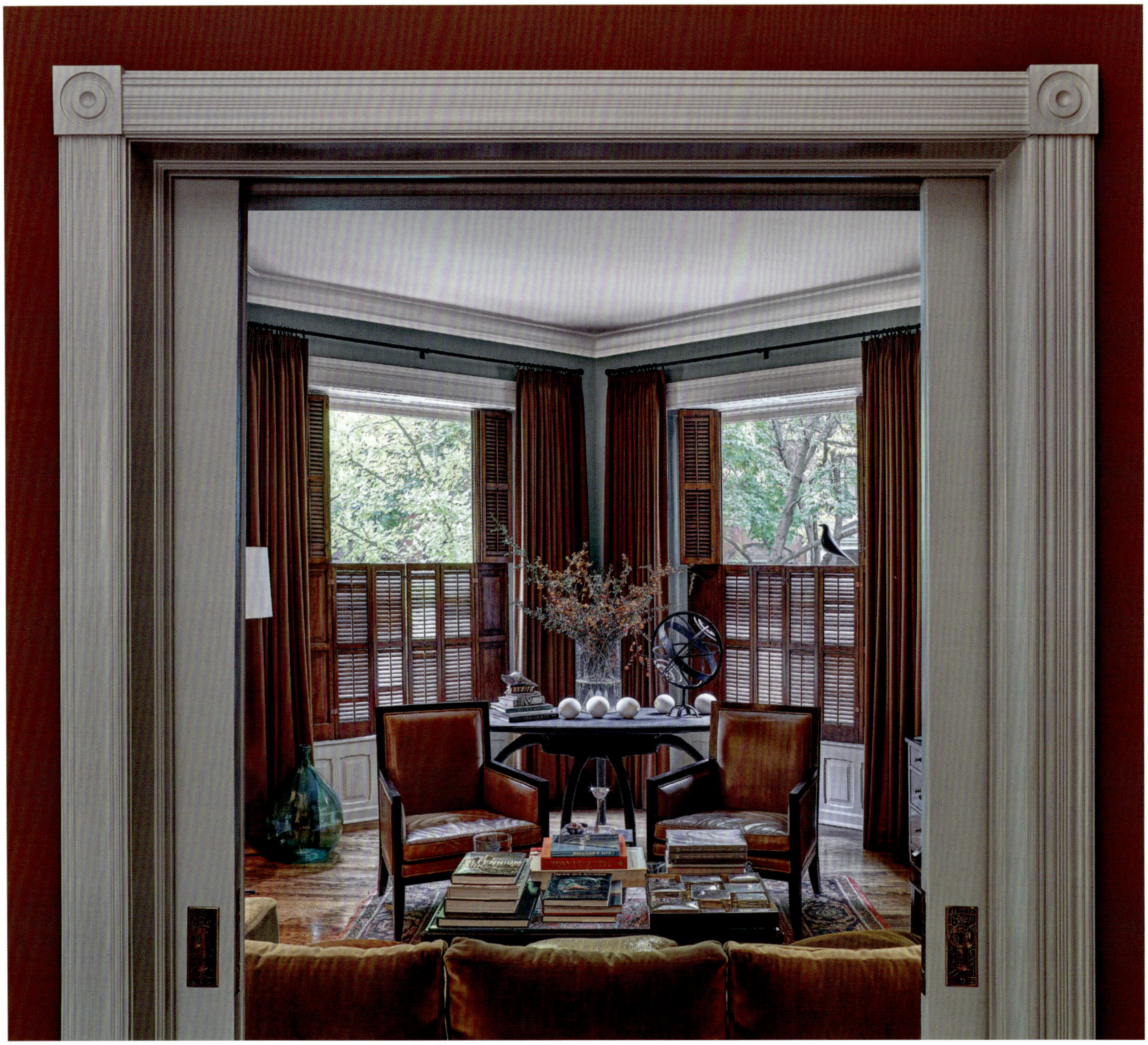

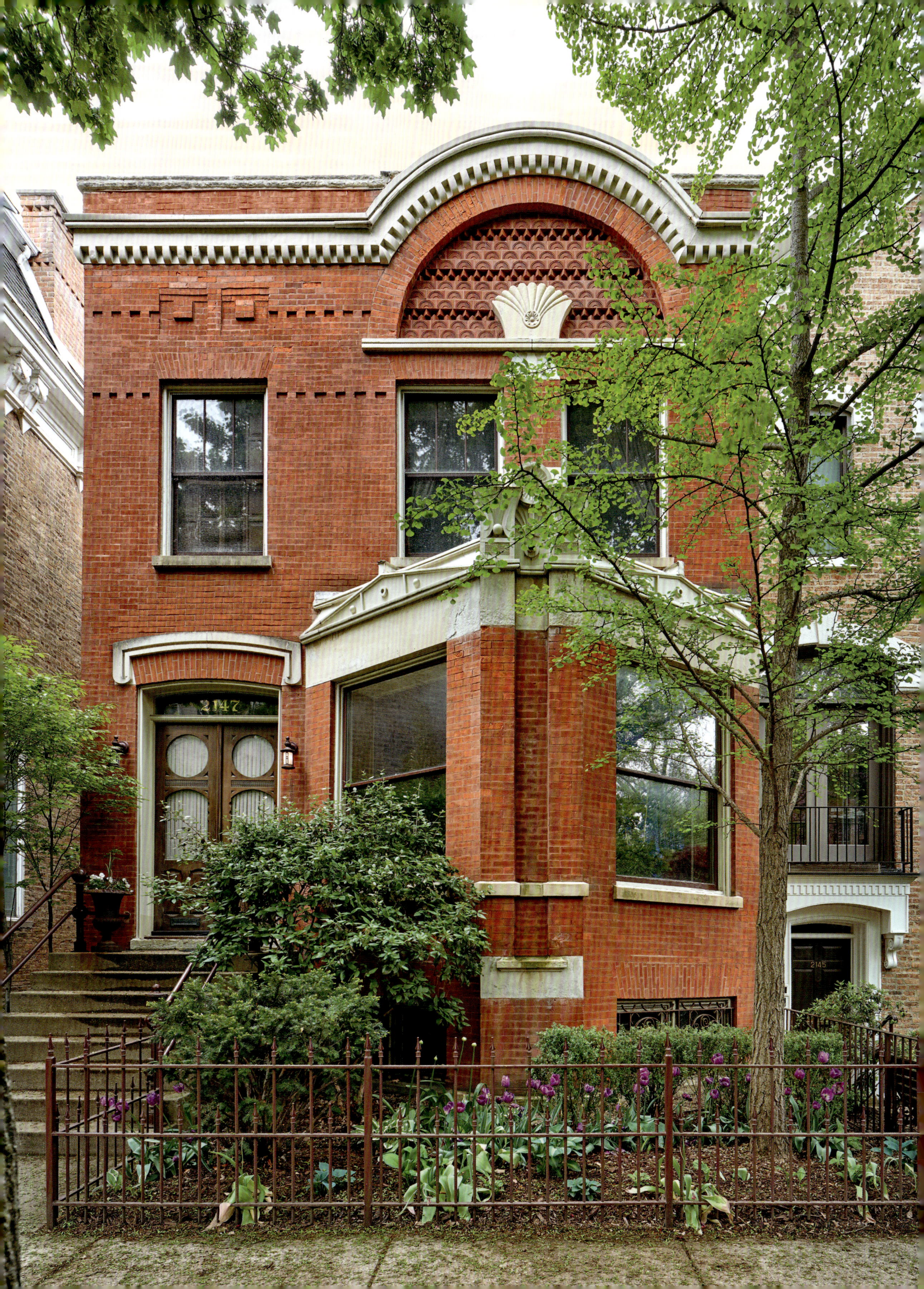
2147
2145

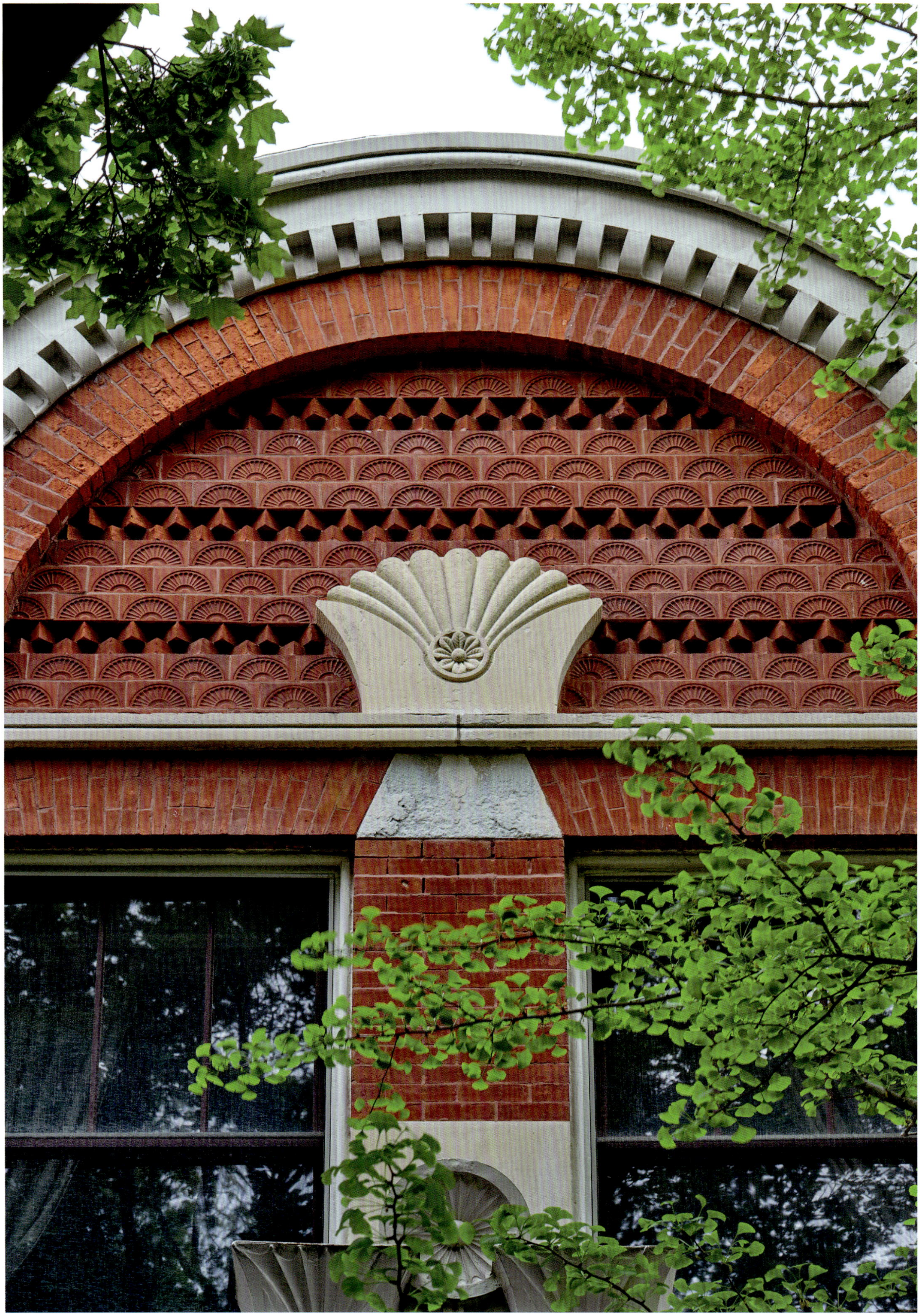

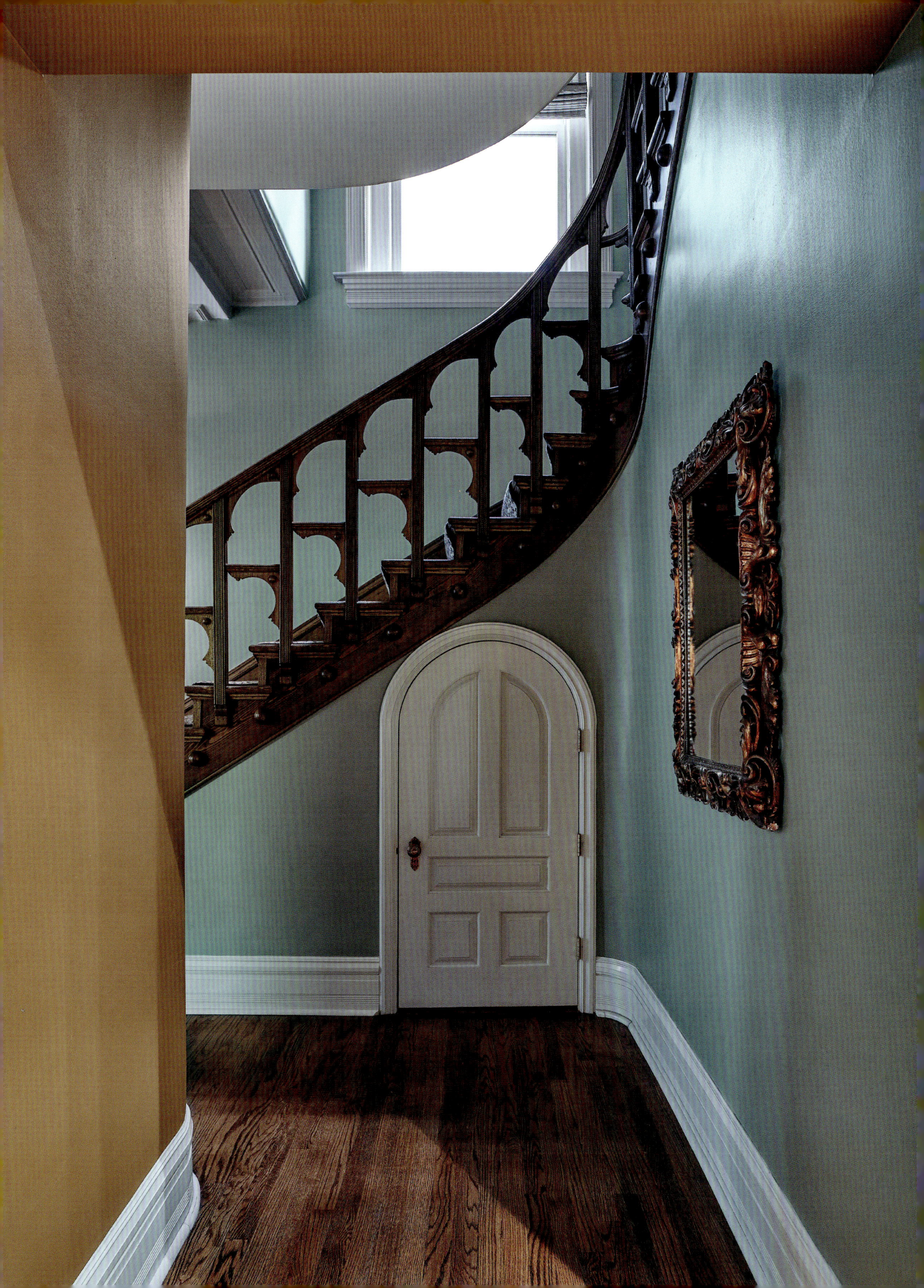

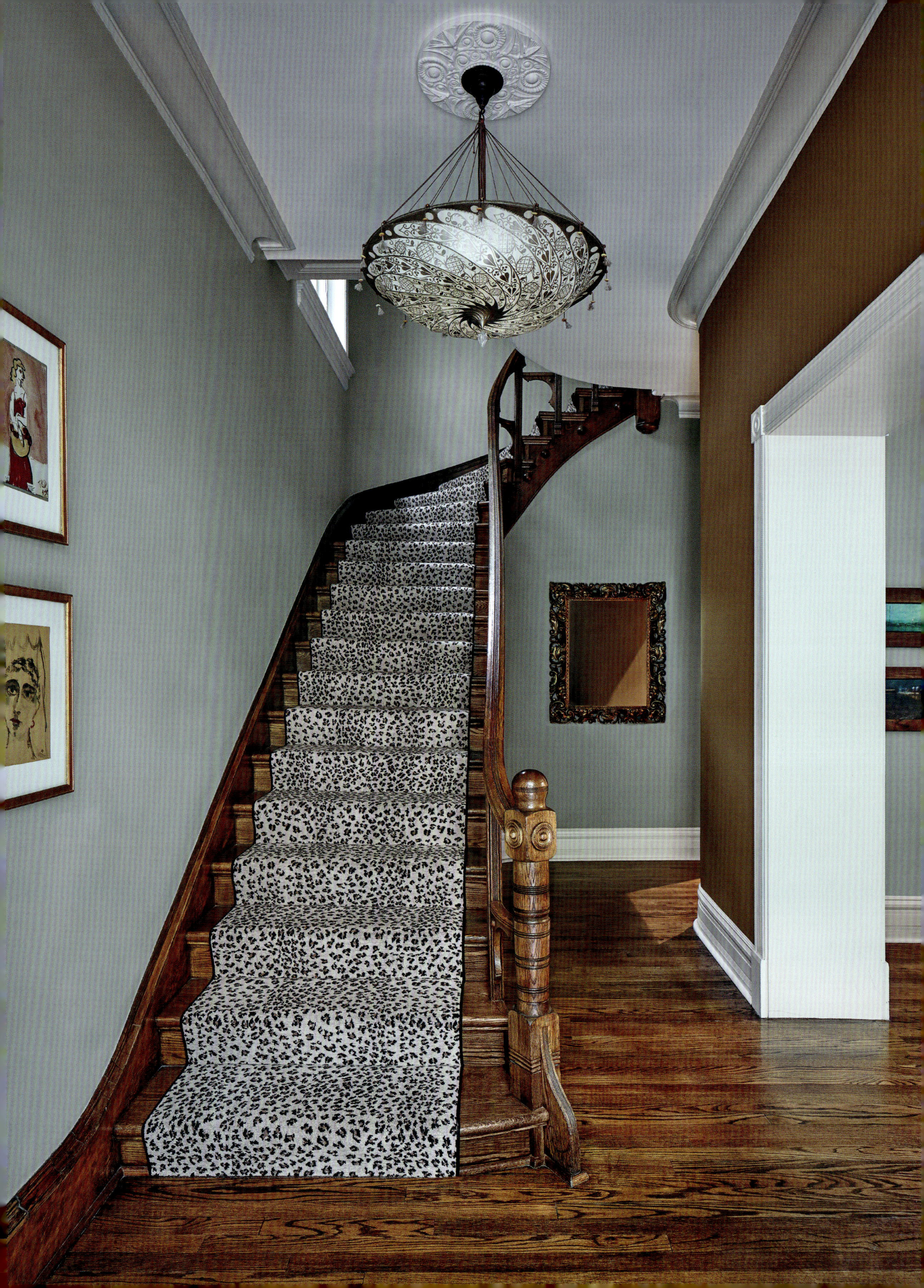

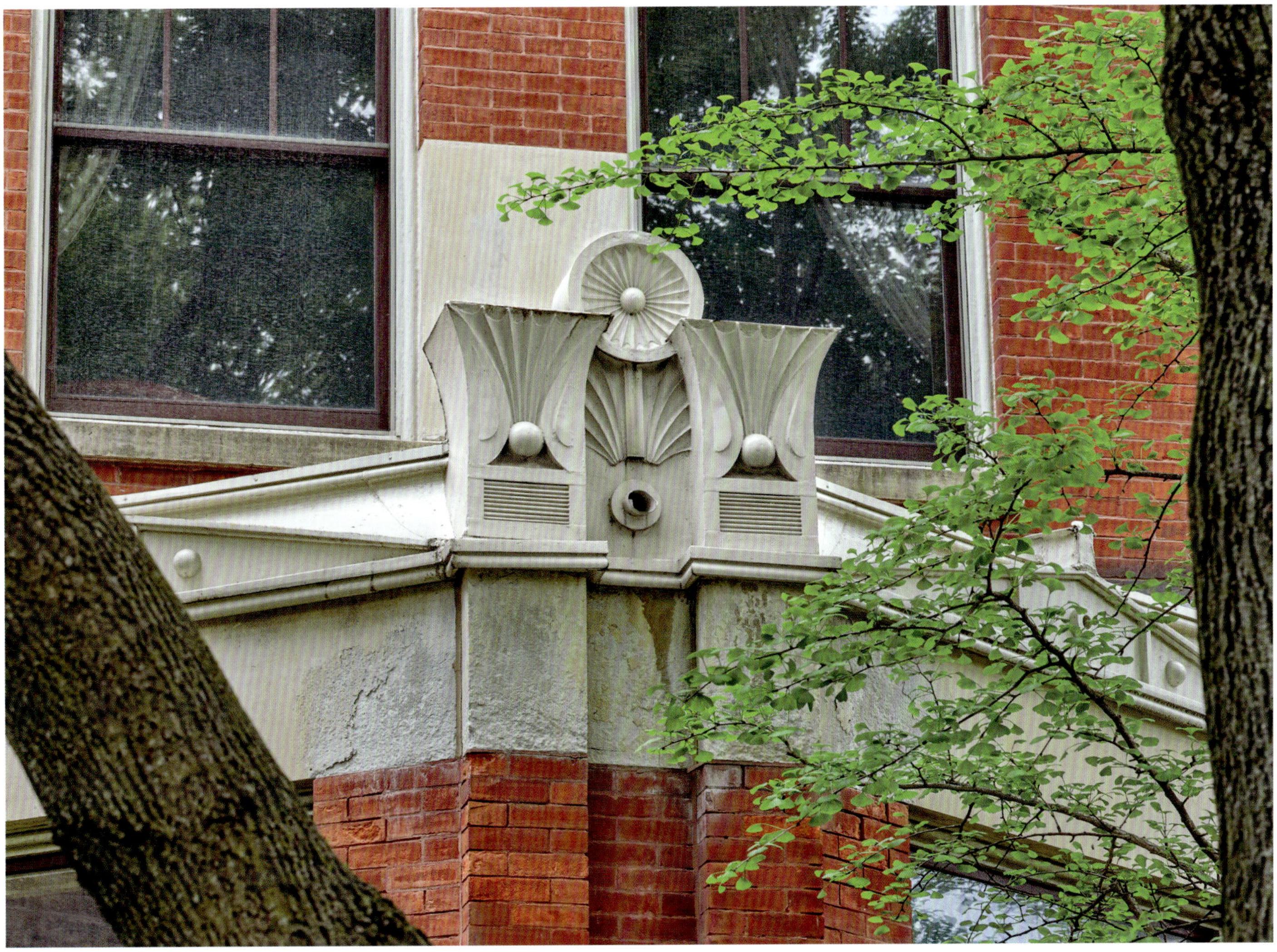

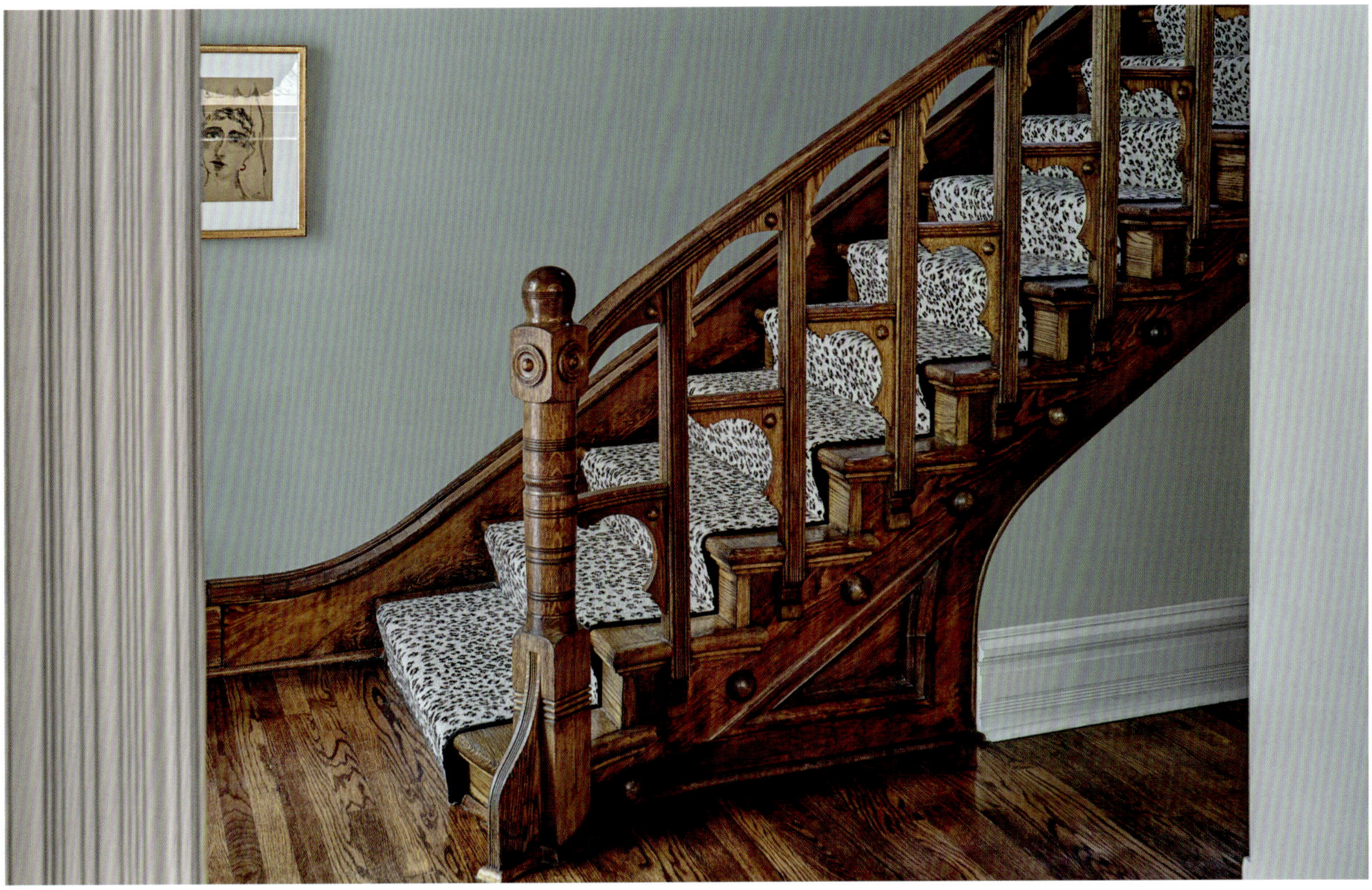

JOSEPH DEIMEL HOUSE

1886, CHICAGO

The Deimel House, like the majority of the firm's residential commissions, was located on Chicago's South Side. The red brick façade, with stone string courses, has its decorative elements limited to the porch pediment and the cornice and balustrade at the top of the two-story bay window. The house is part of Chicago's Calumet-Giles-Prairie Landmark District.

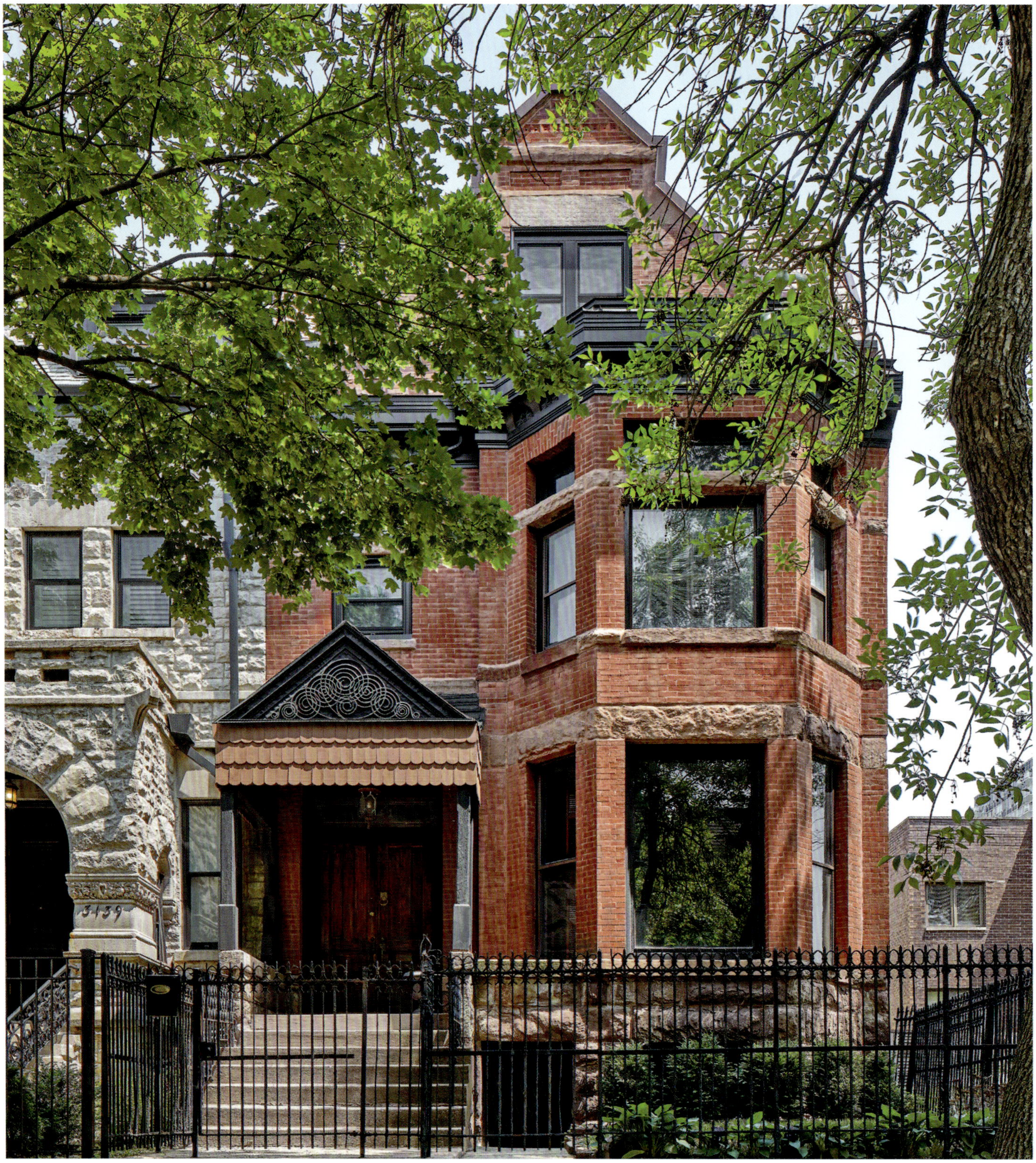

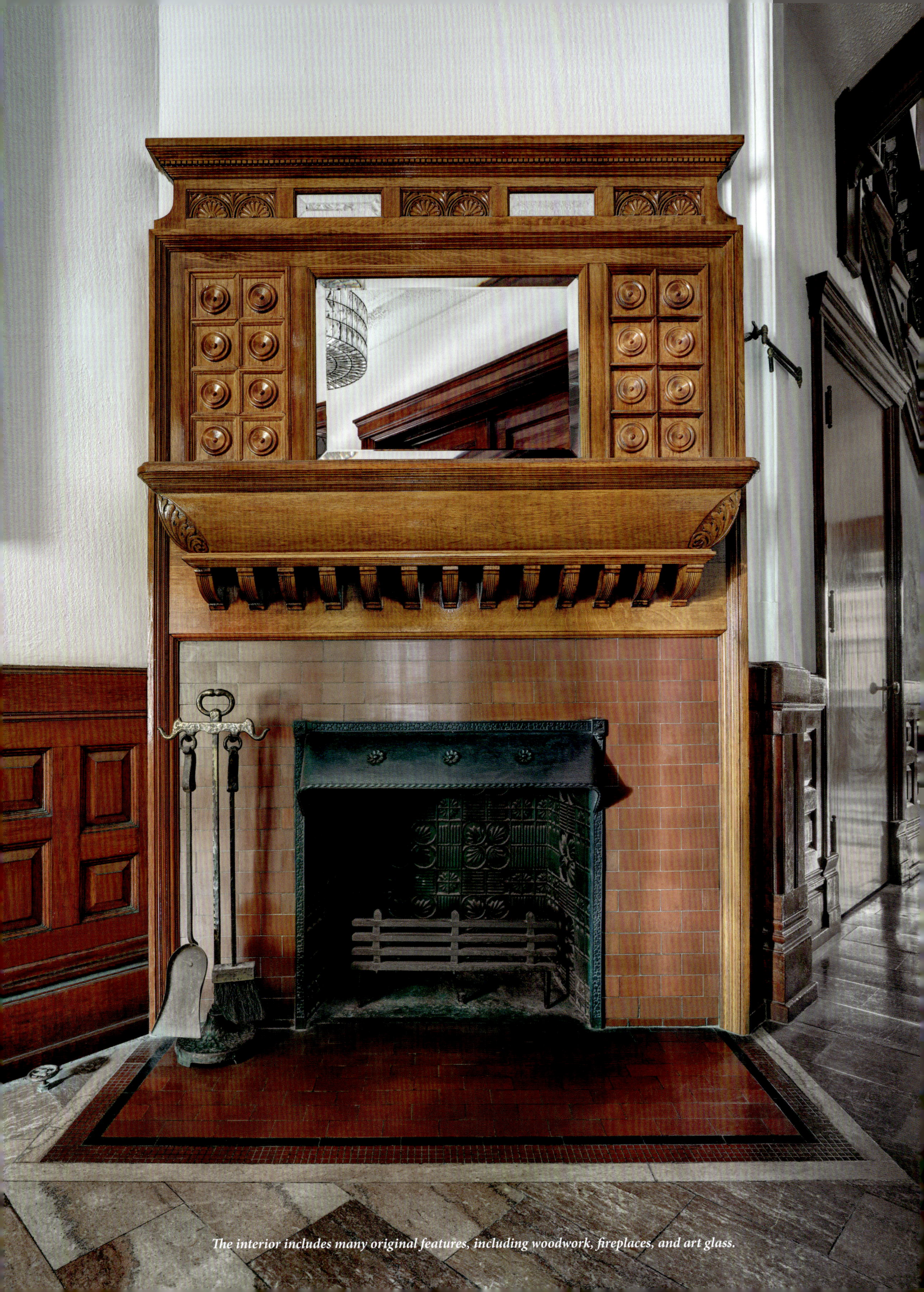

The interior includes many original features, including woodwork, fireplaces, and art glass.

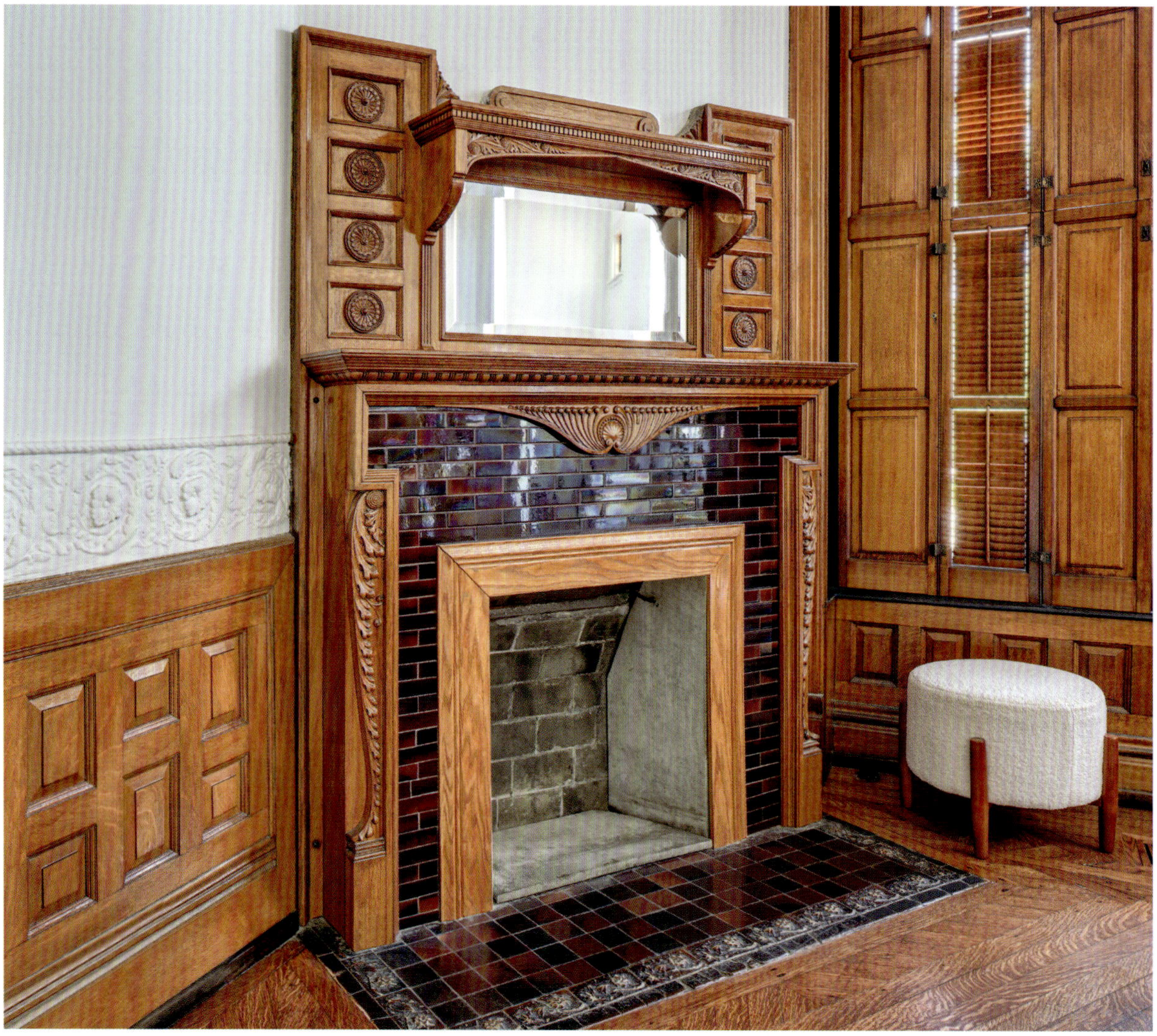

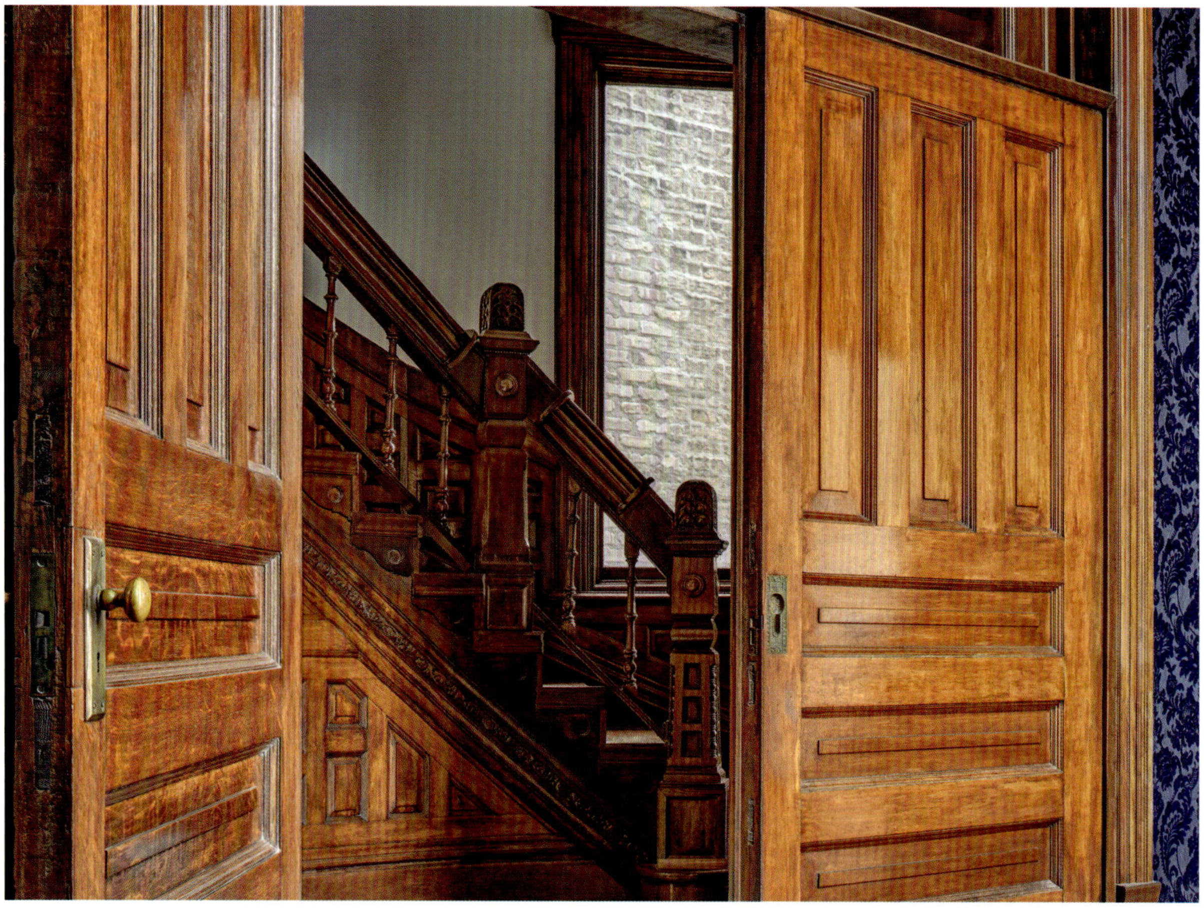

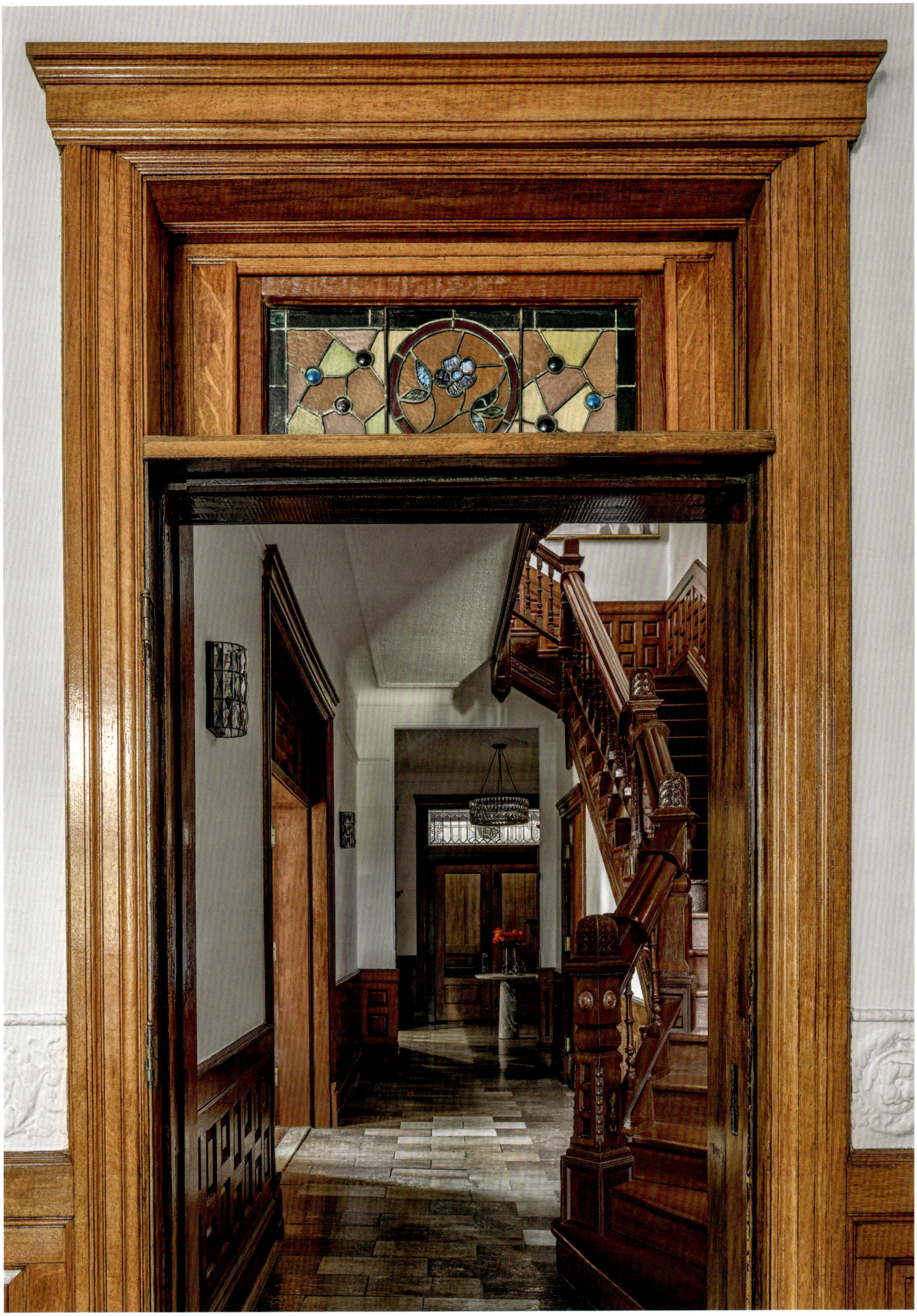

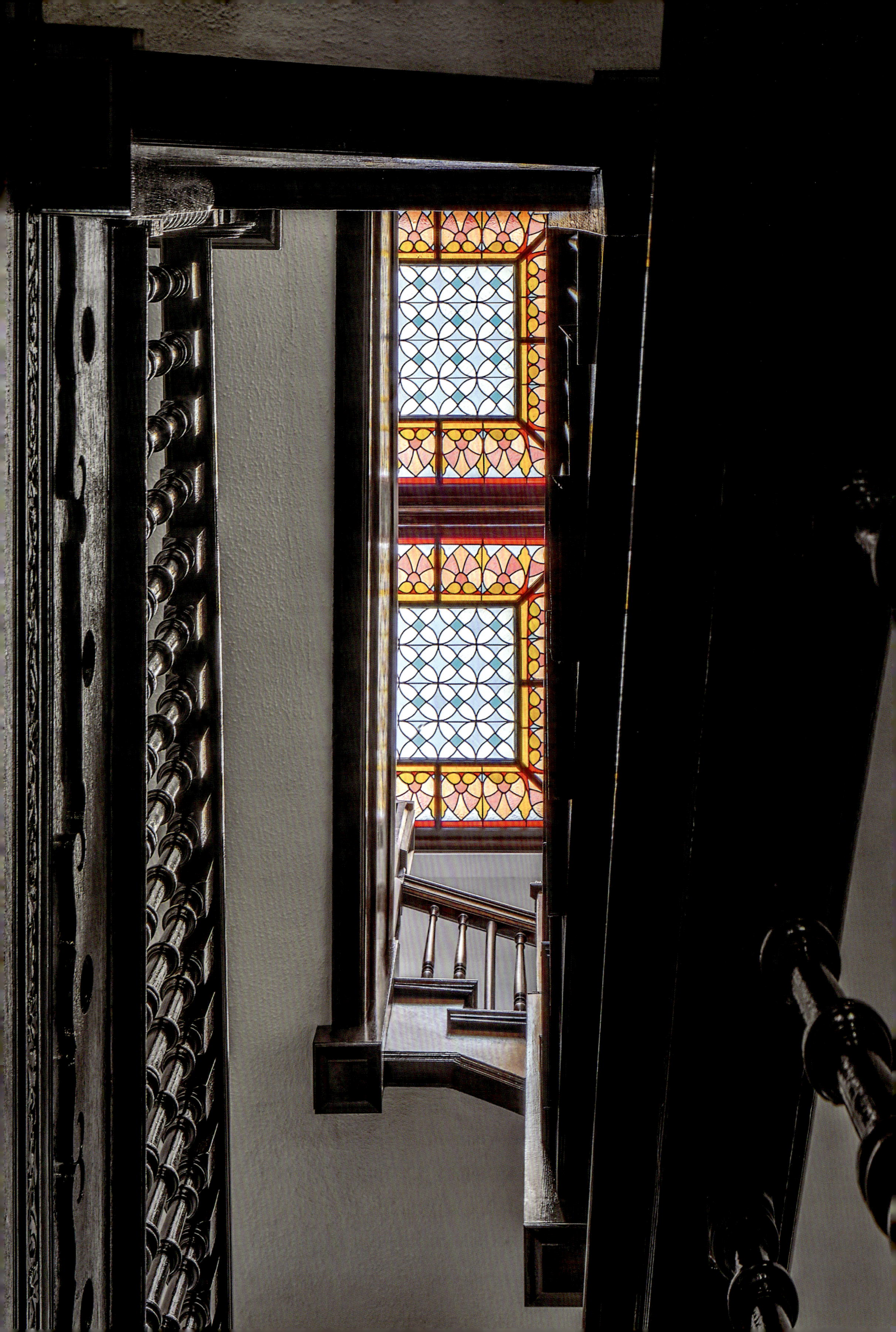

The lunette art glass window is original, but the skylight (opposite), although "Sullivanesque," is thought to be a later addition.

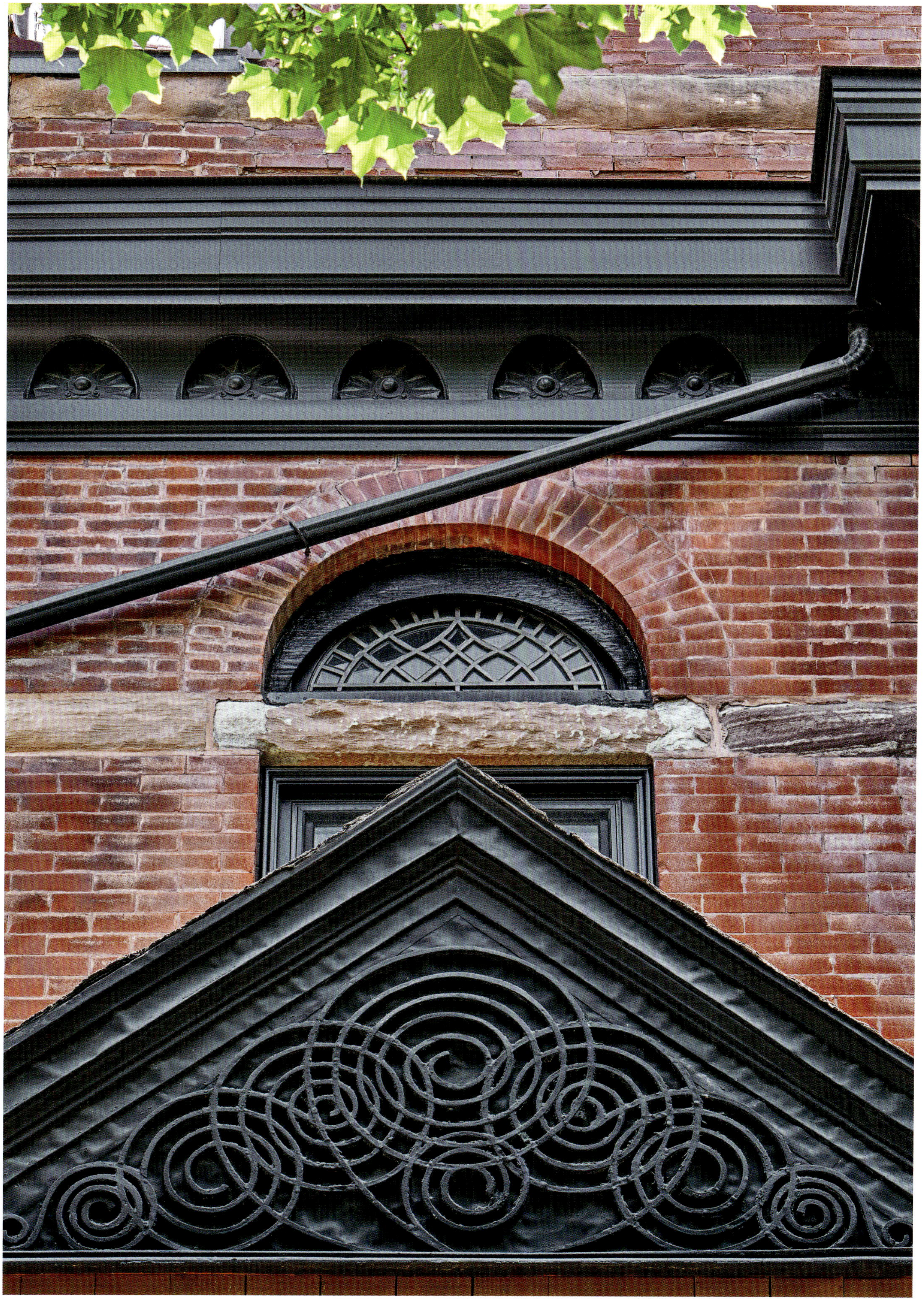

MATHILDE ELIEL HOUSE

1886, CHICAGO

Although the South Side Eliel House survives, its oriel has been re-sided and re-windowed. While the arched window and entrance portal appear original, the porch railings are later additions. The client this time was Dankmar Adler's neice, who was a Chicago school teacher. One of the least expensive of the Adler & Sullivan residentail comissions, it shows great skill in accomplishing a great deal with very little. It was designated as a Chicago Landmark in 1991.

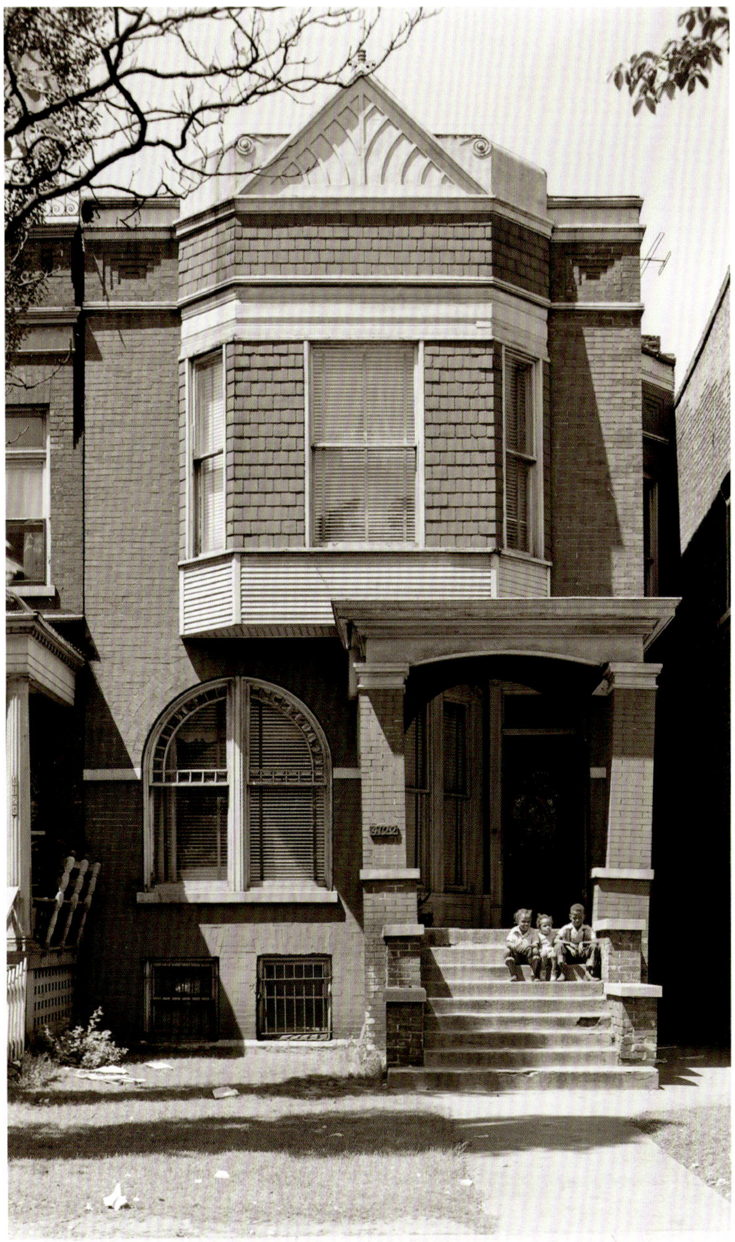

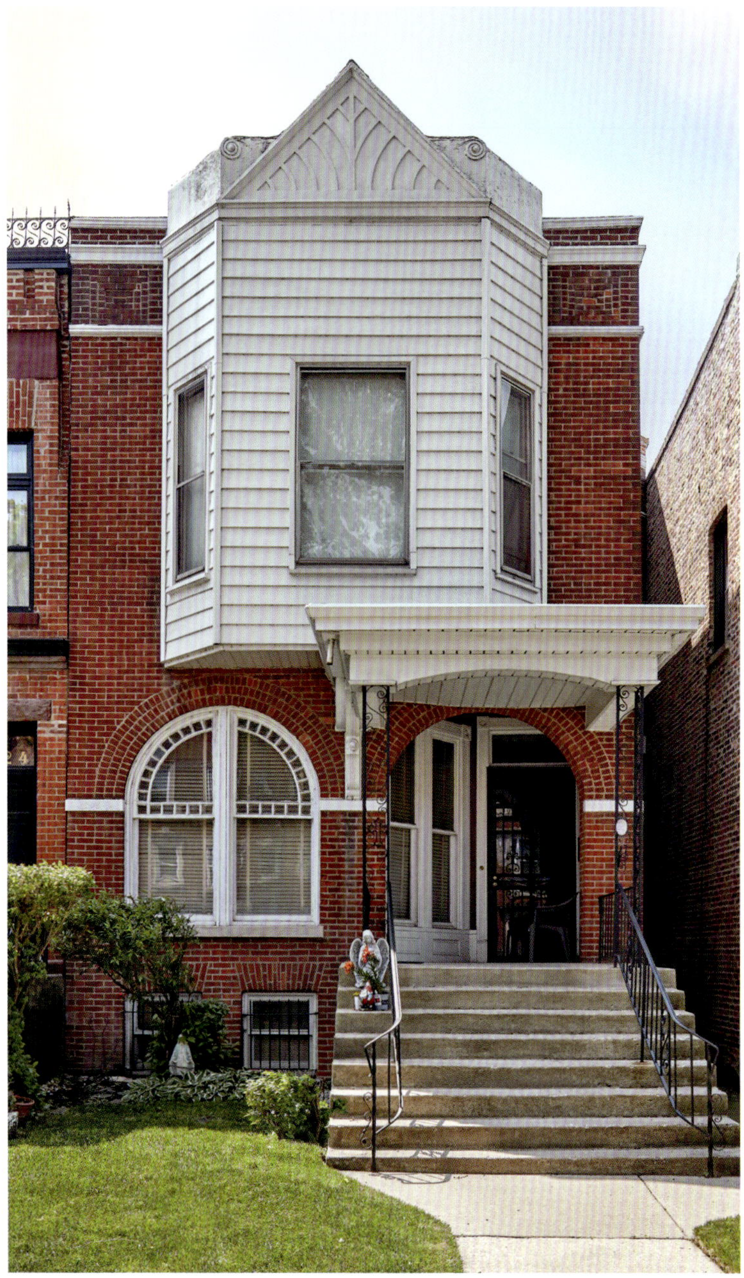

Photo by Richard Nickel, Ryerson and Burnham Libraries, AIC.

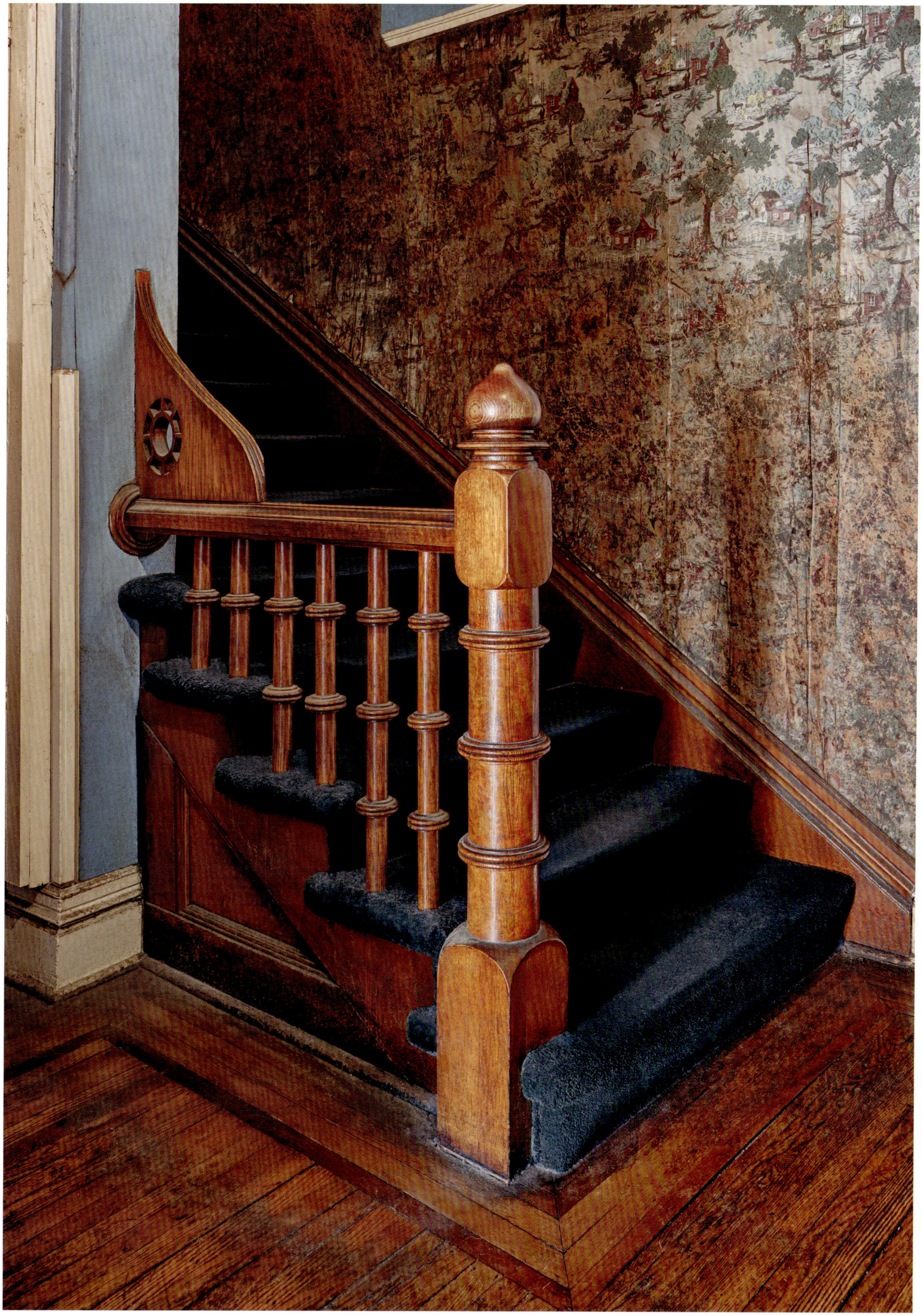

IRA A. HEATH HOUSE

1889, CHICAGO

The Complete Architecture of Adler & Sullivan lists the Heath House as an unbuilt project. Yet, in his biography of Sullivan, Hugh Morrison lists it as a completed project, even claiming a construction cost of $15,000. Frank Lloyd Wright, who claimed to be the author of many of the firm's residences during that period, wrote later that neither Adler nor Sullivan "ever saw the house." But Heath was a friend of Adlers, and it hardly seems necessary to point out that Wright had a very selective memory.

There is undeniably a residence at 3132 S. Prairie Avenue, clearly of the period. Others have commented that its Richardsonian Romanesque design is unlike other Adler & Sullivan houses of the period. It is, however, contemporary with the Romanesque Auditorium Building, and Standard Club. The firm was extremely busy in 1889, and it may be that the job was given to an employee other than Wright. Because there is no convincing evidence that it isn't by Adler & Sullivan, we decided to include it.

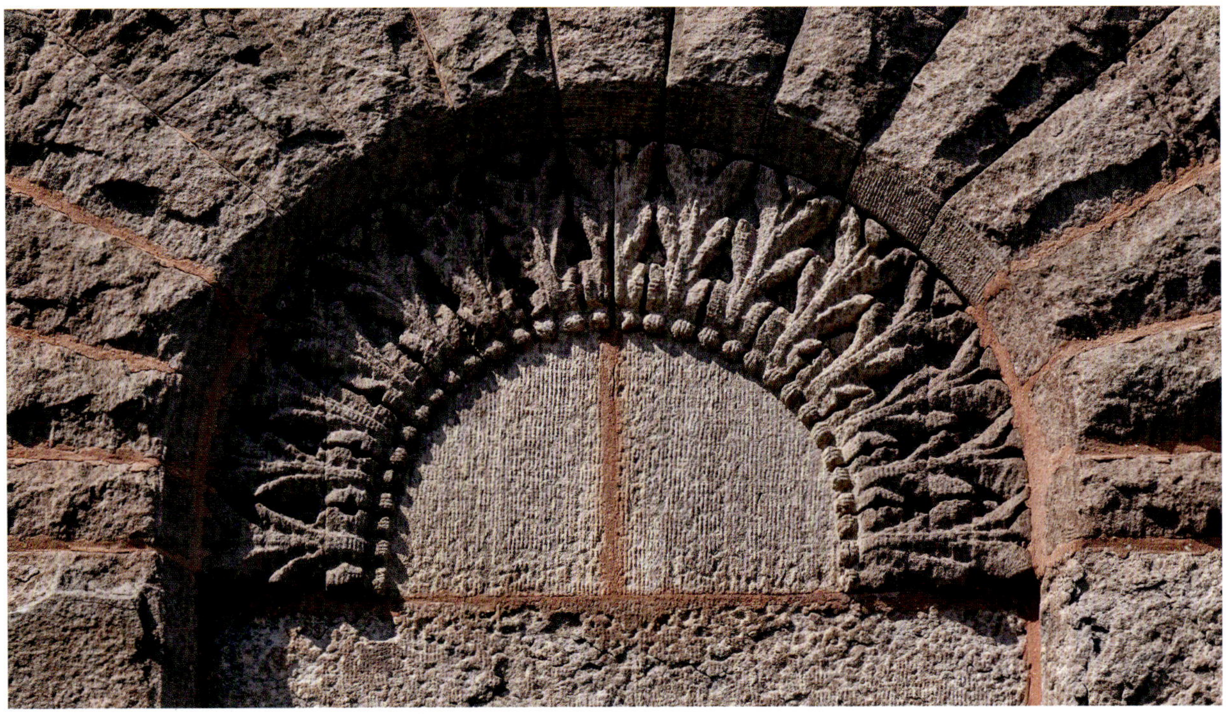

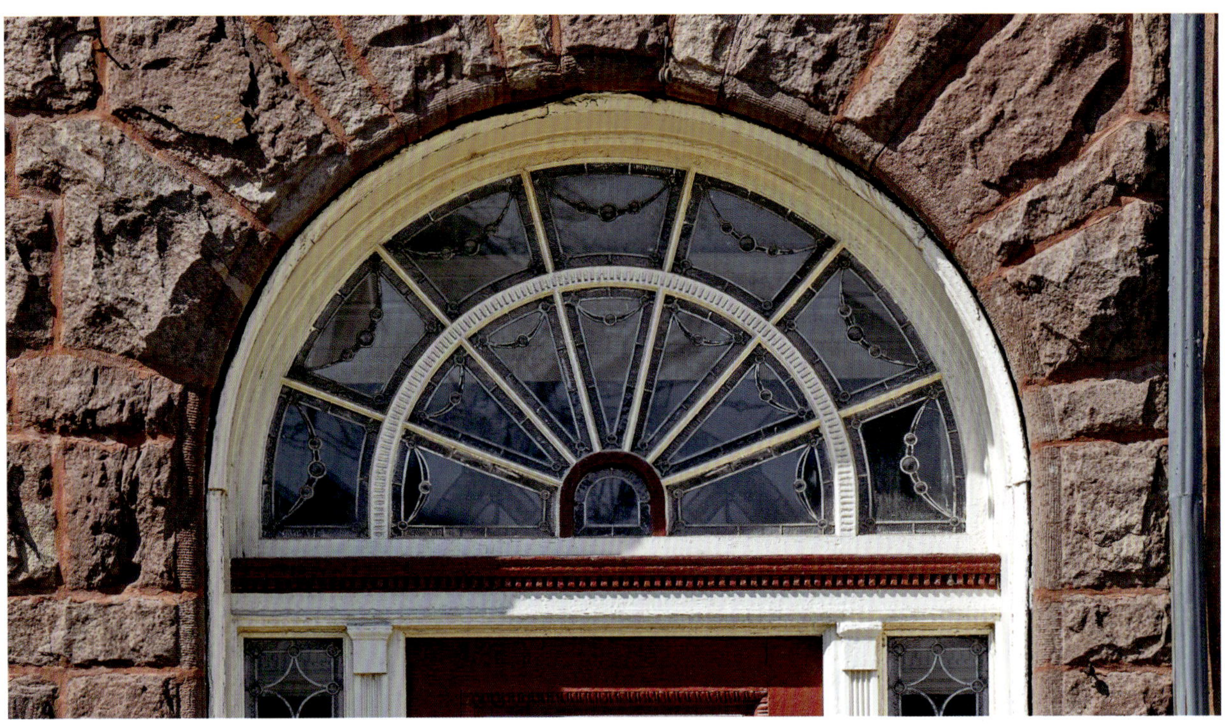

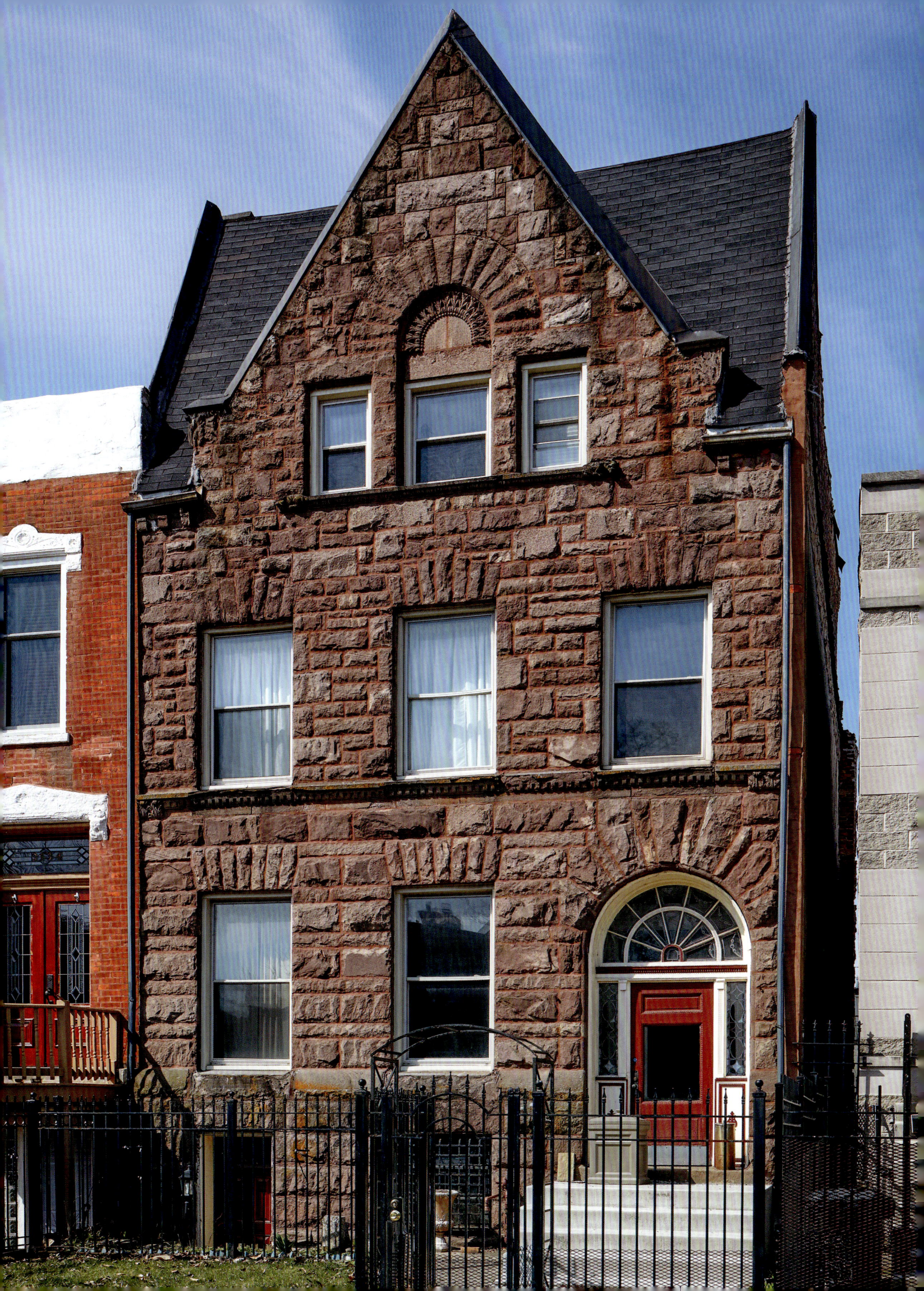

JAMES AND HELEN CHARNLEY HOUSE

1901–02, CHICAGO

The Charnleys were personal friends of Sullivan who had introduced him to his beloved Ocean Springs, Mississippi, where both the Charnleys and Sullivan would have vacation cottages (see **Charnley-Norwood House,** next). The young Frank Lloyd Wright would later claim authorship for both the Sullivan and Charnley Ocean Springs houses. The consensus of scholars today is that Wright was at least responsible for the Chicago house, which graces and contrasts the period mansions and townhouses that line Chicago's still fashionable Astor Street. Despite possibly assigning the house to Wright, Sullivan would certainly have taken more than a passing interest in its design. The restrained exterior decoration on the porch, cornice, and entry door certainly qualify as "Sullivanesque."

It is now known as the Charnley-Persky House in honor of former owner Seymour Persky, who gave it to the Society of Architectural Historians to serve as the organization headquarters. In 1995, Persky purchased the house from the architectural firm of Skidmore, Owings & Merrill (SOM), who had themselves purchased it in 1986. They had removed a 1927 addition and otherwise restored the house, with the intent of using it as a design center. Increasing costs caused a reevaluation and the sale to Persky. The house was added to the National Register of Historic Places in 1970, designated a Chicago Landmark in 1972, and a National Historic Landmark in 1998. For tour information, contact the Society of Architectural Historians.

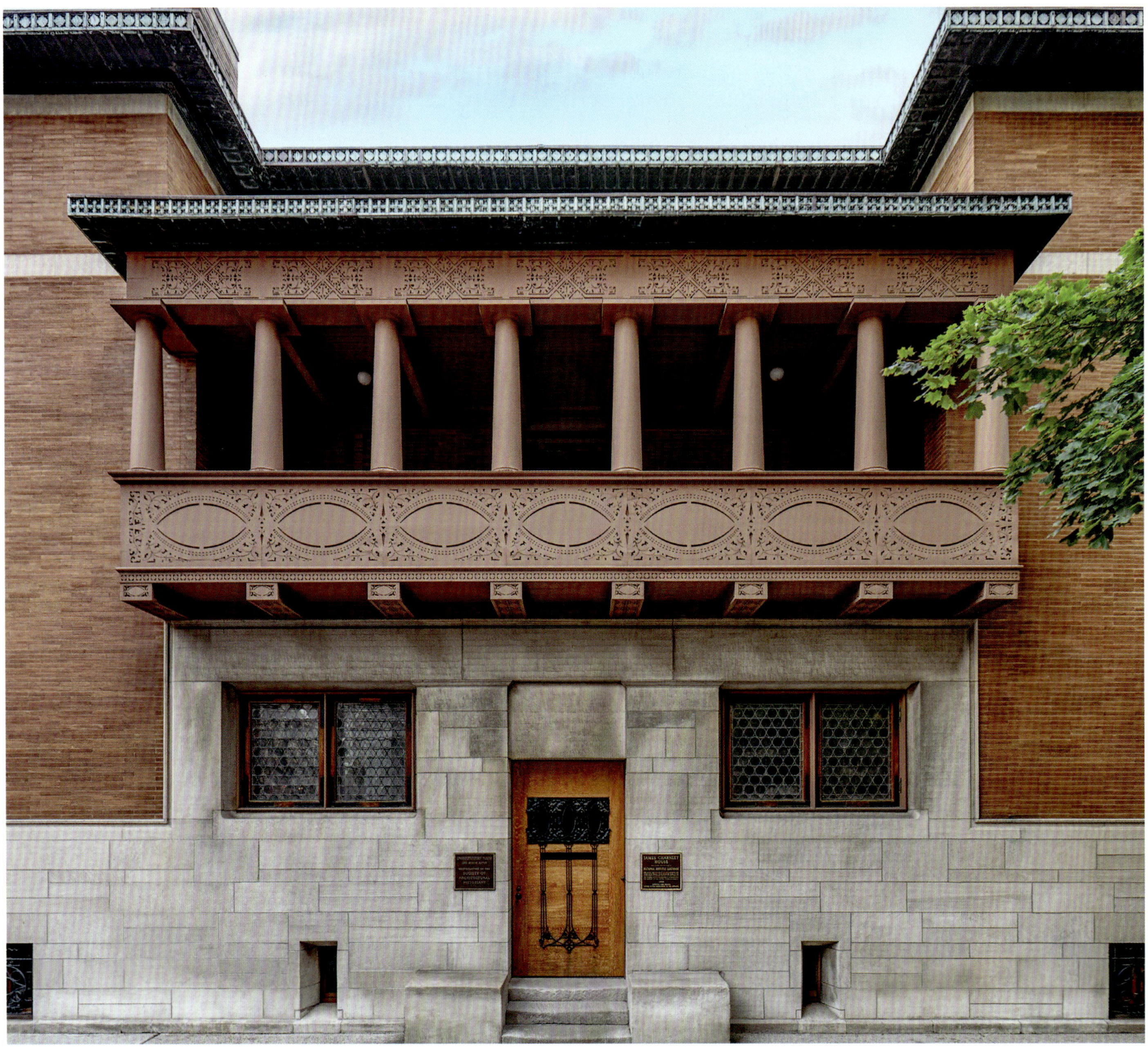

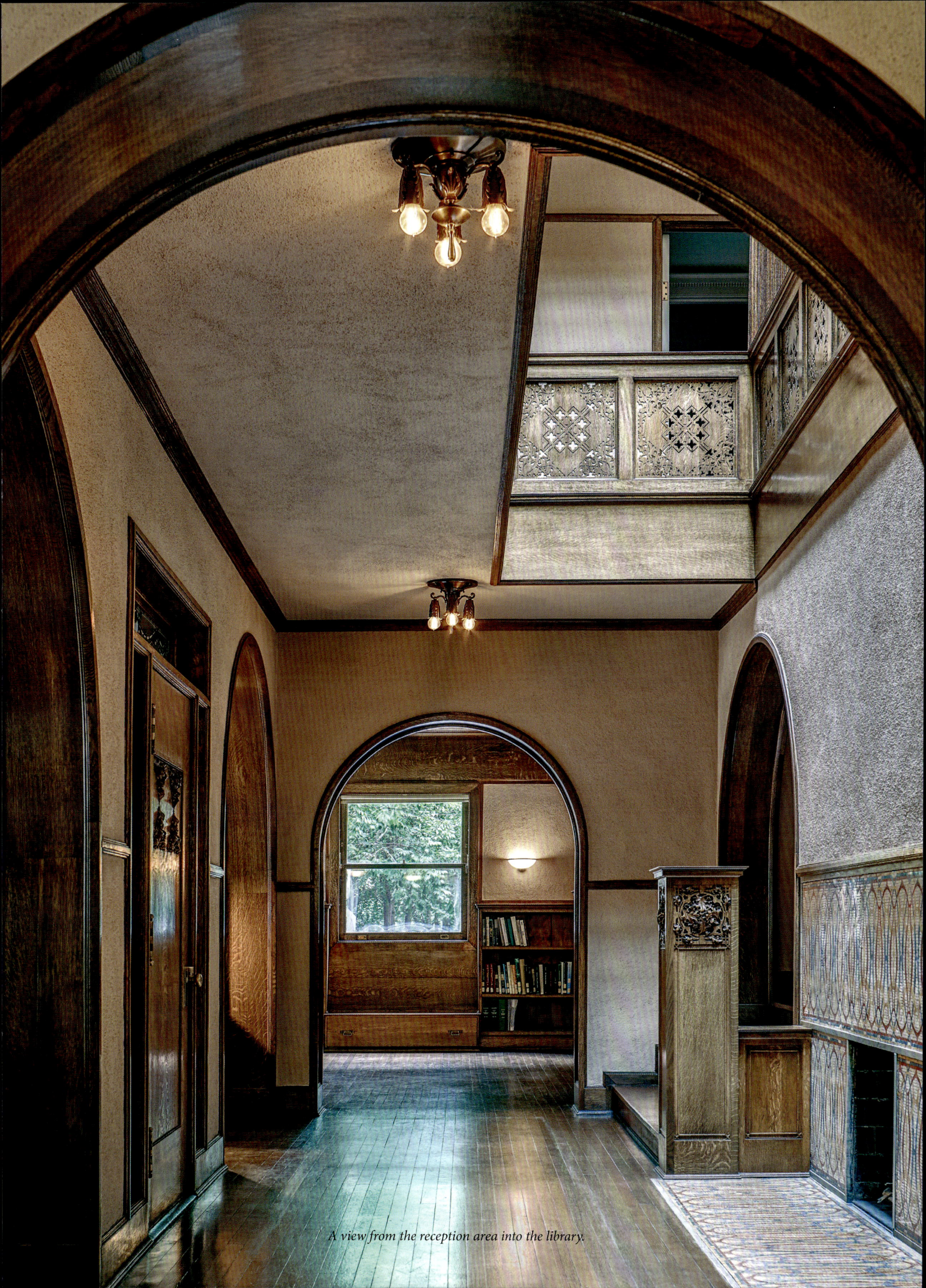

A view from the reception area into the library.

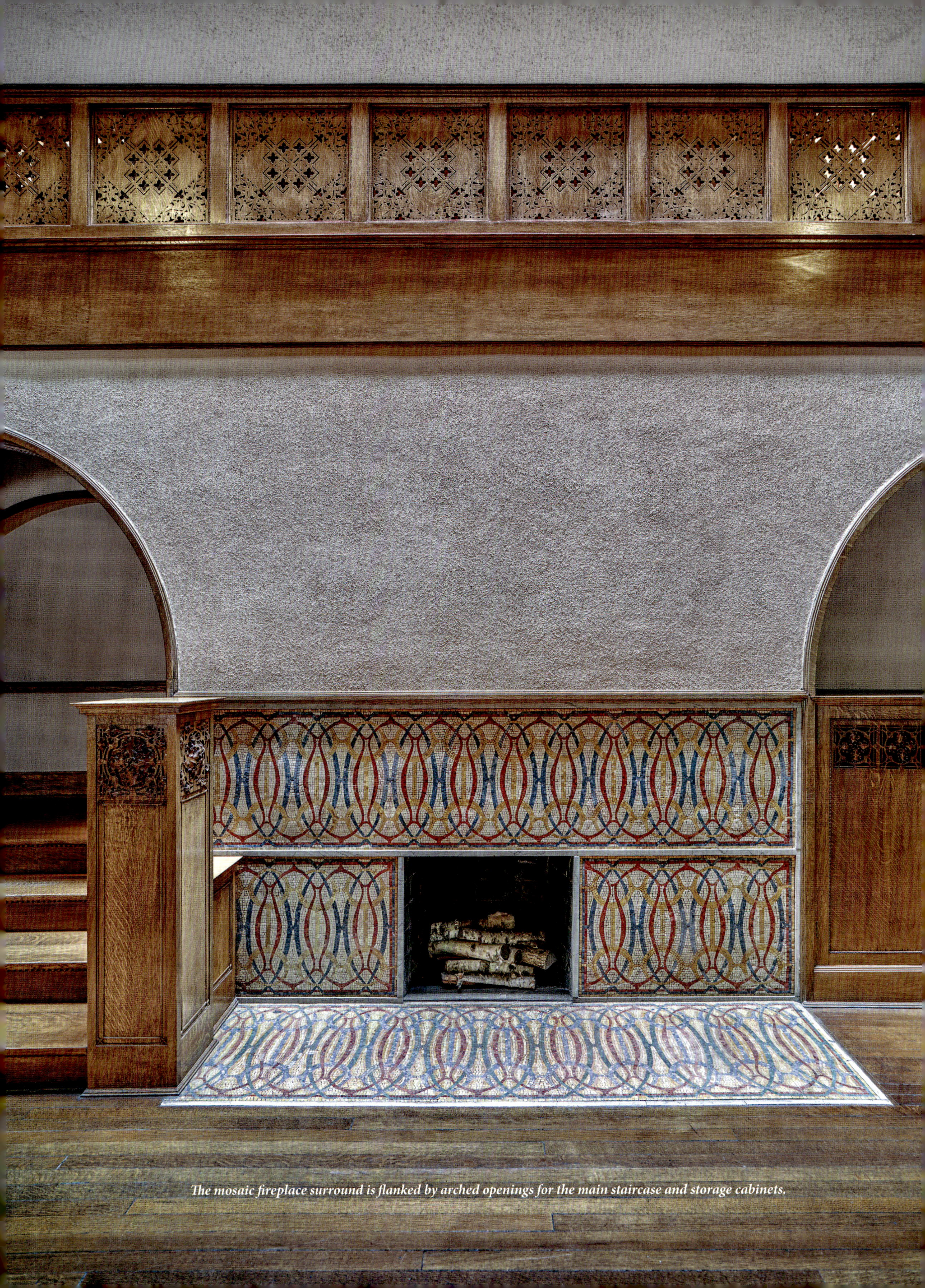

The mosaic fireplace surround is flanked by arched openings for the main staircase and storage cabinets.

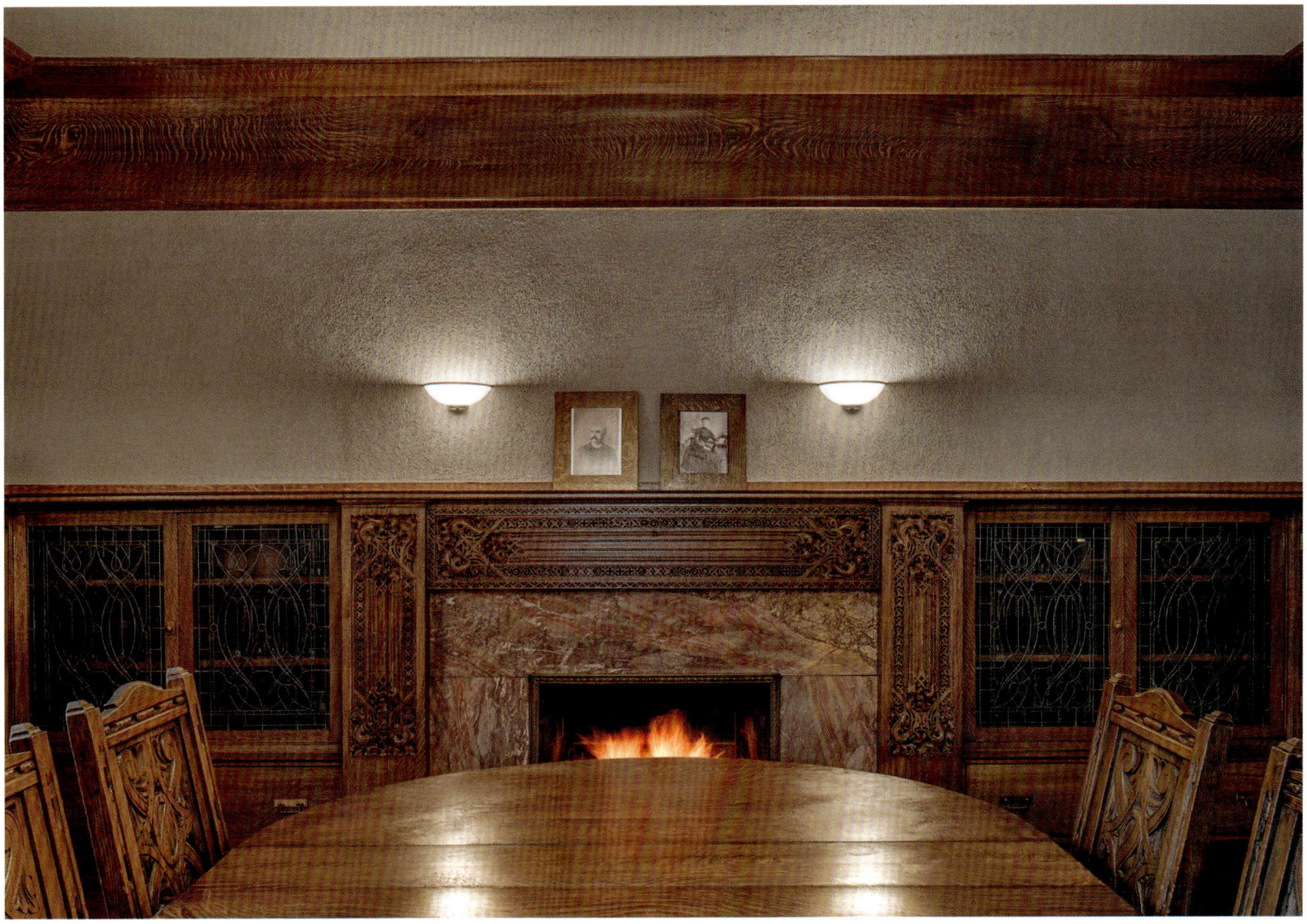

These fireplaces are in the library and the dining room (below).

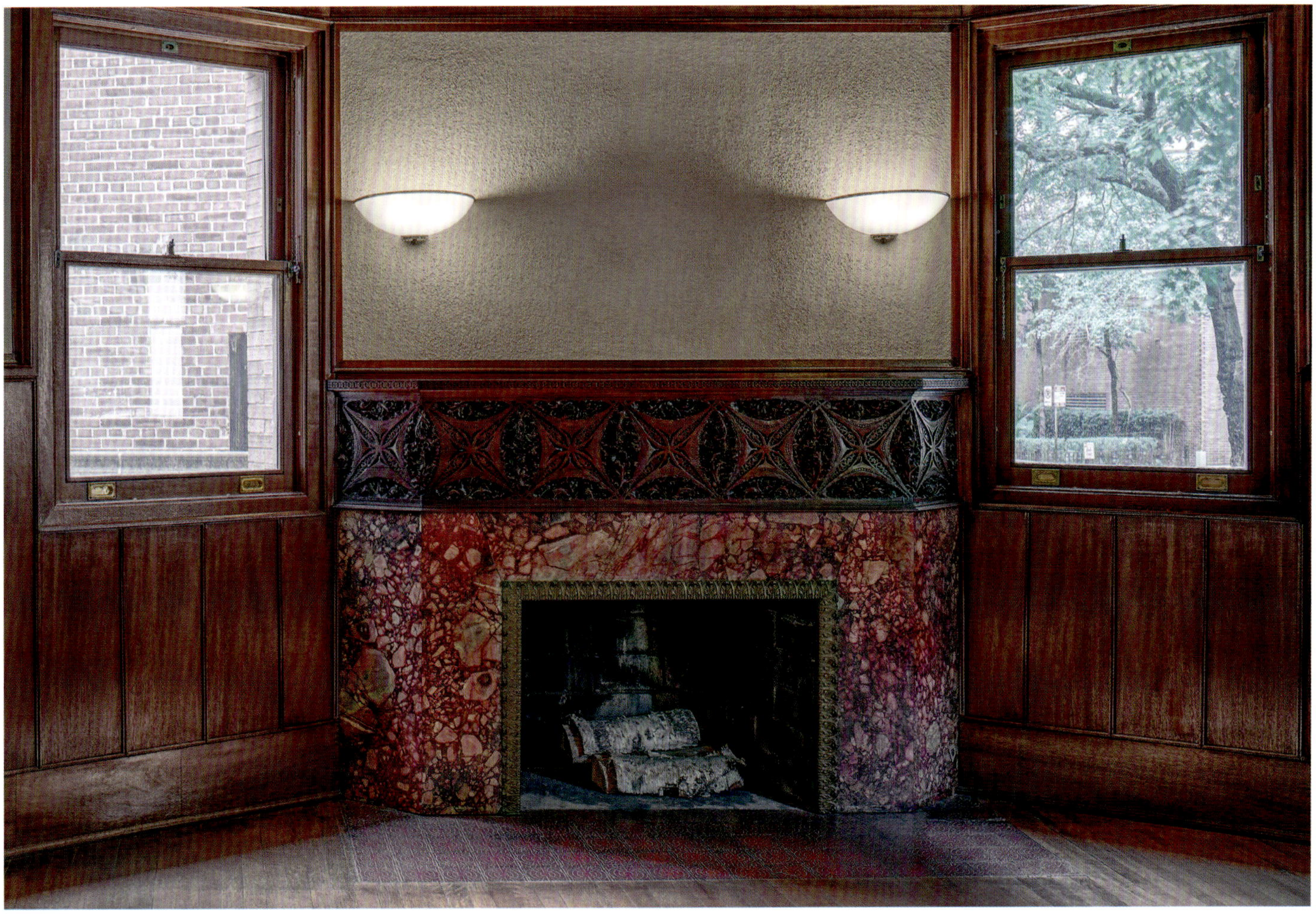

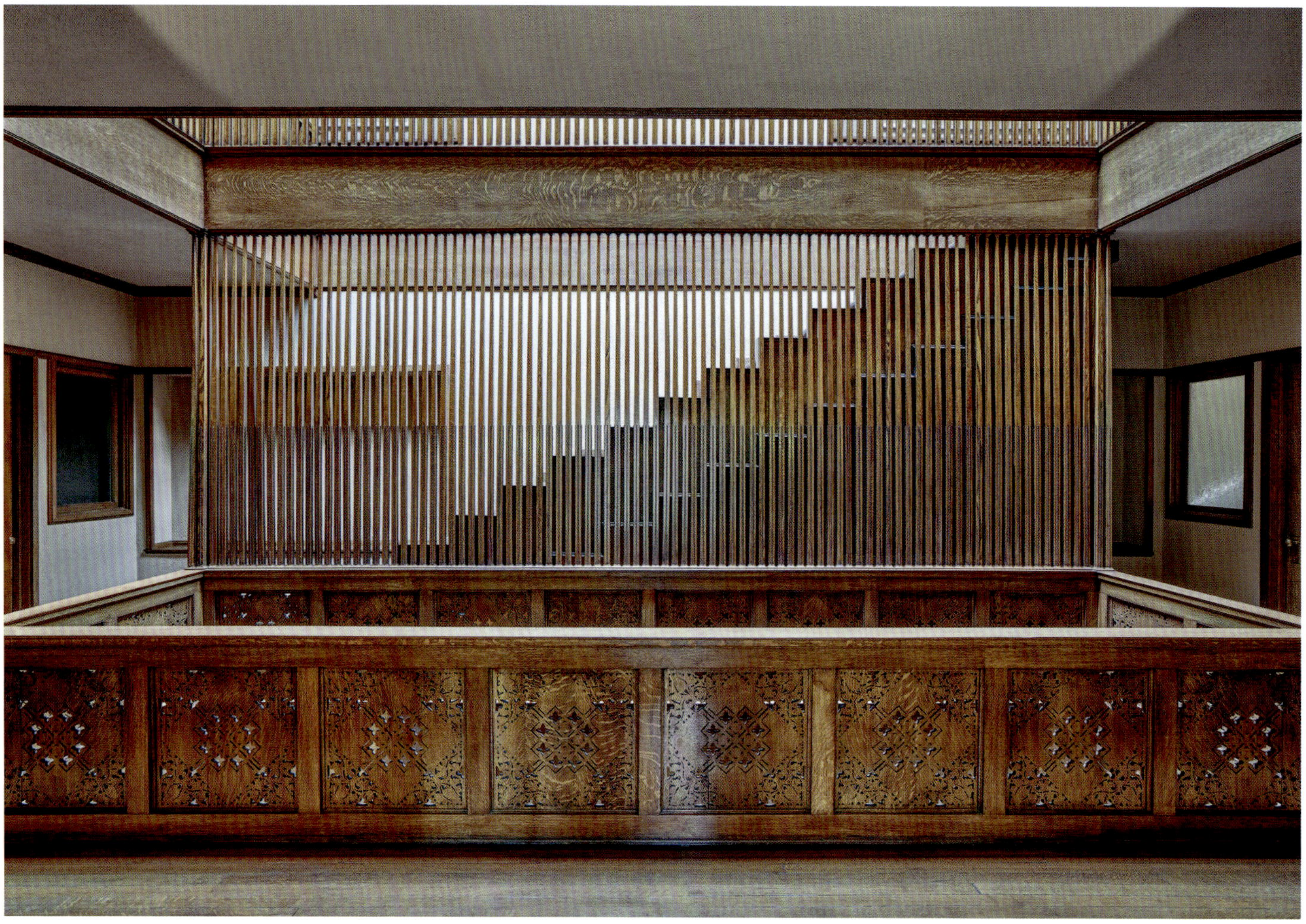

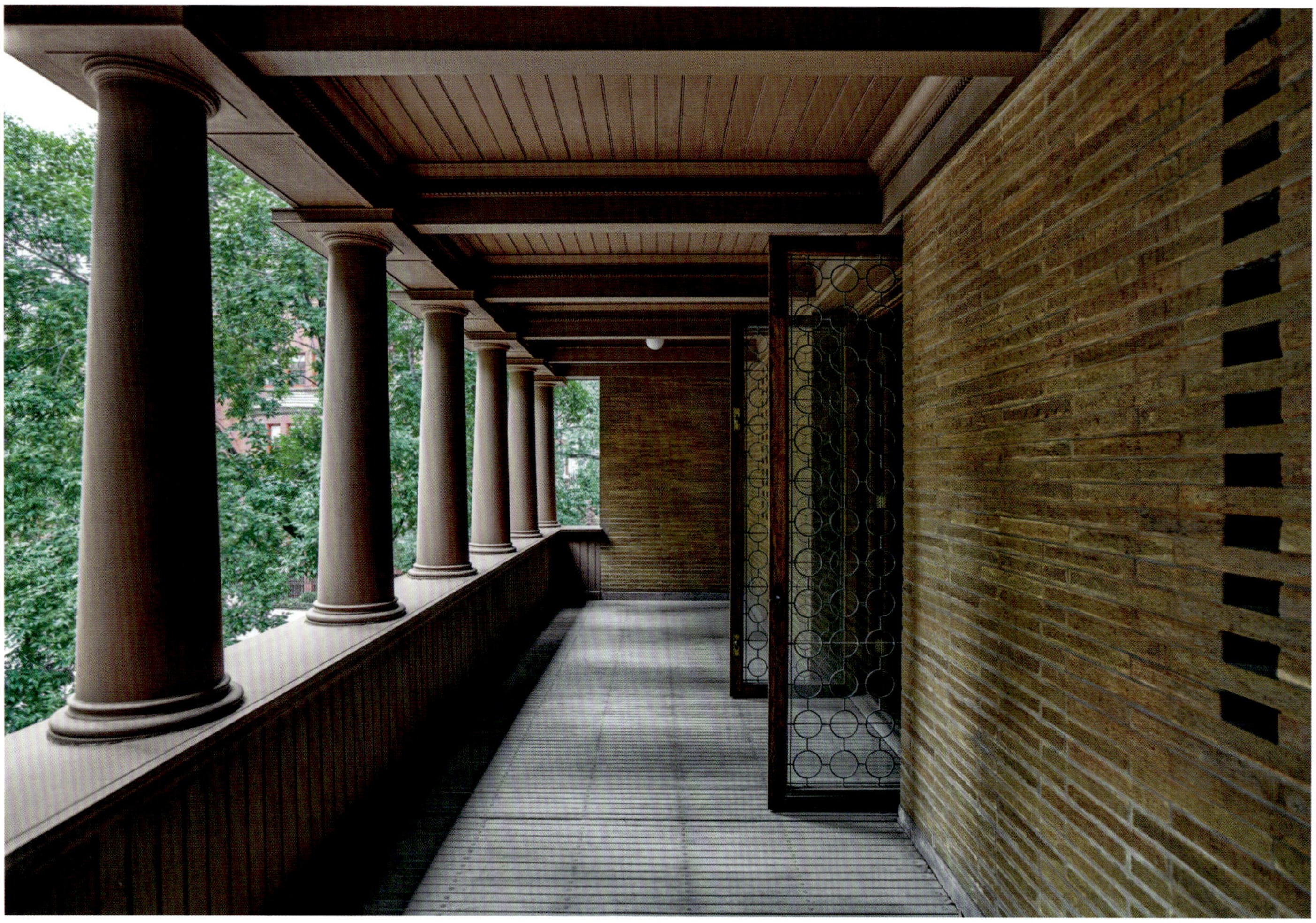

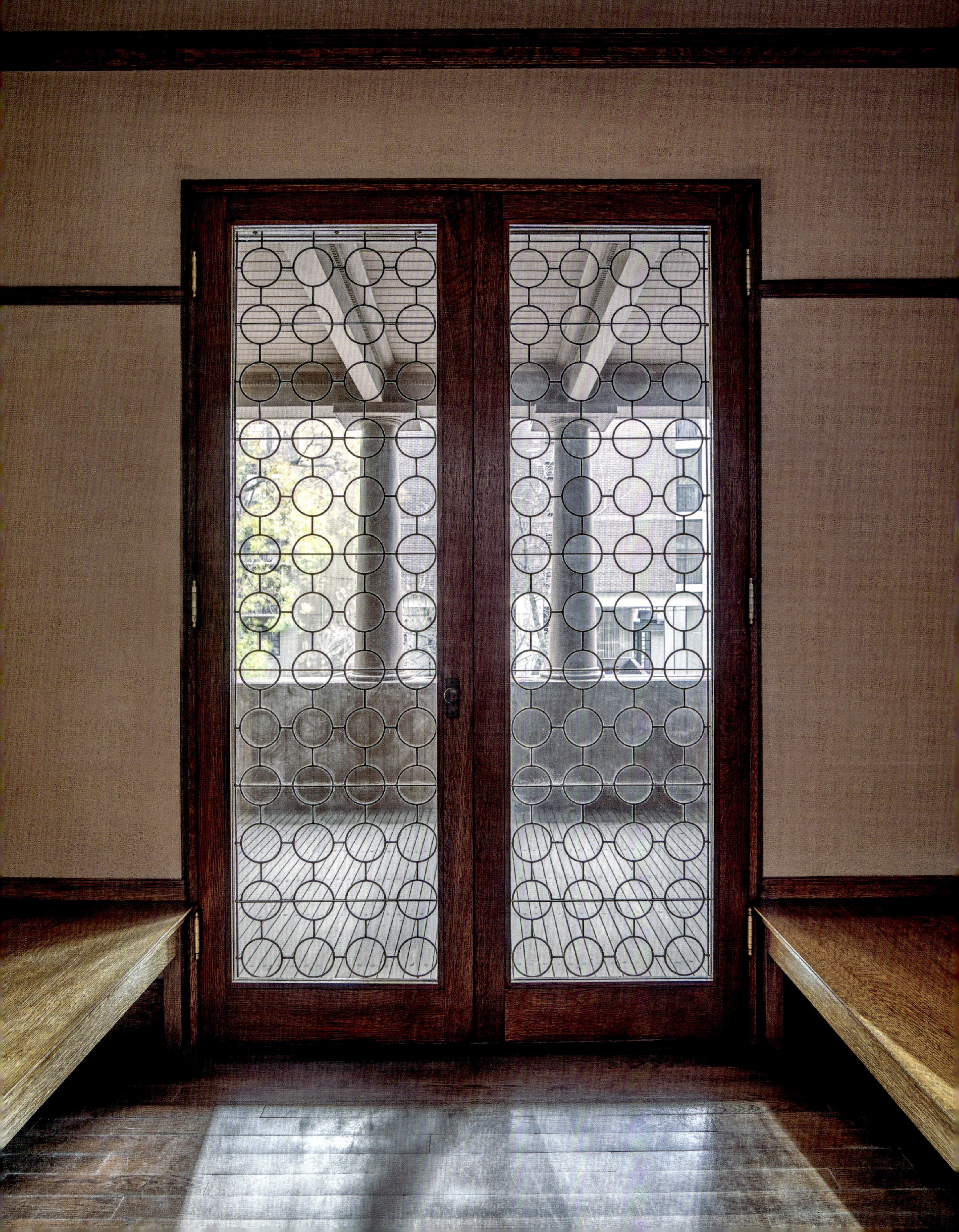

The second floor. The central core of the house is lit by a skylight. Behind the screen are the stairs to the third floor. French doors lead to the balcony, the building's only outside space.

CHARNLEY-NORWOOD HOUSE

1890, 1897 (RECONSTRUCTION) OCEAN SPRINGS, MISSISSIPPI

Sullivan's own similar Ocean Springs home (which he preferred to call his "shack") and associated out buildings were destroyed by Hurricane Katrina in 2005. The neighboring Charnley-Norwood House, which predates the Chicago house, was heavily damaged, but was purchased in 2011 by the State of Mississippi, which chose Larry Albert Associates, Architects of Hattiesburg to restore the property.

As with the Chicago house, Frank Lloyd Wright claimed credit for both the Ocean Springs Sullivan and Charnley houses, a perhaps dubious claim since it involved Sullivan's own house and that of his close friends. If his claim was true, he owed a debt to the bungalows that the British built in India and other Asian colonies to insulate themselves from the tropical heat. In fact, the word bungalow is originally from the Bengali. The low roof, wide overhangs, and deep porches were meant to keep the tropical sun at bay.

Maintenance was kept at a minimum by the use of local woods throughout. Both exterior and interior walls are constructed of southern yellow long-leaf pine. T-shaped in plan, the house was rebuilt by Sullivan, almost as originally designed, in 1897 after a fire and was meant for the new owner, Chicagoan Frederick W. Norwood, who had purchased the property from the Charnleys in 1896. The house was added to the National Register of Historic Places in 1987 as part of the Charnley-Sullivan Historic District. Tour information is available by contacting the Mississippi Gulf Coast National Heritage Area website.

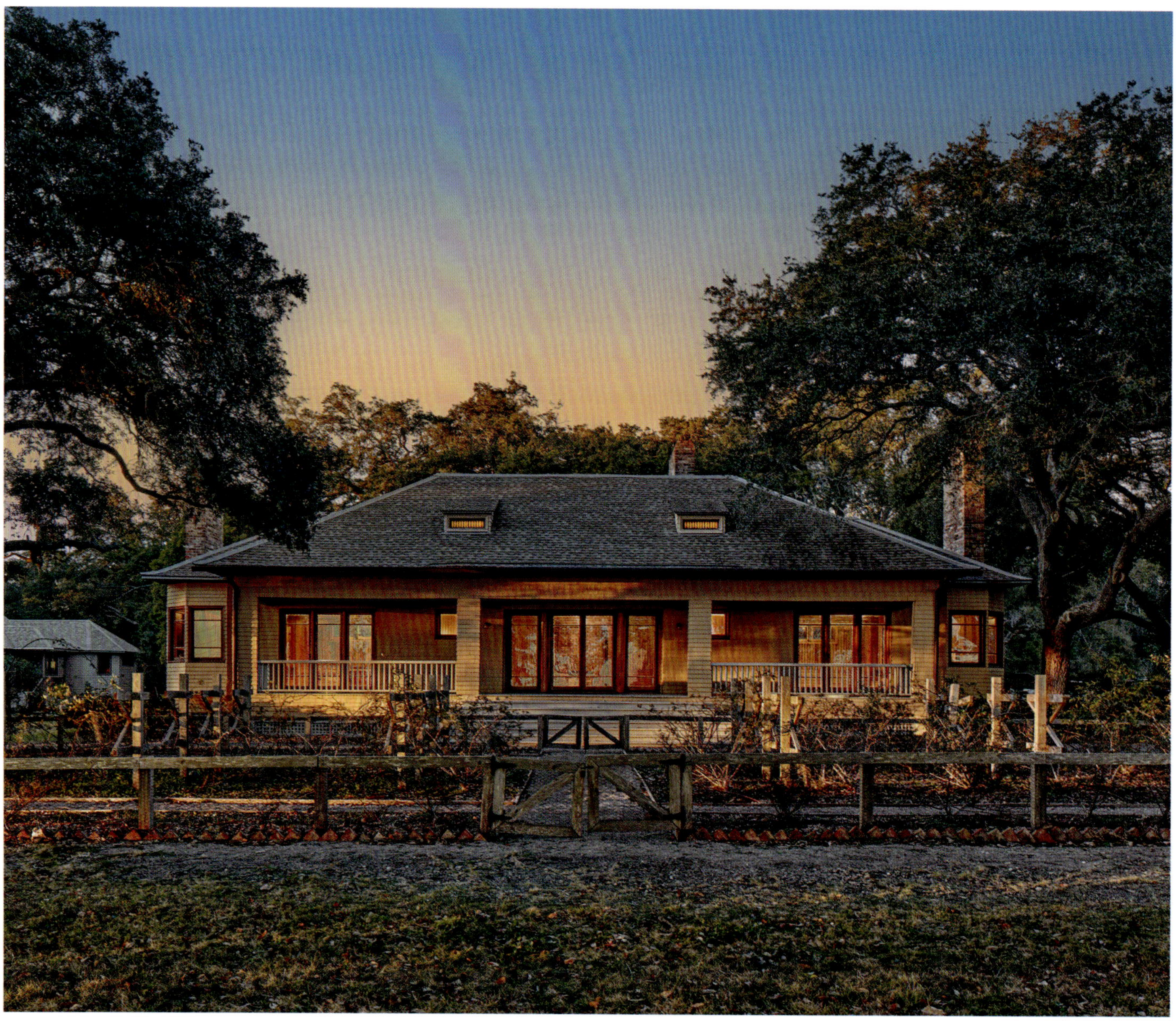

Looking into the dining room from the reception/living room.

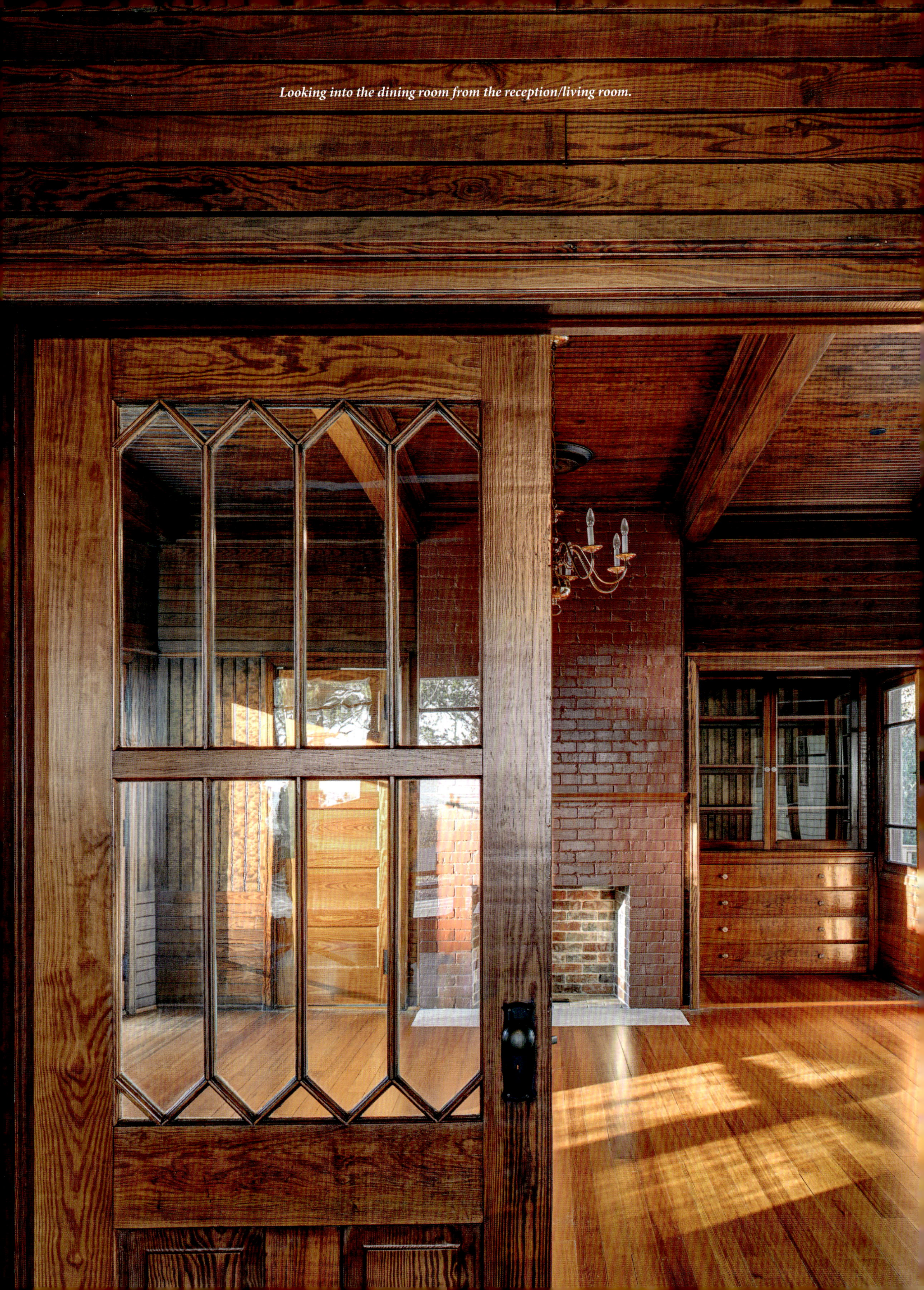

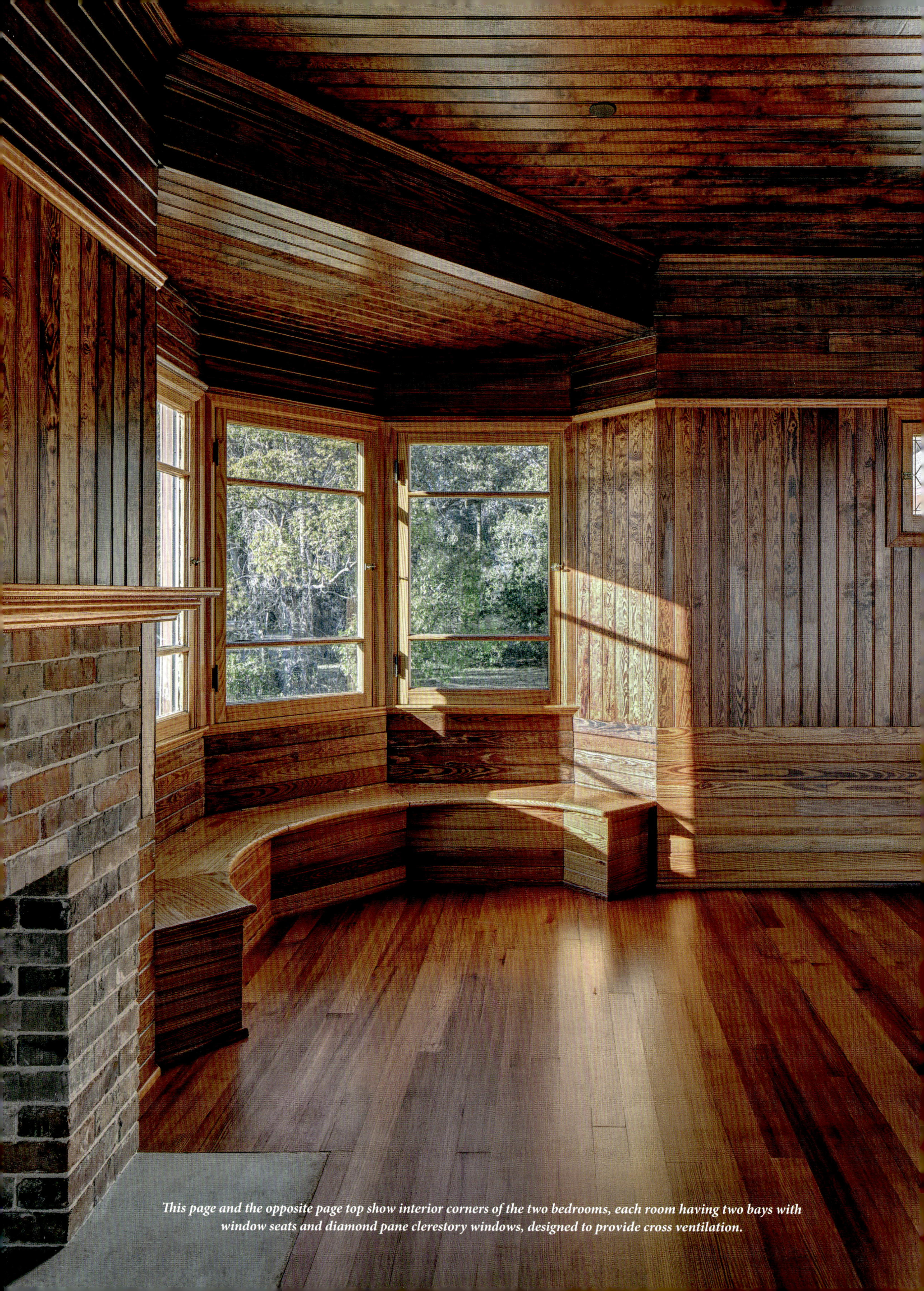

This page and the opposite page top show interior corners of the two bedrooms, each room having two bays with window seats and diamond pane clerestory windows, designed to provide cross ventilation.

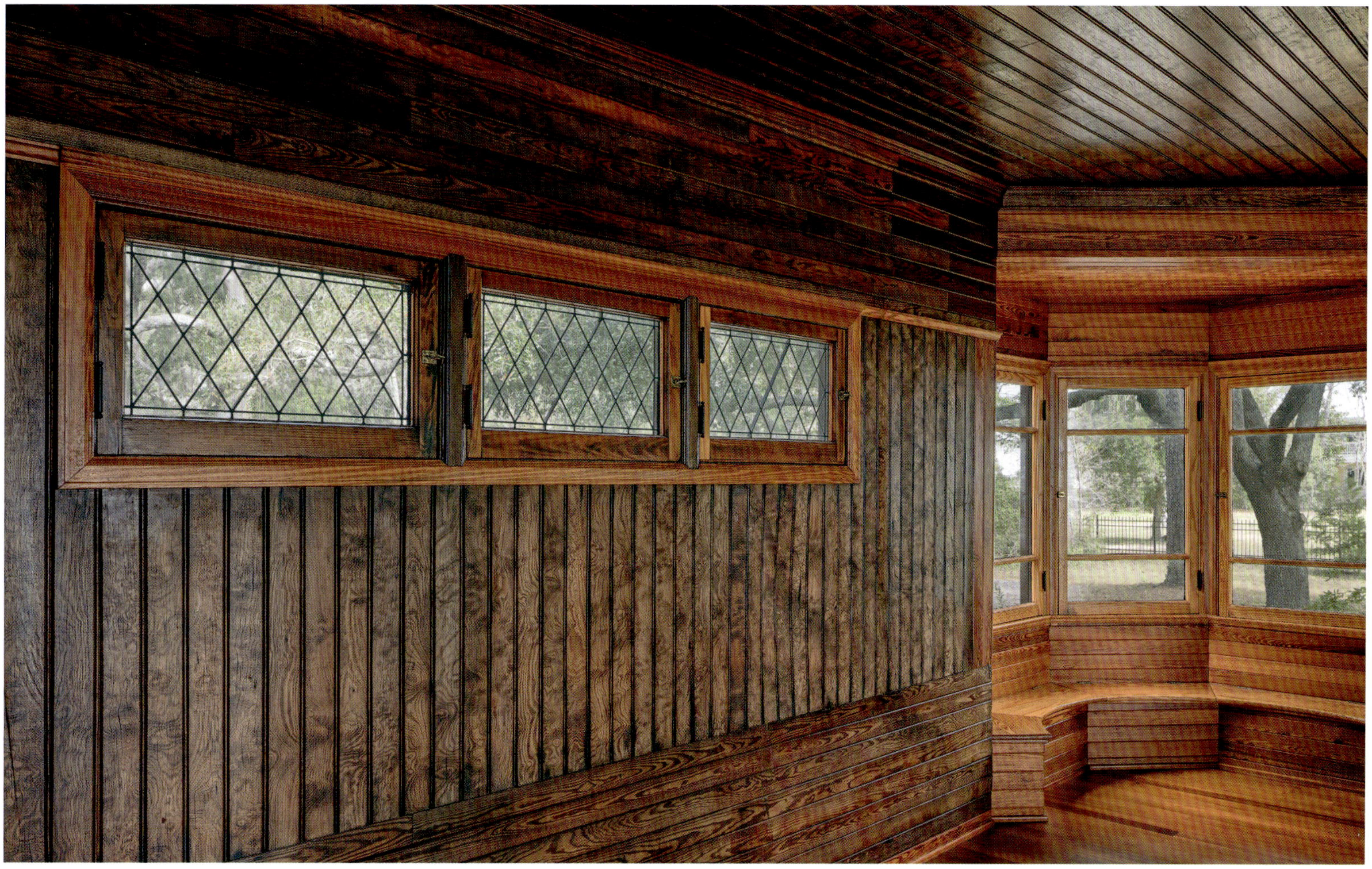

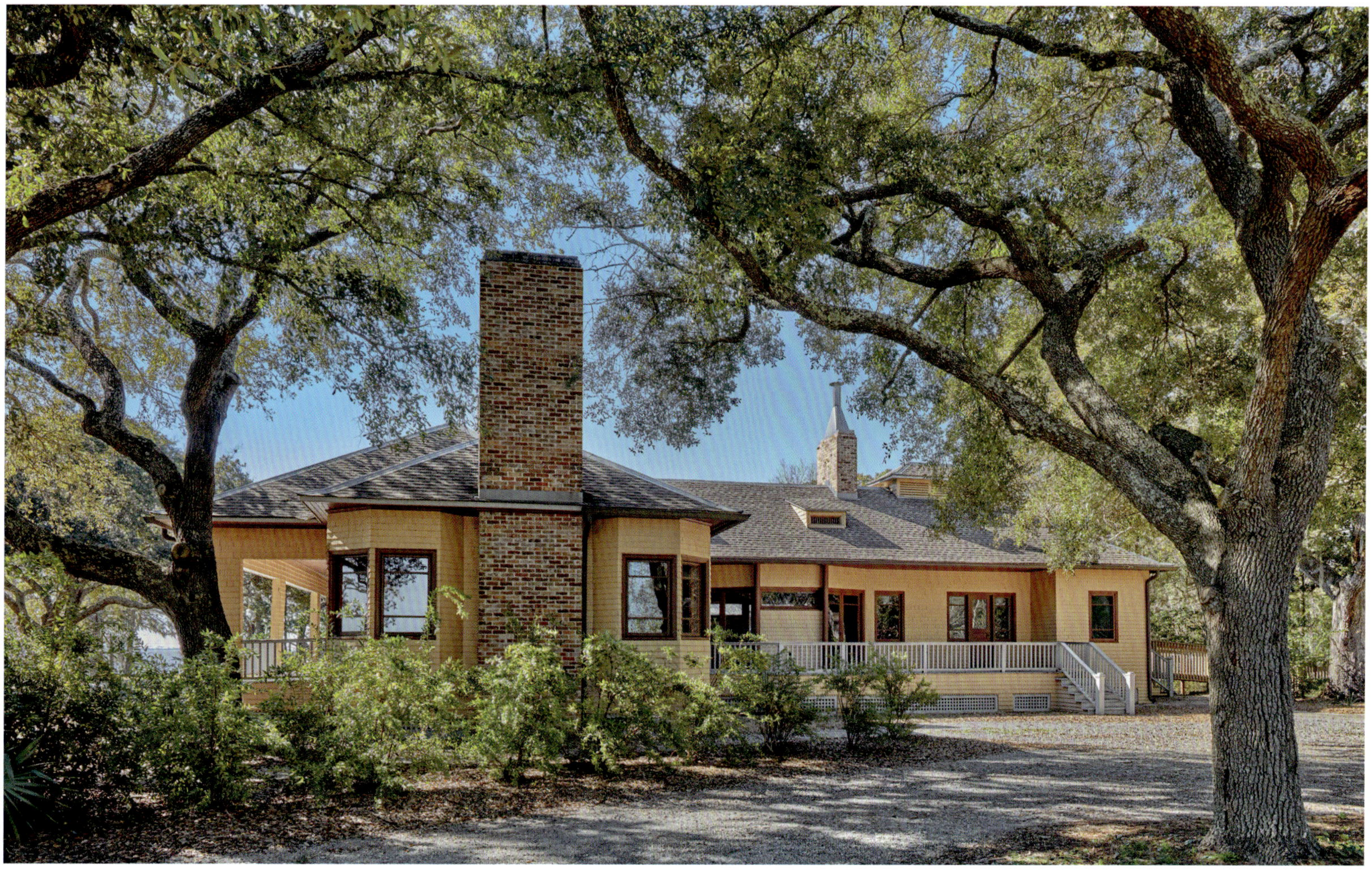

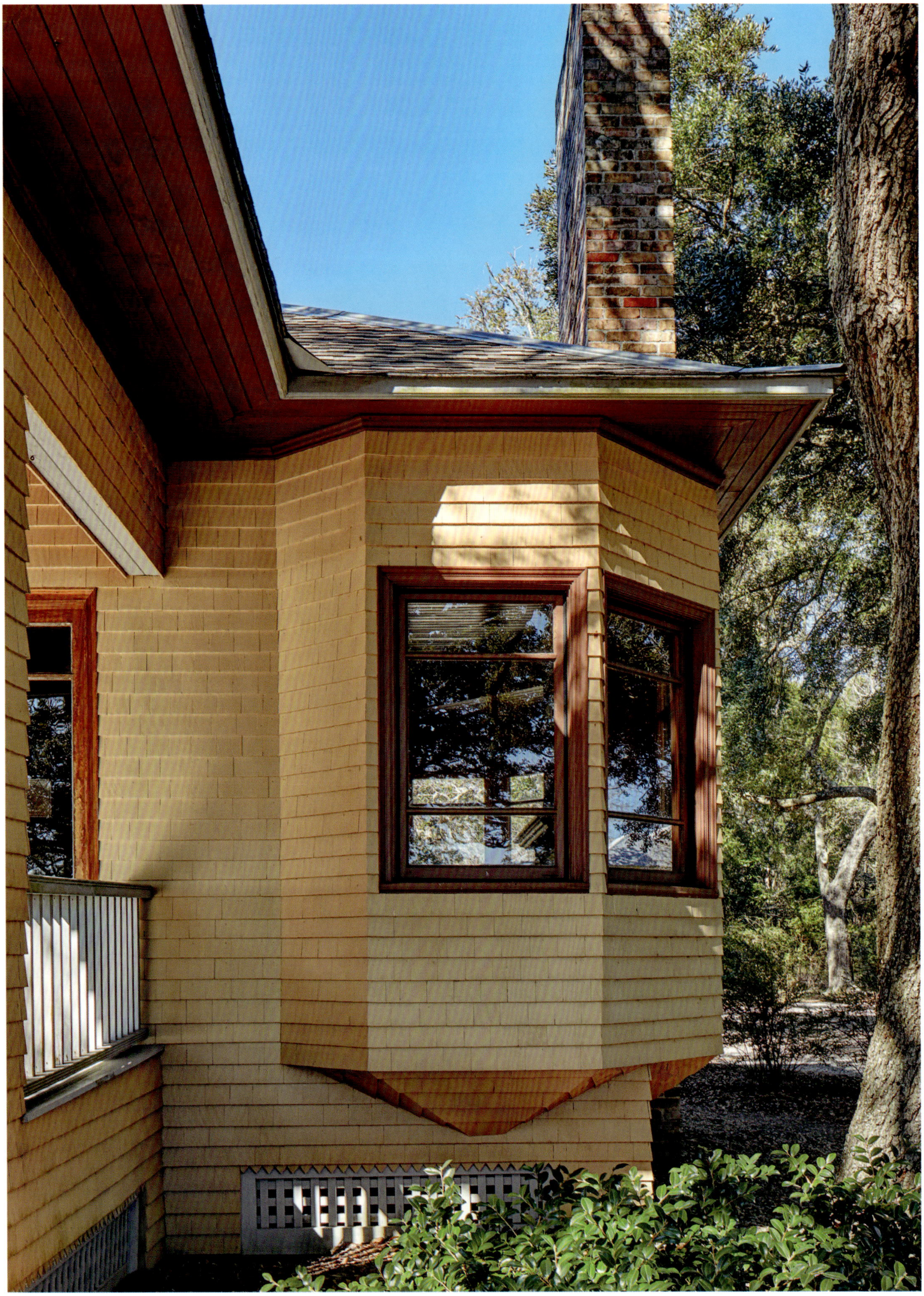

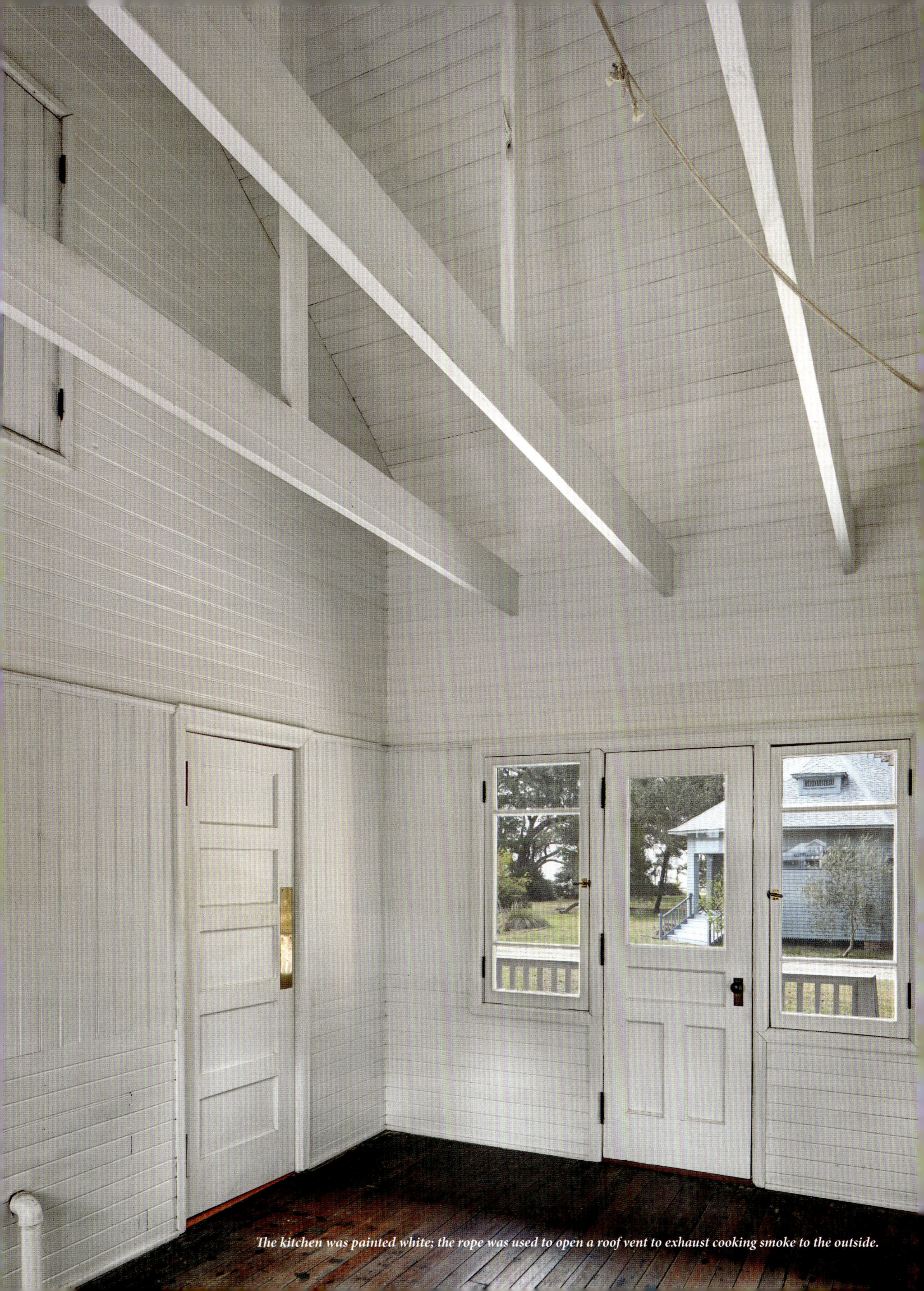

The kitchen was painted white; the rope was used to open a roof vent to exhaust cooking smoke to the outside.

REACHING FOR THE SKY

"Problem: How shall we impart to this sterile pile, this crude, harsh, brutal agglomeration, this stark, staring exclamation of eternal strife, the graciousness of those higher forms of sensibility and culture that rest on the lower and fierce passions? How shall we proclaim from the dizzy height of this strange, weird, modern housetop the peaceful evangel of sentiment, of beauty, the cult of a higher life?"

Louis Sullivan, "The Tall Office Building Considered"
Lippincott's Magazine 57 (*March 1895*): *403–09*

Chicago has long laid claim to being the birthplace of the modern skyscraper. While the genesis of the engineering techniques—including the safety elevator—that permitted buildings to rise ever higher is a long one, there seems little doubt that these techniques came together for the first time in the since-demolished ten-story Home Insurance Building of 1885, designed by William LeBaron Jenney.

Jenney was a trained engineer turned architect. Despite its steel frame and masonry non-bearing curtain wall construction, the Home Insurance Building was just a taller version of its neighbors. No attempt was made to express its verticality; indeed, it had no fewer than four horizontal bands dividing its façade into five separate units.

Many of Adler & Sullivan's office building designs of that time and earlier weren't unlike the Home Insurance Building. But when the firm began to exploit the new structural possibilities available with steel framing, Sullivan began to think seriously about how best to emphasize the most obvious feature of the new buildings—their height.

The late 1880s were busy times for the firm, not least due to the extreme demands of designing and constructing the Auditorium Building, which began in 1886 but was not finished until 1889. The Auditorium had an office tower that rose to seventeen stories but was only five floors above the main building; and like the main building, the office tower was of masonry load-bearing construction. In 1890, the commission for the Wainwright Building in St. Louis was the turning point in the development of a true tall building aesthetic by Sullivan. Frank Lloyd Wright later remembered Sullivan putting a rough sketch of the building on his table, which is when he realized that his master had solved the "problem" of the skyscraper.

To another young architect, Claude Bragdon, Sullivan explained: "As to my buildings, those that interest me date from the Wainwright Building ... It was a sudden and volcanic design (made literally in three minutes) {presumably the sketch he showed to Wright} and marks the beginning of a logical and poetic expression of the metal frame construction ... All my commercial buildings since the Wainwright are conceived in the same general spirit..."

How had Sullivan done it? While he would not have put it in these terms, he had seen the tall building as a column, consisting of a base, a shaft, and a capital. His important tall buildings, save one, follow this pattern: a basement for the furnace and other utilities; a two-story base for shops and similar uses; a sill; then the multi-story main office section, with identically expressed, uninterrupted bearing columns and non-bearing mullions rising to the attic, often highly decorated and capped by an equally highly decorated cornice. Spandrels separating the windows are recessed so that the columns and mullions rise uninterrupted to the cornice.

The two Chicago buildings that best expressed Sullivan's ideas—the Chicago Stock Exchange and Schiller Buildings—have both been demolished, the Schiller in 1961 and the Stock Exchange in 1972. Tragically, photographer and preservationist Richard Nickel was killed while trying to salvage some pieces of the Stock Exchange. Only fragments, stored in museums and private collections, from two of Sullivan's greatest accomplishments remain.

Although the interior has changed significantly, the Wainwright Building in St. Louis largely retains its original exterior. Also in St. Louis, the Union Trust Building of 1893 still stands, although with significant changes to the base. Sullivan's only New York City commission, the Bayard (later Condict) Building exists in largely restored condition, as does the Guaranty Building in Buffalo, which is perhaps Sullivan's best tall building, restored in the 1980s by the law firm that is now its main tenant.

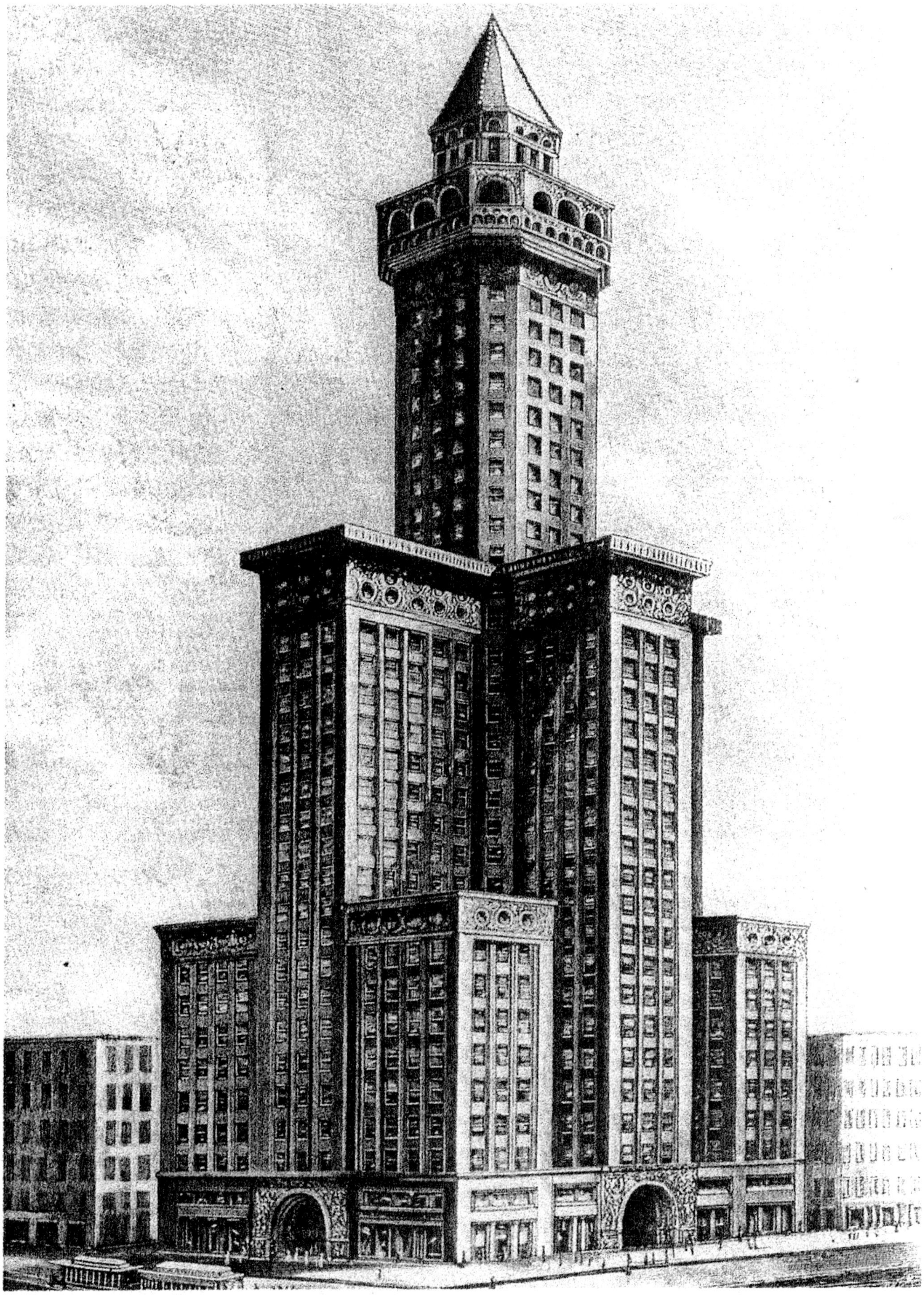

Sullivan's 1891 design for a Fraternity Temple for the Odd Fellows would have been the world's tallest building at 556 feet and thirty-six stories had it been built. Other architects would widely copy his use of setbacks. Difficulties in locating a site, and arranging financing, prevented its realization. (An Alamy image)

JEWELERS BUILDING

1881, CHICAGO

Now known as the Jewelers Building because of the businesses that later became its main tenants, it was commissioned by Martin Ryerson as an income property. The first primary tenant was paper goods retailer S.A. Maxwell, which is the name by which the building was originally known. When completed, Sullivan was still an employee. In May 1883, Sullivan became a partner; thereafter, the firm became Adler & Sullivan.

Exterior materials of the building are pressed brick and Ohio sandstone, with exposed structural cast-iron elements. The first two floors have been extensively remodeled over its long life, primarily due to changing retail tenants, but have recently been modified to suggest the original design; the upper floors, however, are little changed. Most of the decorative flourishes are at the top, with carved stone panels and a fan cornice. The north corner (left in photo) has a chamfered bay since it didn't directly abut the neighboring building, as was the case at the other side. Few original interior details survive. It is now used as a combined commercial space and hotel. The lobby is a circa 1910 alteration by other architects. It was added to the National Register of Historic places in 1974 and became a Chicago Landmark in 1981.

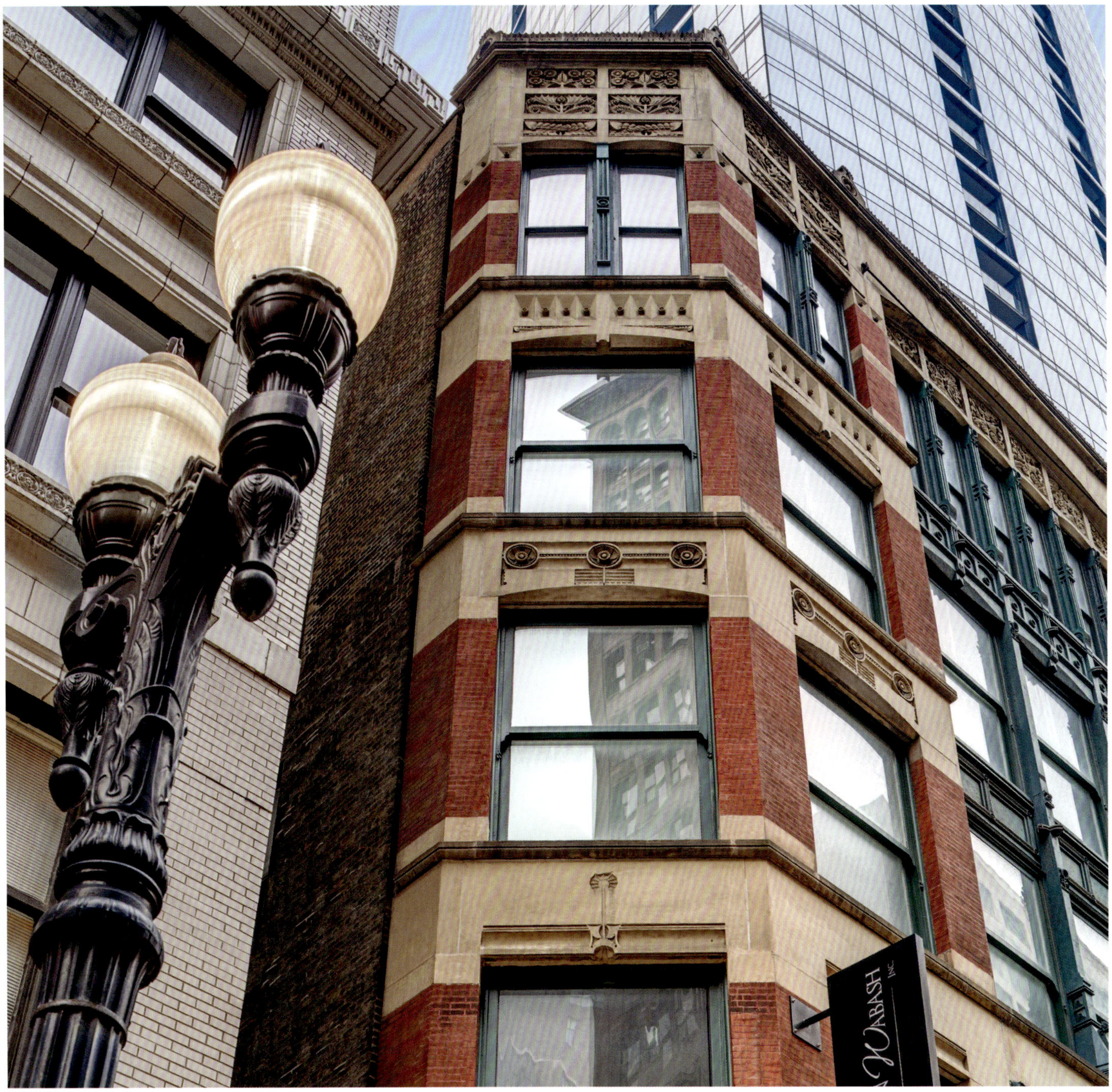

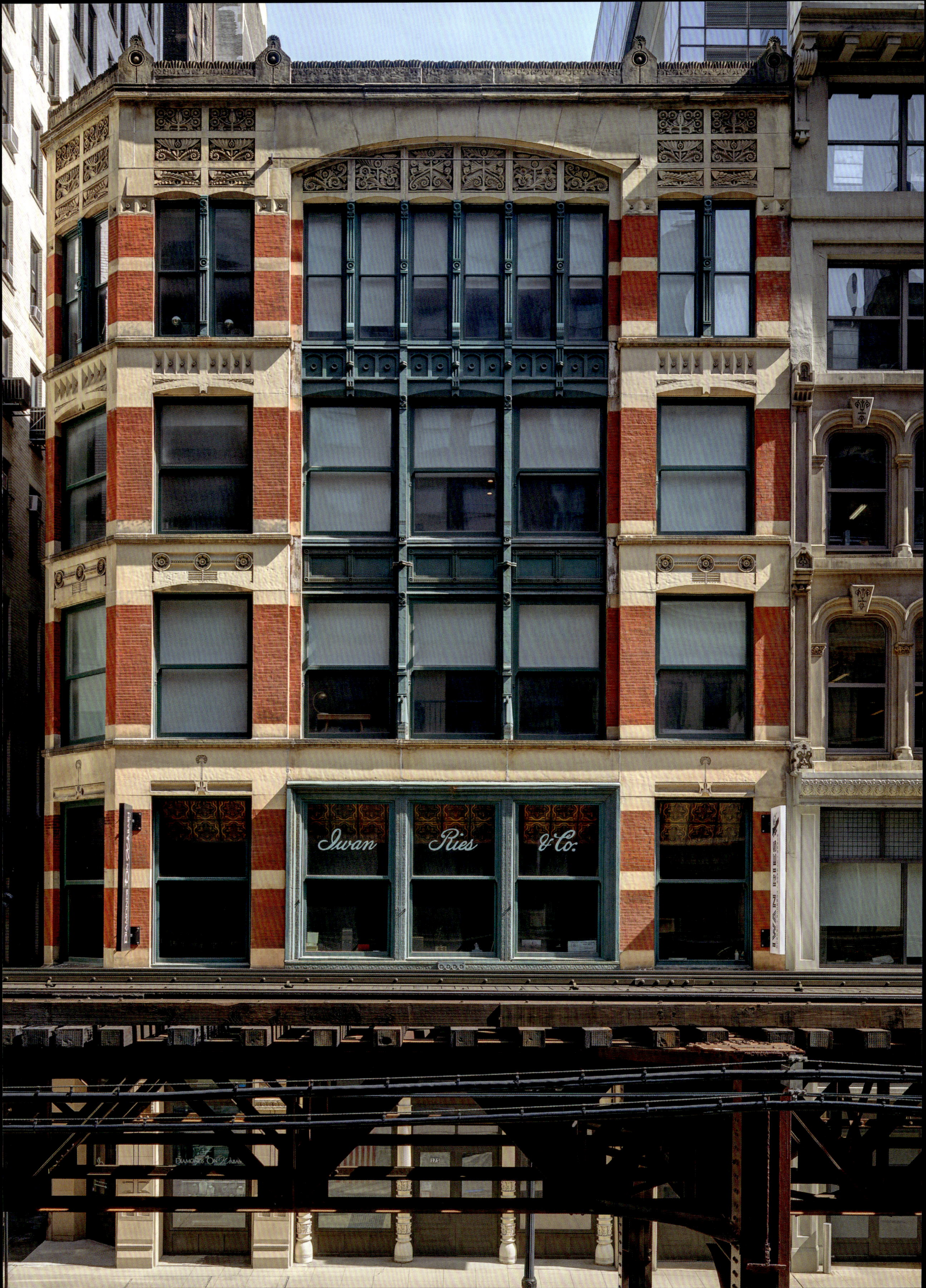

Iwan Ries &Co.

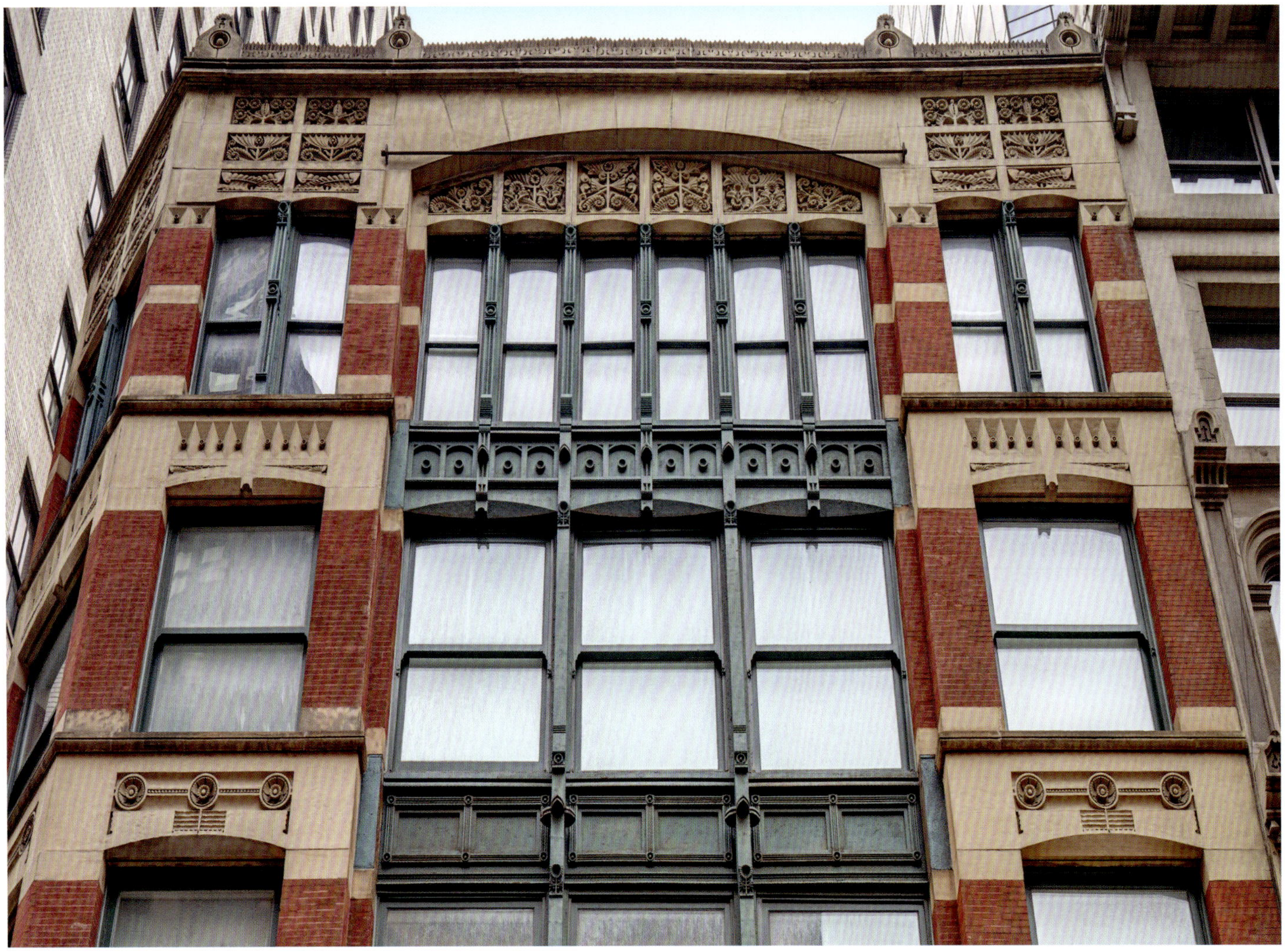

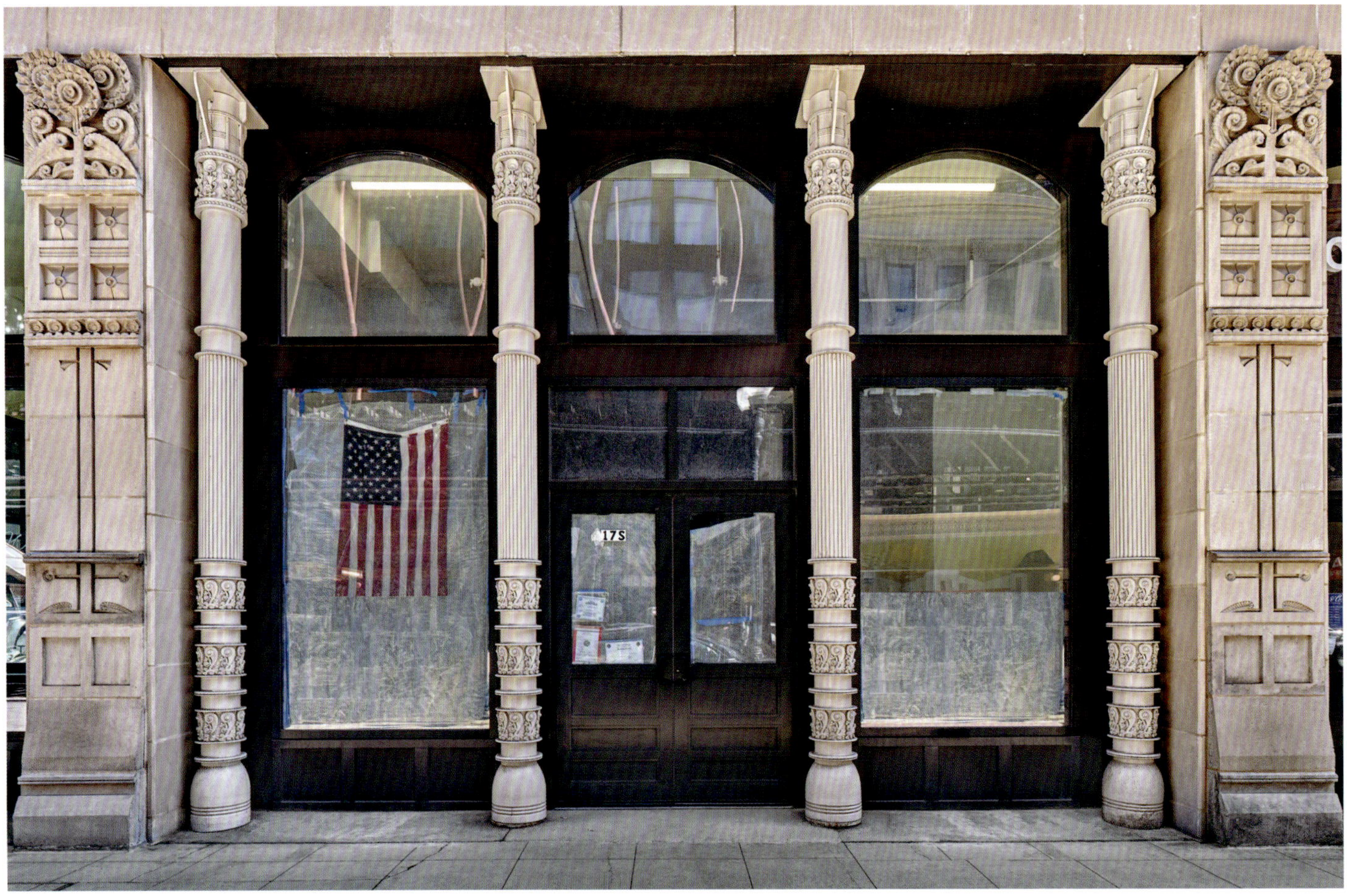

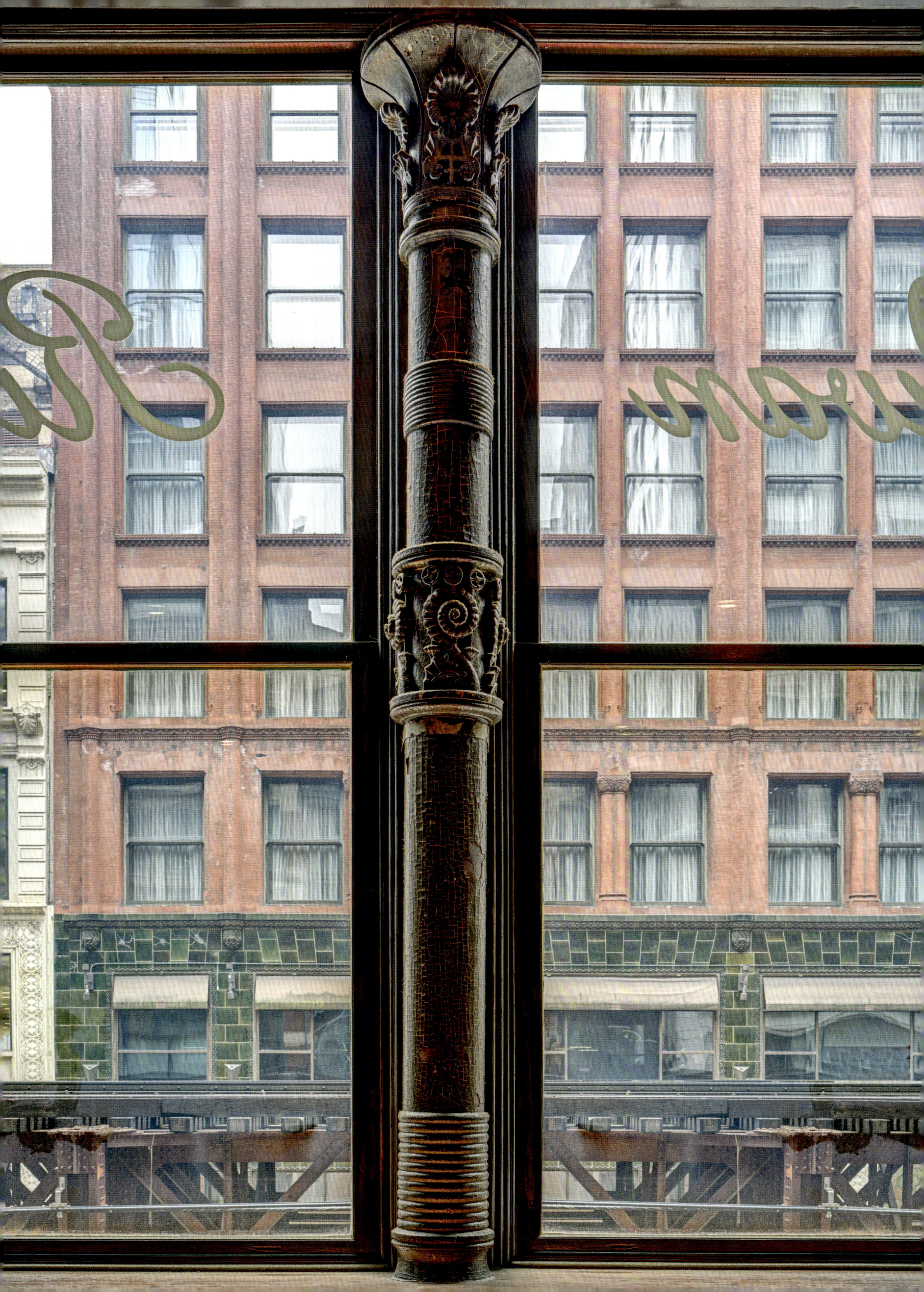

WAINWRIGHT BUILDING

1890, ST. LOUIS, MISSOURI

A true landmark in the history of the skyscraper, the Wainwright Building was commissioned in 1890 by brewer Ellis Wainwright and his mother, Catherine. The original architect chosen for the project was local practitioner Charles K. Ramsey. He designed a conventional building, but Wainwright, a noted art collector, seemingly wasn't satisfied. Adler & Sullivan's Auditorium Building had been dedicated late the previous year to almost universal acclaim, which may well have encouraged Wainwright to enlist Adler and Sullivan to redesign the building. Ramsey would remain as associate architect for this and other St. Louis projects and would supervise its construction. It would be Adler & Sullivan's first steel-framed building.

Frank Lloyd Wright later told the story of Sullivan throwing a sketch of the Wainwright on his drafting table. Wright said he immediately saw that his boss and mentor had "solved" the problem of the tall building. As he did with his later "skyscrapers," Sullivan provided a two-story base—in this case, of reddish granite—above which was a dividing string course, then continuous vertical brick piers and terra cotta spandrels, which are decorated with variations of the hop plant, a reference to Wainwright's business. Massive piers defined the corners. The building's top has a decorative frieze of leaves and interlocking circles, small circular windows to provide light to mechanical spaces, and a projecting cornice. These basic techniques would be used for all of Sullivan's subsequent tall buildings (and, interestingly, for Wright's own early tall-building designs, although none of his were actually built).

Like so many buildings of its vintage, the Wainwright eventually became outdated and was threatened with demolition in the 1970s. Through the efforts of then Governor Bond, the Wainwright was repurposed as a Missouri state office building. In addition to substantial interior modernization, it was expanded with the addition of a new annex. It was added to the National Register of Historic Places and named a National Historic Landmark in 1968 and designated a St. Louis Landmark in 1972.

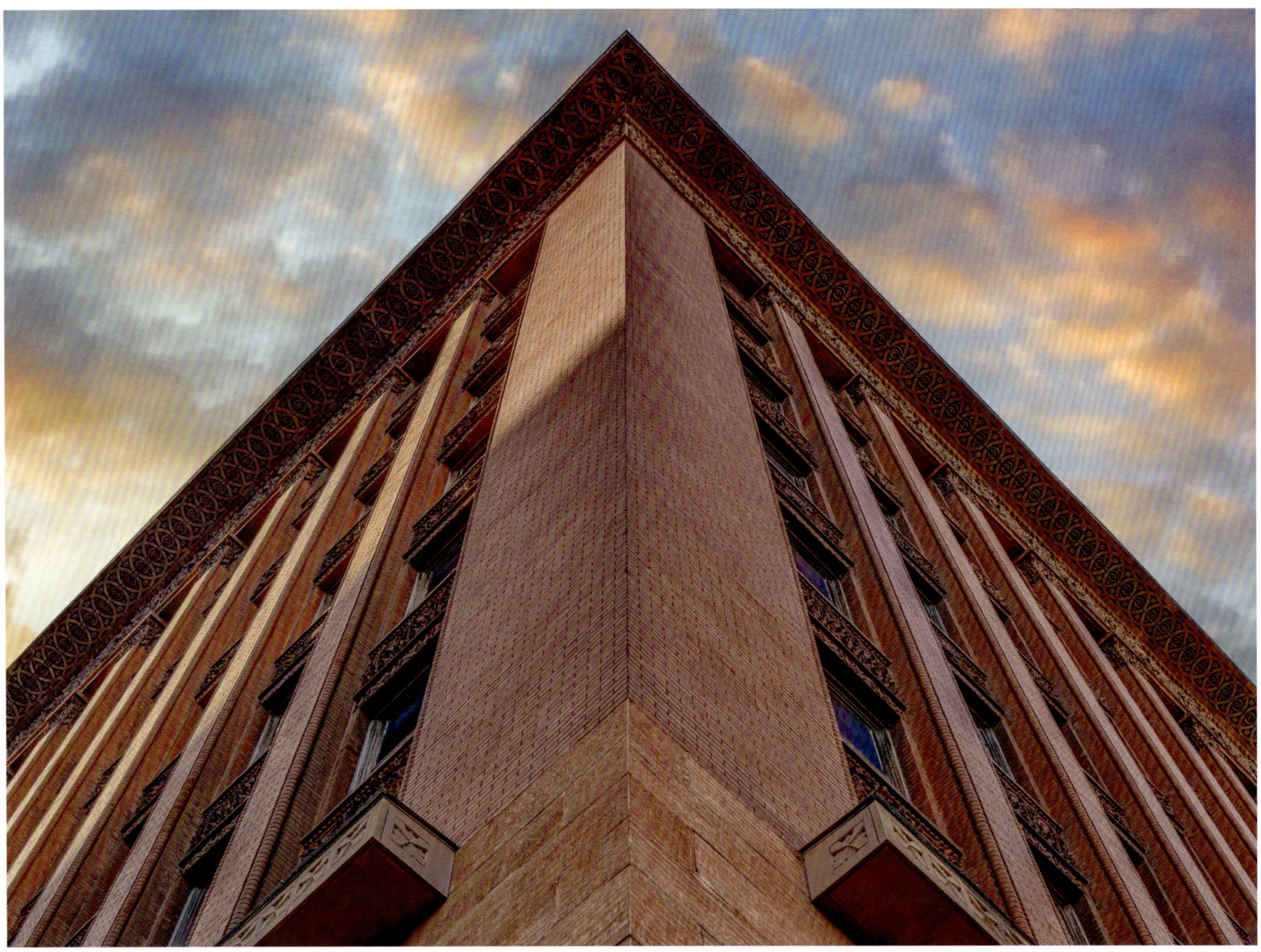

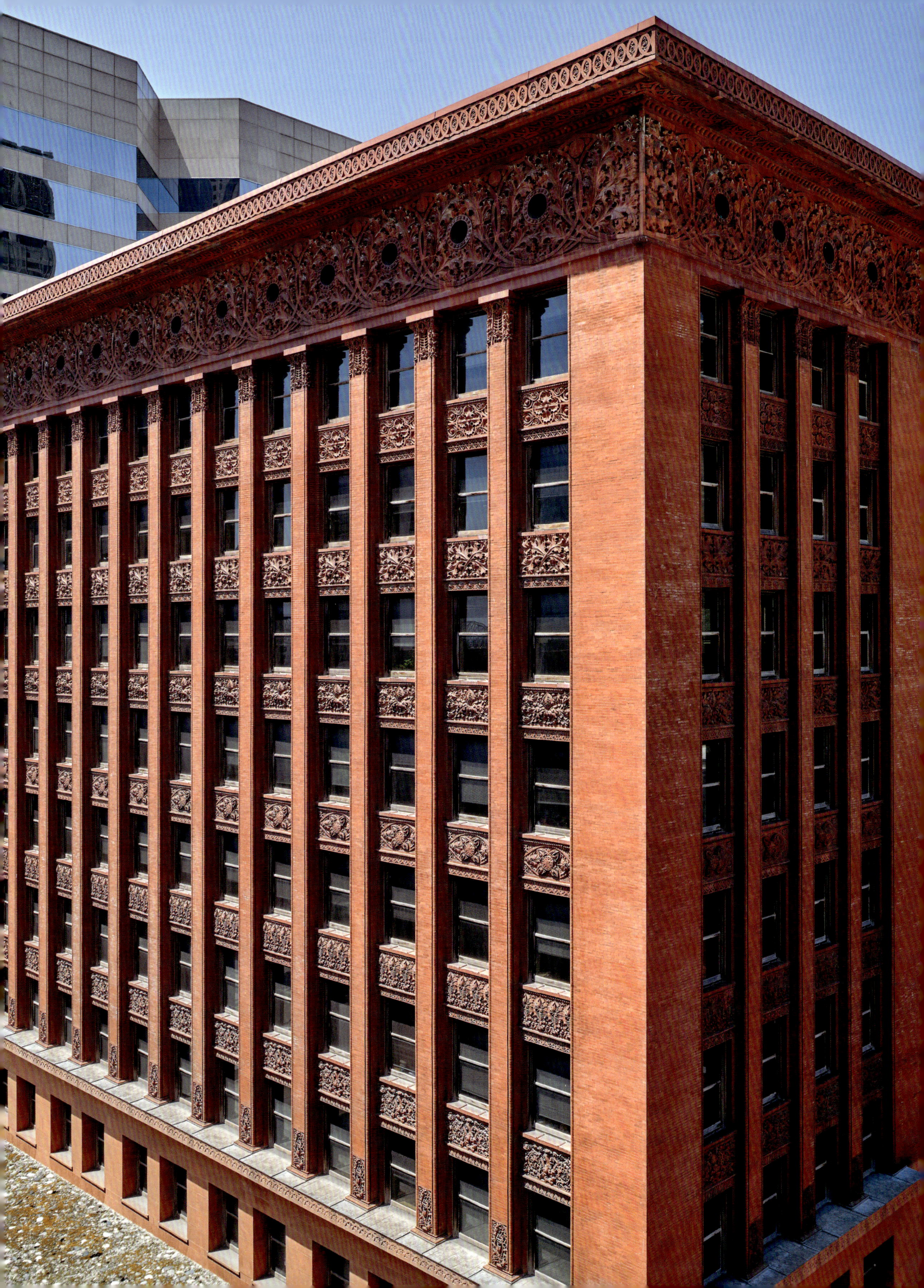

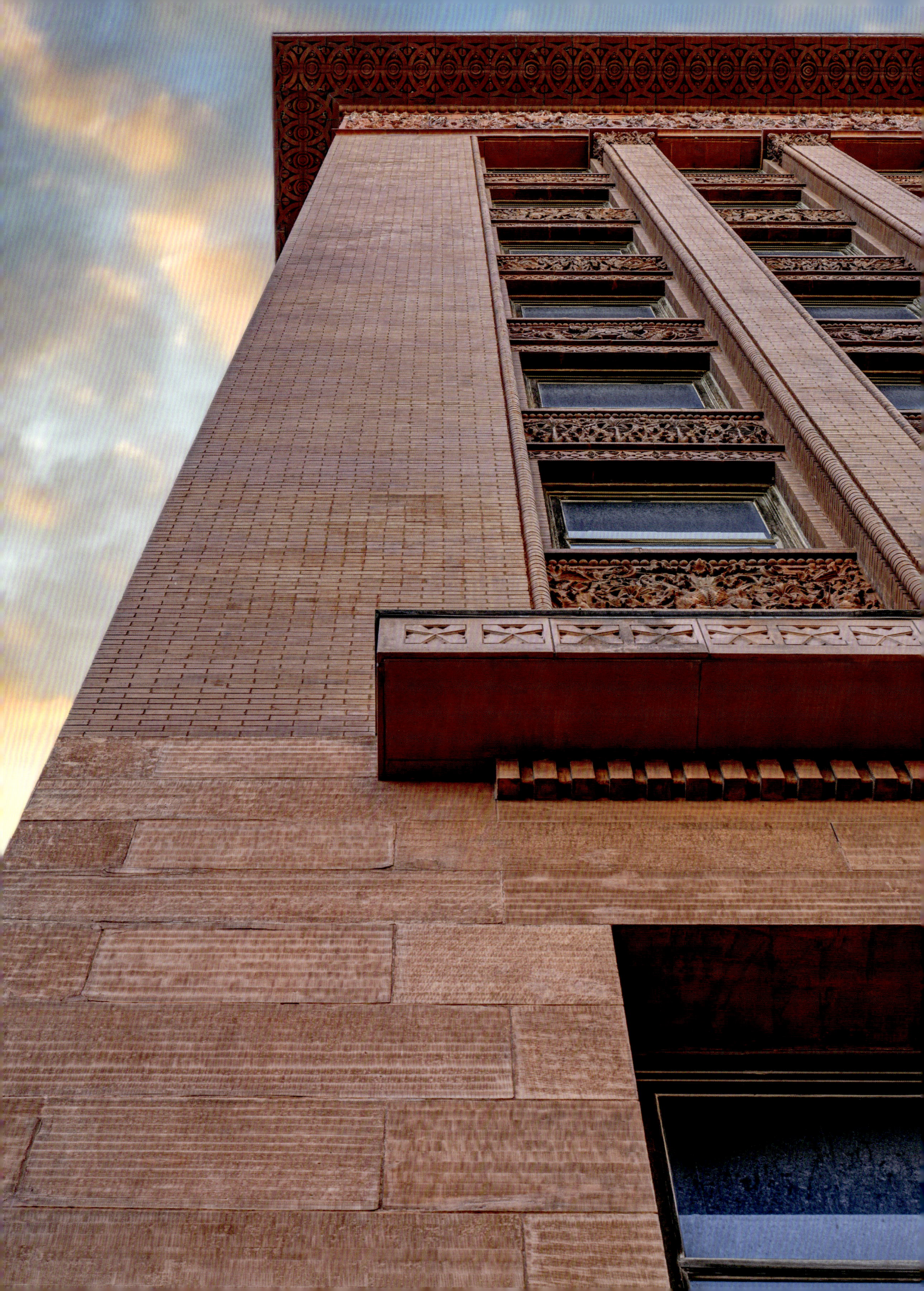

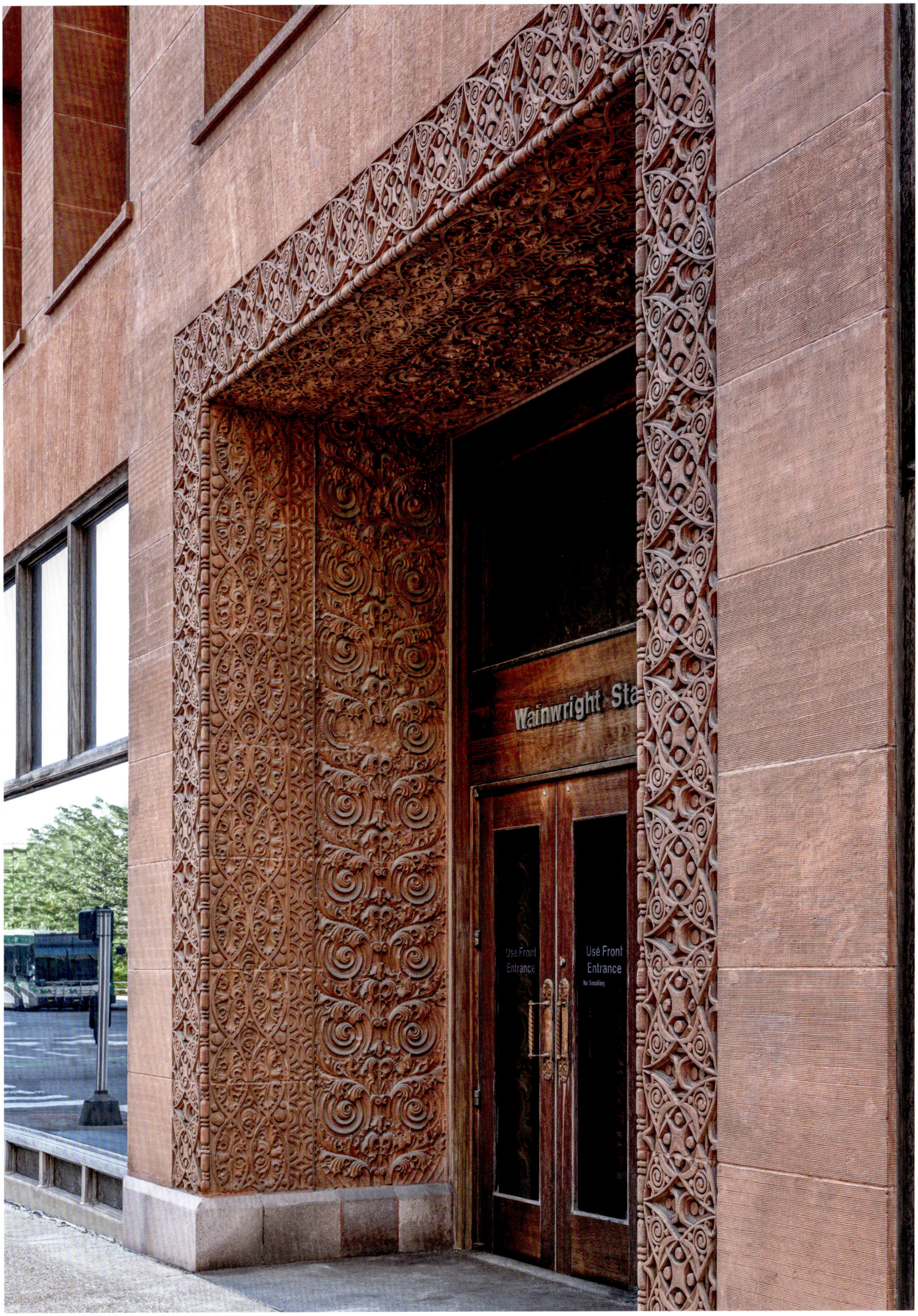
Wainwright Sta
Use Front
Entrance
Use Front
Entrance
No Smoking

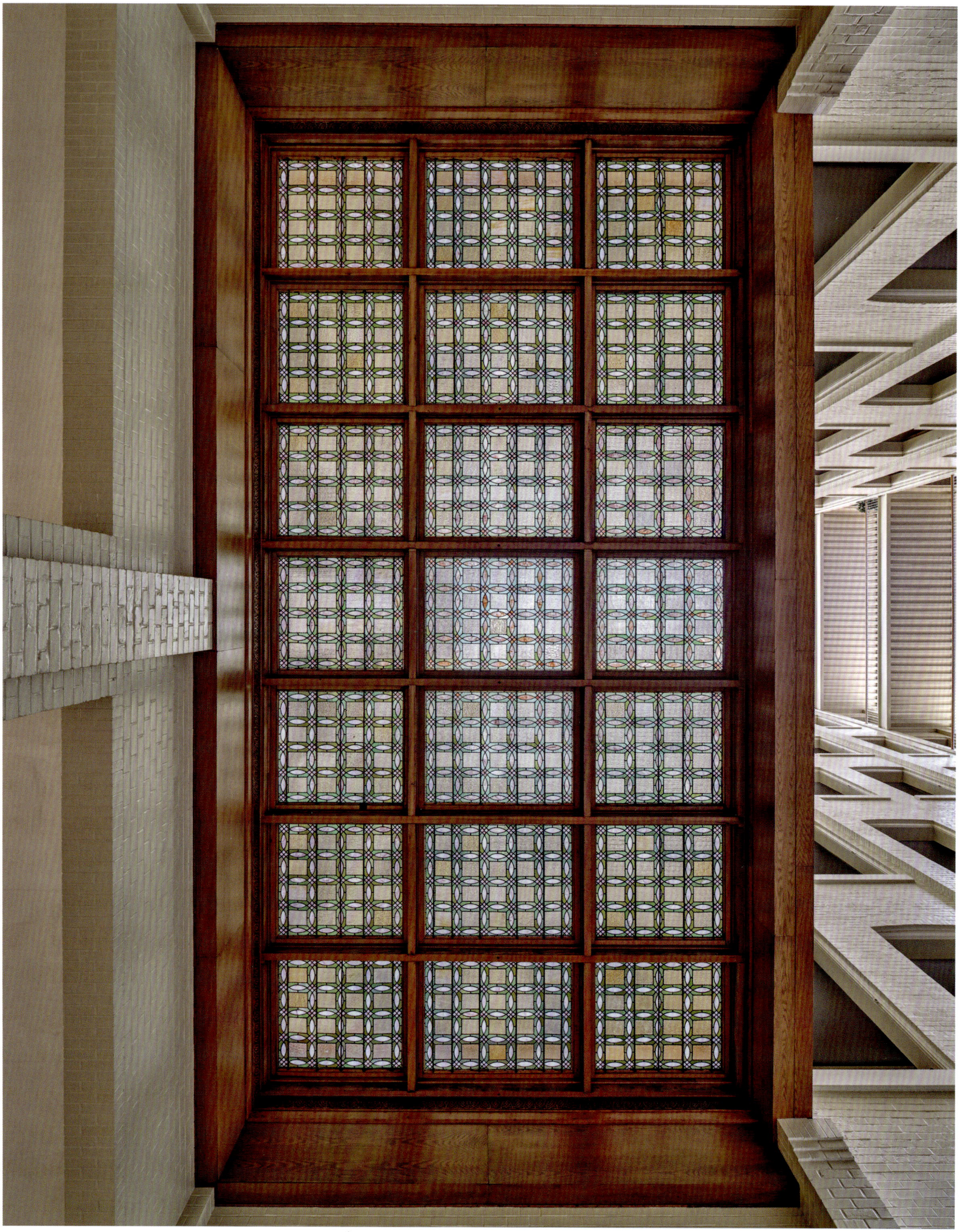

Before electric lighting became more efficient, large buildings typically had central light courts to bring natural light to interior spaces. Often, decorative laylights brought some of this light into lobbies.

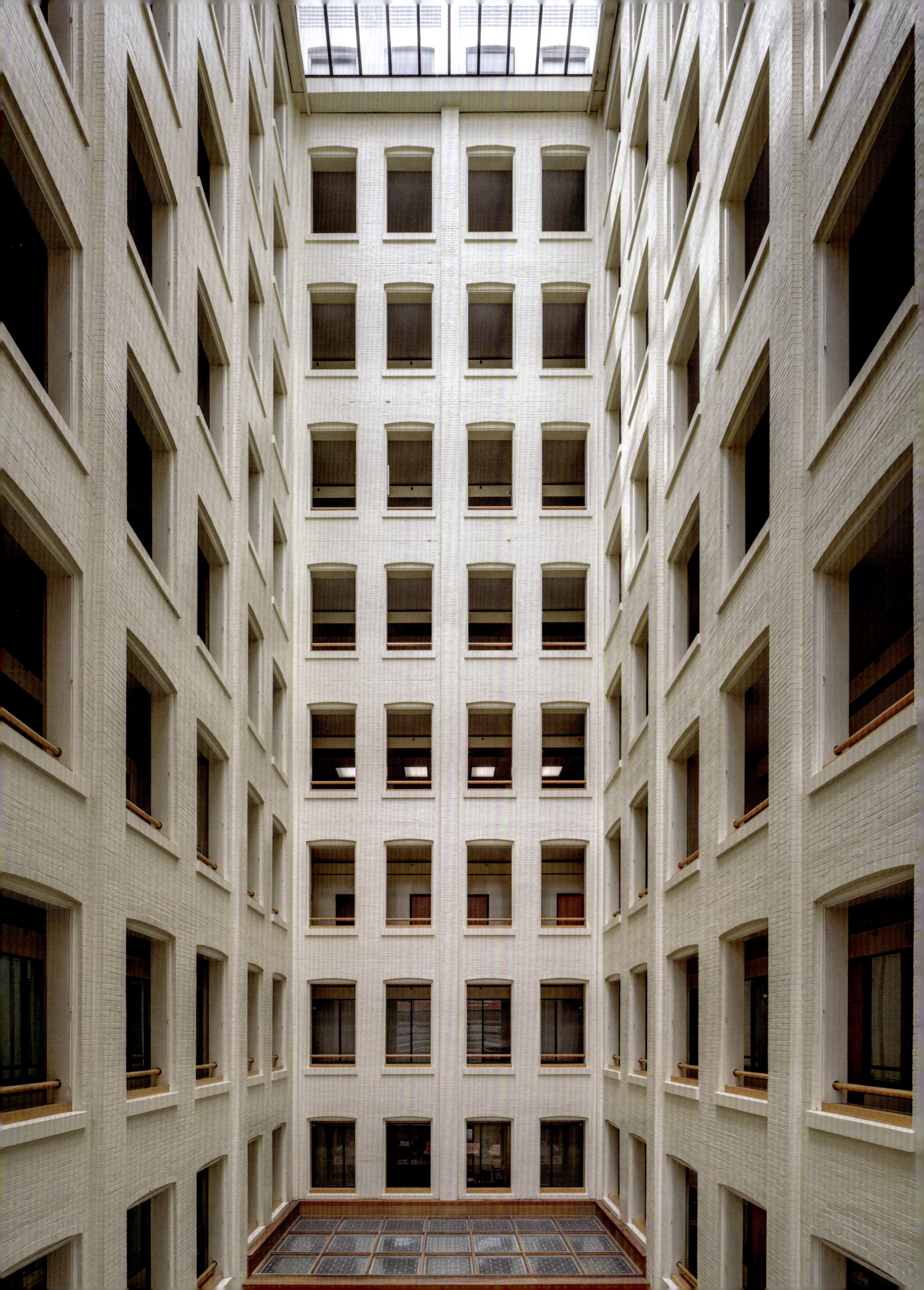

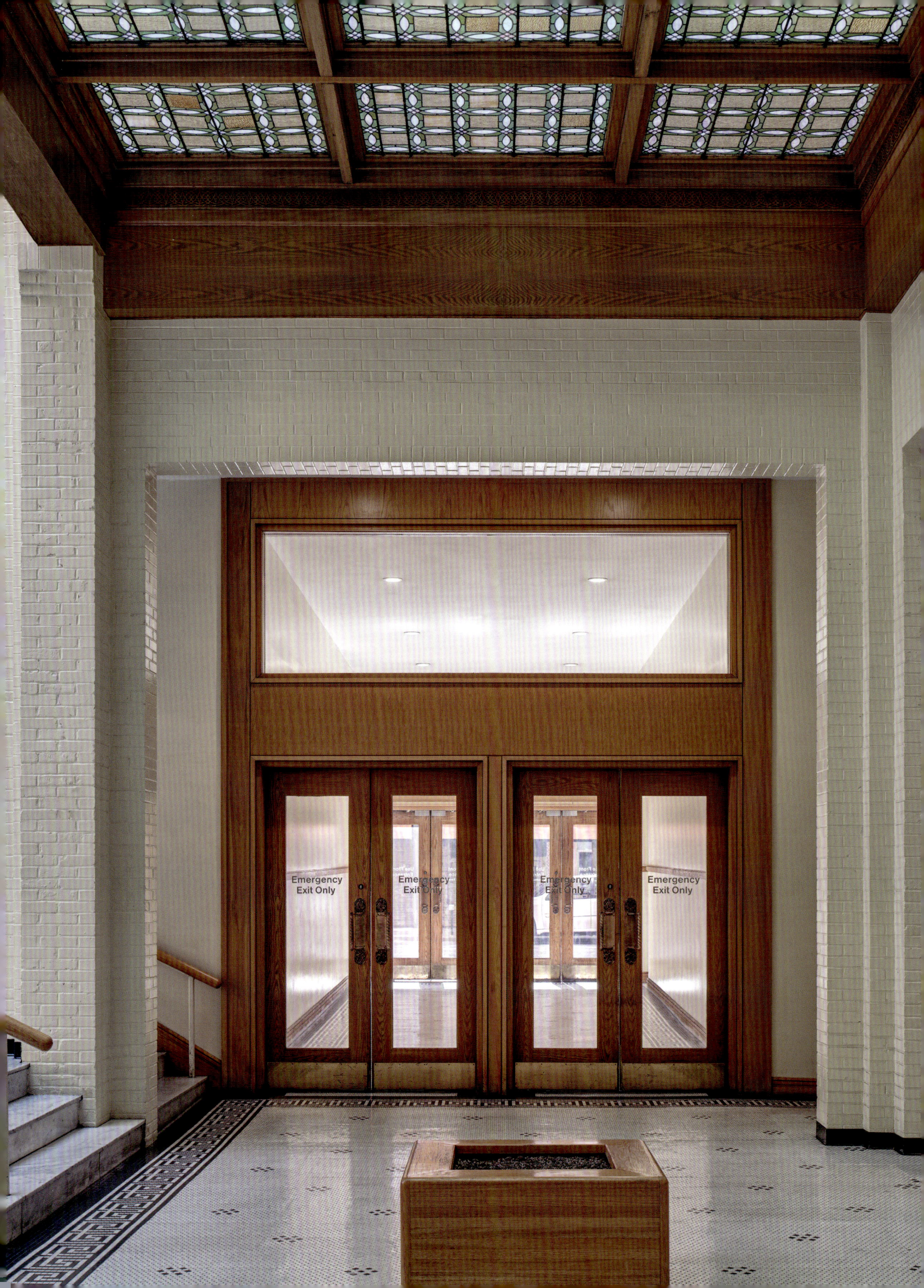
Emergency
Exit Only
Emergency
Exit Only

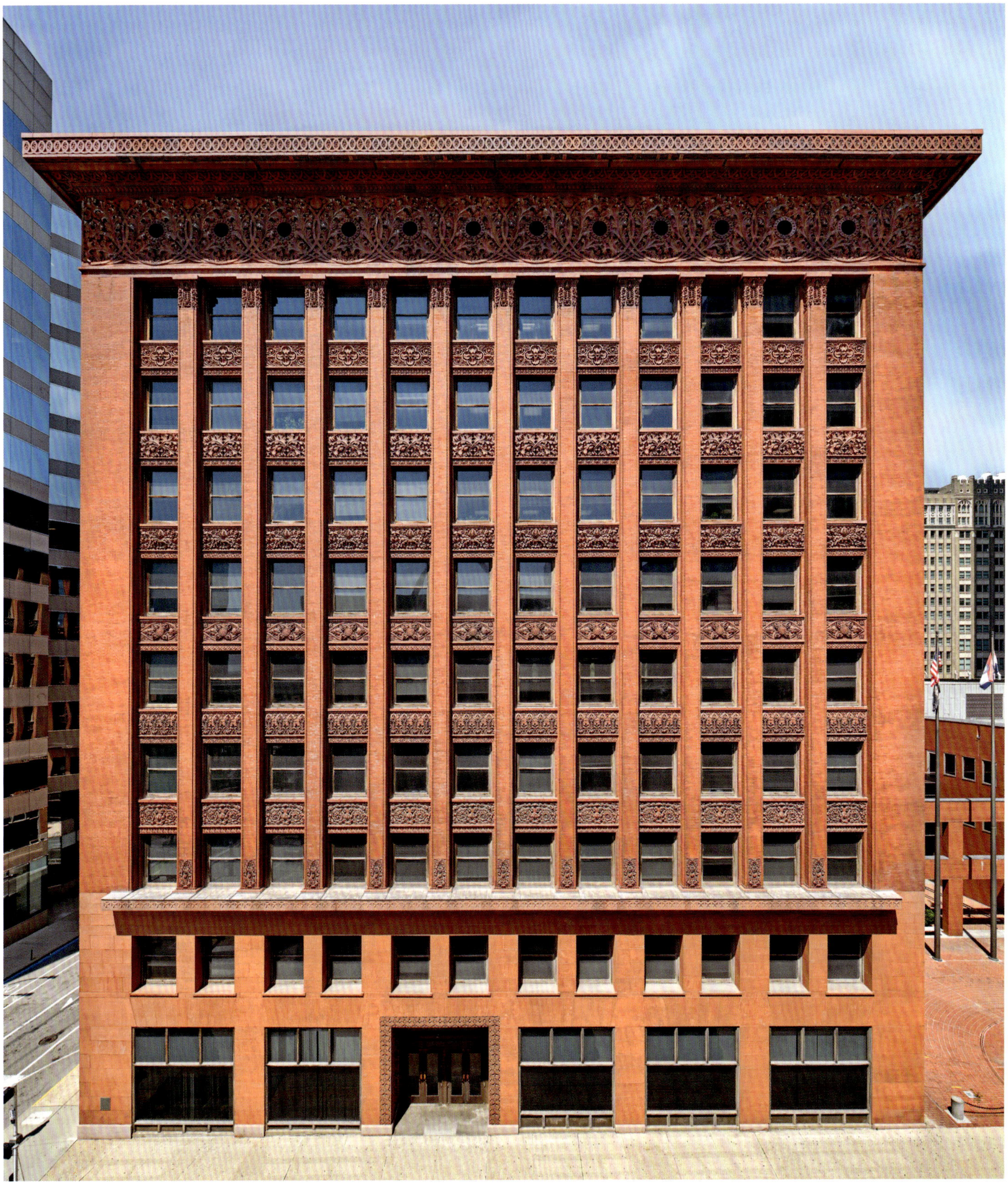

SCHILLER BUILDING

1891, CHICAGO

It could be argued that the demolition of the Schiller Building in 1961 was the most serious loss of the firm's work. Commissioned by members of Chicago's German community as the German Opera House Building, by the time of its completion, it became the Schiller, named for the German poet and playwright Friedrich Schiller (1759–1805). Because it was both an office building and a theater, the Schiller Building is as much a testament to Adler's structural genius as it is to Sullivan's design virtuosity.

The tower rose to seventeen stories (of which the theater took seven), flanked by two nine-story wings. Behind the tower was a fourteen-story wing, forming the base of a T-shaped plan that ensured outside light would reach every office. Directly to the east (right in the illustration)—and in strong contrast to it—was Dankmar Adler's Borden Block of 1880. Sullivan had joined the firm by then, and certainly participated in its design. In this colored postcard image, the gabled building in the distance to the east is Burnham and Root's Masonic Temple Building, which, at twenty-two stories, was the tallest building in the world when it was completed in 1892. (Postcard published by Acmegraph Co., Chicago. Courtesy, Patricia A. Sabin.)

This section of the second-floor colonnade that honored notable German figures is the only major piece of the Schiller Building that survives. It graces the front façade of the famous Second City improv theatre in Chicago.

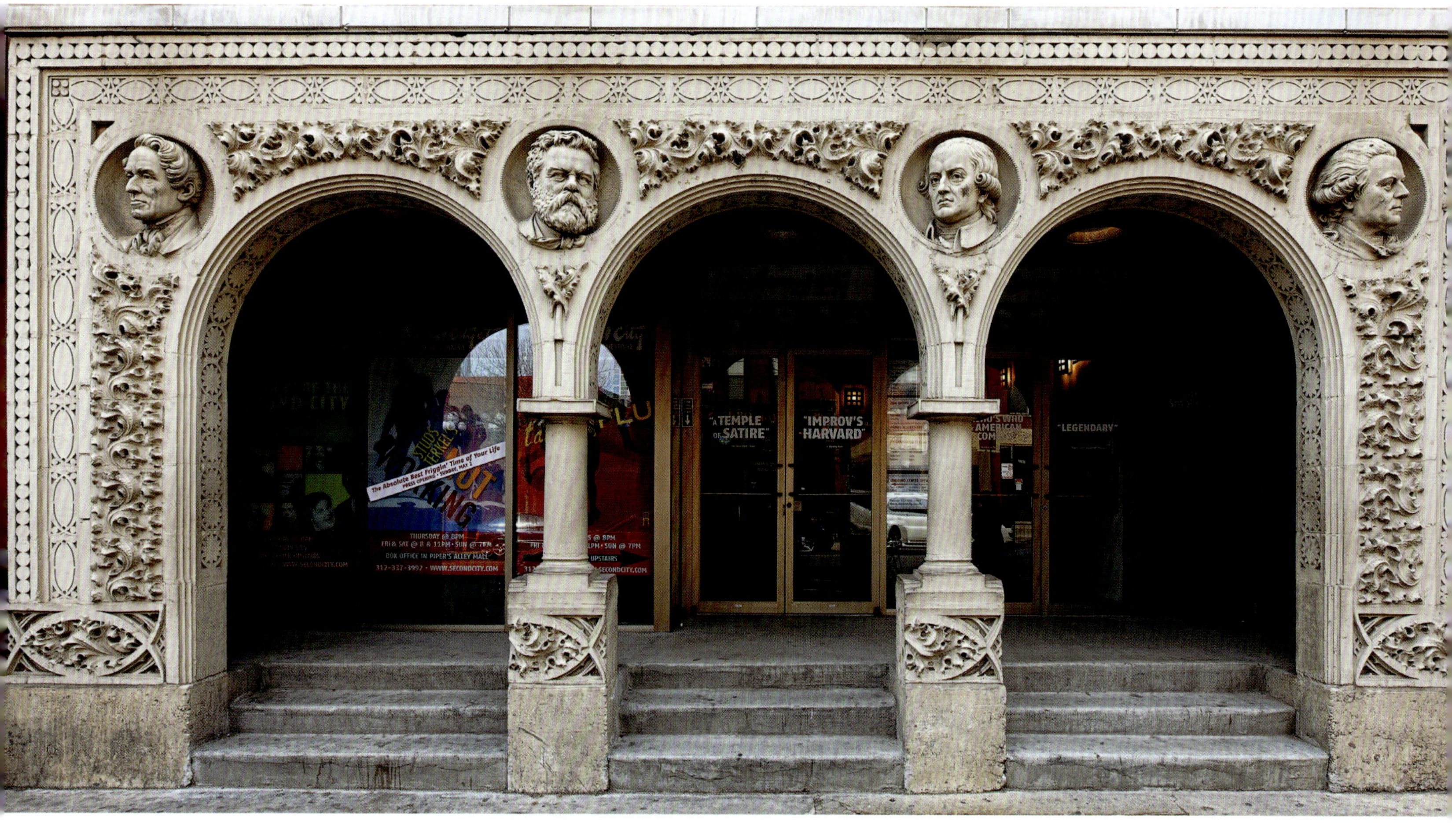

From left to right, they are composer Giacomo Meyerbeer; novelist Fritz Reuter; composer Wolfgang Amadeus Mozart; man-of-letters Gotthold Ephraim Lessing.

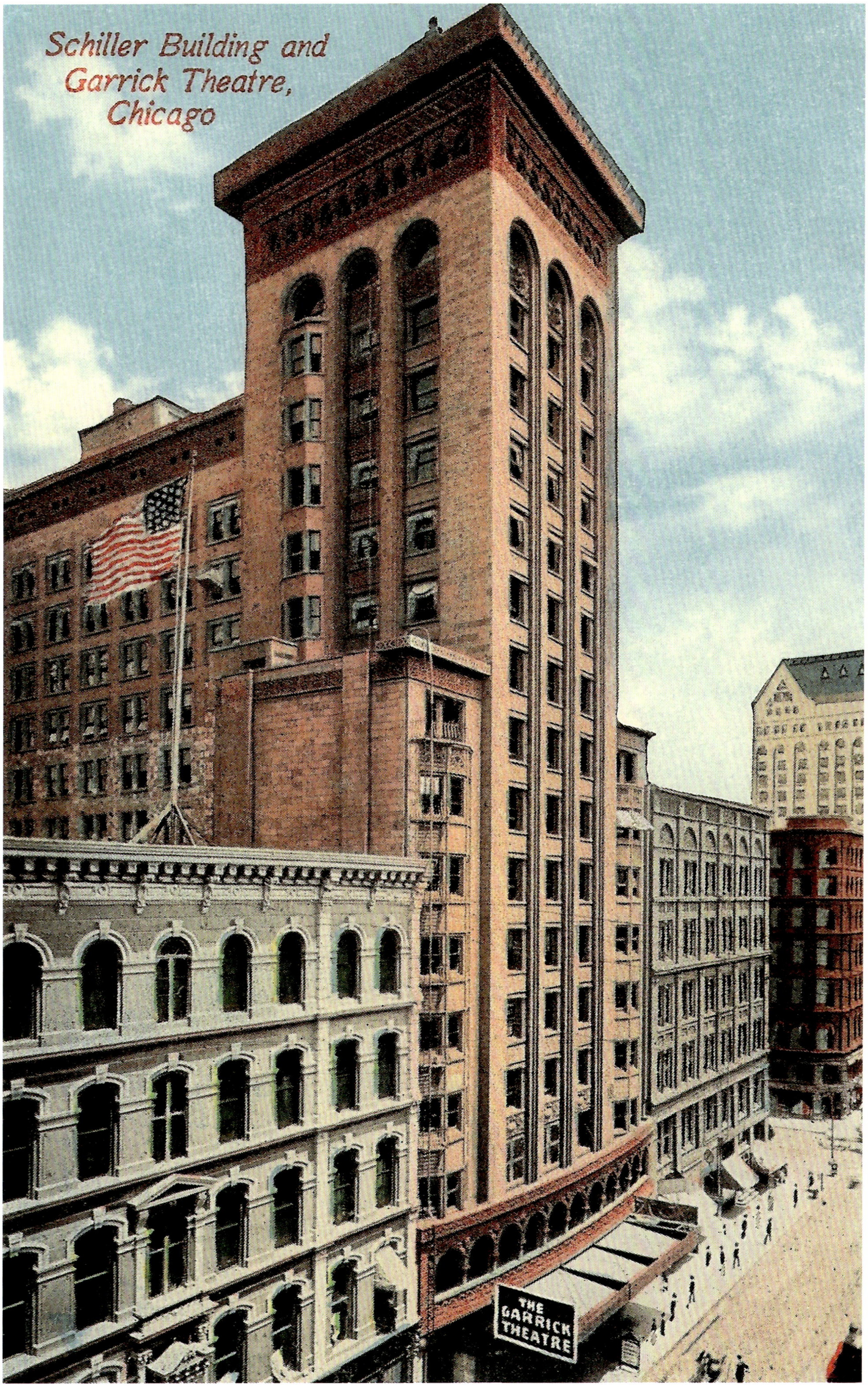
Schiller Building and
Garrick Theatre,
Chicago
THE
GARRICK
THEATRE

UNION TRUST BUILDING

1892, ST. LOUIS, MISSOURI

Originally named for the bank that occupied the first two floors, the Union Trust Building has since been repurposed as the Hotel St. Louis. As was true of most office buildings at the time, it has a U-shaped plan to provide a light court for interior offices, except in this case, the opening is in the front, which visually creates two separate towers of fourteen stories each (when built, it was the tallest building in the city). Prior to a 1924 remodeling, the two-story base had simple rectangular windows on the first floor and a highly-ornamented terra cotta second floor with circular windows and winged lions.

In 1905, the St. Louis firm of Eames & Young added a fourteen-story, four-bay addition on the east side to conform to the original design. Lost during the 1924 remodeling was the arched main entrance, which was similar to the one at Chicago's Stock Exchange. Above the base of the building, the exterior is much as Sullivan designed it. It was designated a St. Louis Landmark in 1971 and was added to the National Register of Historic Places in 2014.

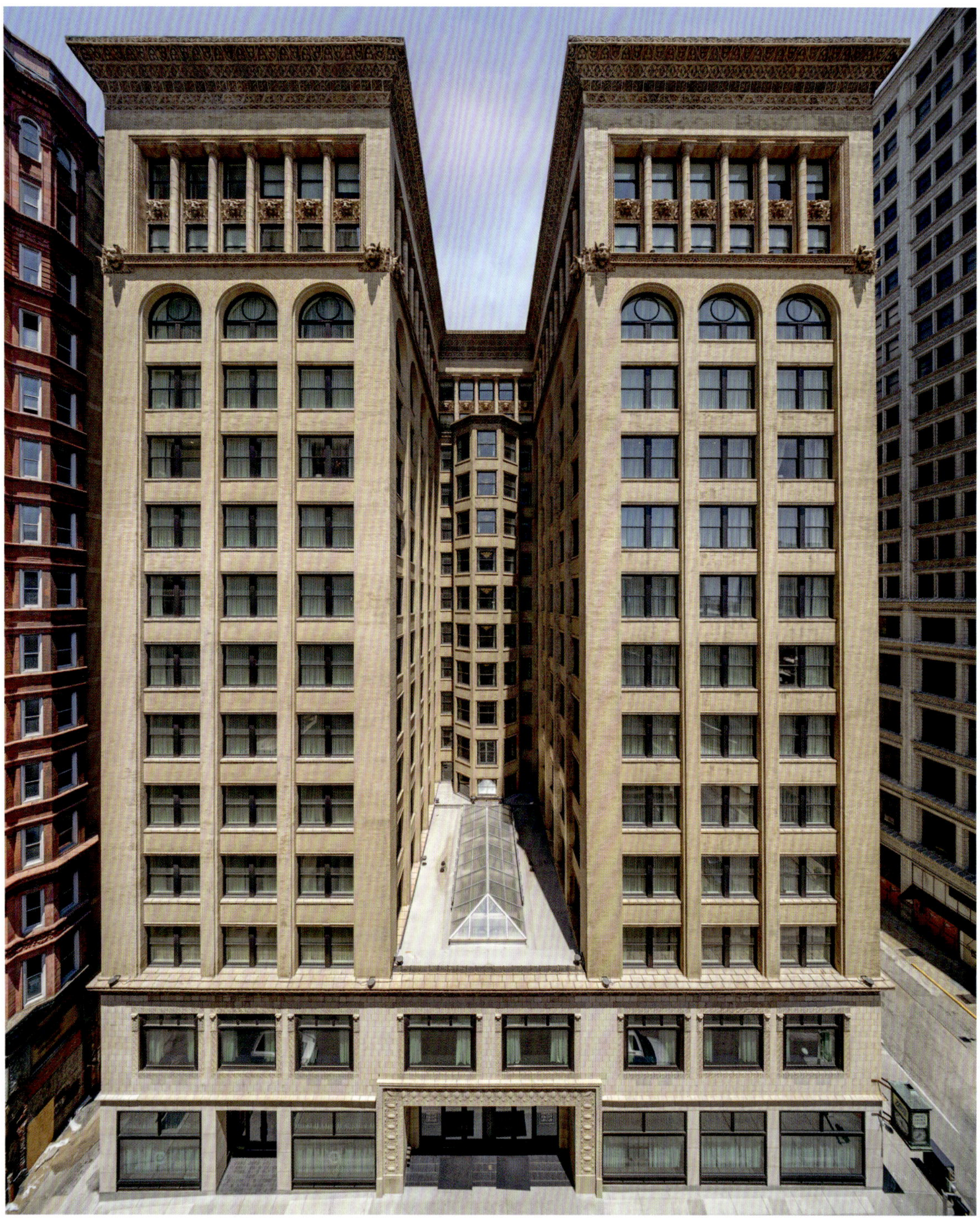

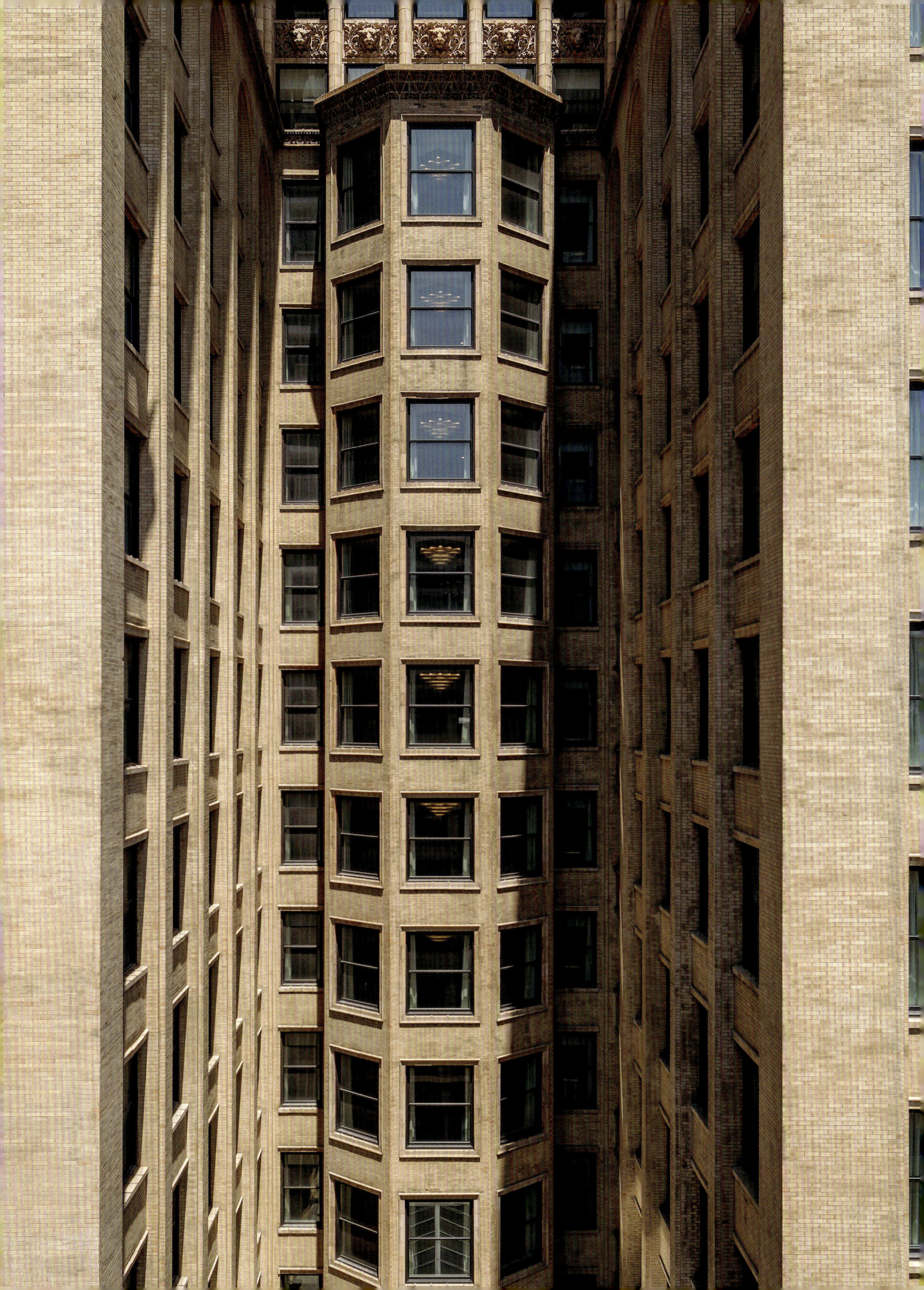

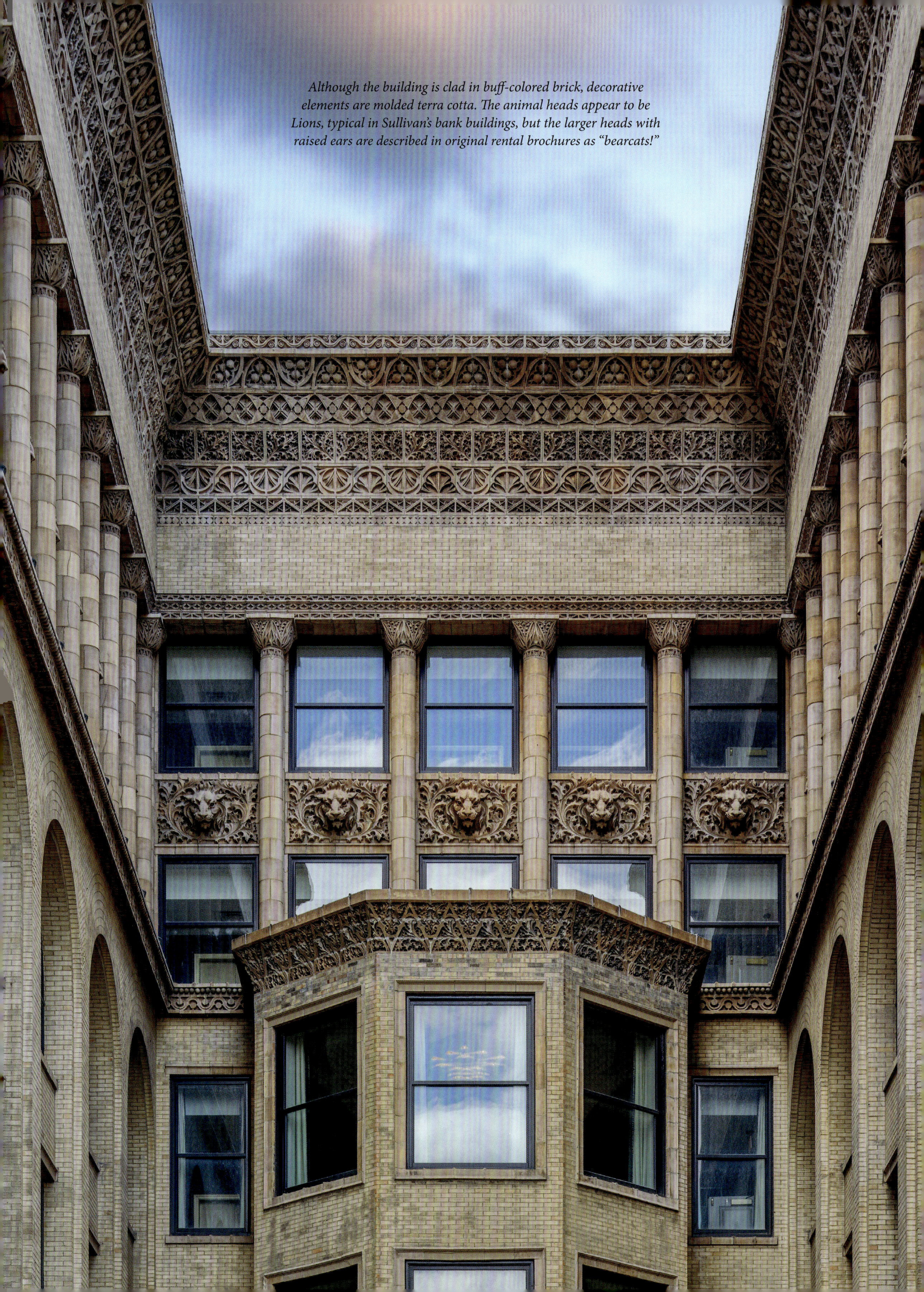

Although the building is clad in buff-colored brick, decorative elements are molded terra cotta. The animal heads appear to be Lions, typical in Sullivan's bank buildings, but the larger heads with raised ears are described in original rental brochures as "bearcats!"

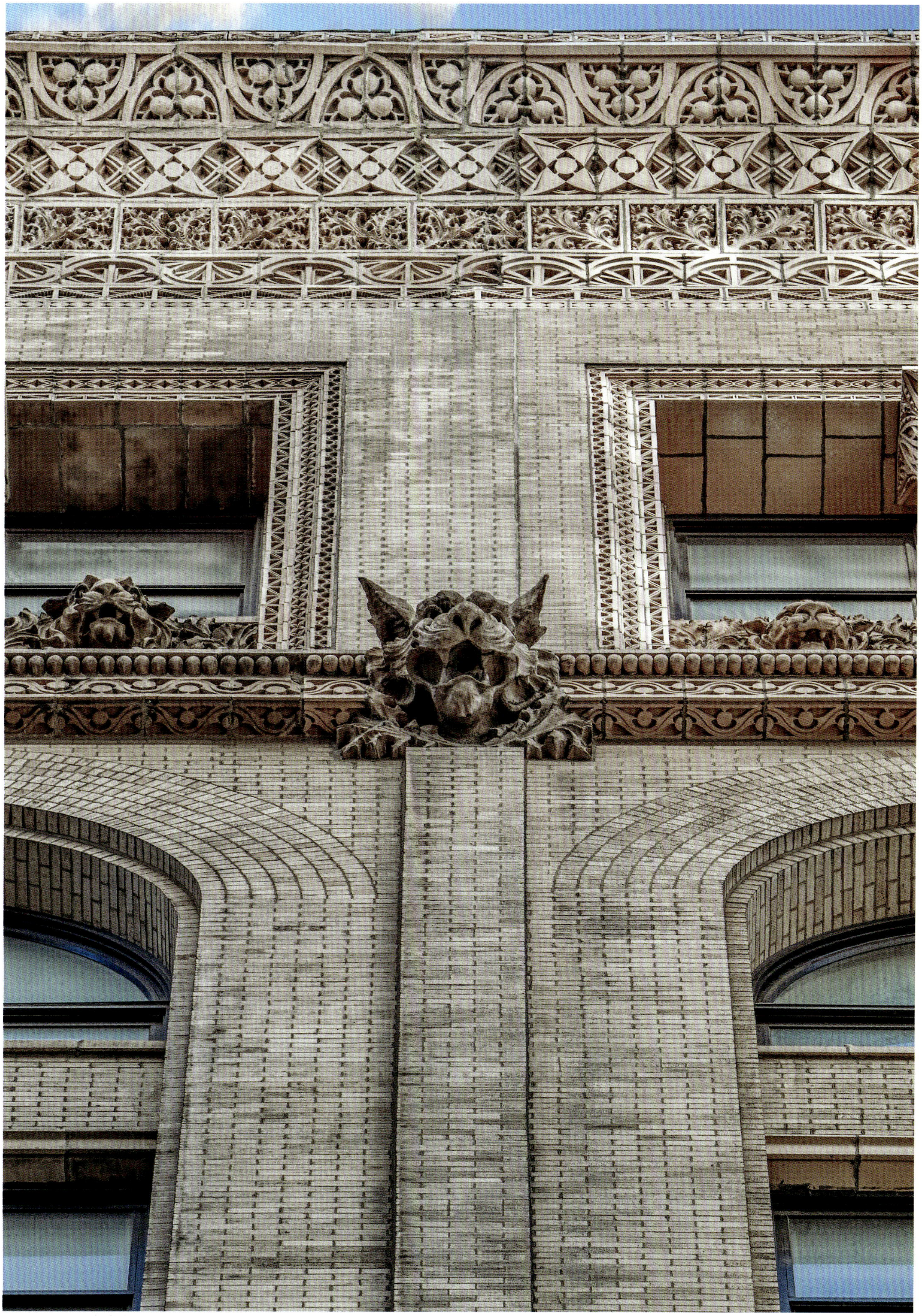

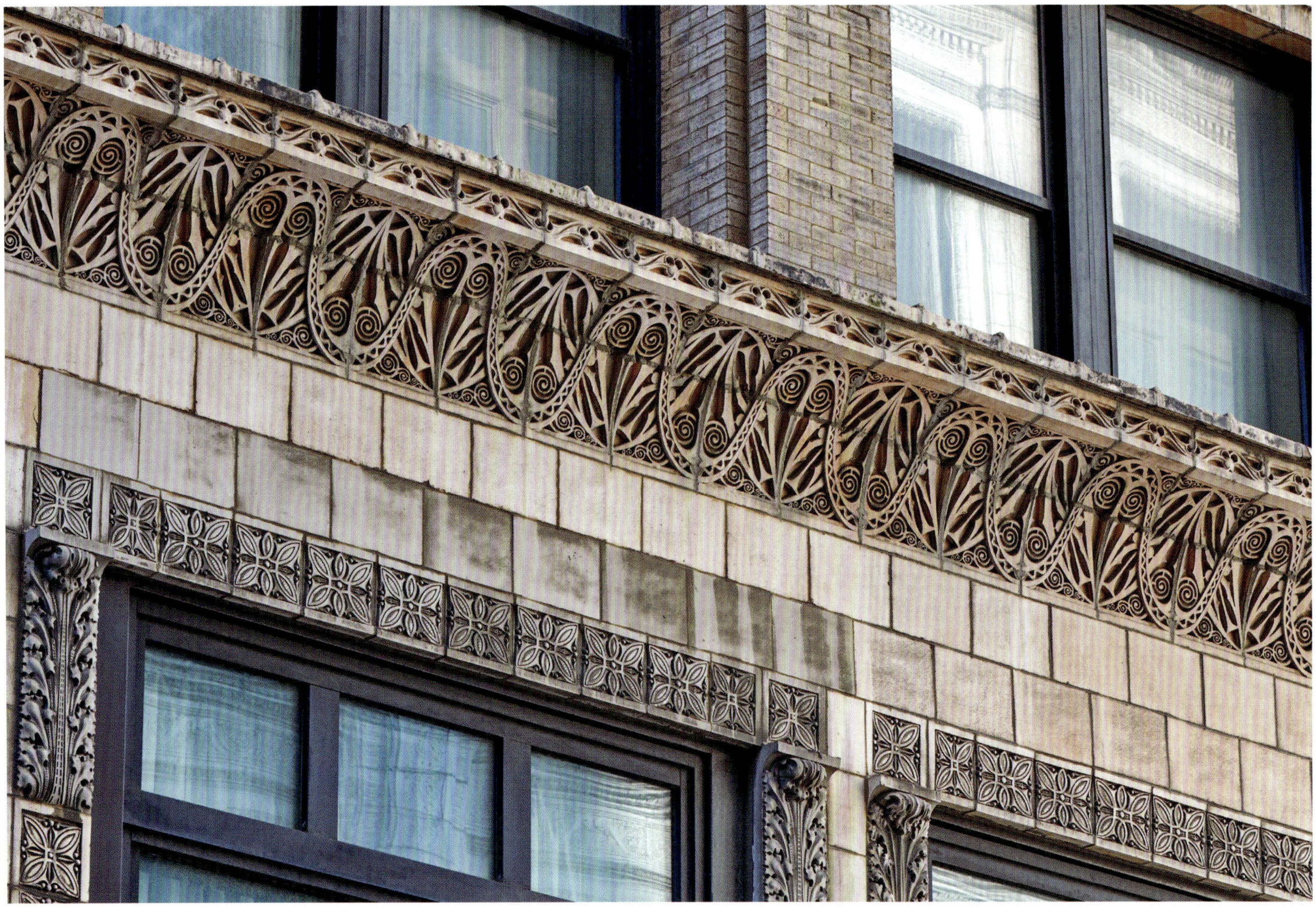

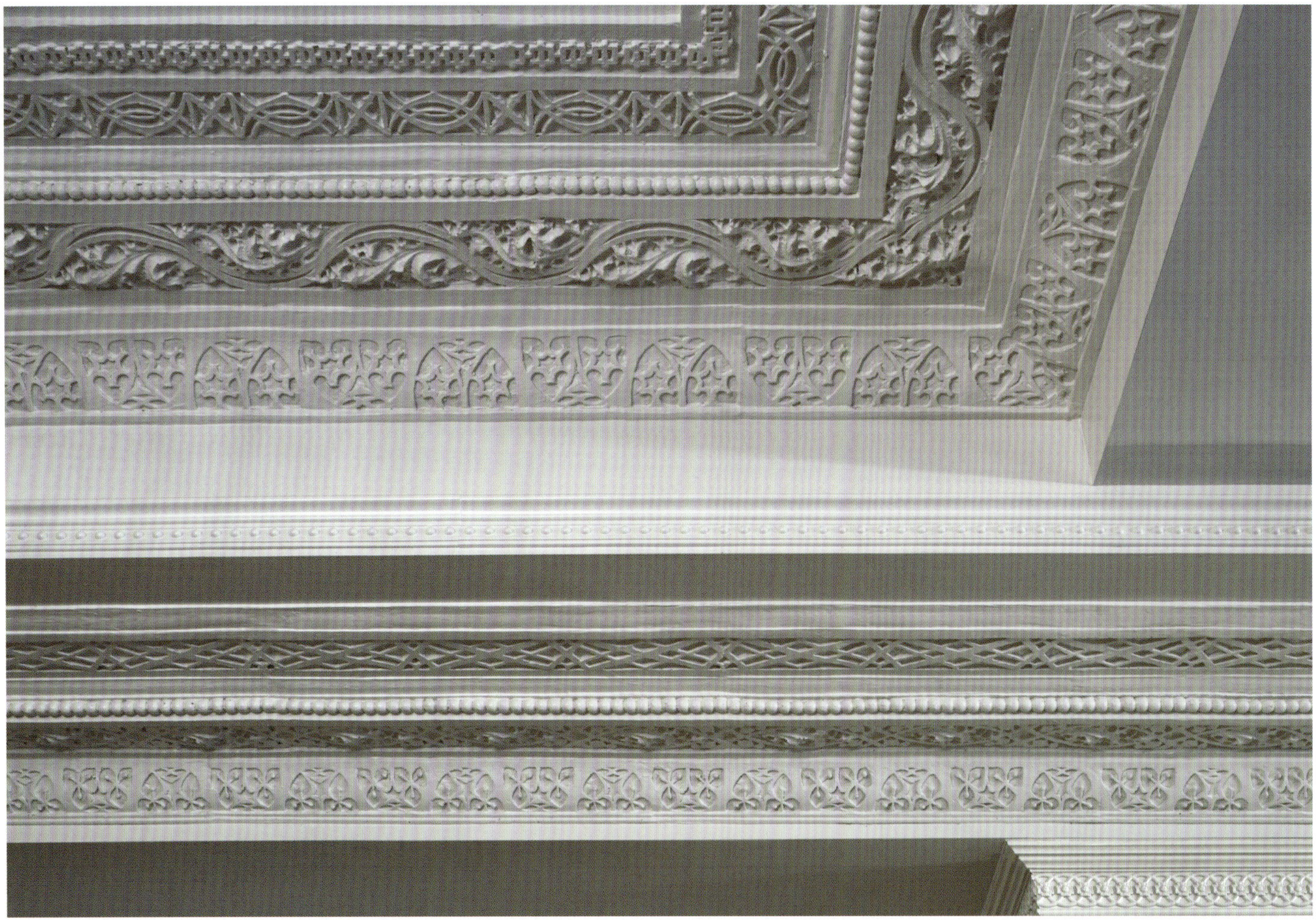

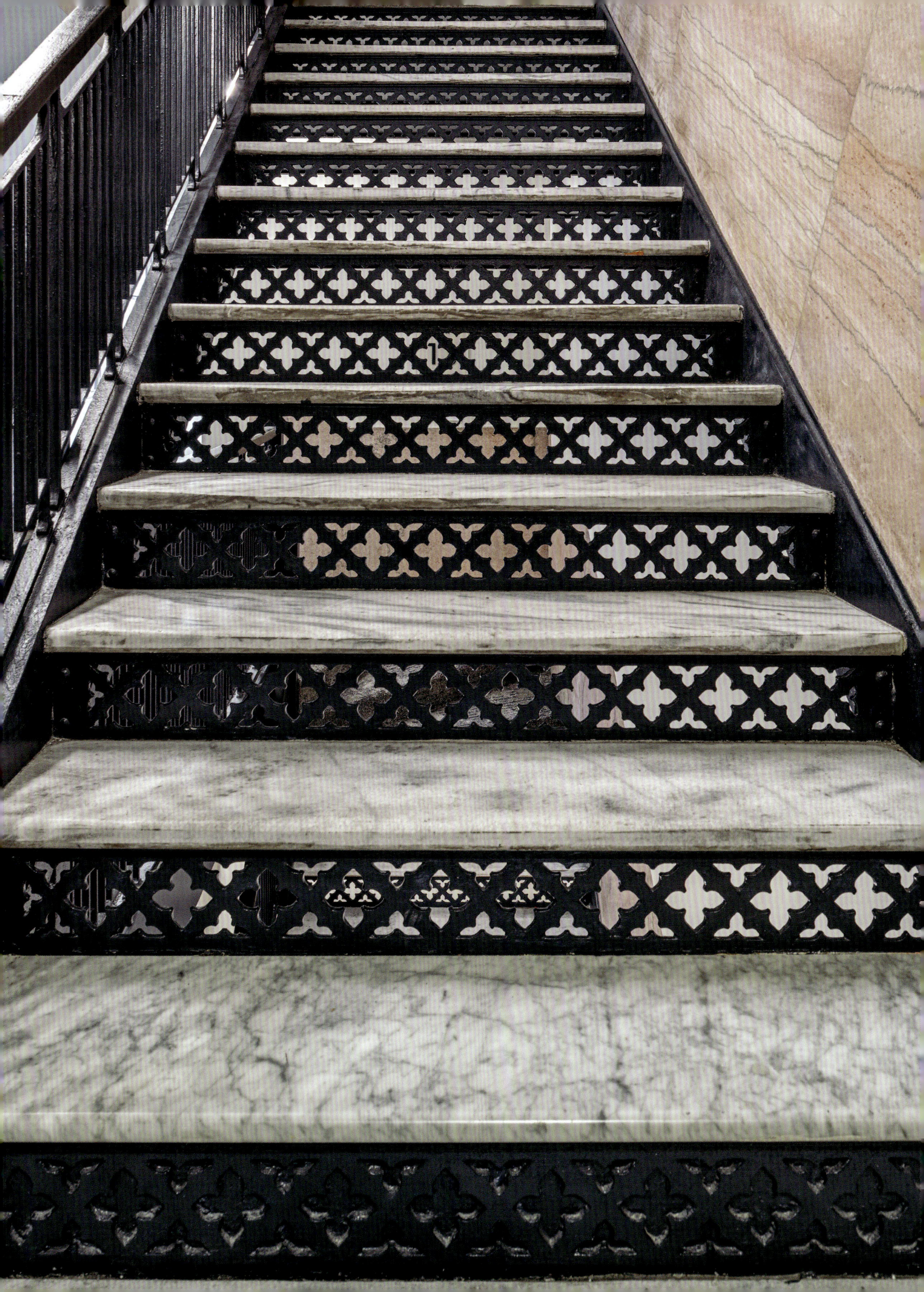

CHICAGO STOCK EXCHANGE

1893, CHICAGO

The Chicago Stock Exchange (1893) achieved its verticality not through the use of uninterrupted columns and mullions but by narrow projecting bays that began at the third-floor sill and ended at the colonnade that rings the building below the cornice. The LaSalle Street façade had six bays, and the Washington Street façade had three. They alternated with particularly large "Chicago" windows, which consist of a large, fixed center light, flanked by movable sashes. The Chicago window was used by many of Adler and Sullivan's contemporaries, most particularly, Holabird & Roche.

Although efforts were made by the local architects and preservationists to save the building, it was demolished in 1972.

This author was working across the street at the time and watched, day by day, as the building came down, only to be replaced by a mediocre steel and glass tower. As mentioned above, Richard Nickel—some of whose photographs appear in this book—died in a fall while trying to salvage some of the building's artifacts.

Fragments of the building are in museums and private collections. The arched entry was reconstructed on the Columbus Drive side of the Art Institute of Chicago, also home to the reconstructed Trading Room, which includes some original fragments and was directed by architects Vinci/Kenney.

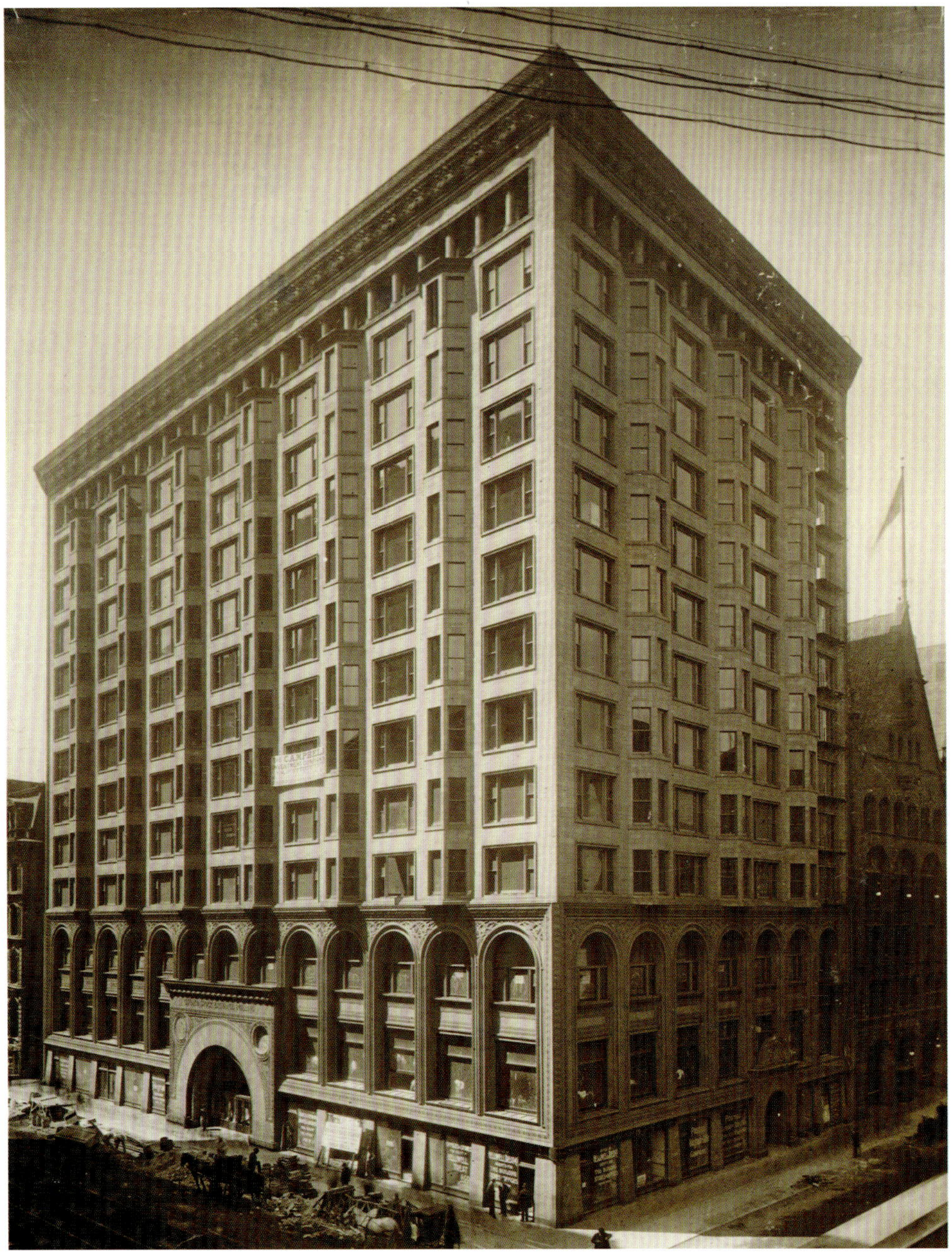

Photo courtesy Ryerson and Burnham Libraries, Art Institute of Chicago

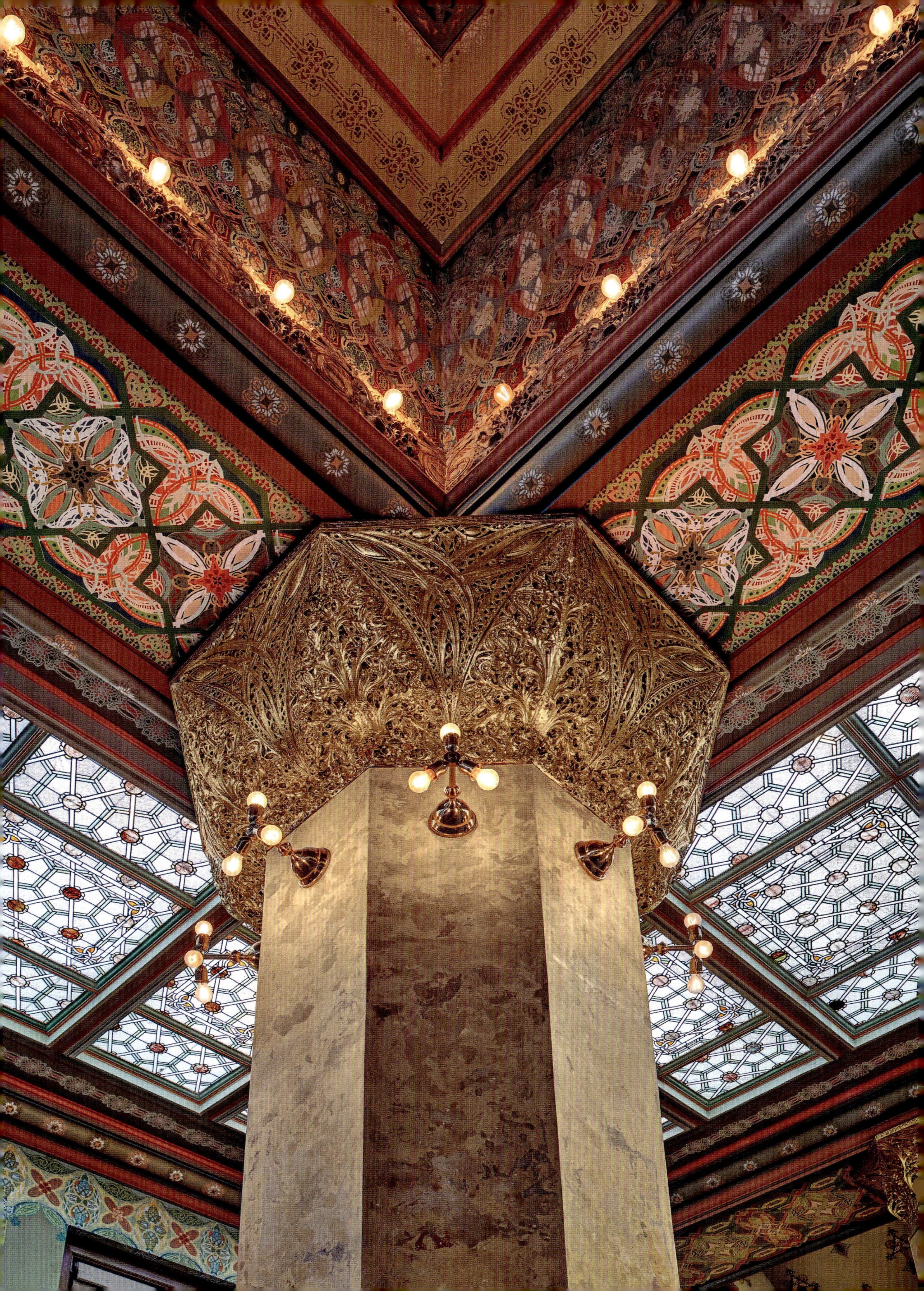

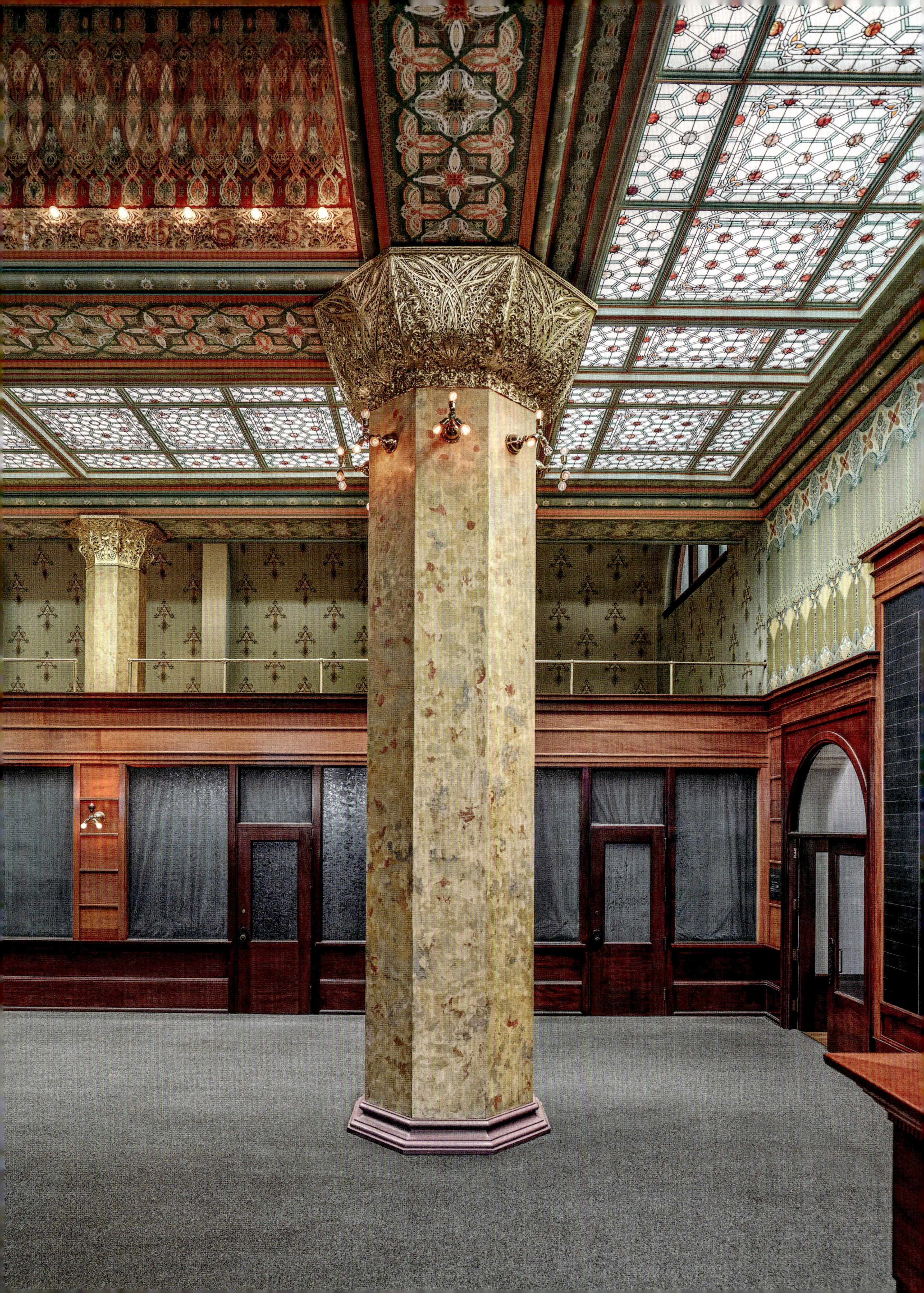

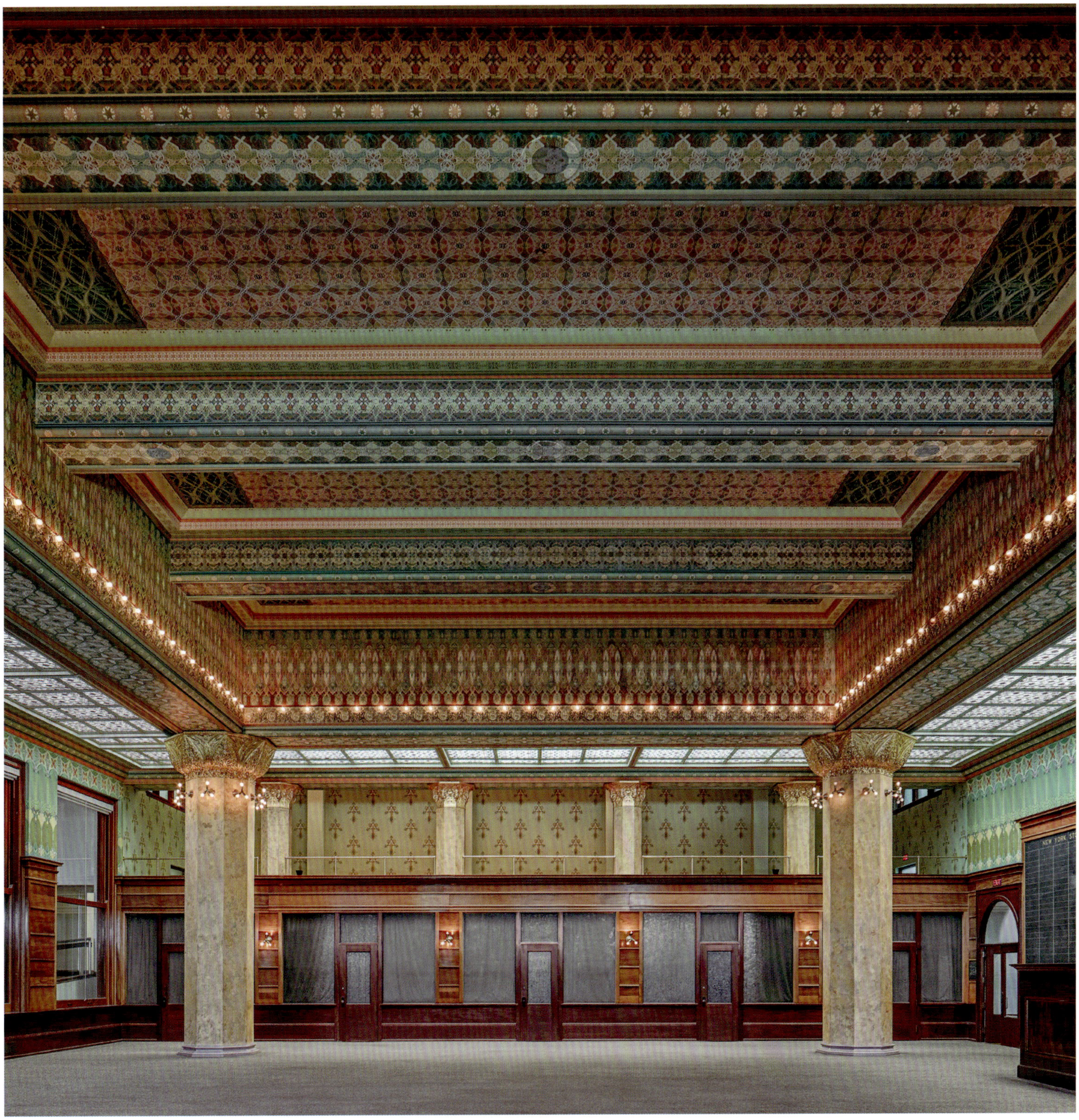

The Stock Exchange Trading Room was reconstructed in 1976–1977 at the Art Institute of Chicago, under the supervision of architects Vinci & Kenney. Some of the stenciled decorations—in as many as fifty-two colors—were saved from the old building, but most are new.

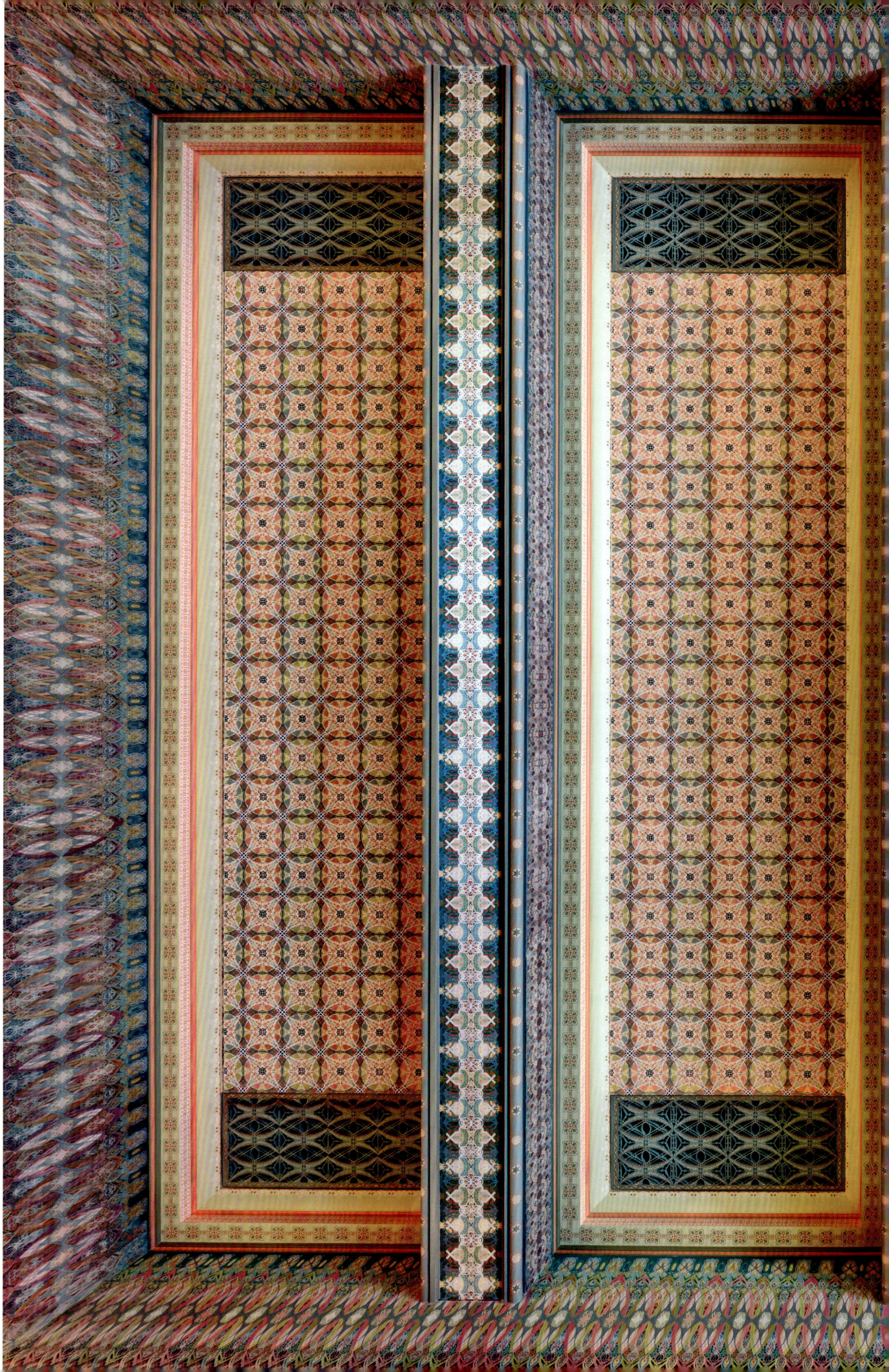

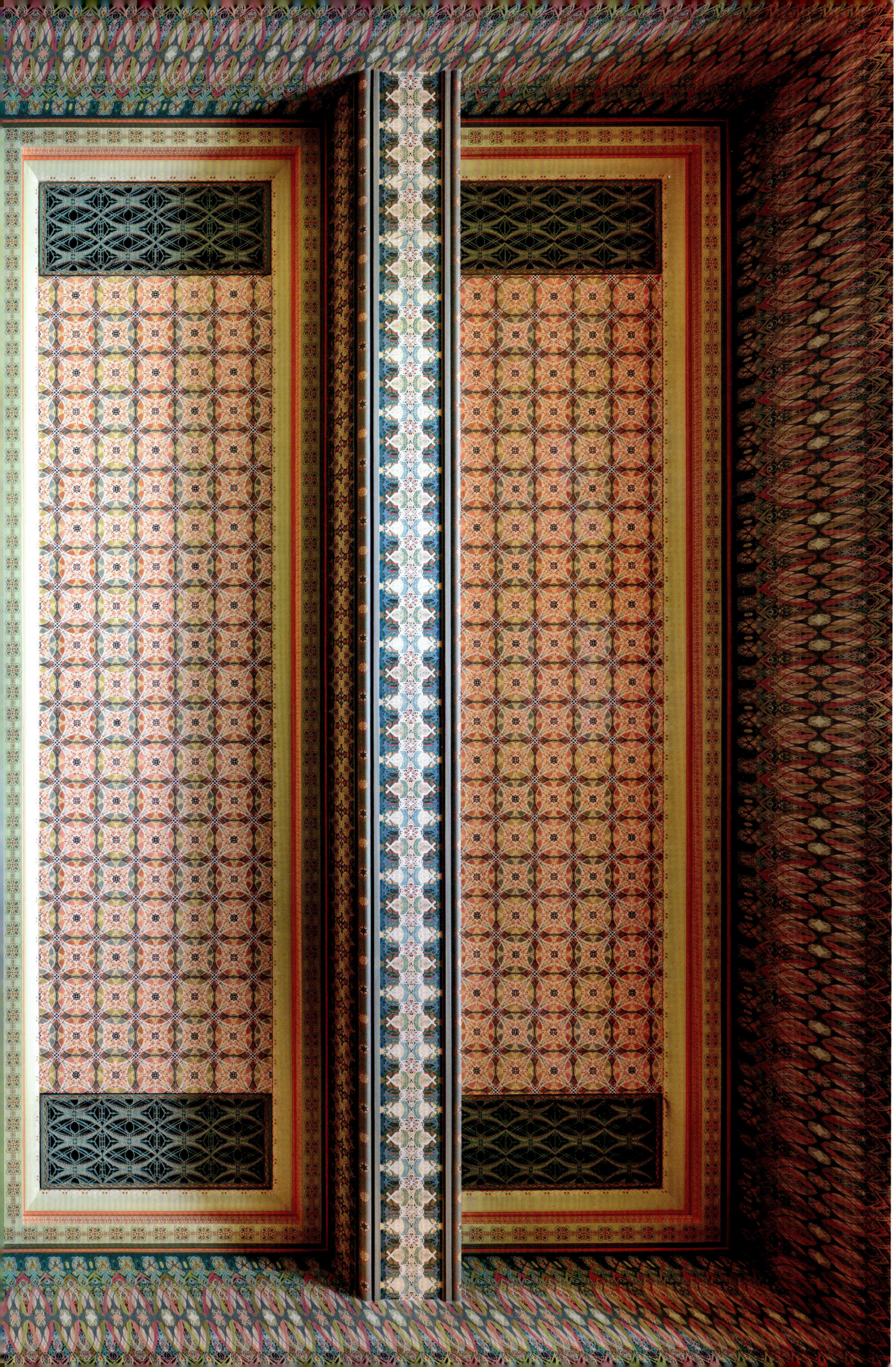

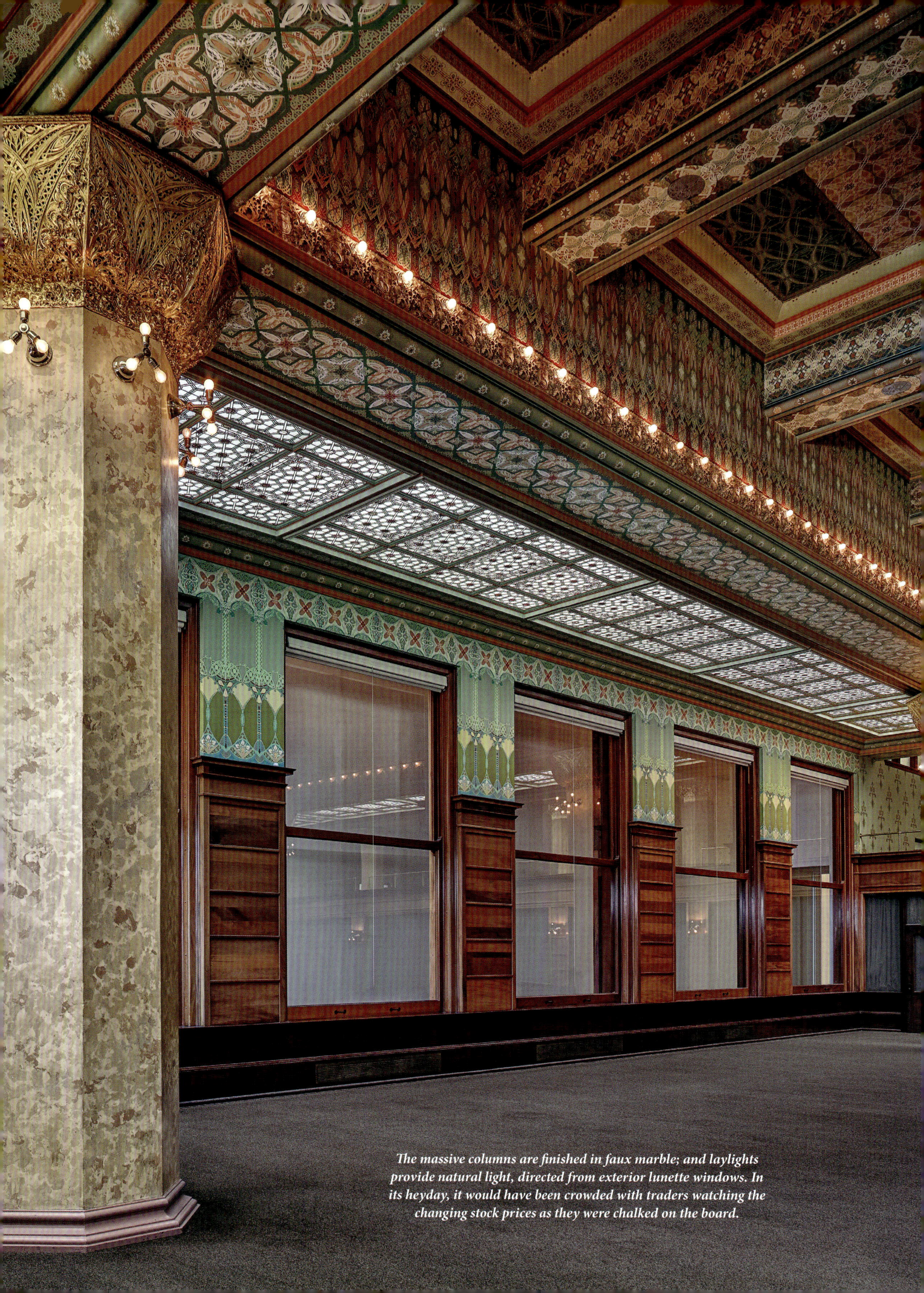

The massive columns are finished in faux marble; and laylights provide natural light, directed from exterior lunette windows. In its heyday, it would have been crowded with traders watching the changing stock prices as they were chalked on the board.

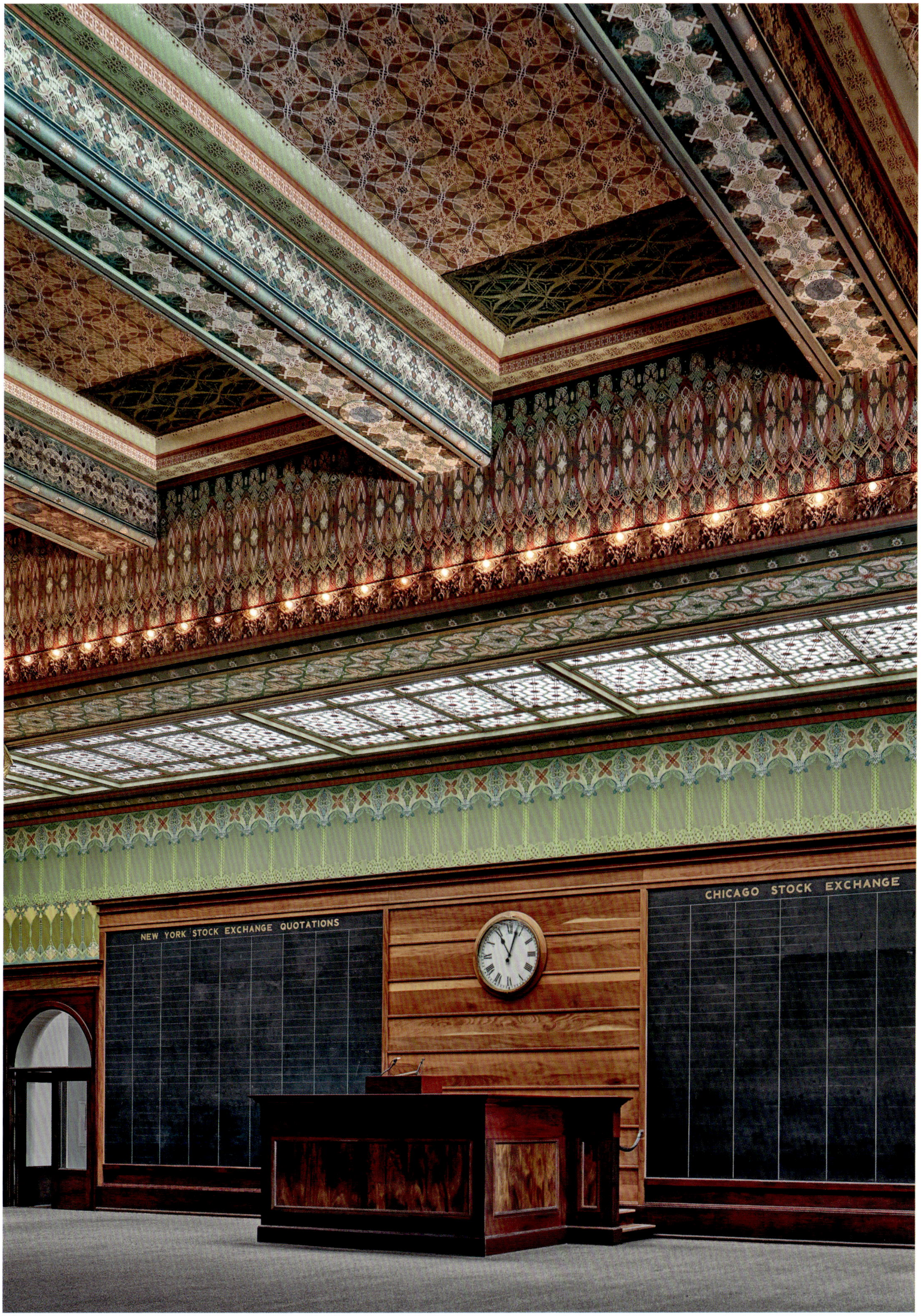
NEW YORK STOCK EXCHANGE QUOTATIONS
CHICAGO STOCK EXCHANGE

GUARANTY BUILDING

1895, BUFFALO, NEW YORK

The Guaranty Building was the last commission completed by Adler & Sullivan before the partnership was dissolved, which occurred when a lack of business caused by the depression that began in 1893 led Adler—who had a family to support—to leave the firm and take a job with the Crane Elevator Company. It may well be the most richly decorated commercial building in America and later became the Prudential Building. A major restoration was completed in 1982. It is now owned by the Hodgson Russ law firm, which is the building's main tenant. The firm, which participated in the preservation and restoration of the building, bought it out of bankruptcy in the 1990s and has lovingly maintained it ever since. It is now known again as the Guaranty Building.

Every inch of the Guaranty, except the glazing, is covered with terra-cotta molding. Sullivan worked out the decorative scheme, then left it to George Grant Elmslie, who had become Sullivan's main assistant after Frank Lloyd Wright left, to execute them. Rather than looking fussy, the building soars gracefully from base to top thanks to the combination of geometric and foliate designs. As quoted in Twombly's biography, critic Montgomery Schuyler wrote at the time that there is "no steel-framed building in which the metallic structure is more palpably felt through the envelope of baked clay." Widely considered Sullivan's best tall building, it was added to the National Register of Historic Places in 1973 and was further honored as a National Historic Landmark in 1975.

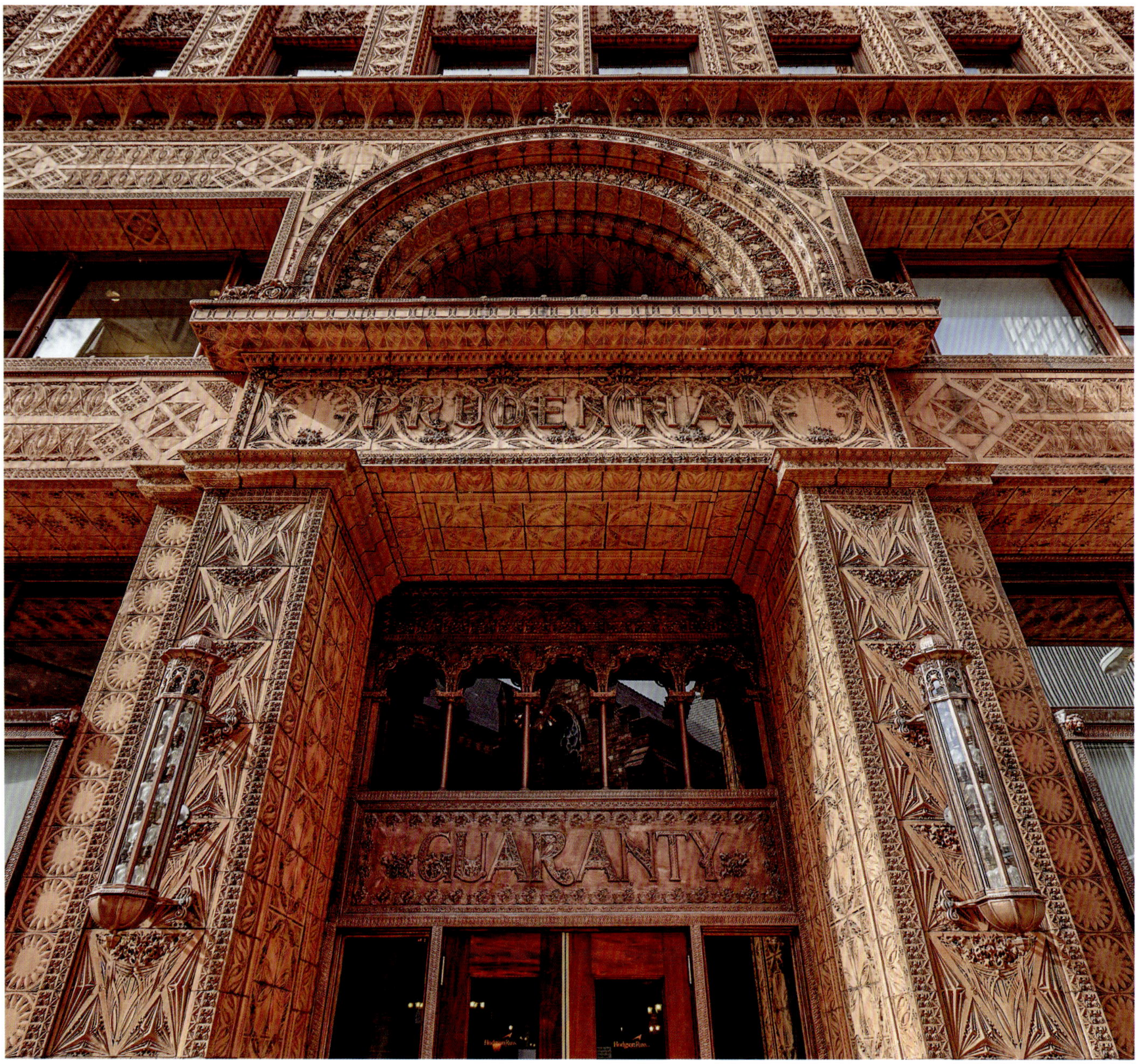

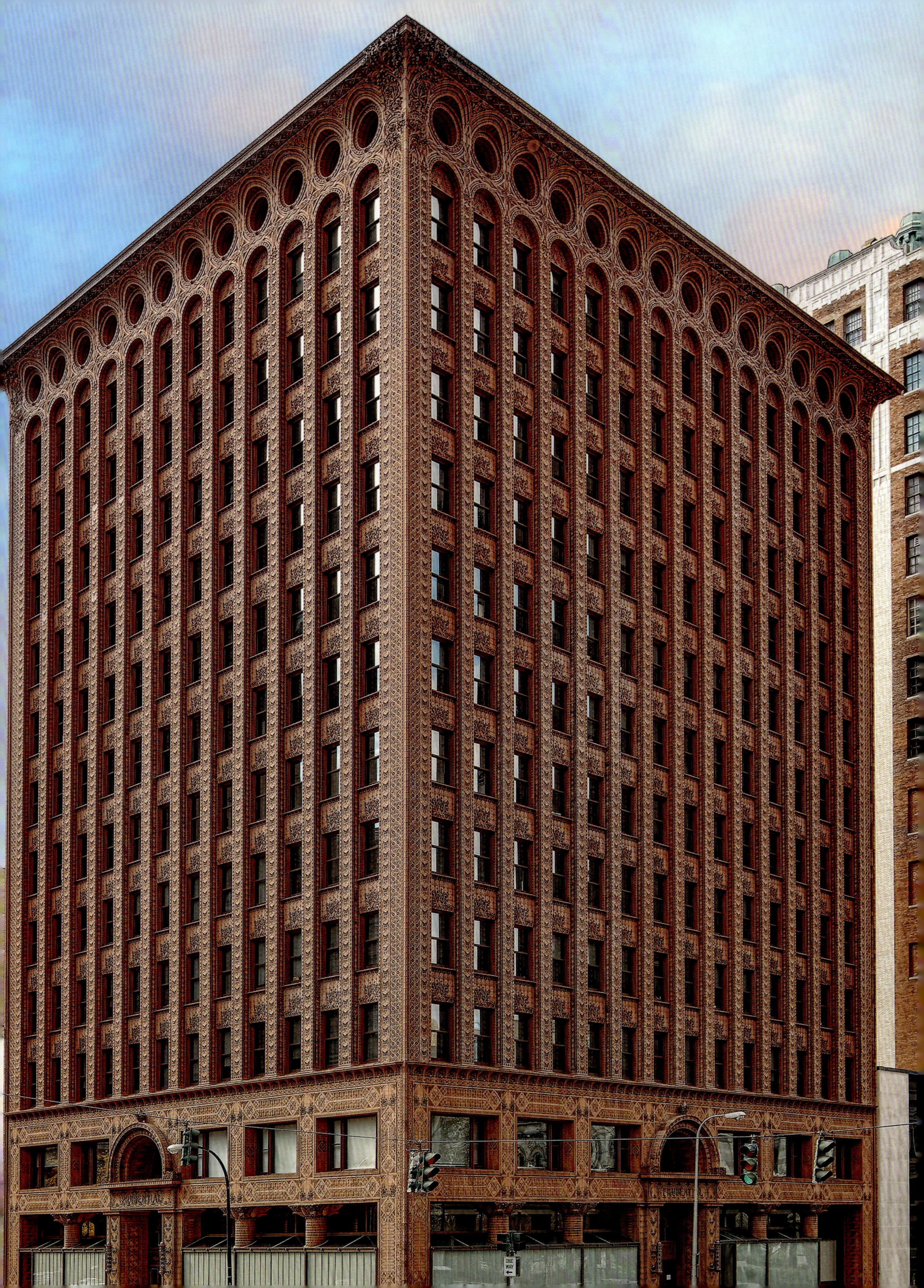

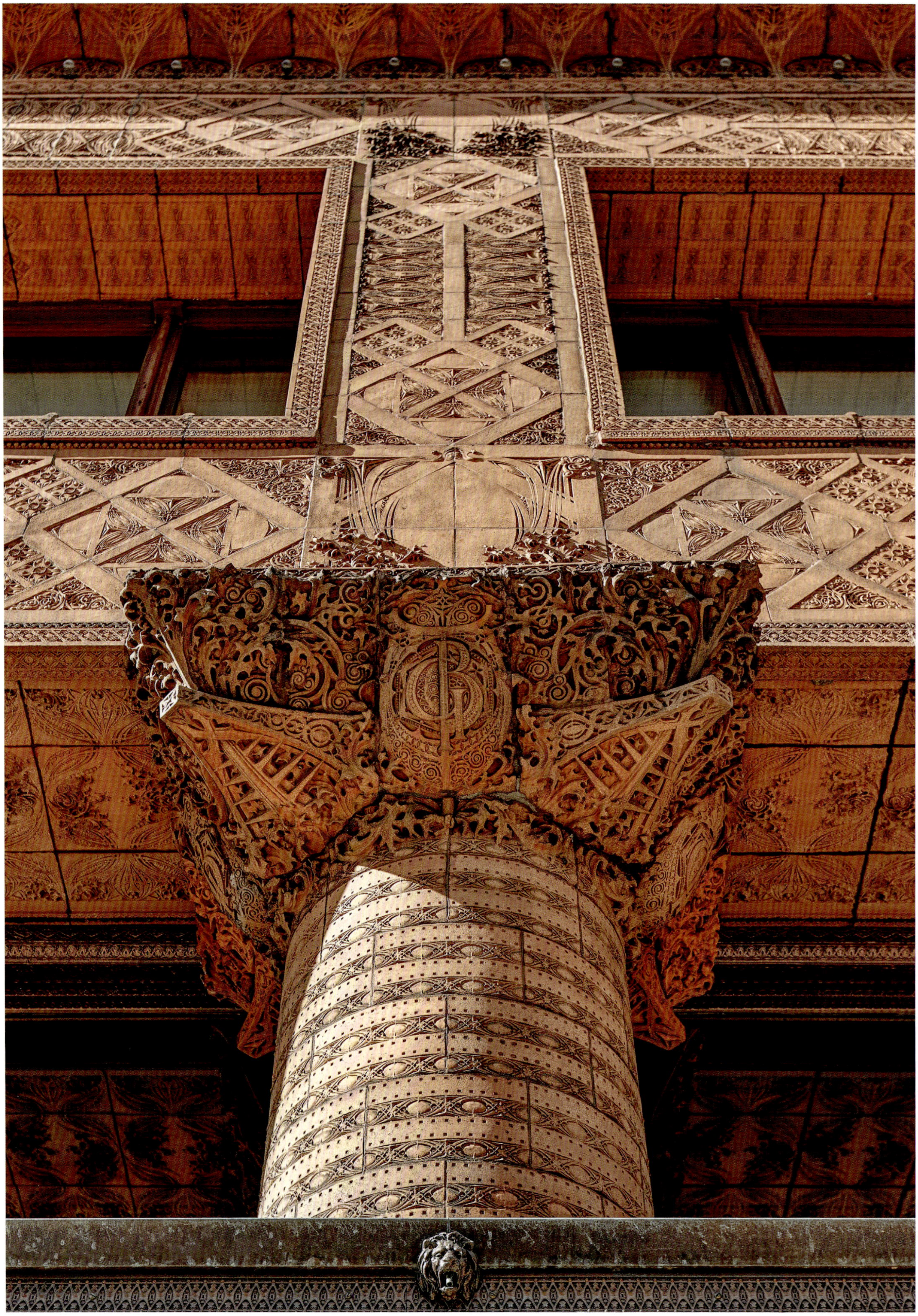

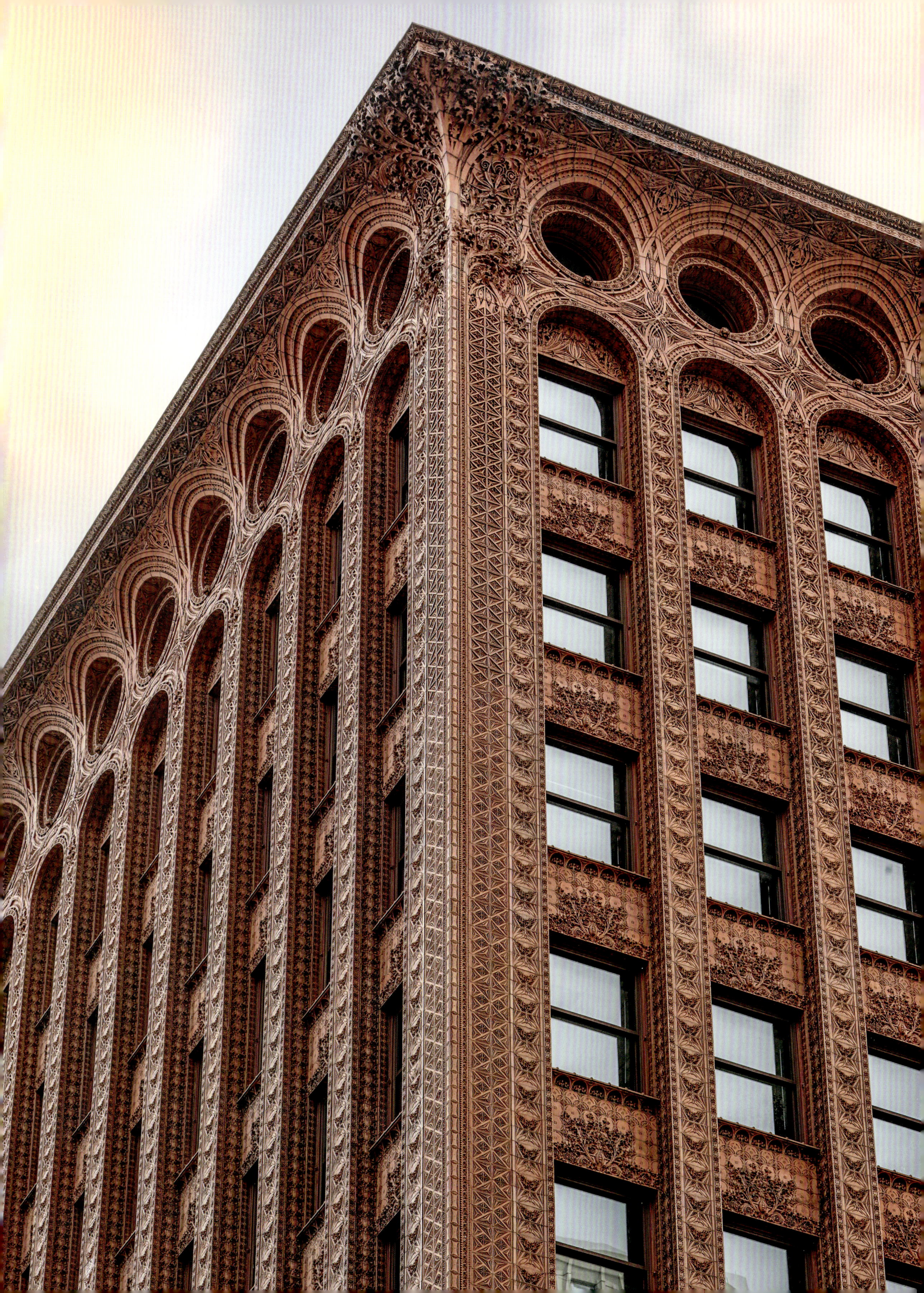

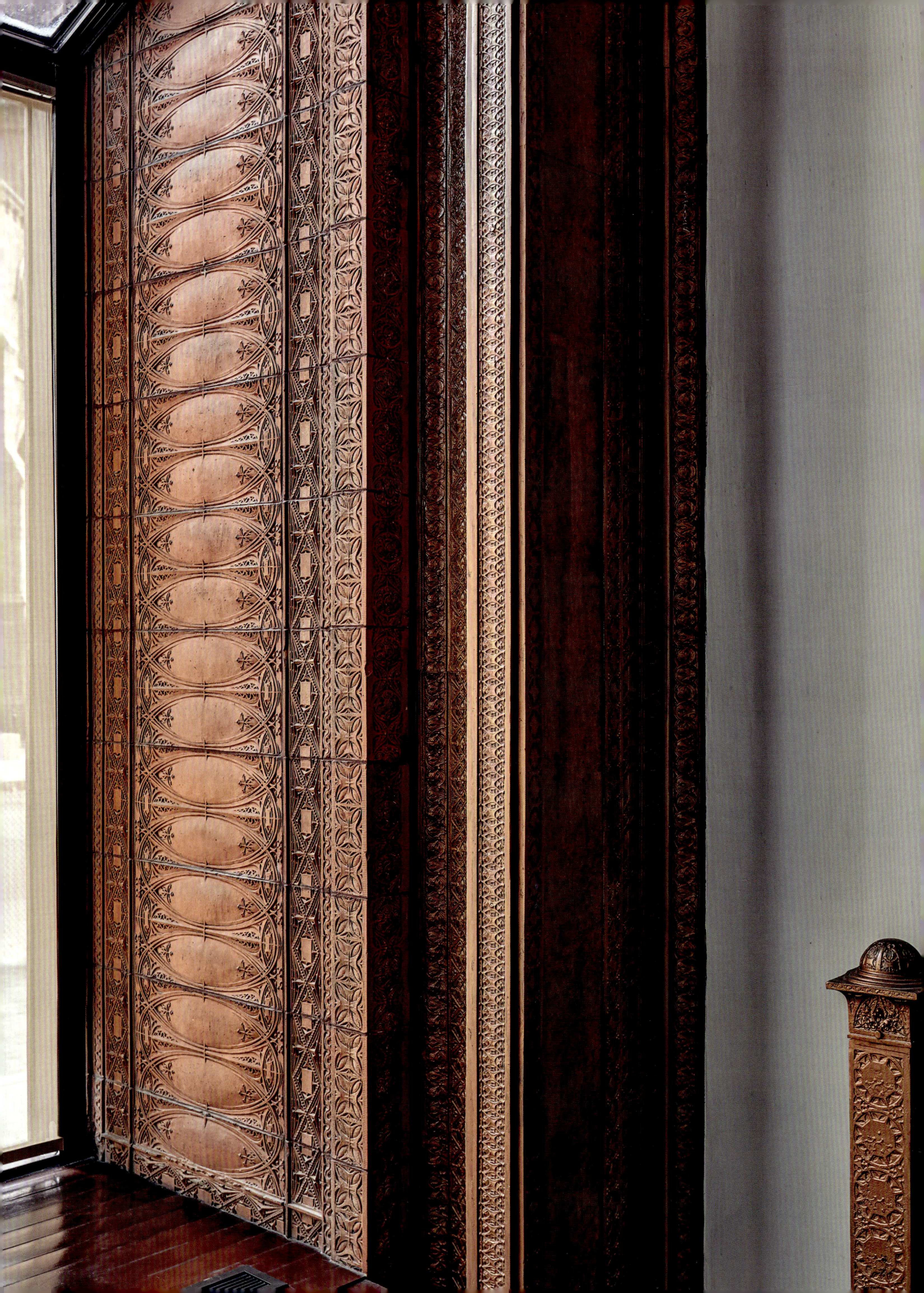

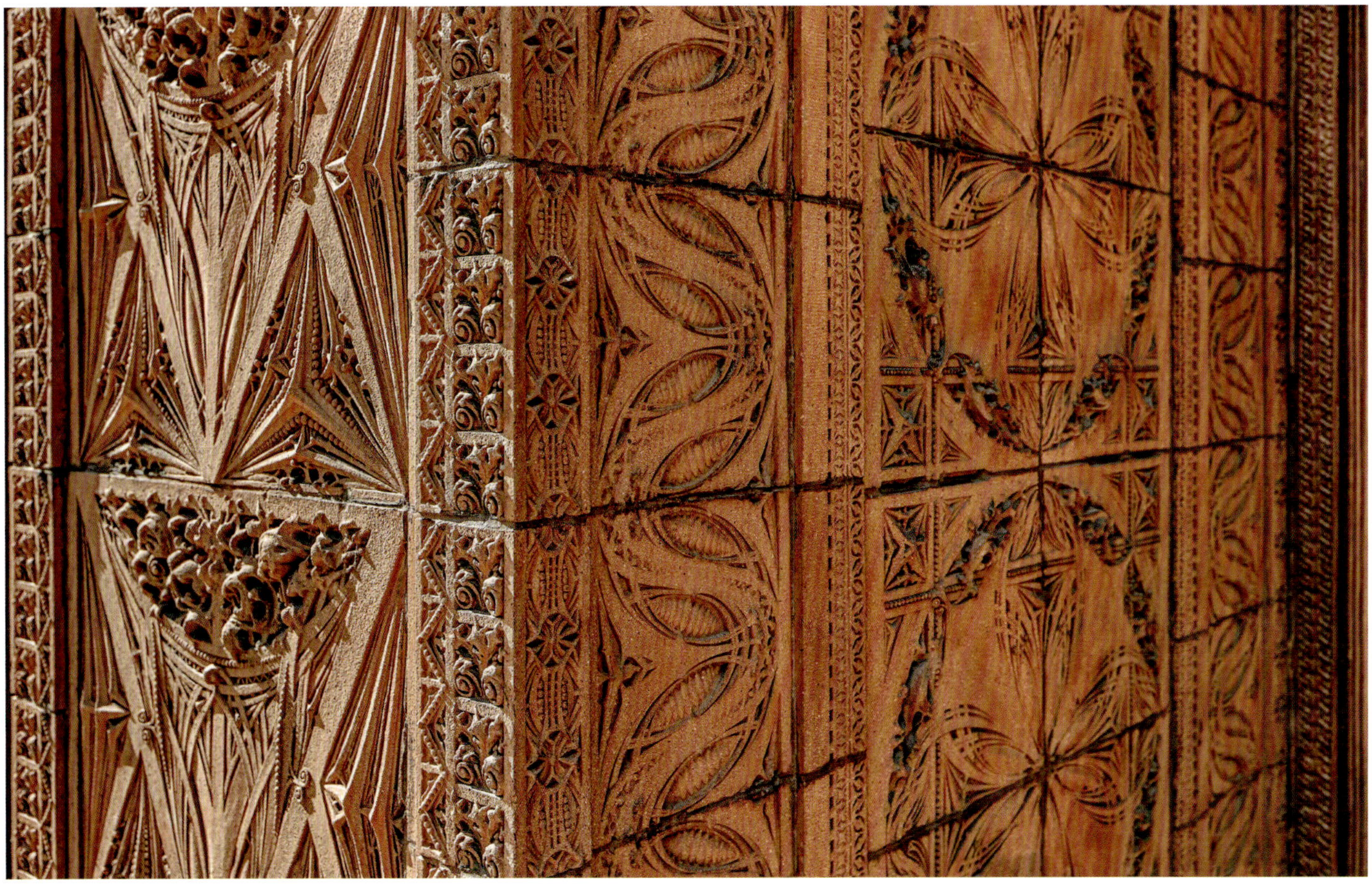

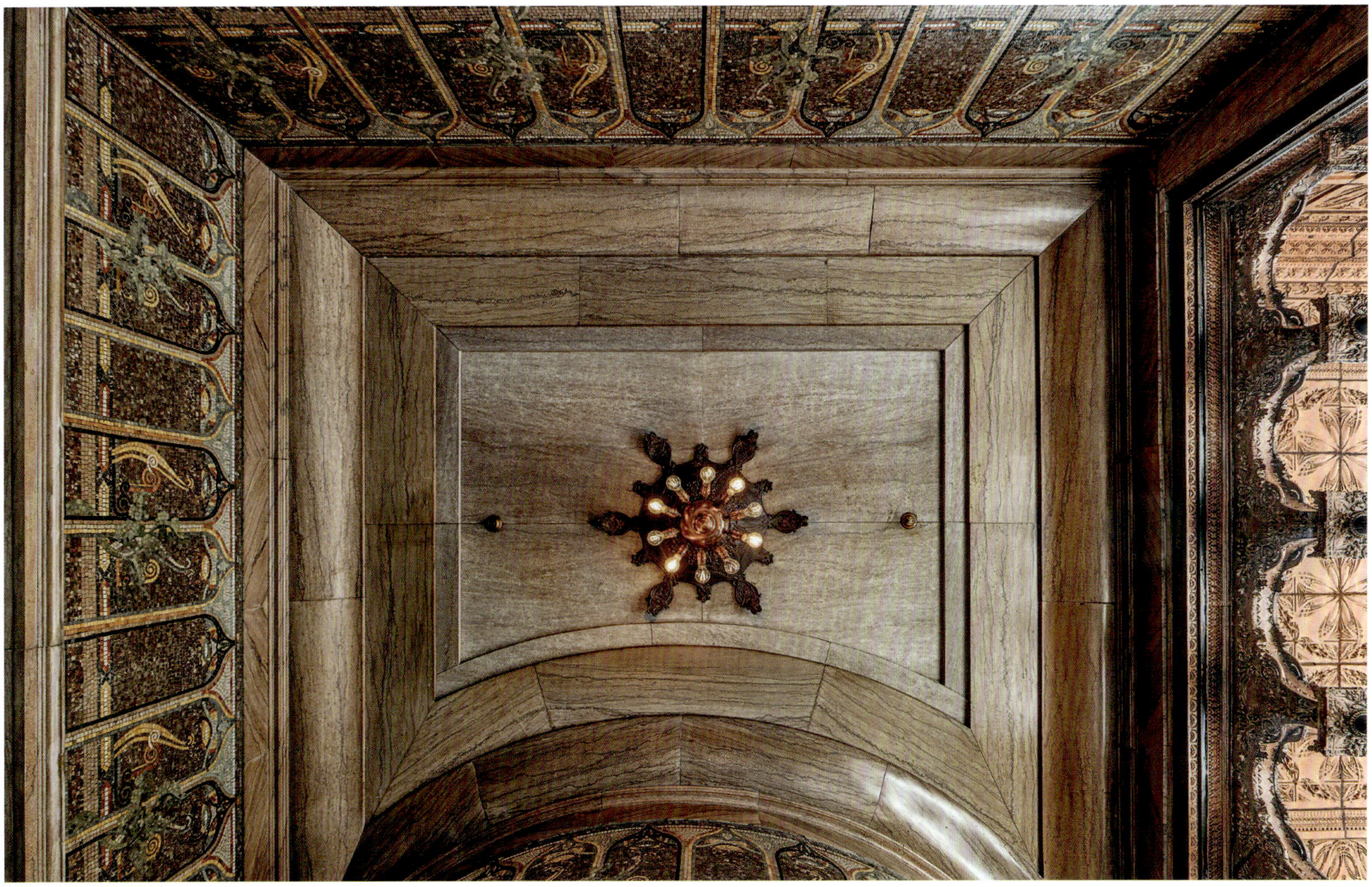

The interior of the Guaranty is as stunning as the exterior.

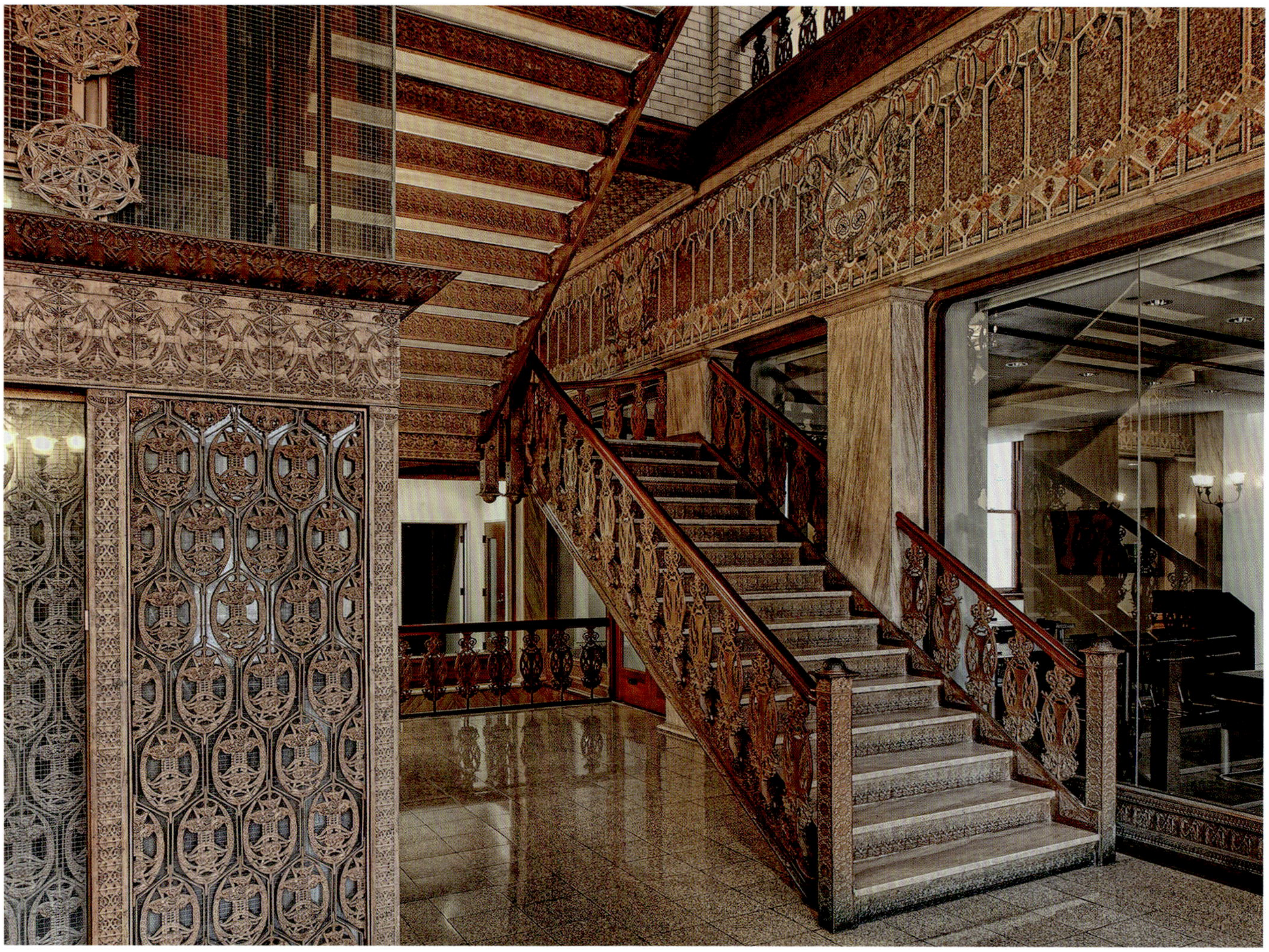

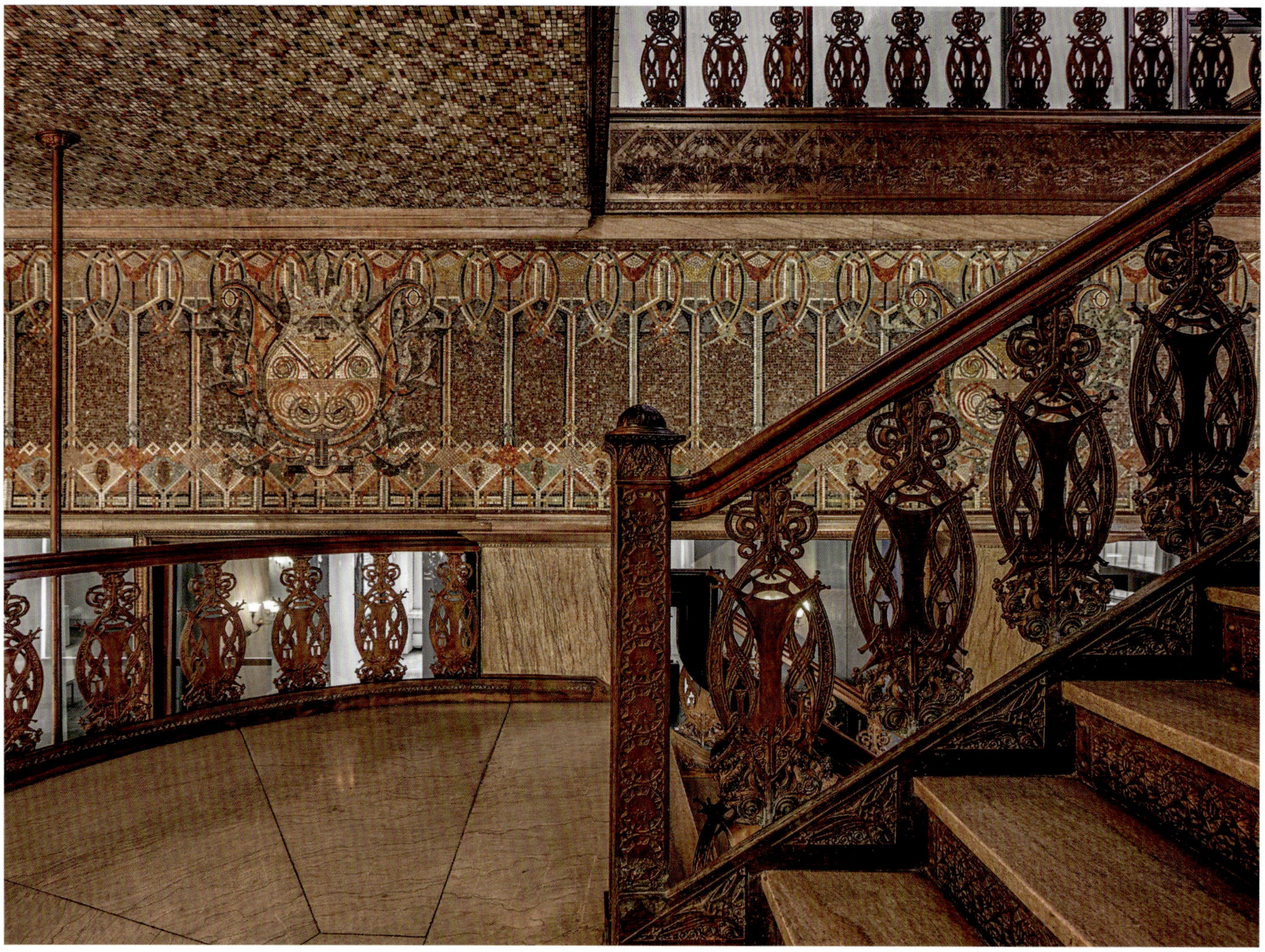

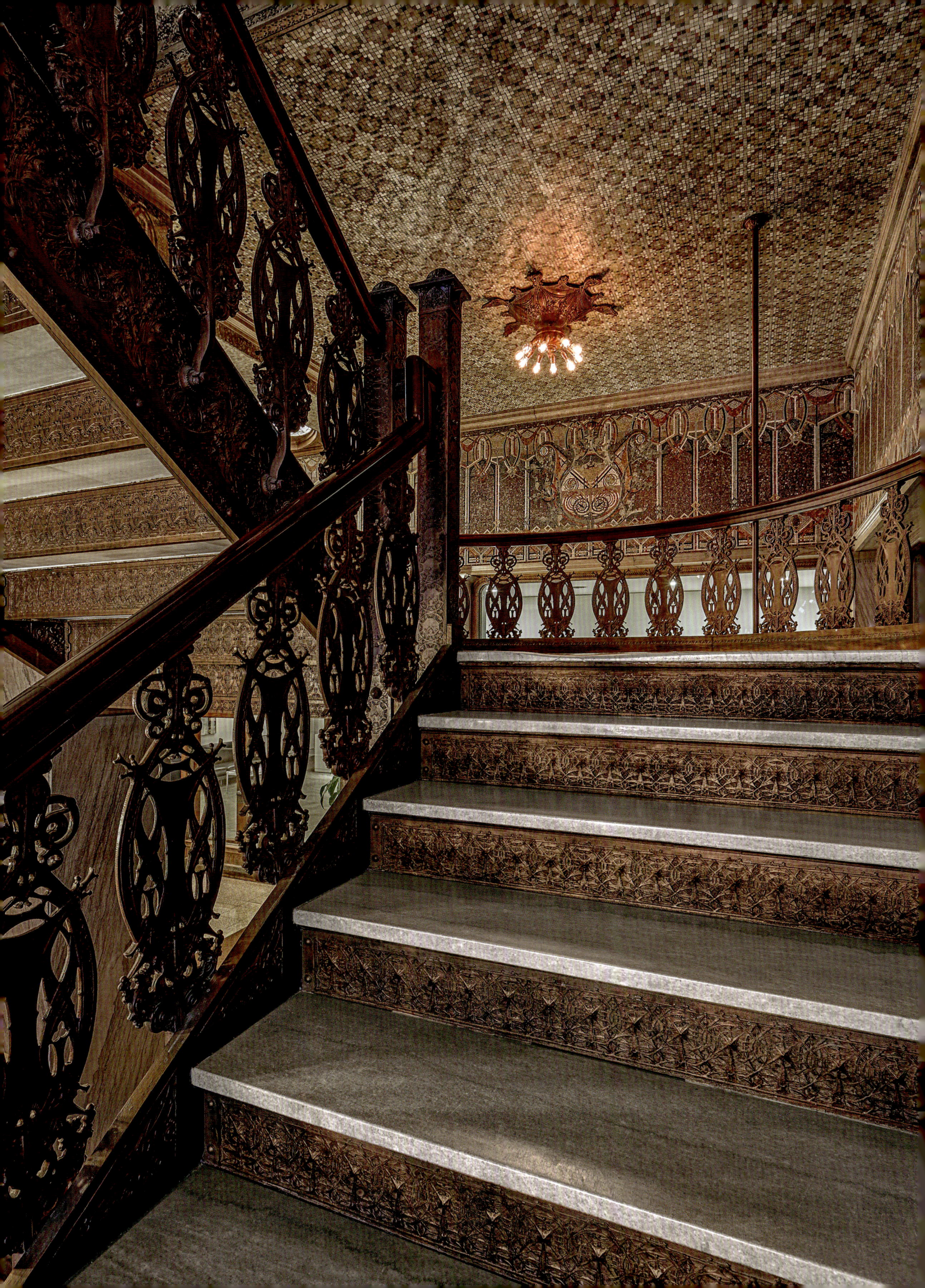

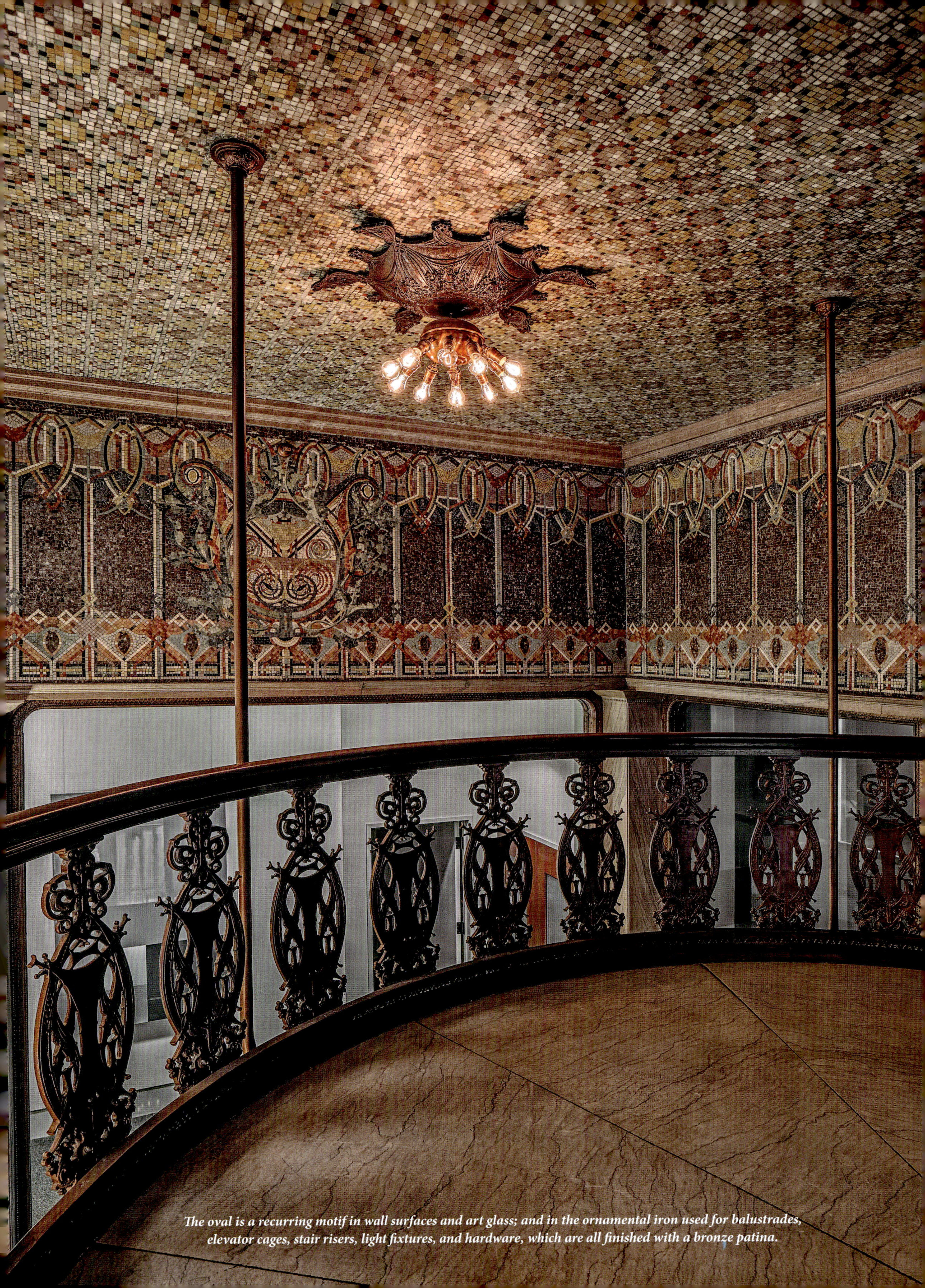

The oval is a recurring motif in wall surfaces and art glass; and in the ornamental iron used for balustrades, elevator cages, stair risers, light fixtures, and hardware, which are all finished with a bronze patina.

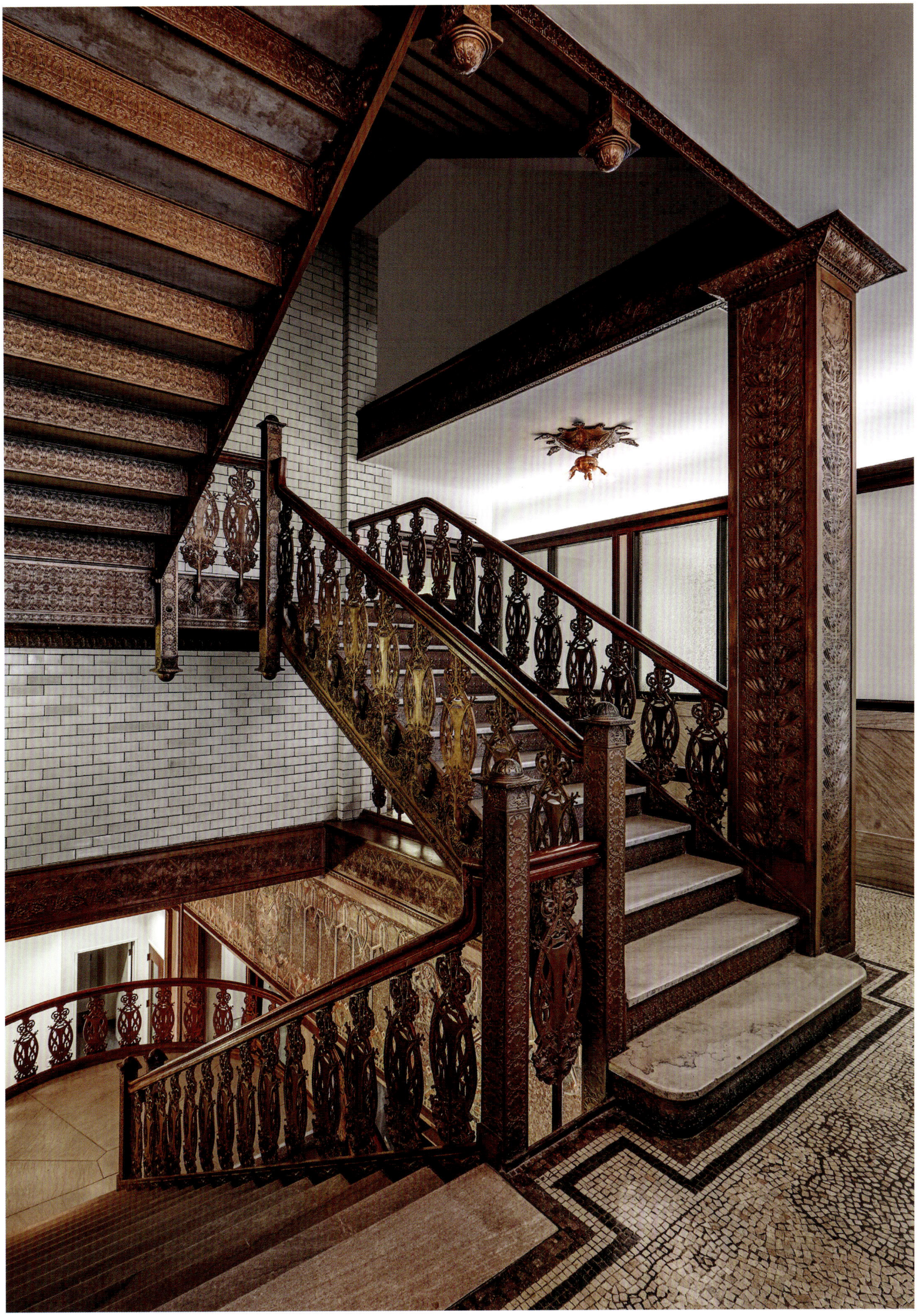

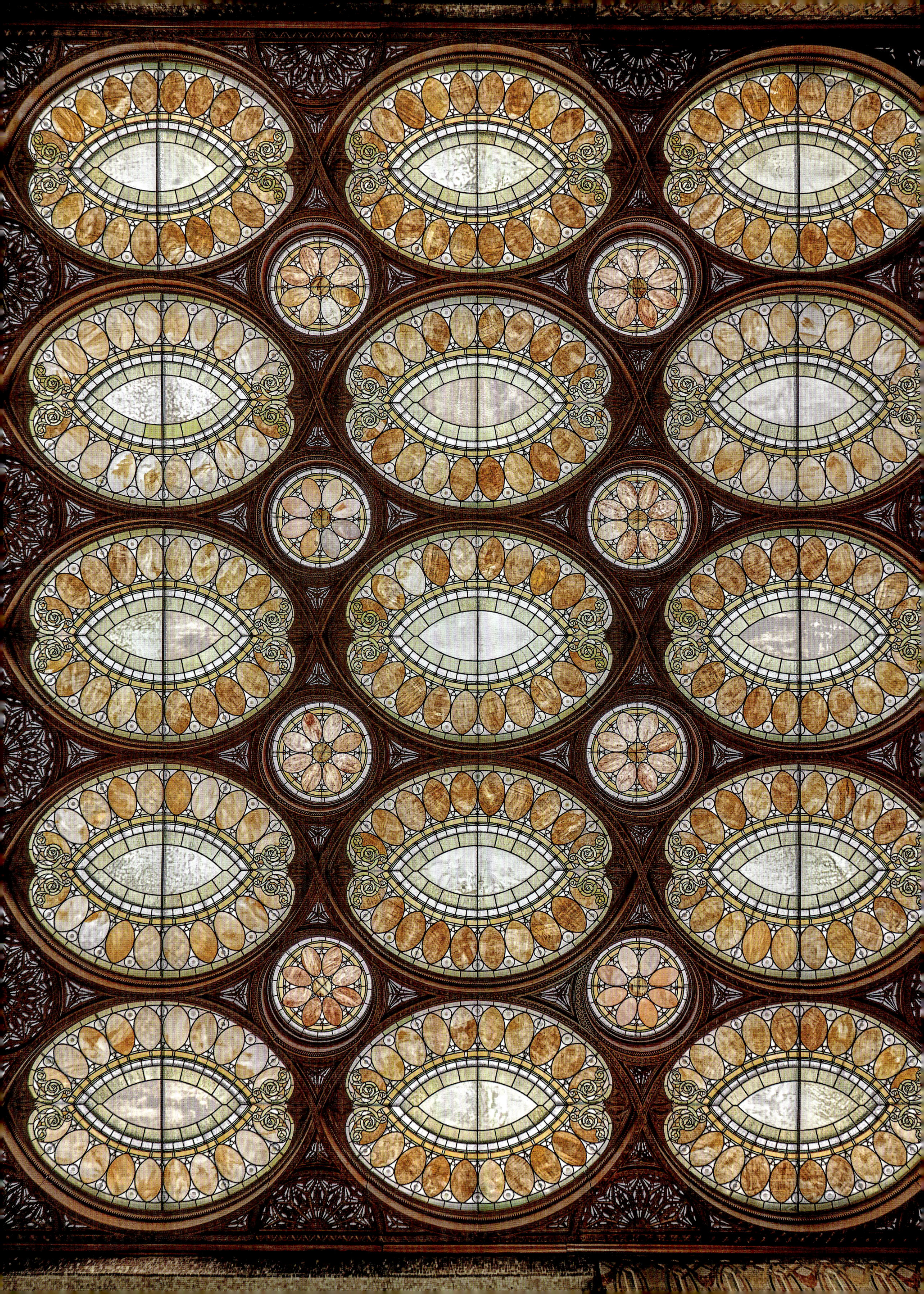

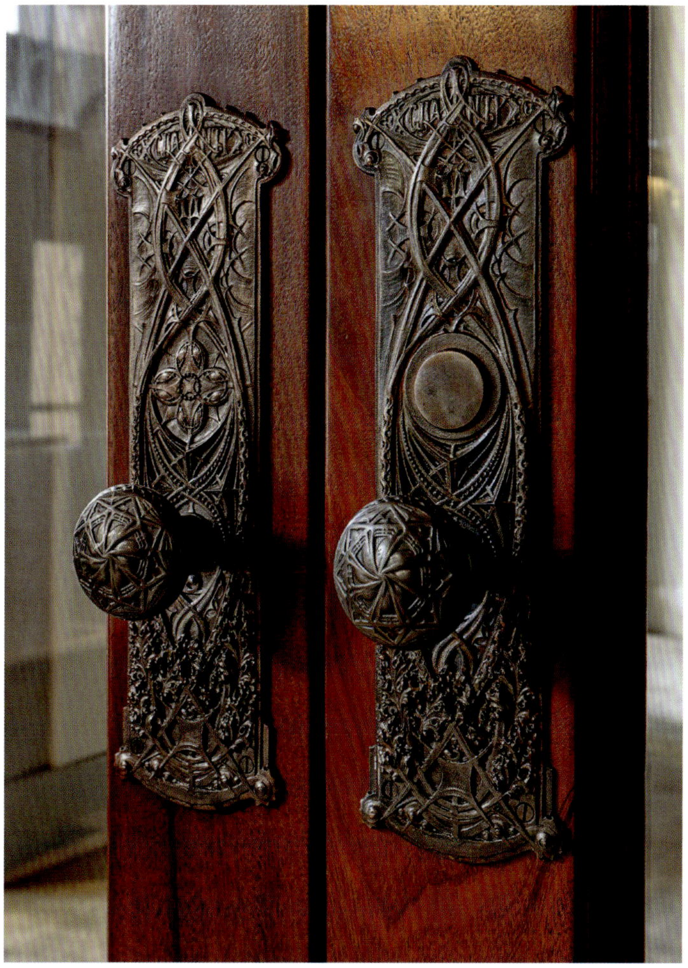

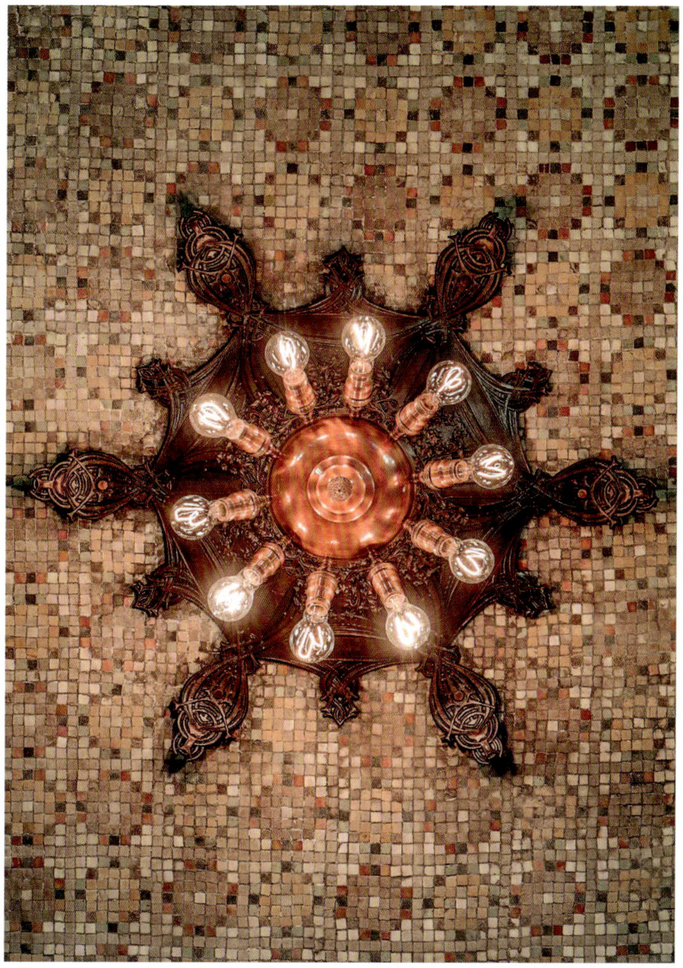

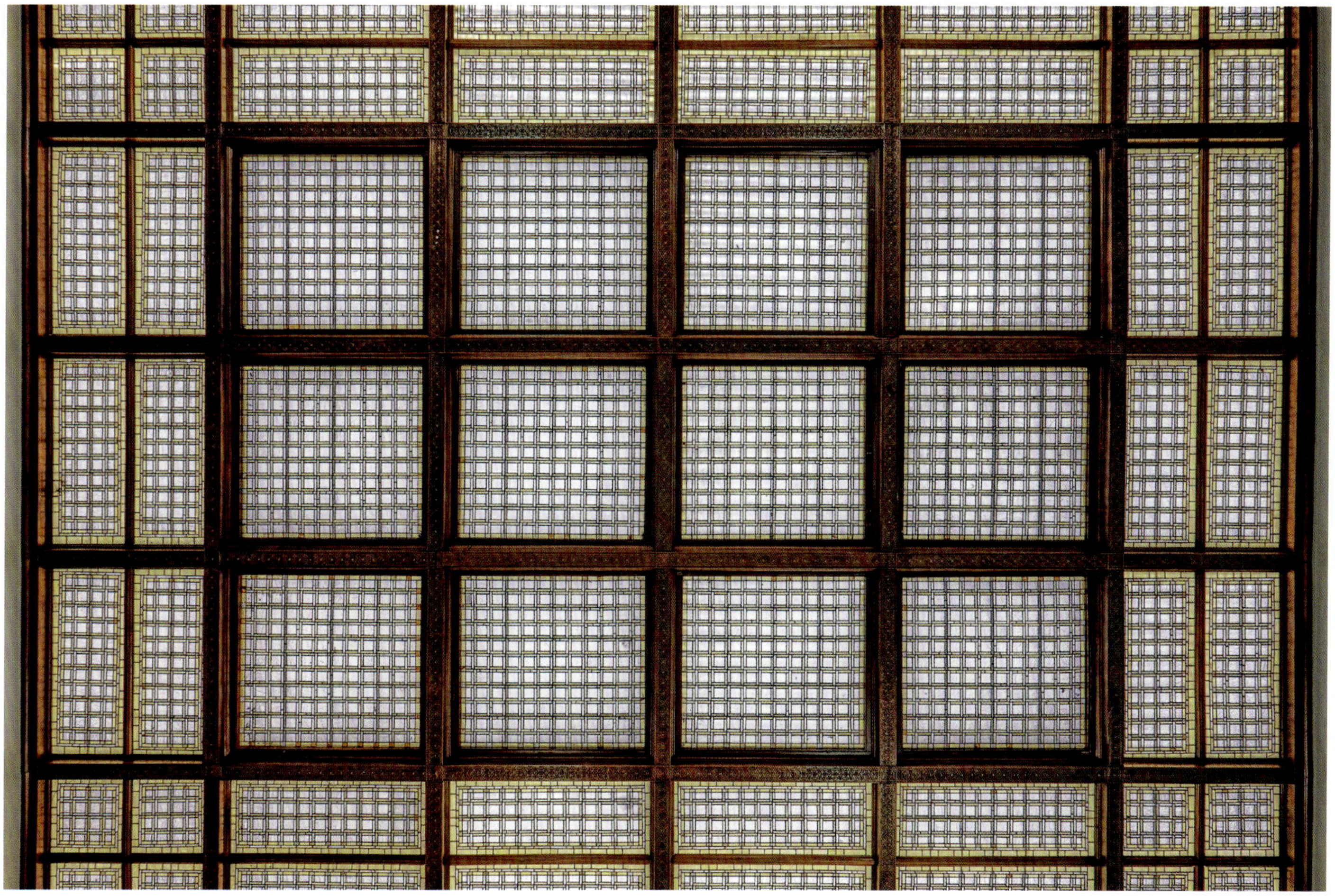

As in most office buildings of that time there was a light court which provided natural light to the lobby through skylights, now laylights.

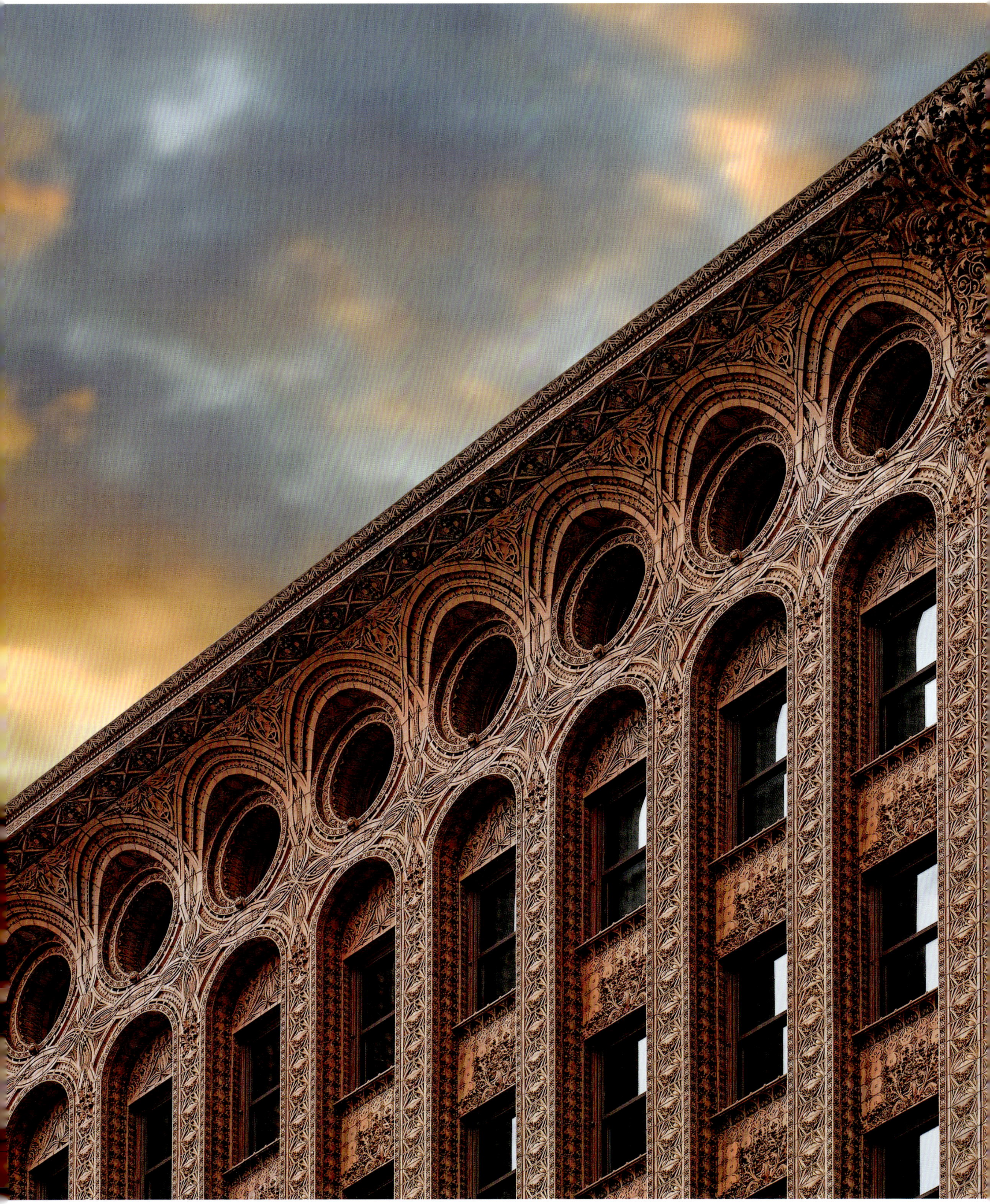

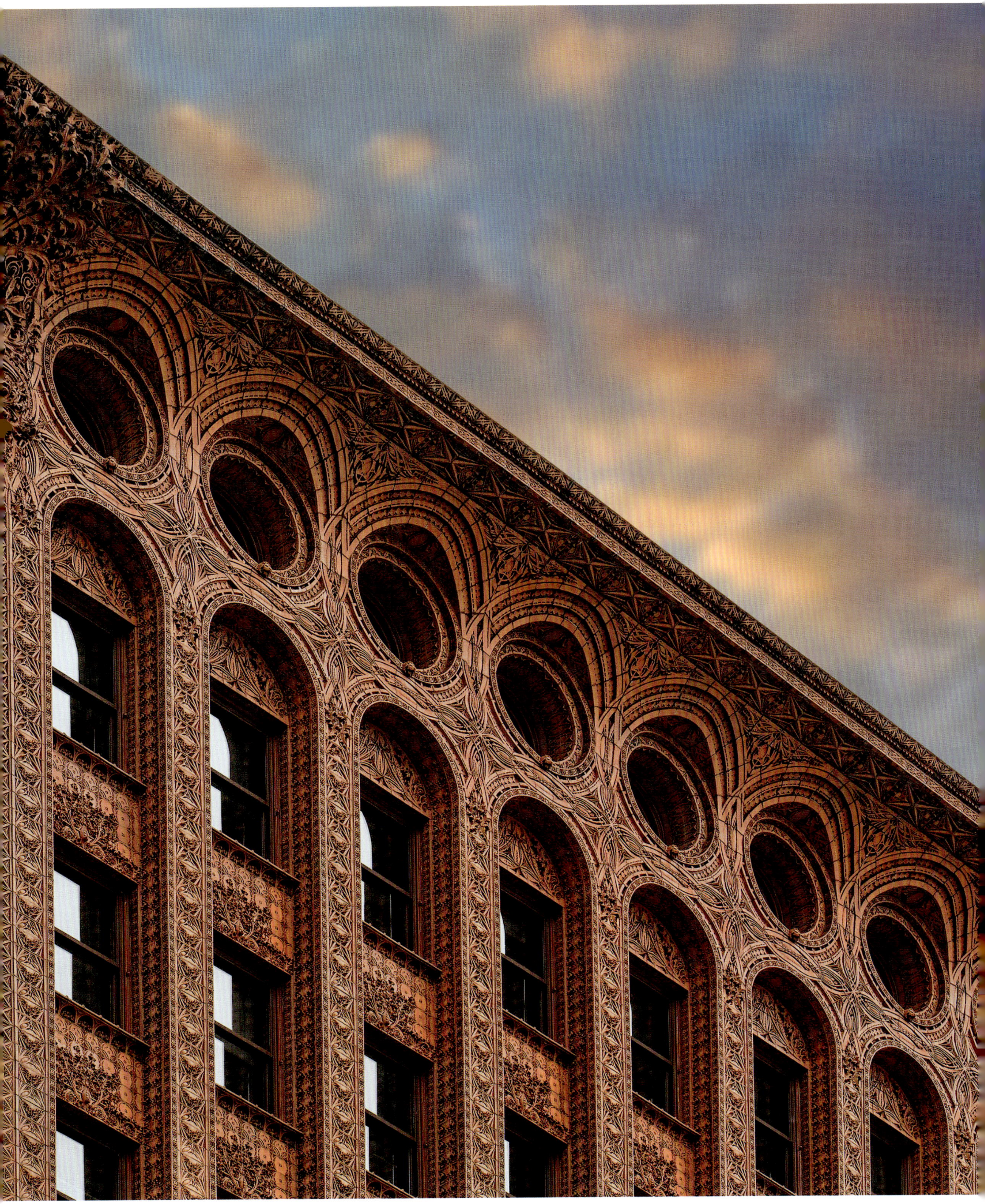

GAGE BUILDING

1888–1900, CHICAGO

The basic building for the Gage Brothers & Company was designed by Holabird & Roche as one of three South Michigan Avenue loft buildings commissioned by Stanley R. McCormick. Sullivan was brought in at the request of the Gage Brothers to give the northernmost of their three buildings a more distinctive facade, trusting that the added expense would result in increased sales. Interestingly, each of the three buildings had a continuous frame, designed to permit generous window openings. Originally, the buildings stepped up in height from six stories at the south to the Gage's original eight stories. The first two buildings were clad in red brick, but the Gage was faced in creamy white terra cotta above a highly ornamental cast-iron base (now lost).

The facade was divided into three bays. Two piers rose from the base and culminated in typical Sullivan organic cartouches at the cornice. The upper sections of the windows were filled with Luxfer prisms, designed to amplify sunlight to the interior. These were later removed. In 1902, Holabird & Roche added four stories to the Gage, carefully removing and reinstalling Sullivan's ornament, although the former symmetry of the group was lost. The Gage was designated a Chicago Landmark in 1976 and was added to the National Register of Historic Places in 1985.

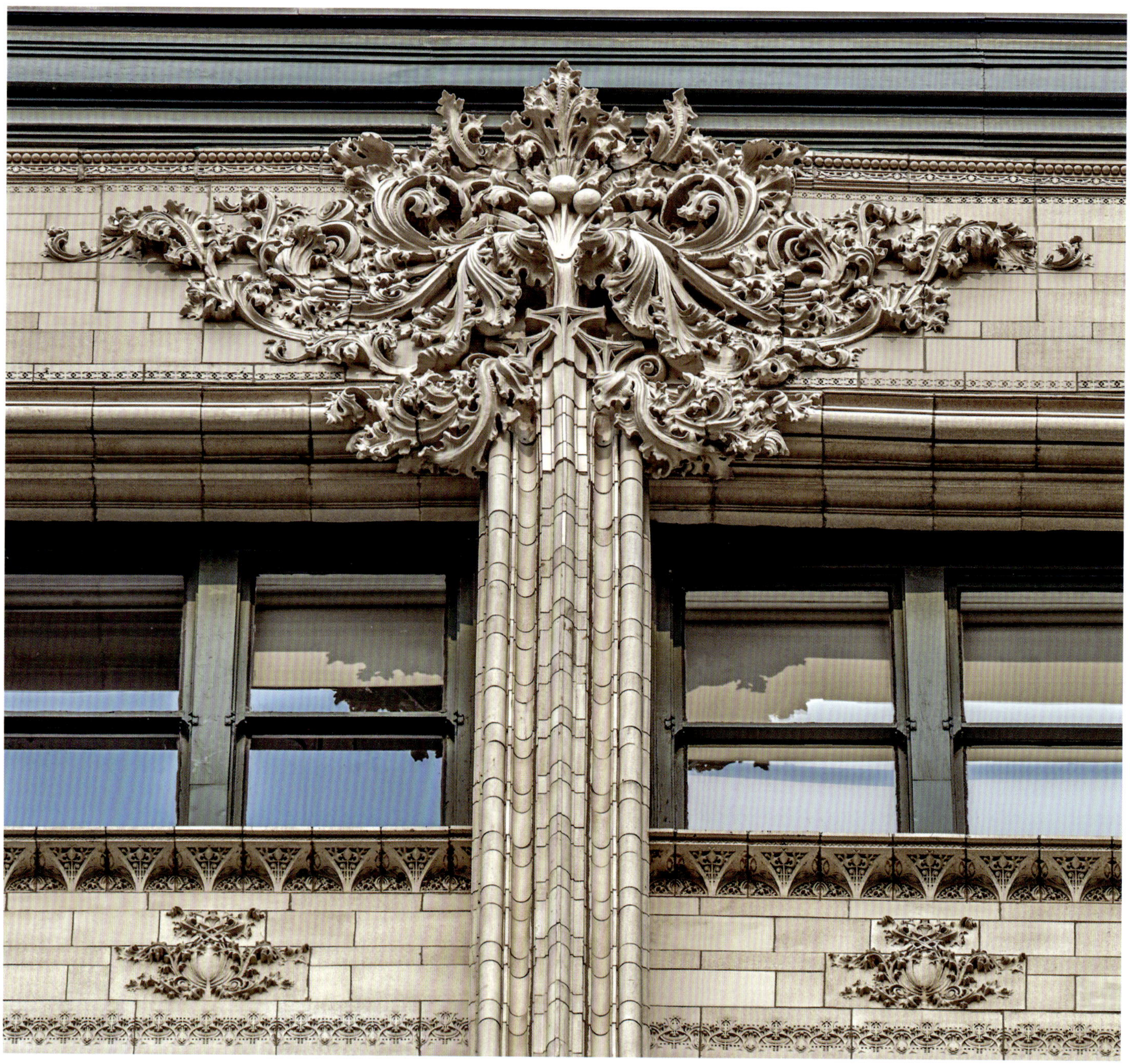

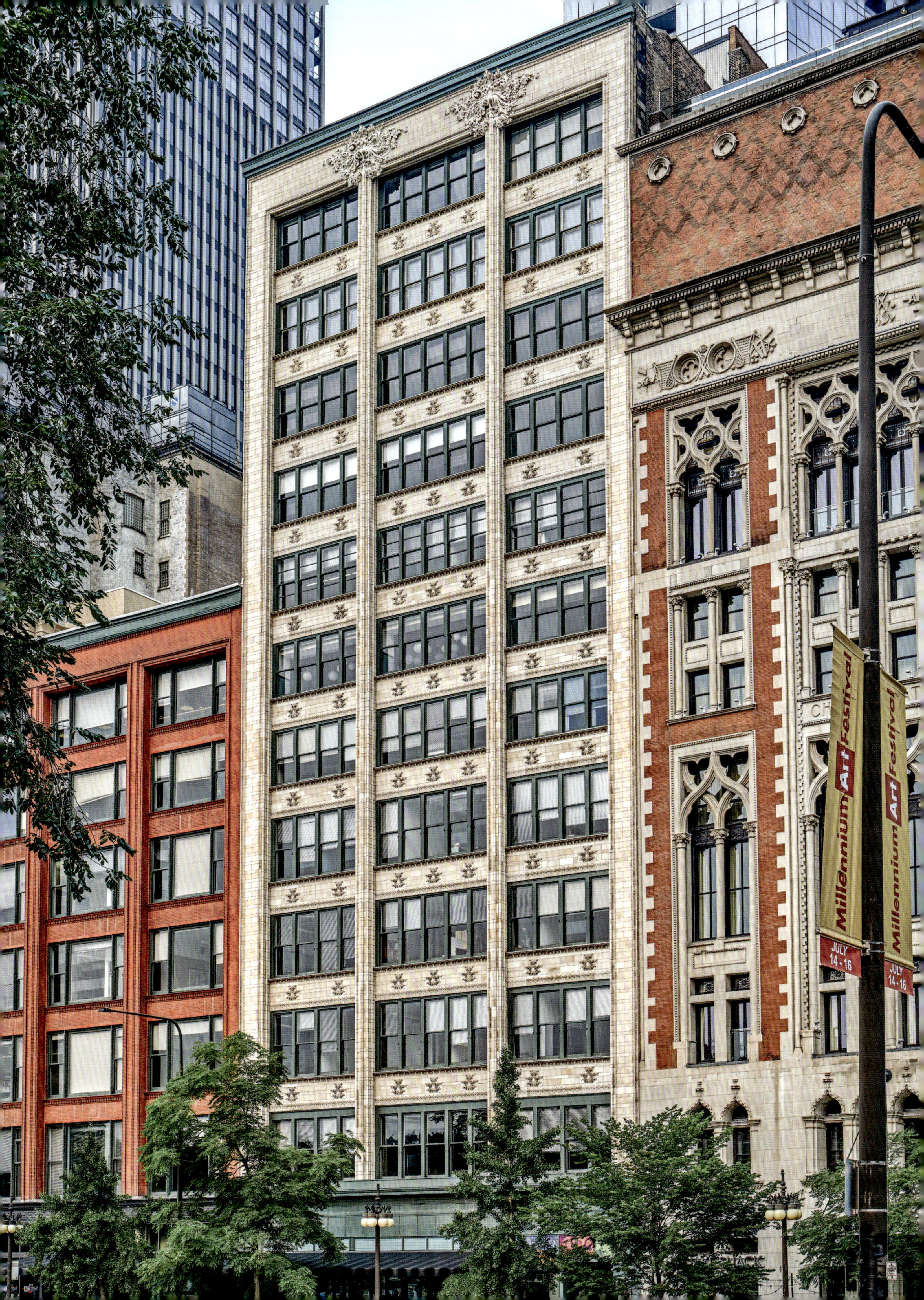
Millennium Art Festival
JULY 14-16

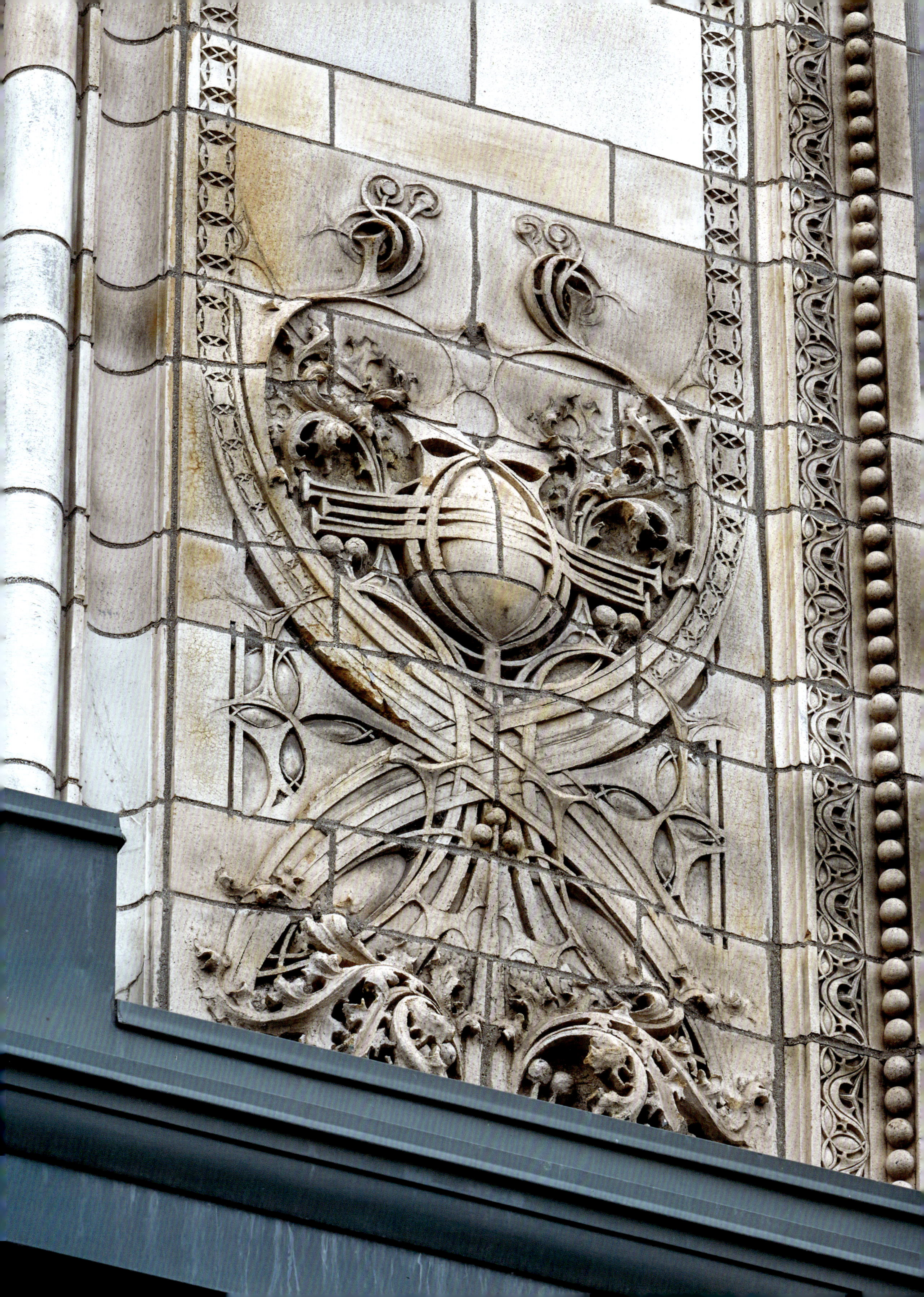

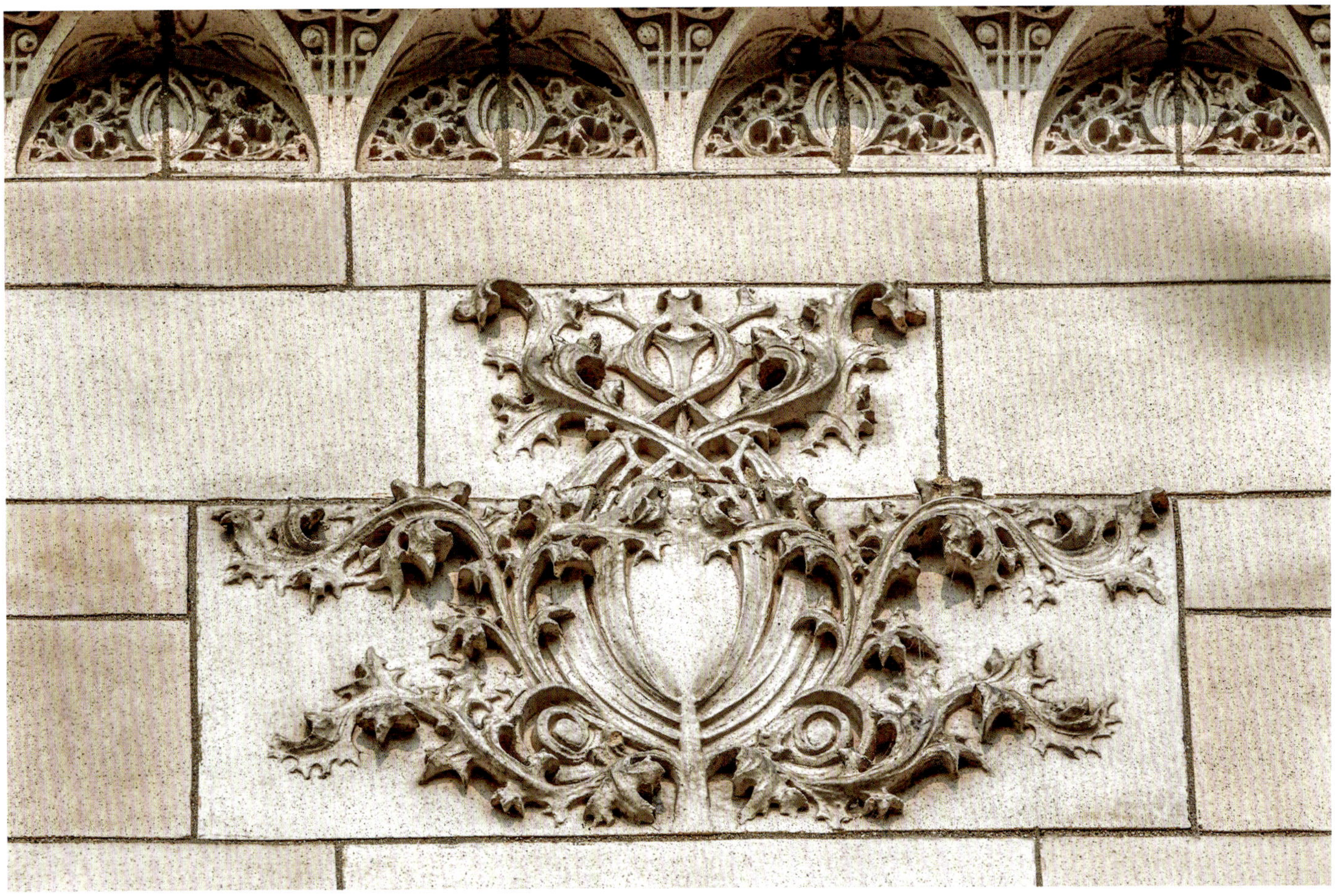

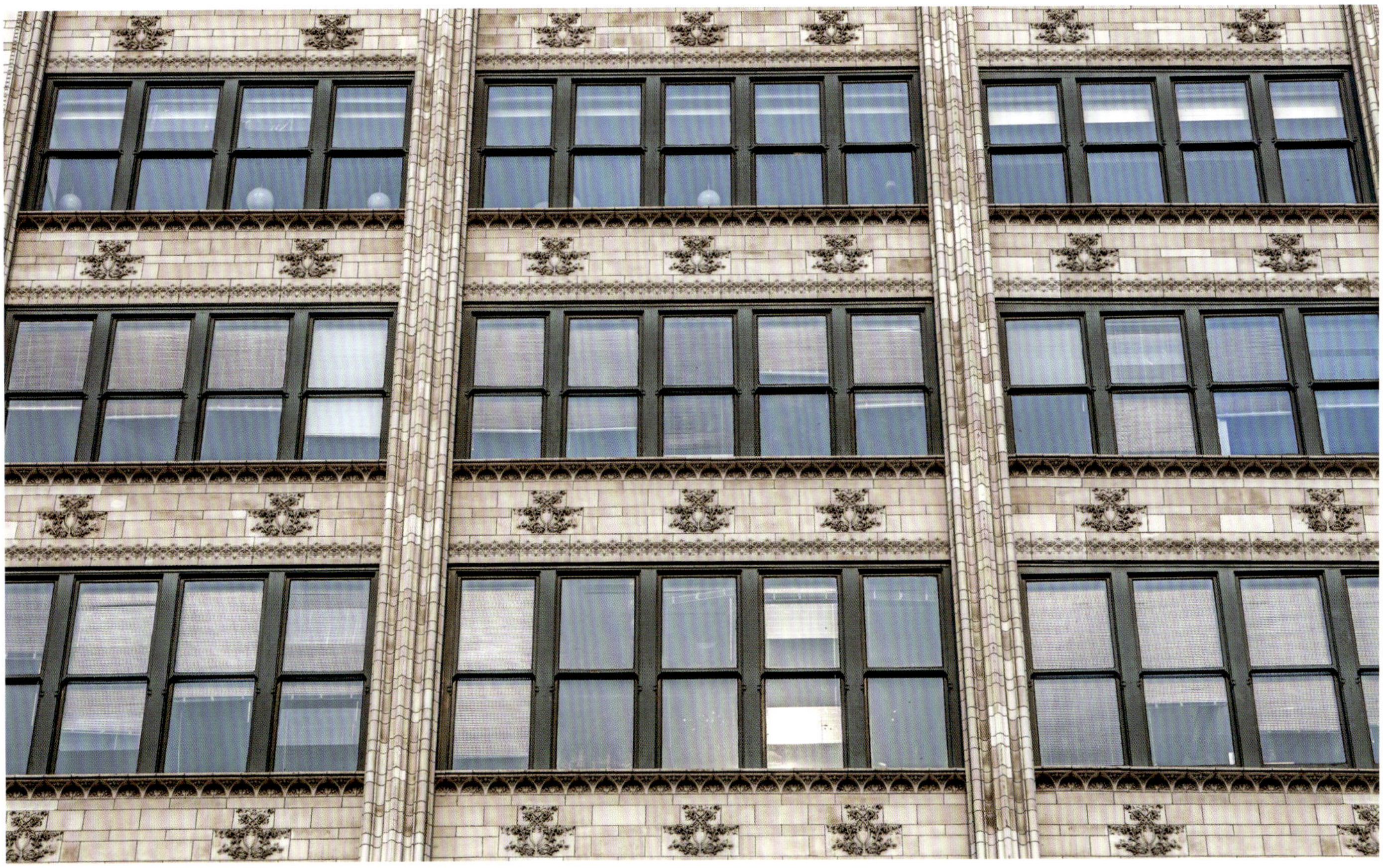

BAYARD-CONDICT BUILDING

1899, NEW YORK CITY

Sullivan's last skyscraper, the Bayard-Condict Building was originally to be called the Mercantile Building, but it briefly became the Bayard and then the Condict, named after the lawyer who ultimately purchased it. Sited in lower Manhattan in an area that was then the location of printing-related companies, the building's open floor plans were meant to provide flexible space for sales, warehouse, and product display. Twelve stories tall, it has a one-story base (not typical for Sullivan), then an eleven-story shaft and a decorative cornice. The curtainwall is glazed terra cotta. In this case, Sullivan added five non-bearing piers, which lead to arches with typical circular windows. According to Frank Lloyd Wright in a 1935 article, Sullivan considered it his best tall building.

An interesting addition to the cornice are the angels whose outspread wings seem to support the roof projection. One source claims that they were added at the client's insistence, but in fact, they are very similar to the angels between the arches on the façade of Adler & Sullivan's Columbian Exposition Transportation Building of 1893. Winged messengers have a long history in myth and, most commonly for us, in the Bible. In Sullivan's mind, the role of the angels may have seemed related to the role of printing as a purveyor of information.

In 2000, the building underwent a substantial restoration, supervised by the New York firm WASA/Studio A. It has been a New York Landmark since 1975 and was added to the National Register of Historic Places and named a National Historic Landmark in 1976.

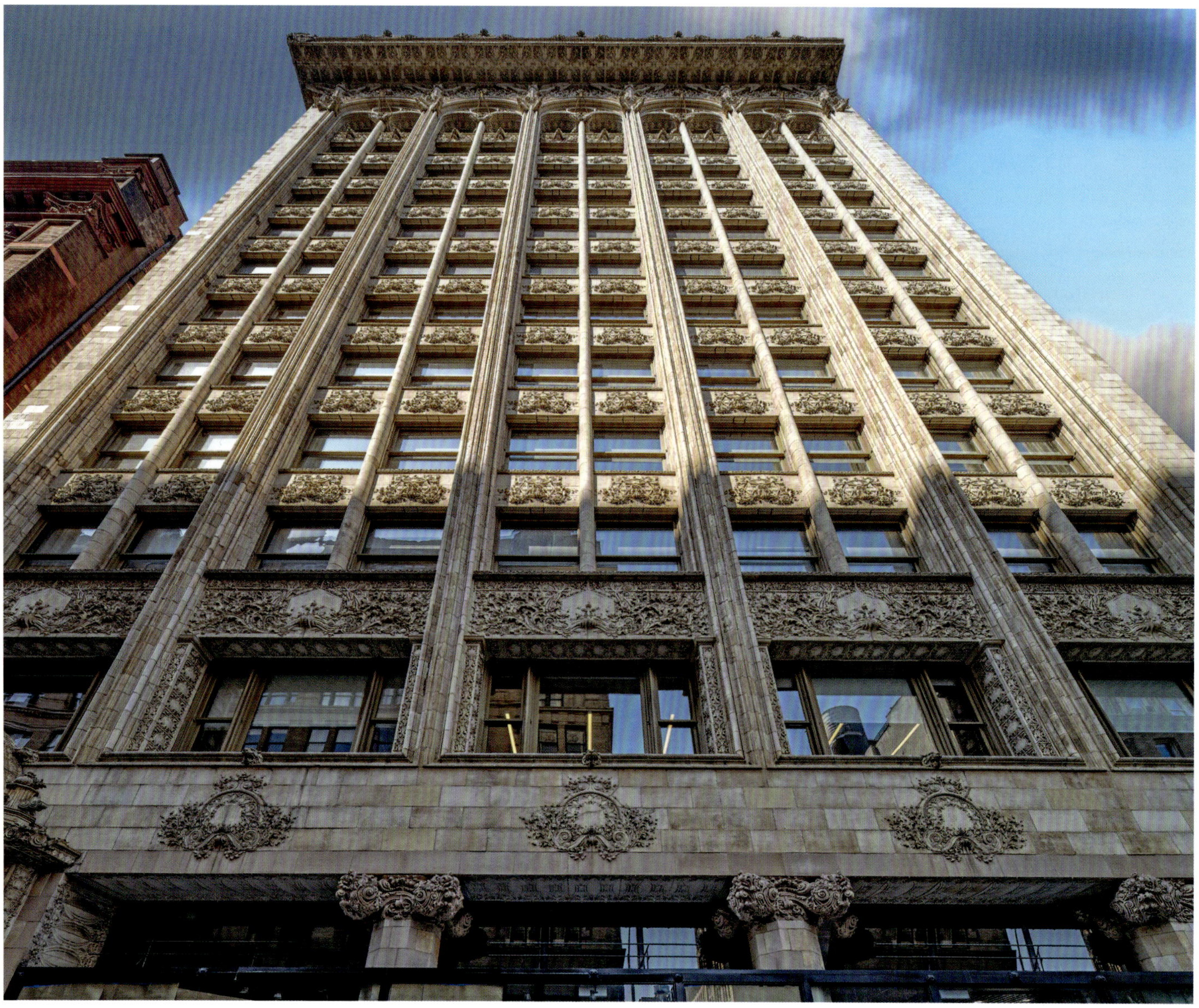

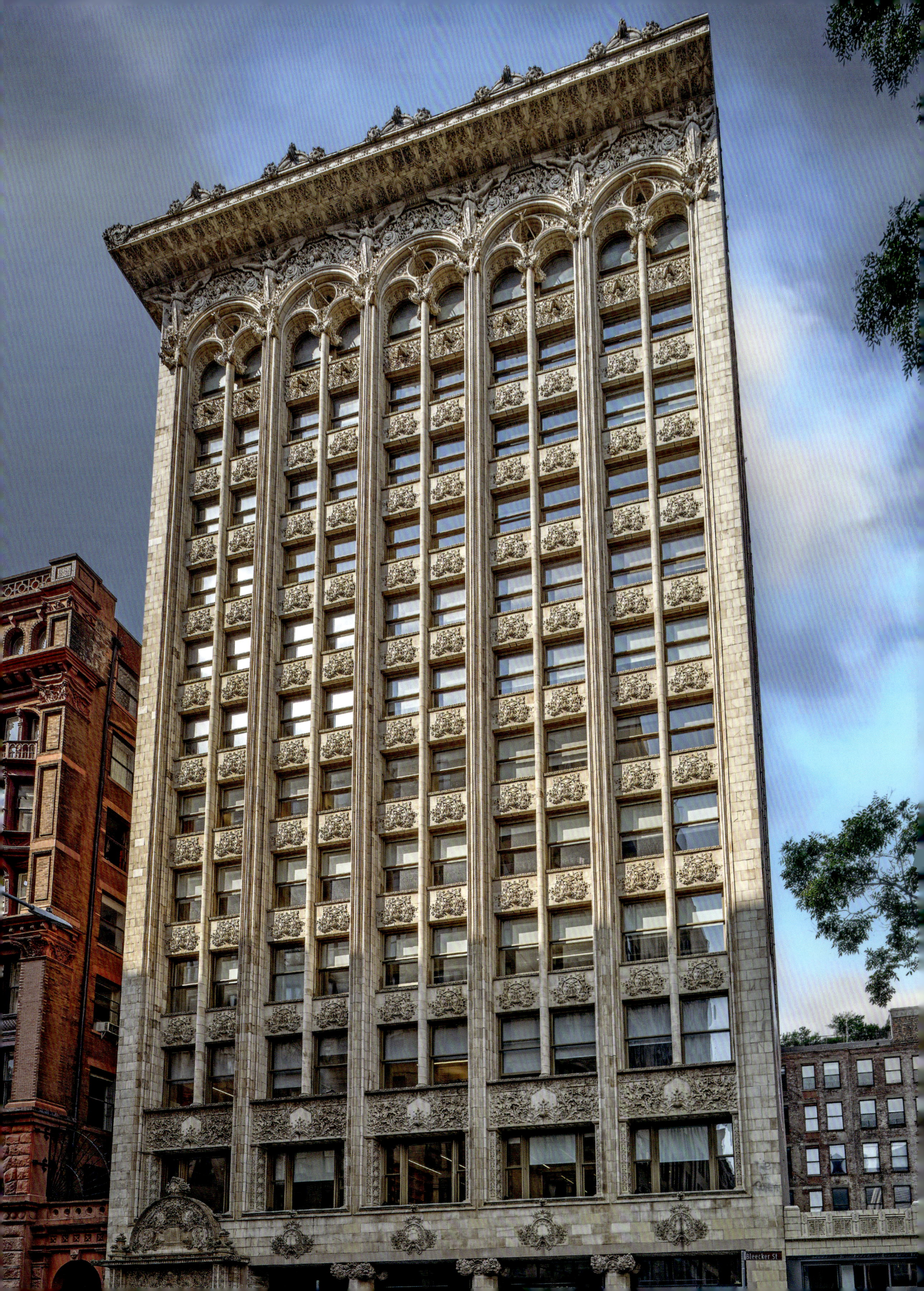
Bleecker St

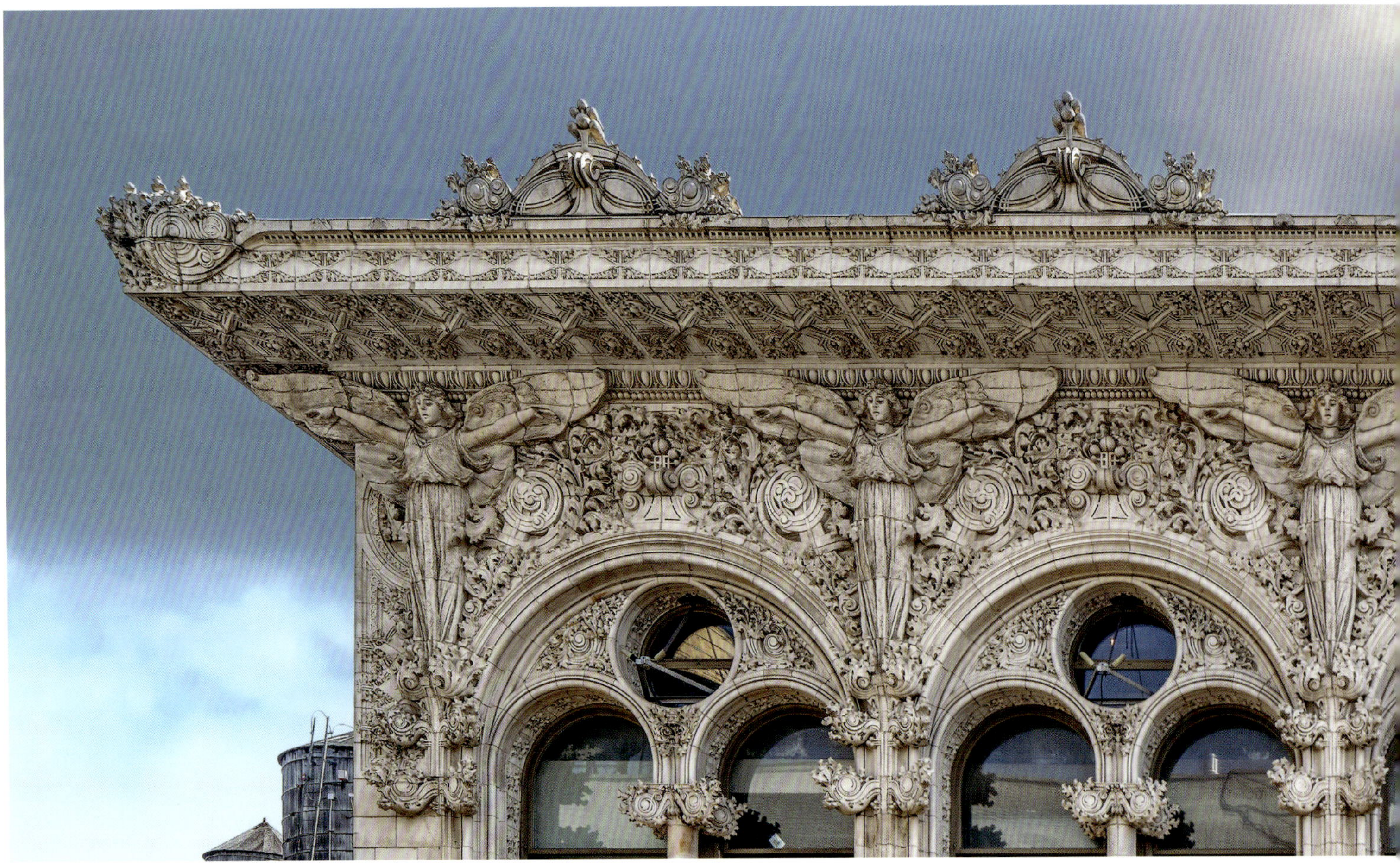

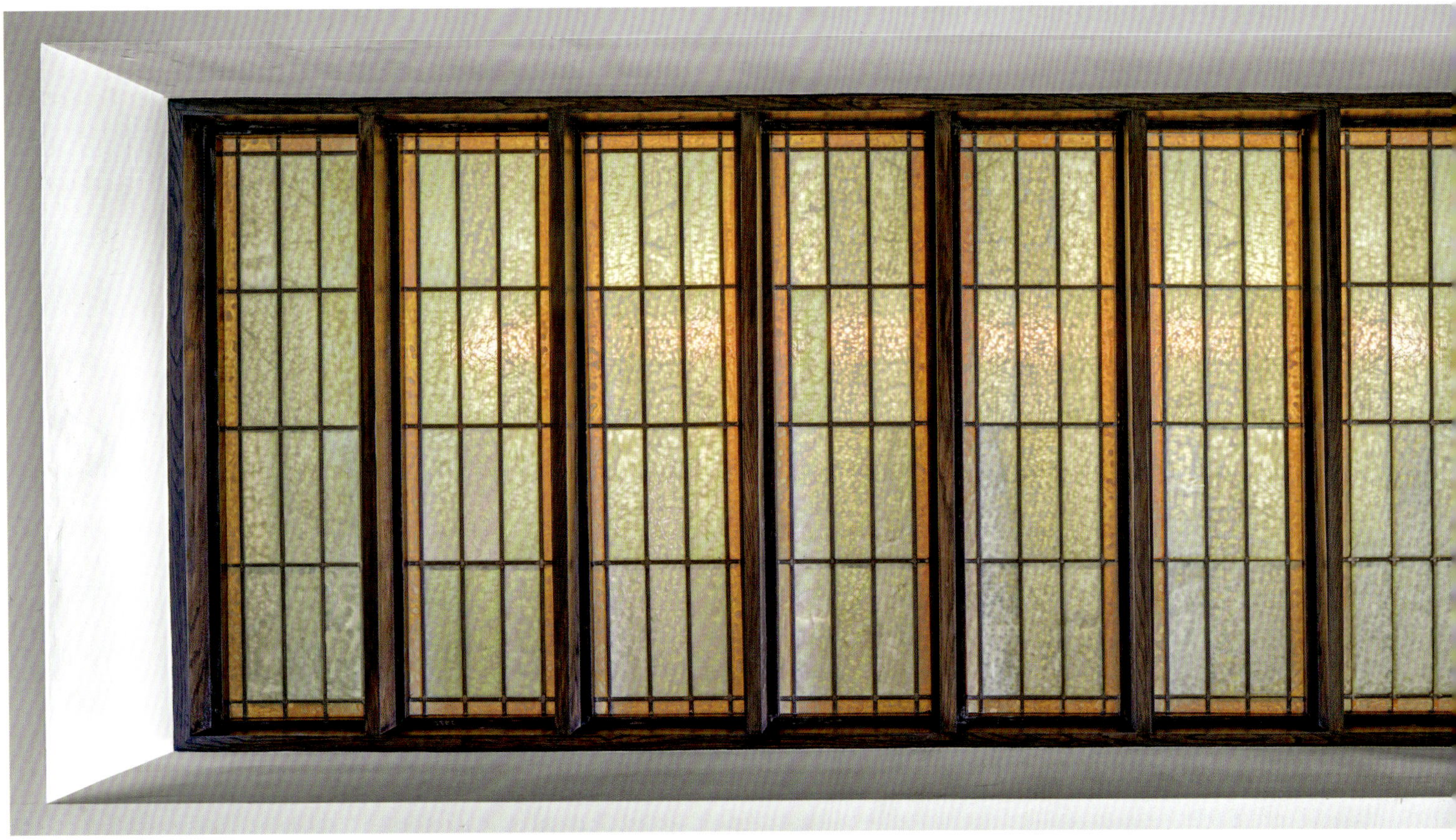

This laylight design in the lobby resulted from a later renovation.

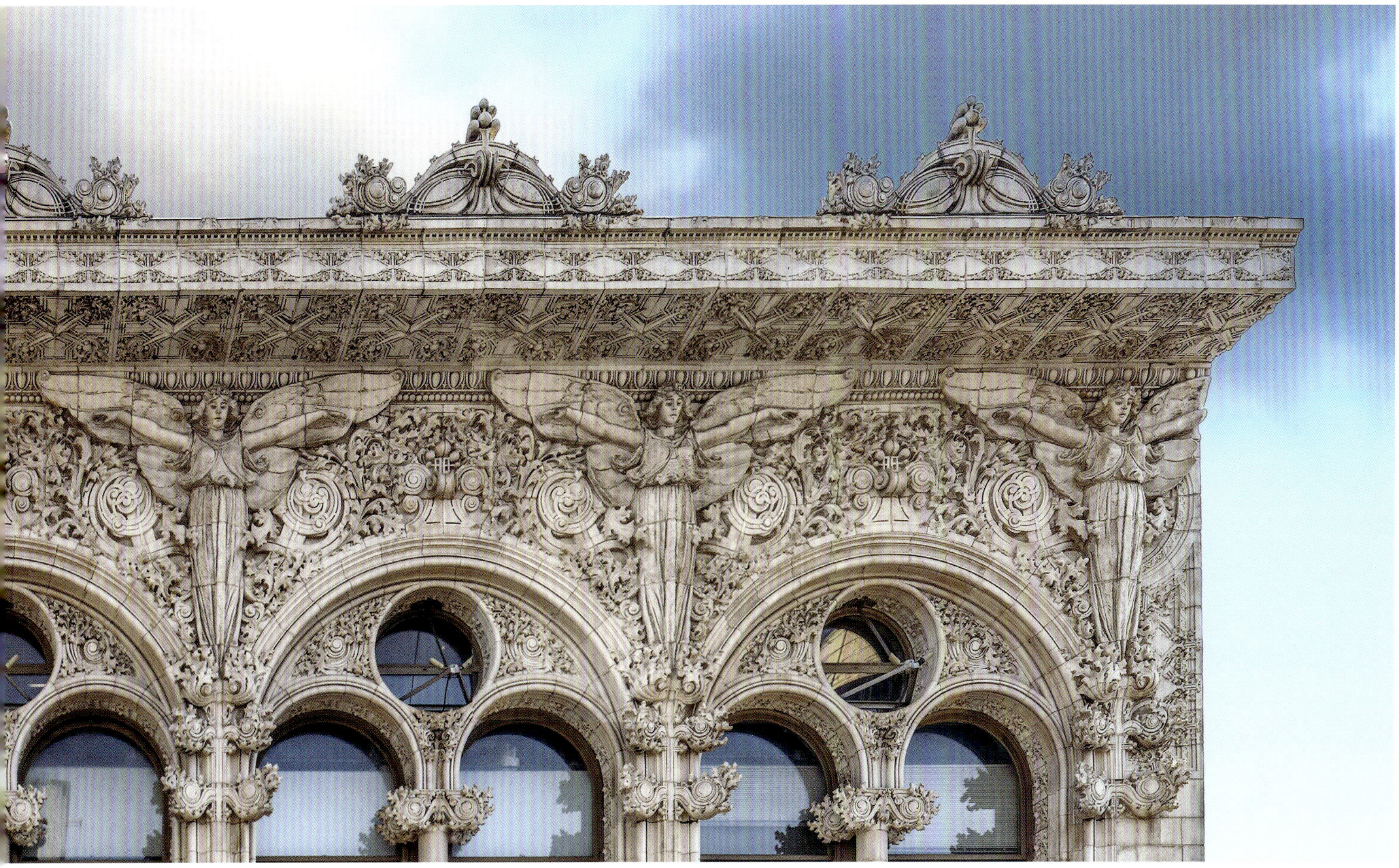

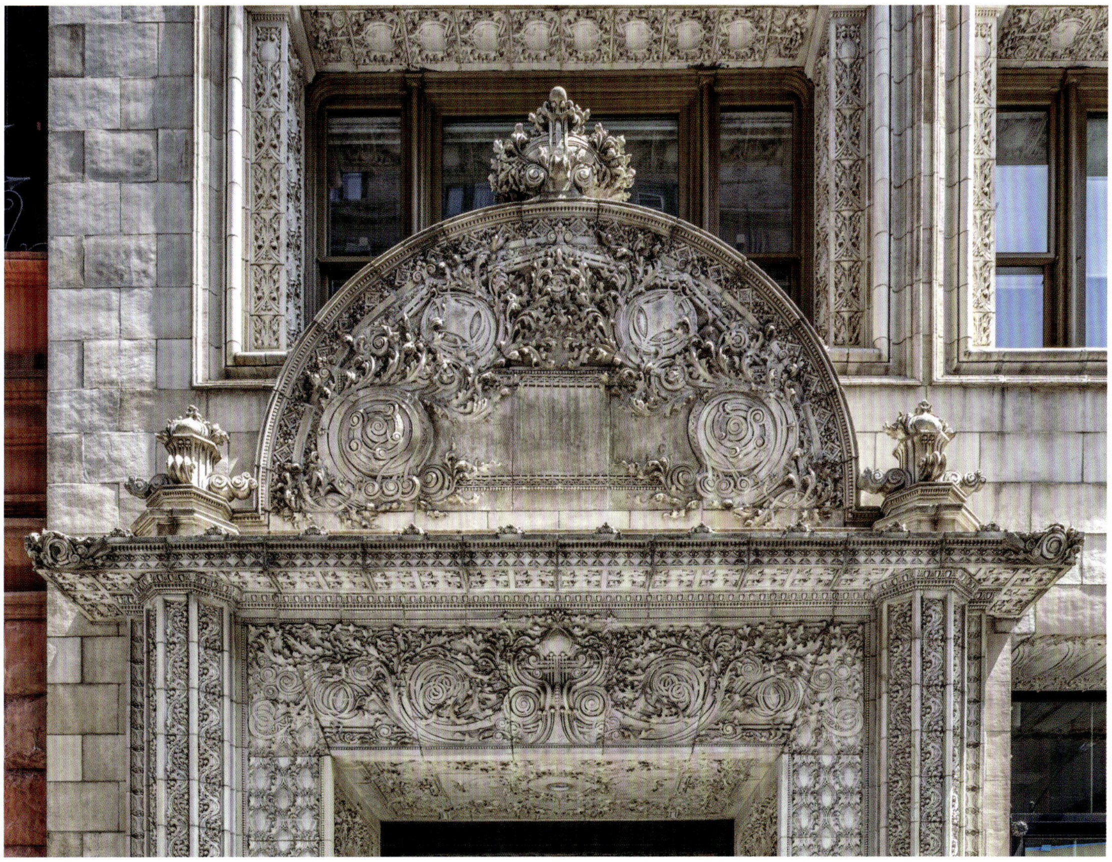

Little survives in the interior except for some staircases, this view from the lobby level.

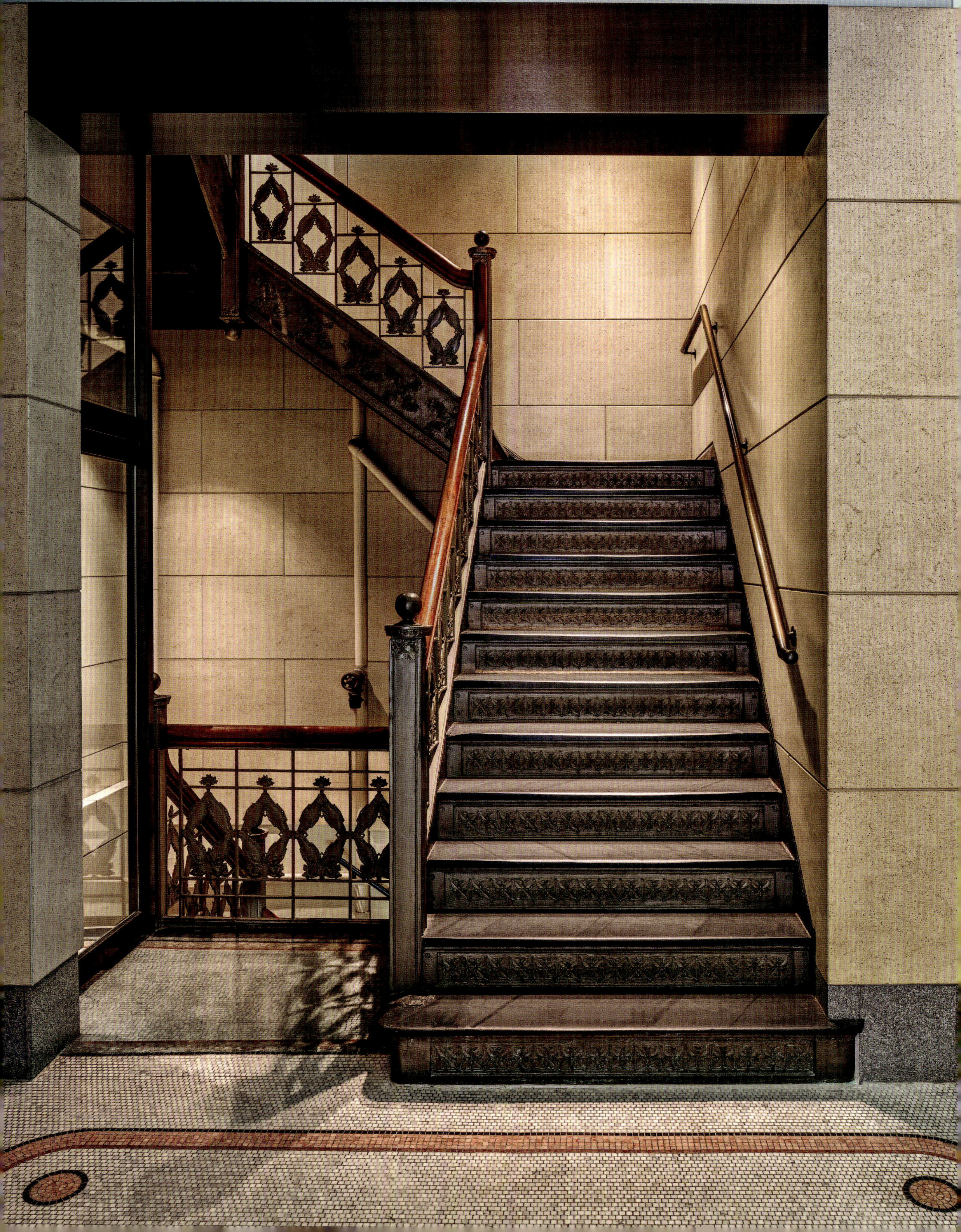

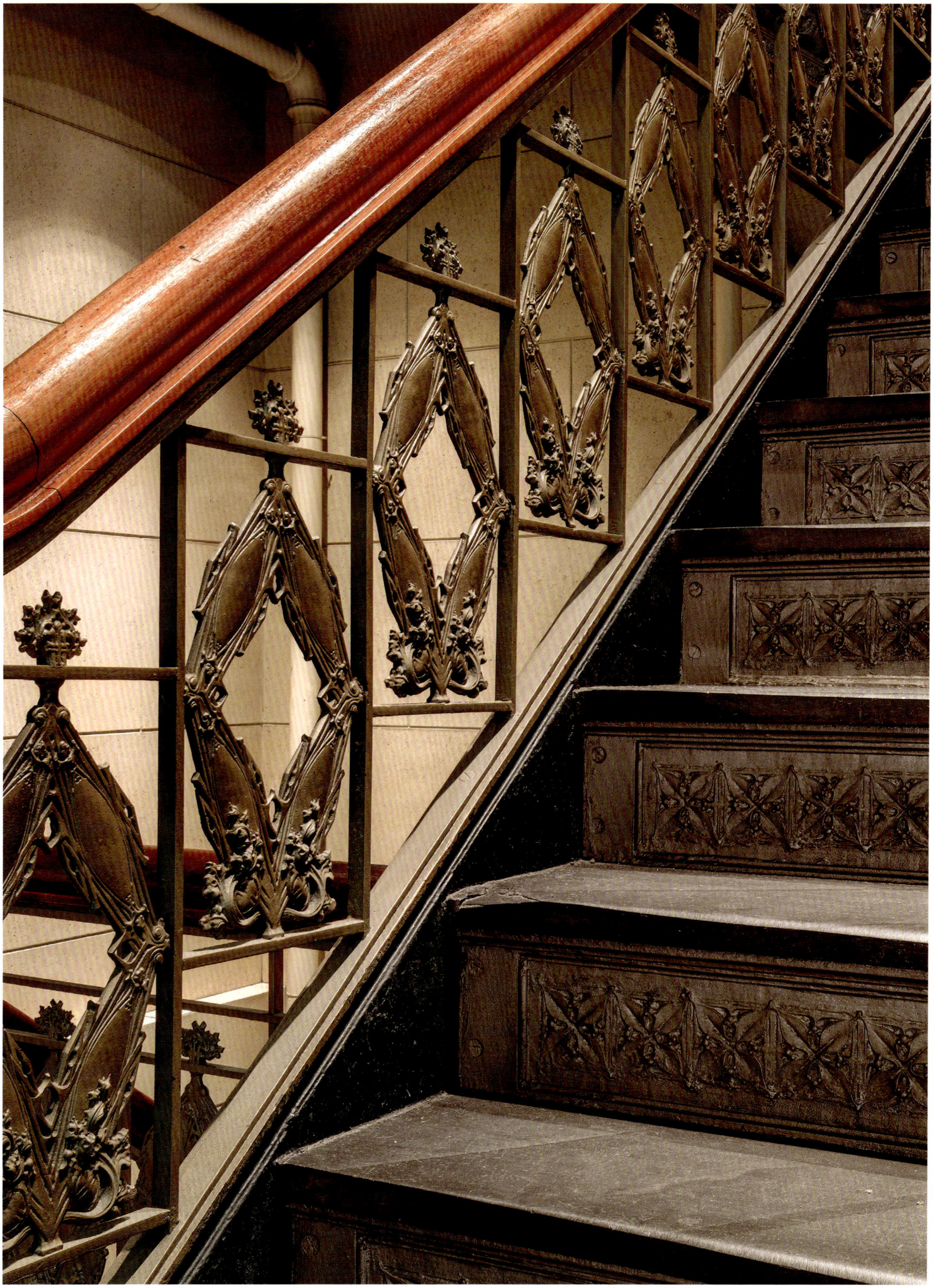

THE WONDER OF THE AGE

"We have in us romanticism, and feel a craving to express it. We feel instinctively that our strong, athletic and simple forms will carry with natural ease the raiment of which we dream, and that our buildings thus clad in a garment of poetic imagery ... will appeal with redoubled power."

Louis Sullivan, Ornament in Architecture

When dedicated on December 9, 1889, the Auditorium Building was hailed as the wonder of the age. Not only was it the largest private building in the country, but its seventeen-story tower was the highest structure in Chicago. A 4,200-seat theater designed to accommodate the most elaborate operatic productions was also the largest permanent facility of its kind in the world. In addition, the structure included a 400-room hotel and abundant retail space. It is no wonder, then, that President Benjamin Harrison decided to attend the dedication.

It was and still is one of Adler & Sullivan's grandest accomplishments. But the real hero may have been the man who spearheaded the effort to build it in the first place, Ferdinand W. Peck (1848–1924). Peck, whose father had made a fortune in what had become the fastest growing city in the world, was an art and music lover who had hired Adler and Sullivan in 1885 to renovate the International Exposition Building to house a hugely successful Opera Festival. Its success encouraged Peck to organize the Chicago Auditorium Association the following year.

Despite the Festival's success—in a two-week run, 90,000 people attended twelve operas—selling Chicago's movers and shakers on building such a large theater wasn't easy, at least not until Adler floated the idea of supporting the opera house with an income-generating hotel, along with office and retail spaces. Mixed-use complexes like the Auditorium are common now, but it was unique for its time.

The association was incorporated in December of 1886, and at a meeting over which Marshall Field presided, Peck was elected president. Adler and Sullivan were chosen as architects, despite some misgivings about the comparative youthfulness of the latter—Sullivan was only thirty. Balancing Sullivan's youth was Adler's acknowledged expertise as both a structural engineer and a builder of acoustically successful theaters. The firm had previously done several, including the McVicker's in Chicago; the Academy of Music in Kalamazoo, Michigan; and others. Adler's skill in acoustics combined with the fame of the Auditorium would later garner the firm a consulting role at Carnegie Hall in New York.

The building would not only be an aesthetic opportunity for Sullivan but also a daunting engineering challenge for Adler. It would not only be the largest building in the country but the heaviest as well, at just over 100,000 tons. And Adler would also have to design a structure within a structure for the theater. While the foundations of large buildings in Chicago would soon consist of caissons drilled to bedrock, the Auditorium is supported by something that resembles a series of rafts floating on the subsoil. The tower, for example, is supported on a raft five feet thick, reinforced with eight layers of timbers, rails, and I-beams. Because of the building's weight, Adler planned for a settlement of no less than eighteen inches.

Sullivan constantly refined his designs, starting with a fussy and picturesque design with a sloping roof, gables, cupolas, oriels, and other decorative touches. Eventually, the design was pared down to the flat-roofed, restrained building we see today. Interiors, of course, are another matter altogether!

The final exterior design owes much to the influence of Henry Hobson Richardson who became one of America's most admired architects before his death in 1886. His Marshall Field & Co. wholesale warehouse was completed in 1887 and had a profound effect on Sullivan and other designers. Designed in a style that has come to be known as Richardsonian Romanesque, the Field had a massive presence and dignity unmatched in Chicago. At the same time, Richardson also designed the famous Glessner House, which still stands as a reminder of Richardson's genius. Sullivan's infatuation with Richardson didn't last long, but in addition to the Auditorium, his influence can be seen in the Walker Warehouse; Standard Club; Kehilath-Anshe Ma'ariv synagogue; and Pueblo, Colorado Opera House, among other buildings.

While the exterior of the Auditorium has its own solid dignity, it is Sullivan's treatment of the interior spaces of the theater and hotel that guaranteed the building's fame. The sheer variety and inventiveness of Sullivan's forms and decorations are unmatched. It is difficult today to imagine assembling the army of artists, artisans and craftsmen that had to be mobilized to execute the architect's elaborate designs. The designs themselves, in their incredible variety, had to progress from Sullivan's mind to final working drawings. For this, Sullivan had another army of draftsmen, including Frank Lloyd Wright and George Grant Elmslie.

This complexity, of both structure and decoration, resulted in a final cost of approximately $3.4 million, an immense sum for the time. While small profits were made in the early years, financial problems eventually became the norm. For example, one of the main tenants was the Chicago Symphony Orchestra. Its director, Theodore Thomas, thought the Auditorium Theater too large for orchestral concerts—he claimed not enough sound returned to the stage—and insisted that a purpose-built auditorium be built. He got his way, and the orchestra moved into the new Daniel Burnham-designed Orchestra Hall—now called Symphony Center after recent renovations and additions—in 1904.

The Auditorium's life as a home for grand opera was also star-crossed. While it did serve as a home for traveling companies like New York's Metropolitan Opera, local opera companies weren't able to survive. One that did have some success in the 1920s, the Chicago Civic Opera Company, was led by utility magnate Samuel Insull, who moved the company to what is now the Civic Opera House, designed by Graham, Anderson, Probst & White and completed in 1929. The Depression led to the failure of both the opera company and Insull's utility empire.

By 1941, the Auditorium Building was operated by the nonprofit Auditorium Music Foundation, which used it as a serviceman's center during World War II. Among its amenities was a bowling alley installed on the theatre's stage!

In 1946, the new Roosevelt University negotiated an agreement to take over the building from the city and convert it to classrooms and offices, with the understanding that the theater would also eventually be restored. Clear title was gained only when the city agreed to forgive back taxes for the right to create an arcaded sidewalk on the north portion of the building and theater to enable the widening of Congress Parkway.

Restoration began in earnest in 1956 and continues to this day. Architects involved in the restoration include Crombie Taylor; Skidmore, Owings & Merrill; Harry Weese & Associates; Danforth, Rockwell, Carow; John Vinci; and Booth Hansen Associates. Despite feeling it necessary to modernize certain areas rather than restore them, in general, the university has done its best to return the complex to its original glories. It was added to the National Register of Historic Places in 1970; named a National Histroic Landmark in 1975; and a Chicago Landmark in 1976.

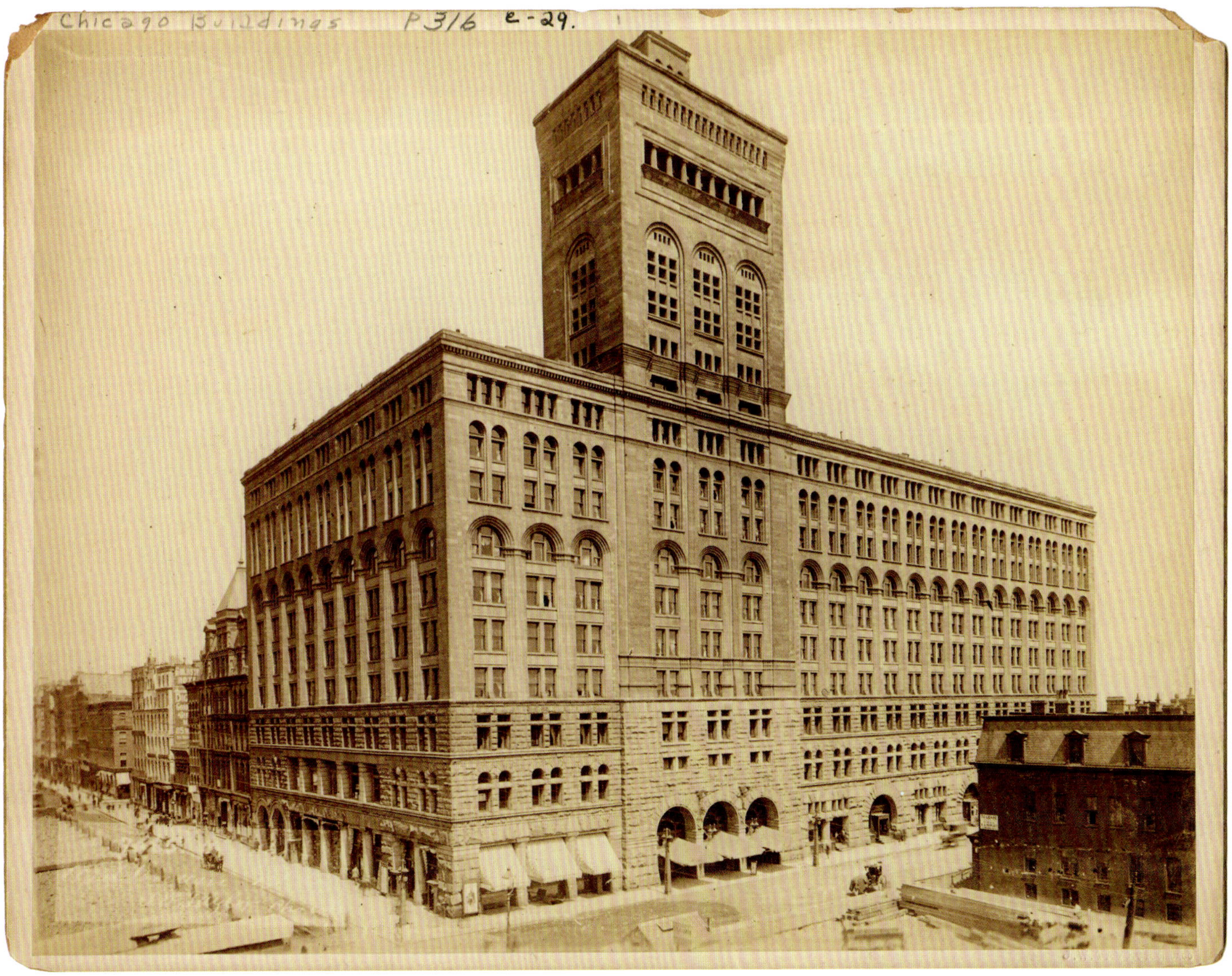

Photo by J.W. Taylor, Chicago History Museum/Alamy Stock Photo

Soon after it was completed Adler & Sullivan moved their offices to the tower. Sullivan was forced to leave his reduced office space there in 1918 when he could no longer afford it.

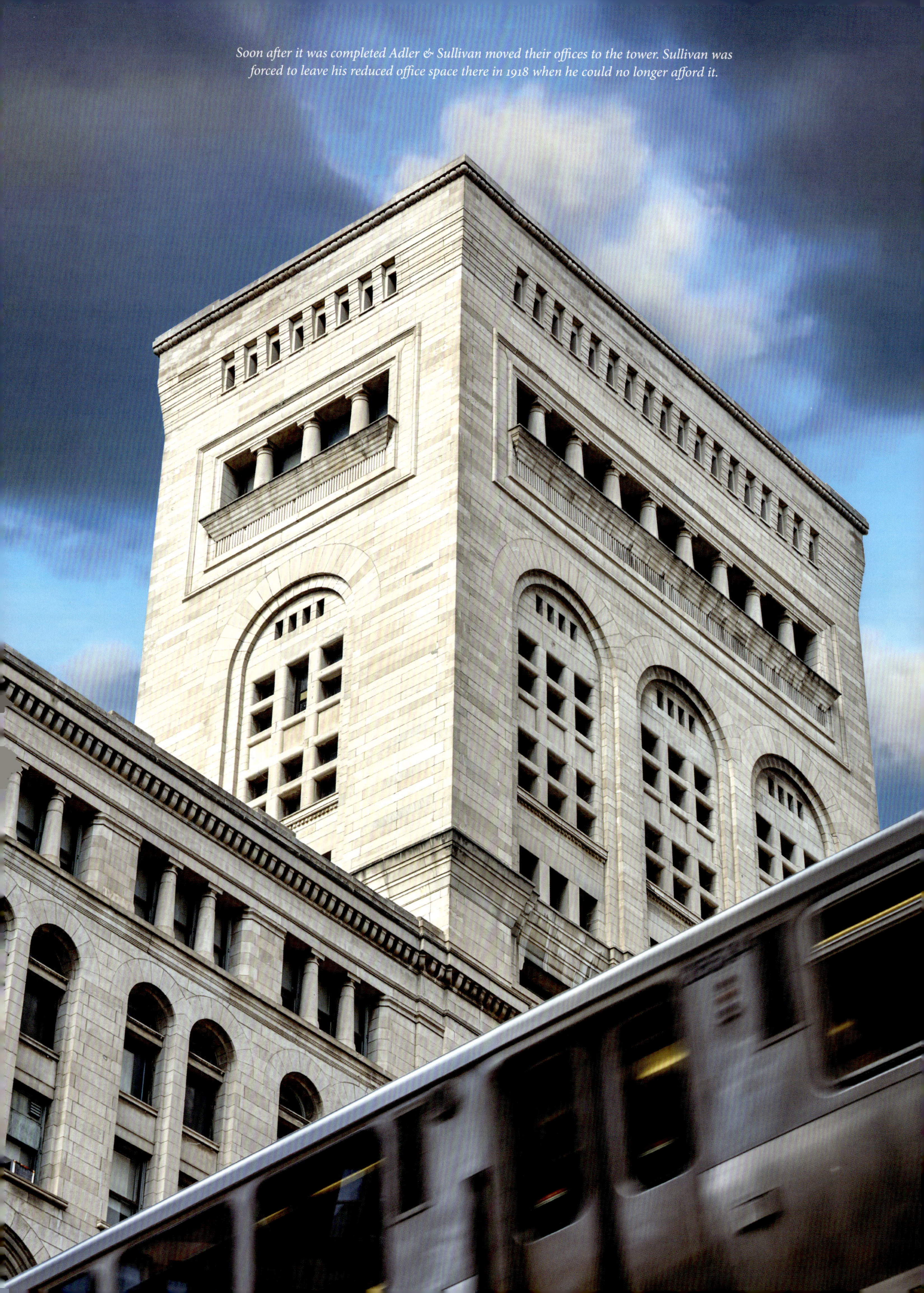

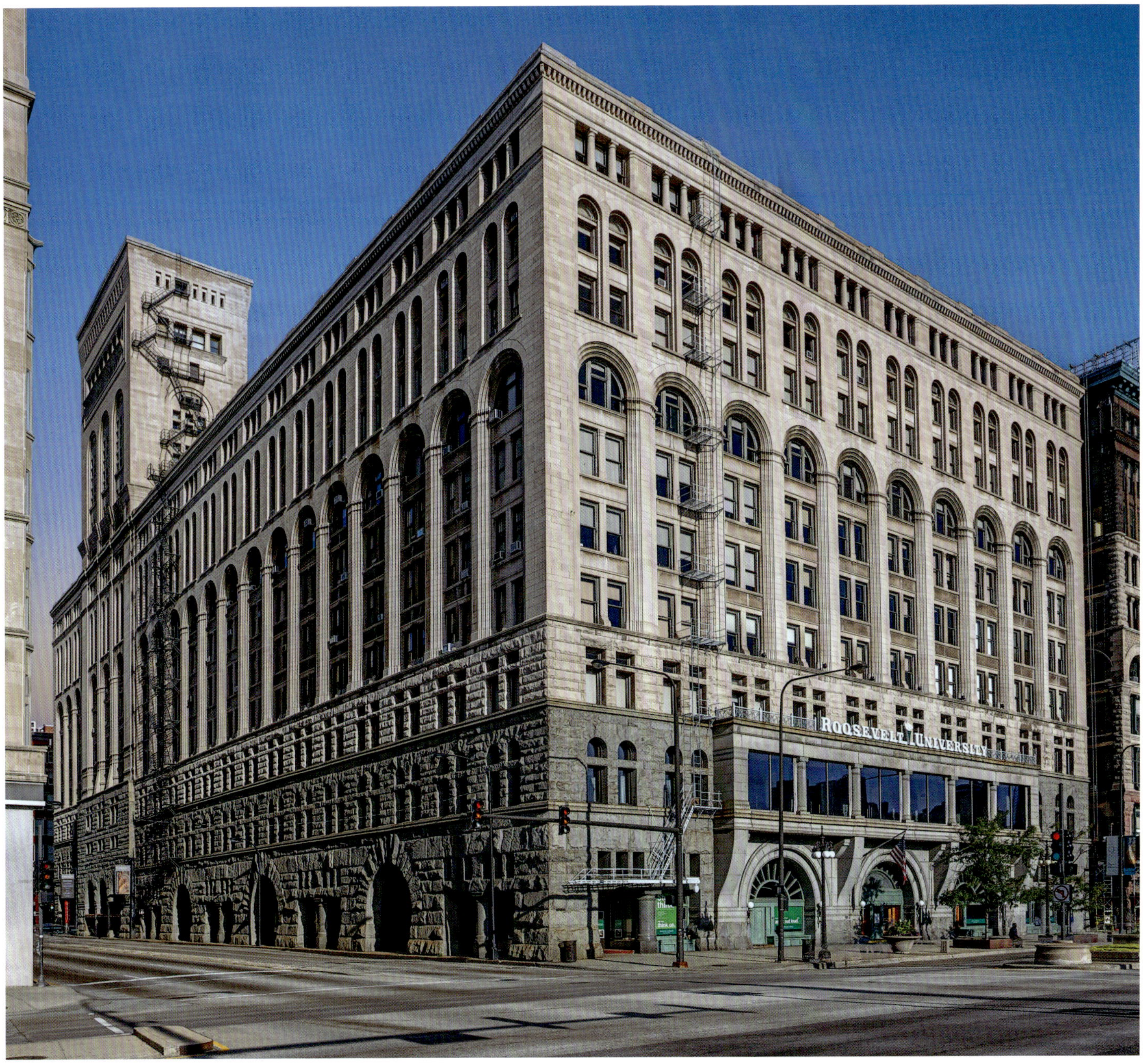
ROOSEVELT UNIVERSITY

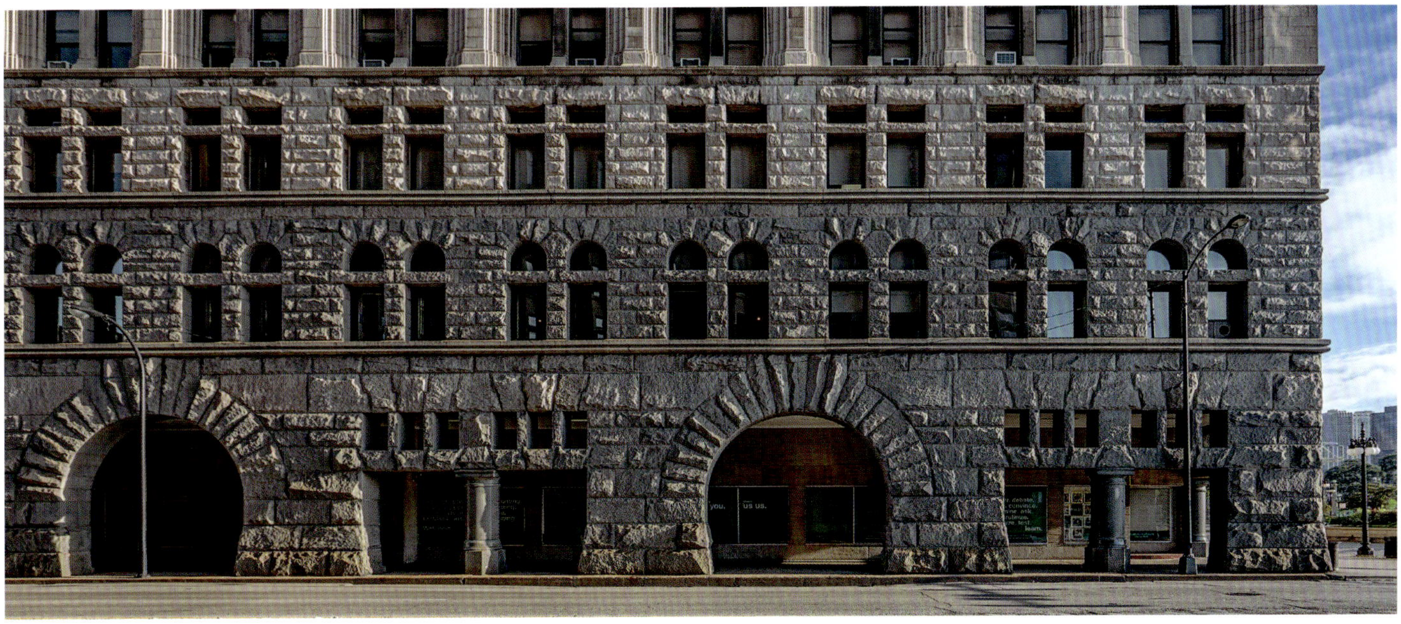

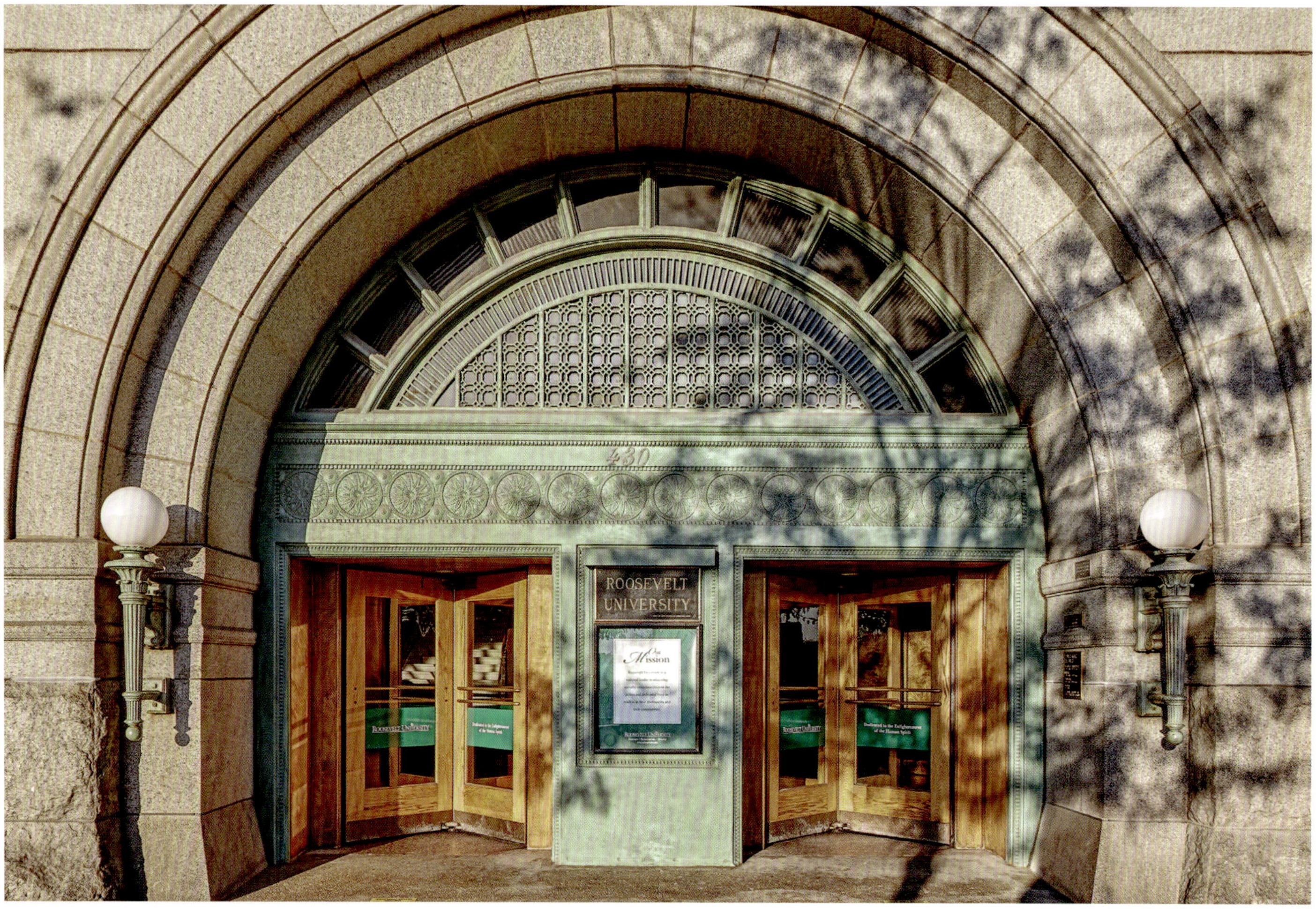
ROOSEVELT
UNIVERSITY

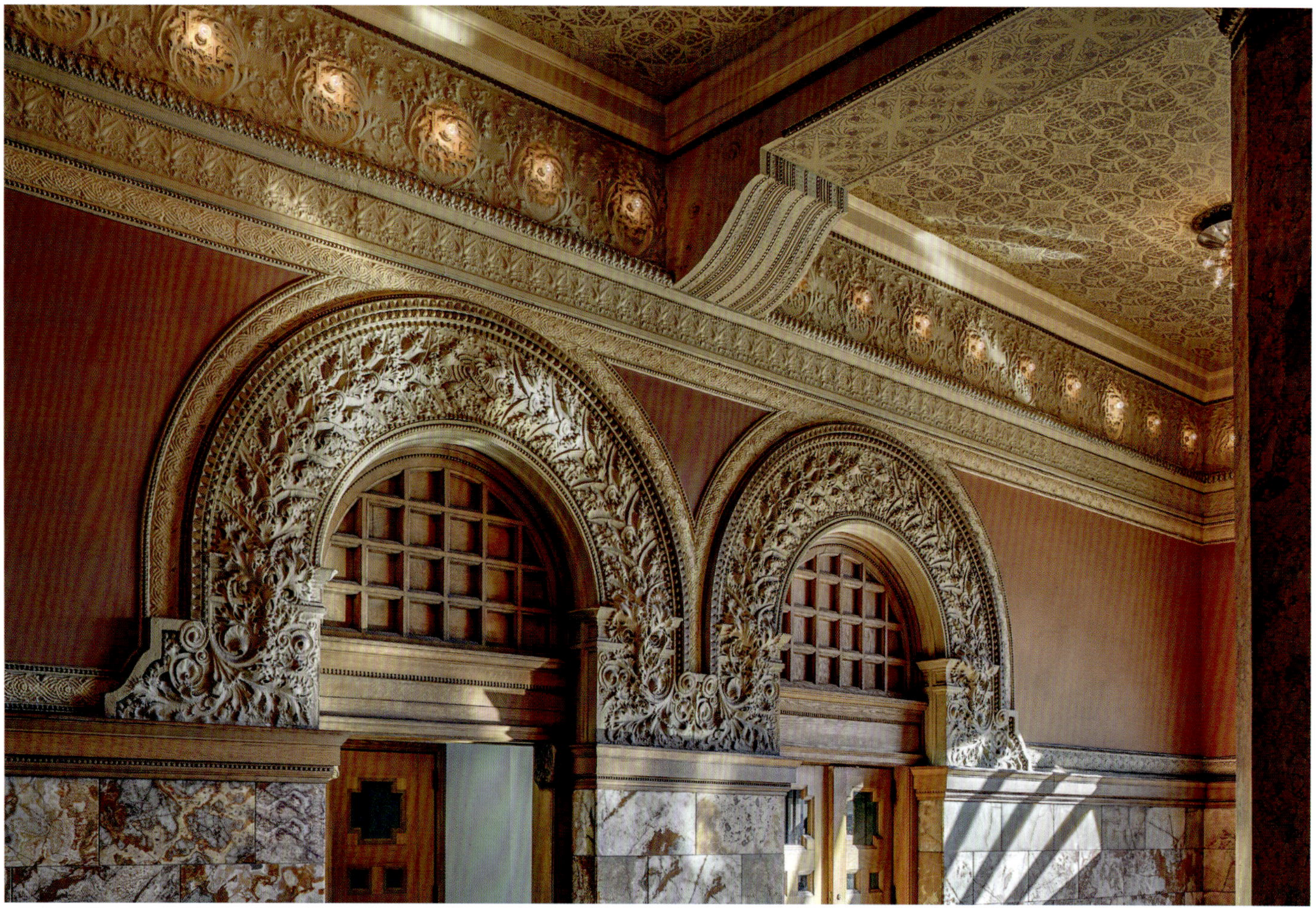

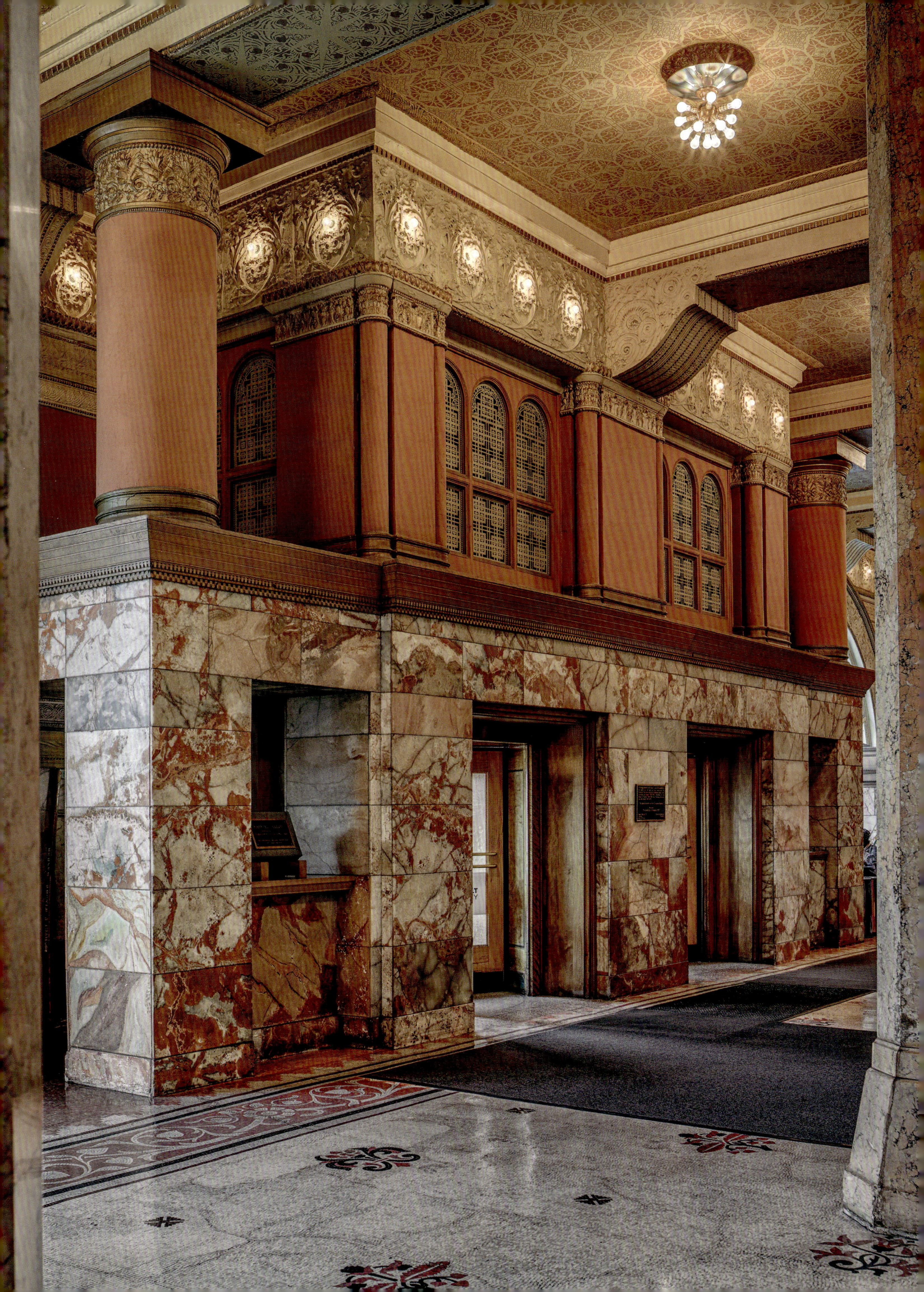

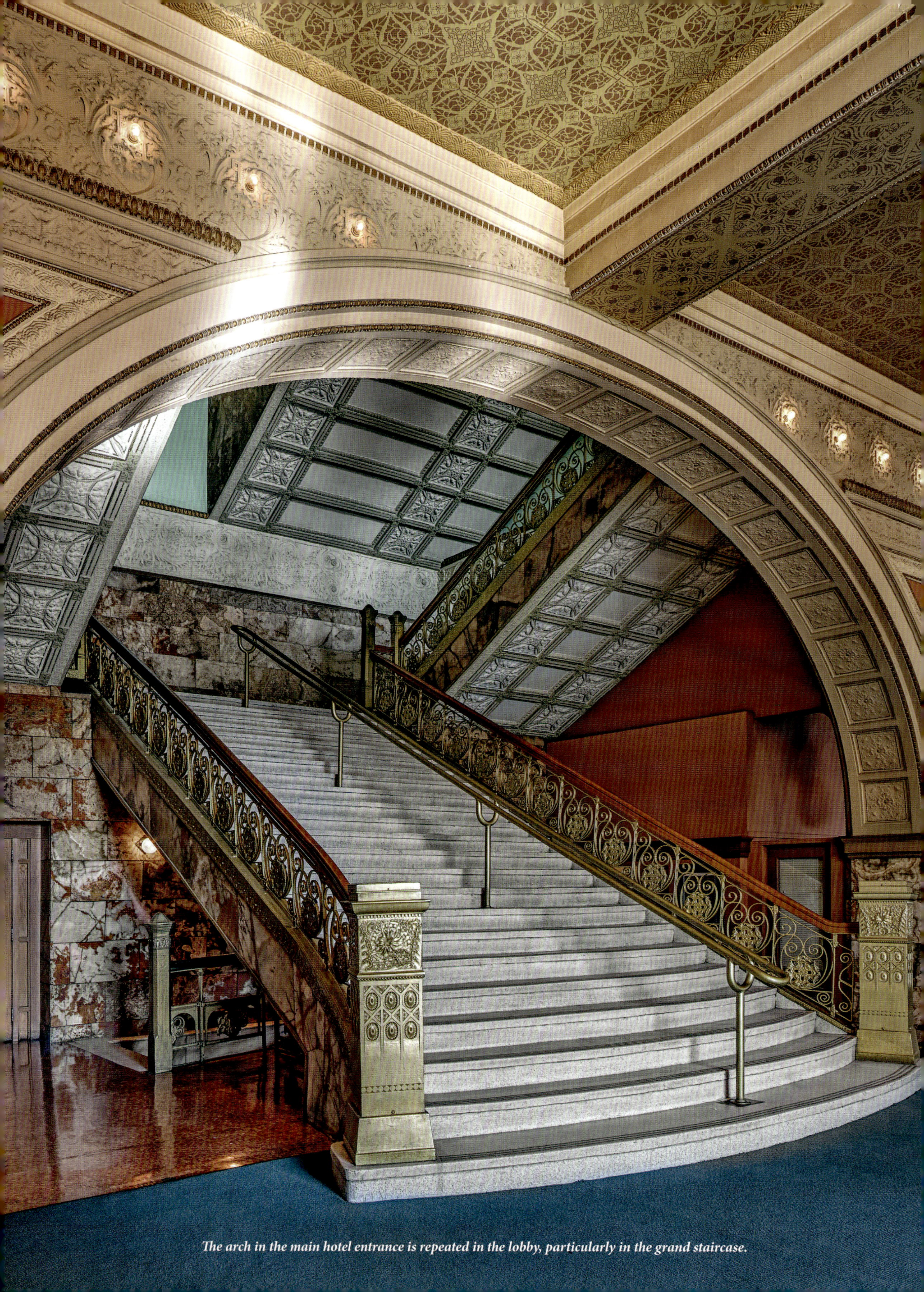

The arch in the main hotel entrance is repeated in the lobby, particularly in the grand staircase.

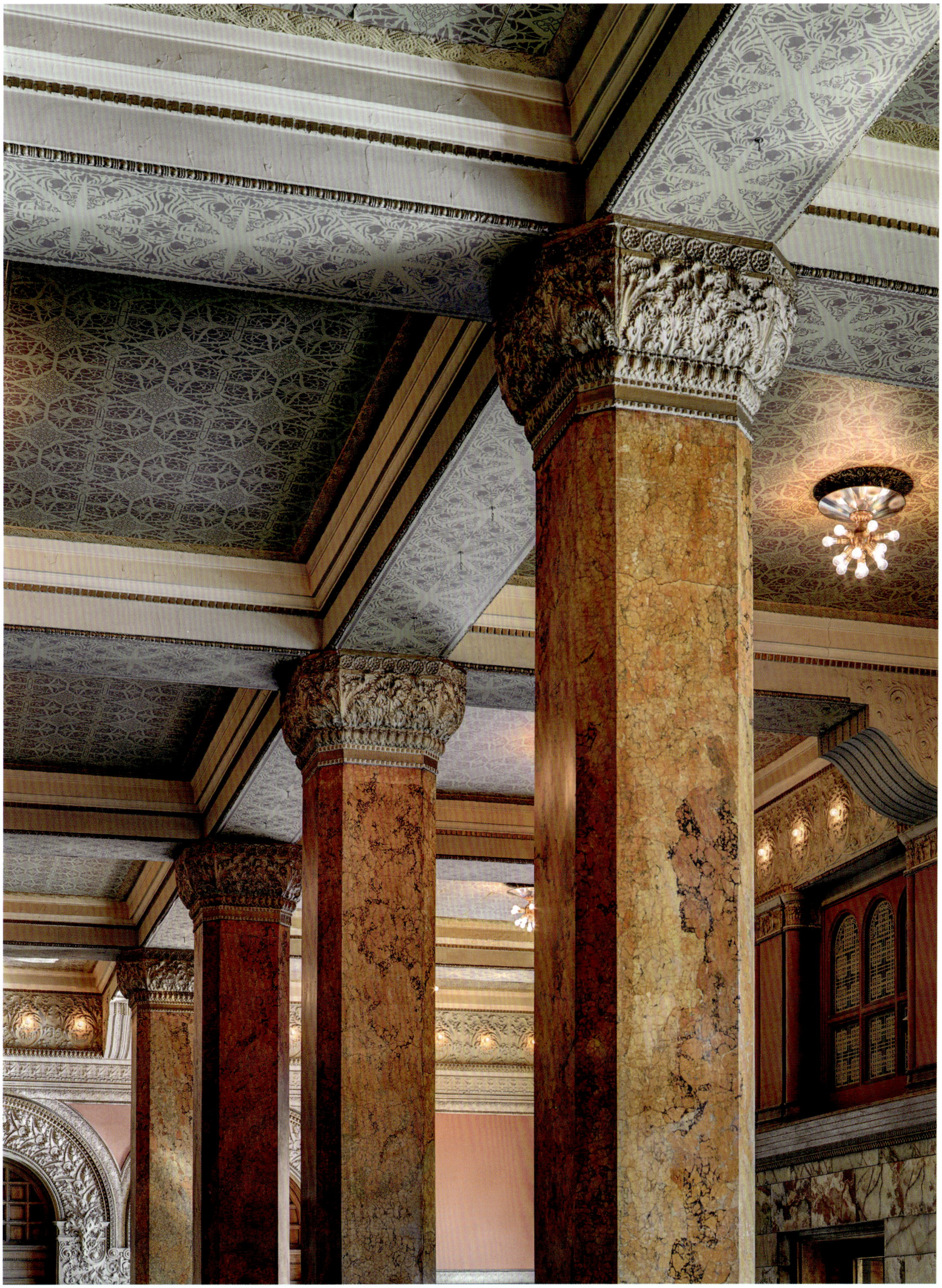

While real onyx is used for the inside of the entrance, the columns are finished with faux marble.

The grand staircase rises three stories and is capped by an art glass laylight.

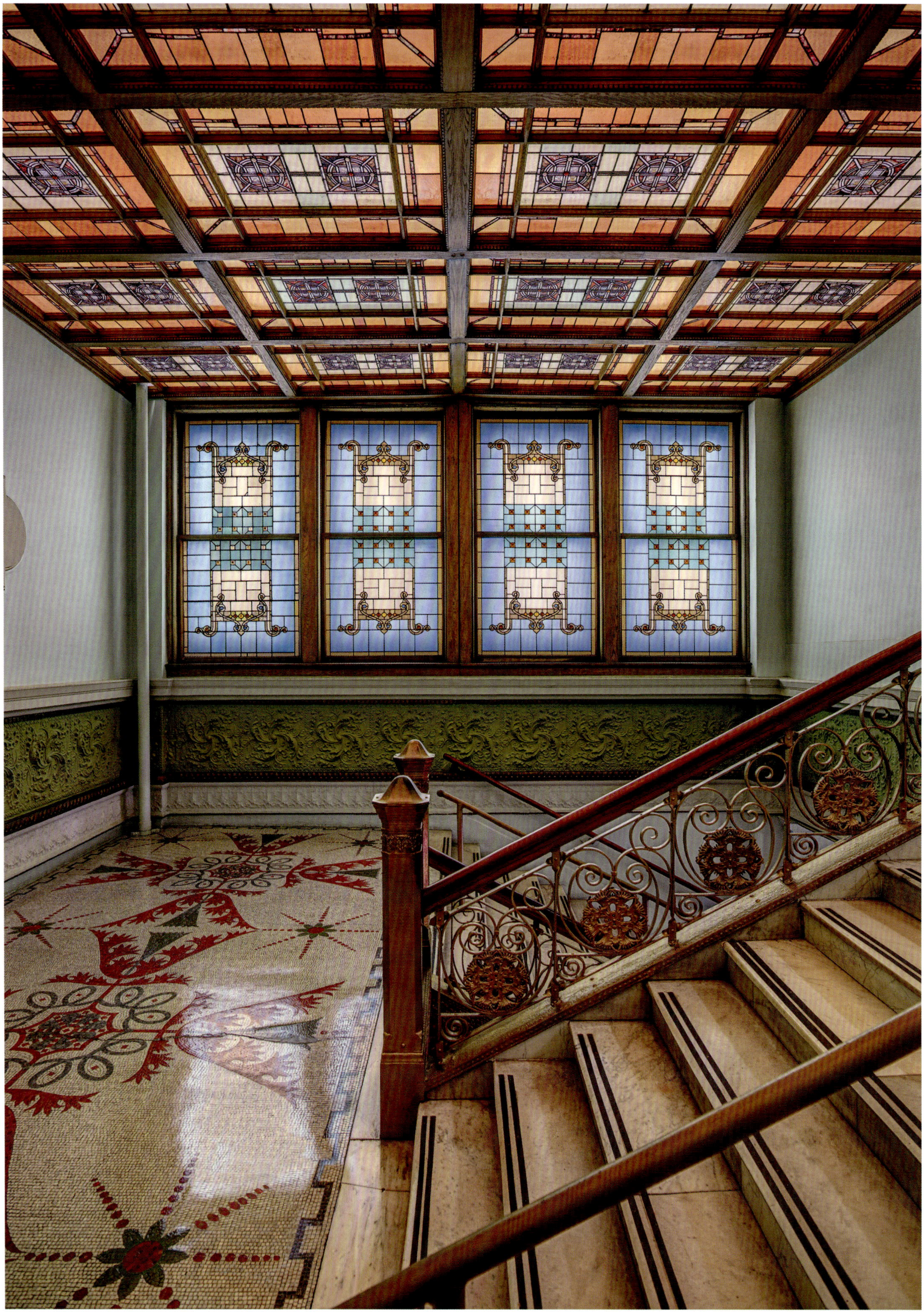

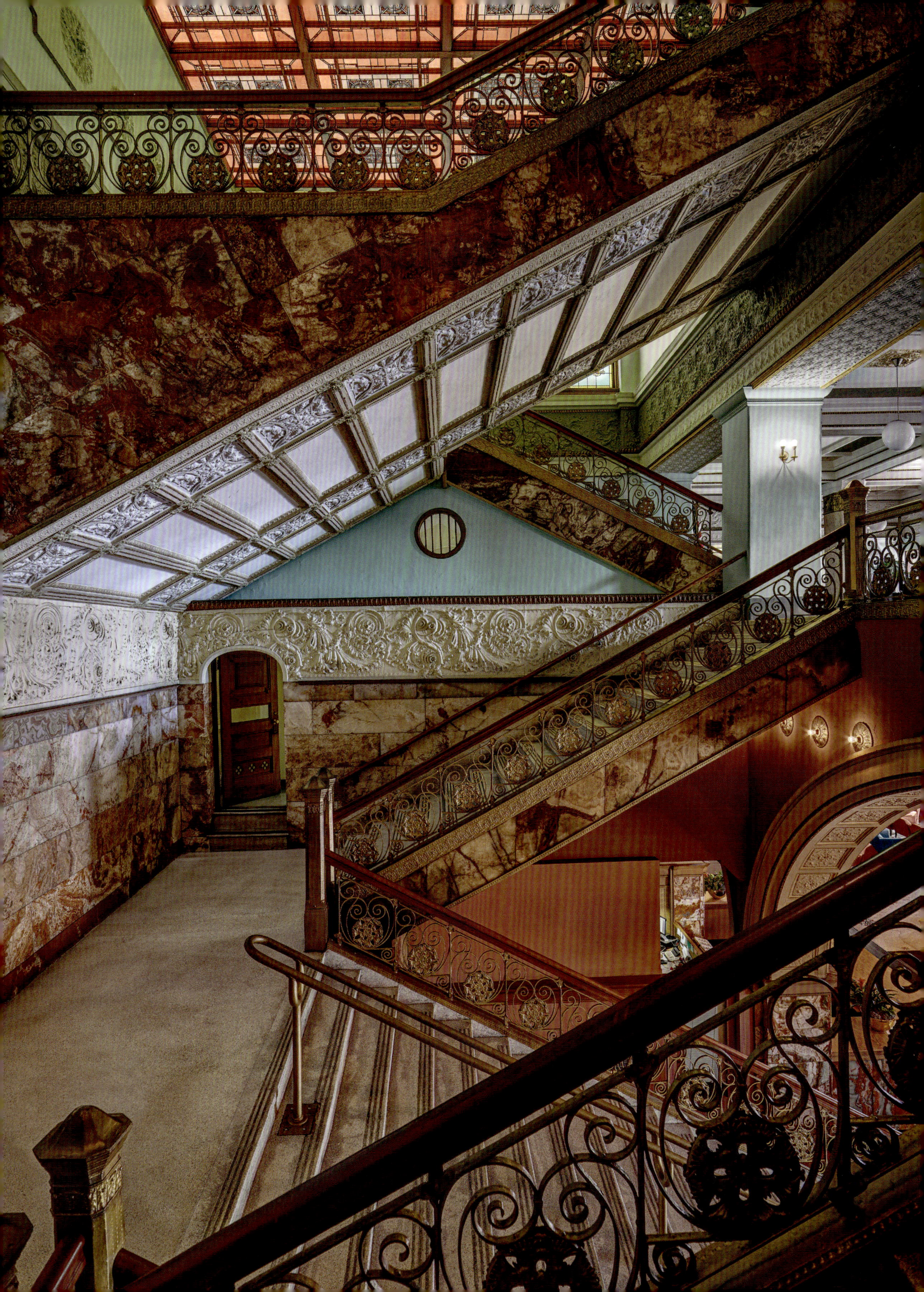

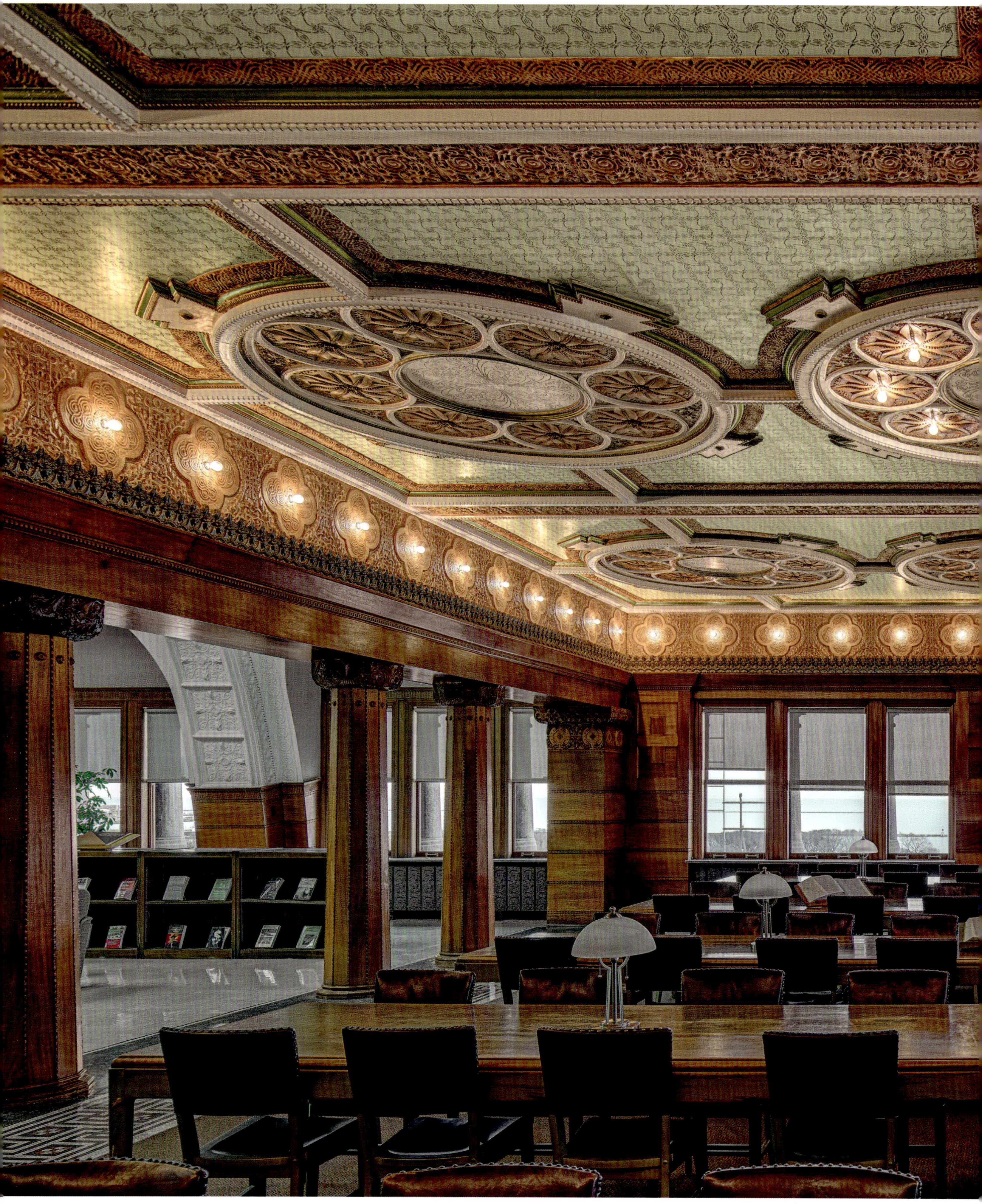

The hotel's main dining room—now Roosevelt University's library—was on the top floor. This is a view of the side room.

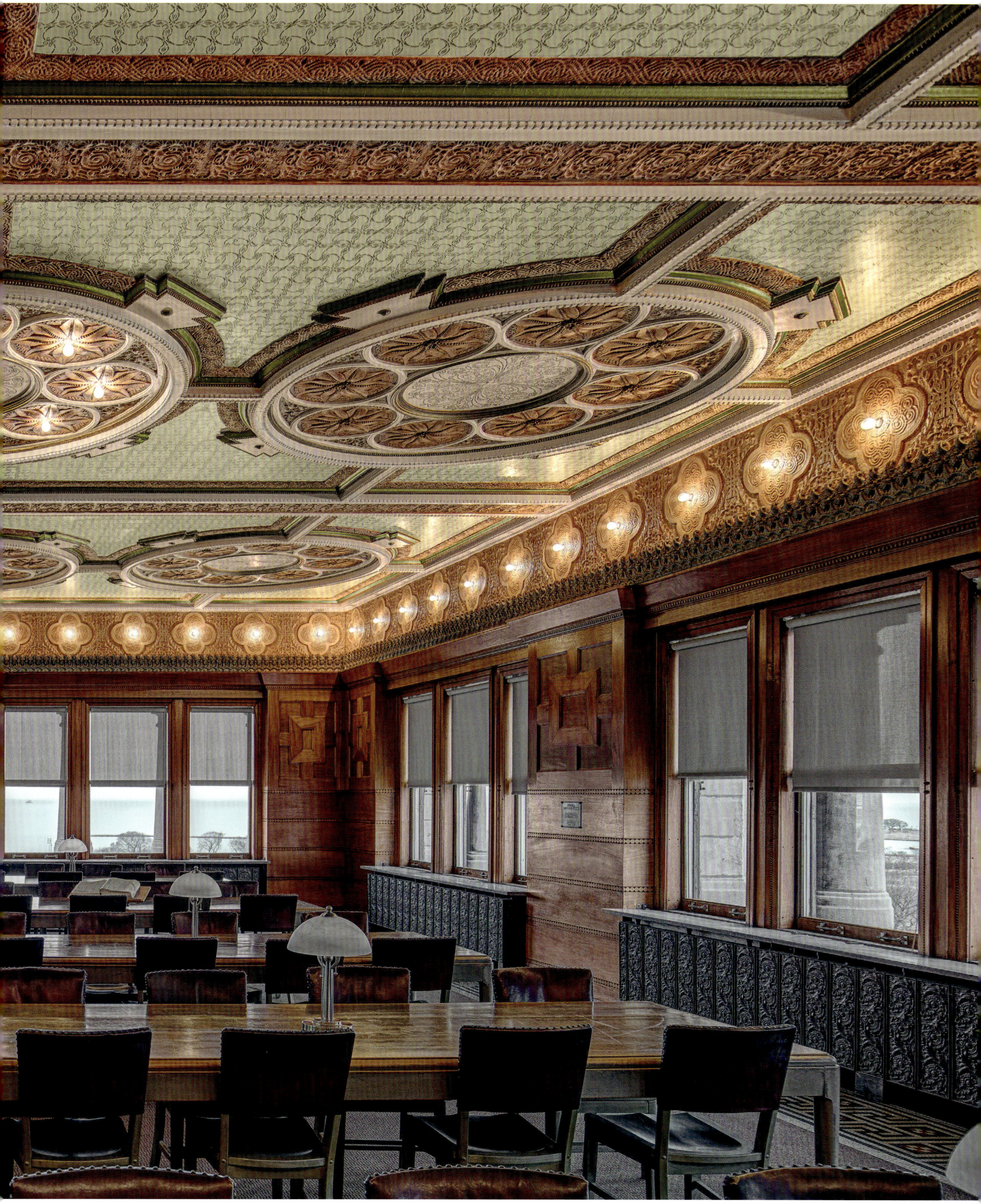

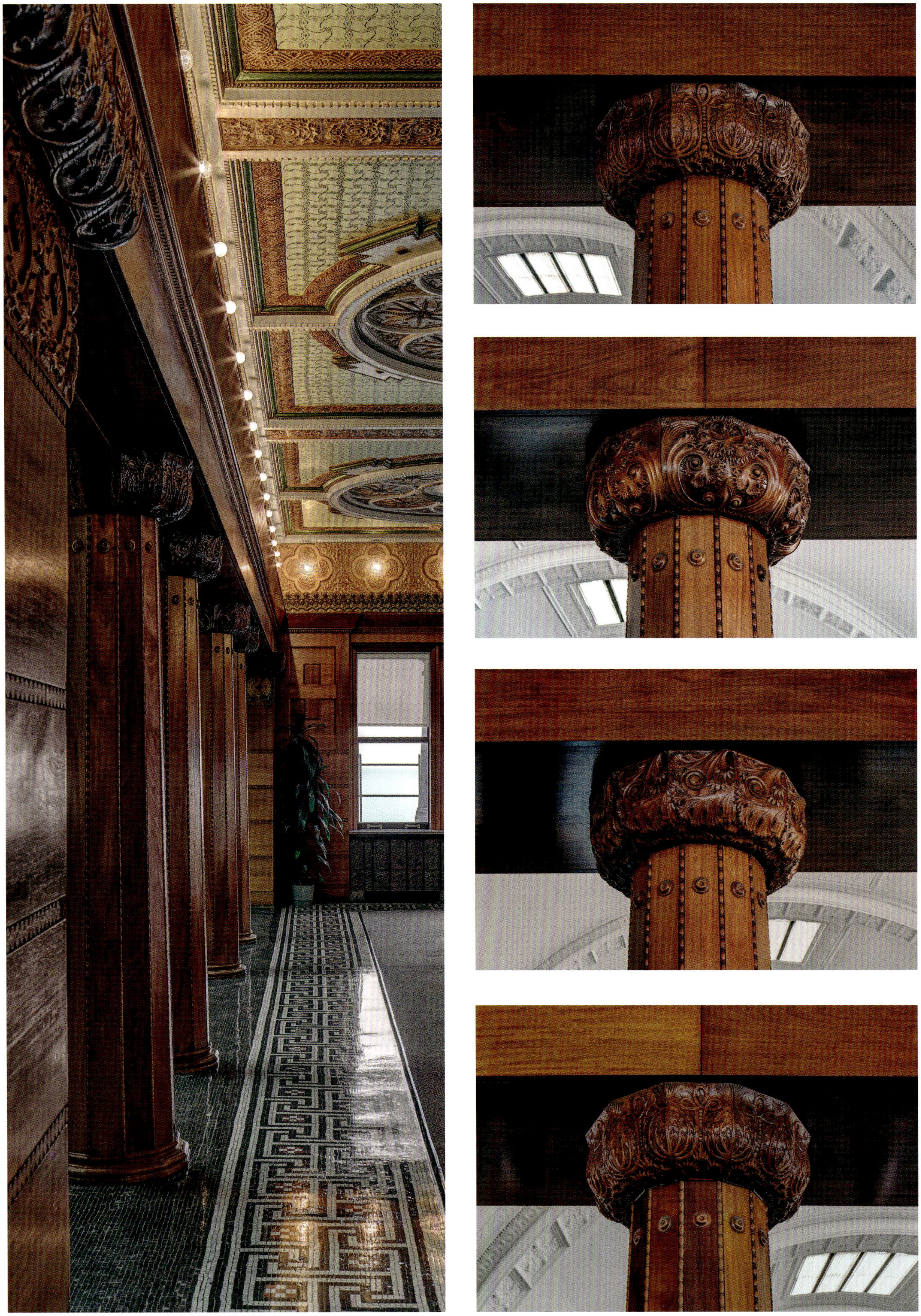

Each of the capitals on the wood columns is different. Richard W. Bates executed them to Sullivan's design.

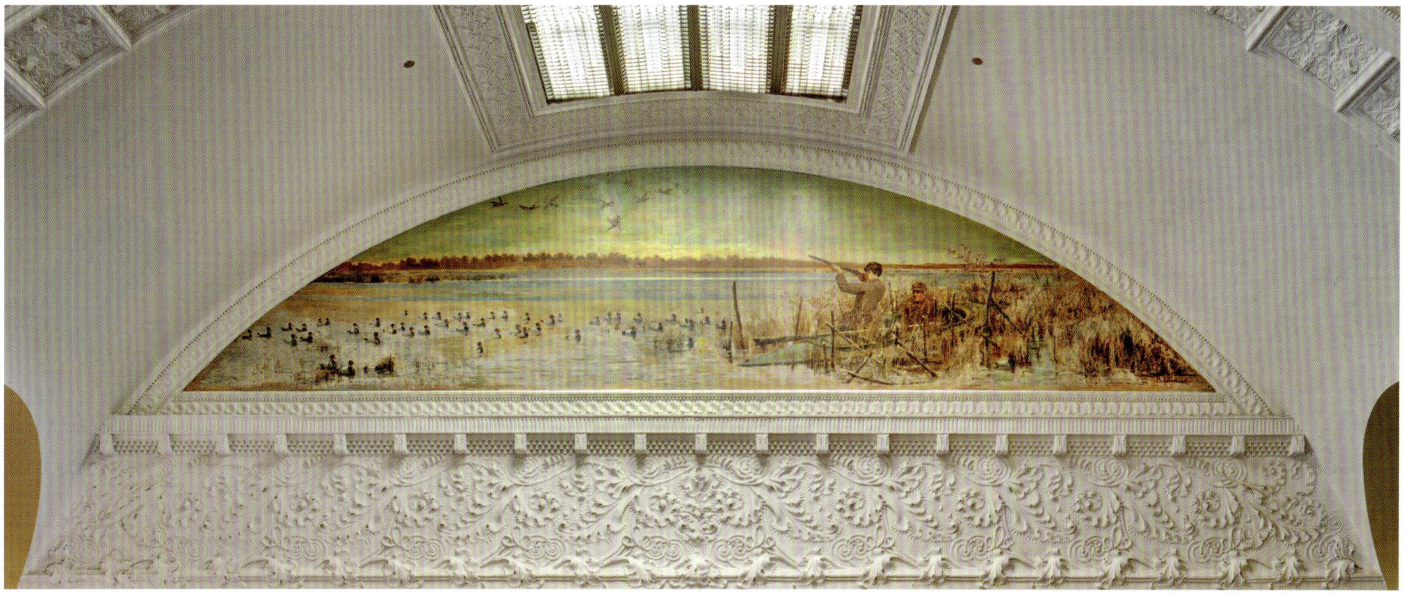

The main dining space has a barrel-vaulted ceiling.

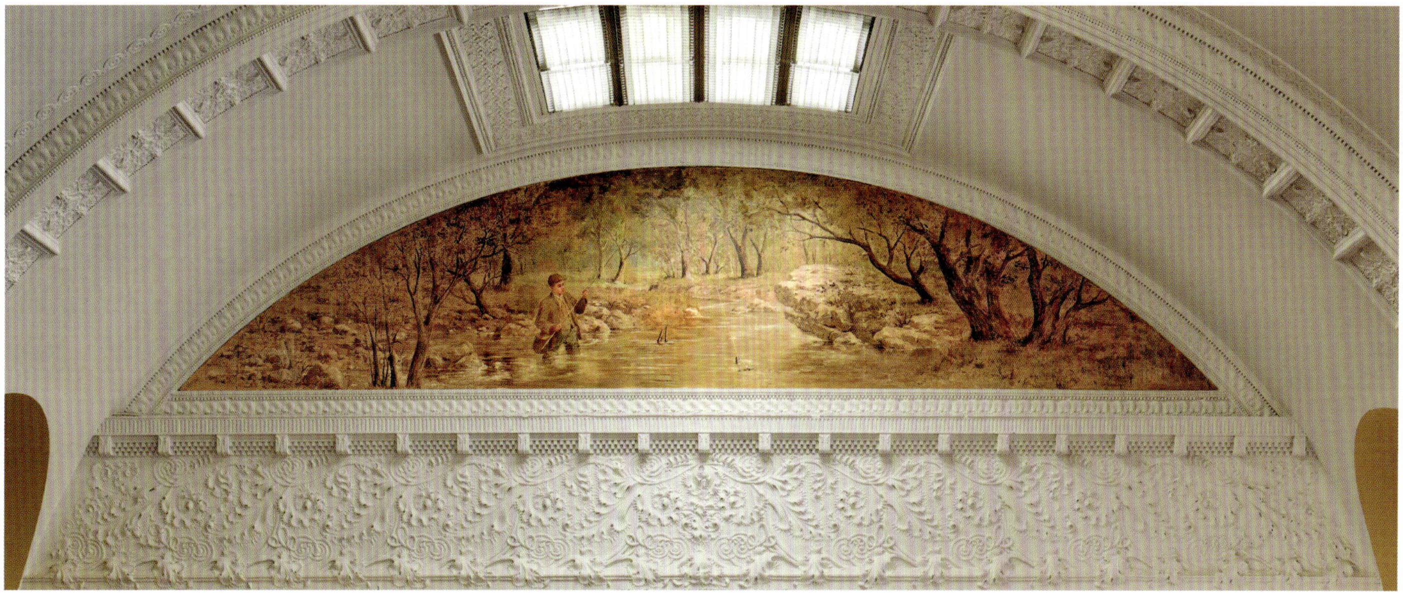

Murals by Oliver D. Grover on opposite ends show hunting and fishing scenes.

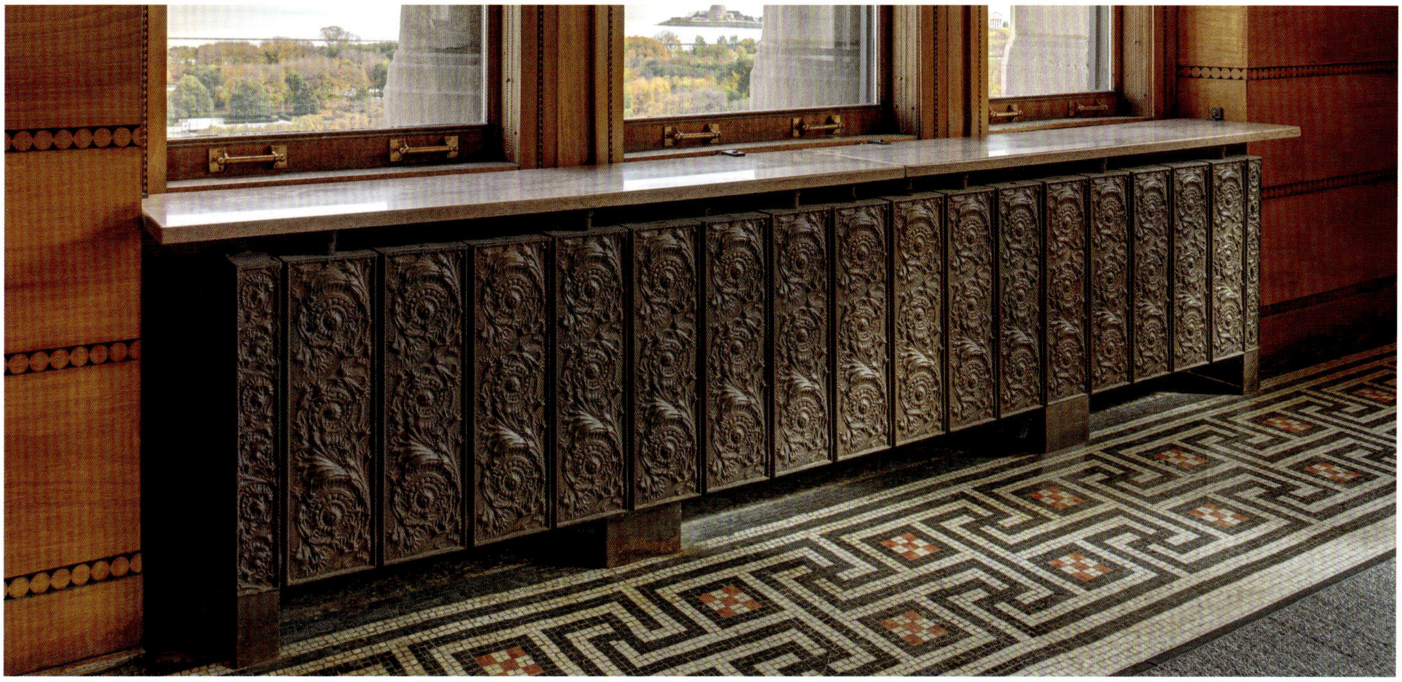

Now known as Ganz Hall and used as a recital venue, it was originally the hotel's banquet hall. Sullivan designed the elaborate electroliers.

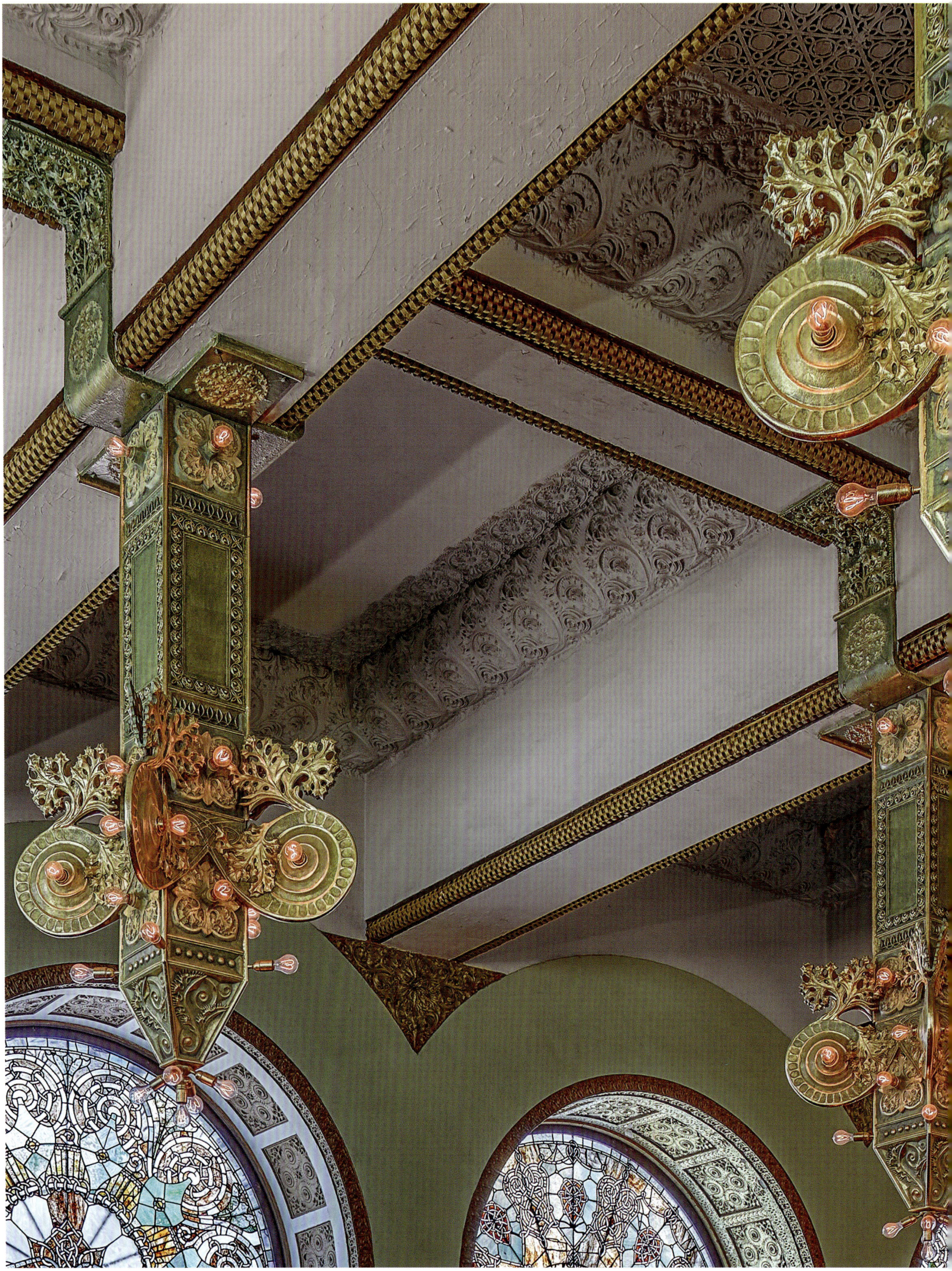

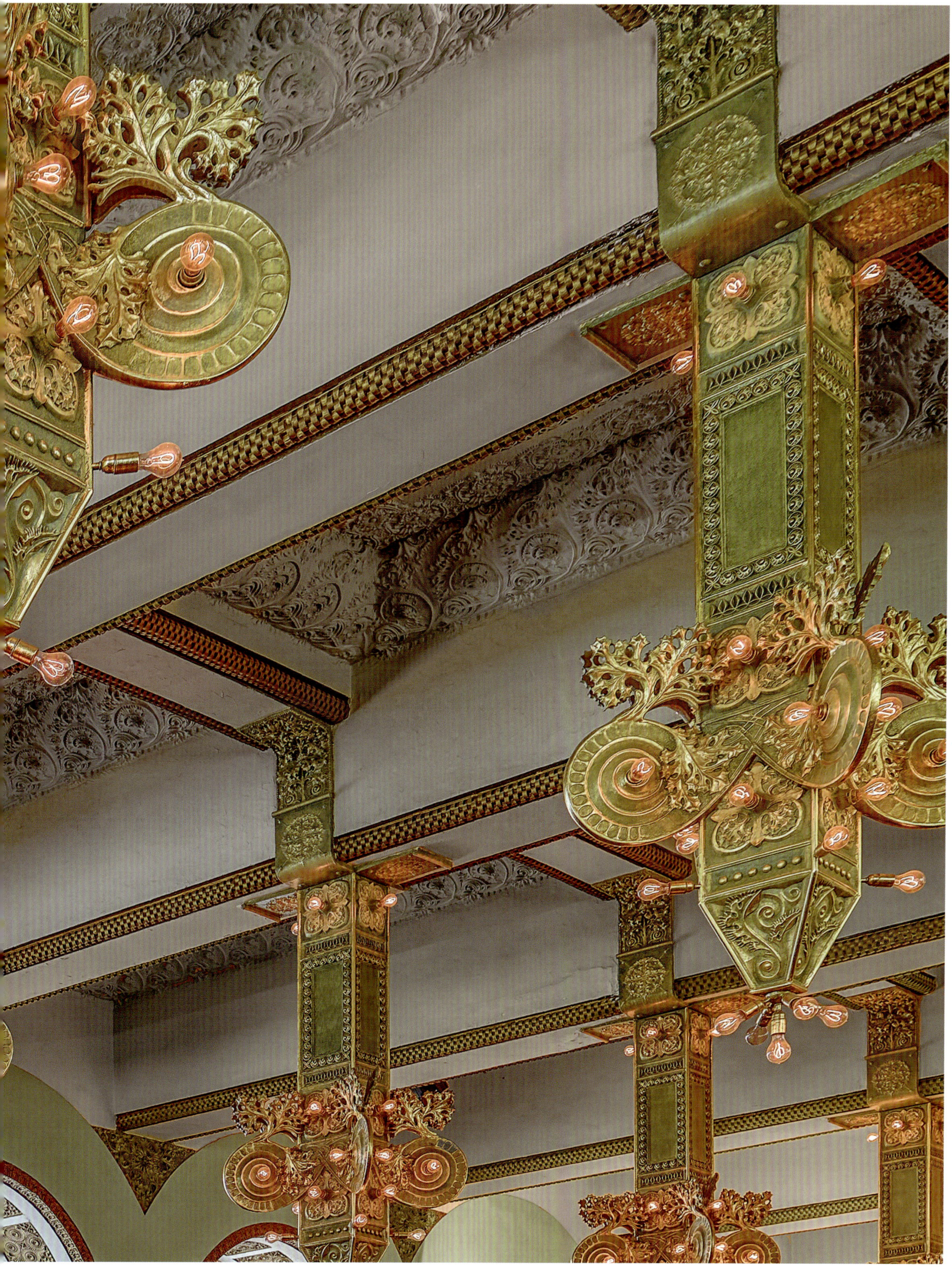

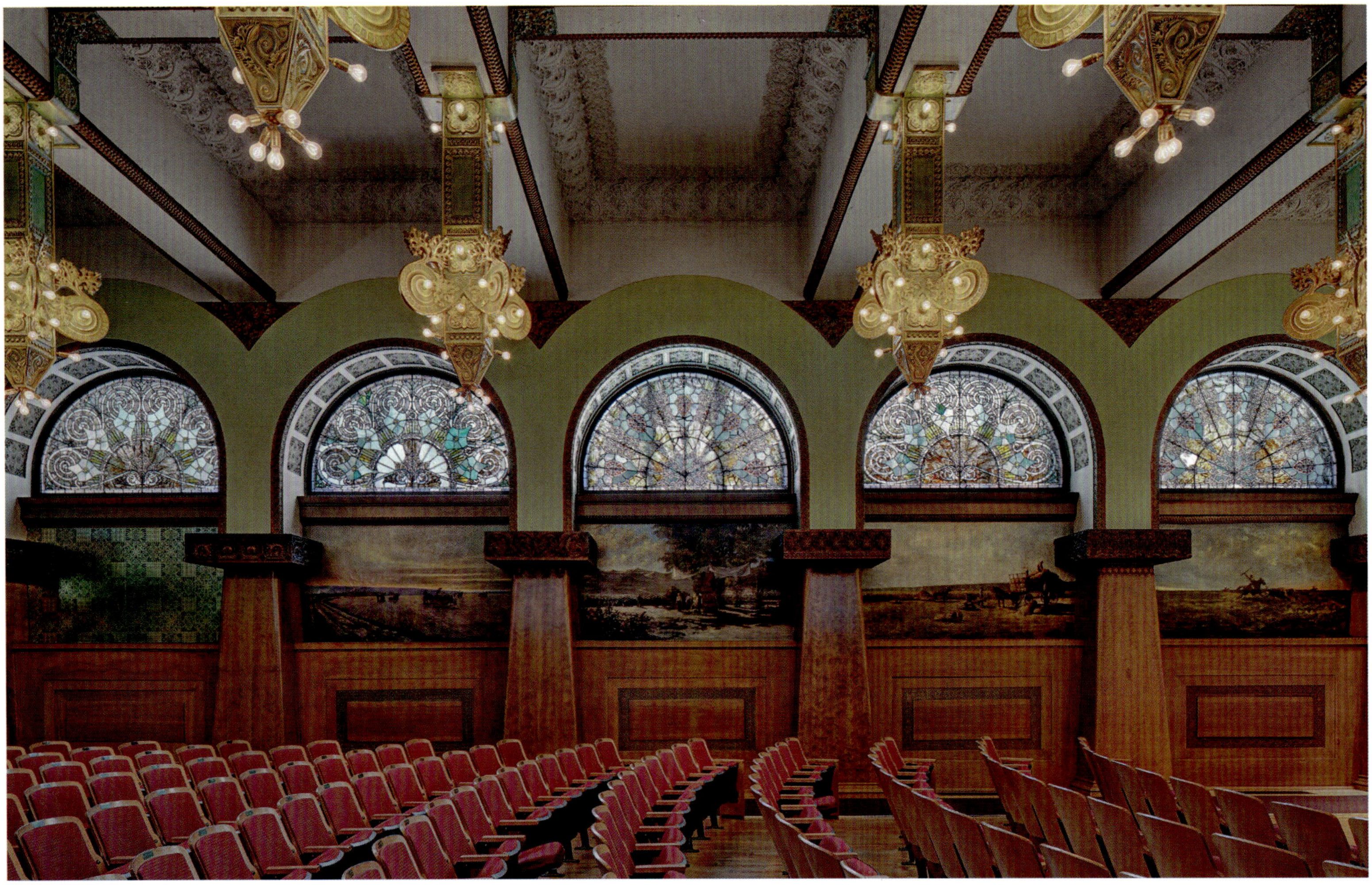

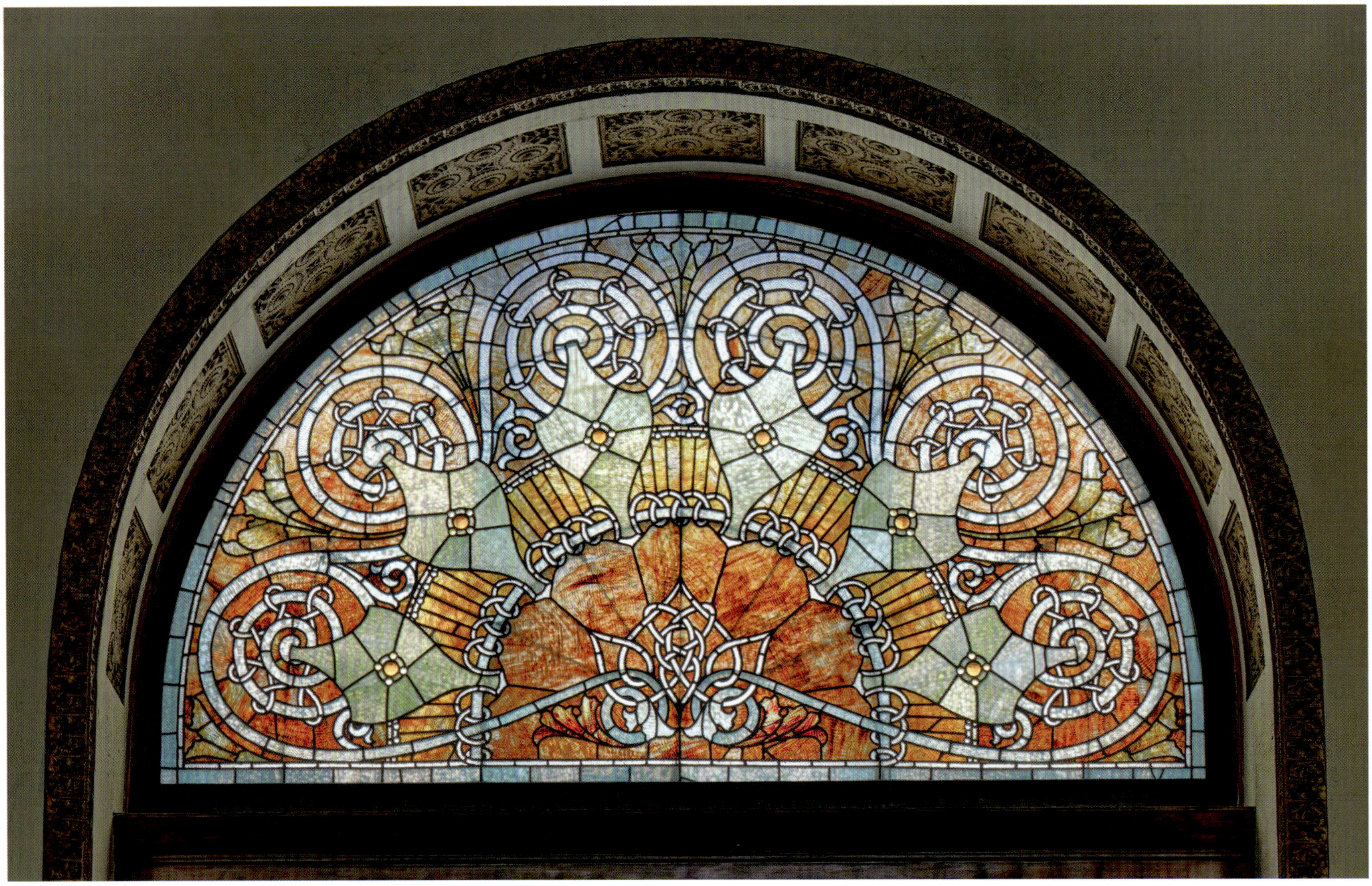

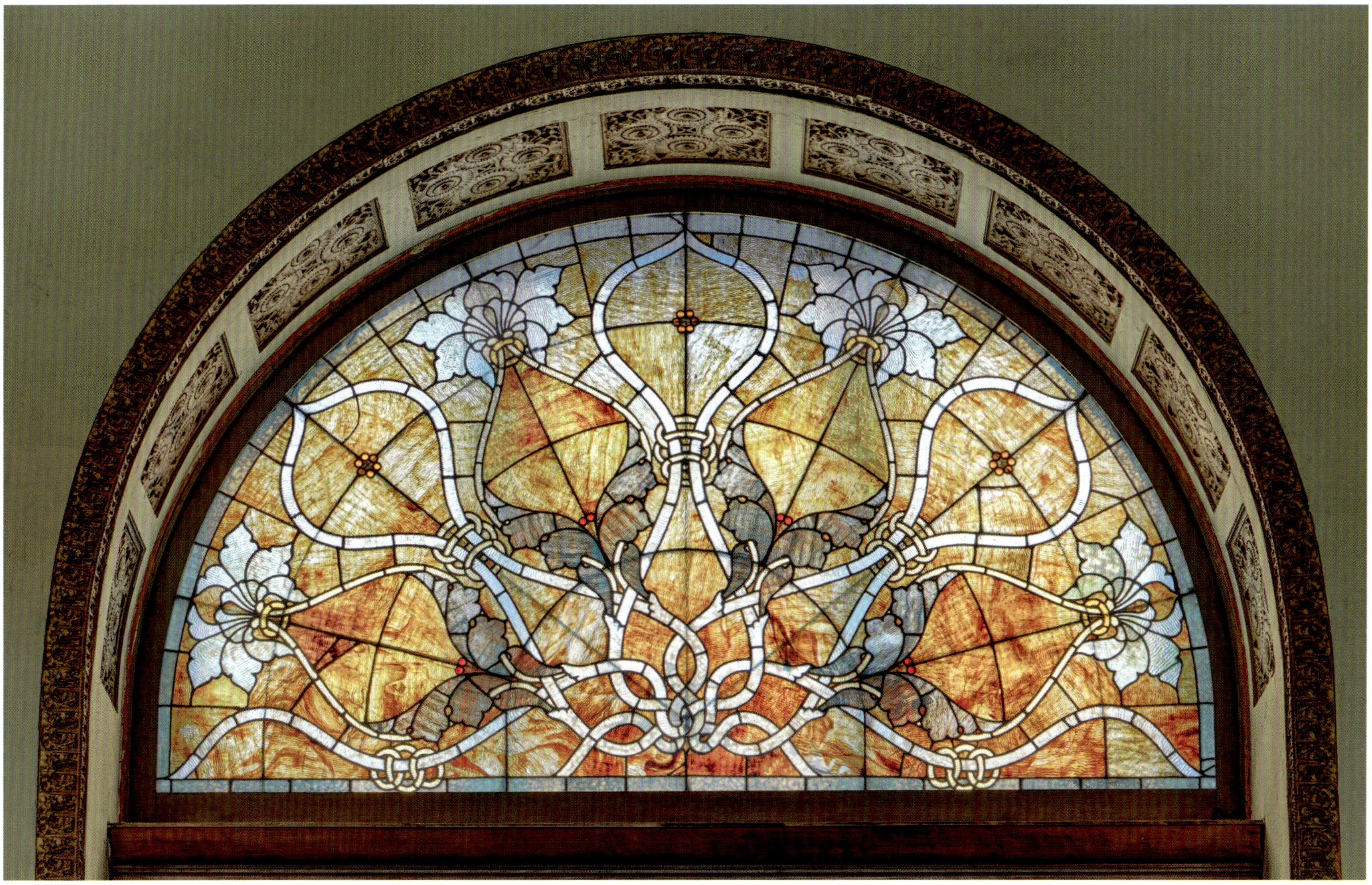

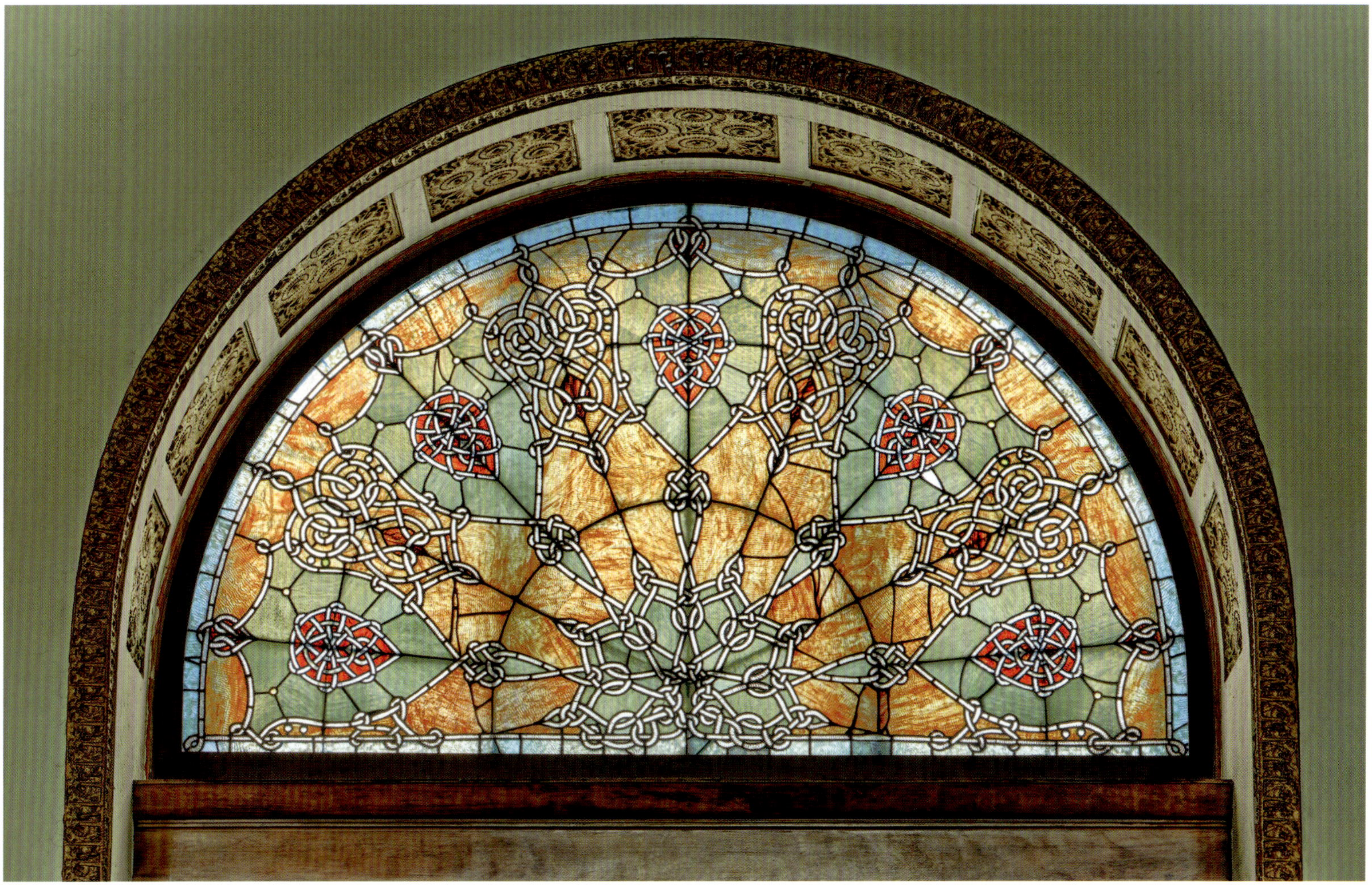

The clerestory windows and murals are by Healy & Millet.

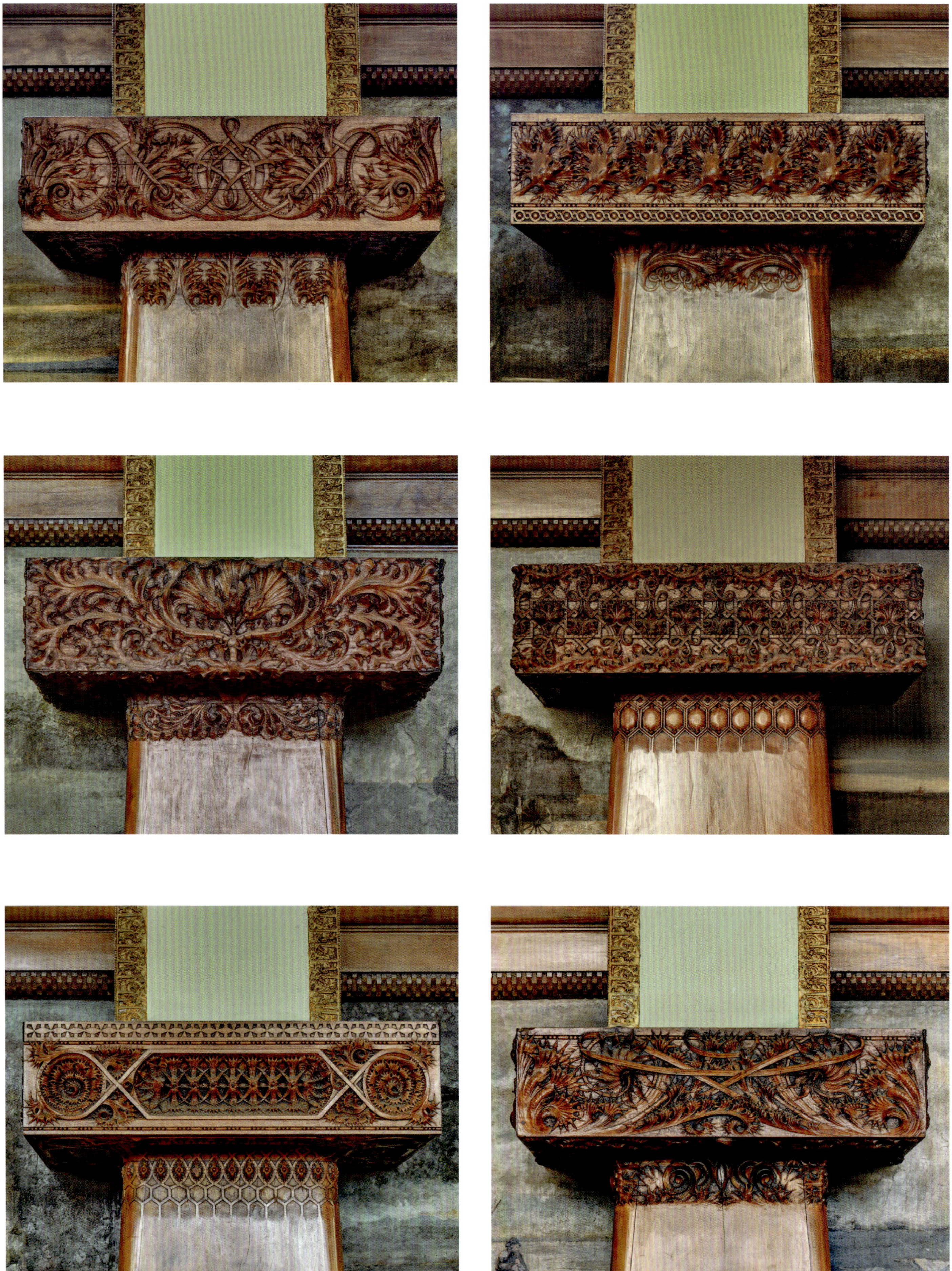

There are no fewer than twenty carved column capitals, all different, again executed by Richard W. Bates.

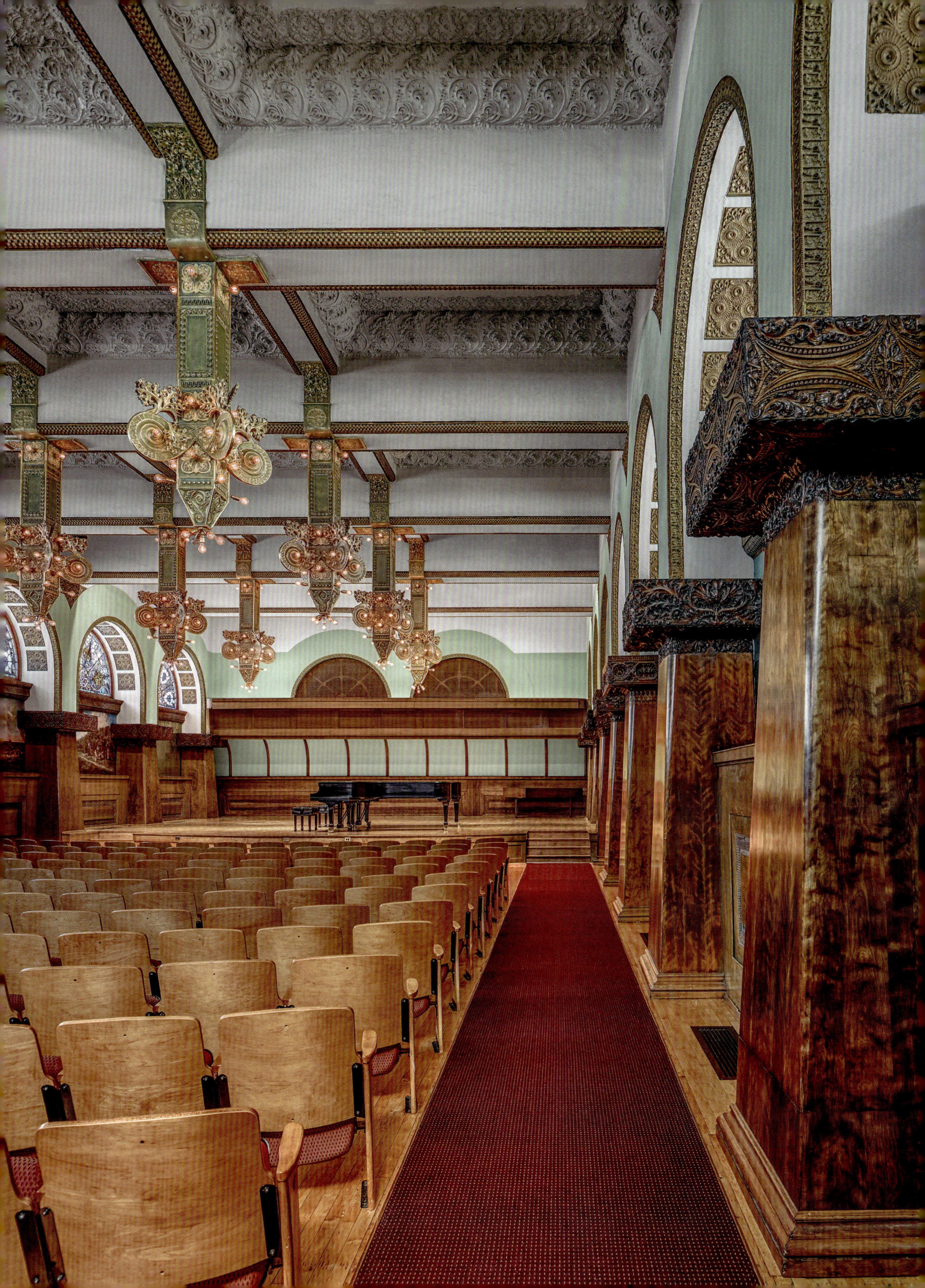

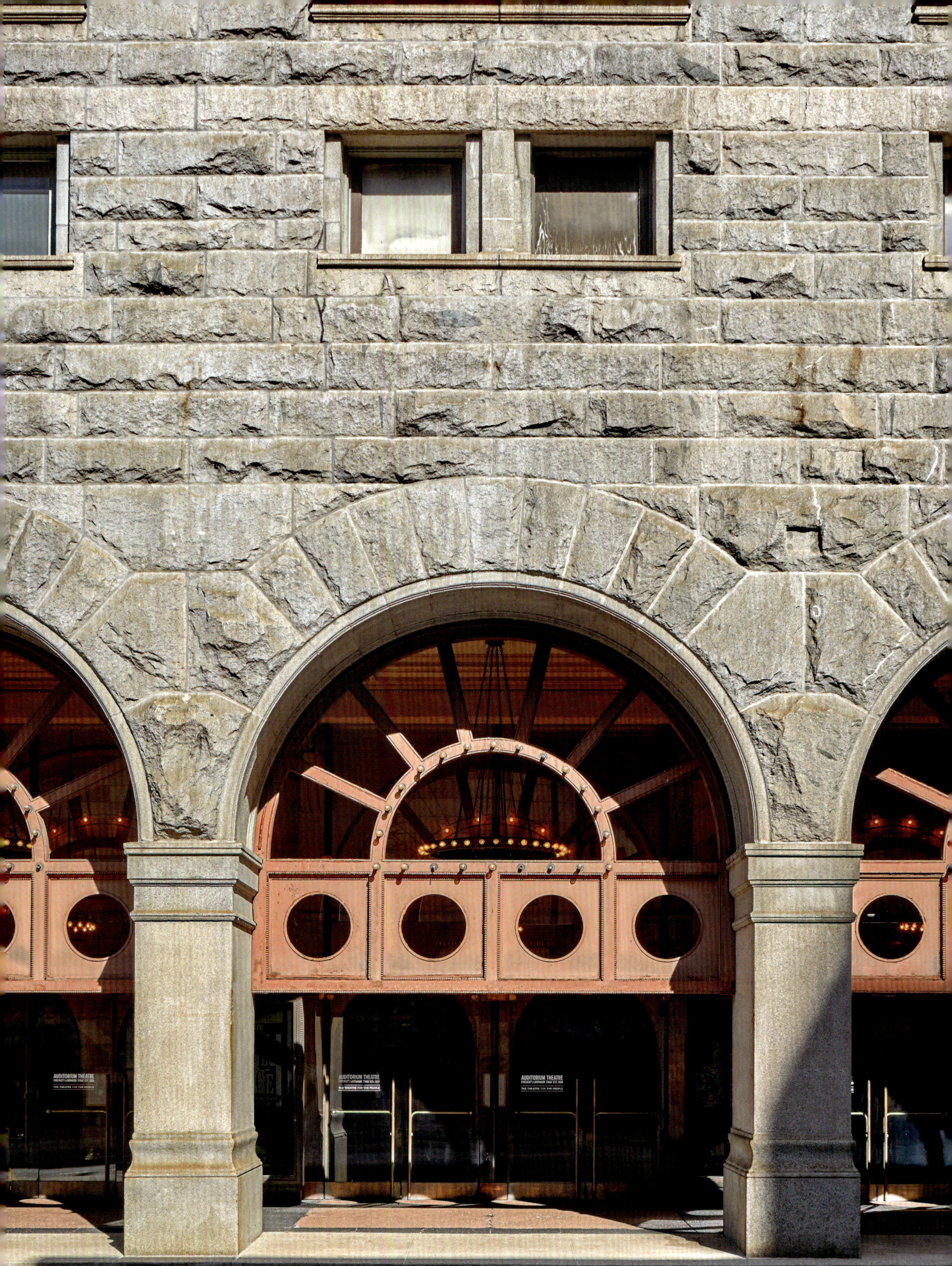

When Ida B. Wells Drive (formerly Congress Parkway) was widened, an arcade was created from what was formerly enclosed space.

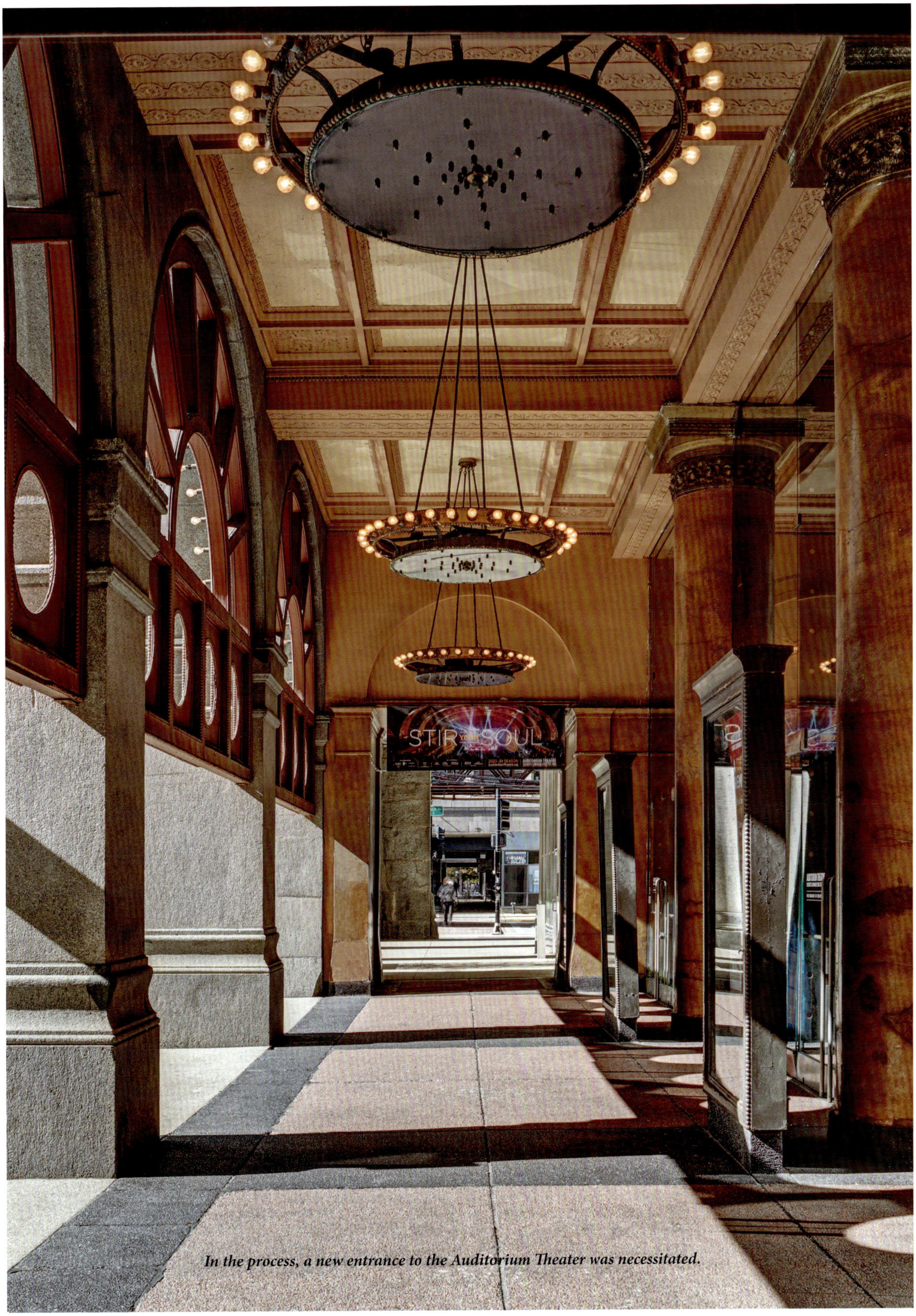

In the process, a new entrance to the Auditorium Theater was necessitated.

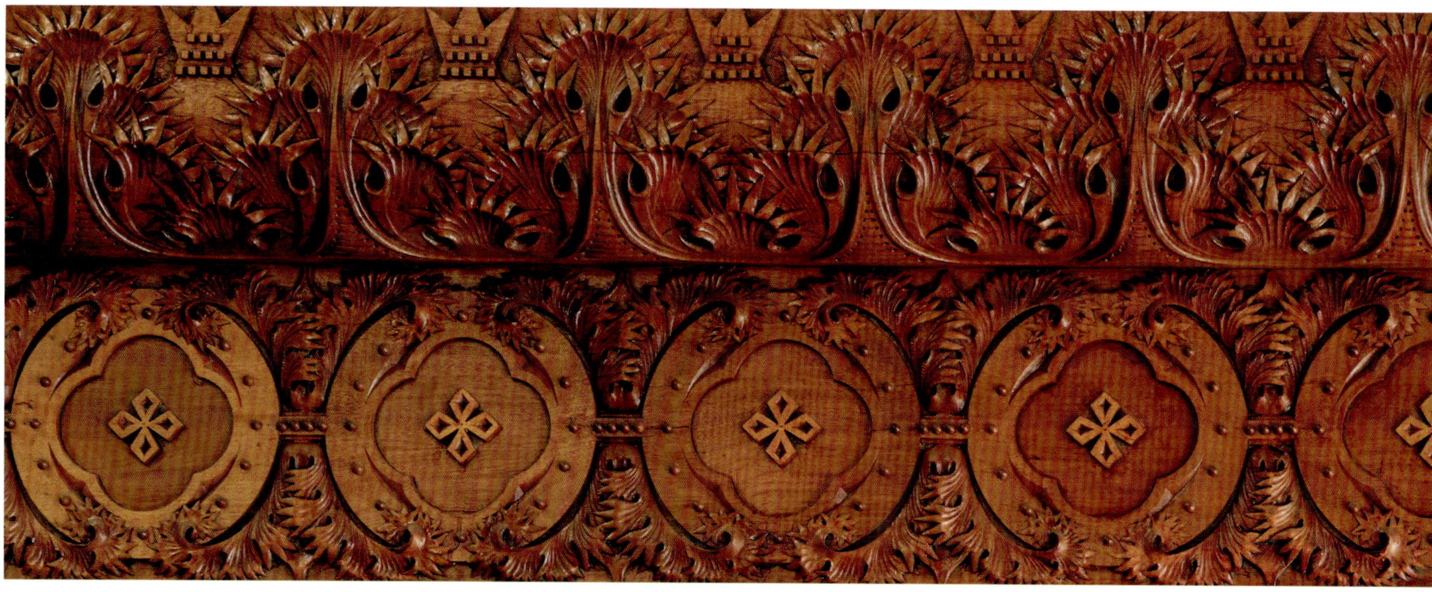

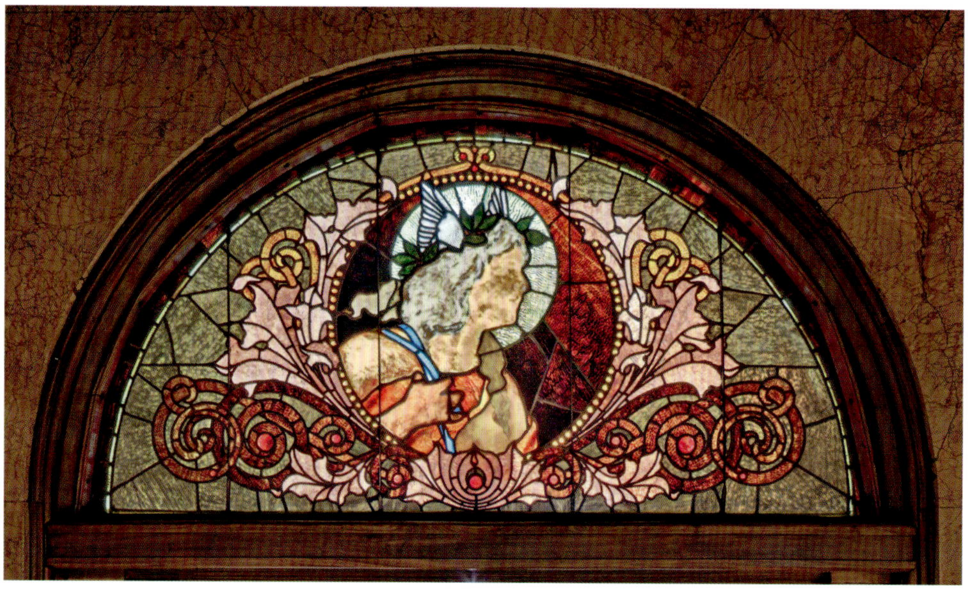

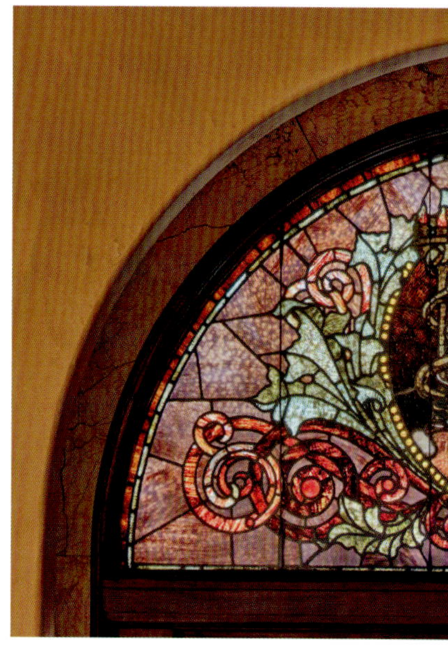

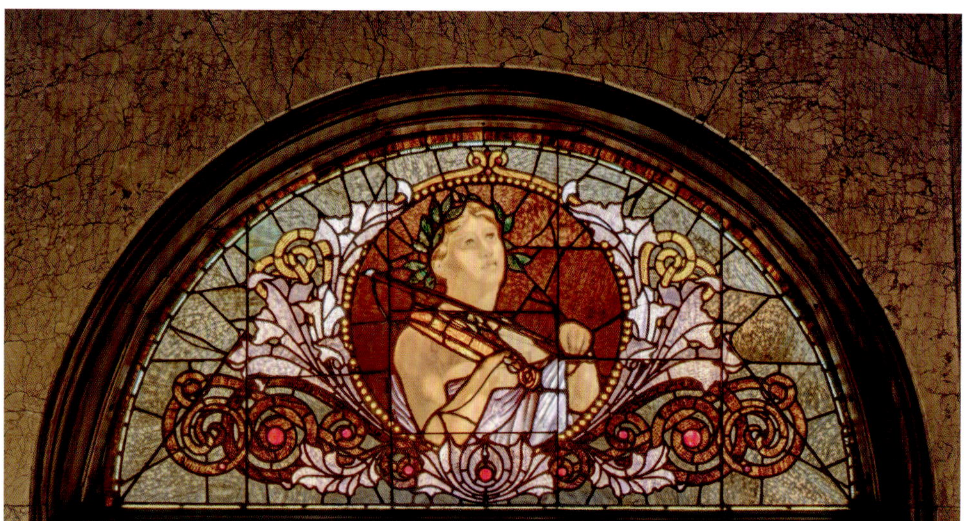

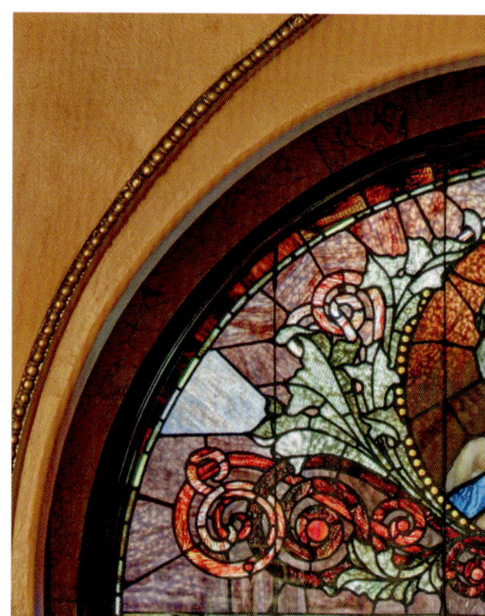

Inside the entrance are six art glass windows by Healy & Millet representing the various arts.

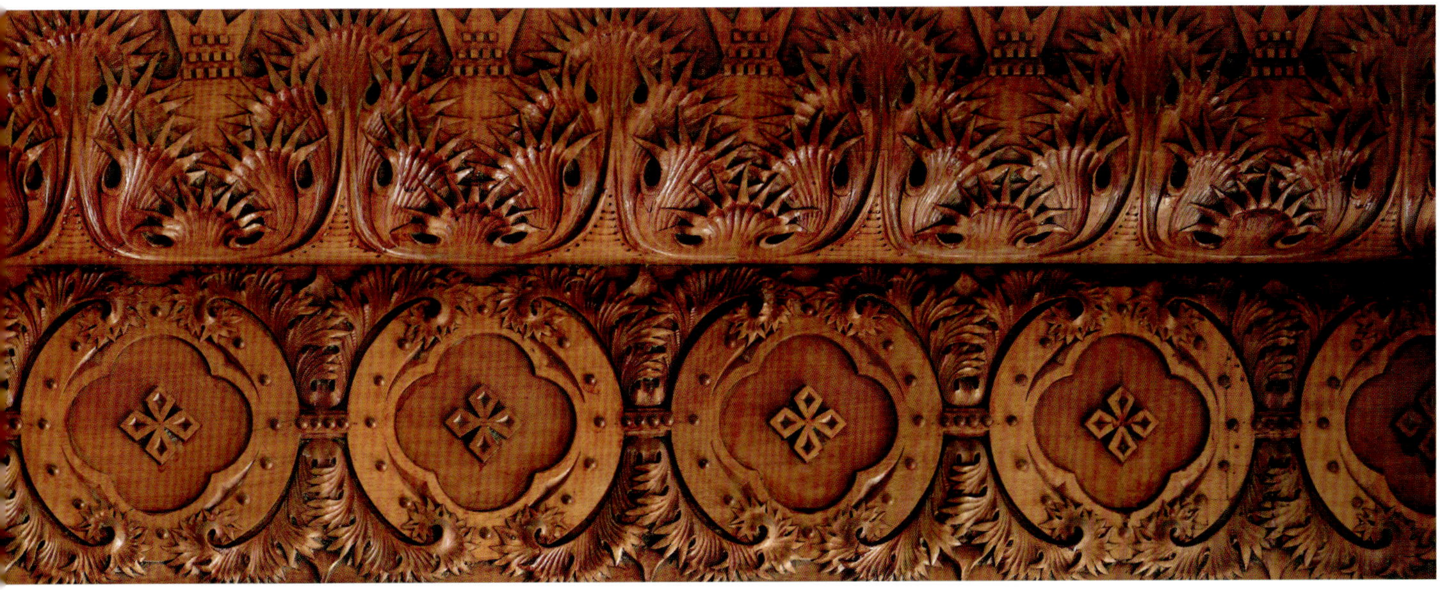

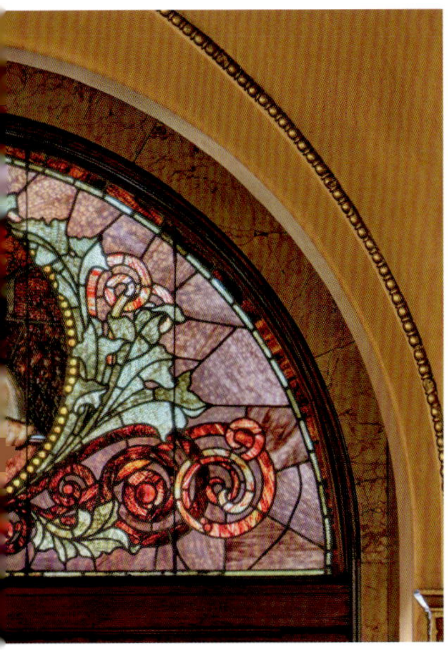

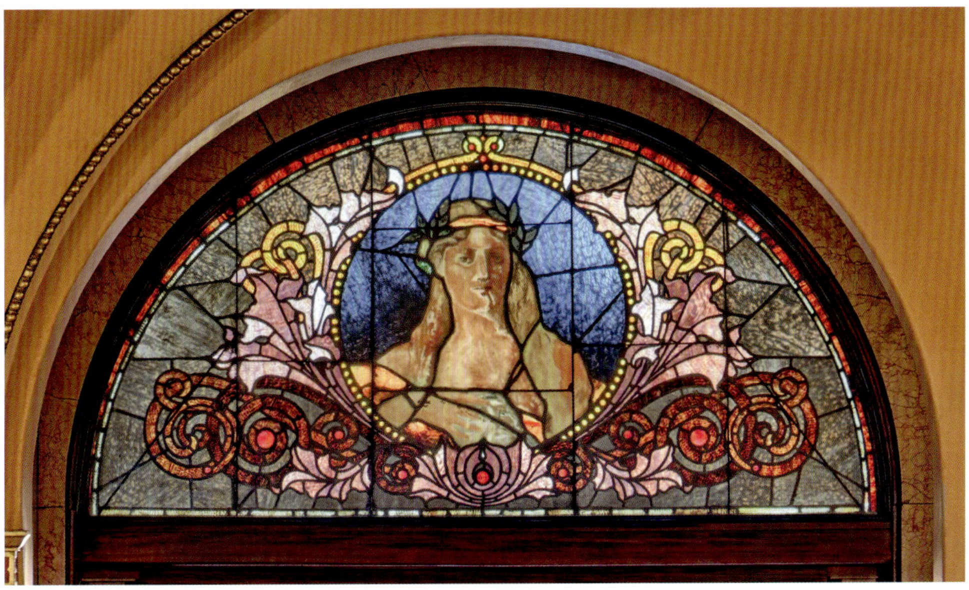

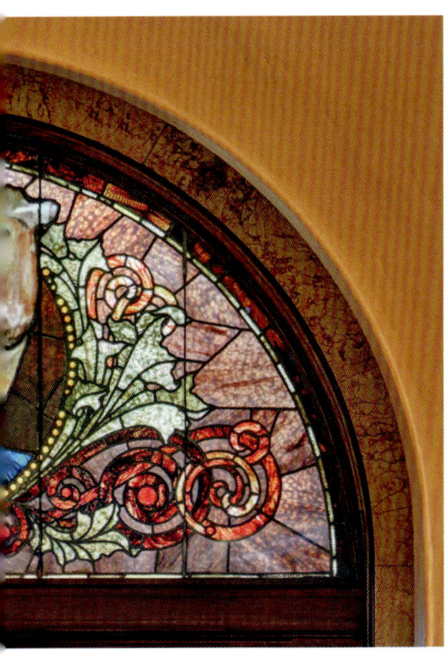

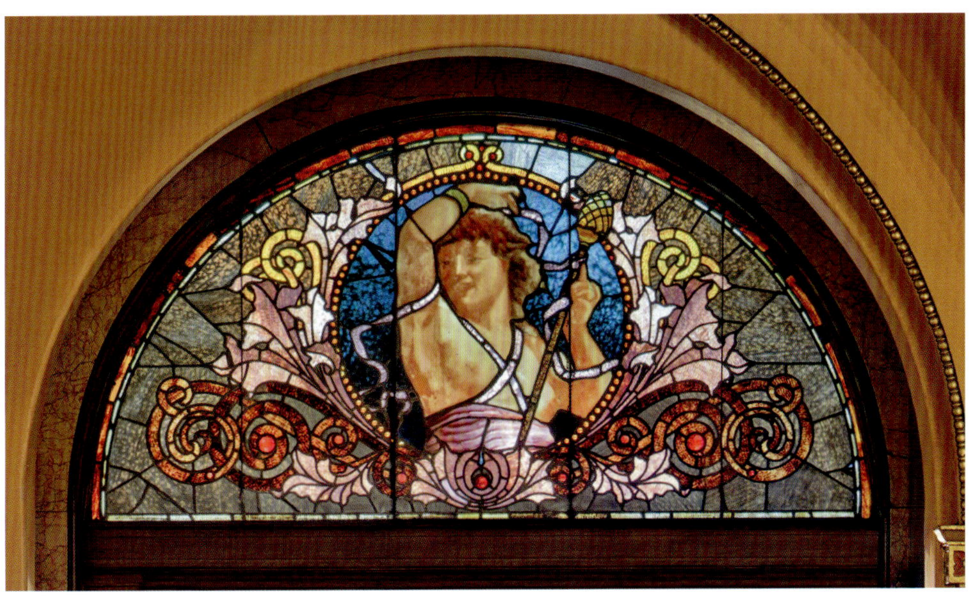

They are (clockwise from top left): poetry, wisdom, drama, music, oration, and dance.

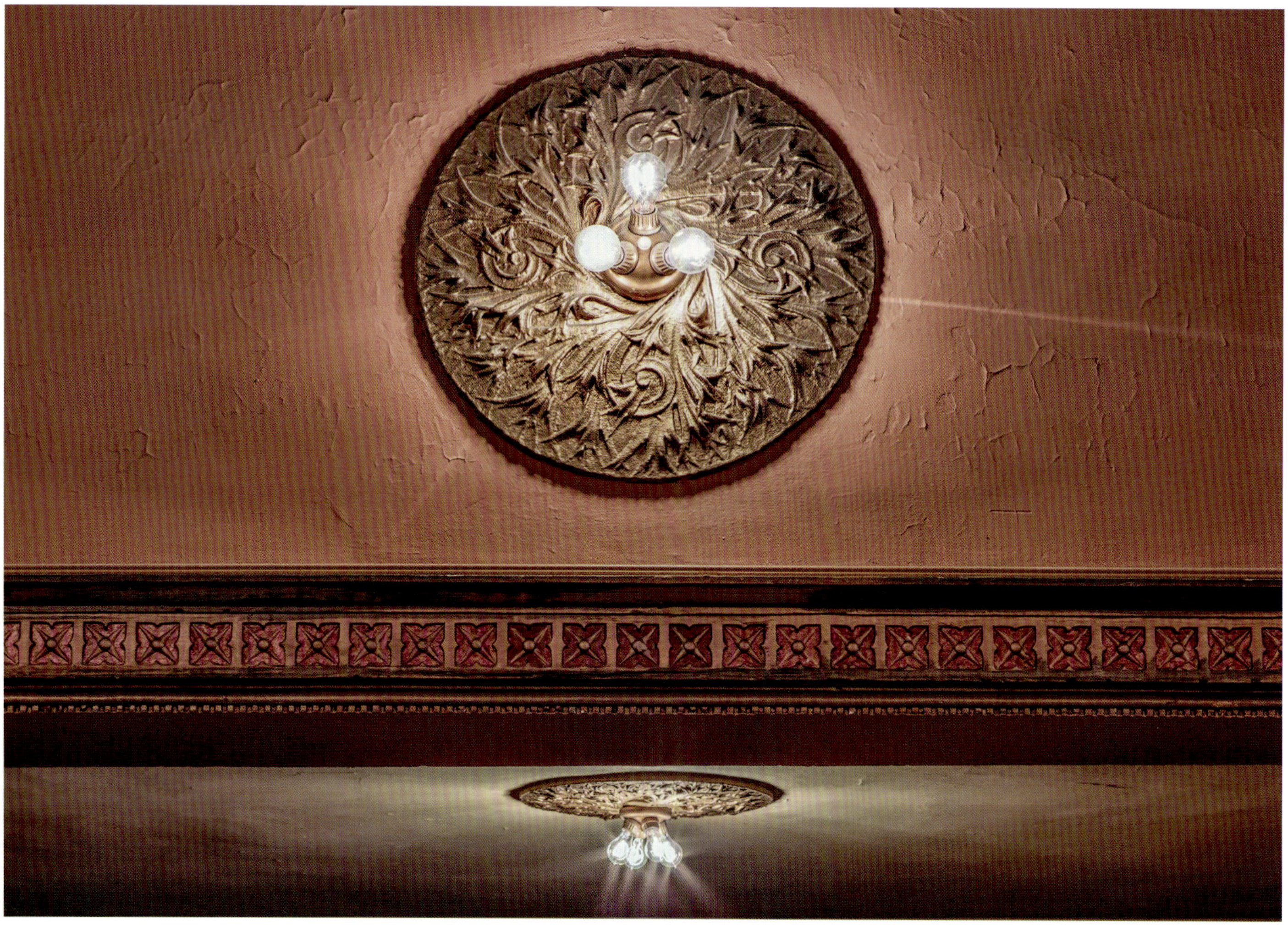

A coat-check room was located next to the main theatre entrance.

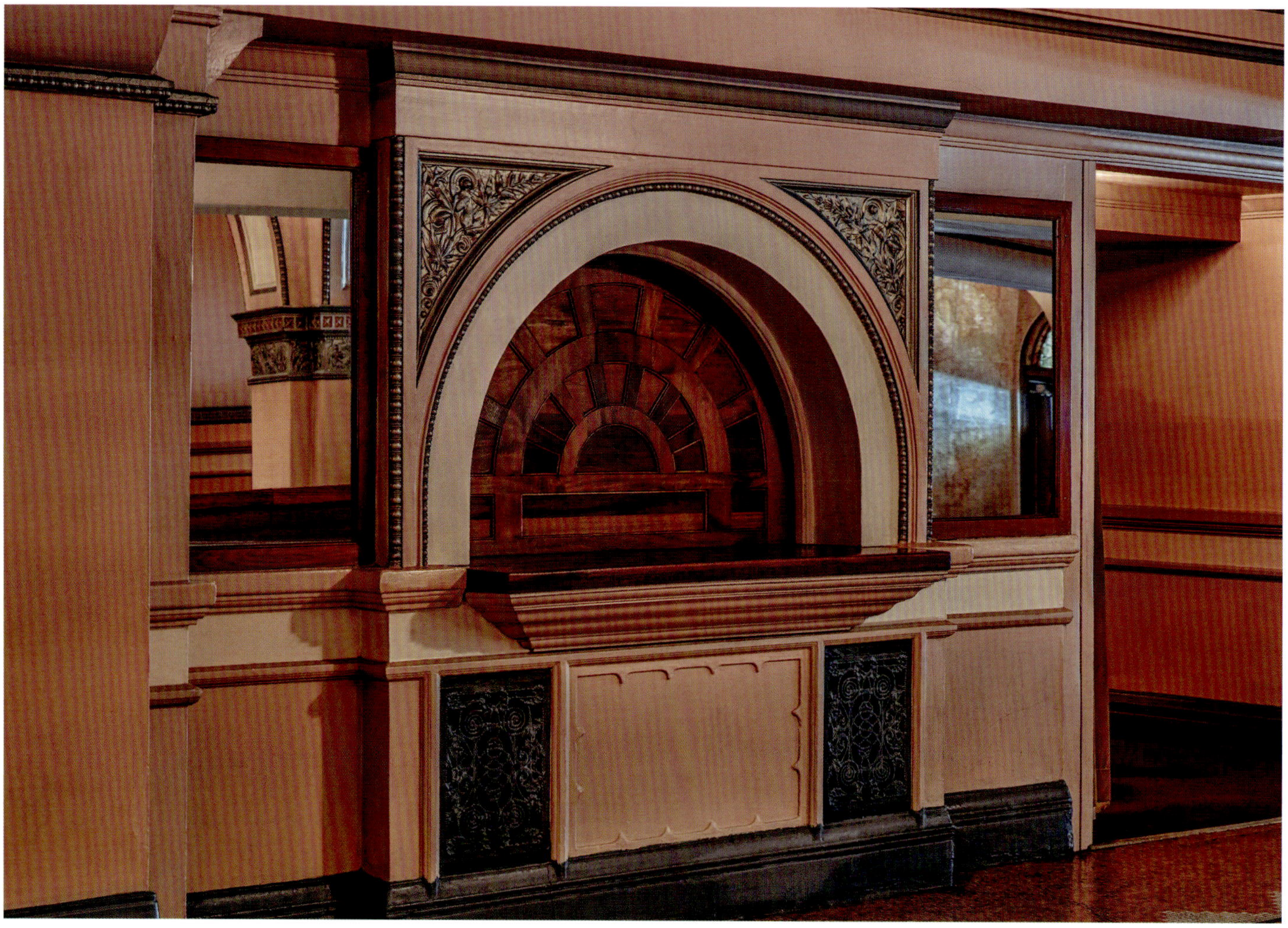

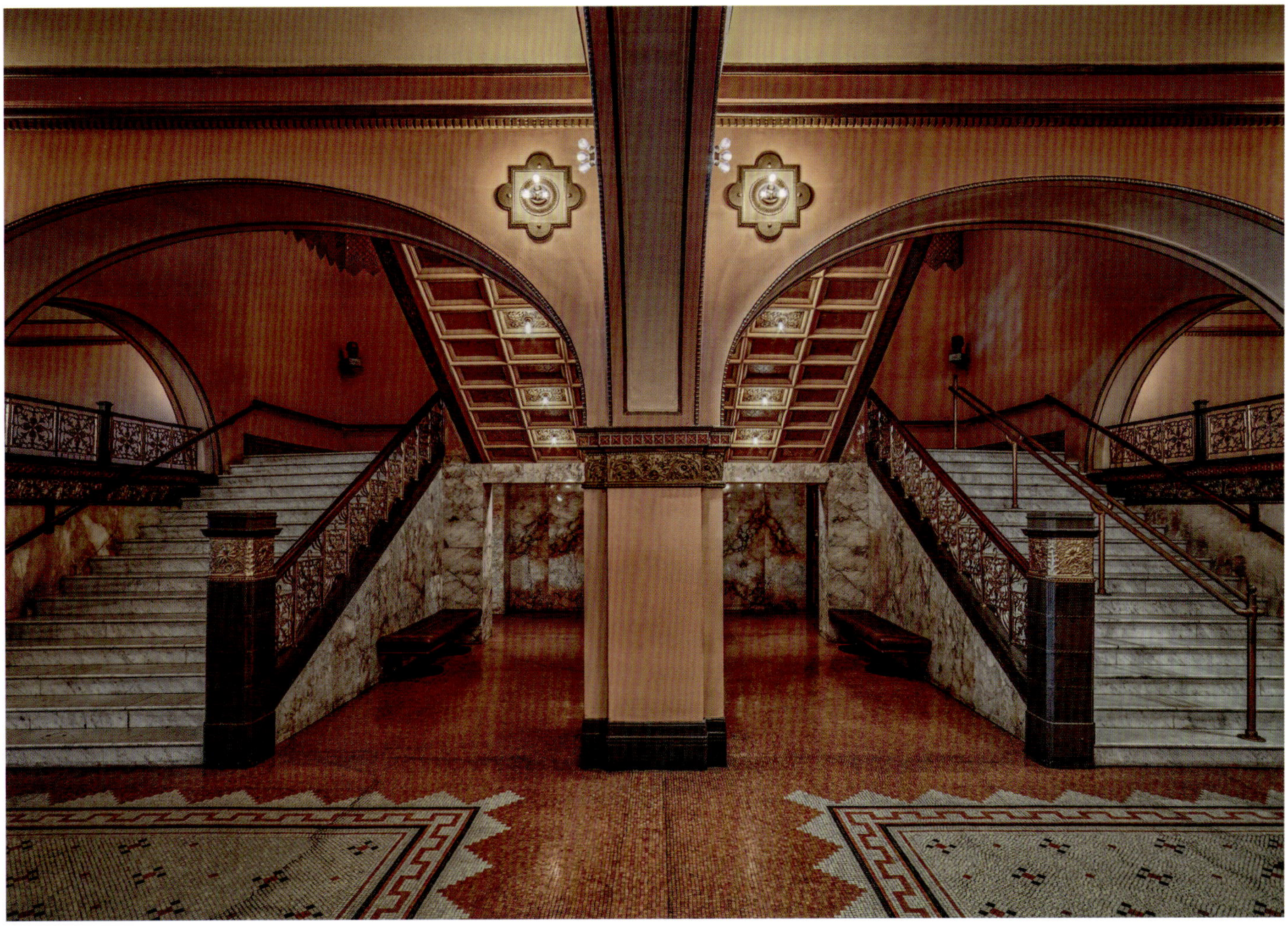

As in the hotel lobby, the arch is dominant. The floor mosaics are meant to suggest oriental rugs.

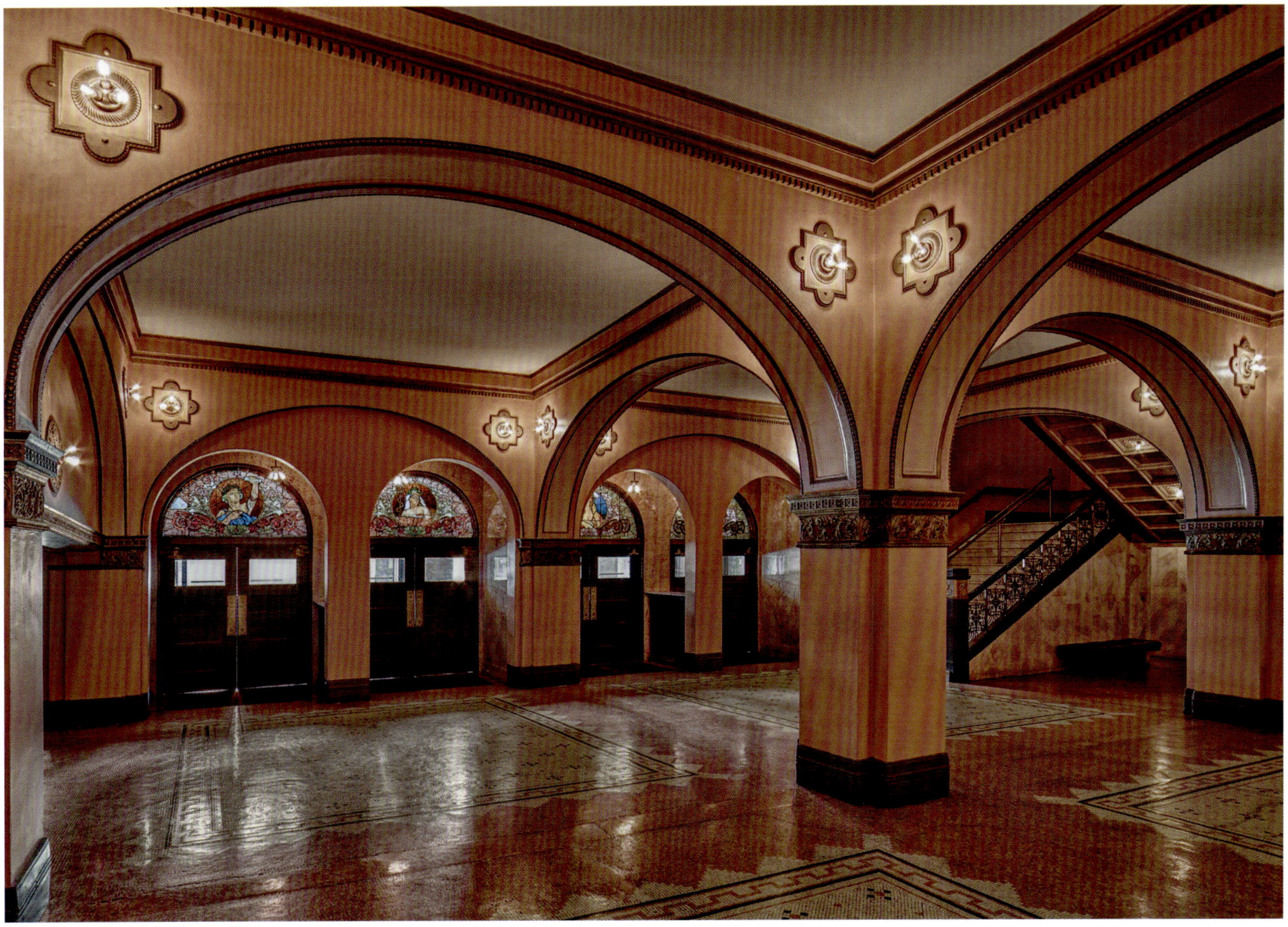

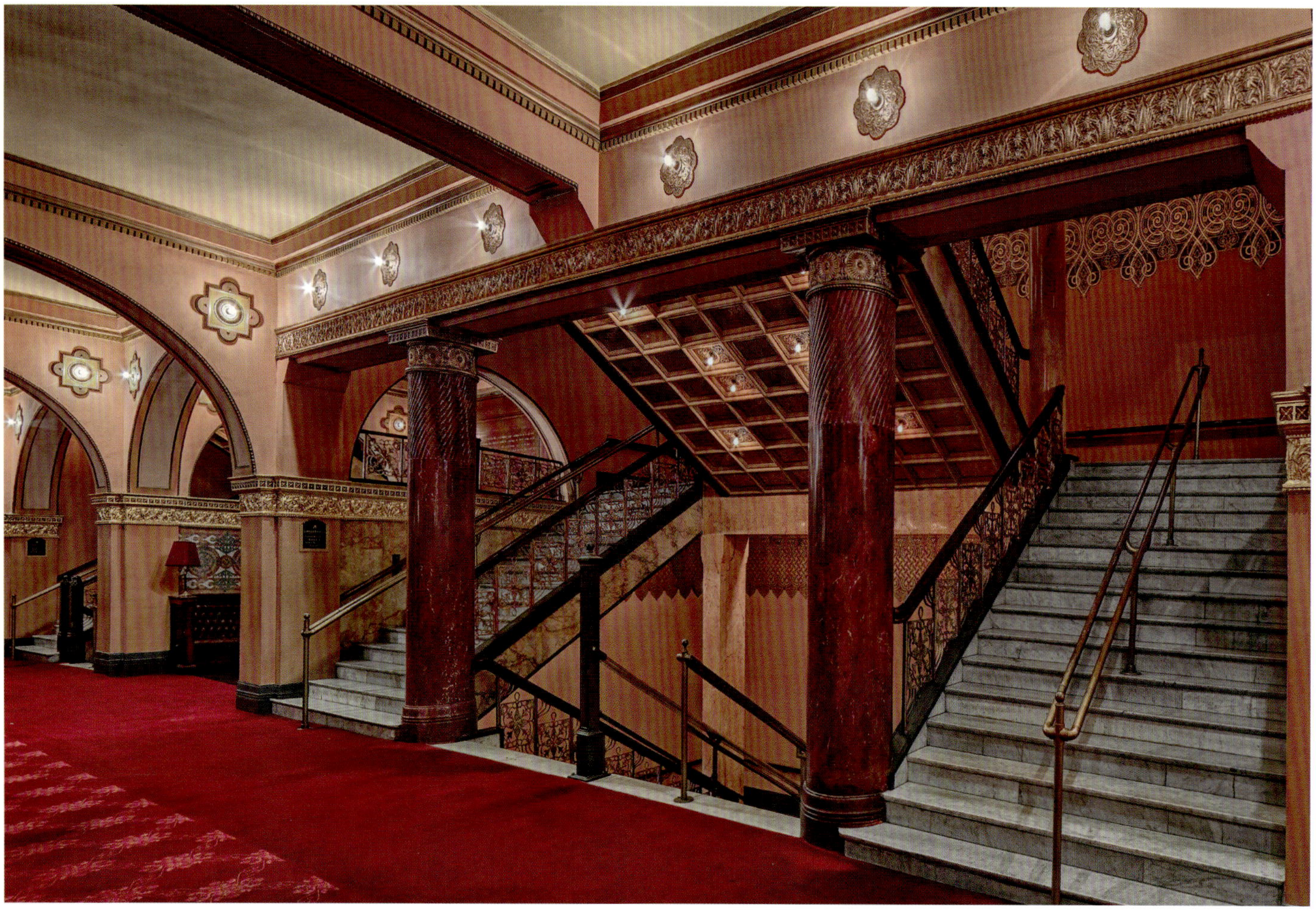

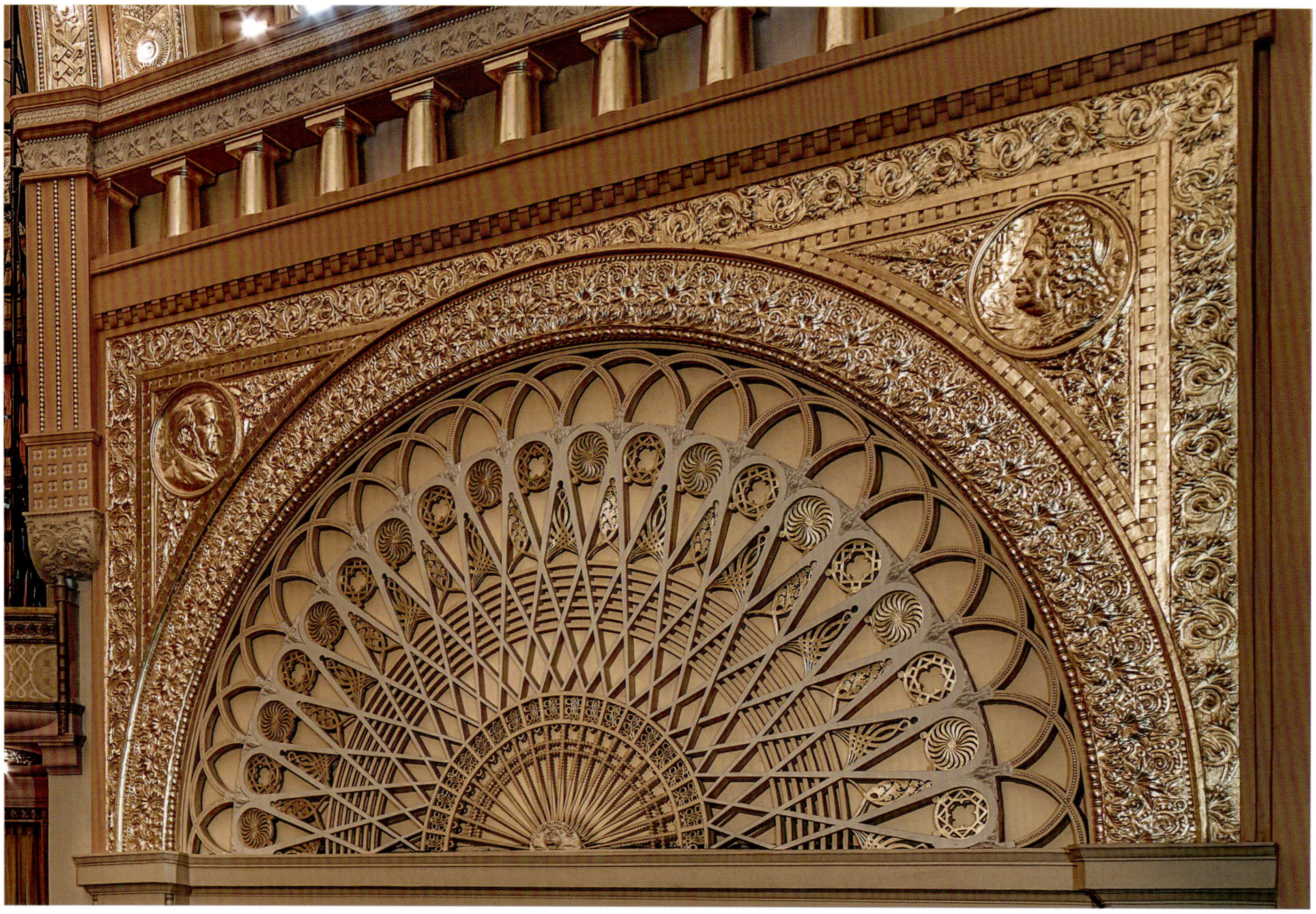

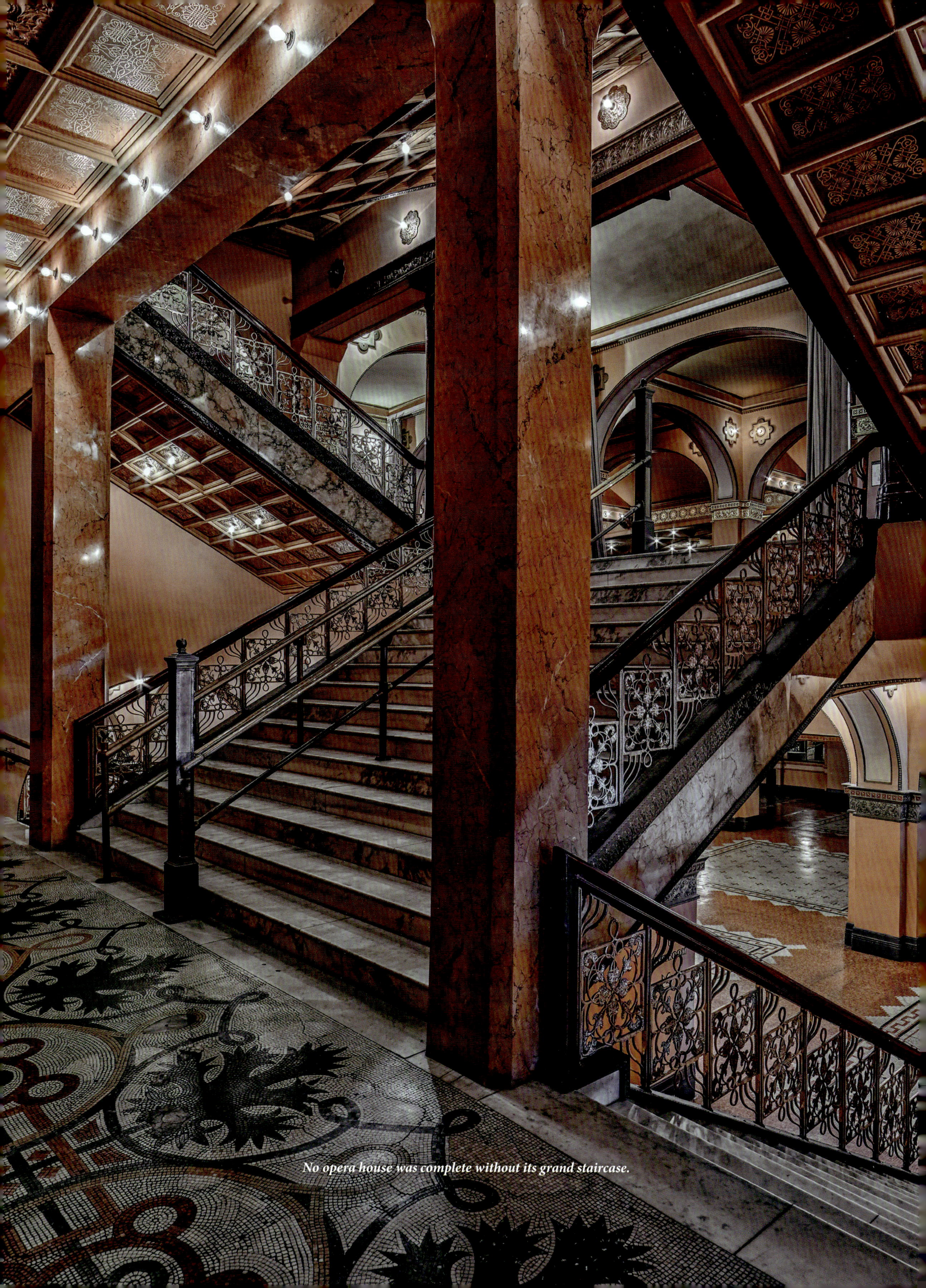

No opera house was complete without its grand staircase.

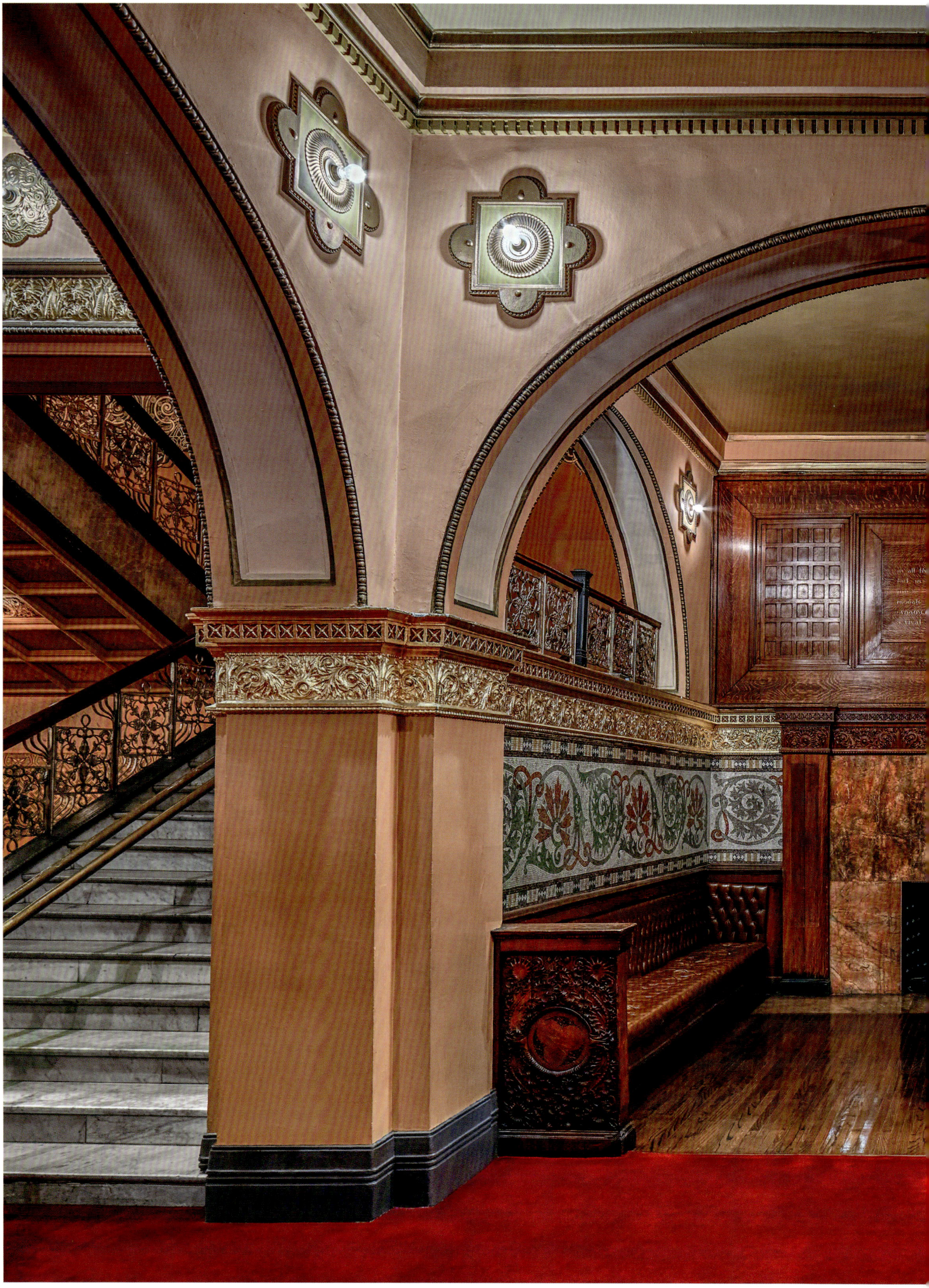

An inglenook with a working fireplace and built-in seating provided a convenient gathering place.

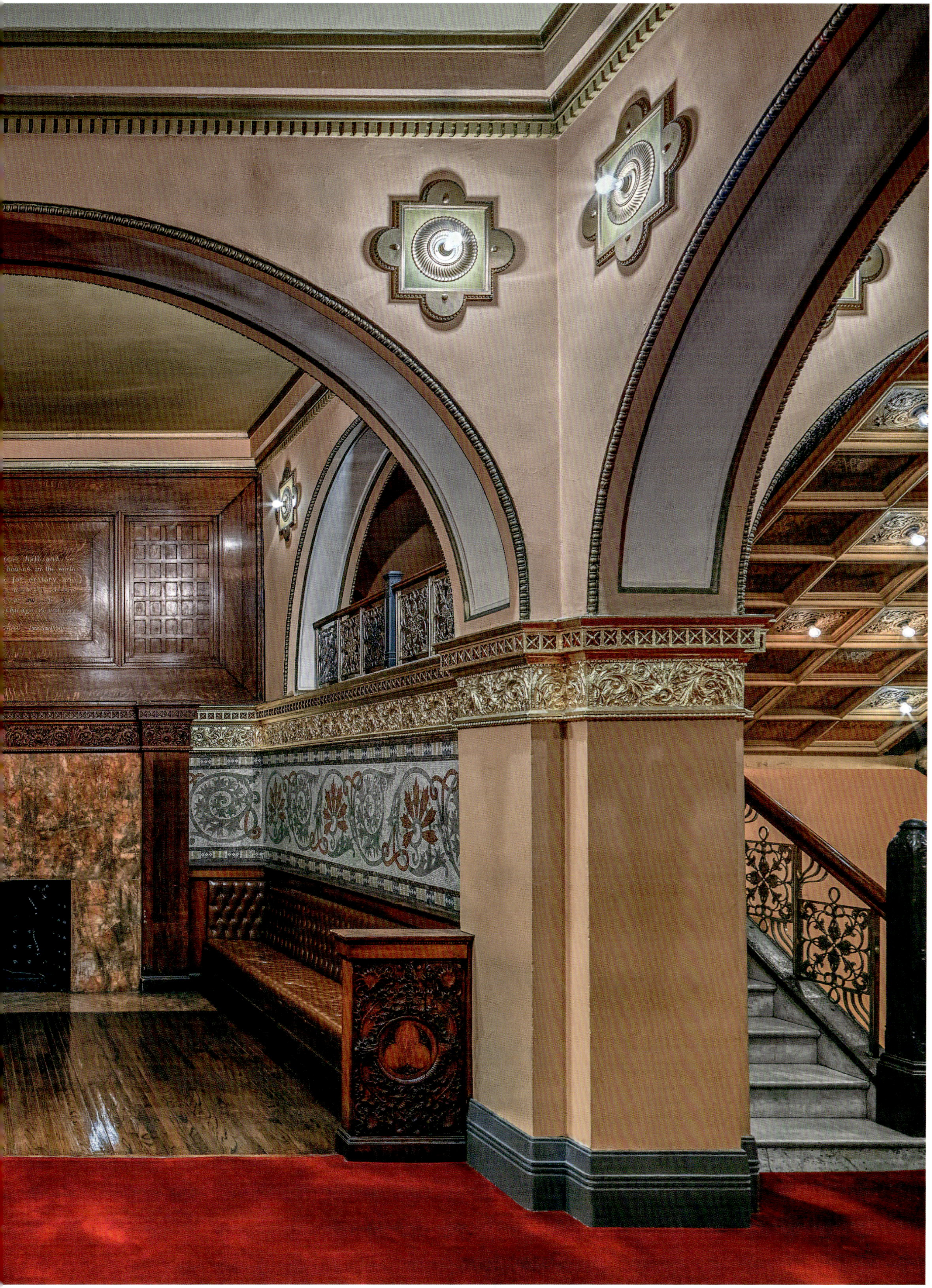

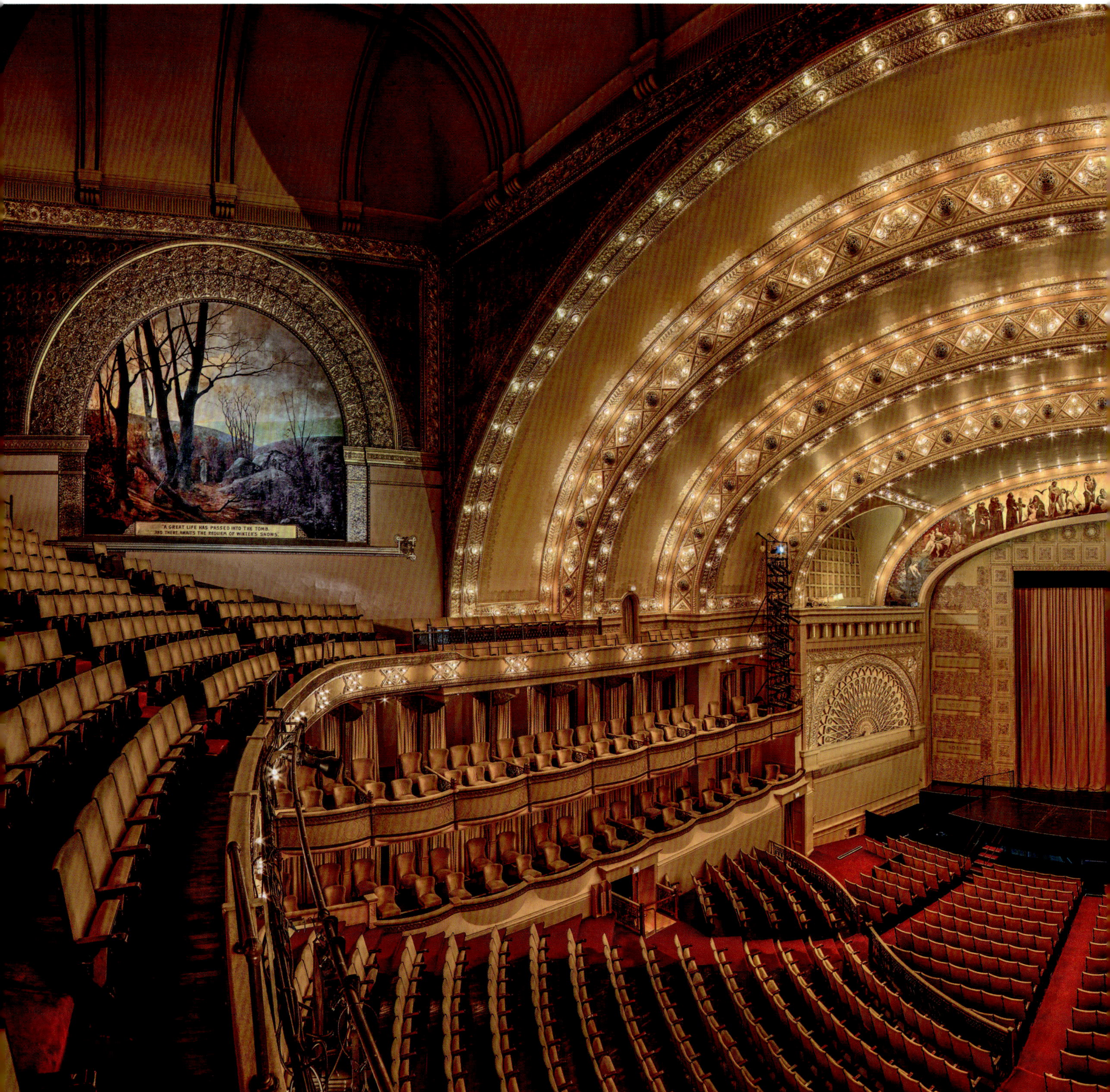

The Auditorium Theatre is one of the grandest spaces in America. Seating approximately 4,000, its acoustics—an Adler specialty—are unrivaled. Sullivan's decorative genius is everywhere apparent. He was assisted by Healy & Millet, who chose Charles Holloway to execute the mural above the proscenium arch; and Albert Fleury to do the side murals.

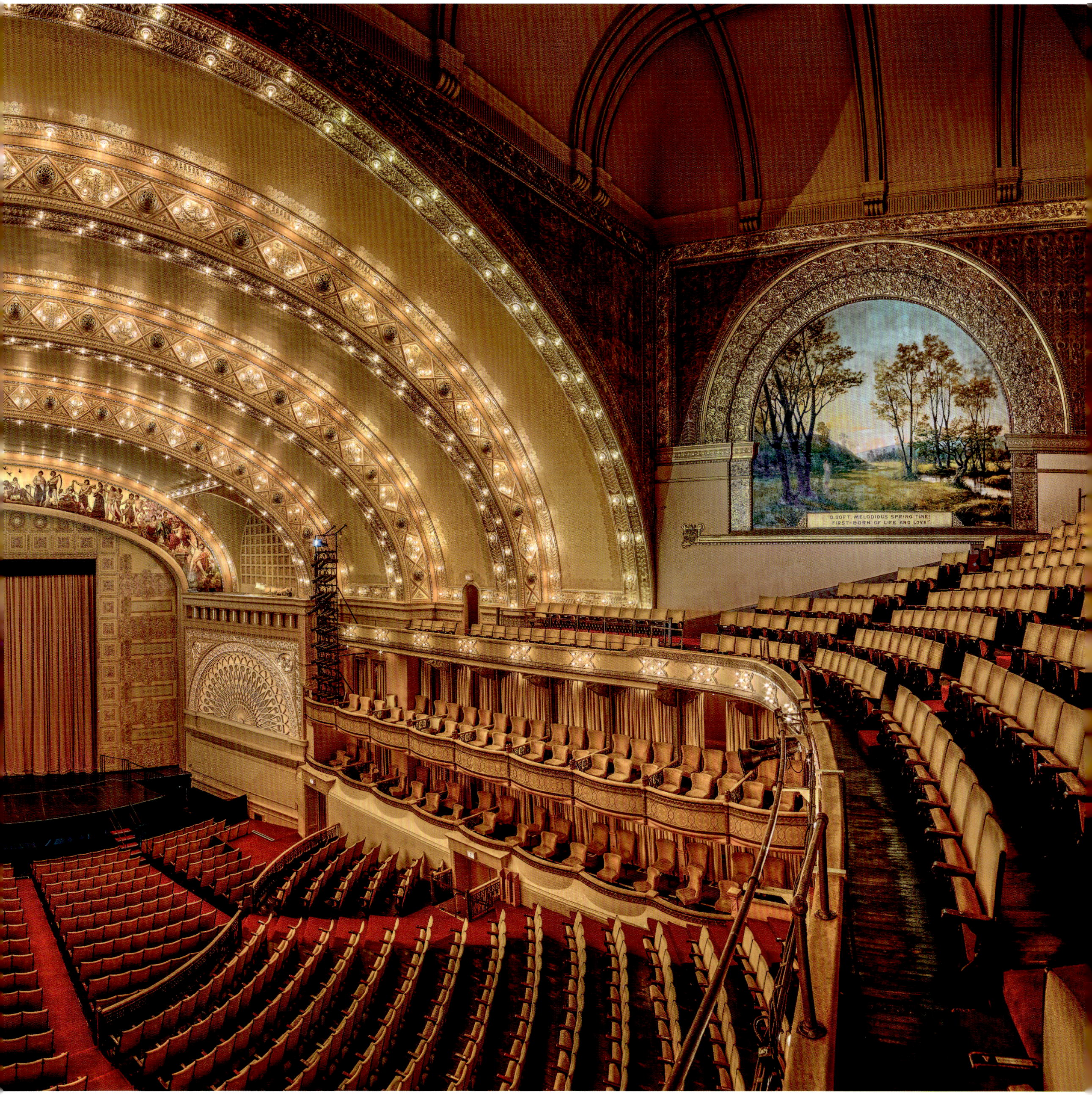
"O, SOFT, MELODIOUS SPRING TIME!
FIRST-BORN OF LIFE AND LOVE!"

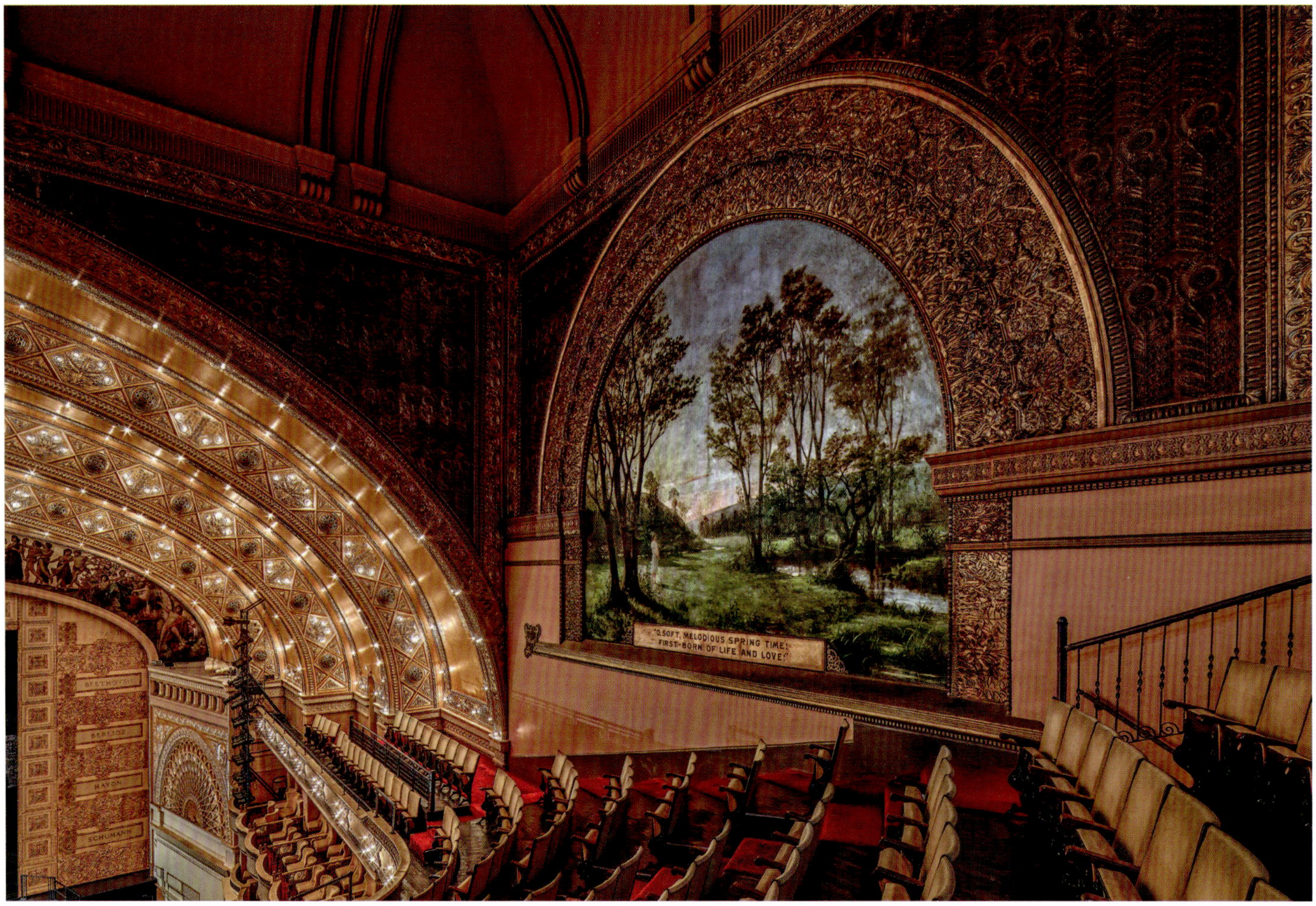
"O SOFT, MELODIOUS SPRING TIME!
FIRST-BORN OF LIFE AND LOVE!"

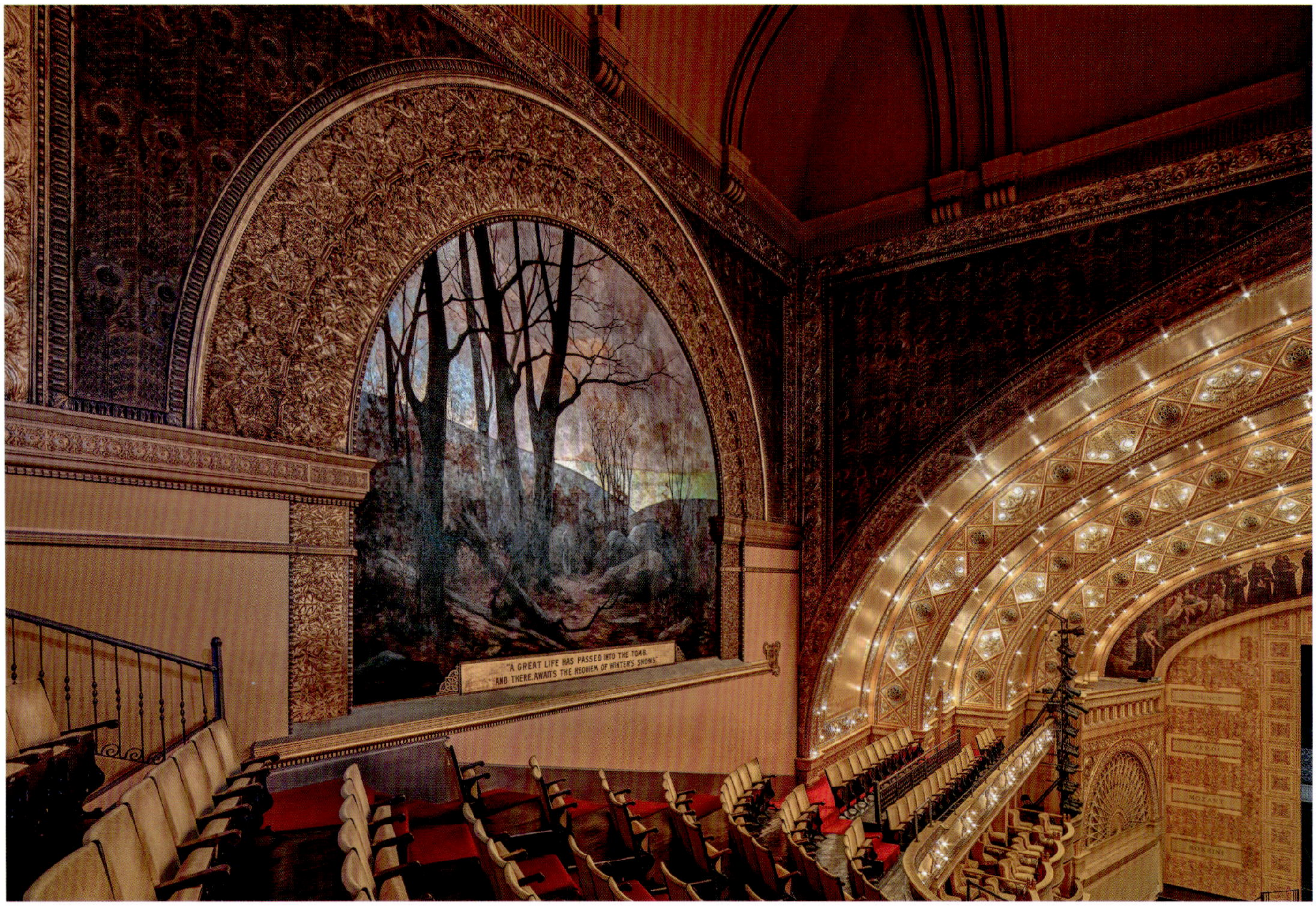
"A GREAT LIFE HAS PASSED INTO THE TOMB,
AND THERE AWAITS THE REQUIEM OF WINTER'S SNOWS."

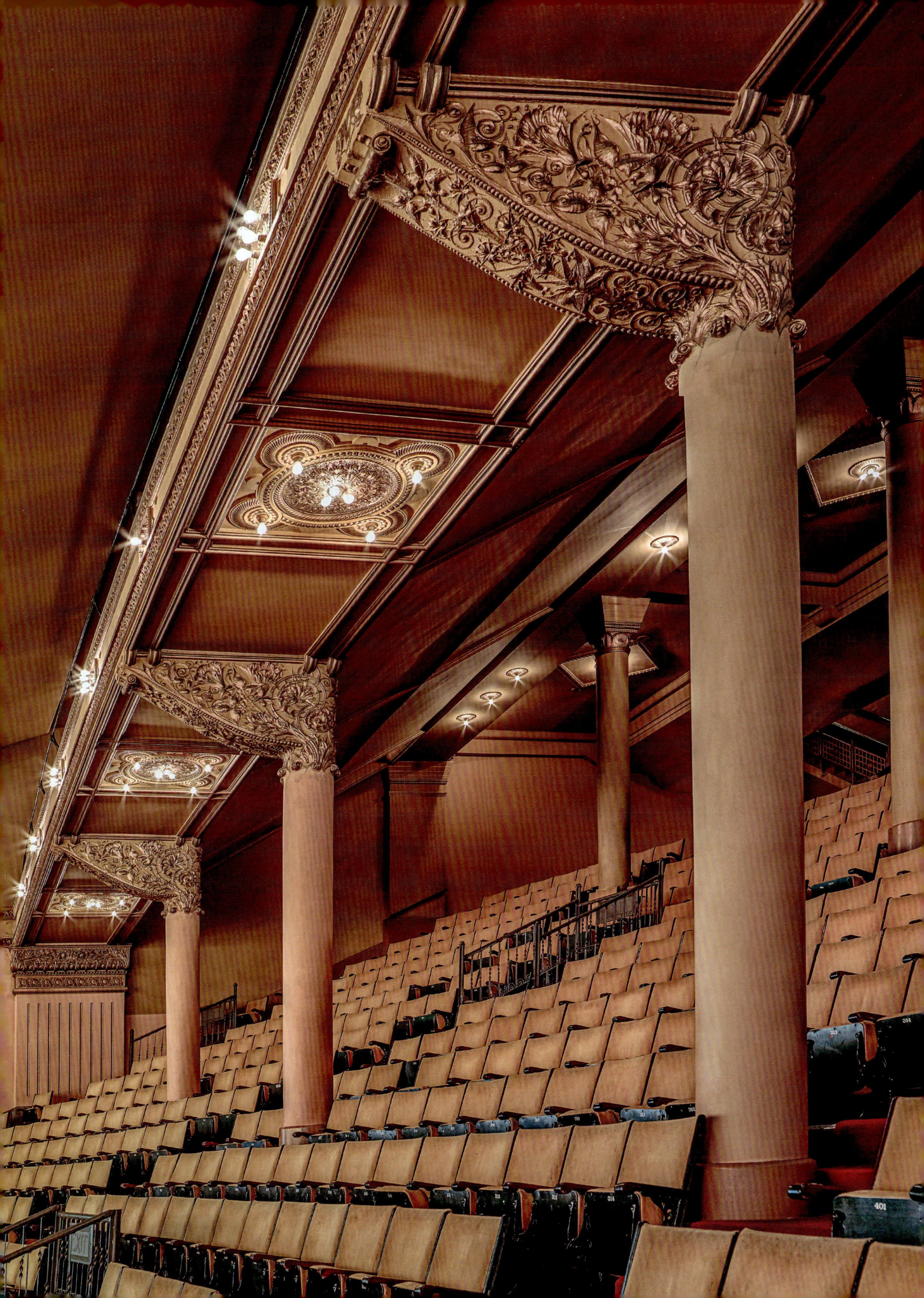

TEMPLES TO GOD, TEMPLES OF COMMERCE

"I do not see and cannot comprehend how anyone who truly reveres the great works of the past can for a moment dream of imitating them ... you will wish ... to do what they did, namely ... to produce ... to interpret, the life of your own people."

LOUIS SULLIVAN, Kindergarten Chats

Adler & Sullivan had what we would now call a general practice. Although best known for their theaters and tall office buildings, they also received commissions for stores, factories, churches, synagogues, and even mausoleums. After the practice dissolved in 1895, Sullivan continued to gain similar commissions, adding small banks as his practice began to decline after 1904. Sullivan's last design was for a terra-cotta front for the small Krause Music Store on north Lincoln Avenue in Chicago, a far cry from the extensive work he did in the late nineteenth and early twentieth centuries for the Schlesinger & Mayer department store in Chicago's loop.

In the late nineteenth century, Chicago was the fastest growing city in the world. Between the Chicago fire in 1871 and the 1929 stock market collapse that led to the Depression of the 1930s, building in Chicago was (with the exception of the usual periodic recessions) substantial and almost continuous. Housing was a large part of this, as the population swelled and the city expanded to its current borders. Adler & Sullivan had their share in this, as we have seen.

They also had their share of the manufacturing plants that rose on the city's Near North, West, and South Sides, conveniently adjacent to railroad tracks and the Chicago River. Many of these multi-story factories still stand, although many have been converted to other uses, including loft housing. Many more have been lost, as land near the central business district has been found desirable for new high rise and town-house developments.

The new residential areas required service from commercial centers, which included not only smaller versions of downtown merchants but also neighborhood department stores and the usual banks, groceries, butchers, druggists, restaurants, and shoe stores. Many of the buildings had retail on the ground floor, with offices or flats above. The more important centers had multi-story office buildings (in most cases, elaborately clad in terra cotta) to provide space for doctors, dentists, lawyers, and other professionals. But the tallest structures in most neighborhoods would have been (and still are) church spires. Many of them were built to serve immigrant communities, whose services were conducted in Polish, Italian, German, Greek, and many other languages.

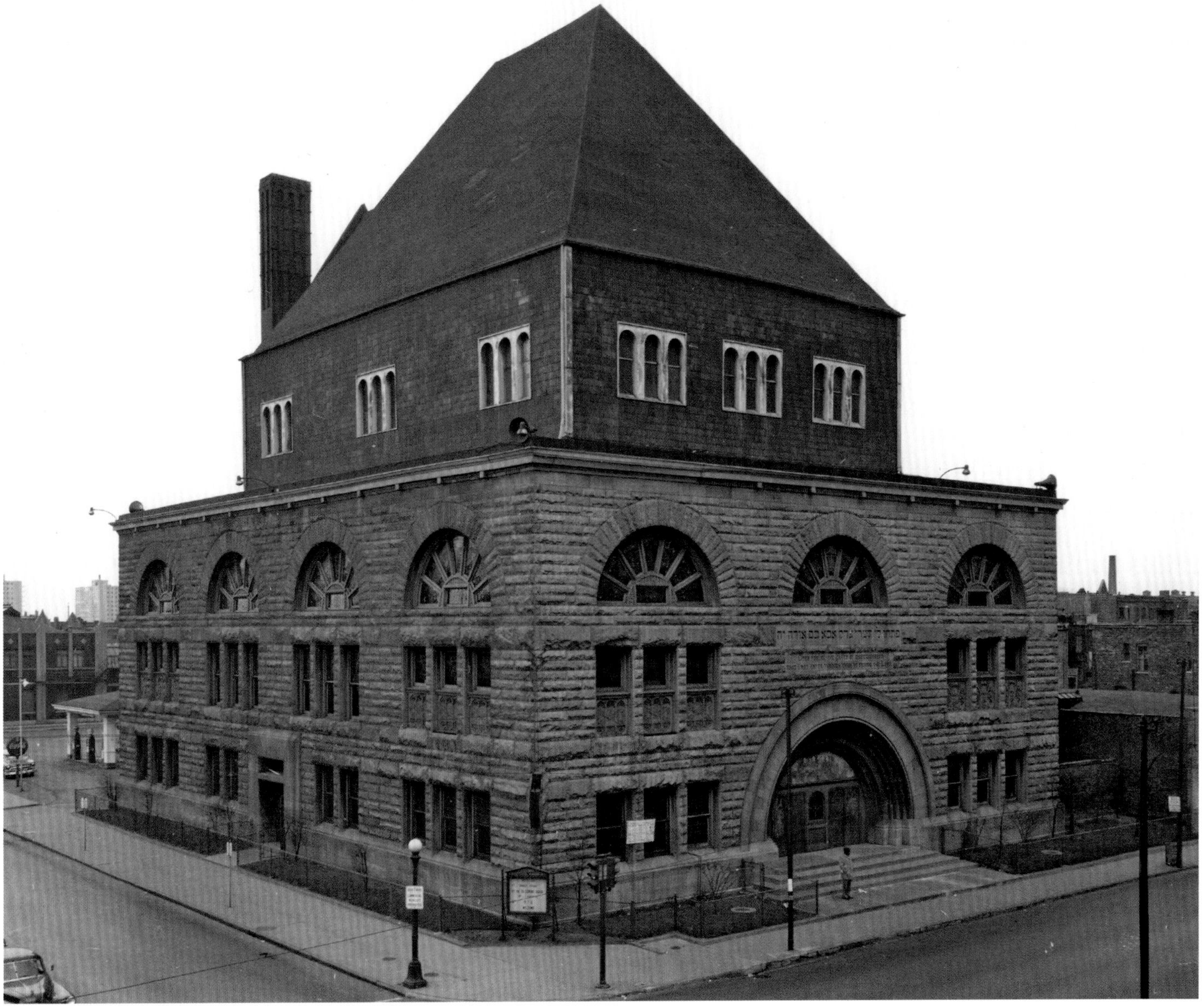

The Kehilath Anshe Ma'ariv Synagogue, 1890–91. Richard Nickel, photographer. Courtesy of the Ryerson and Burnham Library, Art Institute of Chicago.

KAUFMANN STORE AND FLATS

1883, 1887, CHICAGO

Located on Chicago's busy Lincoln Avenue, it was built in two stages for druggist Ferdinand Kaufmann. The 1883 first (south) section was only three stories. In 1887, a four-story addition was added to the north, a fourth story was added to the original, and the whole structure was now topped with a mansard roof. This building type, with shops on the ground floor and flats above, was common on Chicago's main streets (and, of course, in other towns and cities as well). In recent years, there has been a revival of this rational combination. It was designated a Chicago Landmark in 1996.

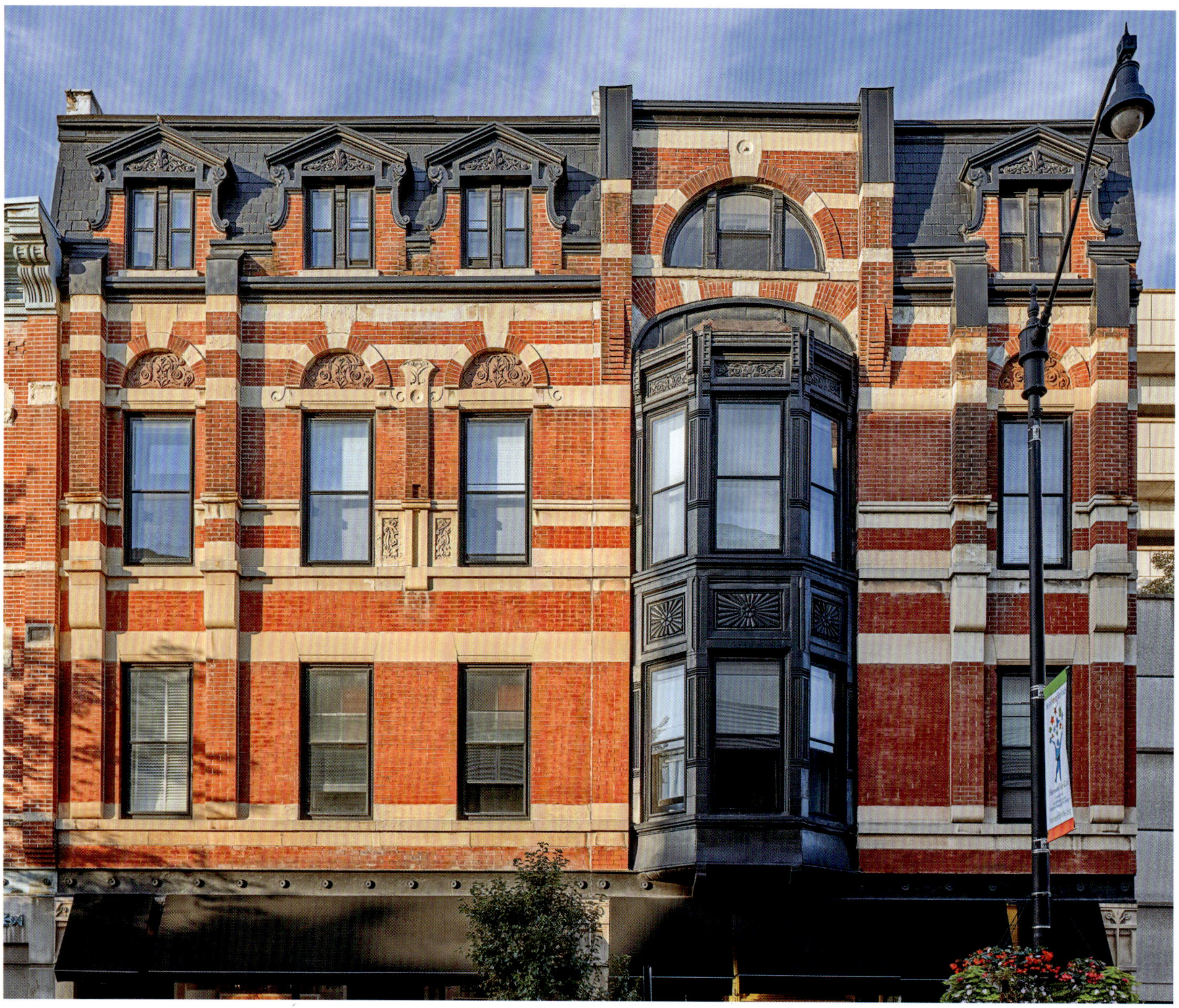

The Kaufmann retains most of its original fabric, including entrances to retail stores.

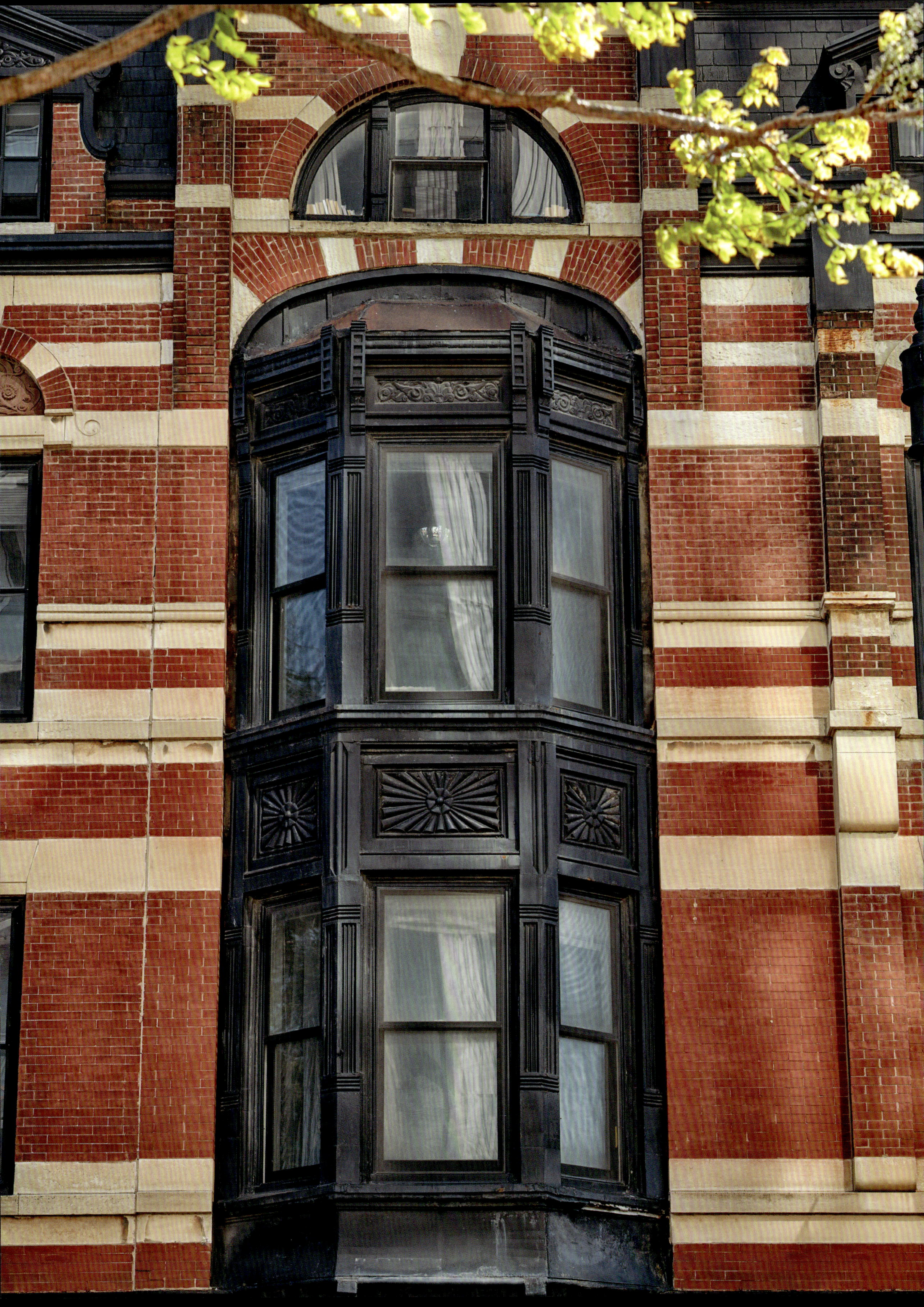

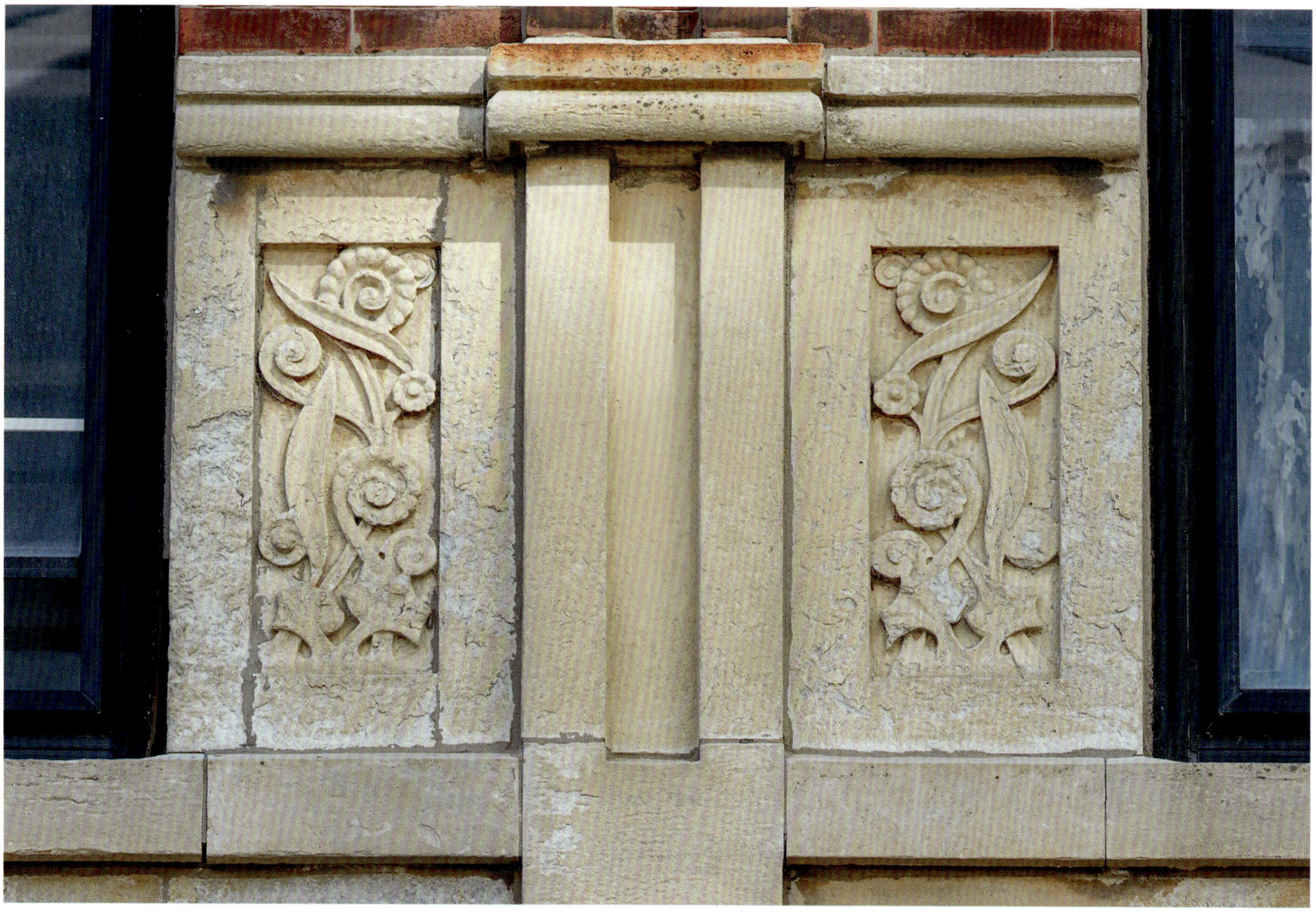

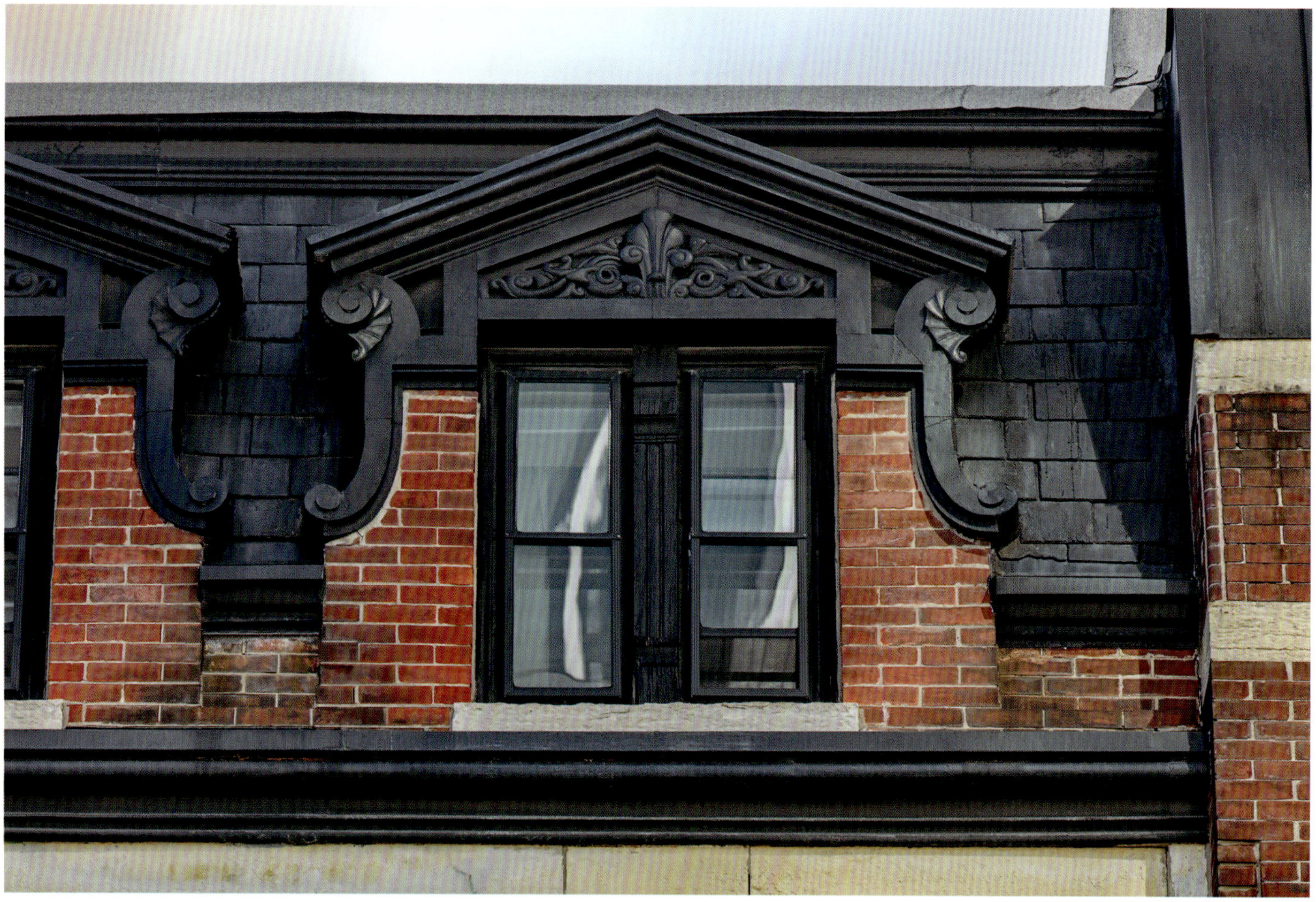

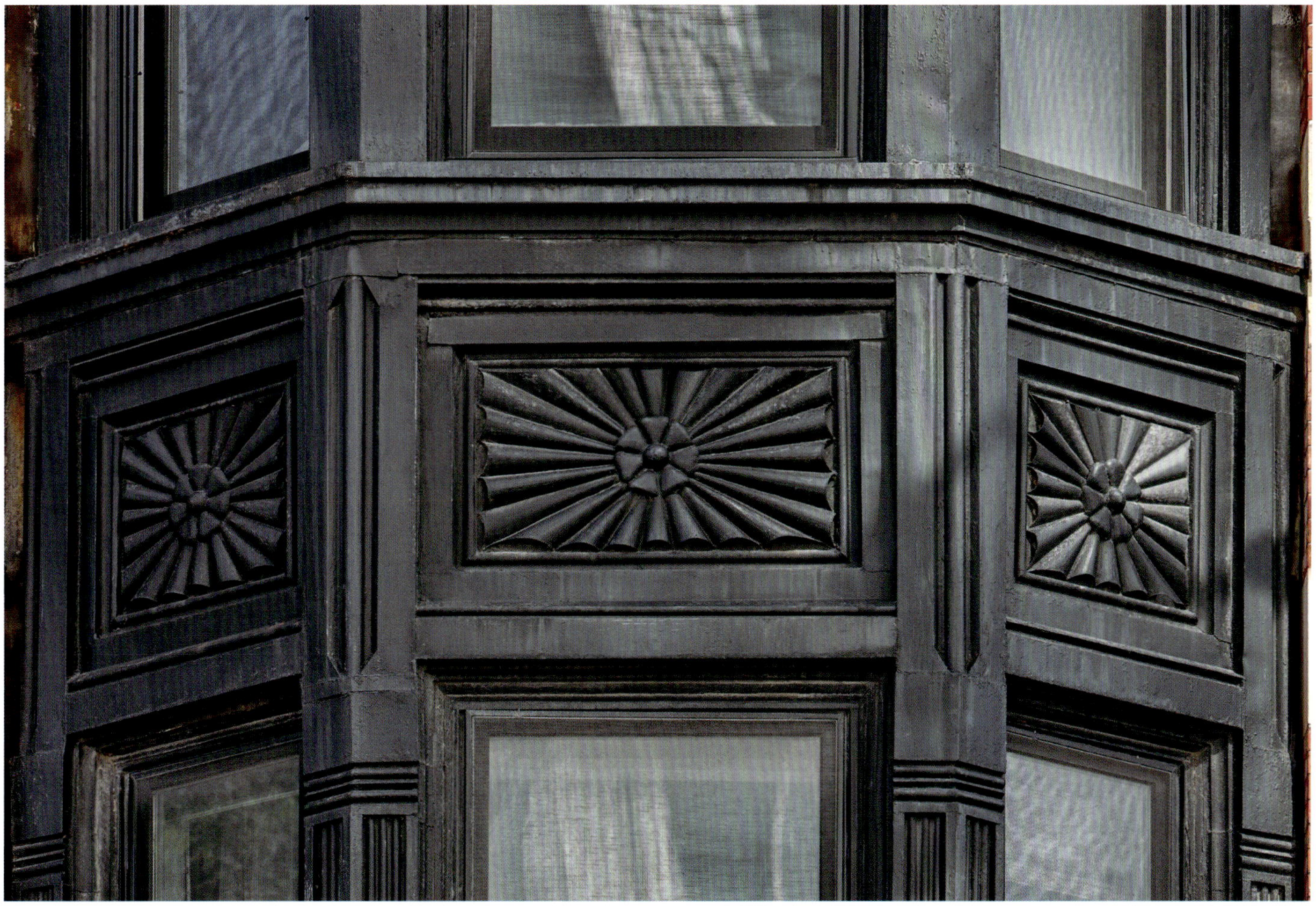

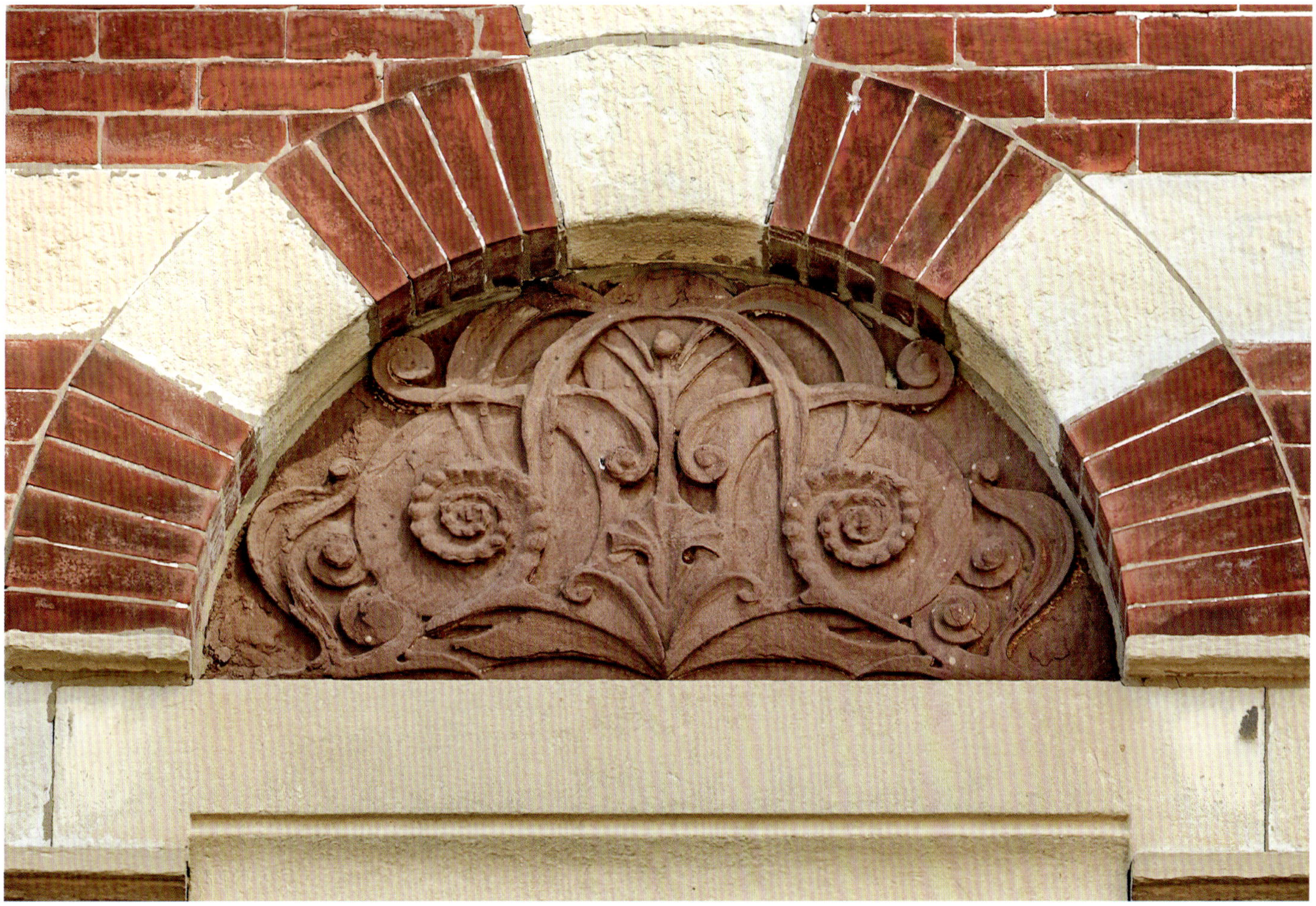

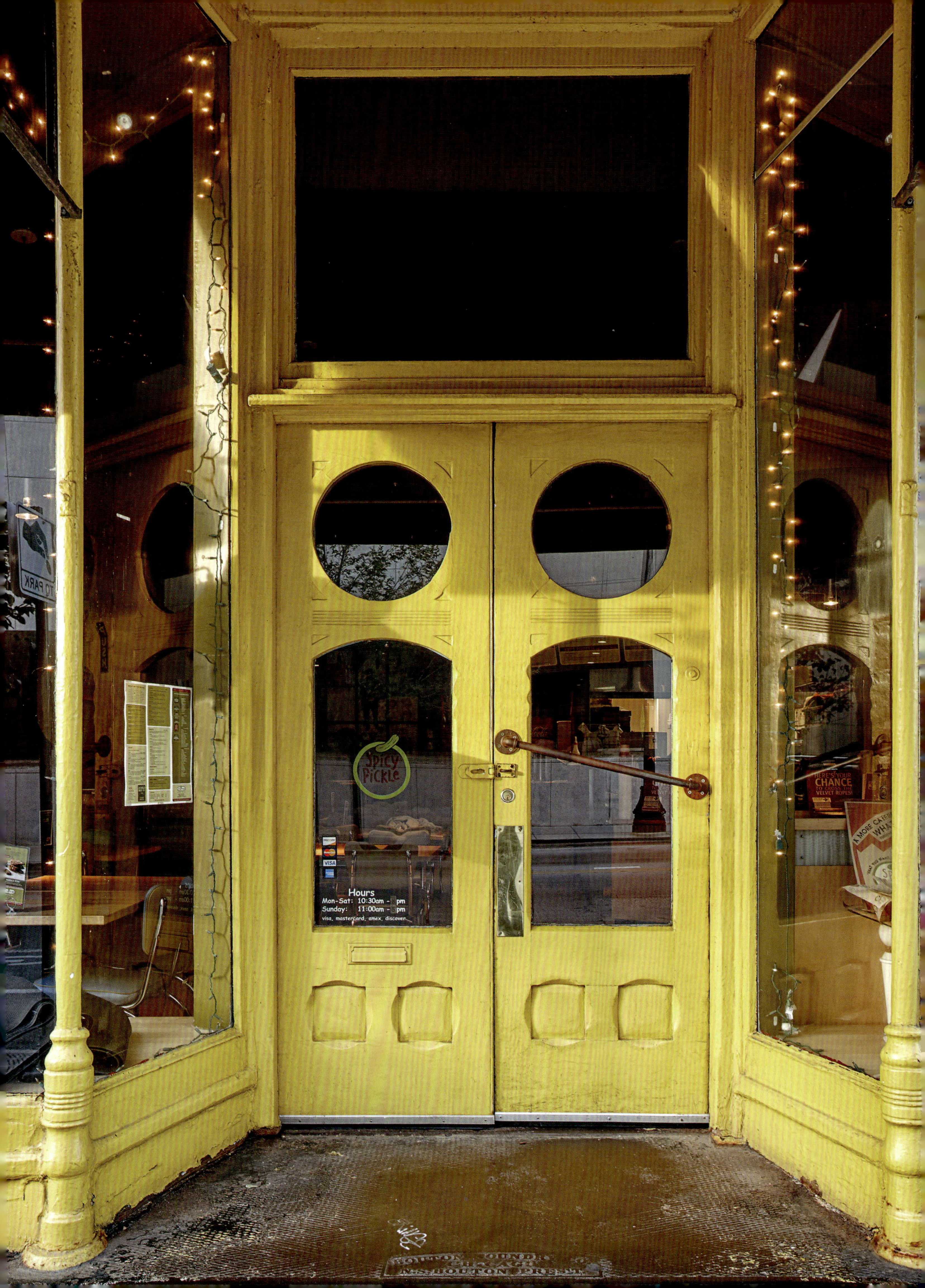
Spicy Pickle
VISA
Hours
Mon-Sat: 10:30am - pm
Sunday: 11:00am - pm
visa, mastercard, amex, discover
HERE'S YOUR CHANCE
VELVET ROPES!

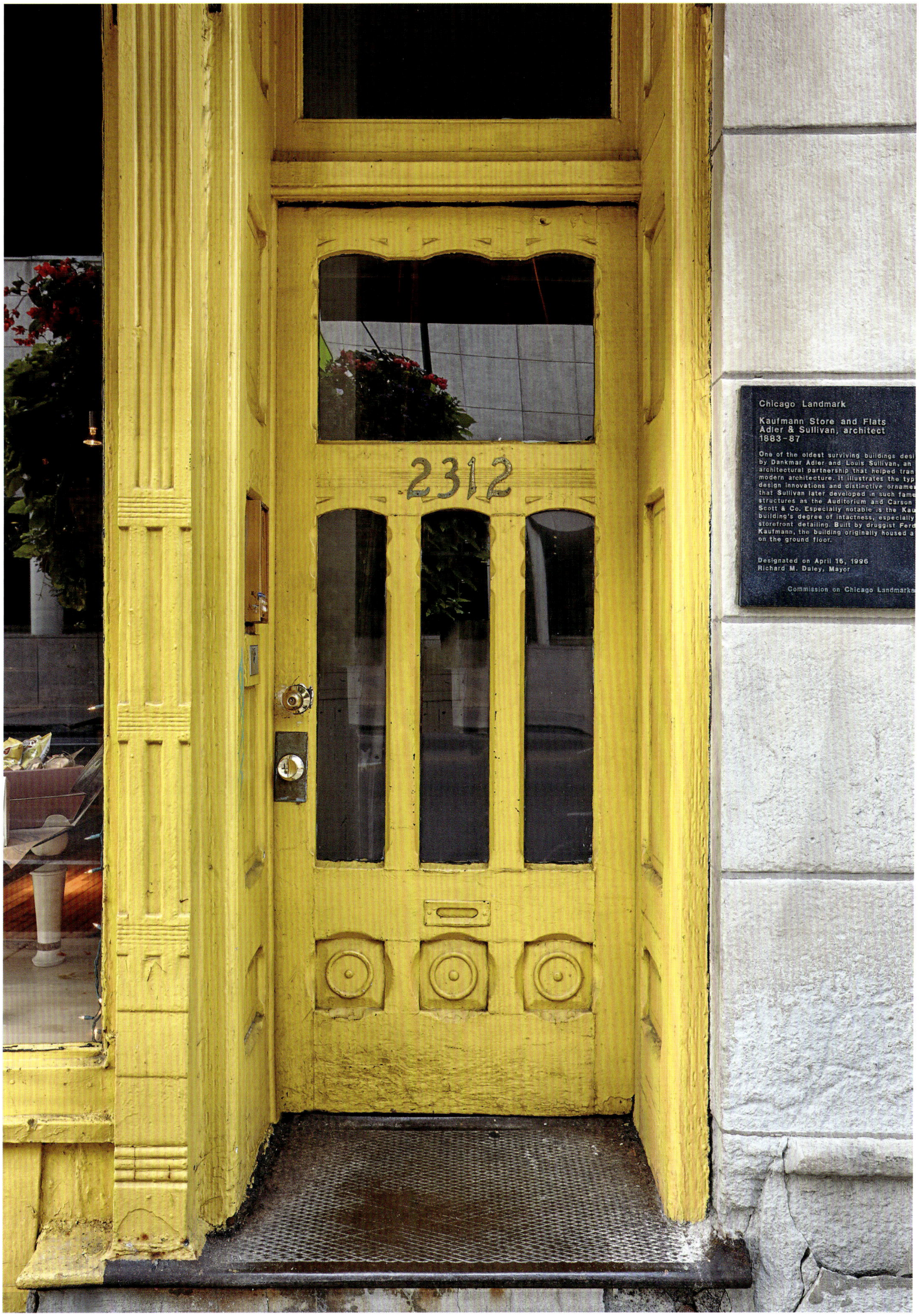
2312
Chicago Landmark
Kaufmann Store and Flats
Adler & Sullivan, architect
1883-87
One of the oldest surviving buildings
by Dankmar Adler and Louis Sullivan, an
architectural partnership that helped
modern architecture. It illustrates the
design innovations and distinctive
that Sullivan later developed in such
structures as the Auditorium and Carson
Scott & Co. Especially notable is the
building's degree of intactness, especially
storefront detailing. Built by druggist
Kaufmann, the building originally housed
on the ground floor.
Designated on April 16, 1996
Richard M. Daley, Mayor
Commission on Chicago Landmarks

B. DESENBERG & COMPANY

1886, KALAMAZOO, MICHIGAN

This modest three-story store and loft was built for a wholesale grocery and tobacco company. Materials included reddish-orange brick, Bedford limestone, and terra-cotta trim.

In the early 1980s, several buildings along Michigan Avenue, including the Desenberg, underwent restoration, which was supervised by architects Gordon Rogers & Associates, with the assistance of Western Michigan University professor of architecture Dr. Elizabeth Dull. The building was added to the National Register of Historic Places in 1979 and is now used as an event venue.

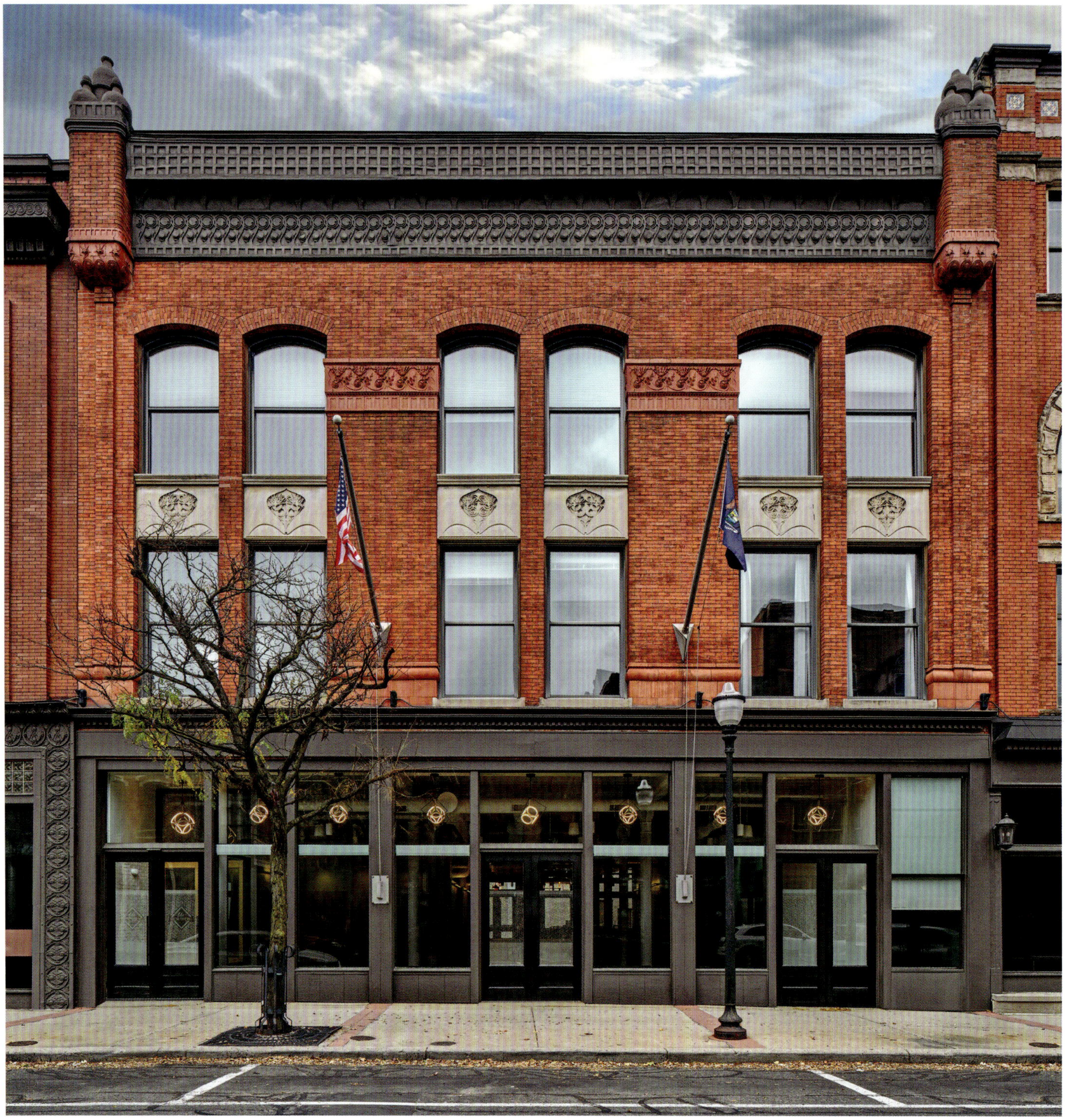

With a symmetrical façade and restrained decoration, the Desenberg has been repurposed as an event space.

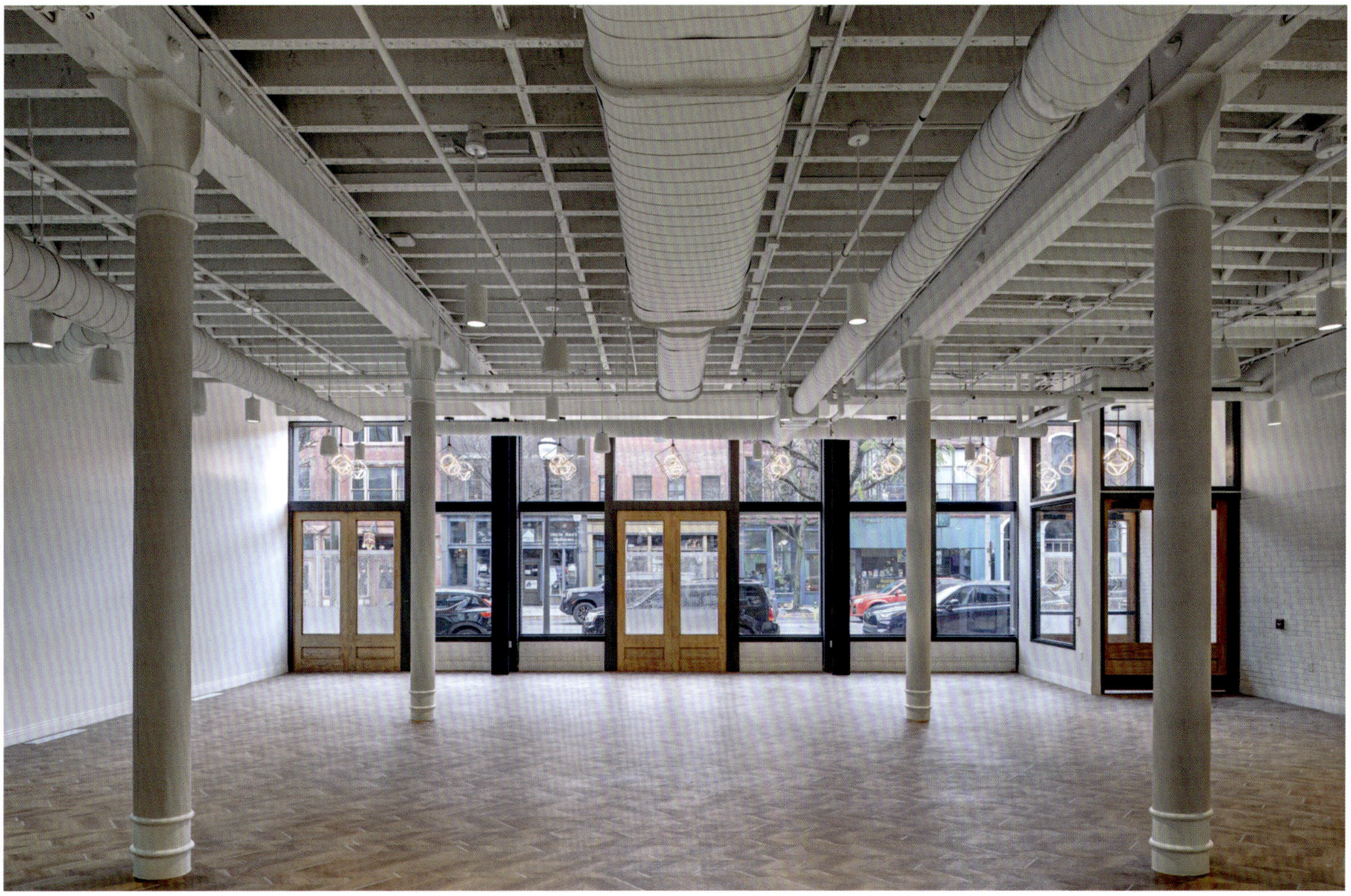

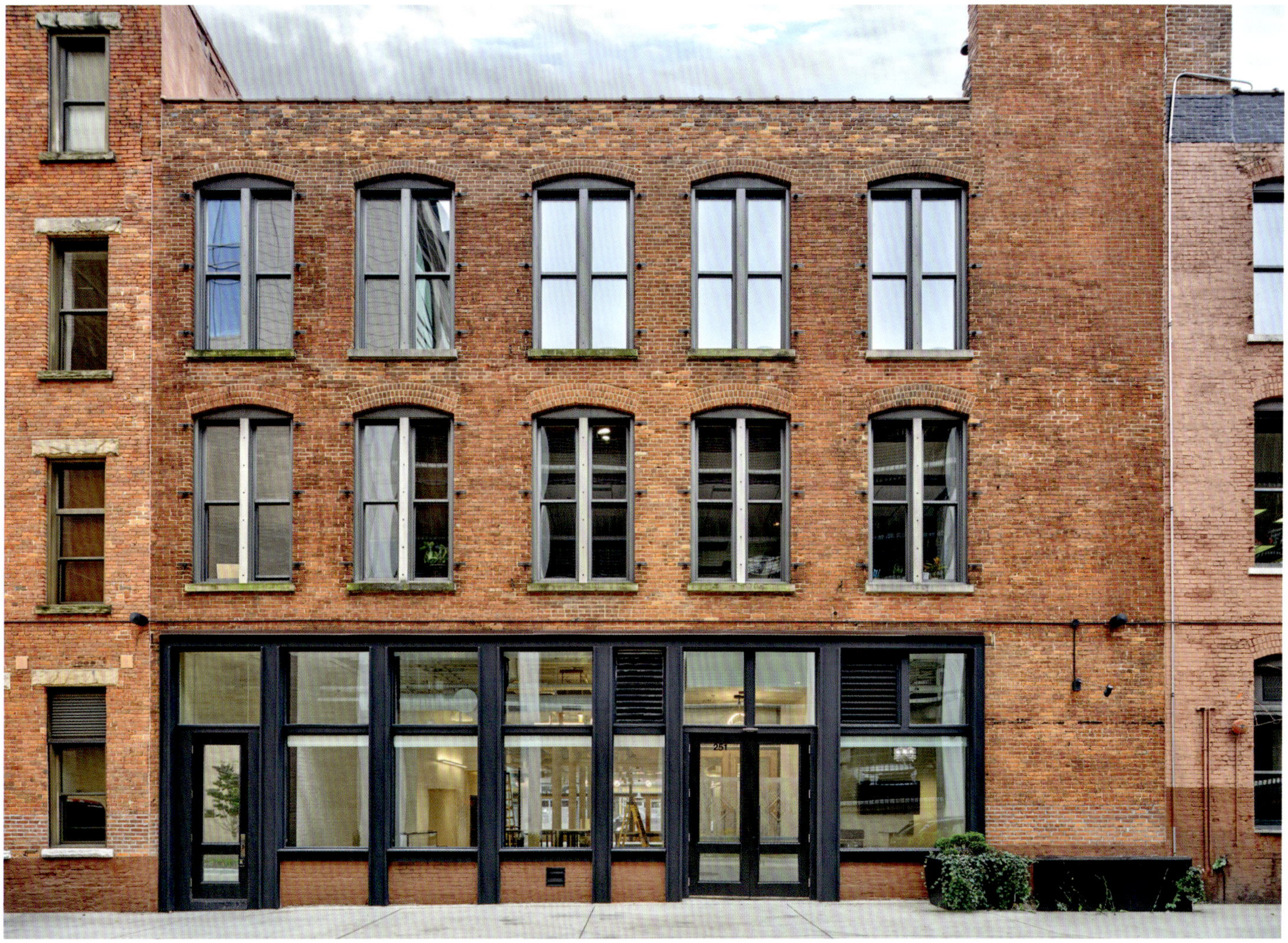

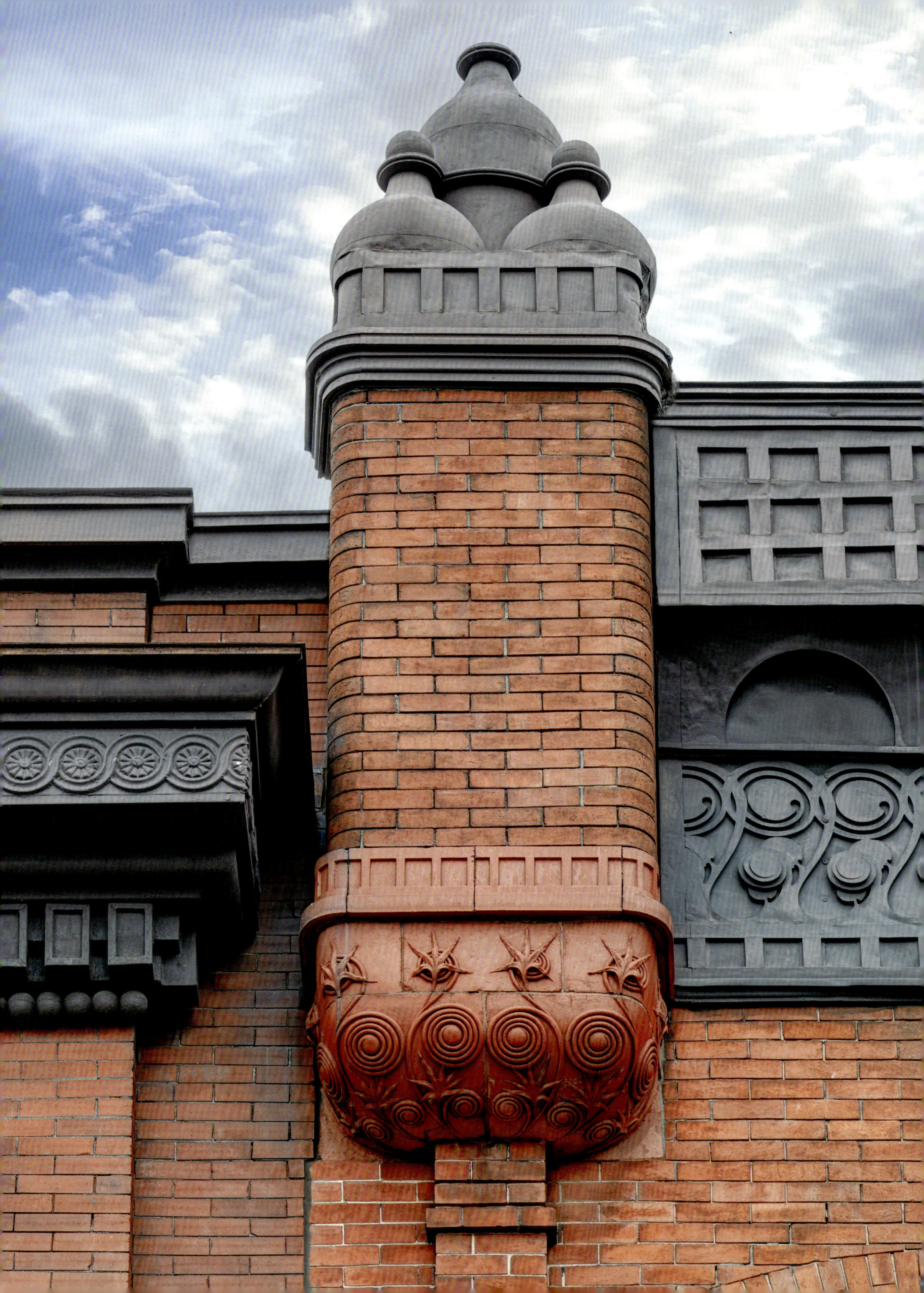

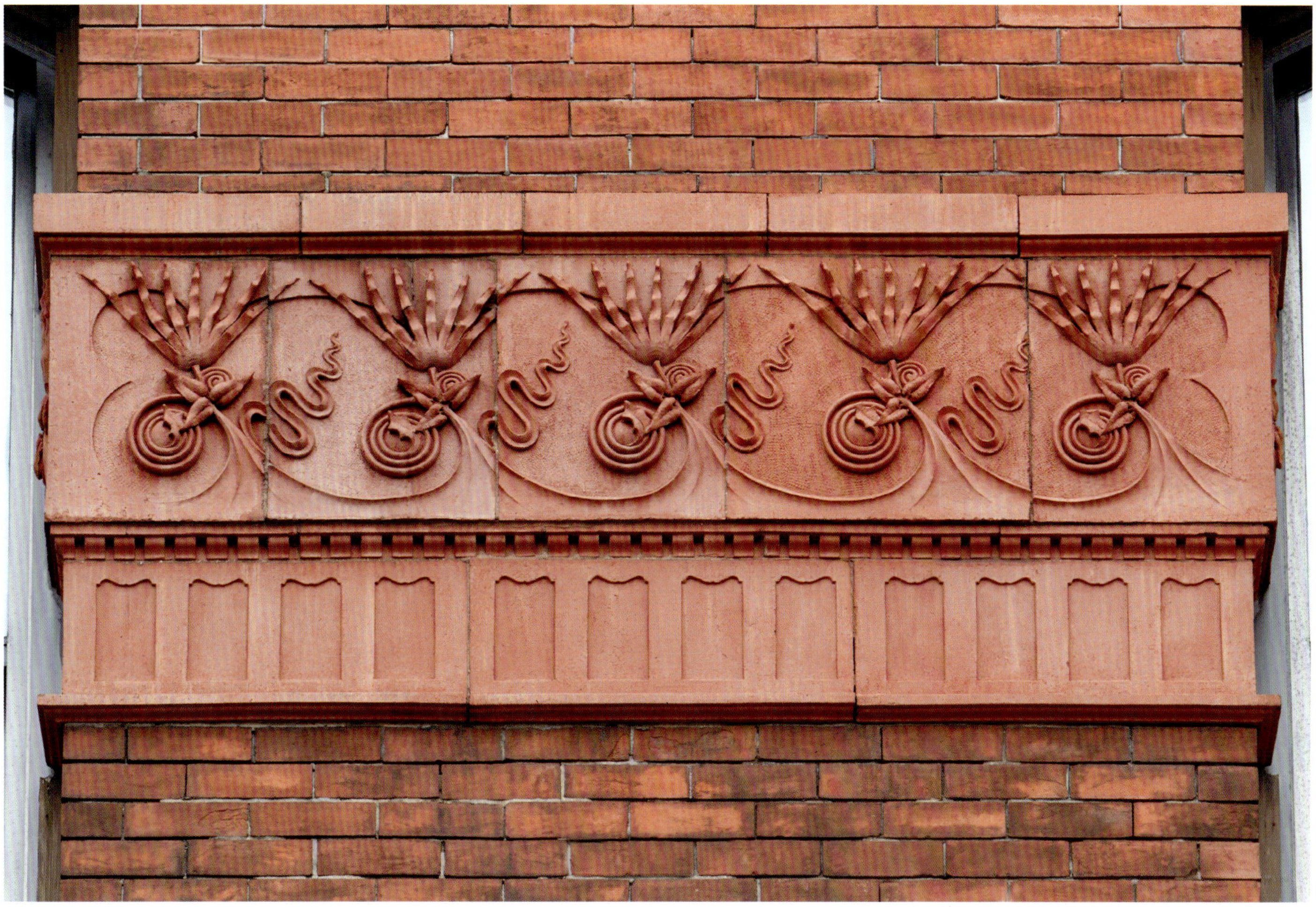

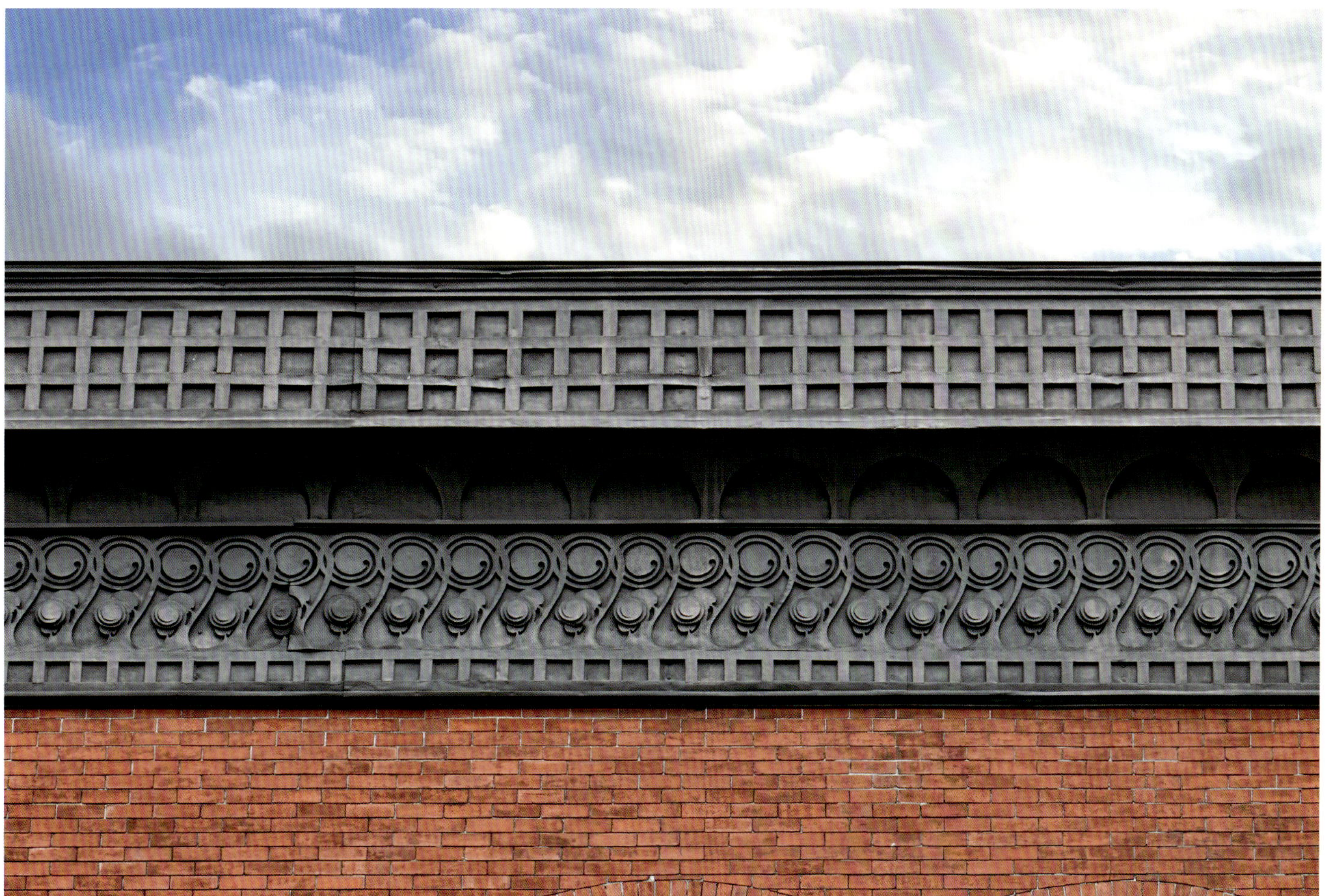

ADOLPH LOEB FACTORY

1888, CHICAGO

There are no existing original photographs, plans, or illustrations of the original design for a small factory for the real estate developers, Adolph Loeb & Brothers. The factory was converted to apartments in 1894, when an additional story was added. It was reduced to its original three stories after a 1946 fire. Although the building survives, it likely looks nothing like Adler & Sullivan's original design.

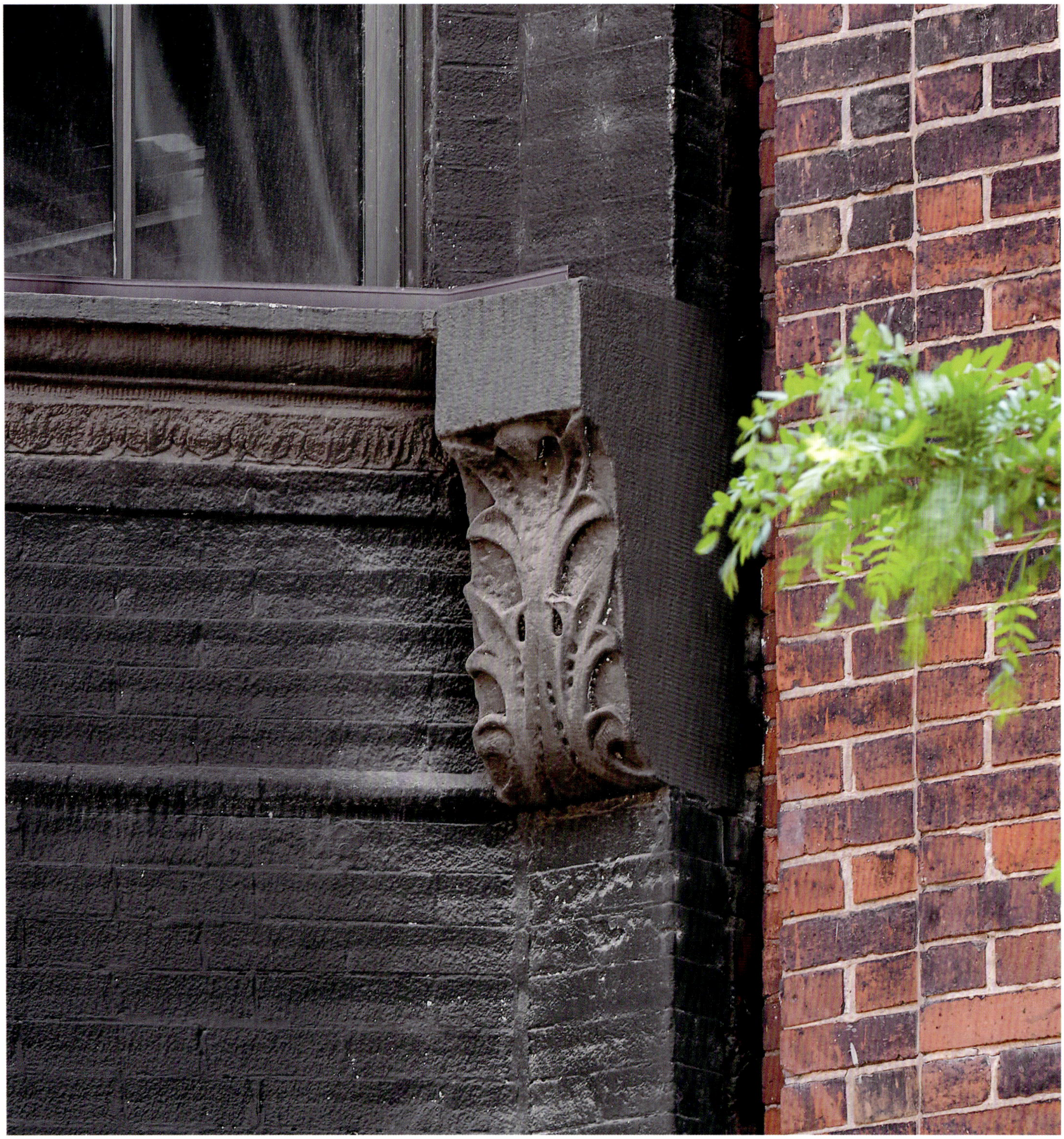

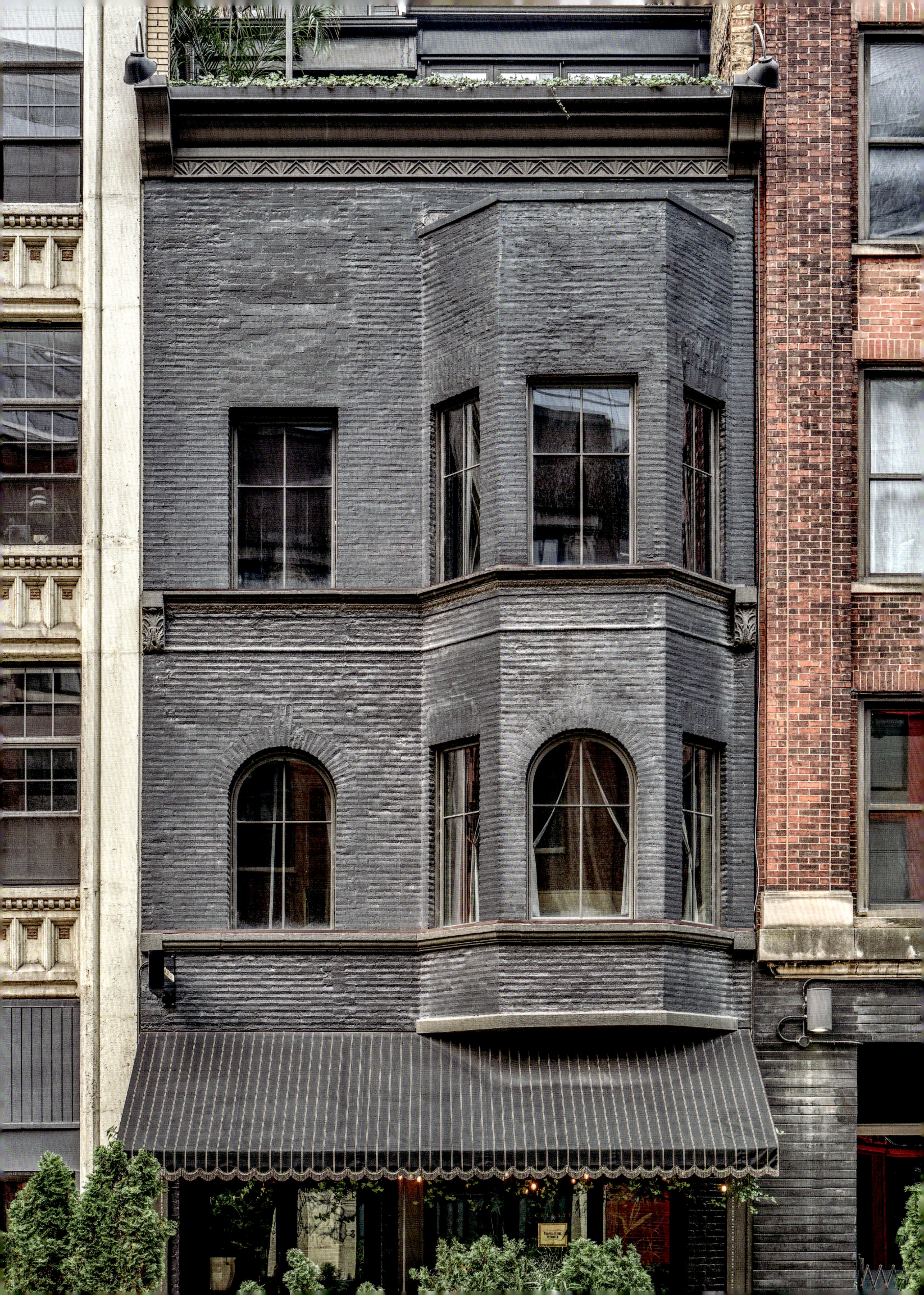

KEHILATH ANSHE MA'ARIV (KAM) SYNAGOGUE

1890–91, CHICAGO

Dankmar Adler's father, Liebman, was the rabbi for the KAM synagogue, Chicago's oldest Jewish congregation, founded in 1847. It was only logical then that Adler & Sullivan would be chosen to design the synagogue's new home on South Indiana Avenue. Constructed largely from rusticated Bedford limestone, the synagogue was the firm's final foray into what has come to be known as Richardsonian Romanesque, used more famously by the firm in the Auditorium Building (1889) and the earlier Standard Club (1888).

The first floor in the 91 by 115-foot building was used for classes and offices, with the barrel-vaulted sanctuary on the second floor. Like the Auditorium, the main entrance of the synagogue was a large arch, and arches were repeated in the lower sanctuary windows. Additional natural light in the barrel-vaulted space was provided by rows of clerestory windows; all the art glass was executed by old friends and collaborators, Healy & Millet. When the congregation moved to Kenwood in 1924, the building was sold to the Pilgrim Baptist Church, famous as the home of gospel music.

A 2006 fire destroyed everything but the exterior shell. In 2020, a storm crumbled the south wall. Plans to restore the exterior and create a gospel museum in a new interior are ongoing. As the Pilgrim Baptist Church, the building was added to the National Register of Historic Places in 1973 and was designated a Chicago Landmark in 1981.

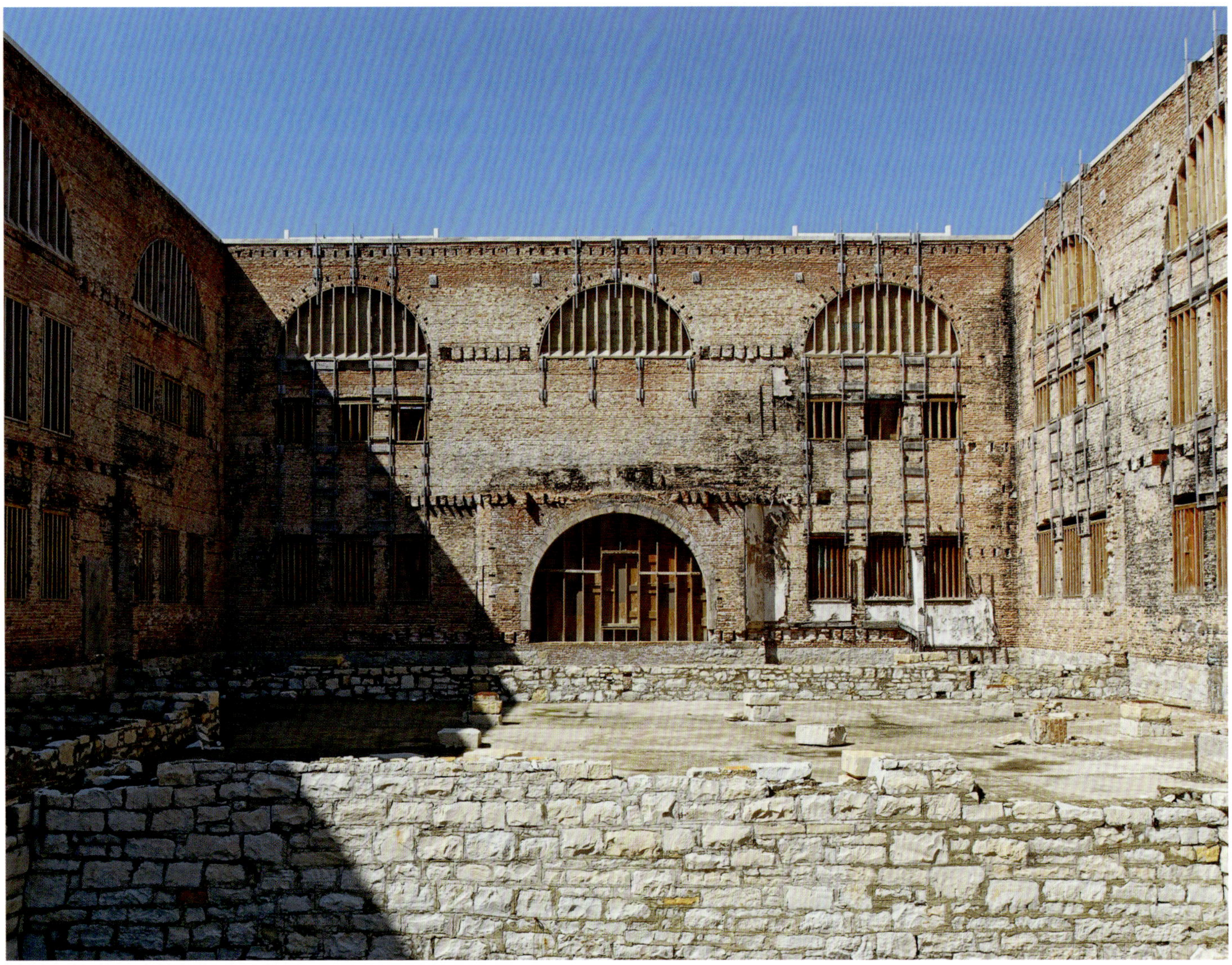

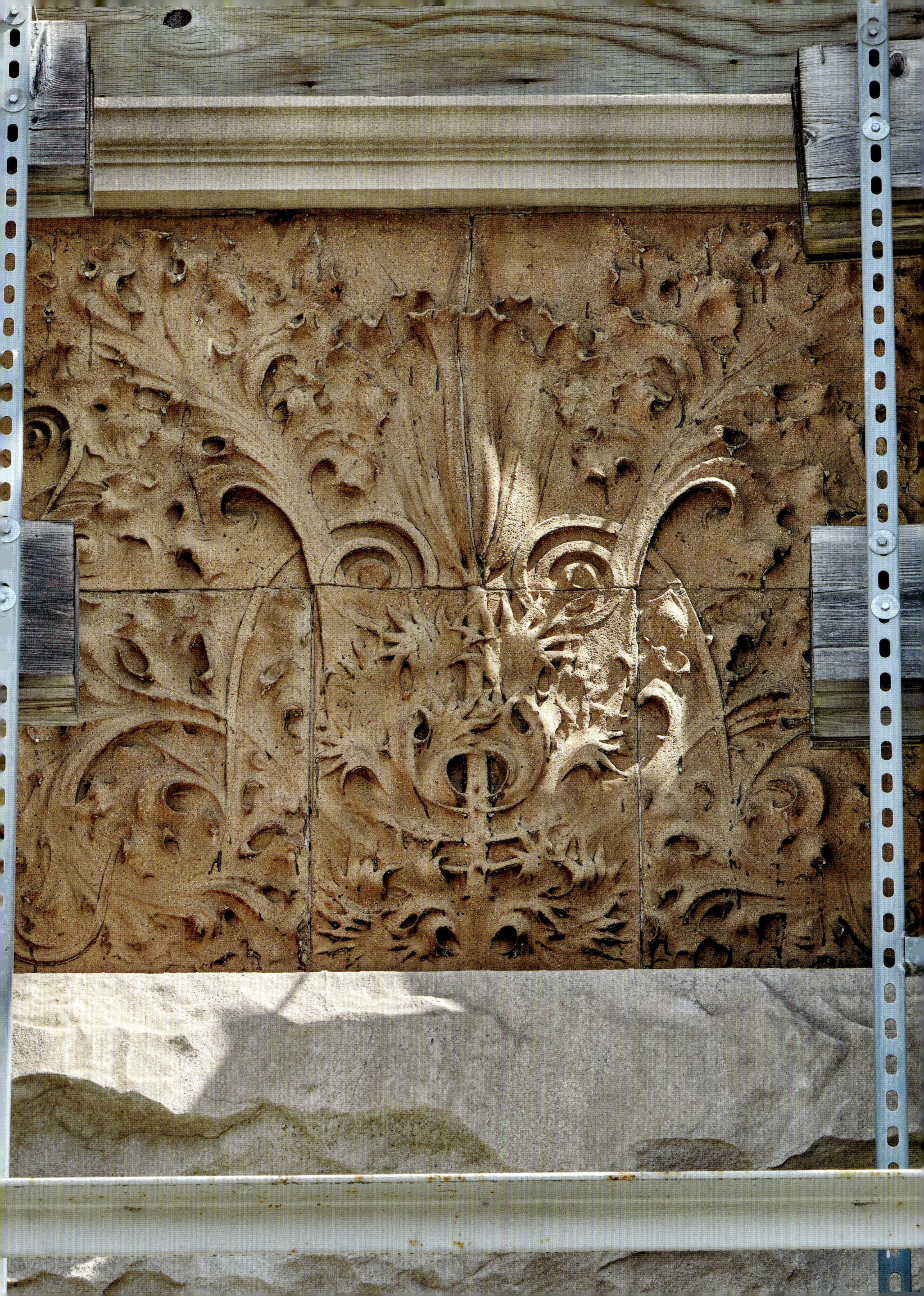

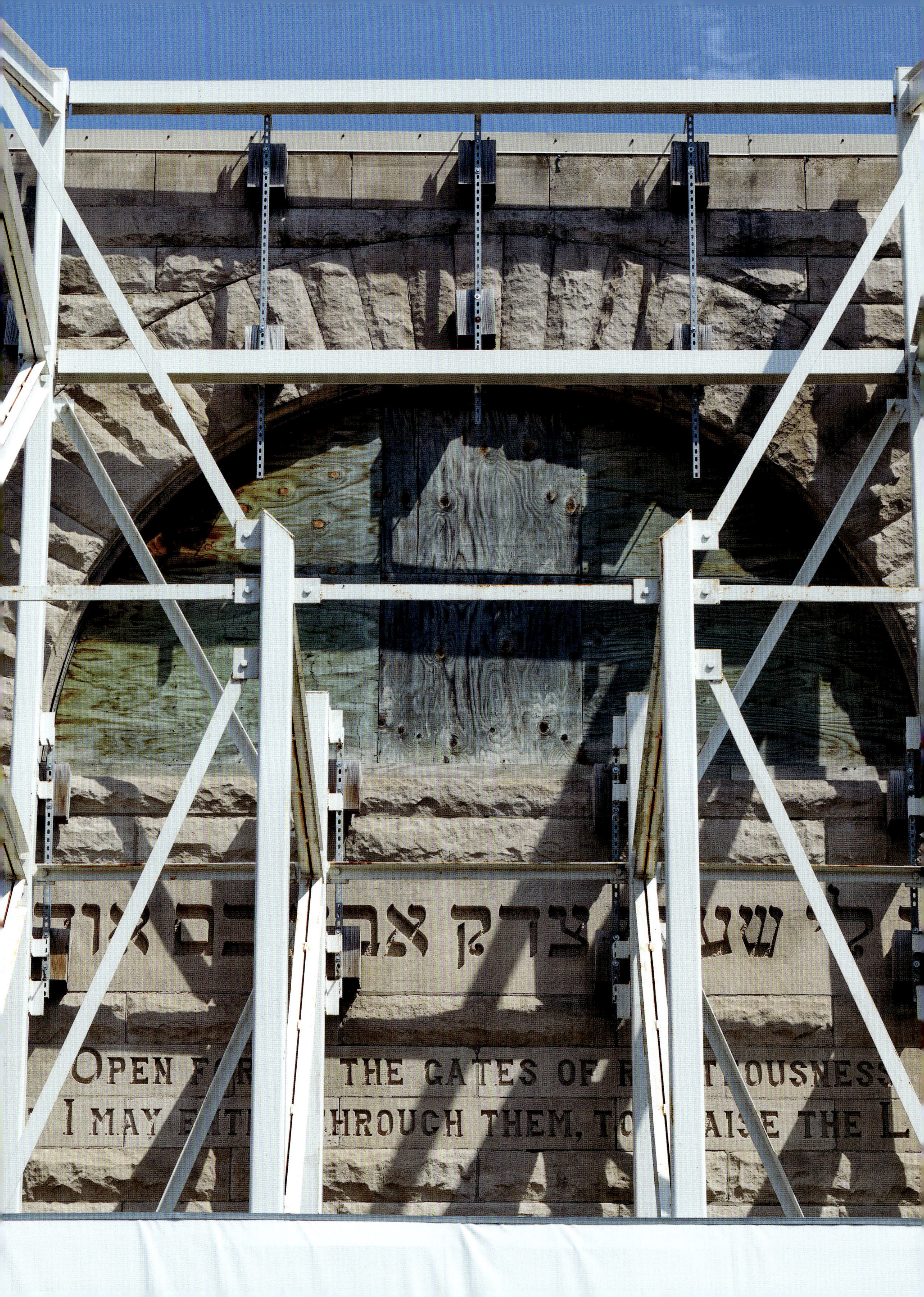

צדק
OPEN THE GATES OF
I MAY THEM, TO THE

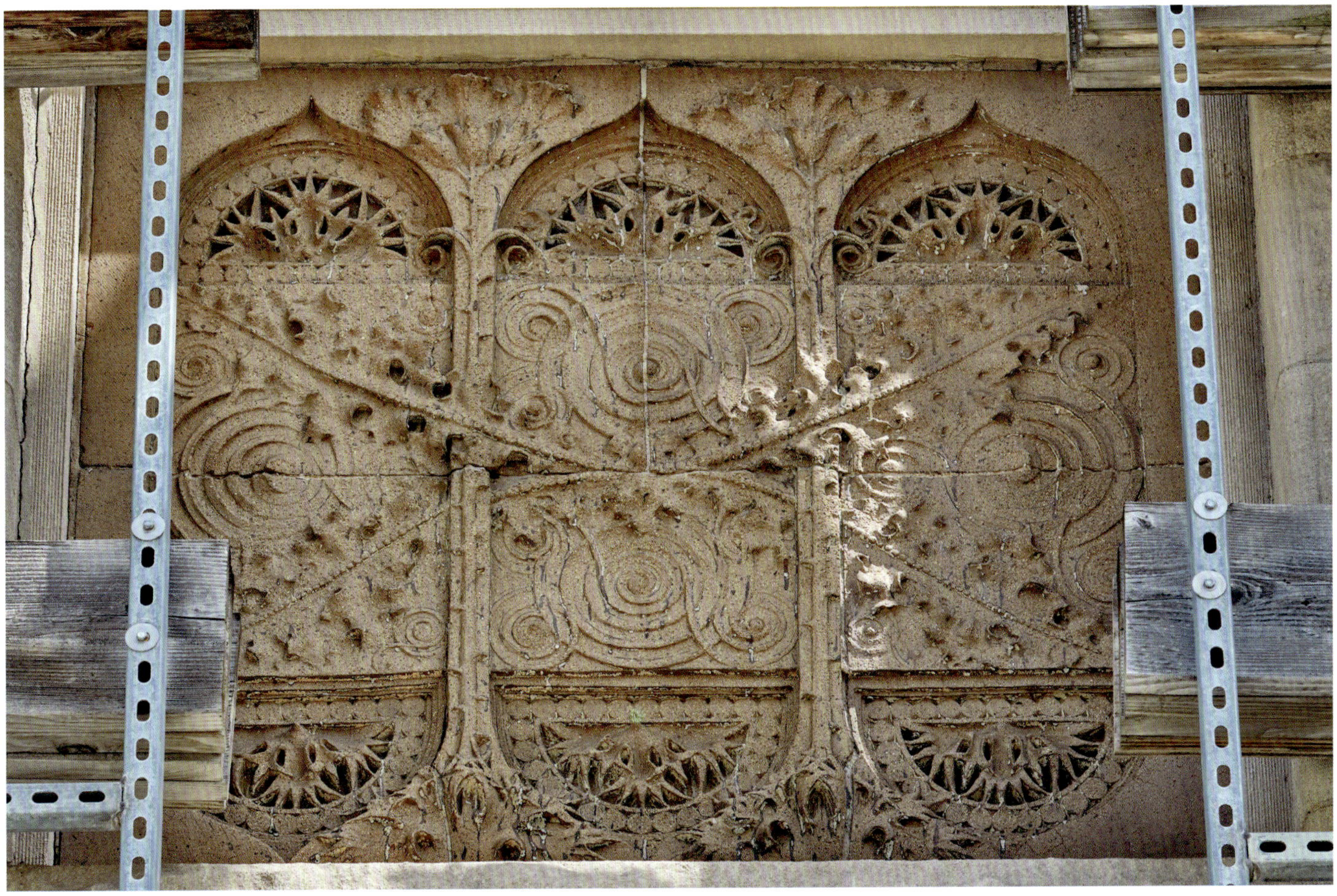

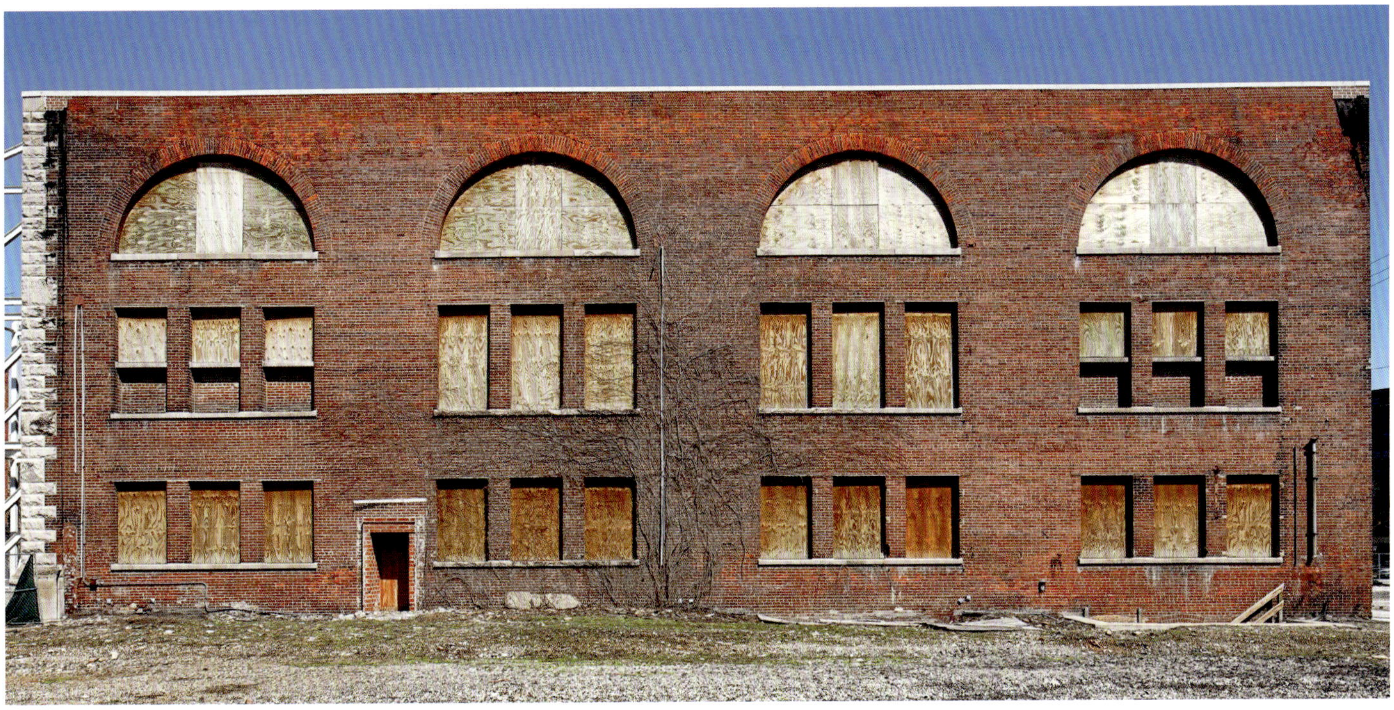

RYERSON TOMB

1887–90, GRACELAND CEMETERY, CHICAGO

The Ryerson family commissioned six buildings from Adler & Sullivan, although only the Jewelers Building (see page 64) survives. So, it was logical that Martin A. Ryerson (1856–1932) would ask the firm to design a tomb for his father, Martin L. Ryerson (1818–1887). When he himself died, the younger Ryerson would be entombed with his father.

The elder Ryerson was originally from Michigan, where he made his fortune in the lumber industry, part of which he used to invest in Chicago real estate. In addition to being "Hog Butcher for the World, Tool Maker, Stacker of Wheat …" as Carl Sandburg described it in his famous poem, Chicago was also a major center for the lumber industry. In an amazing piece of luck, Ryerson's was the only lumber yard to survive the 1871 fire. Ryerson's son carried on the family businesses and was once said to be the city's richest man. A graduate of Harvard Law, he briefly practiced law before joining his father. He was one of the founders of the University of Chicago. He left his considerable collection of French Impressionist paintings, including those of Renoir and Monet, to the Art Institute.

The tomb is in an Egyptian Revival style, expressed in highly polished blue-gray Quincy (Massachusetts) granite. Above the flared base is a clerestory, topped with a pyramid-shaped hipped roof. It is bereft of decoration, except for the ornamental bronze gate and the grilled opening at the rear. The interior features an arched niche with a bronze bust of the elder Ryerson, and stone-fronted vaults for other family members. It is a contributing structure to Graceland's 2001 listing in the National Registry of Historic Places.

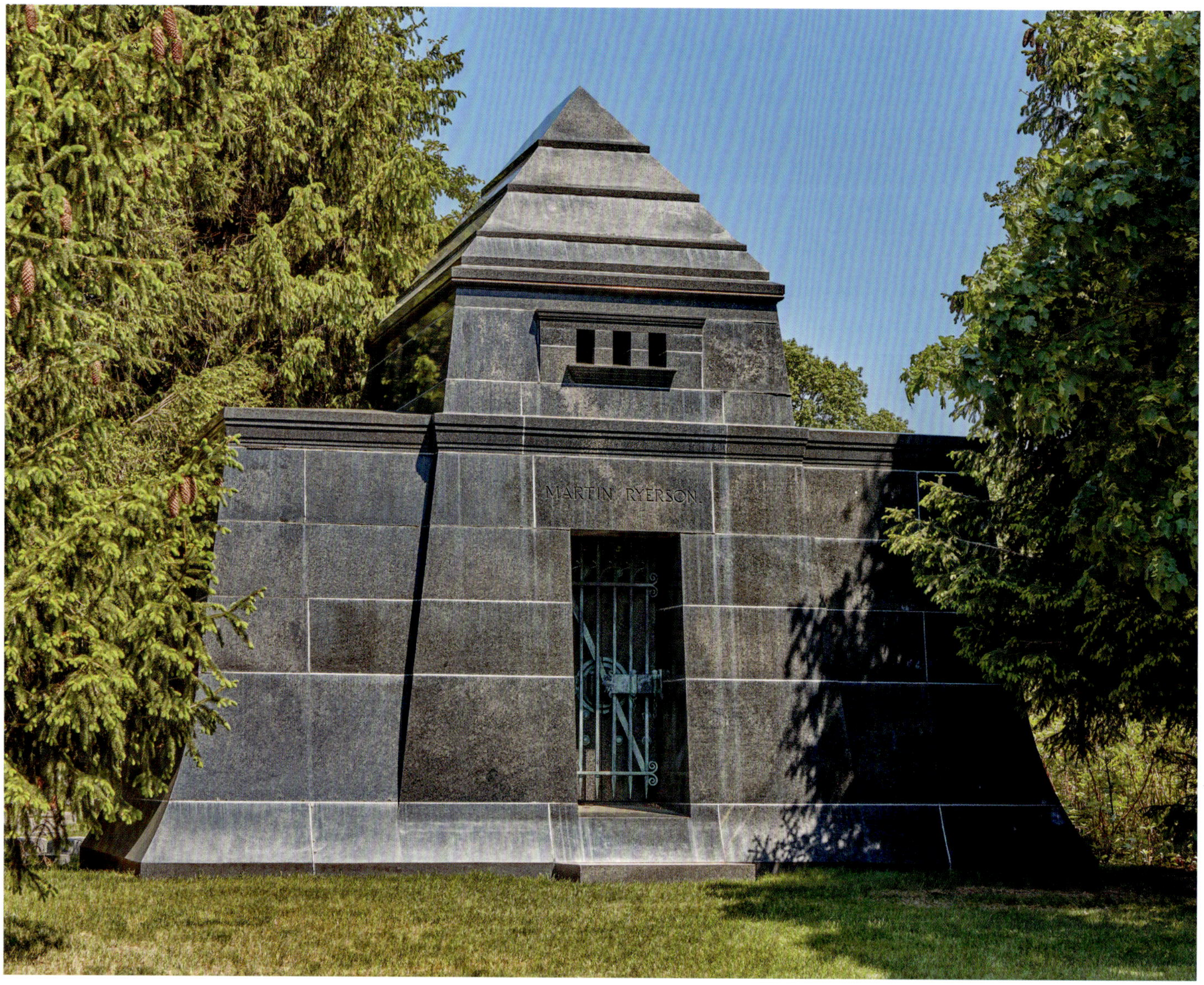

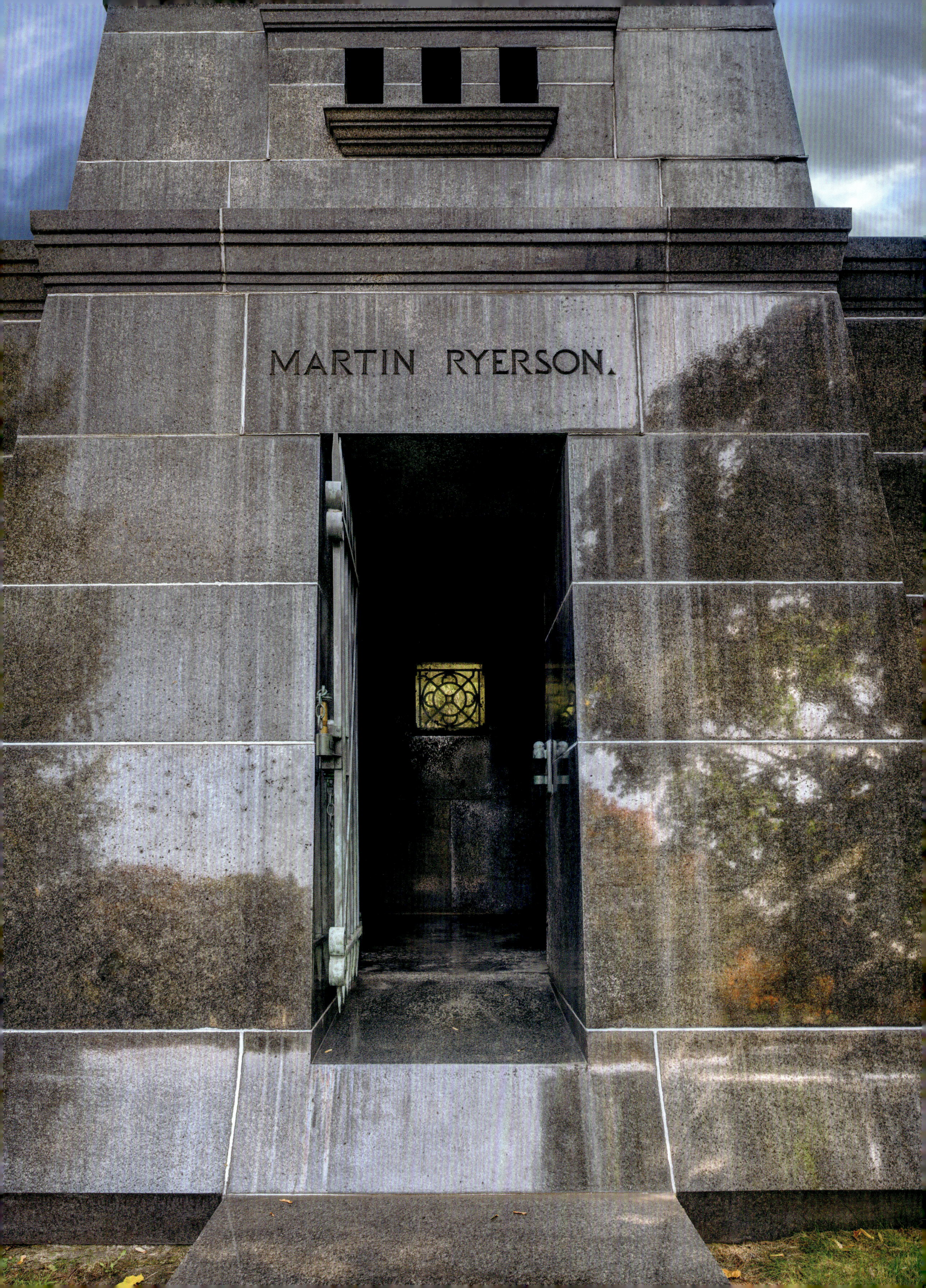
MARTIN RYERSON.

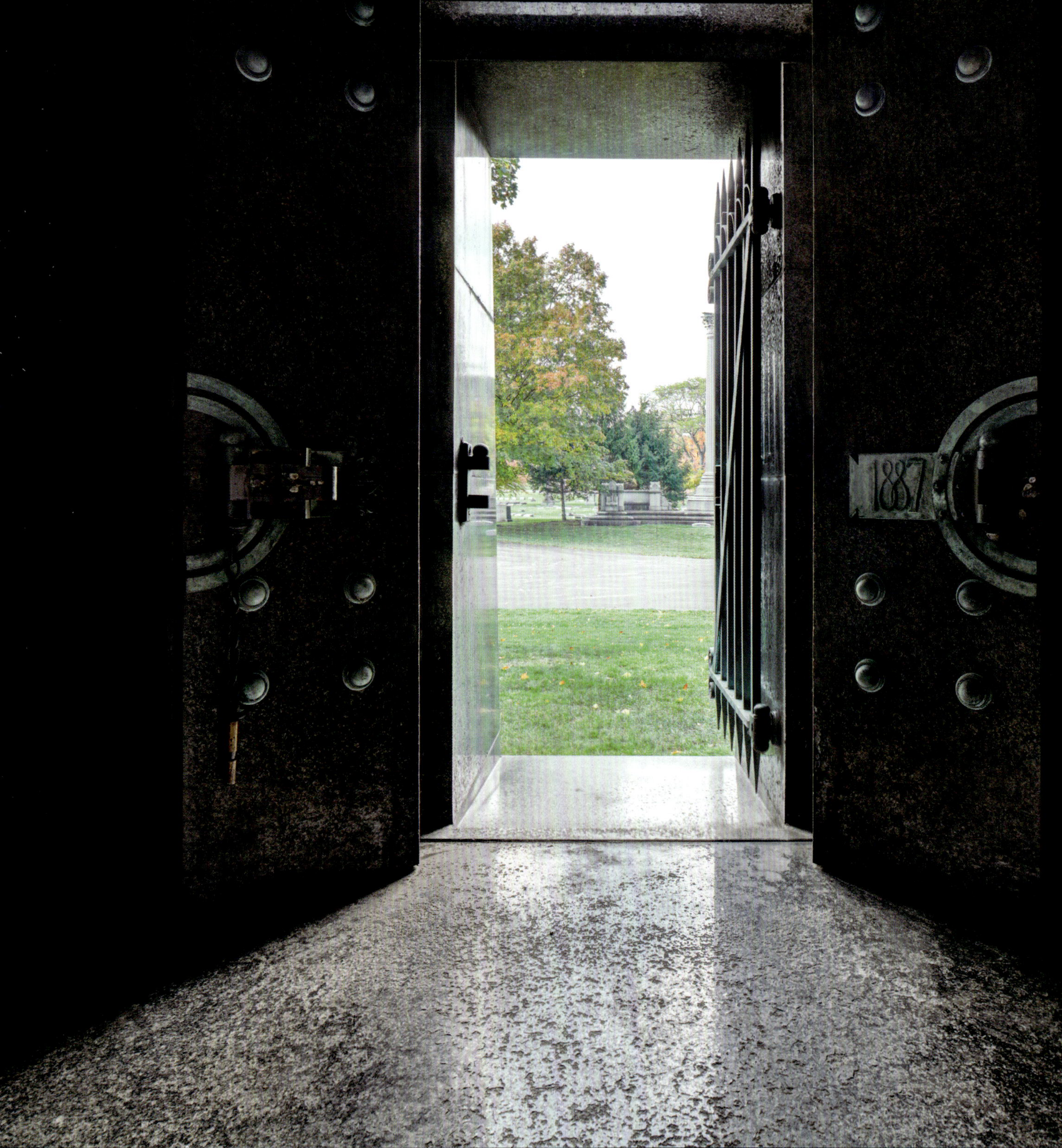
1887

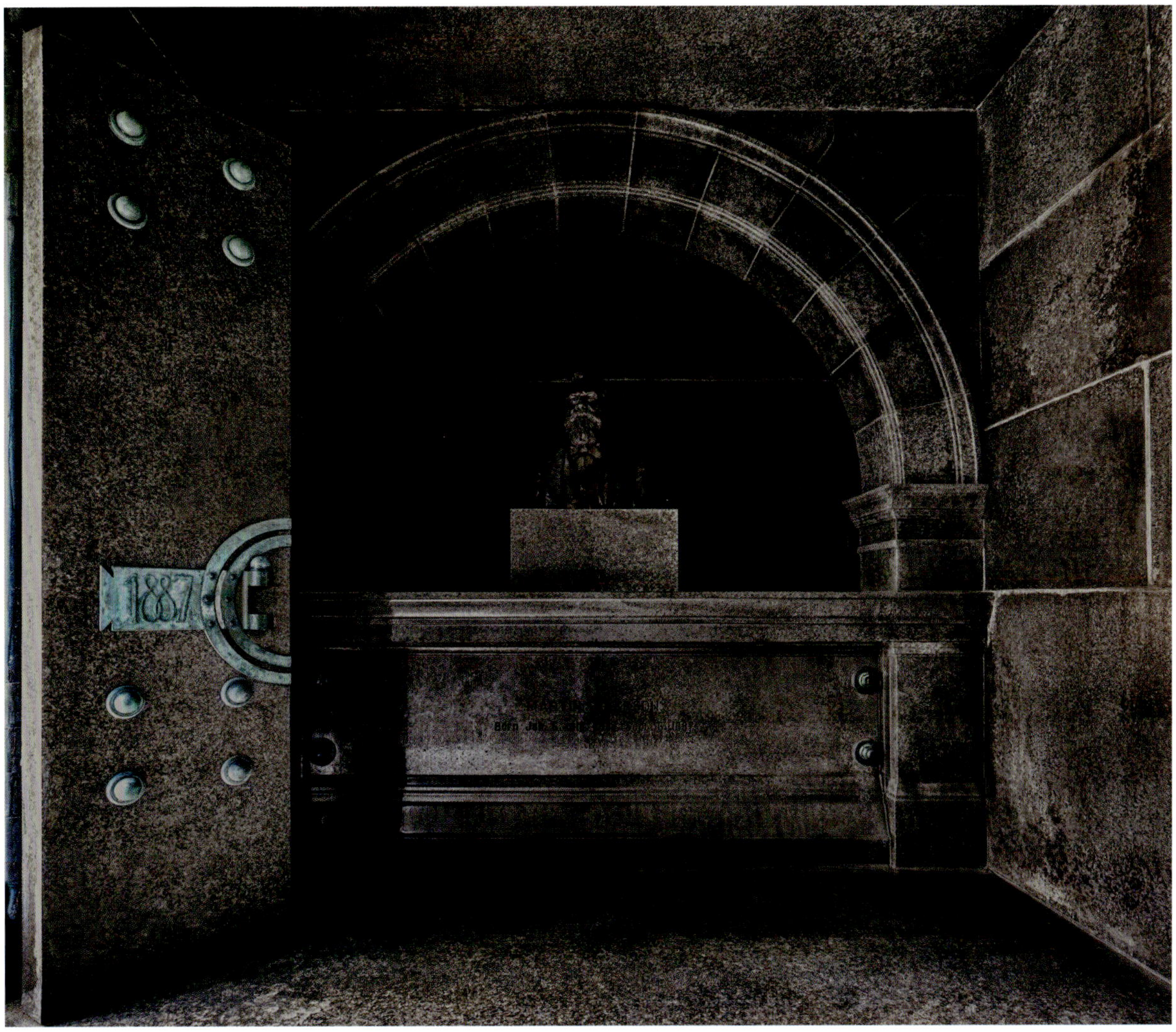
1887

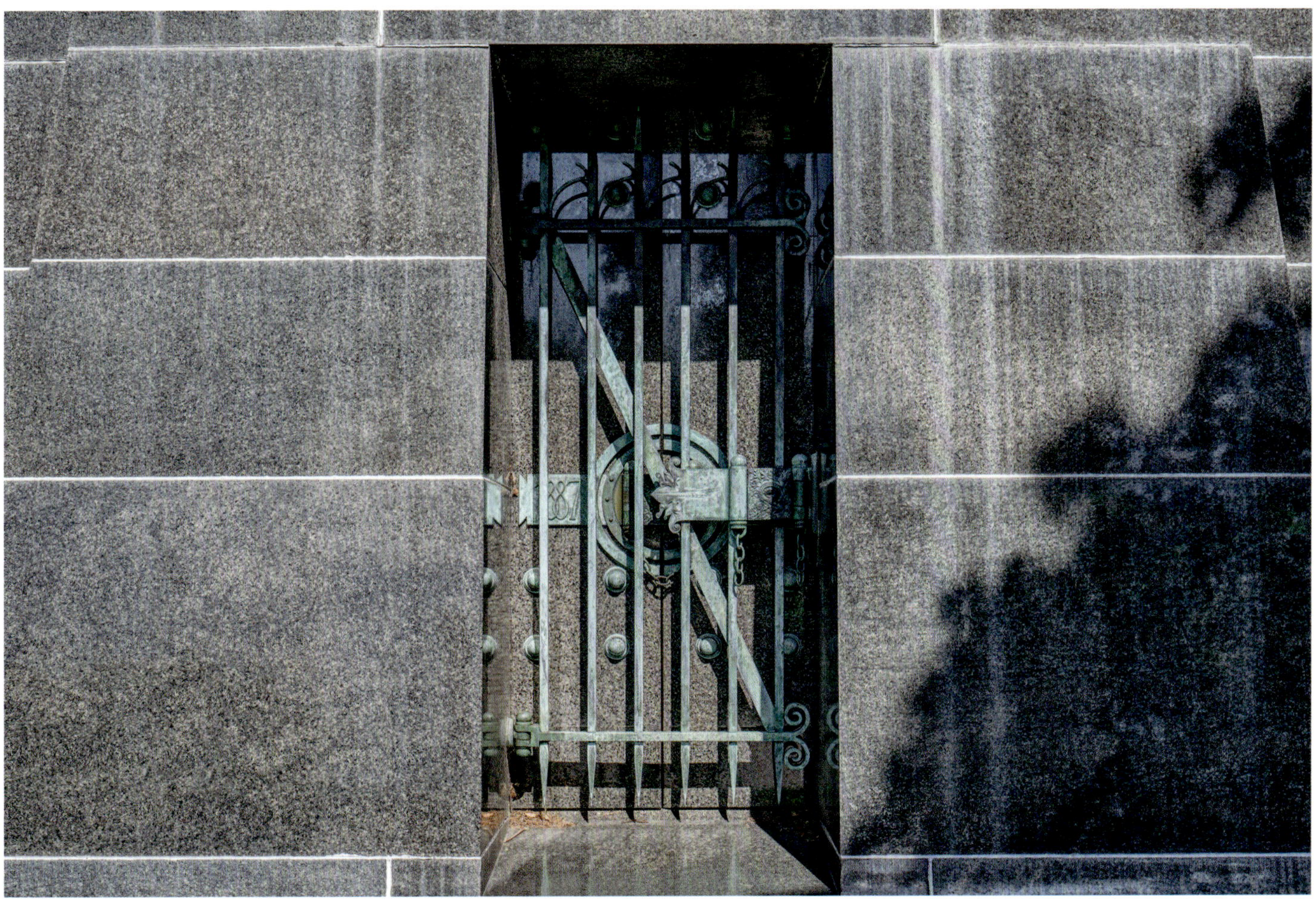

CARRIE ELIZA GETTY TOMB

1890–91, GRACELAND CEMETERY, CHICAGO

The tomb was commissioned by Henry Harrison Getty (1836–1919) for his wife Carrie Eliza (1843–1890). Getty was a partner with the Ryersons in the lumber business and almost certainly chose Adler & Sullivan after seeing the tomb they designed for his partner's family. Henry joined his wife in the tomb when he died (in Paris) in 1919; the couple's only child, Alice, was entombed in 1946.

One of Sullivan's greatest designs, the tomb is both simple and complex—simple in form but complex in decoration. Basically a cube with a slightly projecting cornice, it has an arched entry with elaborate bronze doors, protected by equally elaborate gates. The arch is repeated on the sides, here with bronze-framed lunette windows. The basic decoration is a repeated pattern of octagons, enclosing star bursts. The cornice is decorated with a typical Sullivan combination of geometric and foliate patterns. The interior is much simpler, expressed in white marble, with a white mosaic floor with black border.

Since the tomb was much admired from its beginning, plaster casts of the door were exhibited at the Art Institute and at the Musee des Arts Decoratifs in Paris. The tomb was declared a Chicago Landmark in 1971 and was added to the National Register of Historic Places in 1974.

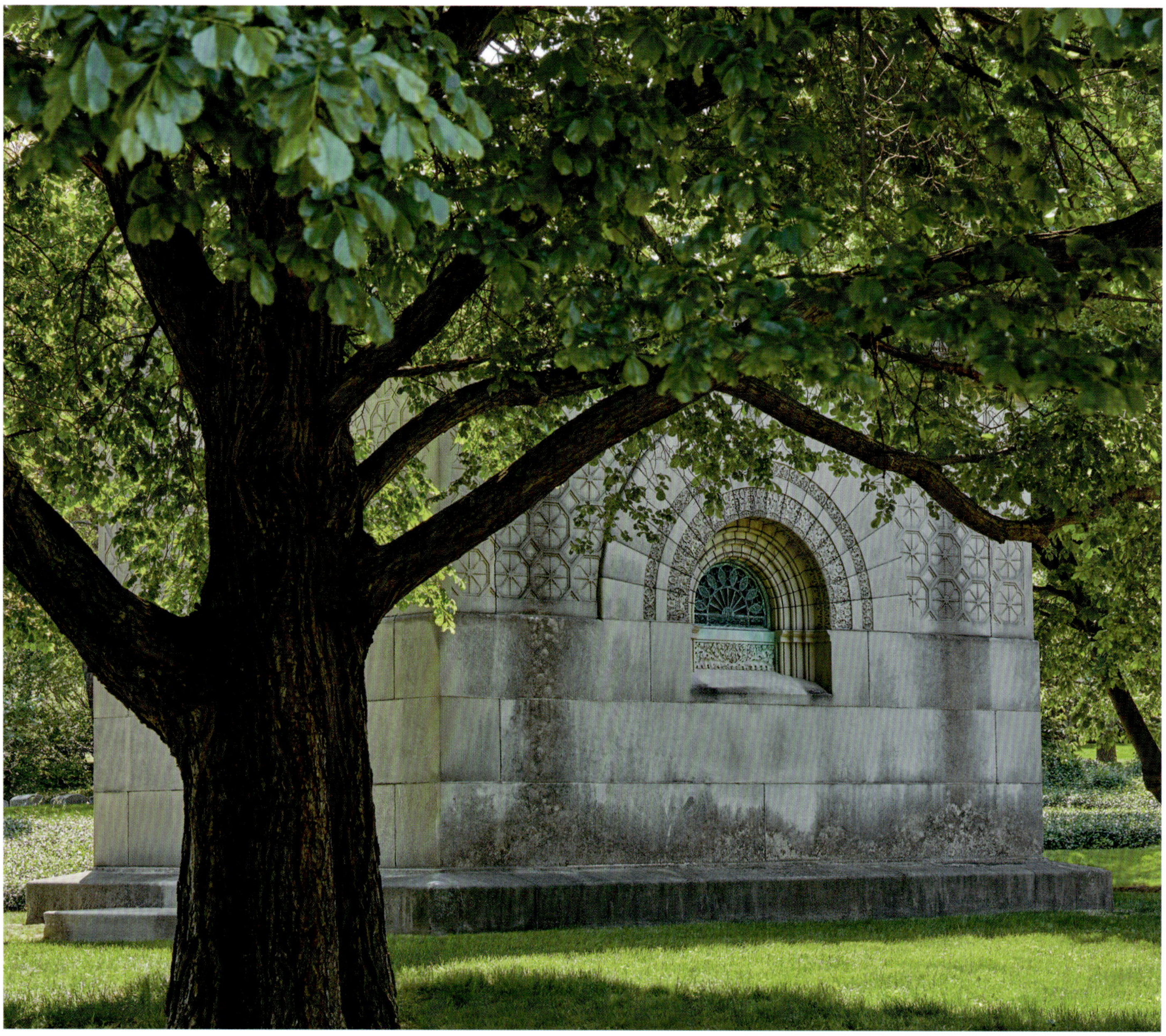

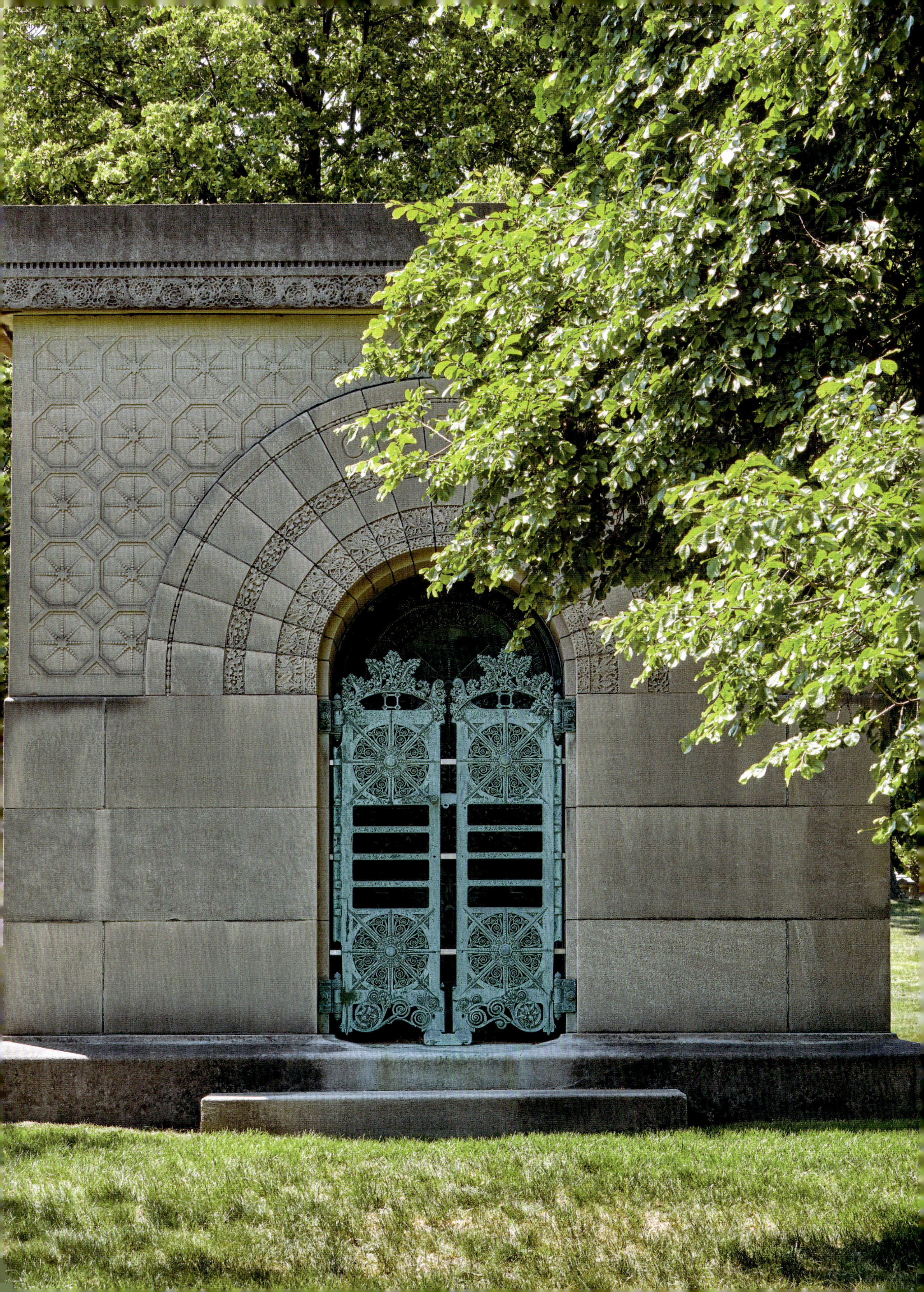

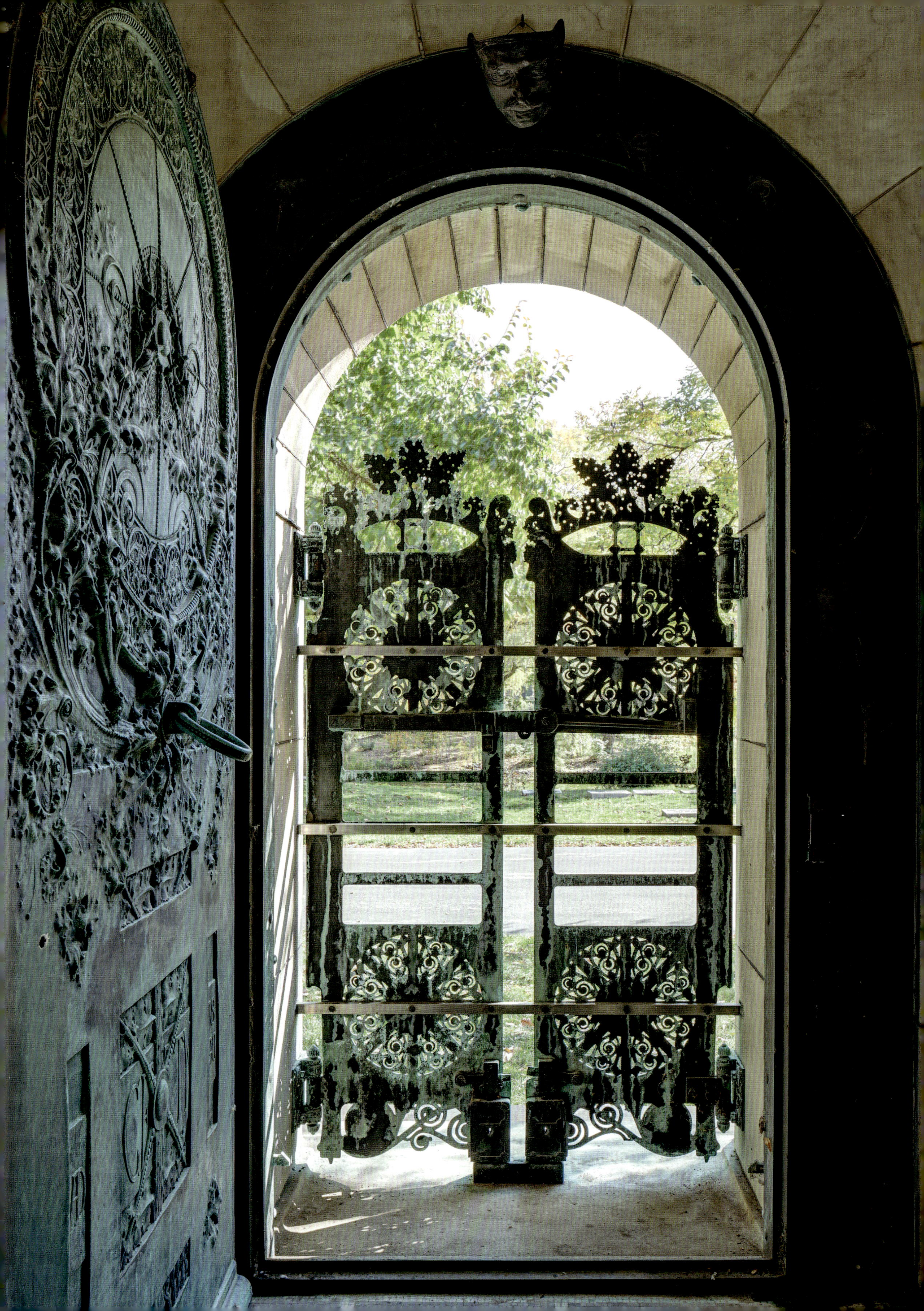

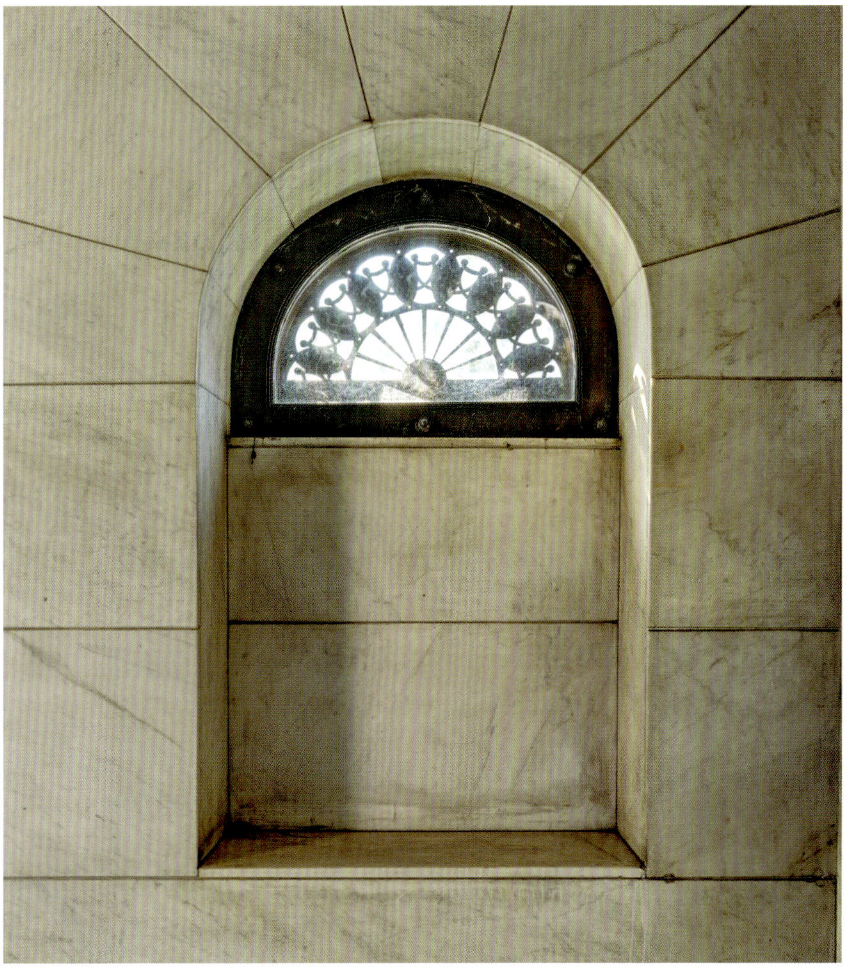

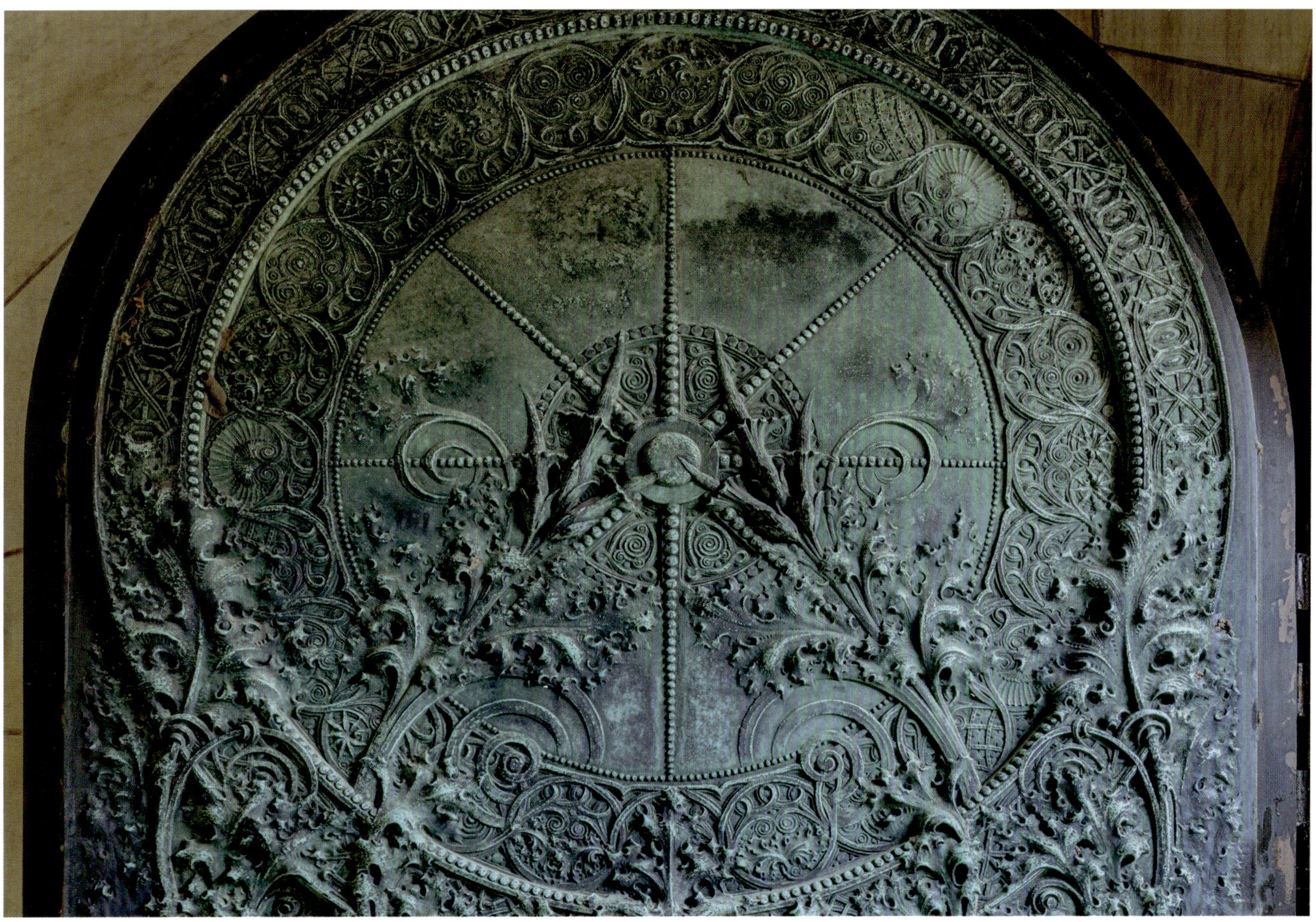

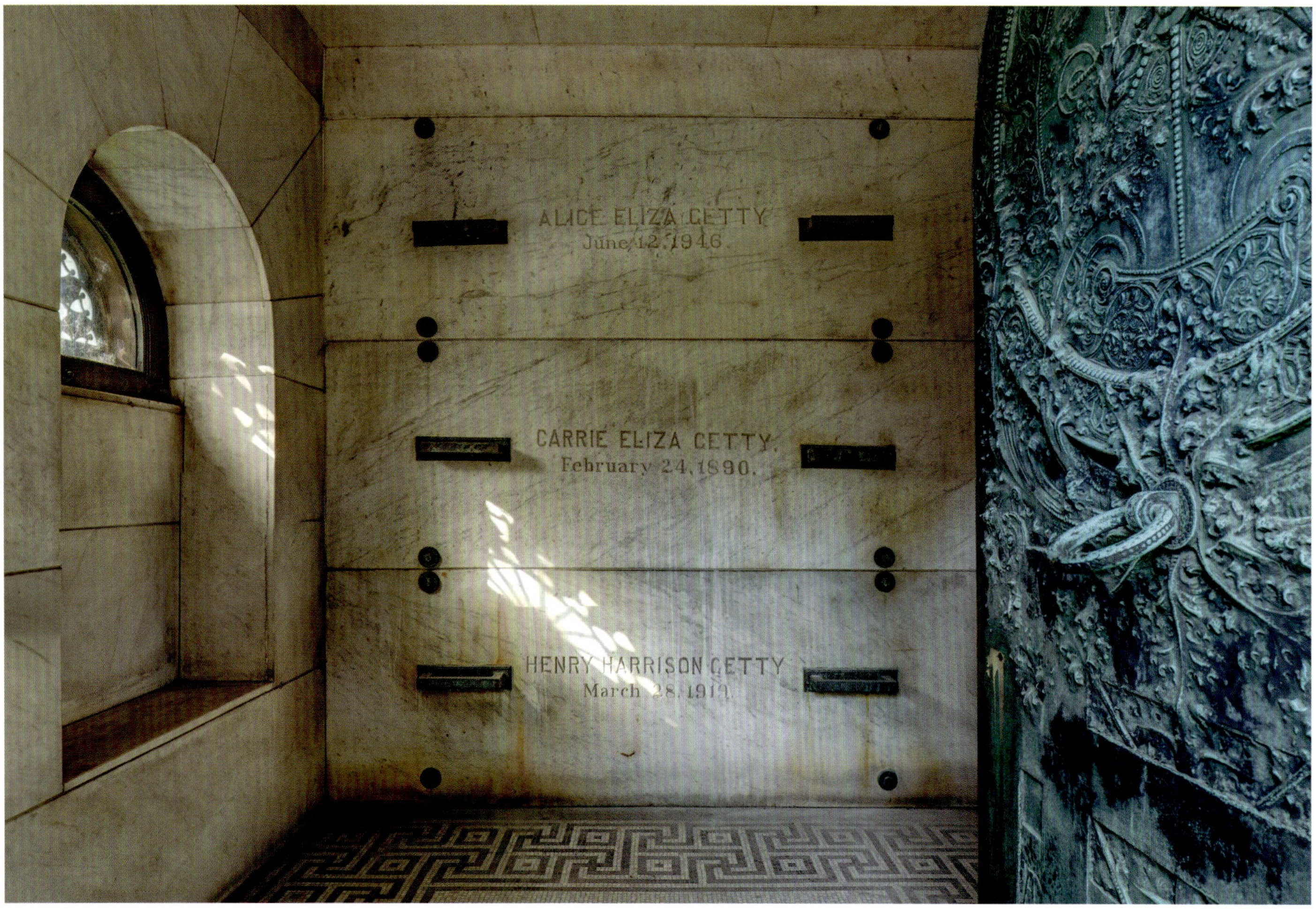
ALICE ELIZA GETTY
June 12, 1946
CARRIE ELIZA GETTY
February 24, 1890.
HENRY HARRISON GETTY
March 28, 1919

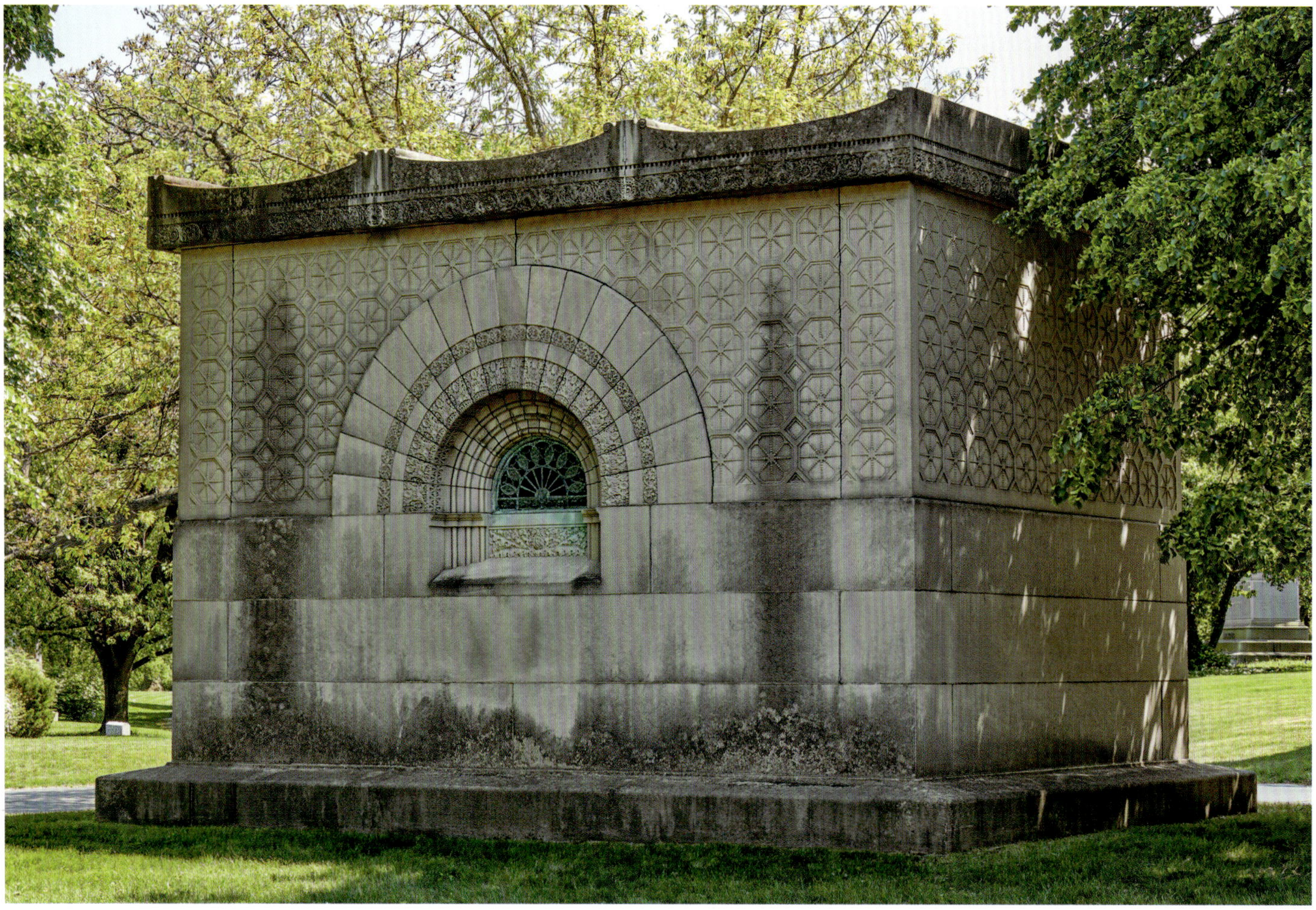

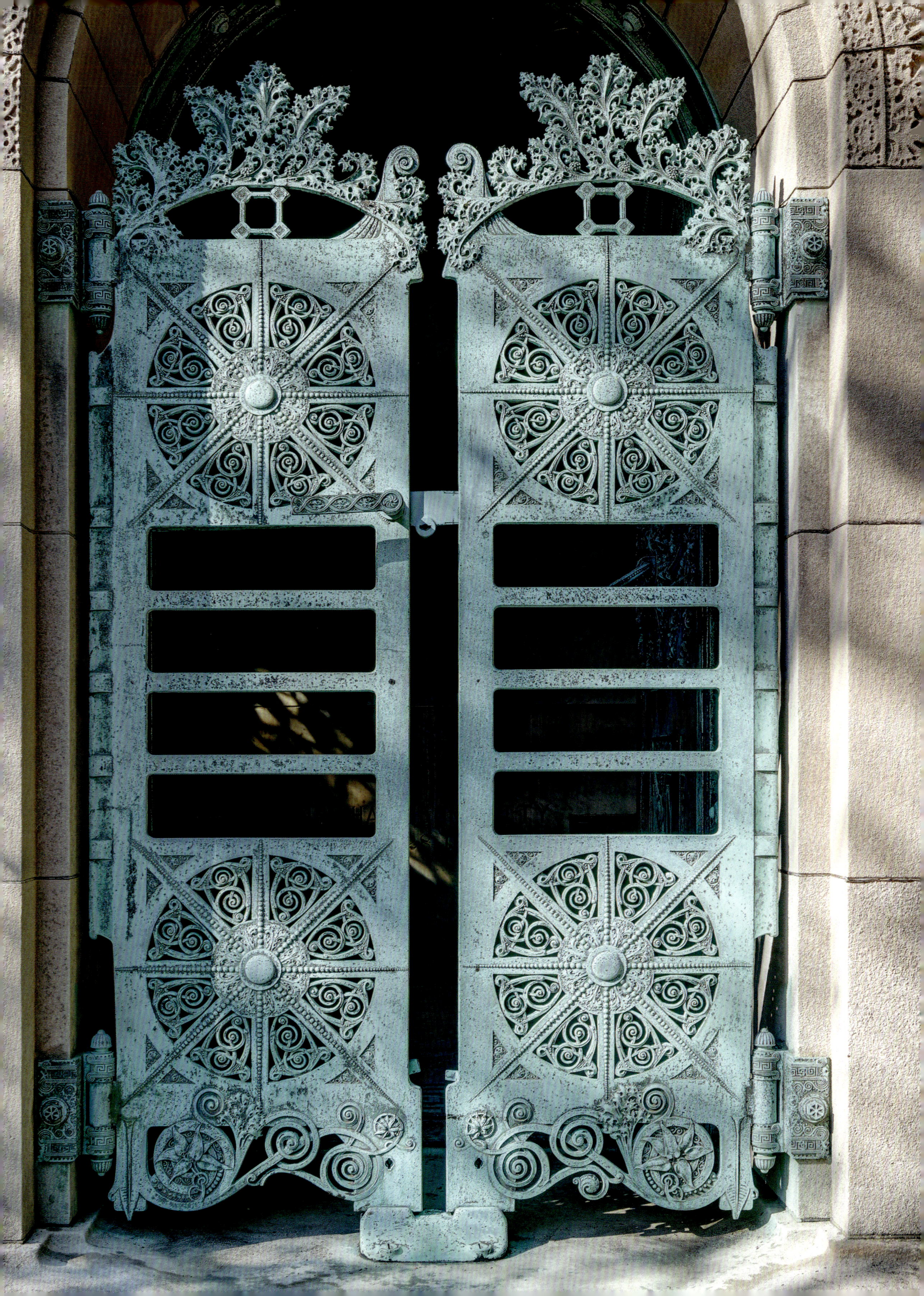

WAINWRIGHT TOMB

1892–93, ST. LOUIS, MISSOURI

Having hired Adler & Sullivan to design his groundbreaking office building, Ellis Wainwright also chose the firm to design a tomb for his wife Charlotte, who died tragically young at thirty-four before the building was completed. The basic shape of the Wainwright Tomb, like the Getty Tomb, is a cube, consisting of Bedford limestone in this case, but Sullivan had added a dome and a porch whose parapets include built-in benches. "All the walls are decorated outside," as described by Robert Twombly in his biography of Sullivan, "by bands of rich, exquisite ornament along the top, down the corners to the parapet in the front and the sills on the sides, then across the facades to rise over the doors and windows, returning on itself in an endless chain."

The bronze doors and protective grill have yet another ornamental band. Side windows are also protected by bronze grills. Inside are rich mosaics, including a ceiling covered with angels, with a gold star at the peak. The floor has two burial slabs, the original one for Charlotte and the other for Ellis, added when he died in 1924. Locals have often called it the St. Louis Taj Mahal. It was added to the National Register of Historic Places in 1970.

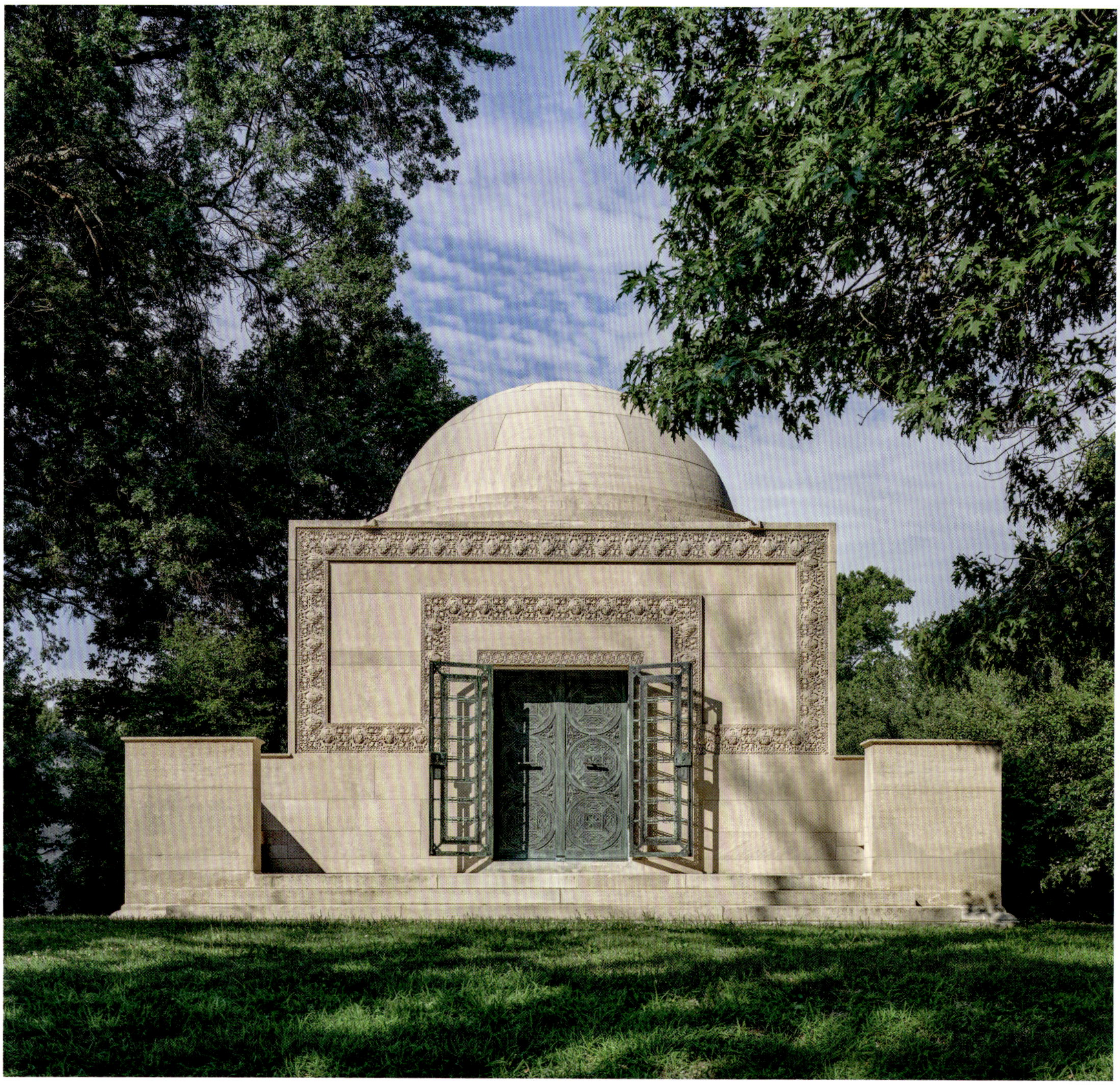

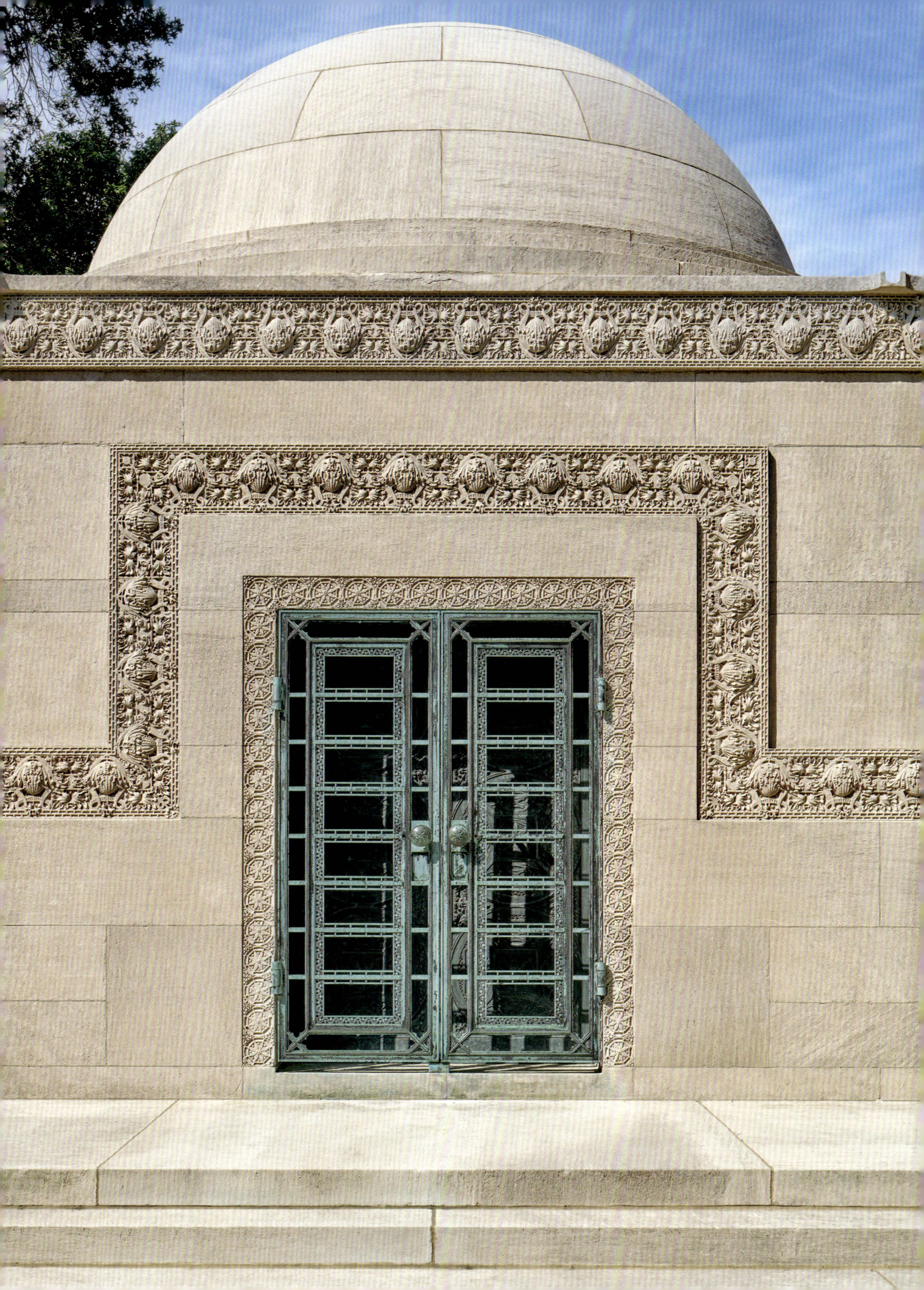

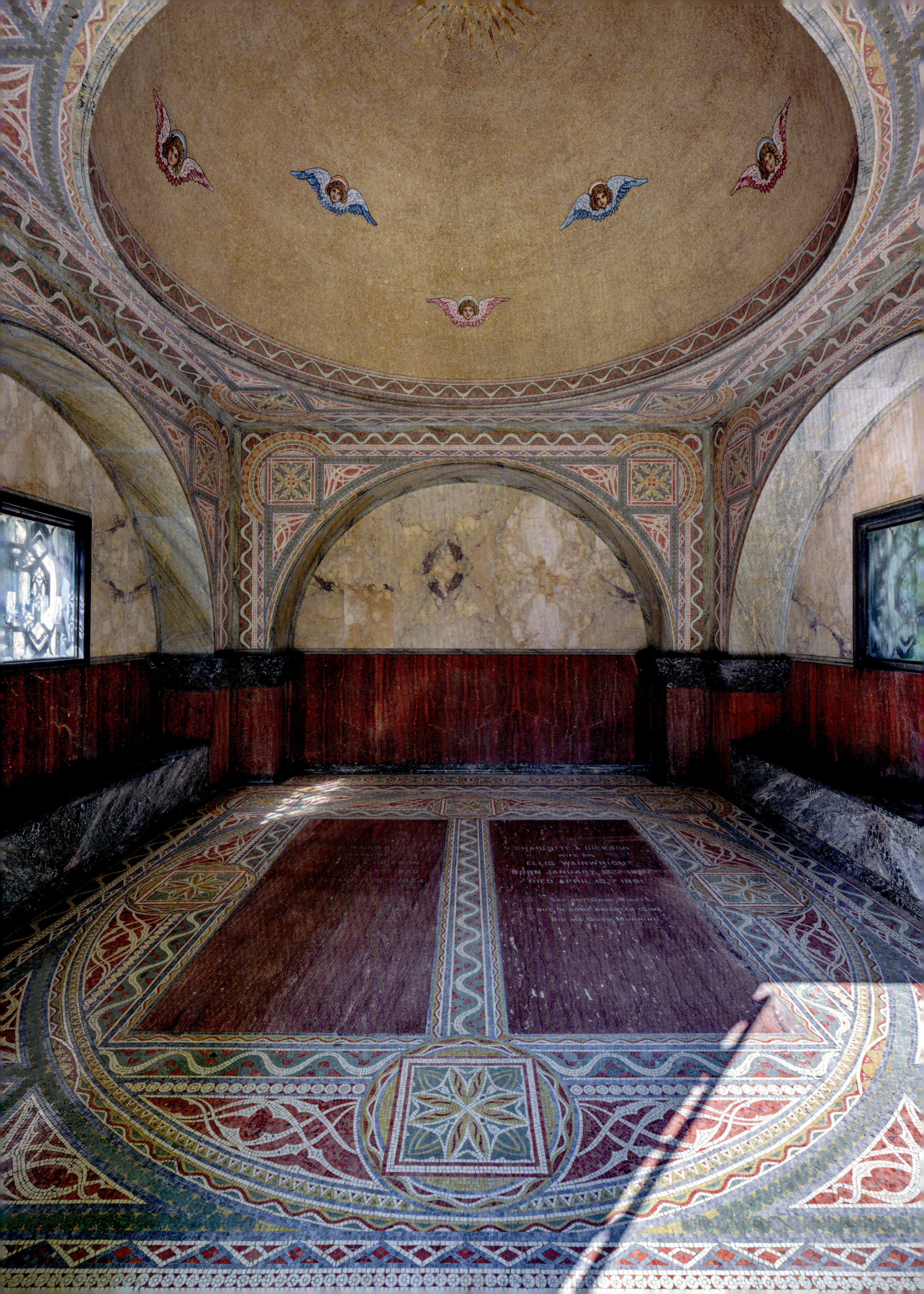
CHARLOTTE A DICKSON
WIFE OF
ELLIS WAINWRIGHT
DIED APRIL 15TH 1891
SAY NOT GOOD NIGHT
BUT IN SOME BRIGHTER CLIME
BID ME GOOD MORNING

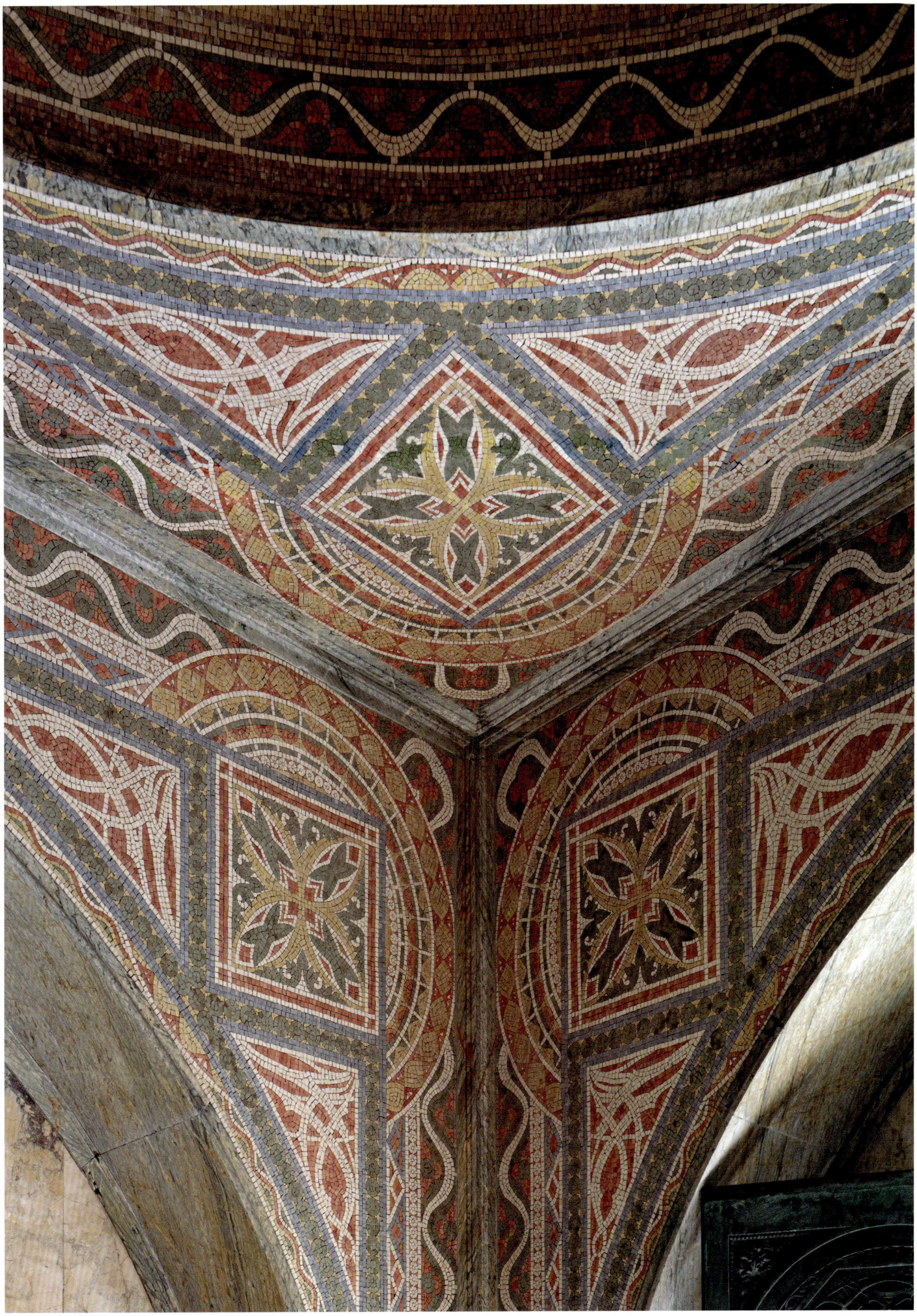

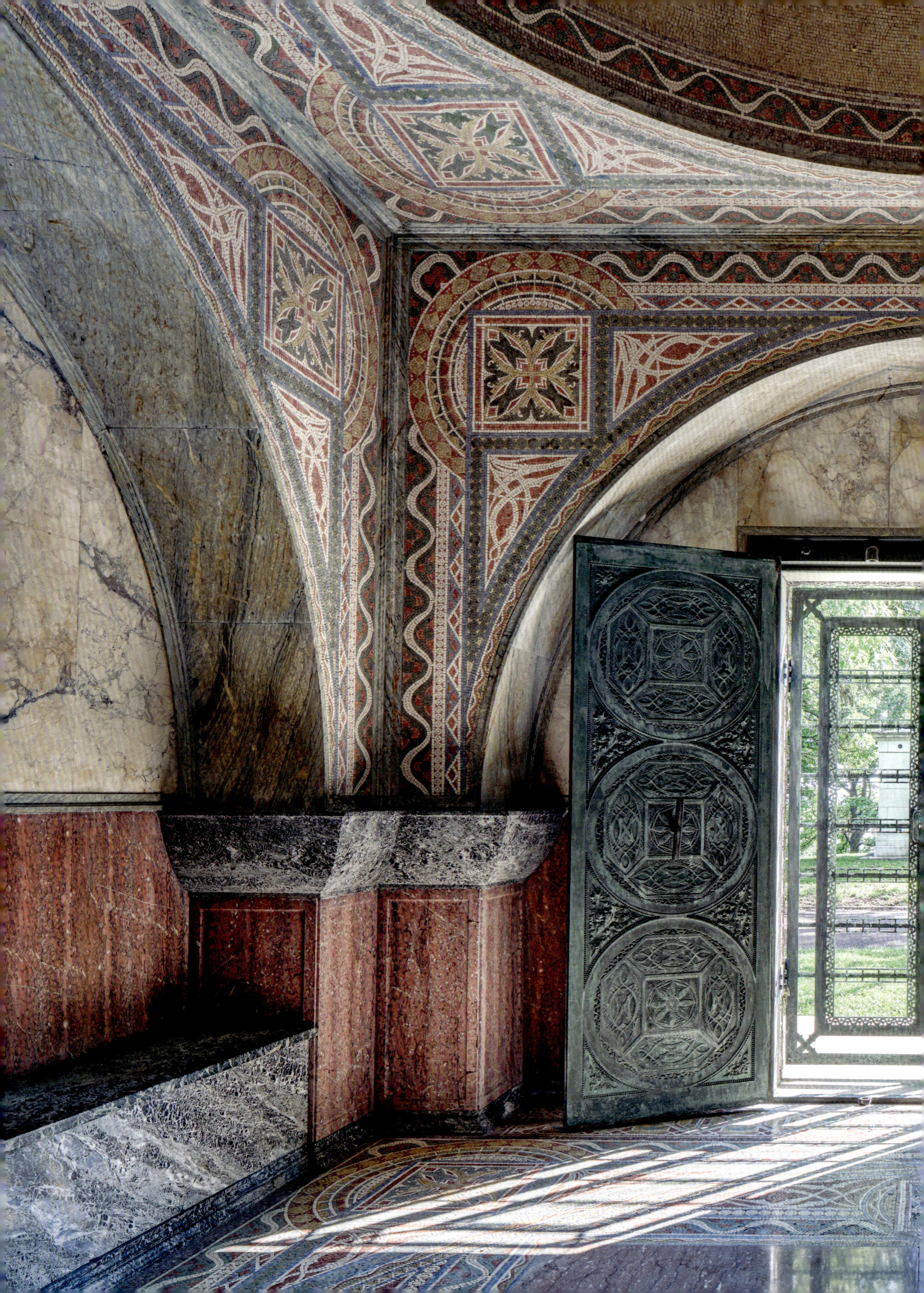

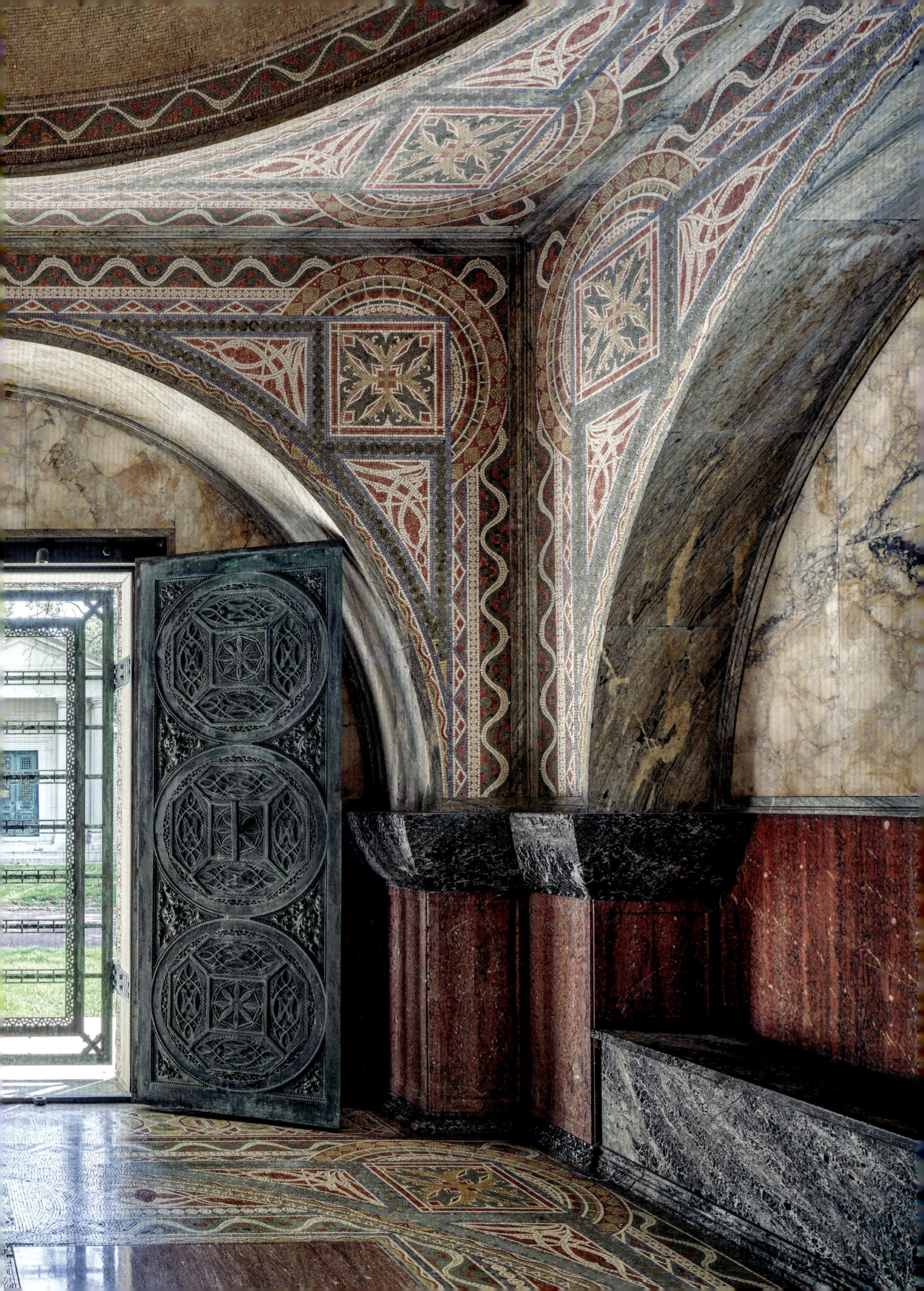

SCHLESINGER & MAYER STORE

1897–1903, CHICAGO

Known as Carson, Pirie, Scott and Company for most of its life, Sullivan's masterpiece of retail design was originally designed and built in stages for retailers Schlesinger & Mayer. Financial difficulties related to the construction of the store forced its sale in 1904 to former Marshall Field's executive Harry G. Selfridge, who sold it to Carsons before moving to London to build and open the famous department store under his own name.

The building, as we see it today, was completed by 1903, with the exception of the last three bays on State Street, which were added in 1961 by Holabird & Root. The stunning corner pavilion and other ironwork were worked out by Sullivan's assistant, George Grant Elmslie, and executed by the Winslow Brothers, who fabricated ornamental iron for many of Chicago's buildings. The building frames large display windows that were originally topped with Luxfer Prism panels, since removed. The rest of the building is clad in white terra cotta panels.

To bring maximum natural light to the selling floors, Sullivan designed oversize so-called Chicago windows for the upper floors, which feature a fixed center pane, flanked by double-hung sashes. According to architectural historian Carl Condit, "... The elevations above the base have a cleanliness and precision so nearly absolute that the most minute change in proportions could be detected. There is not better revelation of the architecture of modern industry and commerce."

In 1979, John Vinci's firm restored the terra cotta, the store fronts, and corner entry. In 2003, Harboe Architects began to restore the top floor and cornice; this and other work continued after Carsons closed the store in 2007. Now known as the Sullivan Center to honor its architect, it survives as a mixed-use building, with retail on the first floor and offices above. It was added to the National Register of Historic Places in 1970 and was declared a Chicago Landmark the same year. It was designated a National Historic Landmark in 1975.

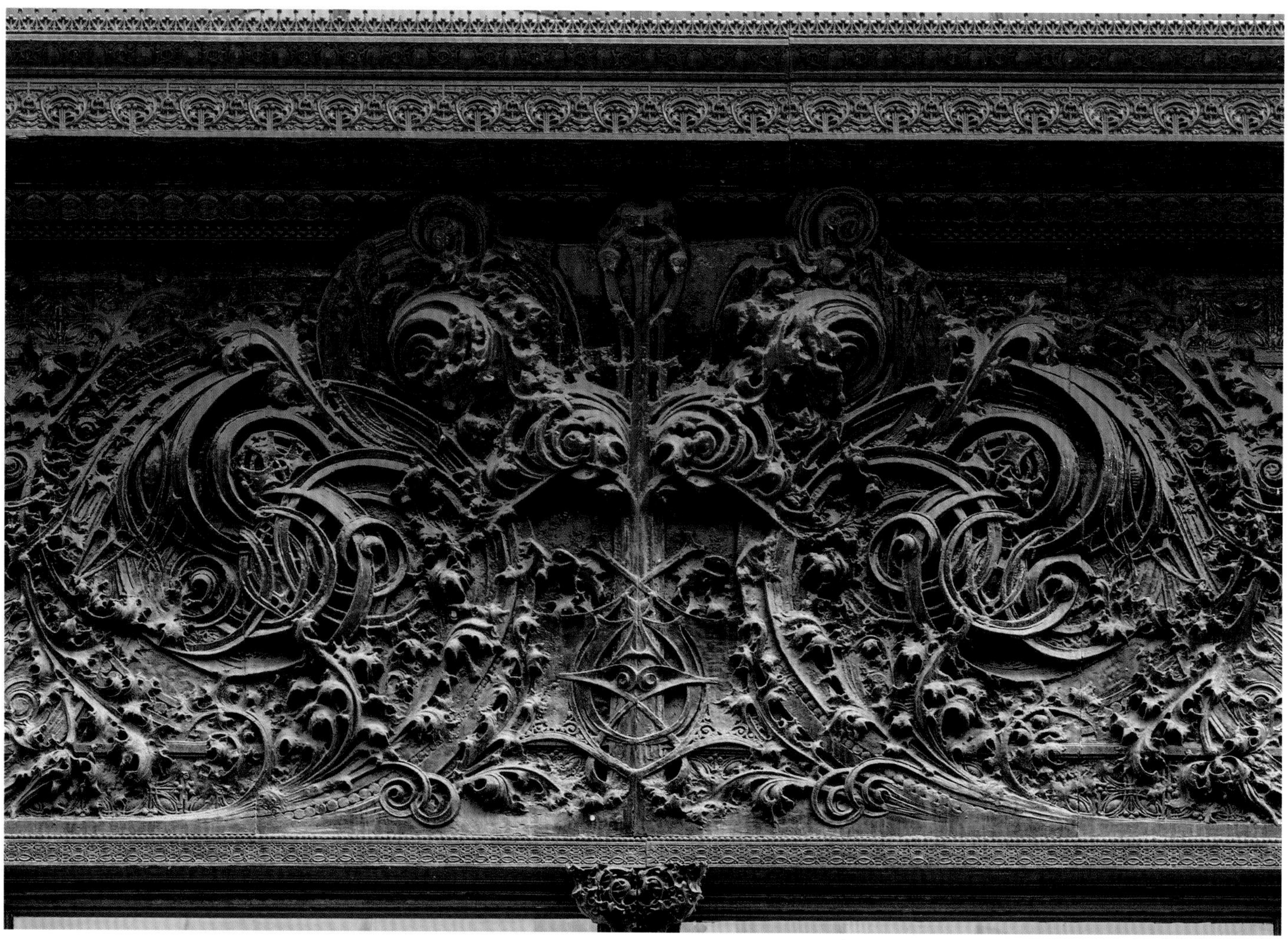

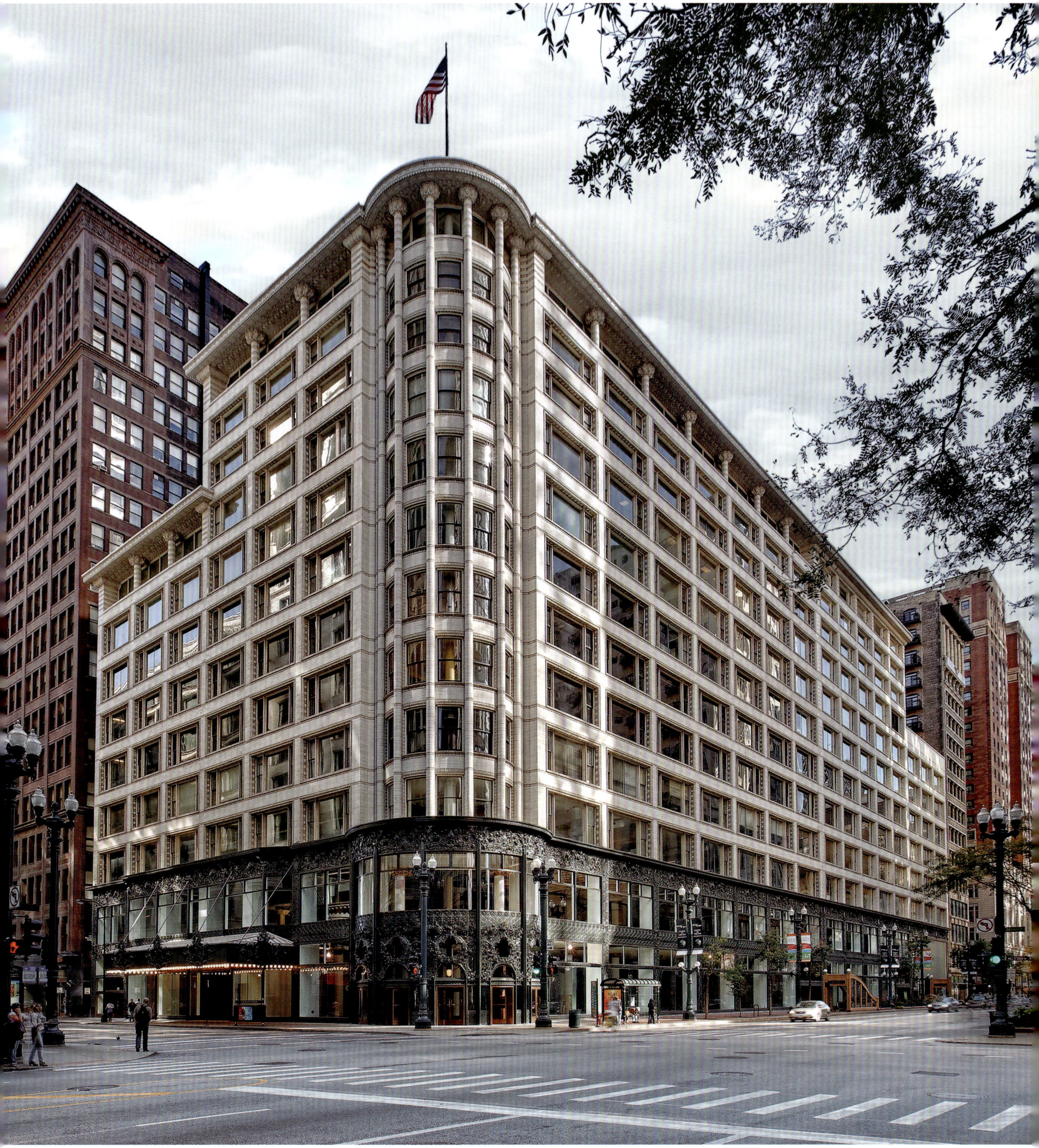

Sullivan's designs for the stunning ornamental ironwork were developed by his primary assistant, George Grant Elmslie; and executed by the Winslow Brothers Company.

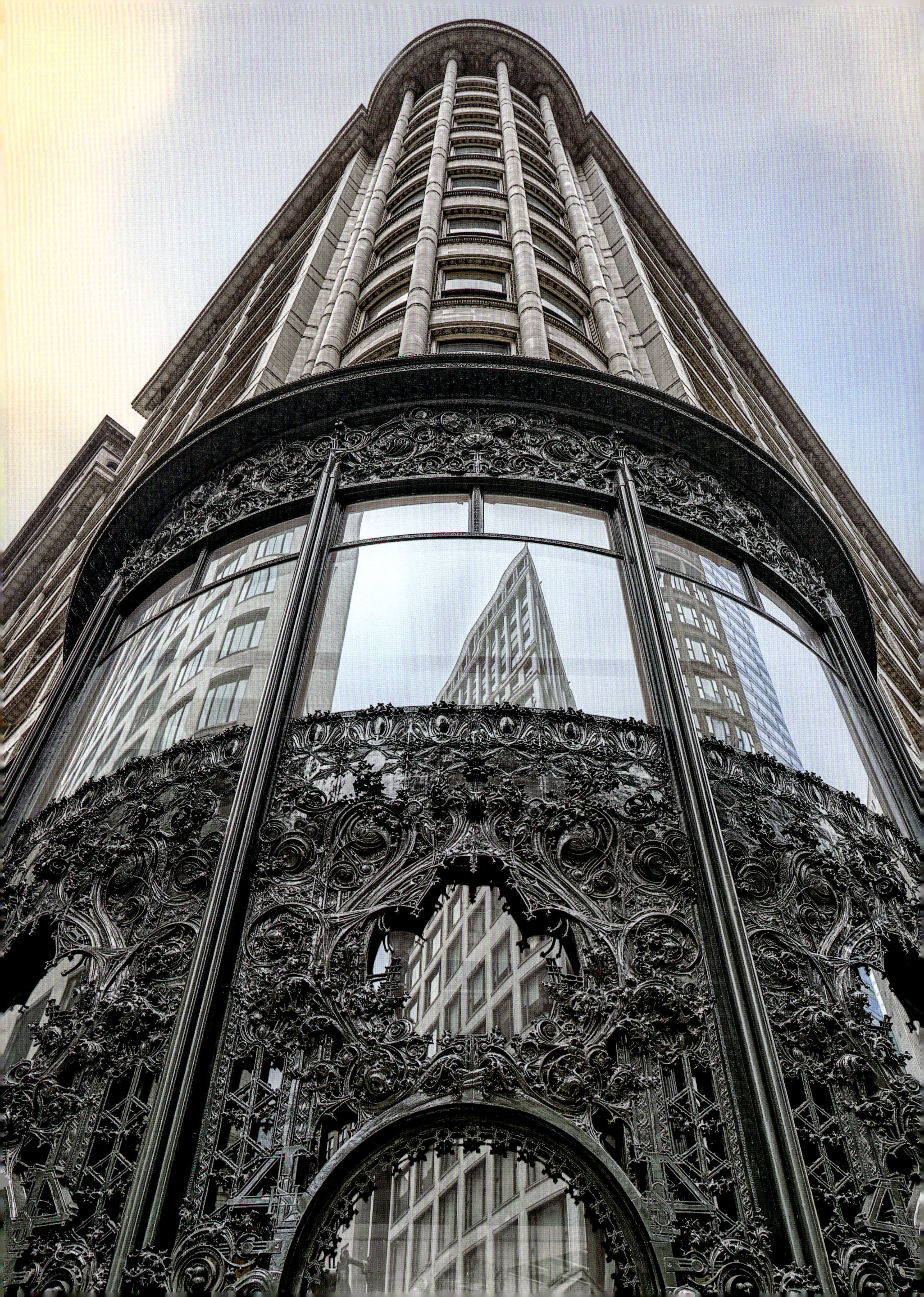

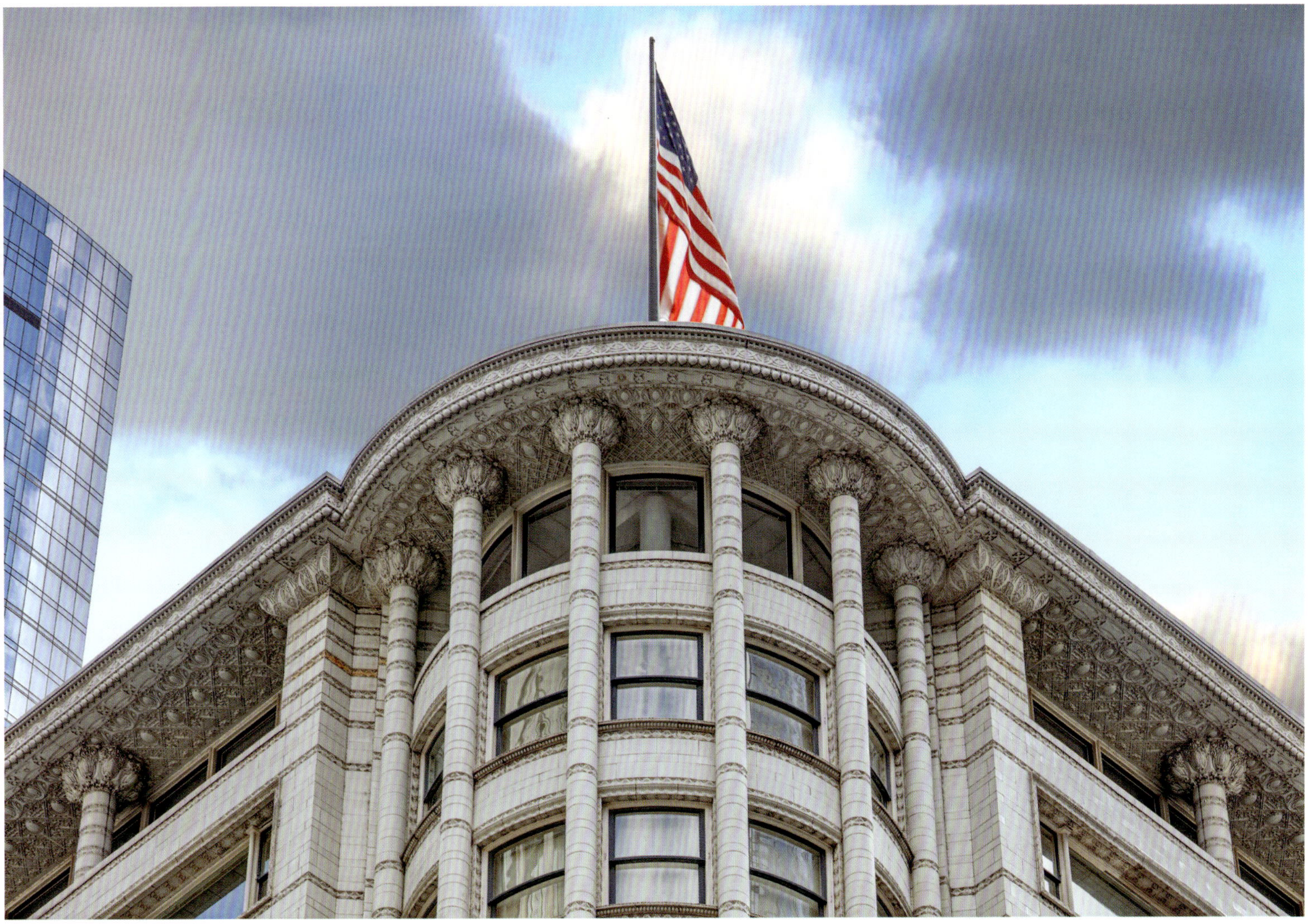

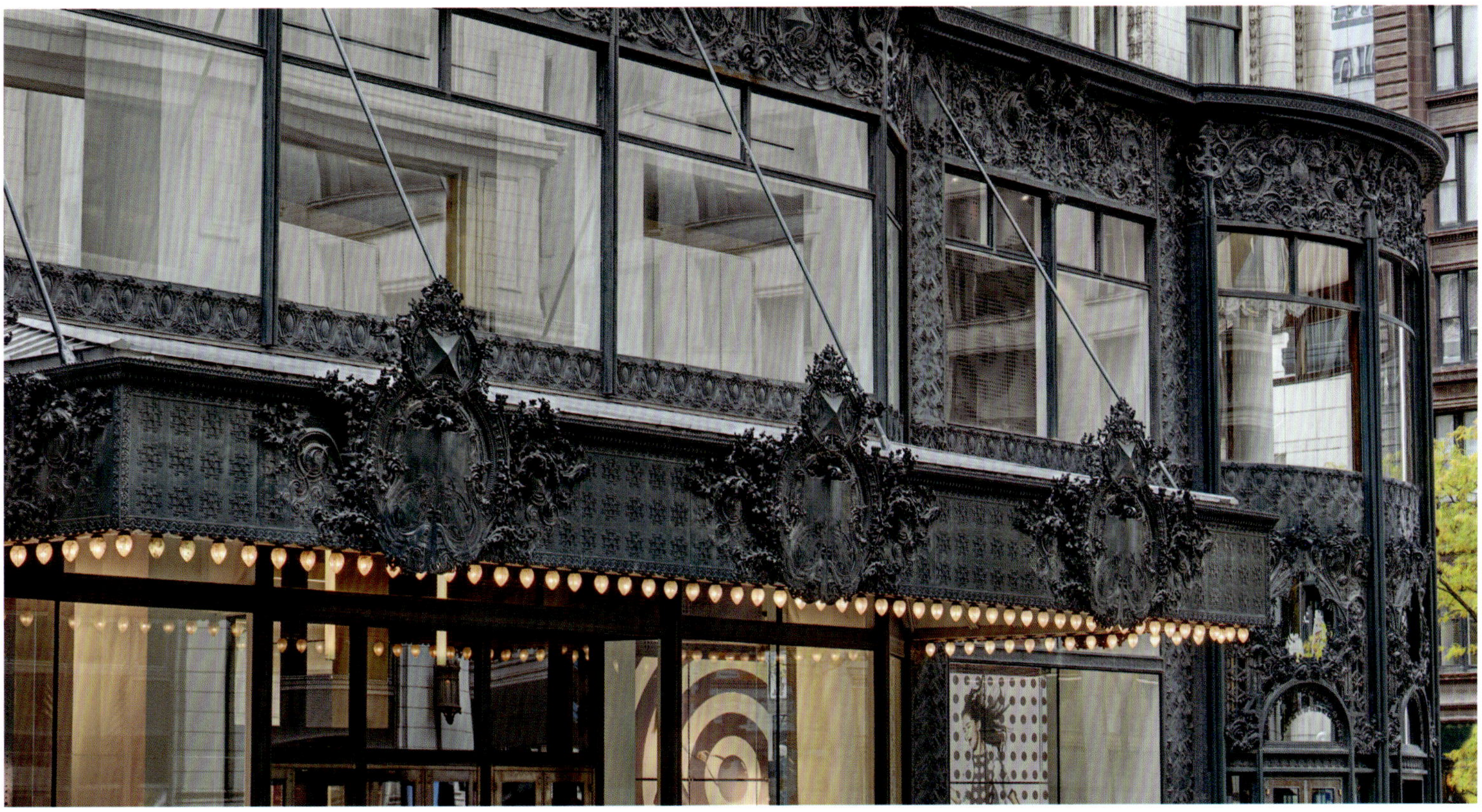

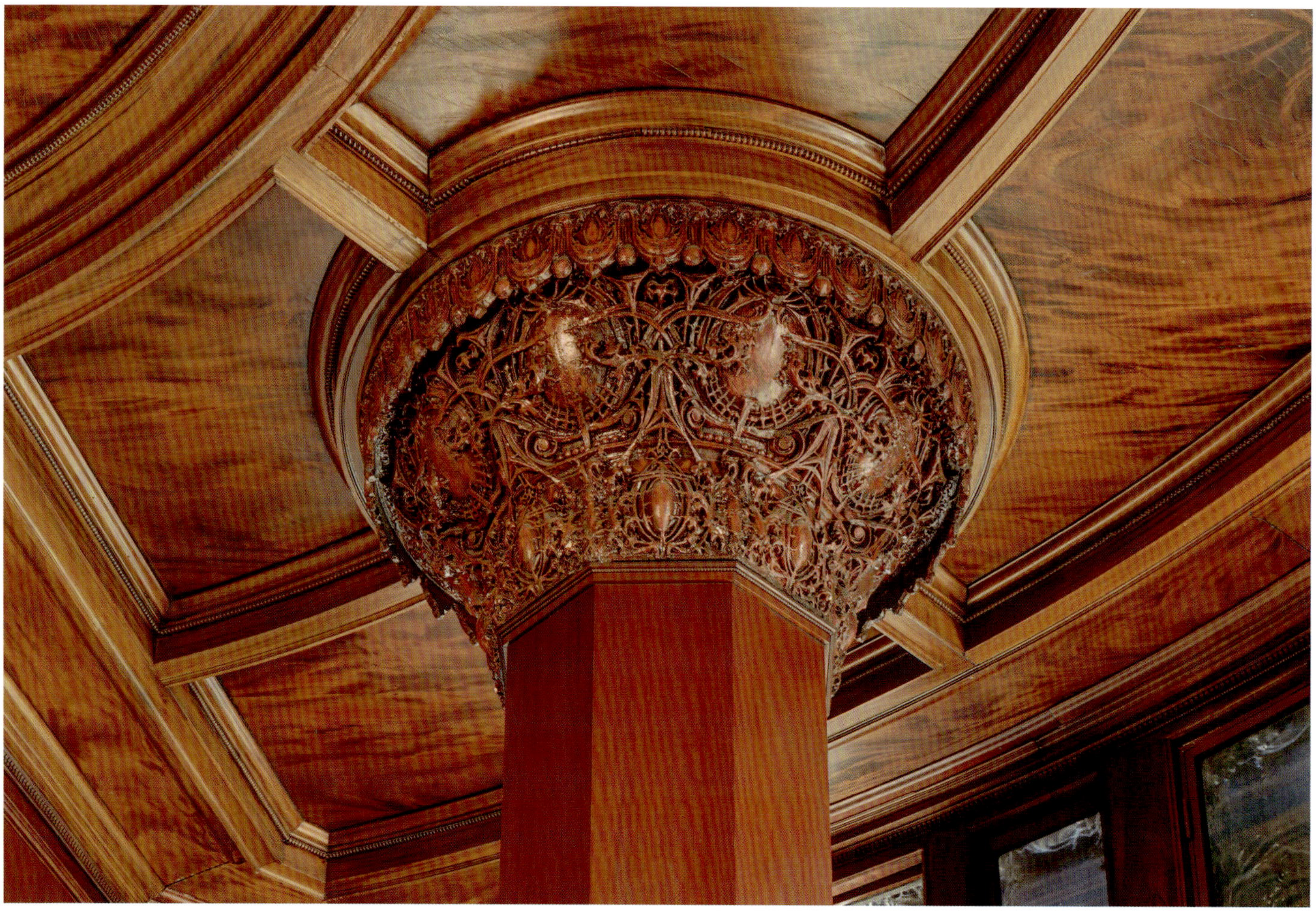

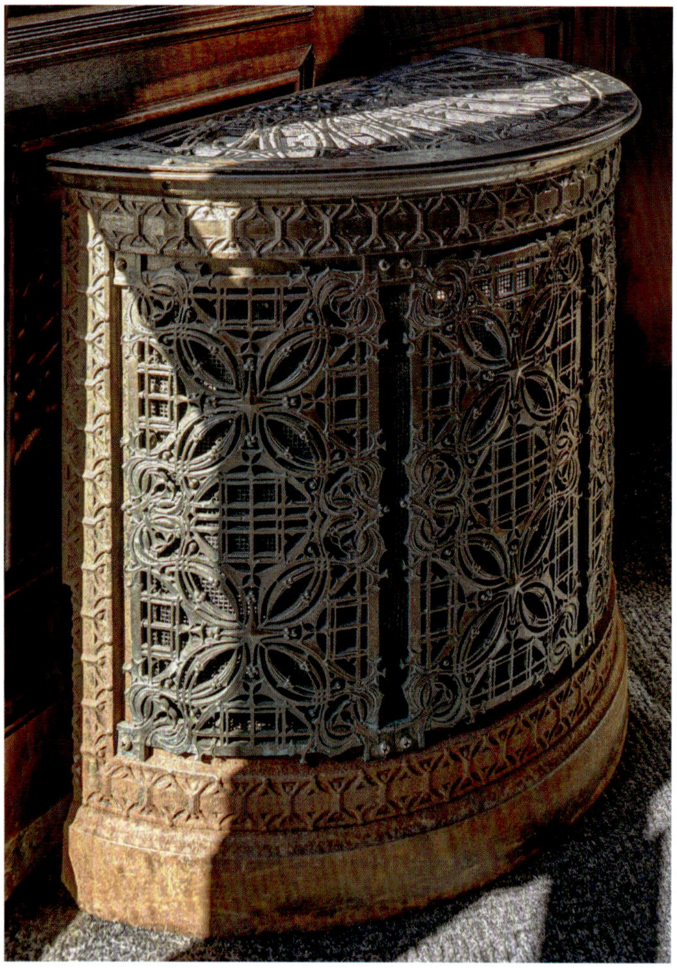

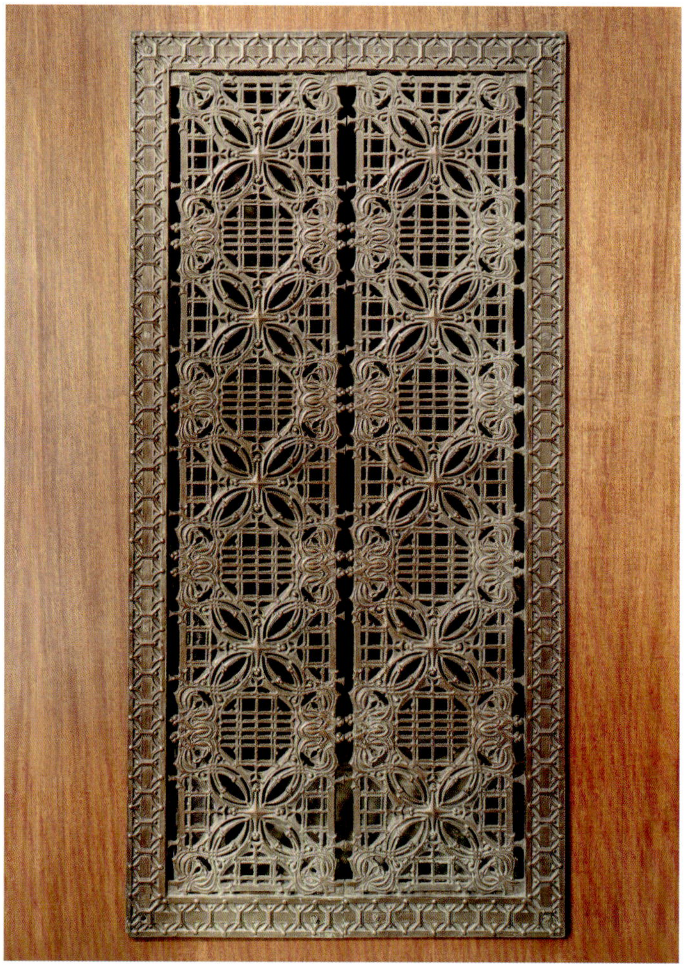

While much of it was lost during later "remodelings", fine wood and metal work were also interior features of the store.

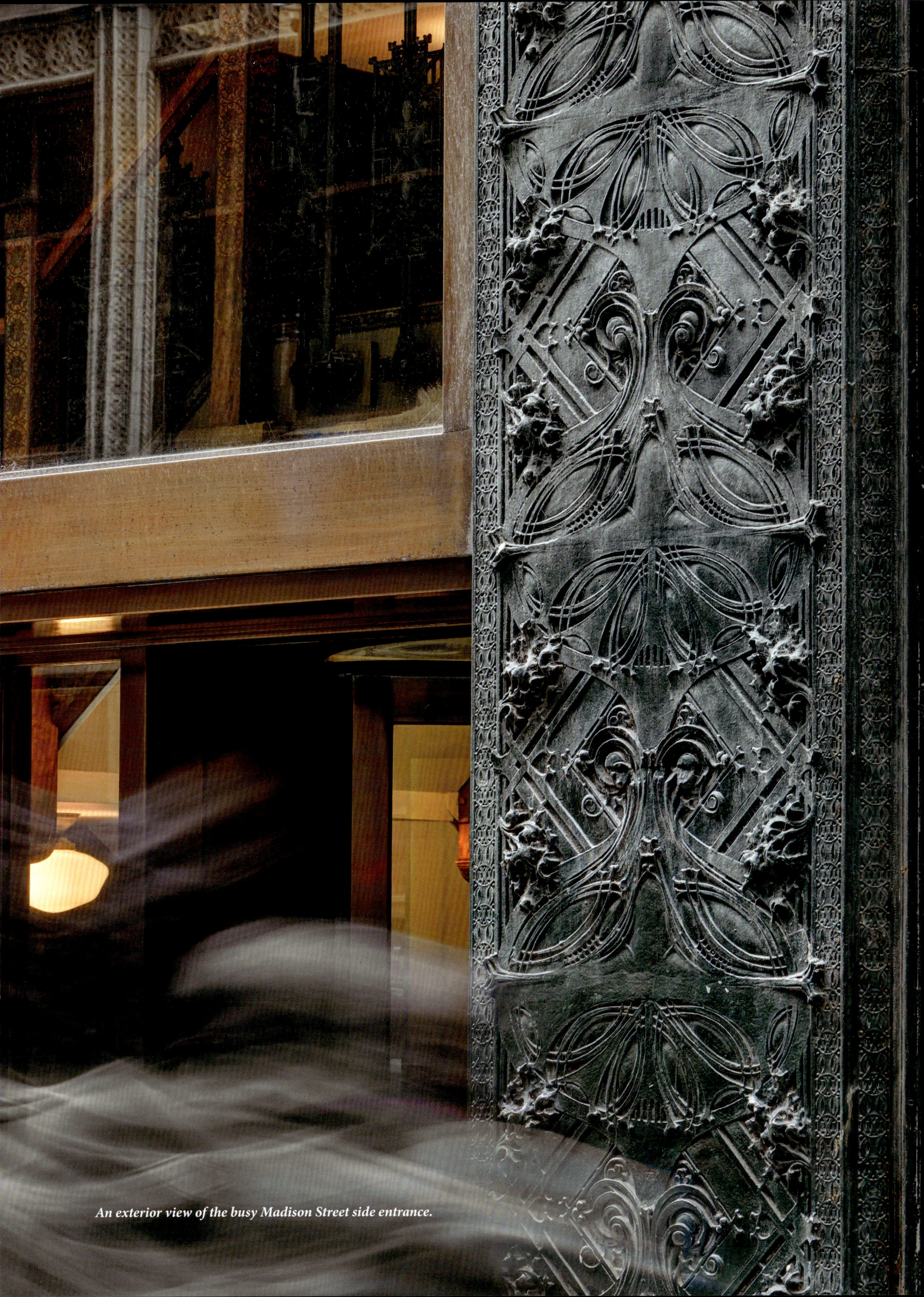

An exterior view of the busy Madison Street side entrance.

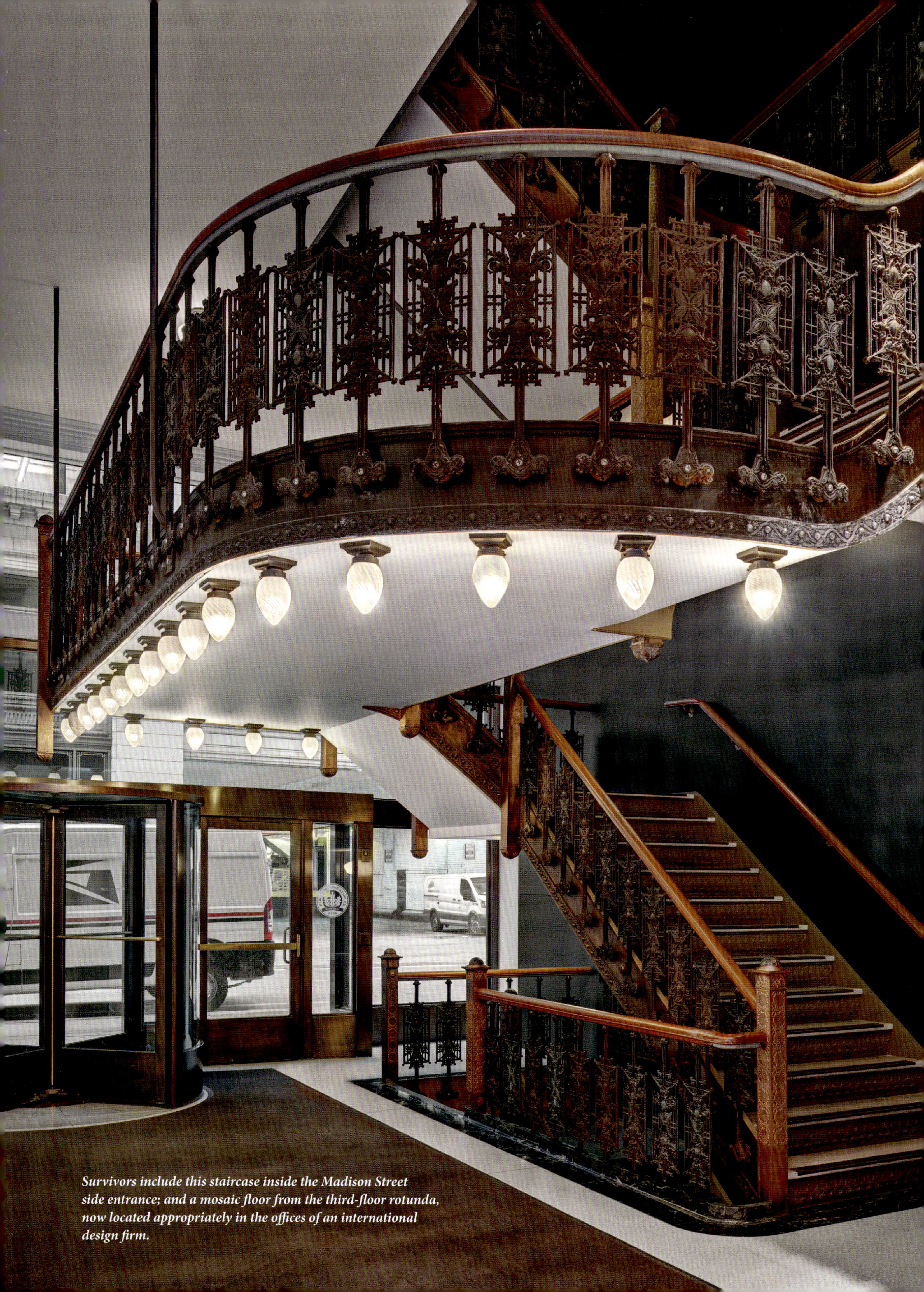

Survivors include this staircase inside the Madison Street side entrance; and a mosaic floor from the third-floor rotunda, now located appropriately in the offices of an international design firm.

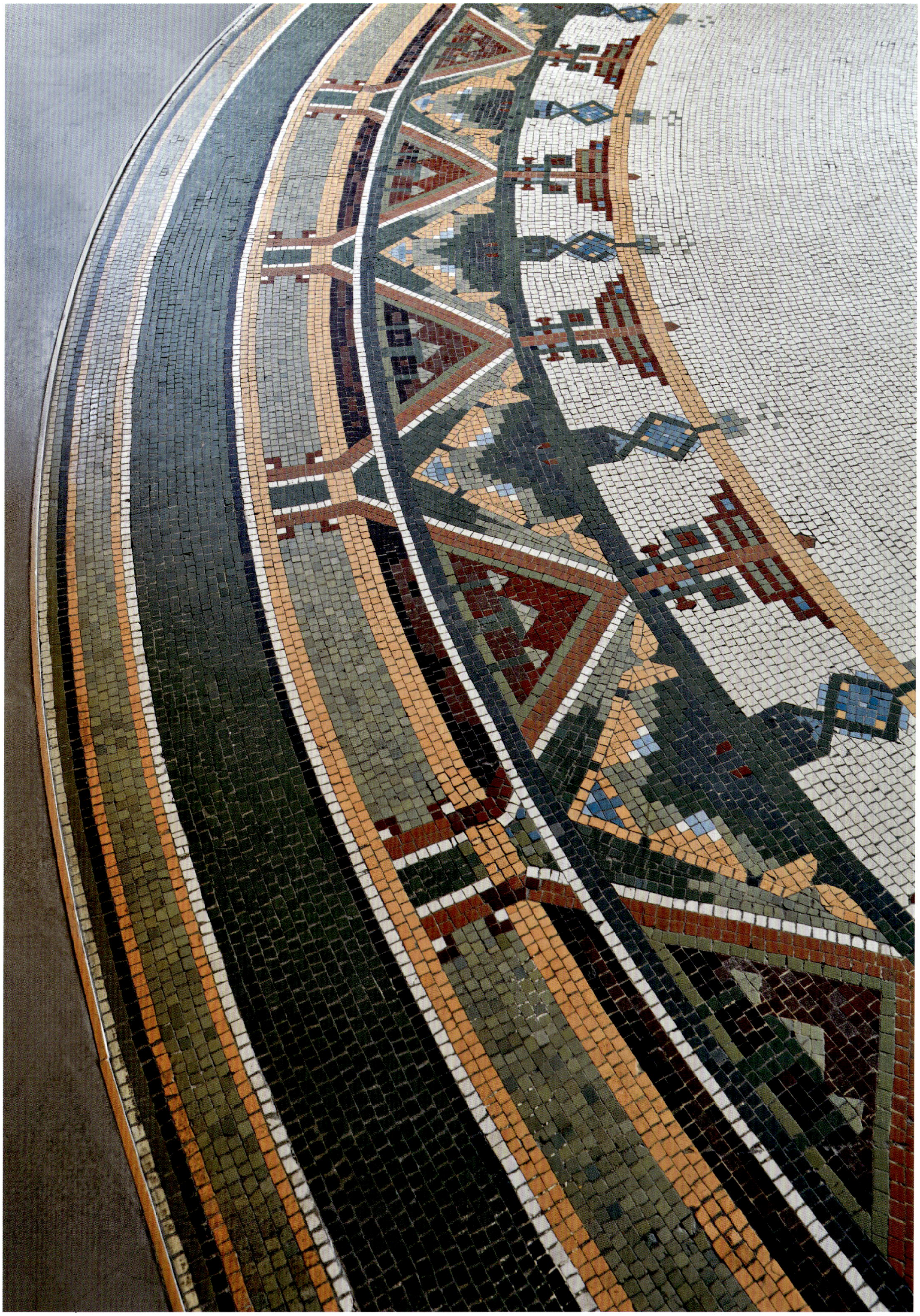

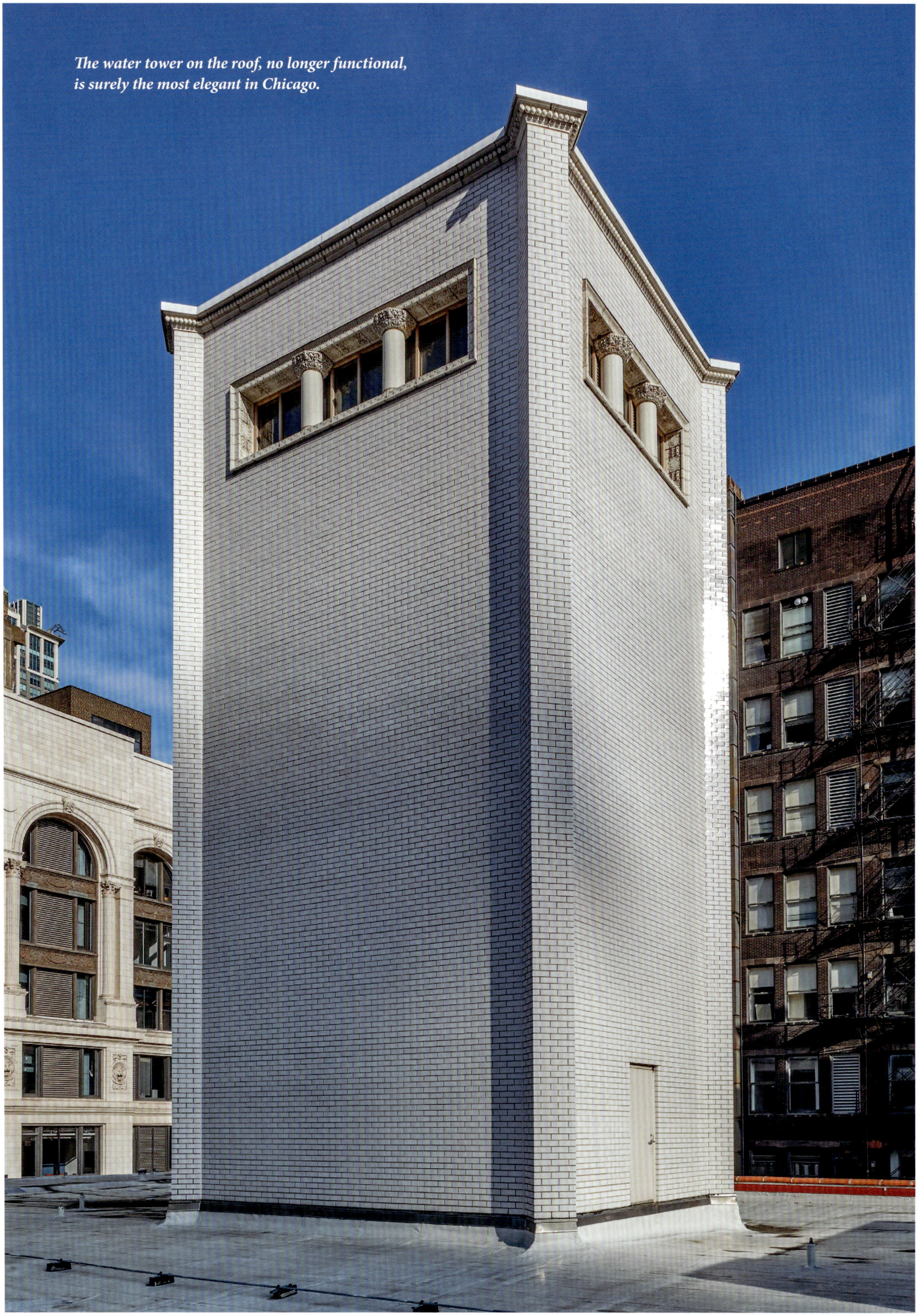

The water tower on the roof, no longer functional, is surely the most elegant in Chicago.

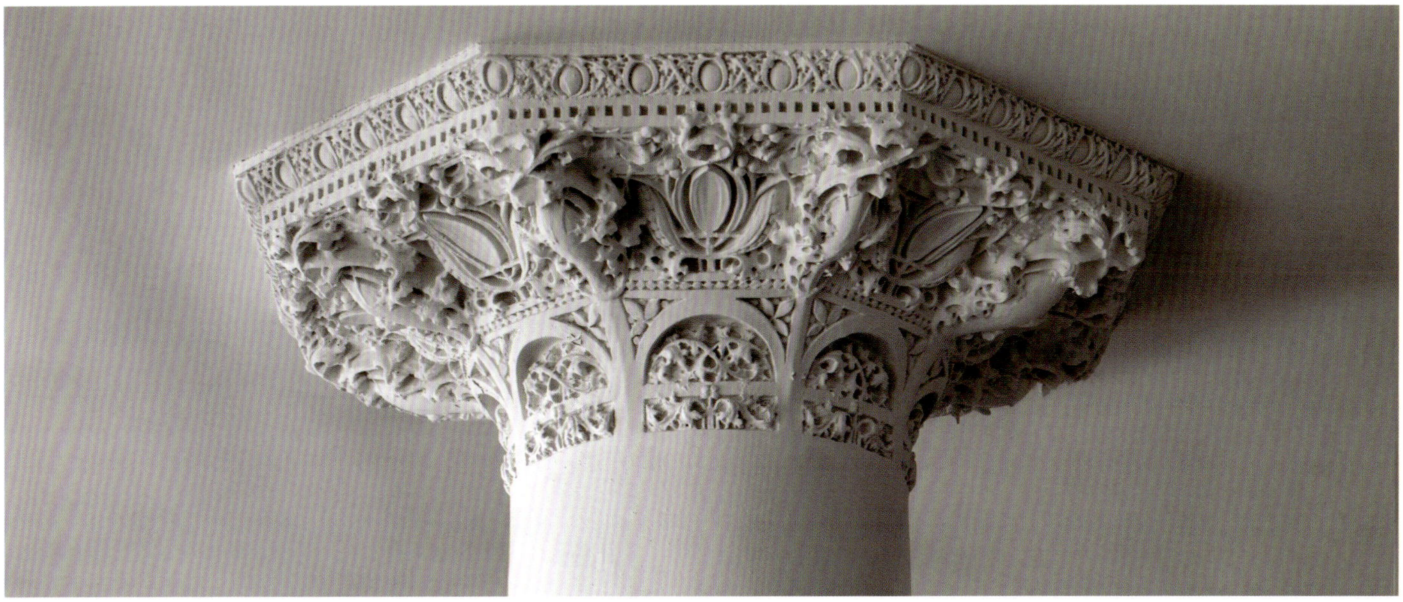

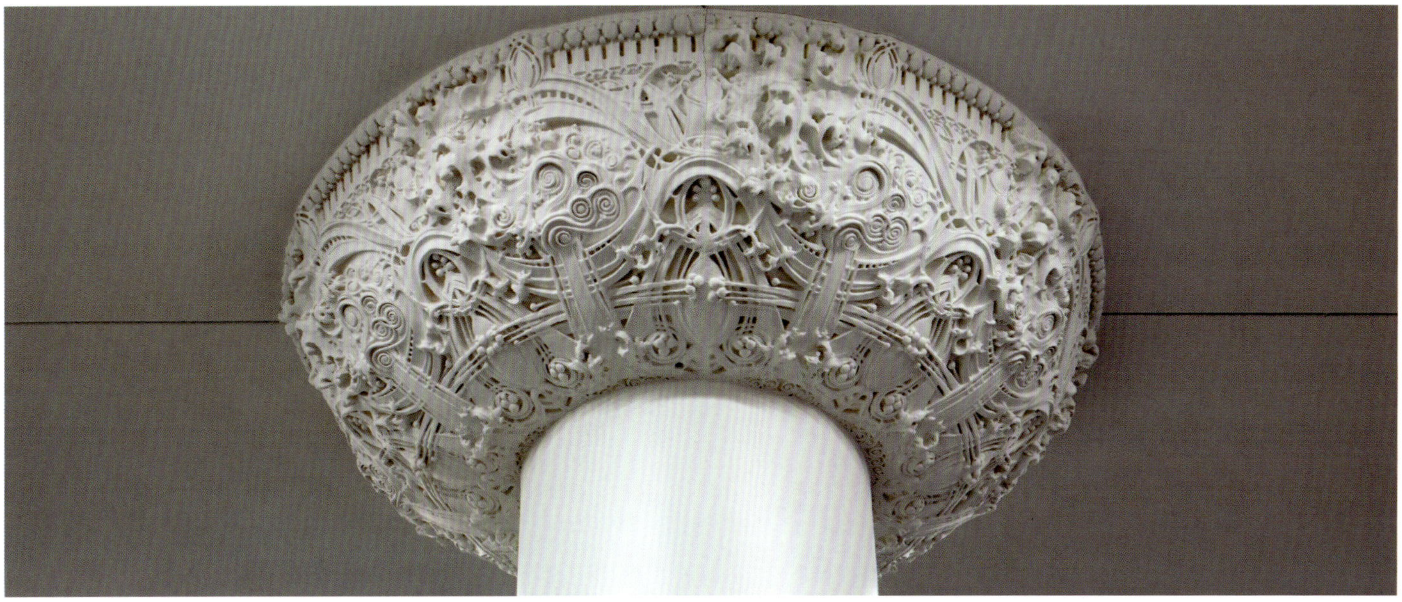

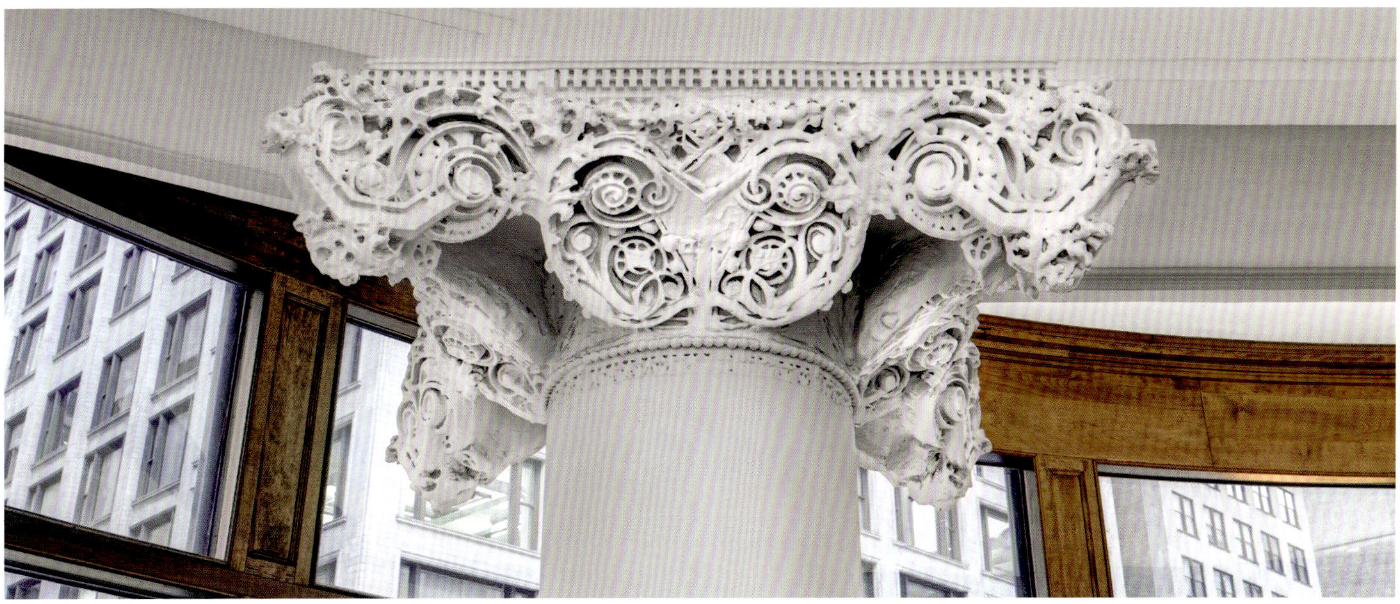

The interior columns were painted with calcimine, a kind of whitewash. Because they capture the light differently, the capitals sometimes appear to be a darker shade.

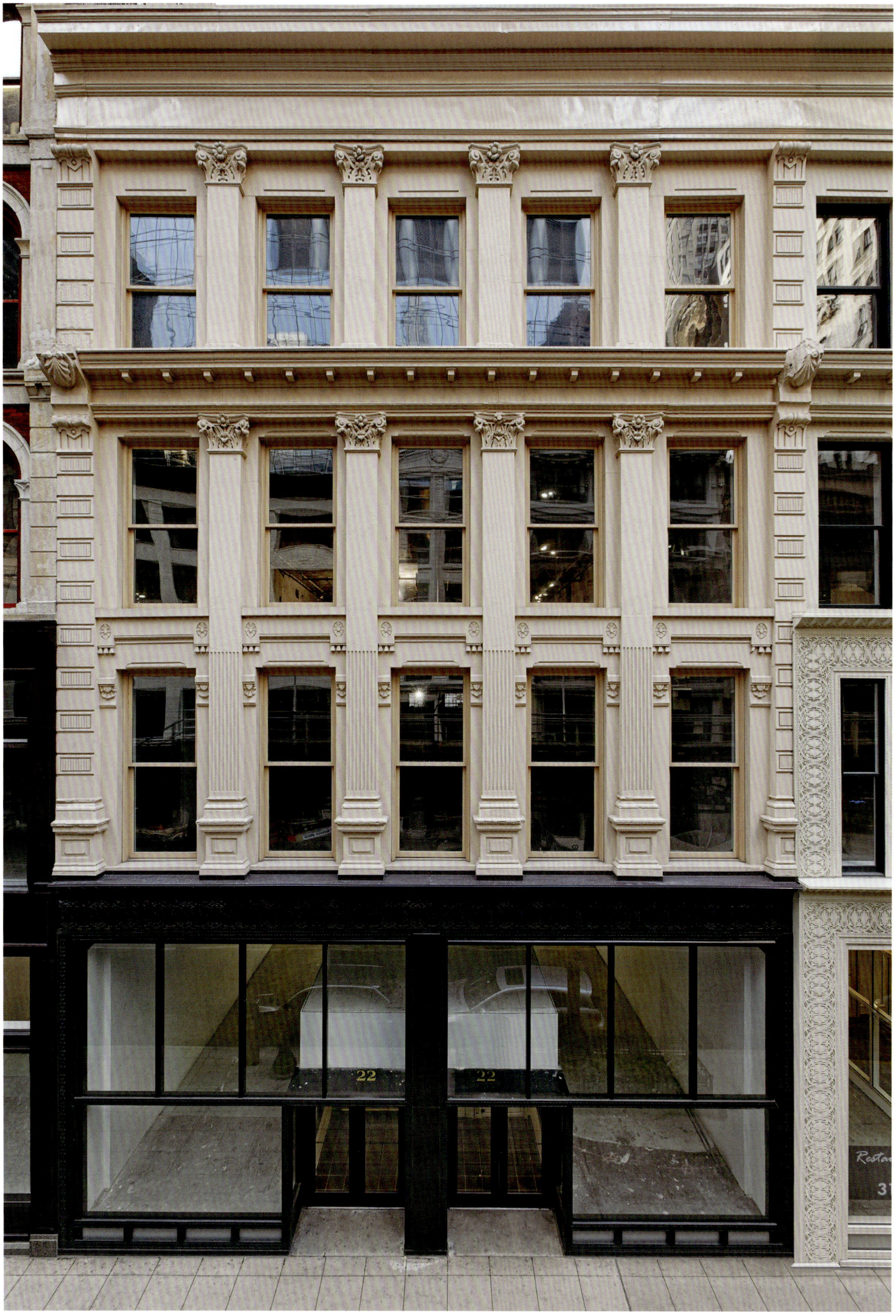

Sullivan redesigned the storefronts at 18 and 22 S. Wabash in 1903 for Schlesinger & Mayer, which became part of the main store.

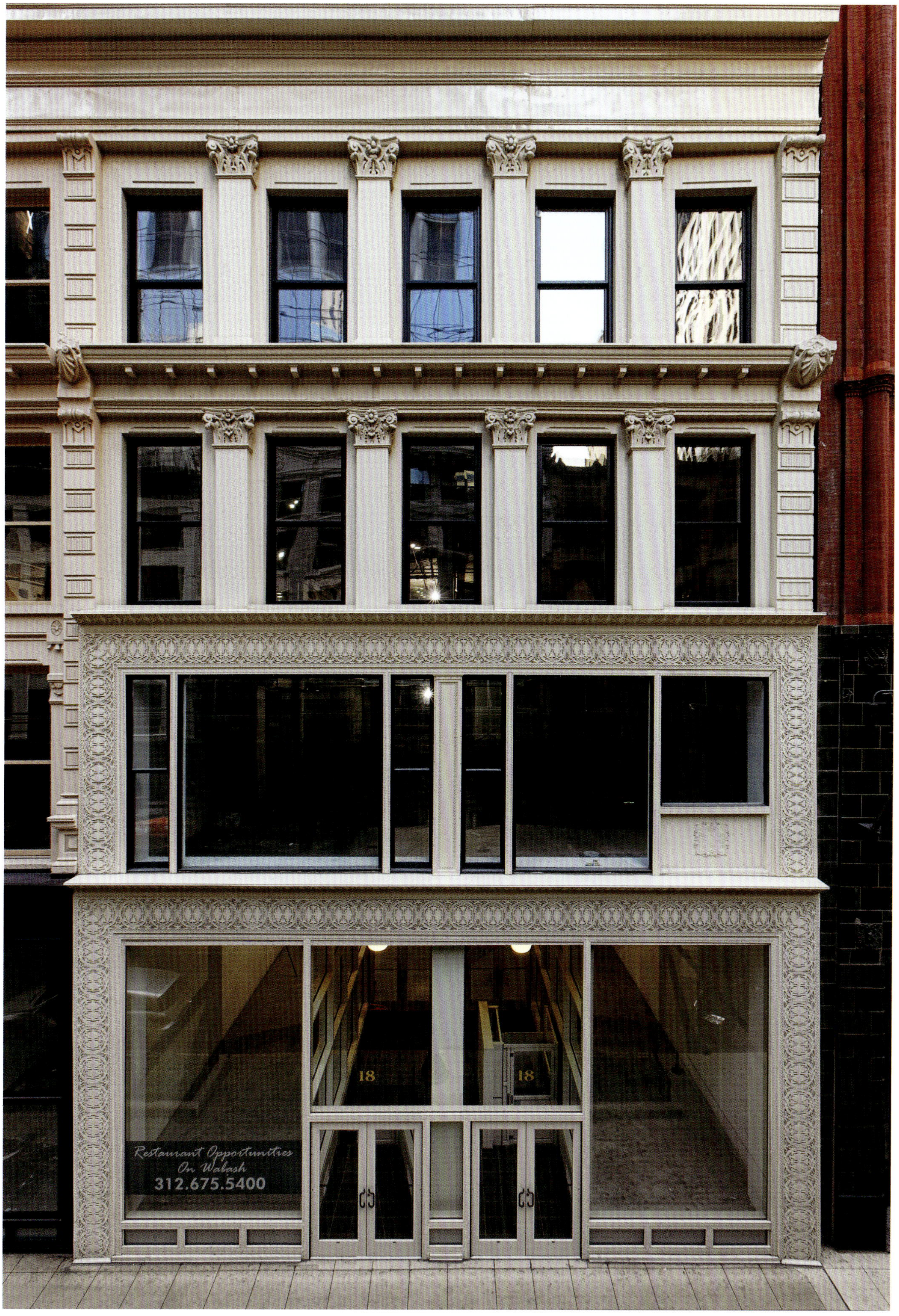

A bridge, also designed by Sullivan, connected the second floor of 18 S. Wabash with the adjacent El station.

VIRGINIA HALL AT TUSCULUM COLLEGE

1901, GREENEVILLE, TENNESSEE

If you were to visit the campus of Tusculum College in the foothills of the Smokey Mountains, you would be unlikely to single out its former women's dormitory, Virginia Hall, as a typical Louis Sullivan design, since it lacks the decorative flourishes that were the architect's hallmarks. Yet, he never intended them for this building, which was commissioned by Nancy "Nettie" Fowler McCormick, the widow of farm machinery mogul Cyrus Hall McCormick.

Founded as early as 1794 by Presbyterian ministers to bring higher education to the southern mountains, the McCormicks were responsible in the late nineteenth and early twentieth centuries for funding several classroom buildings and the president's residence. In 1878, the college started admitting women, who, by the turn of the century, composed half of the student body, so there was a clear need for housing. Sullivan, who had designed a cottage for Mrs. McCormick (not built), received the commission and intentionally kept the design simple, since the $20,000 budget was modest and because it would be built with local materials. Nevertheless, it was the first building on campus to have baths with hot and cold running water, central heating, and fire escapes! No longer a dormitory, it now houses administrative offices and the English Department. It was added to the National Register of Historic Places in 1980.

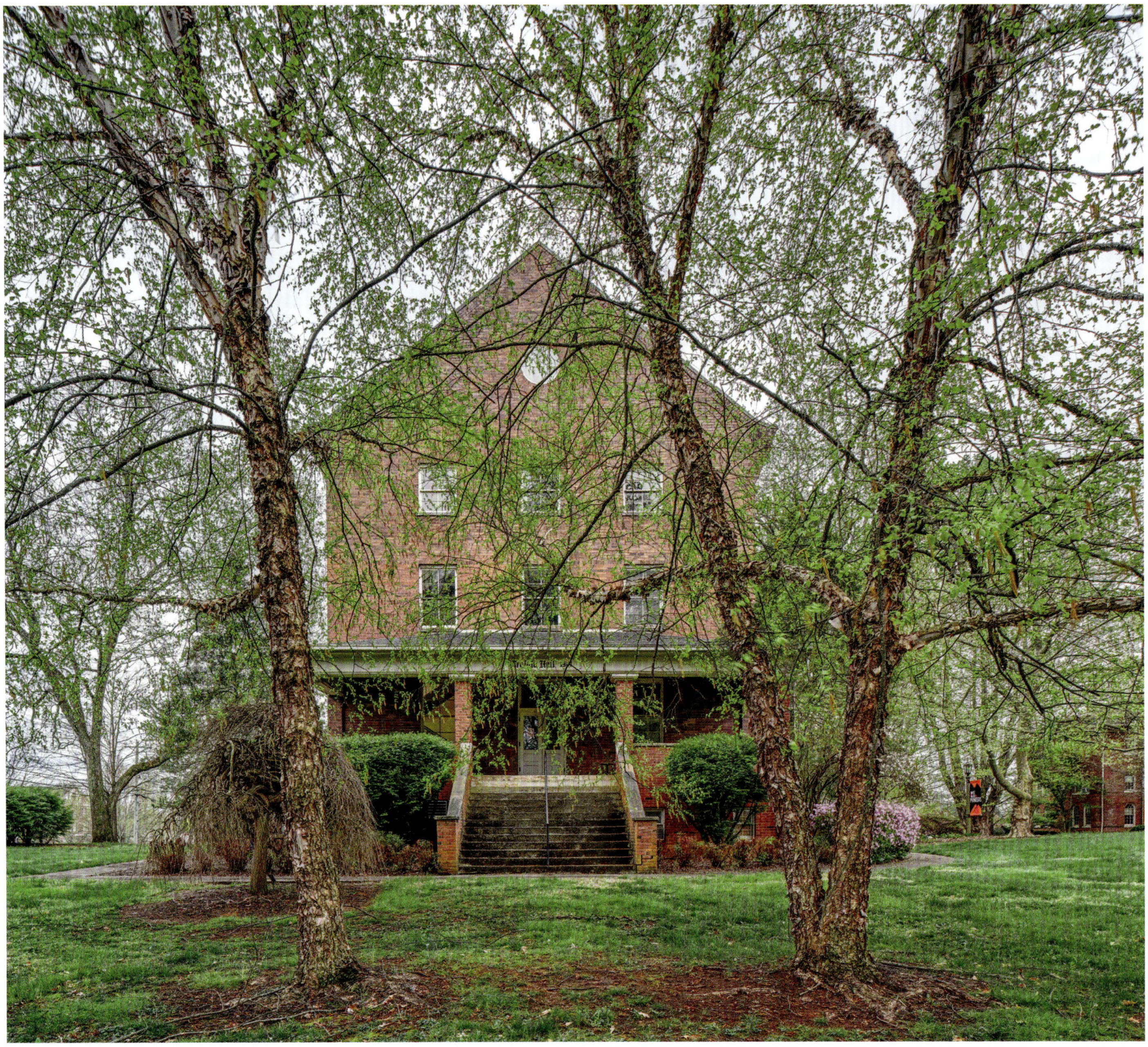

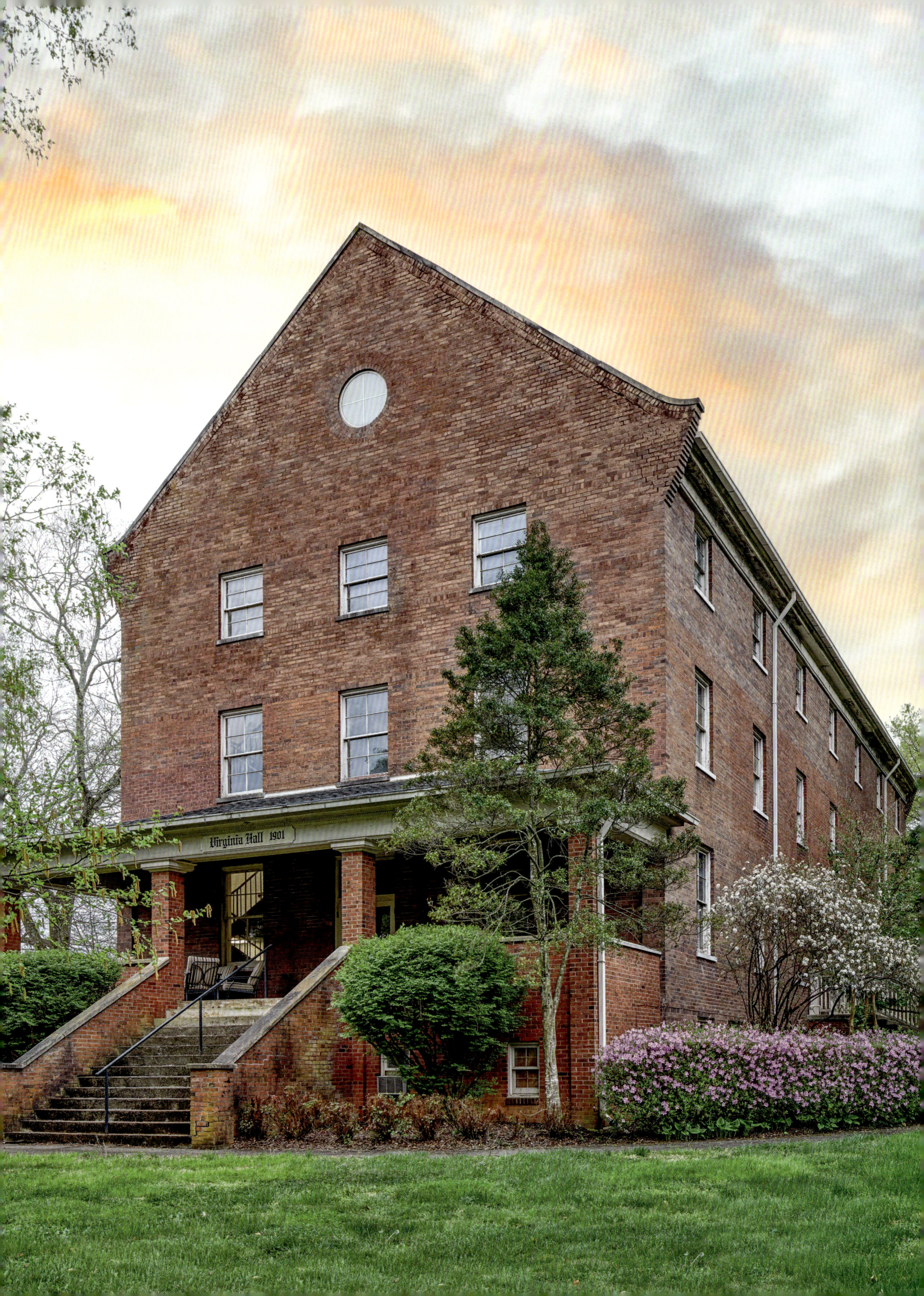
Virginia Hall 1901

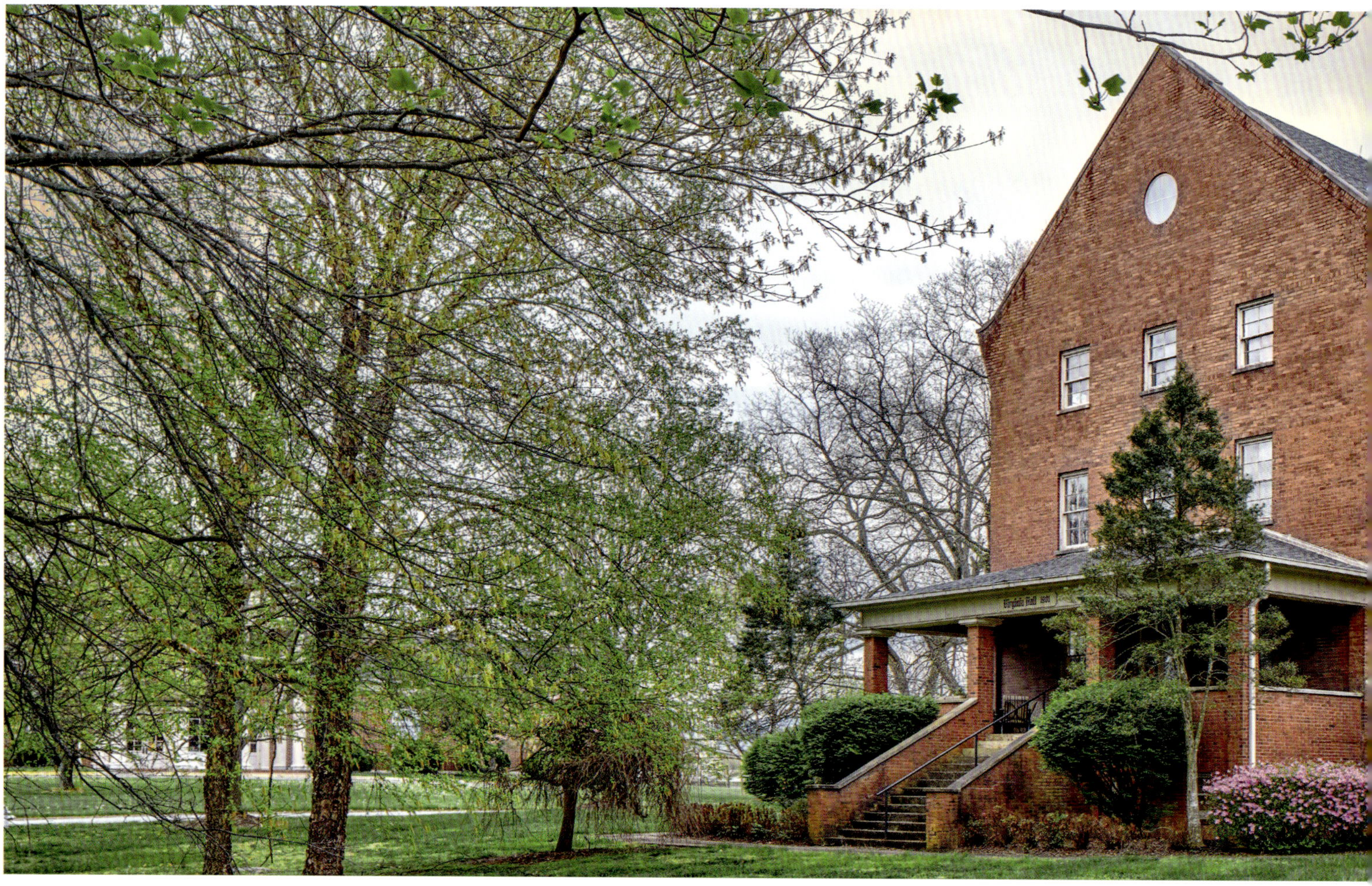

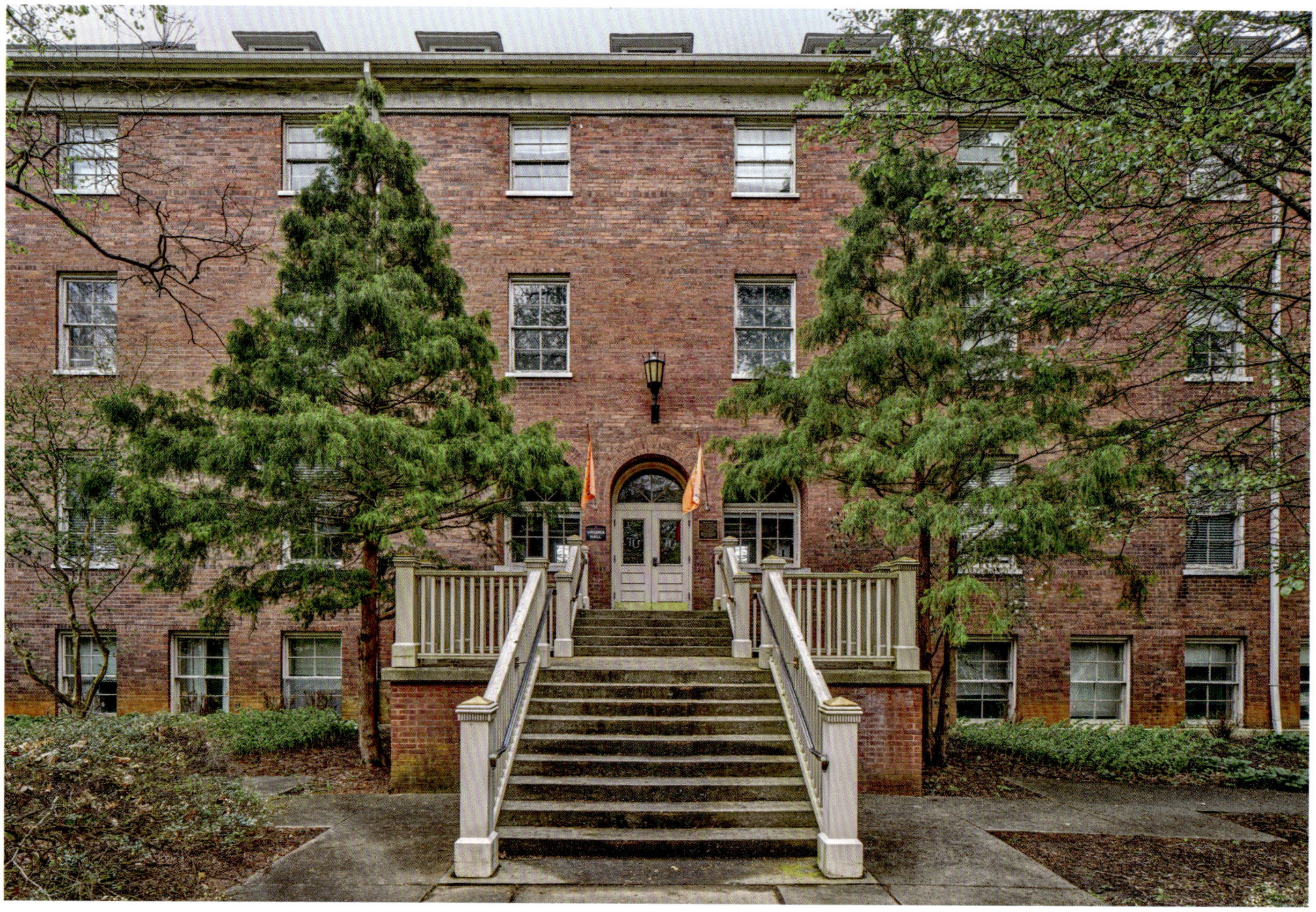

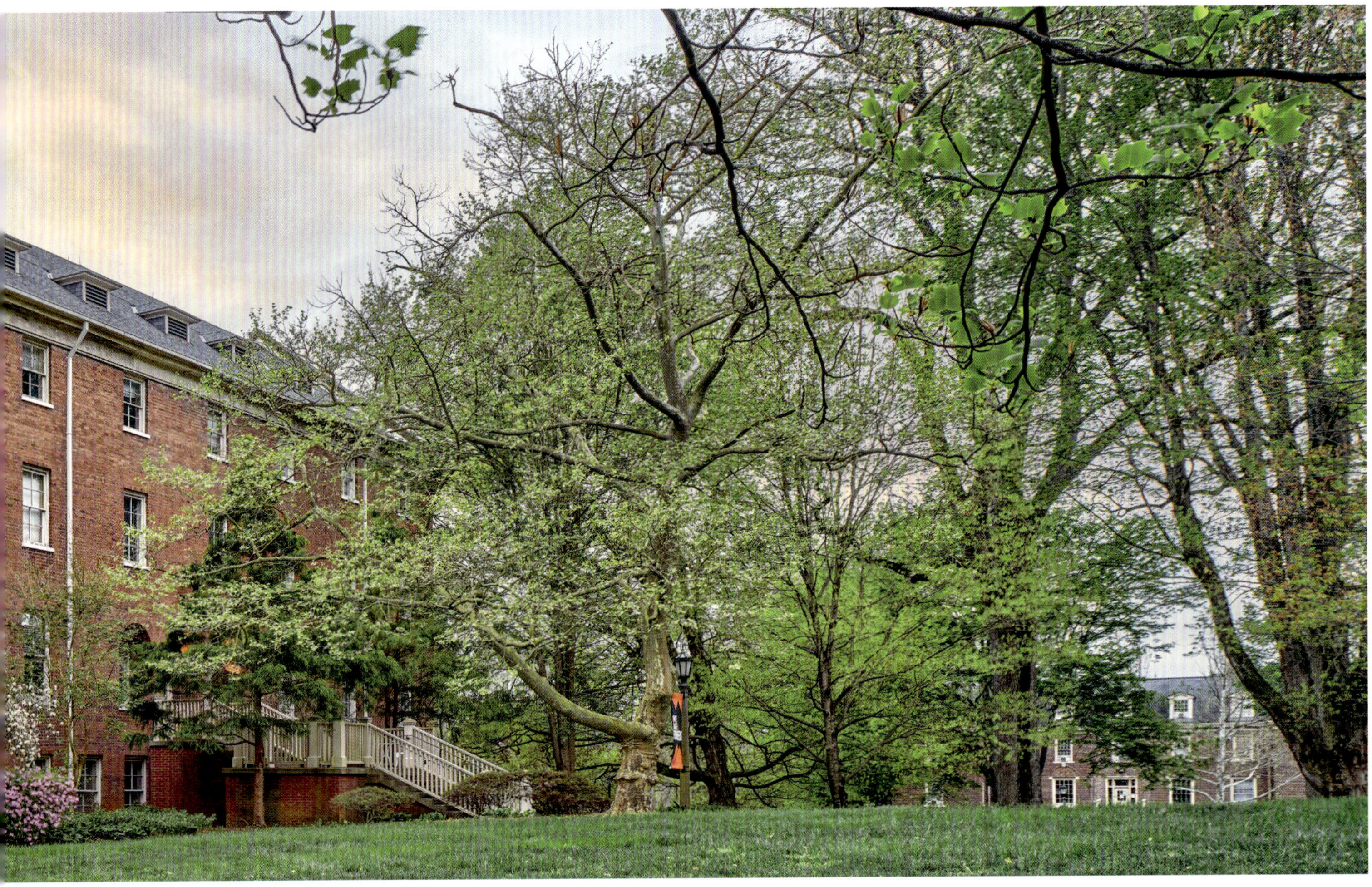

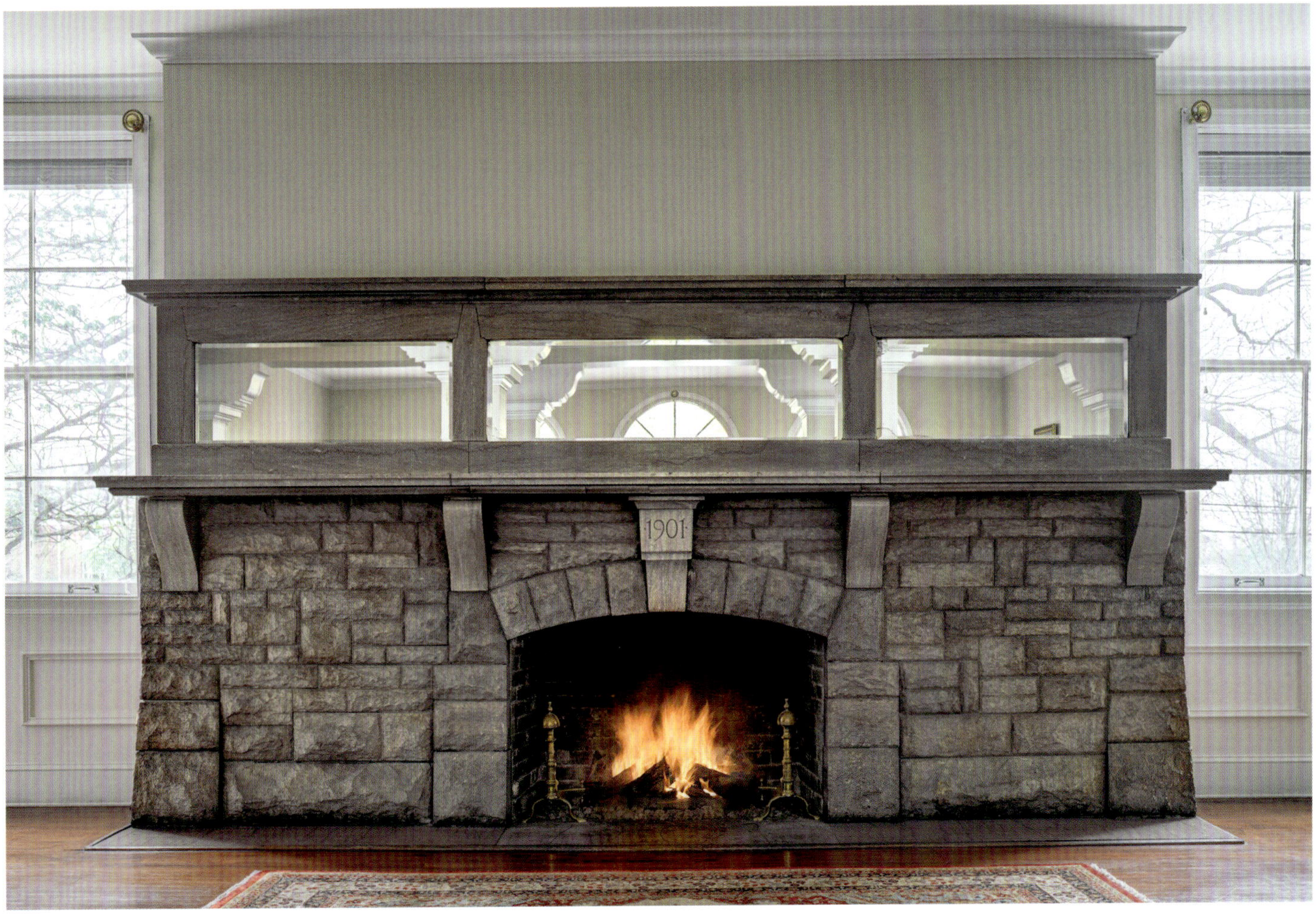

JOHN D. VAN ALLEN & SON STORE

1911–14, CLINTON, IOWA

John D. Van Allen (1850–1928) began his retail career in Chicago with Field, Leiter & Company before moving to New York, where he worked in retailing and, finally, as the Midwest representative for an import company. He returned to retailing and chose the growing Clinton, Iowa, as a place to invest in his own store. When the business outgrew its existing spaces, Allen decided to commission a new building. At the suggestion of Frederick H. Shaver, for whom Sullivan had designed the Peoples Savings Bank in Cedar Rapids, Allen contacted Sullivan.

Although far more modest in size as befitted its small-town location, the building shares several features with Chicago's Schlesinger & Mayer store, including its generous window openings, large selling and display areas, and clear expression of its underlying steel frame. The upper stories are faced with grayish Roman brick. The first-floor display windows were framed with black marble, with grids of Luxfer prisms above to amplify light to the interior, just as had been done for Schlesinger & Mayer. Decorative touches include string courses of light gray terra cotta, but the primary decorations on the main facade are the non-bearing mullions, which rise from ornamental corbels below the second story and terminate at highly decorated festoons of green terra-cotta foliage on blue and white panels.

After the store closed, as detailed in *The Complete Architecture of Adler & Sullivan*, "California architect Crombie Taylor … founded the Van Allen Foundation to protect the building and restore its first floor … with the help of architects John Vinci and Gyo Obata … Its rededication in 1991 included a program featuring architects, architectural historians and politicians." The foundation eventually failed, and the building was later converted to affordable apartments. It was added to the National Register of Historic Places in 1976.

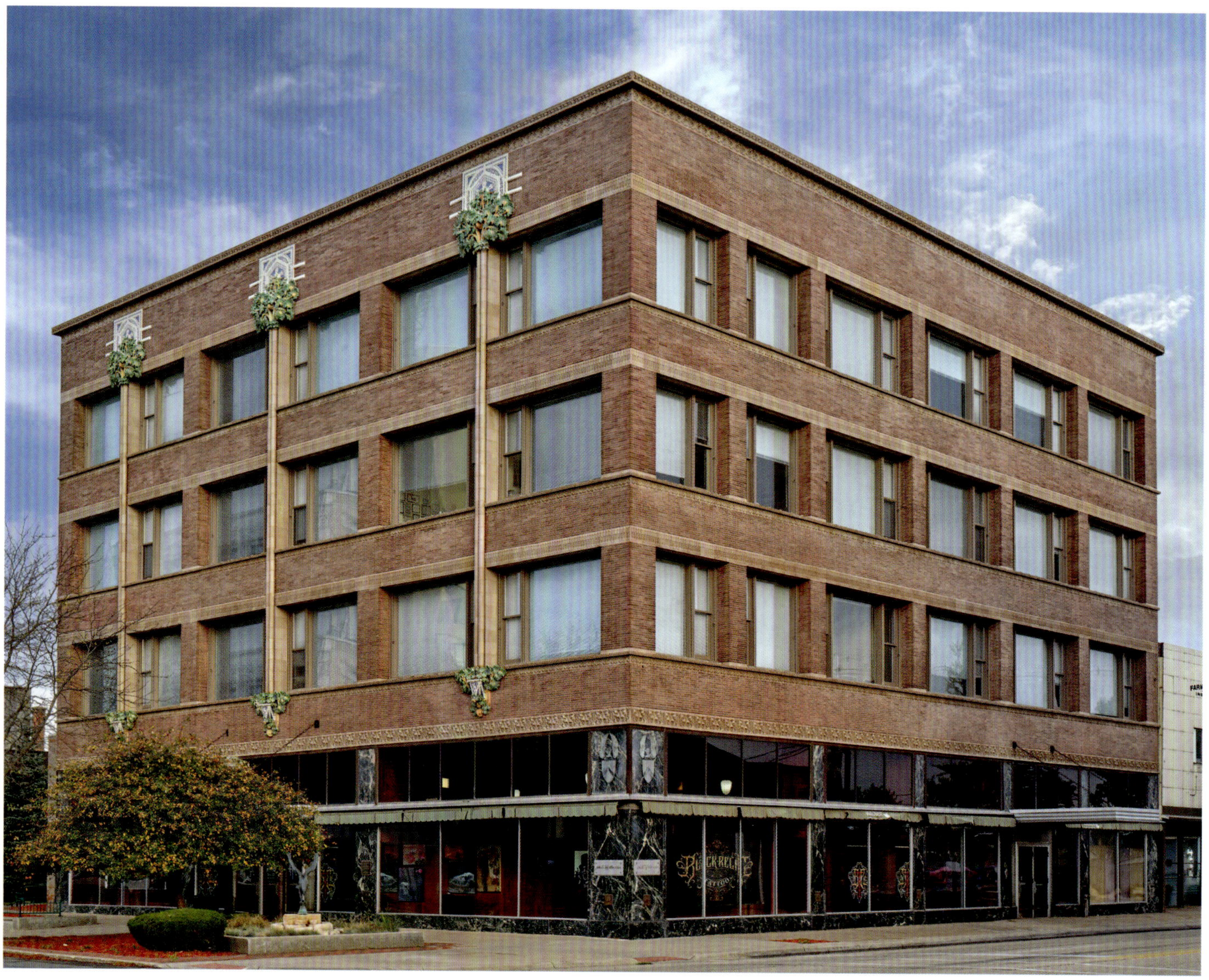

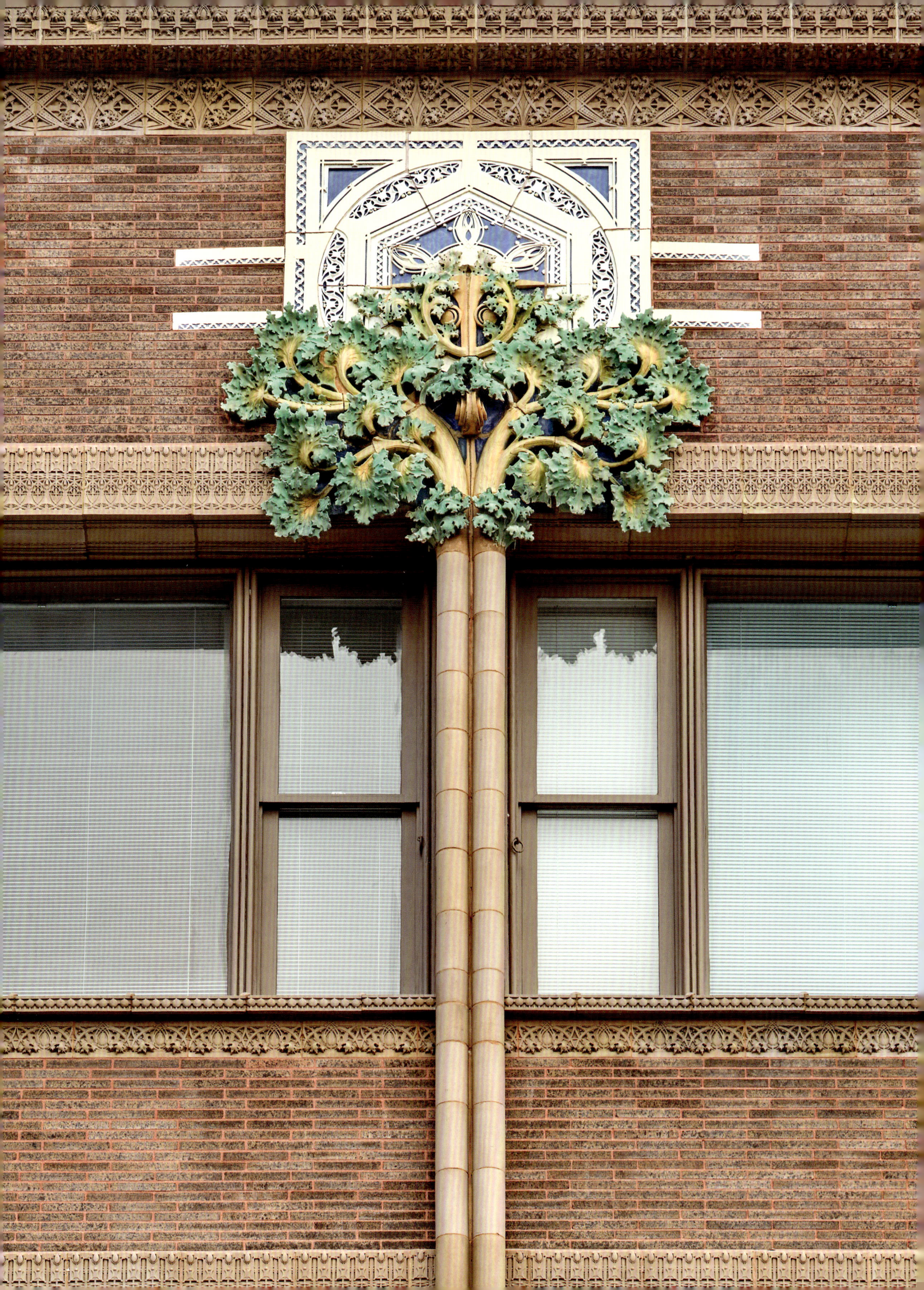

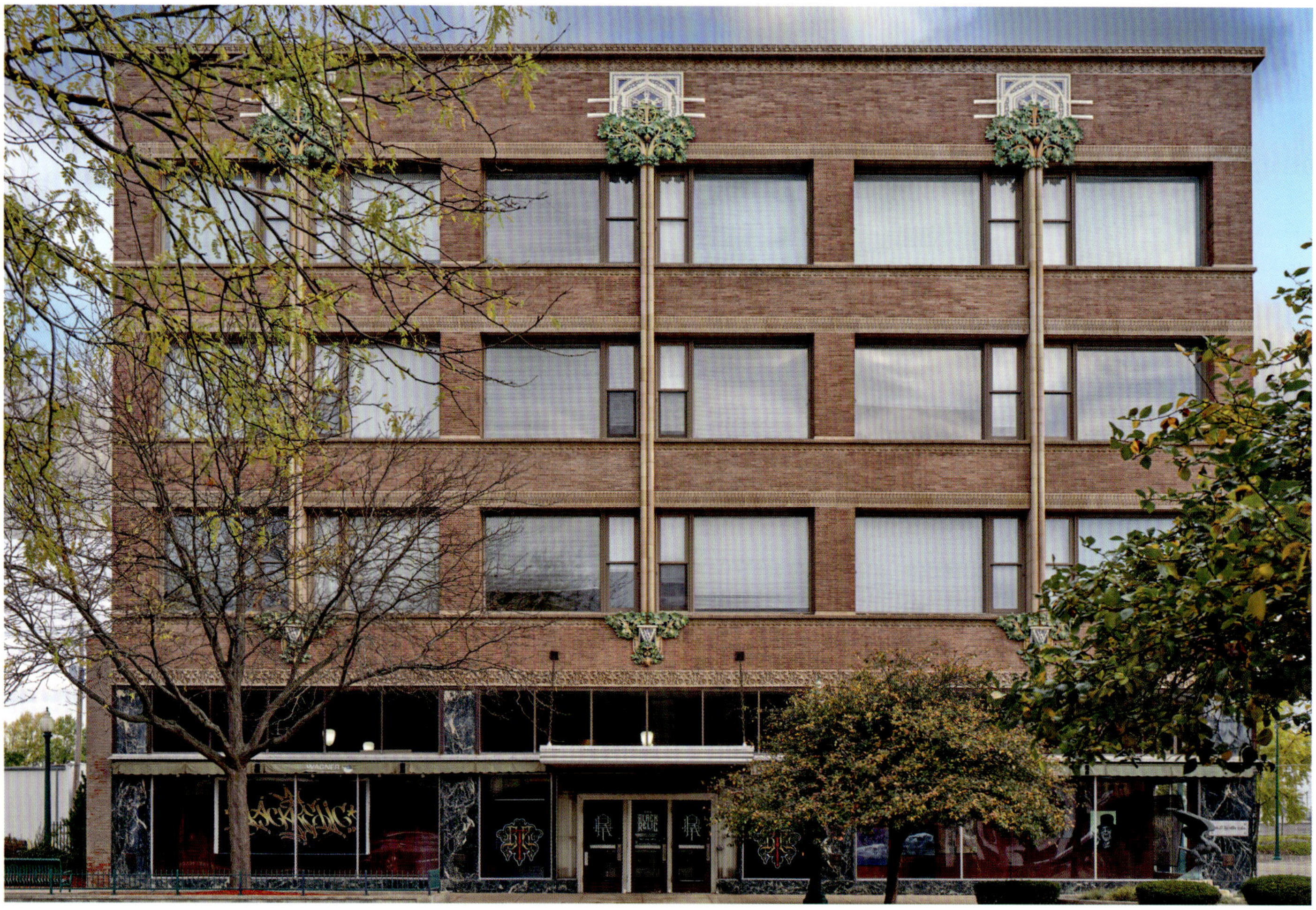

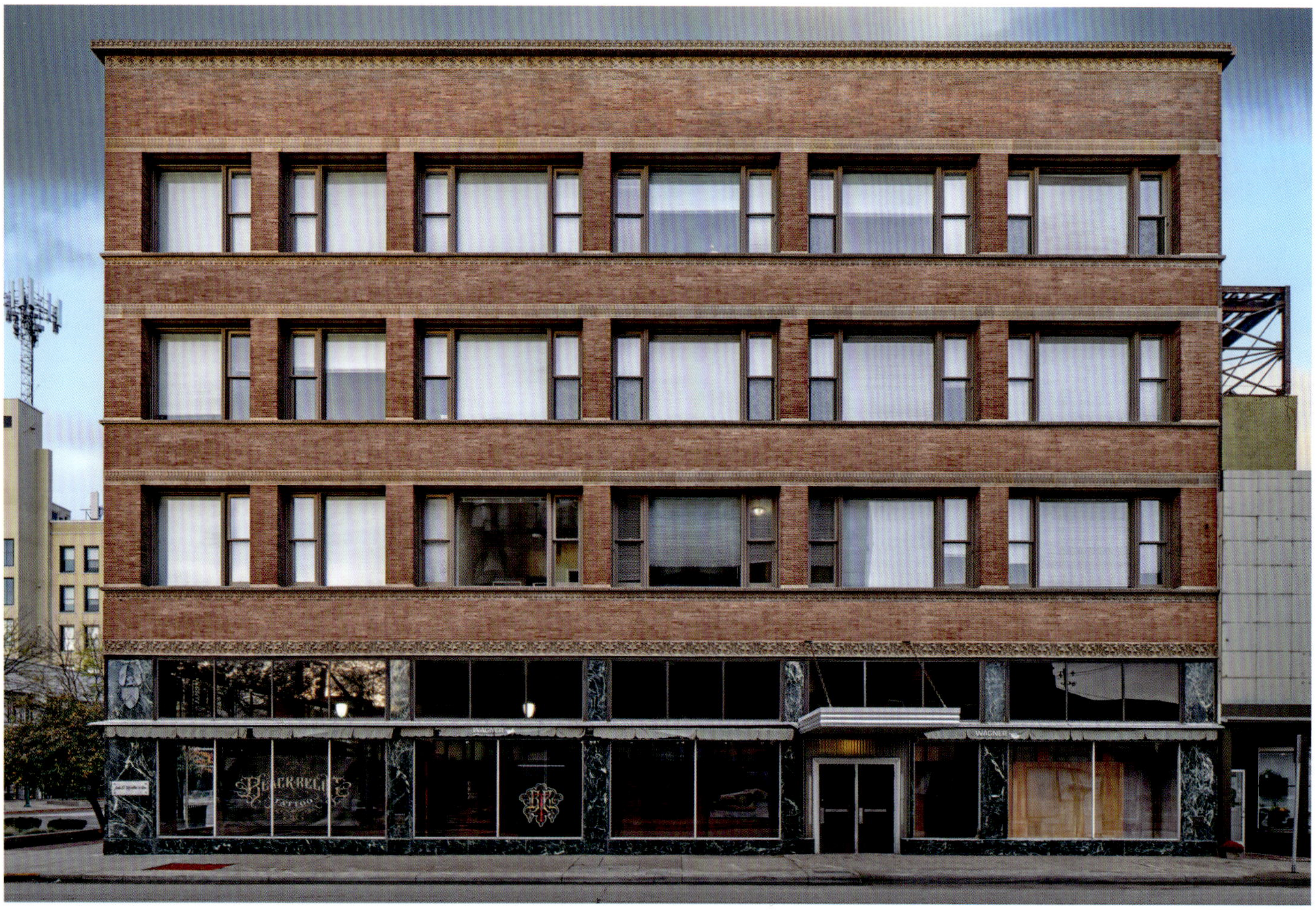

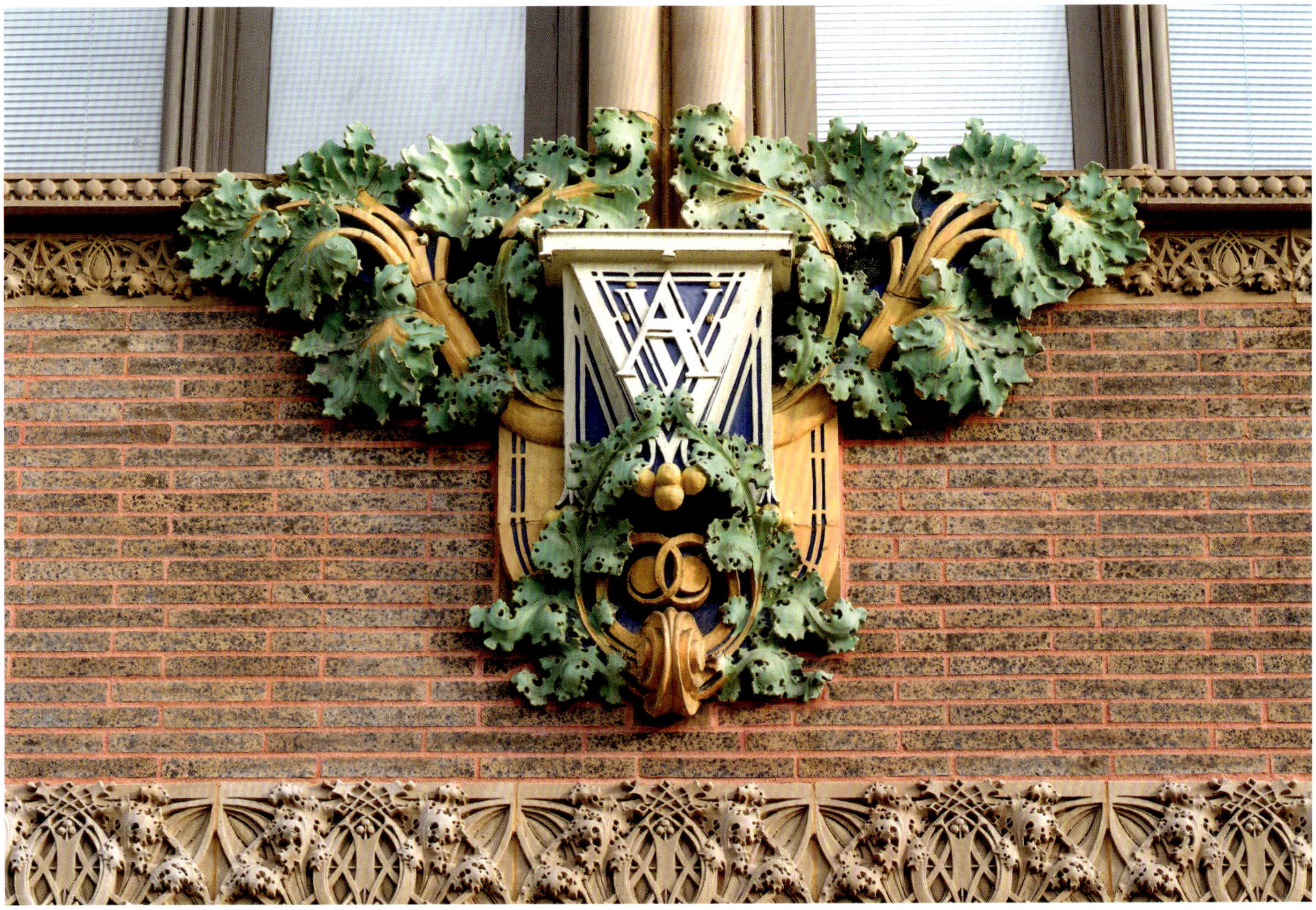

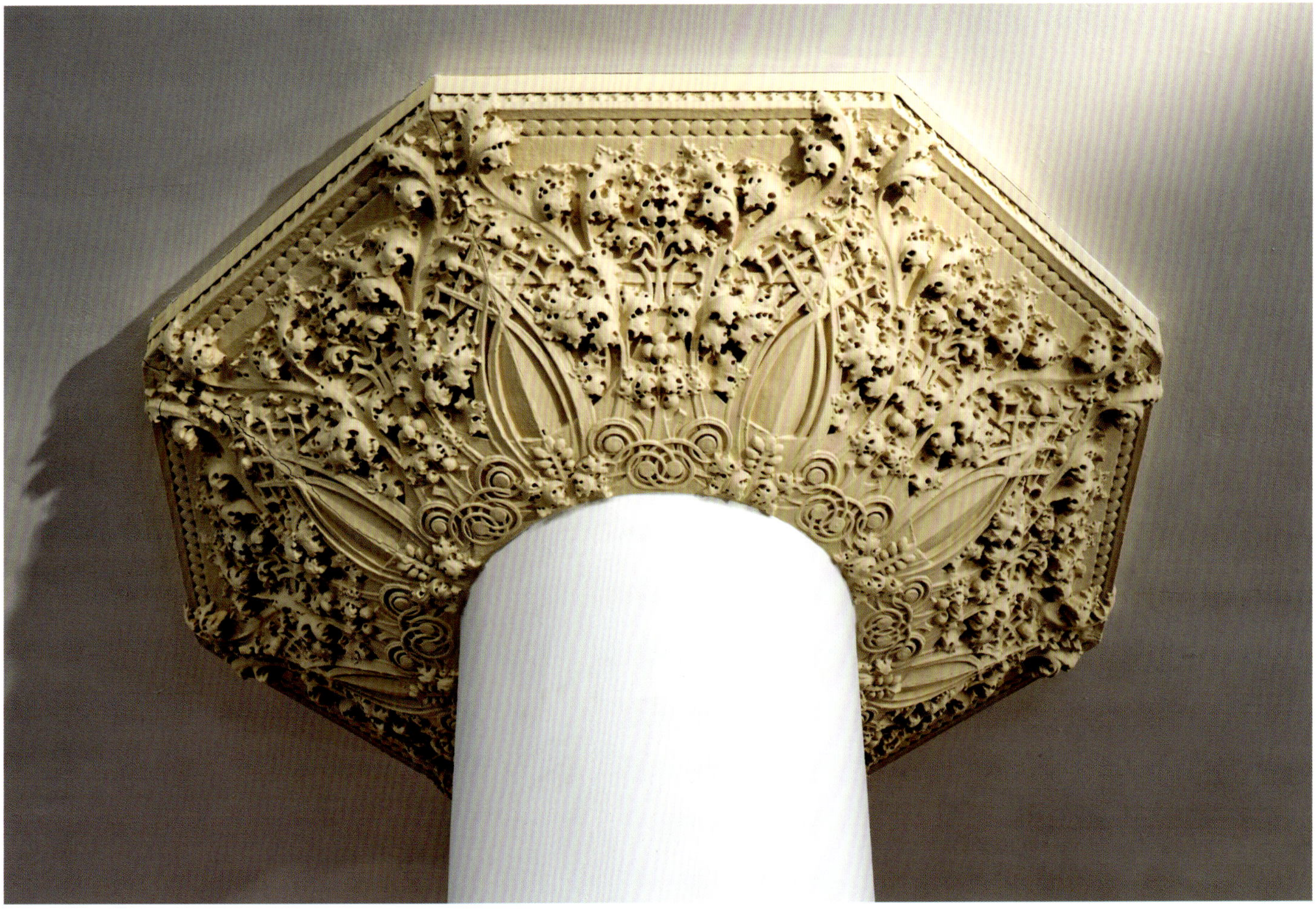

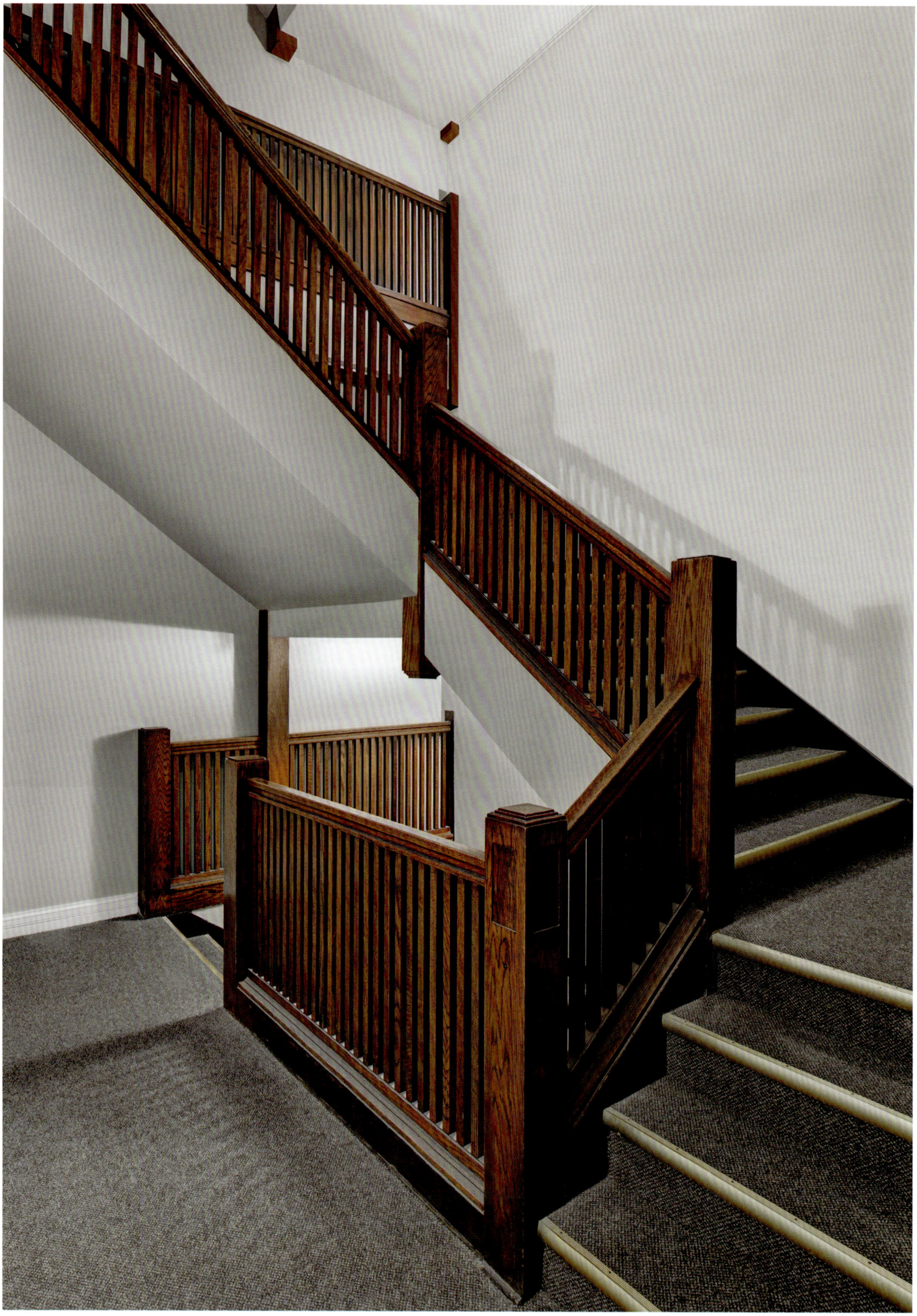

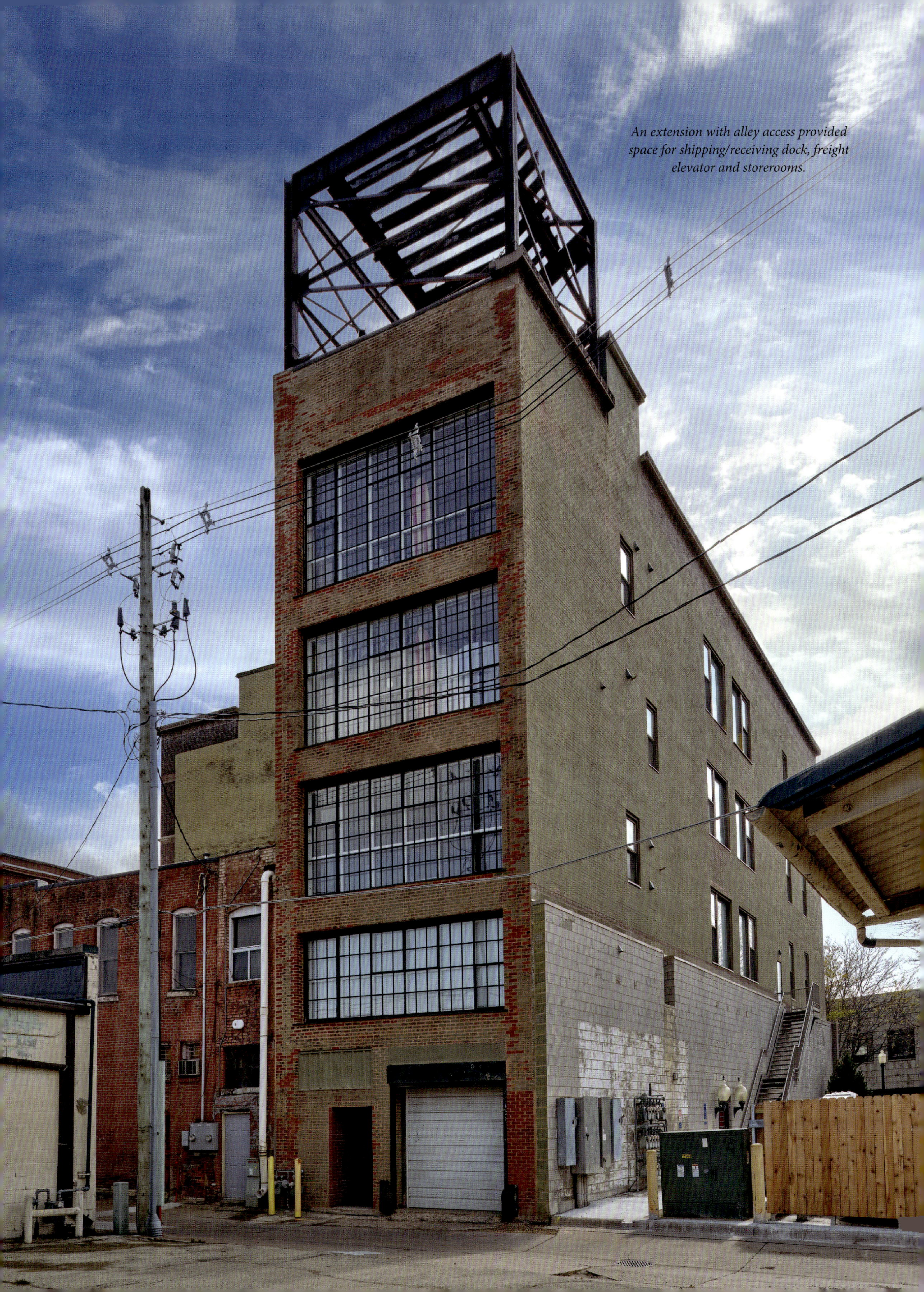

An extension with alley access provided space for shipping/receiving dock, freight elevator and storerooms.

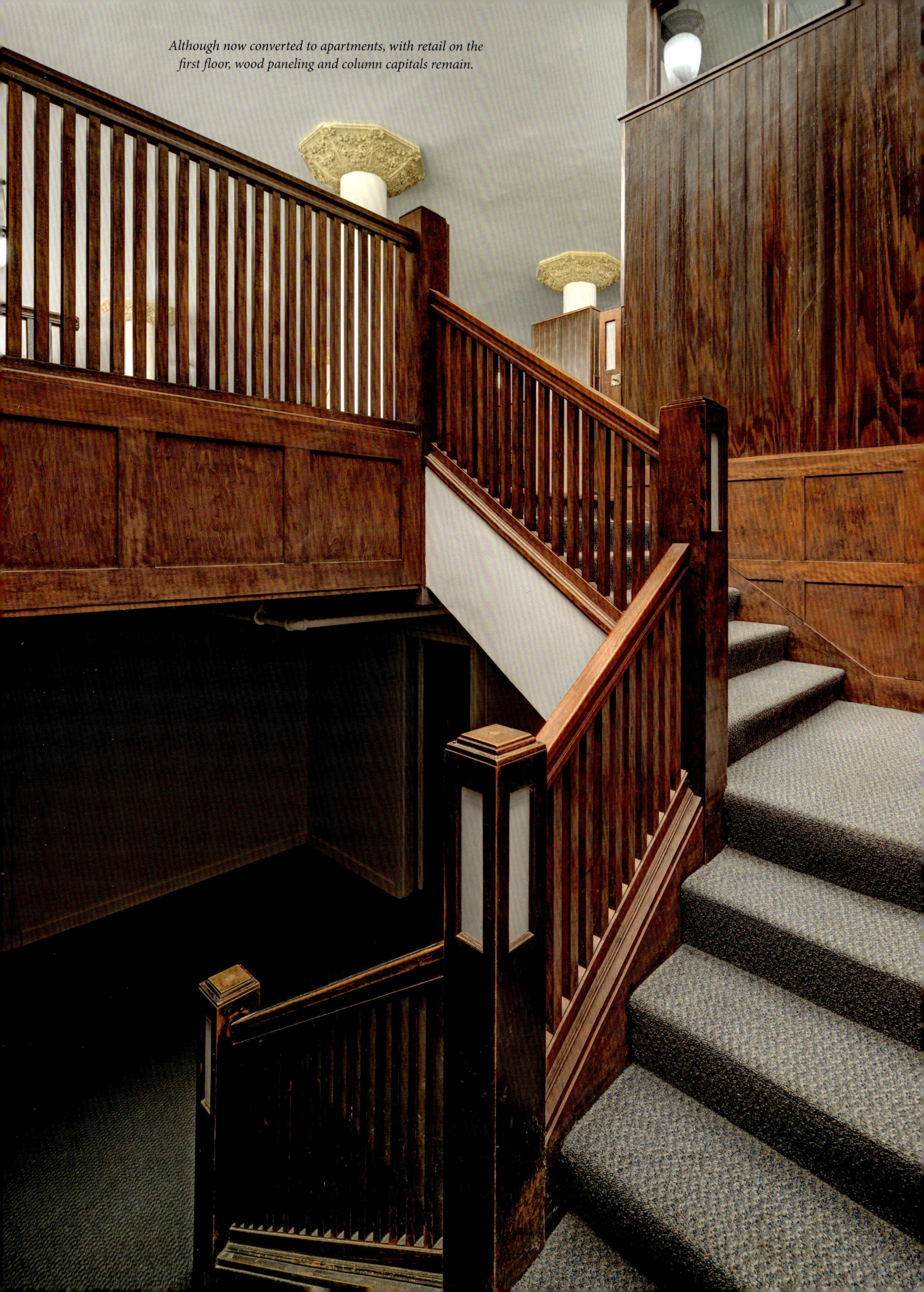

Although now converted to apartments, with retail on the first floor, wood paneling and column capitals remain.

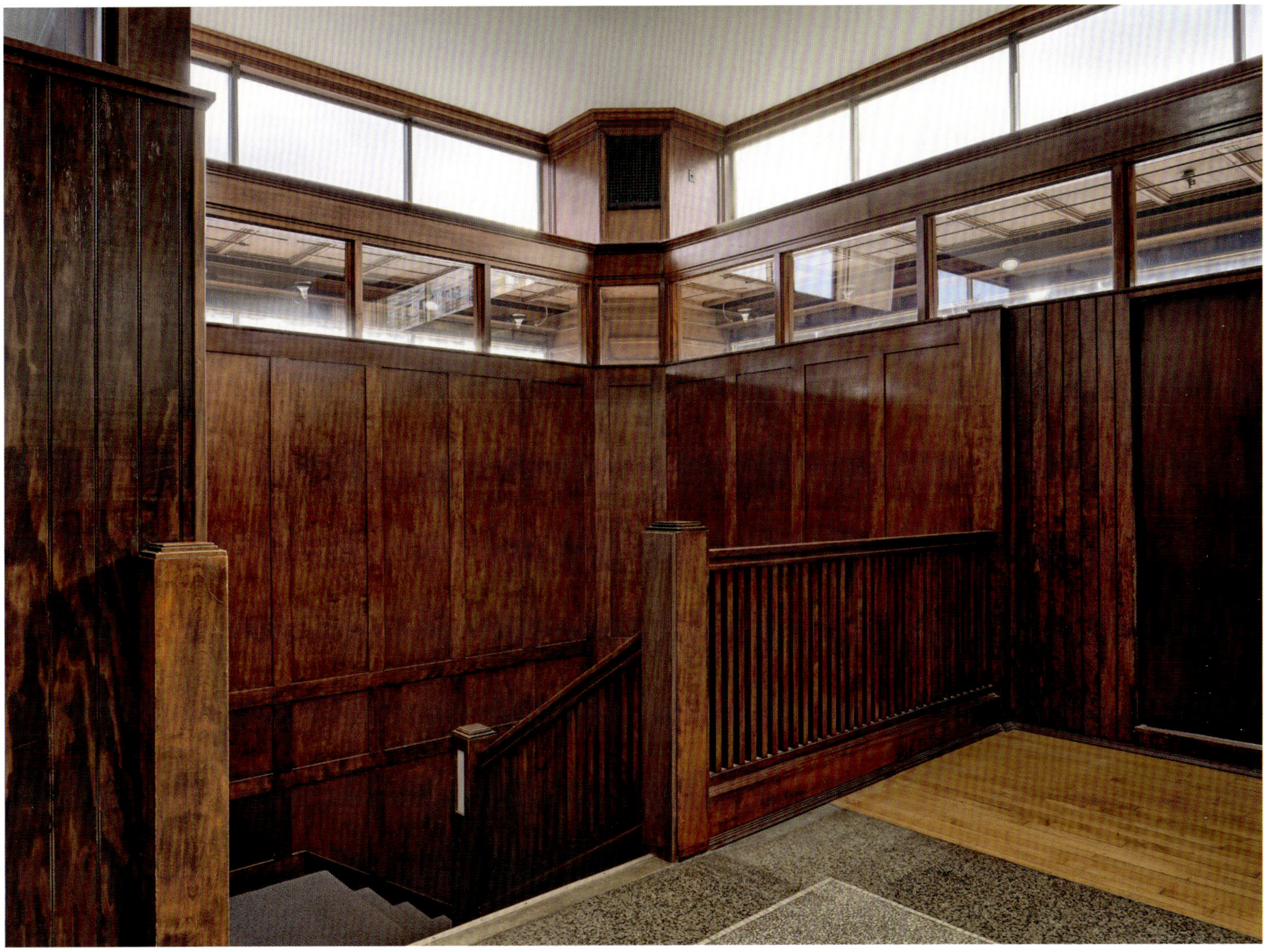

These stairs lead down to the "bargain basement". The clerestory windows and paneling are all original.

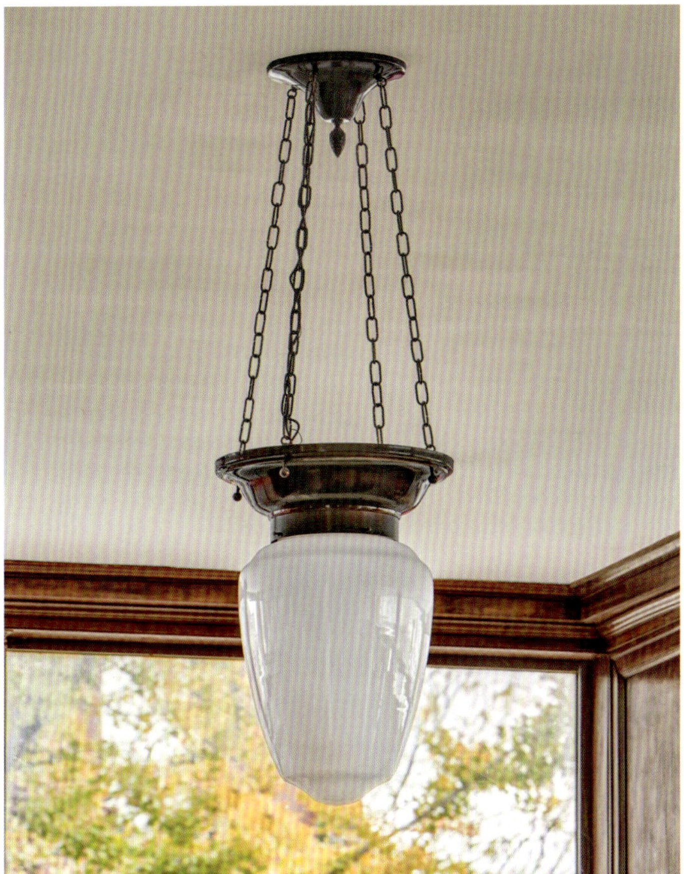

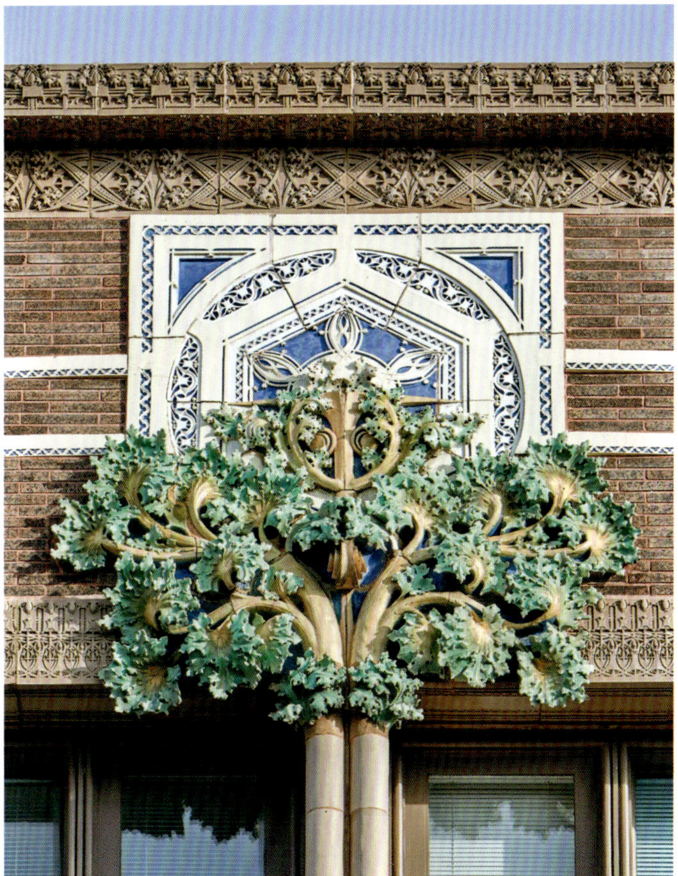

HOLY TRINITY ORTHODOX CATHEDRAL

1900–03, CHICAGO

Although Adler & Sullivan designed several Jewish synagogues and related buildings—Adler's father was a well-connected rabbi—Sullivan later received commissions for two Christian churches. The first of these, Holy Trinity, came to Sullivan from a former client, Charles R. Crane, whose father was the plumbing manufacturer, Richard T. Crane. The younger Crane was a Russophile who had been involved in the construction of the Trans-Siberian Railway. A significant donation from Czar Nicholas II in 1898 made it possible for the congregation to build a permanent home.

Although Sullivan provided several proposals, the final design included the church and neighboring rectory on a near northwest side site in what is now known as Ukrainian Village. He went to some pains to suit his design to its religious heritage, basing it on small Orthodox churches like one in Tatarskaya in Siberia, which had similar four-part windows in the nave and broad gabled eaves in the tower. Sullivan had hoped to have the exterior surfaces stenciled with elaborate designs, but they were never executed for lack of funds. The church and rectory have undergone several restorations, most recently in 2021, when cracked stucco walls were repaired, metal ornamentation was refurbished in the church, the wood floor was replaced, and new windows were installed in the rectory. It was elevated to cathedral status in 1923, added to the National Register of Historic Places in 1976, and designated a Chicago Landmark in 1979.

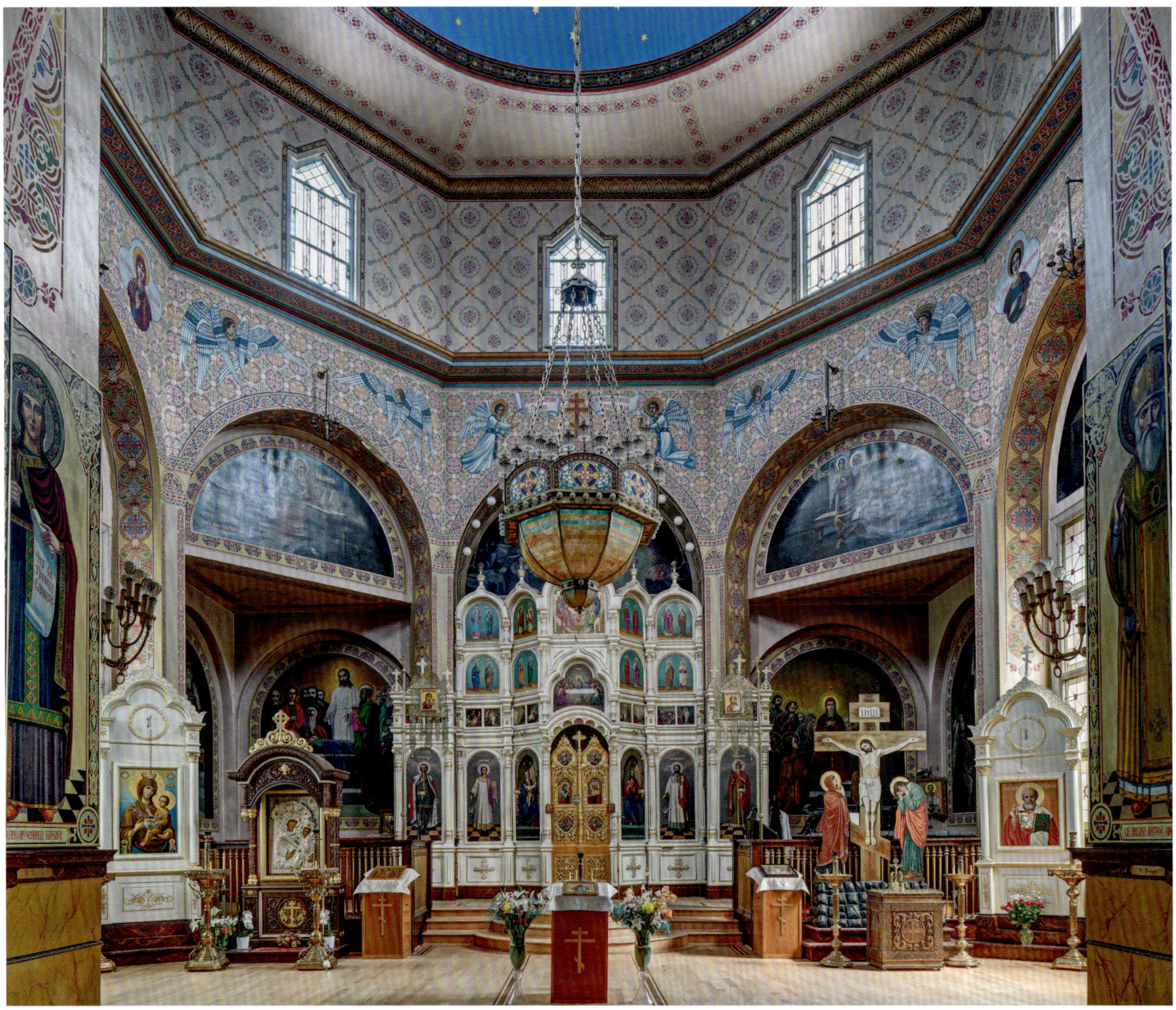

While some of the basic decoration, including windows and stenciling, was Sullivan, much of what now exists was added over the years.

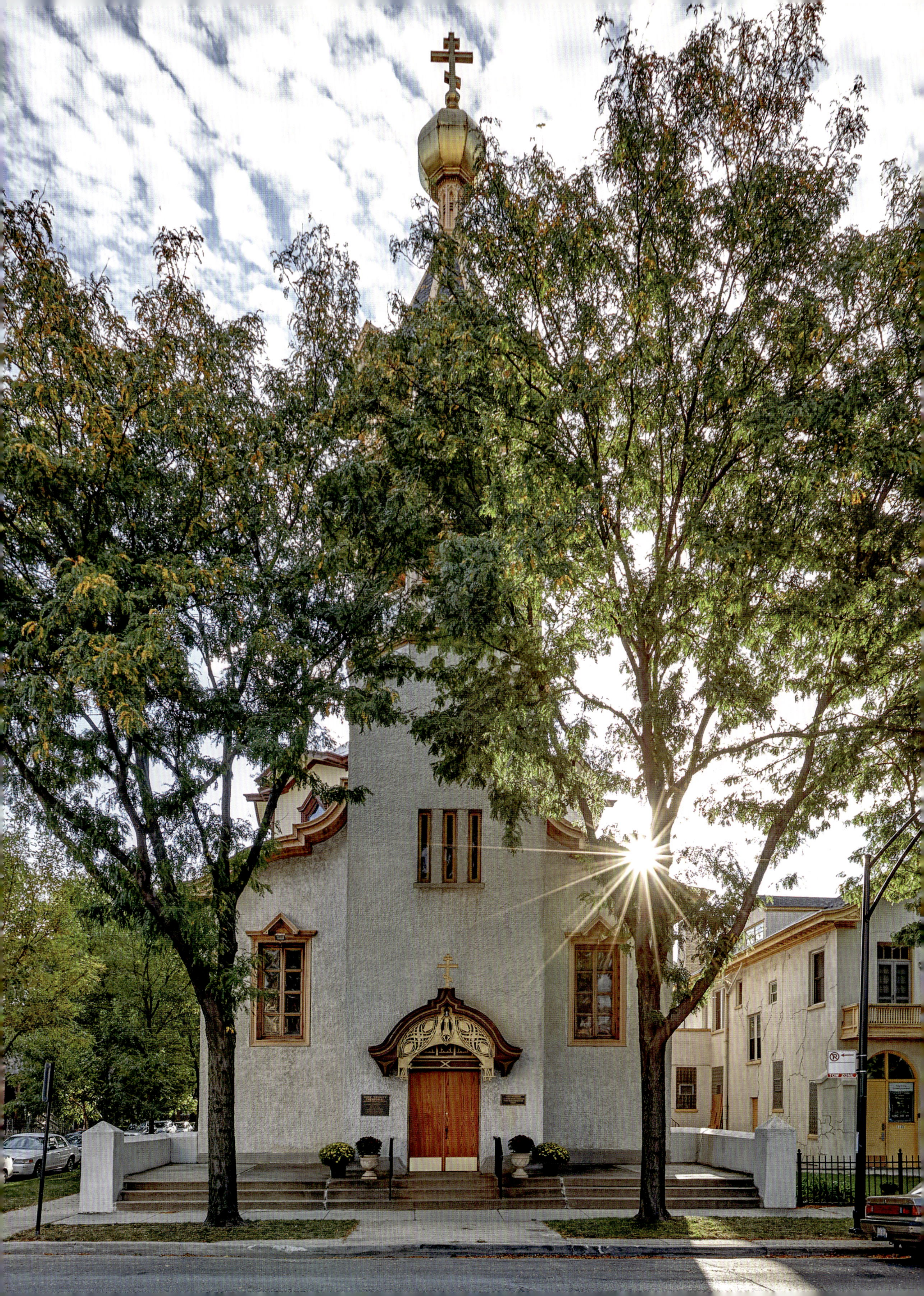
TOW ZONE

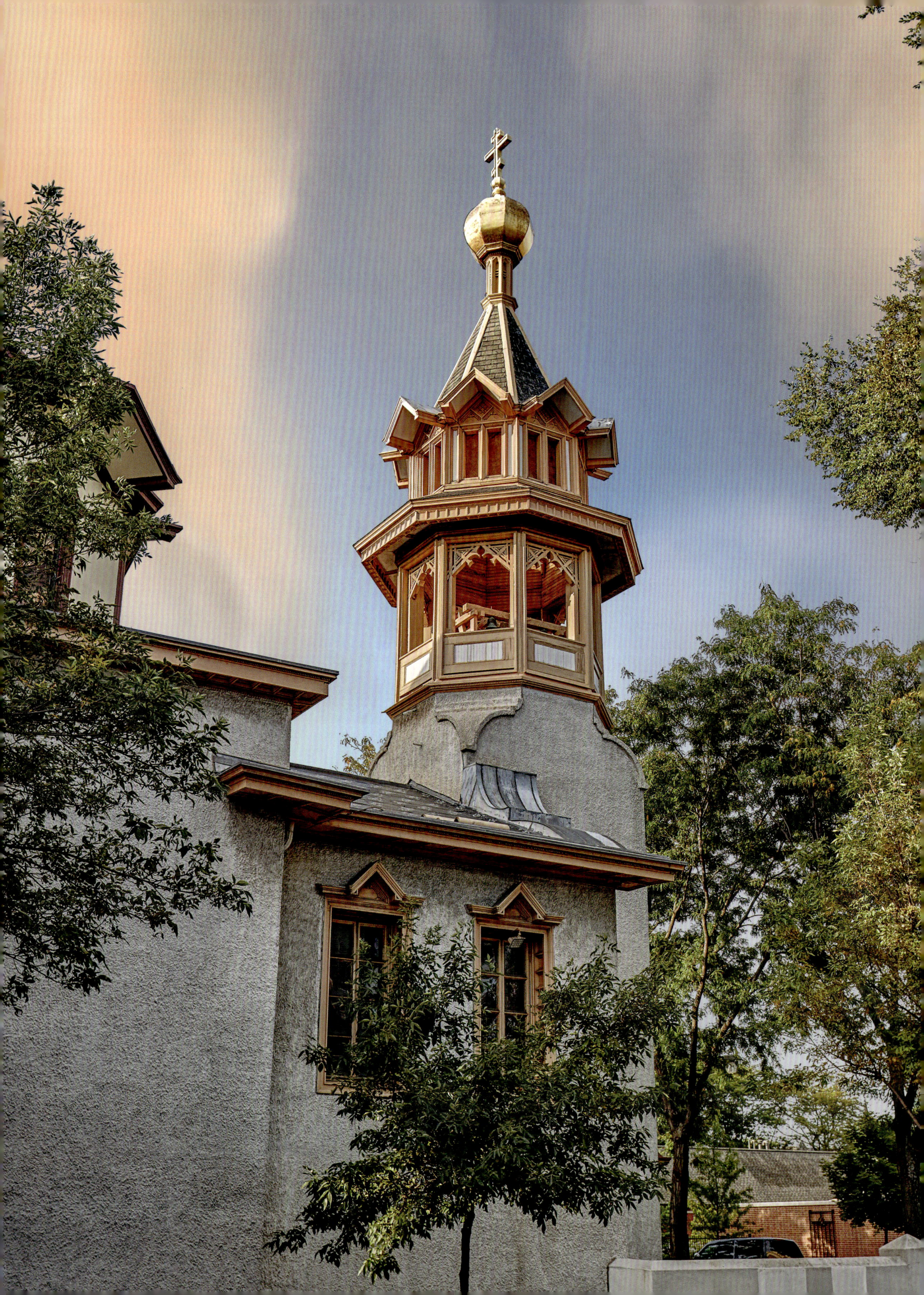

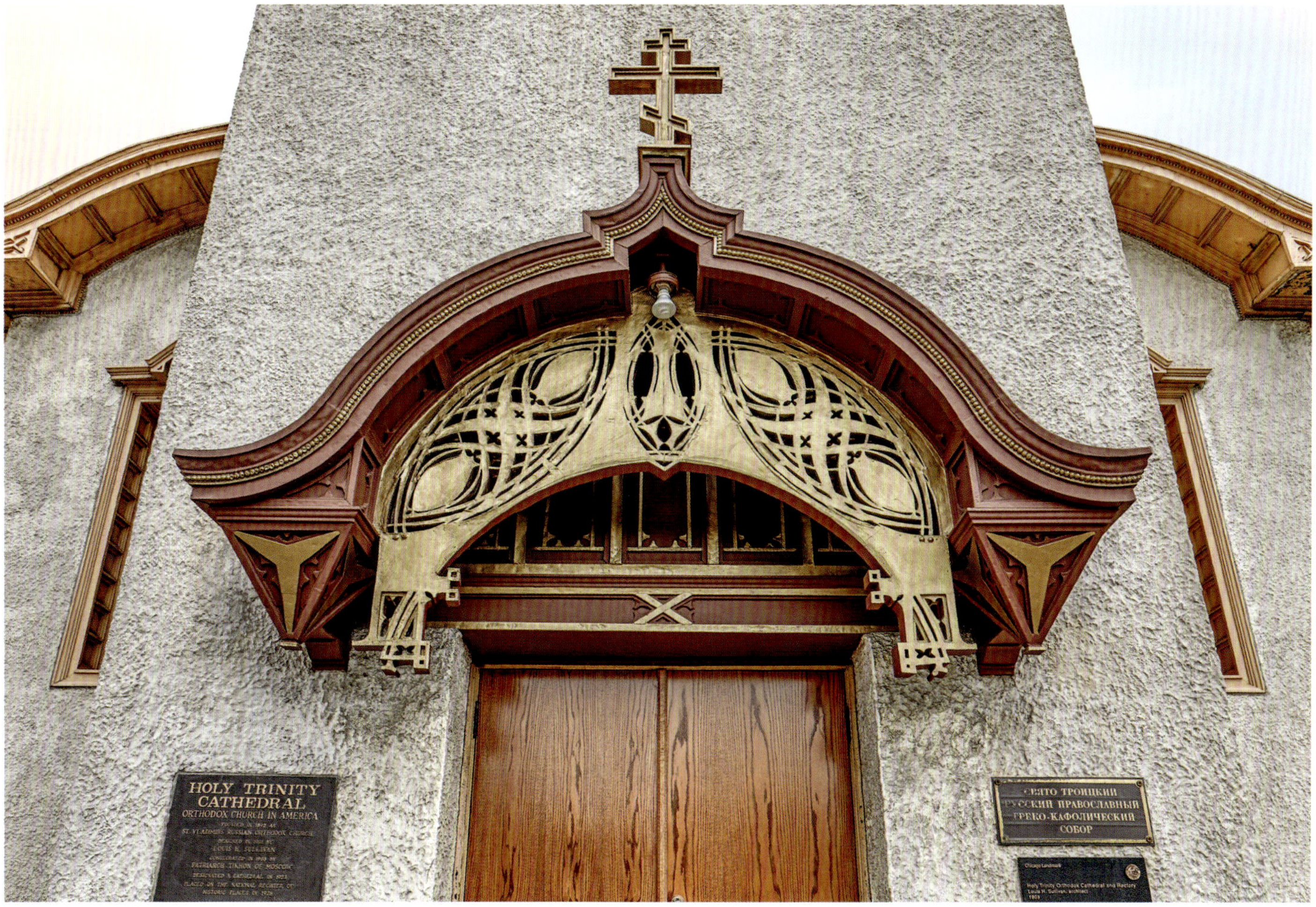
HOLY TRINITY
CATHEDRAL
ORTHODOX CHURCH IN AMERICA
СВЯТО ТРОИЦКИЙ
РУССКИЙ ПРАВОСЛАВНЫЙ
ГРЕКО-КАФОЛИЧЕСКИЙ
СОБОР
Holy Trinity Orthodox Cathedral and Rectory
Louis H. Sullivan, architect

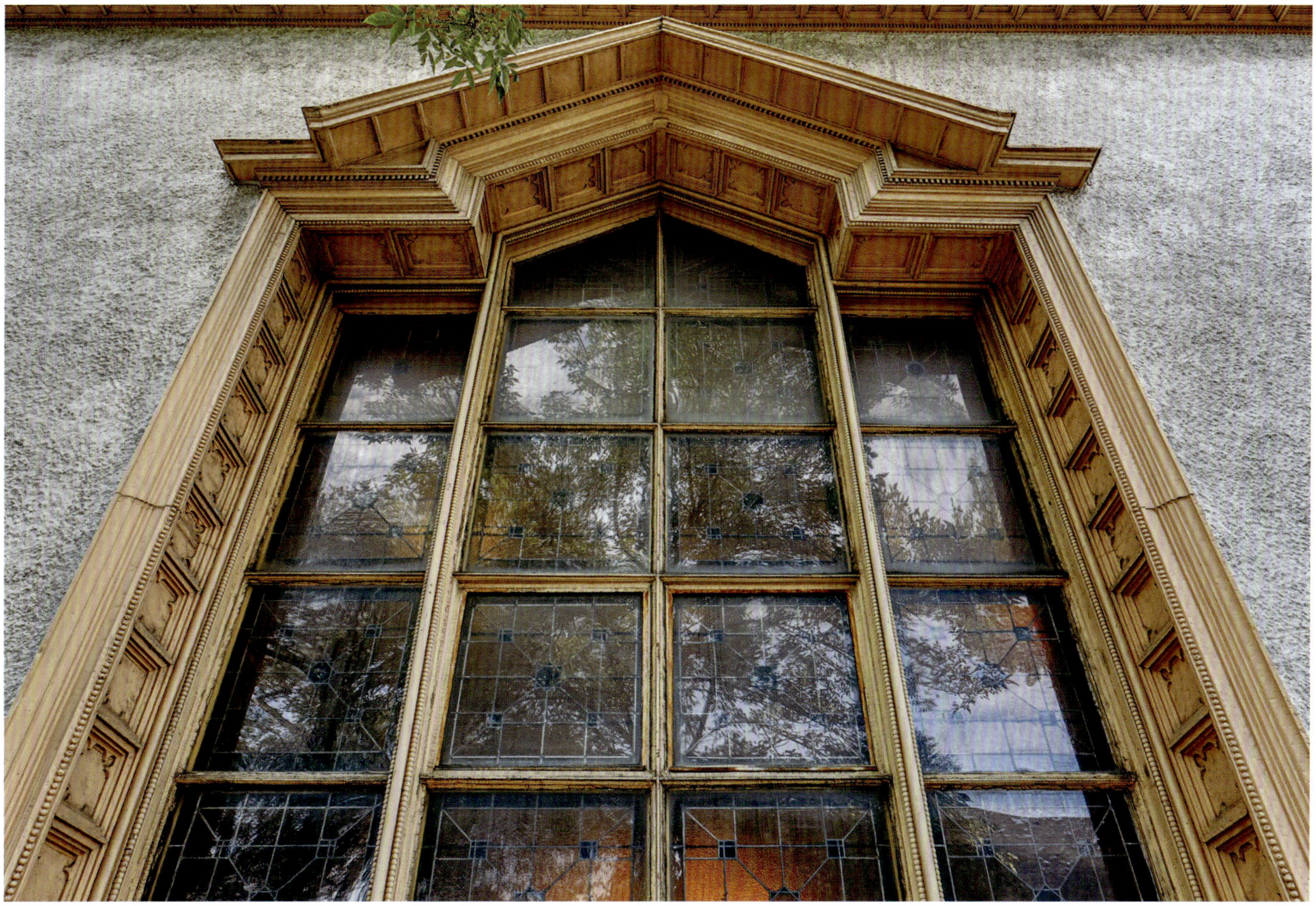

Healy & Millet did the chandelier and assisted in other details.

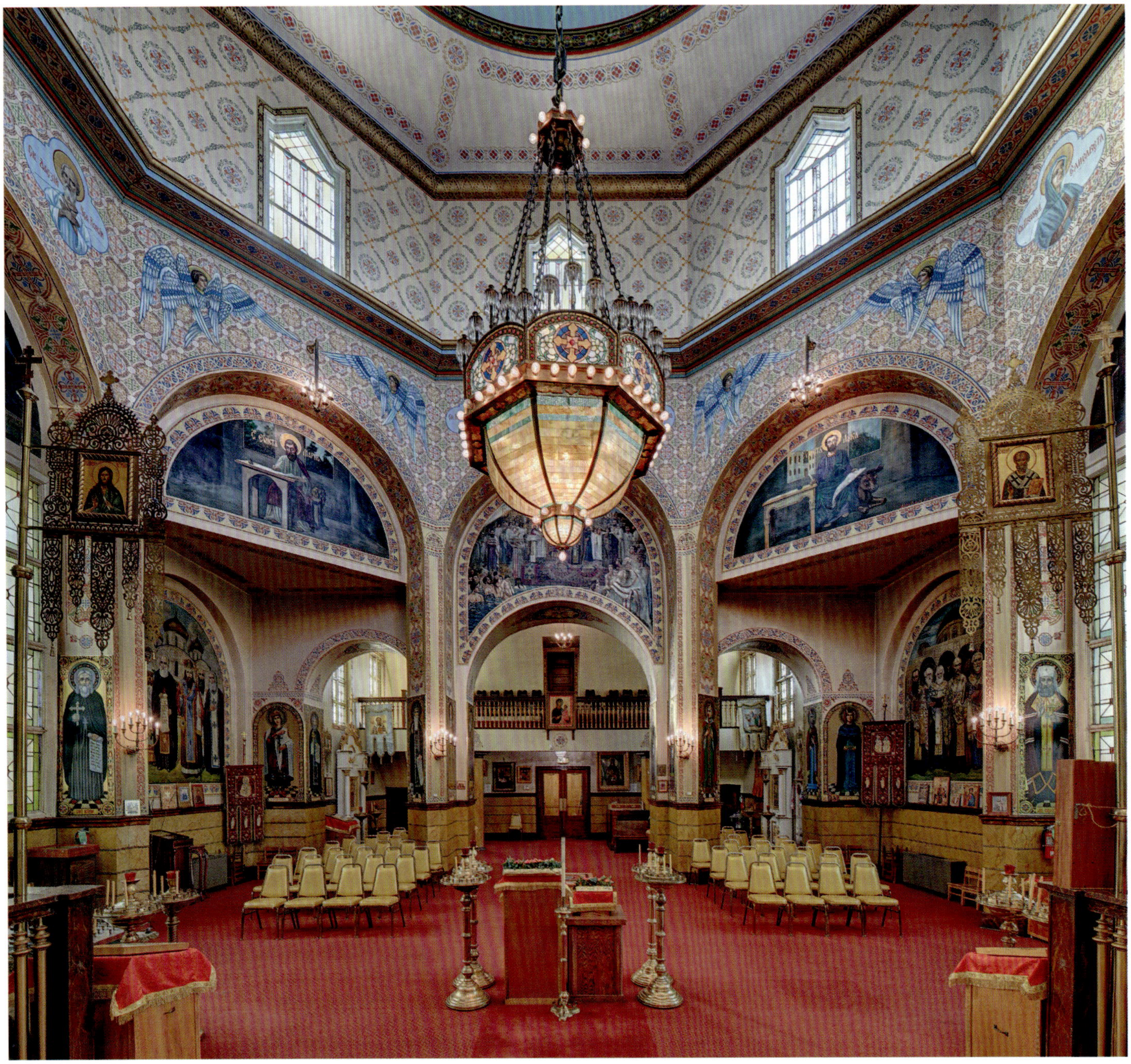

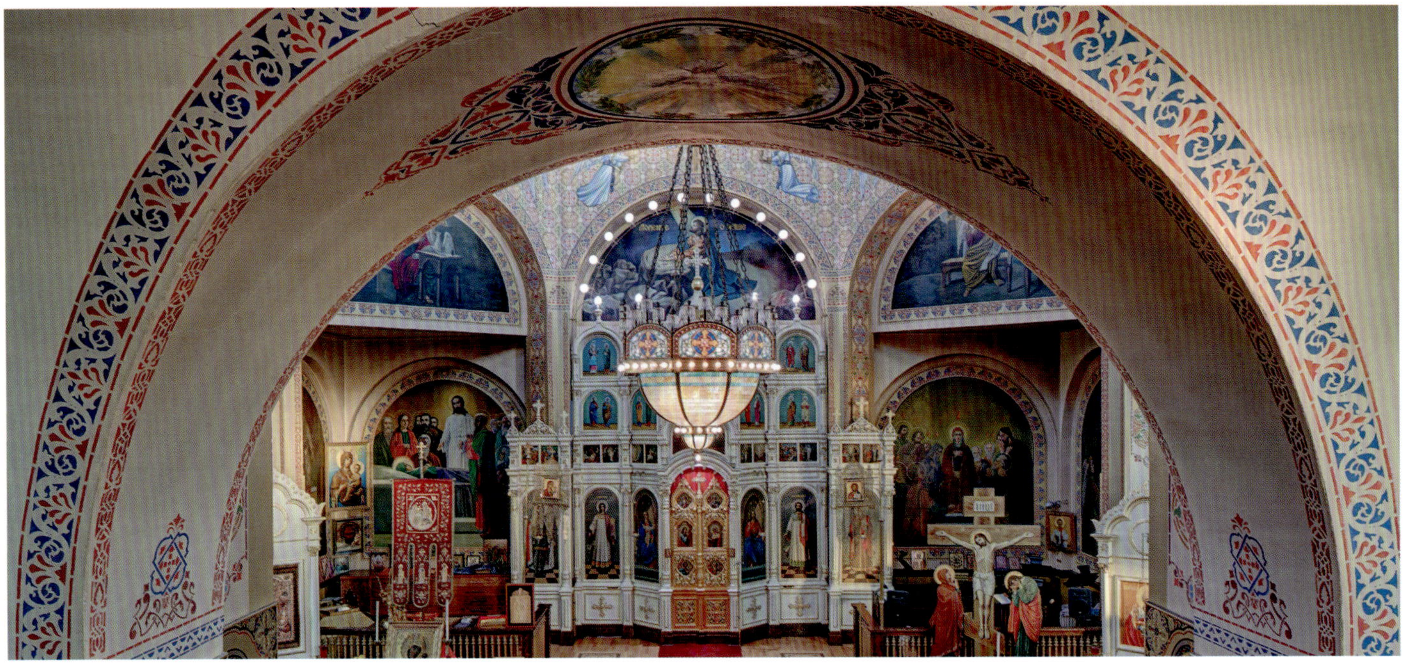

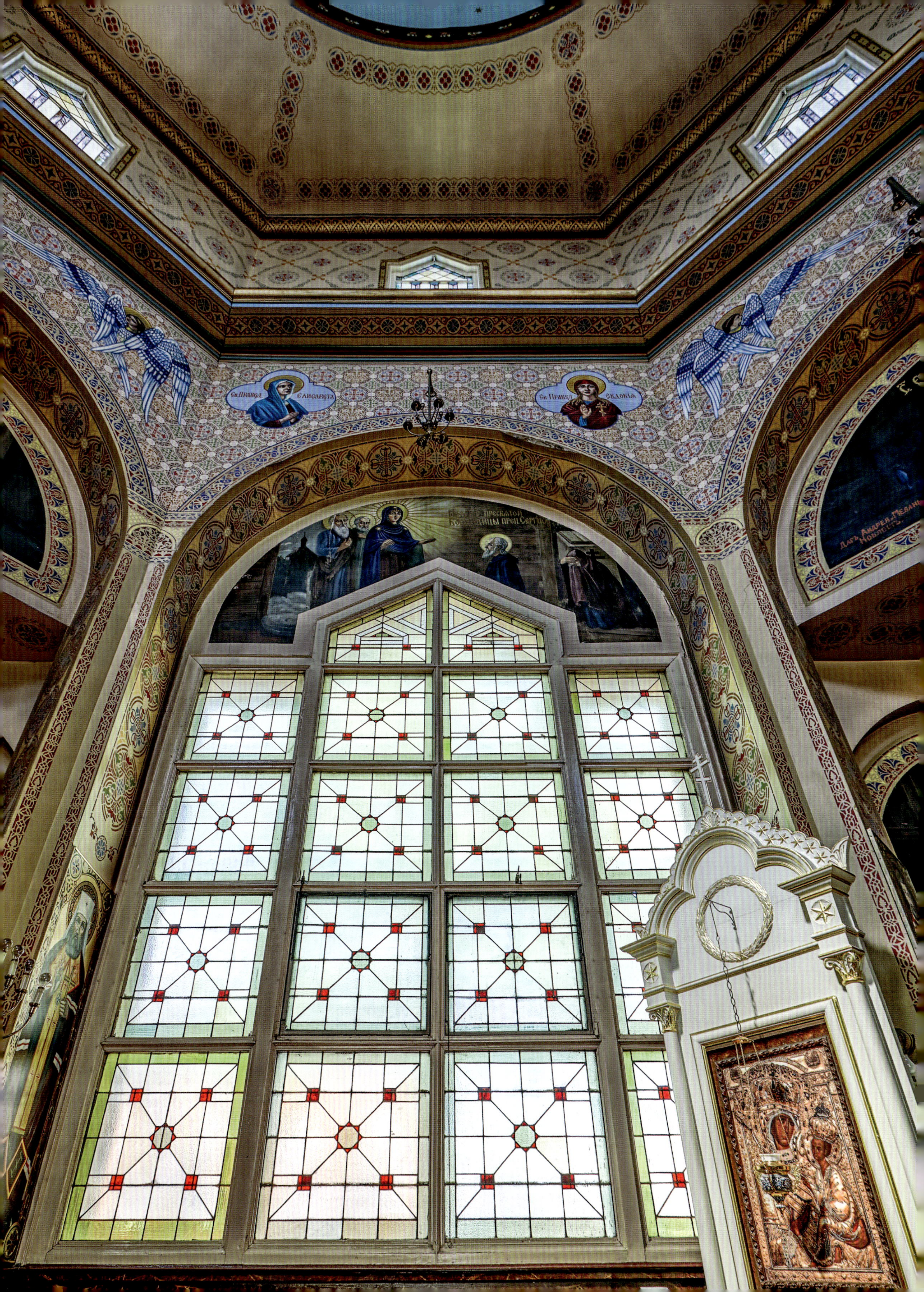

ST. PAUL'S UNITED METHODIST CHURCH

1910–14, CEDAR RAPIDS, IOWA

There is more than one possible reason why Sullivan either quit or was removed as the architect of this building, which was meant to combine a church and related functions. Although the budget was considerably larger than any other that Sullivan was receiving by then, his original design exceeded the allocated funds, as did two revisions that he reluctantly made. What is certain, however, is that he refused to make additional changes that he felt would compromise the building's integrity.

The design was then turned over to Chicago architect W. C. Jones in November 1912. His efforts were apparently so clumsy that Sullivan's former assistant, George Grant Elmslie, spent several days going over the plans to ameliorate at least some of the damage Jones had done. For his efforts, Elmslie refused any payment.

As it now stands, the building's basic form is much as Sullivan intended. It includes a rectangular school and social building, with a semi-circular auditorium on one side. A square bell tower rises above the platform and altar, which are at the midpoint of the semi-circle. Seven sections contain 700 seats, with an additional 400 in the gallery. While such an arrangement no longer seems radical, it certainly was for the time. What was lost, of course, was the rich ornamentation that Sullivan intended. Nevertheless, it was added to the National Register of Historic Places in 1985.

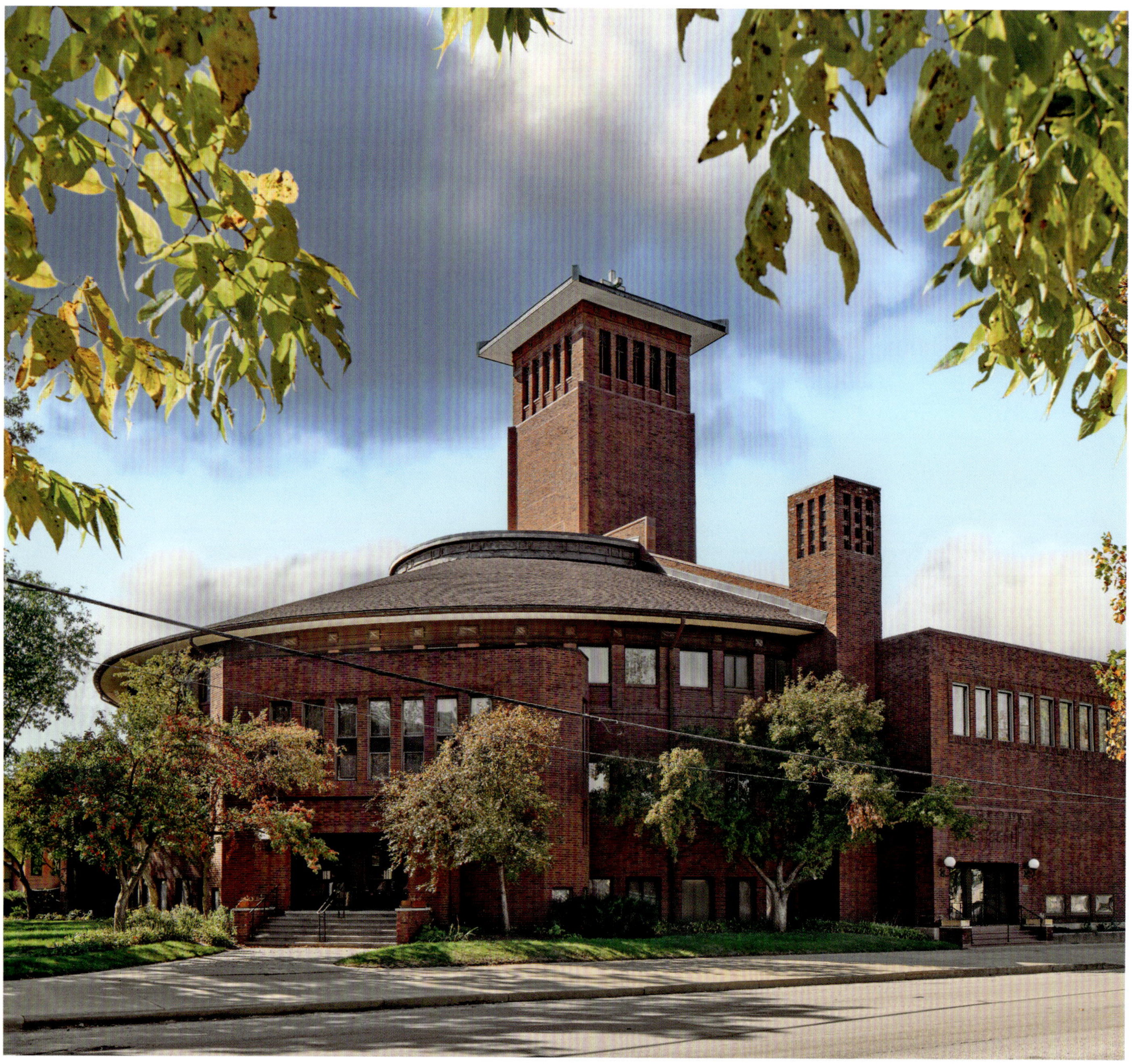

The church tower is like the water tower Sullivan designed for Chicago's Schlesinger & Mayer department store (see page 192).

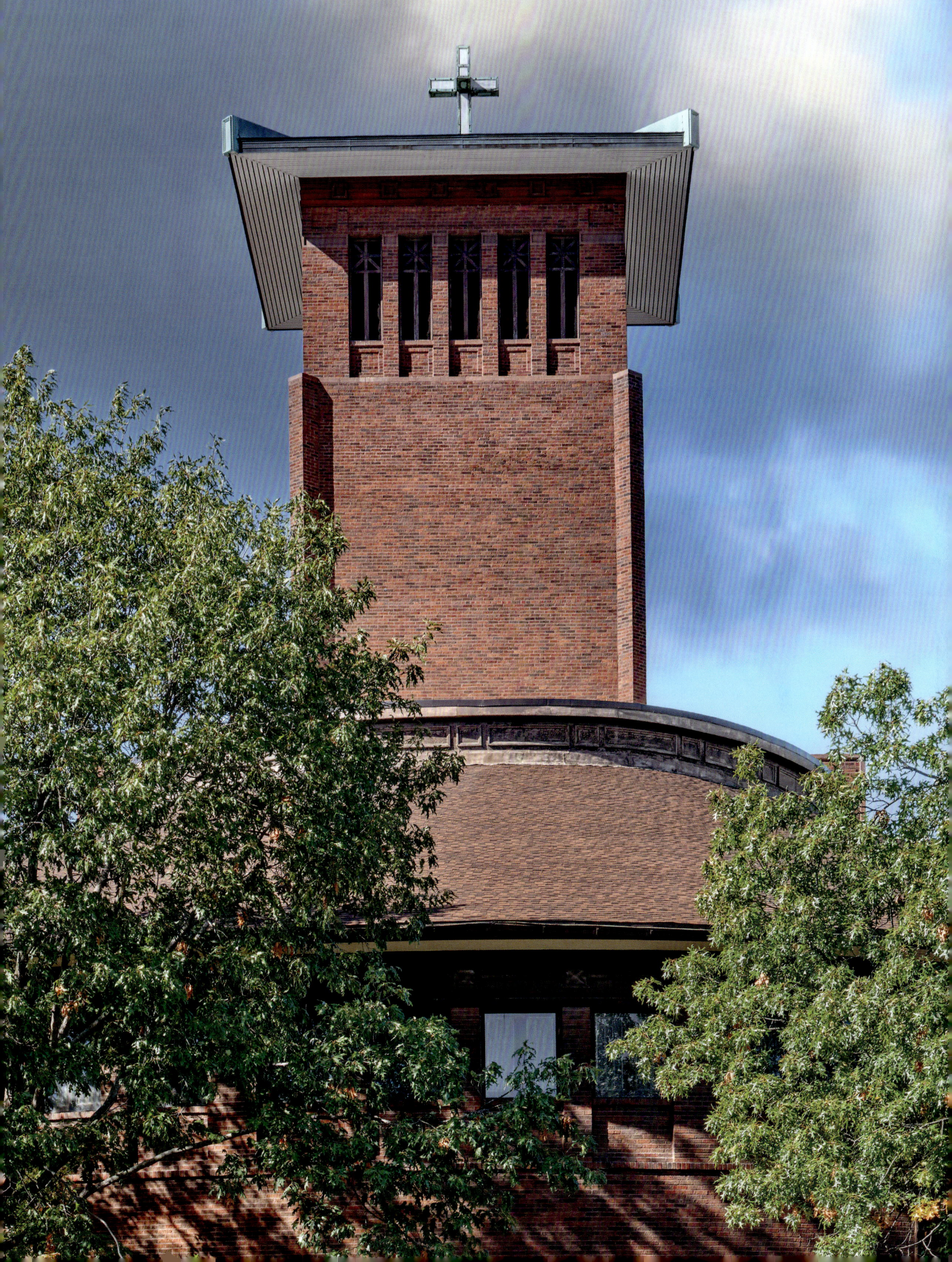

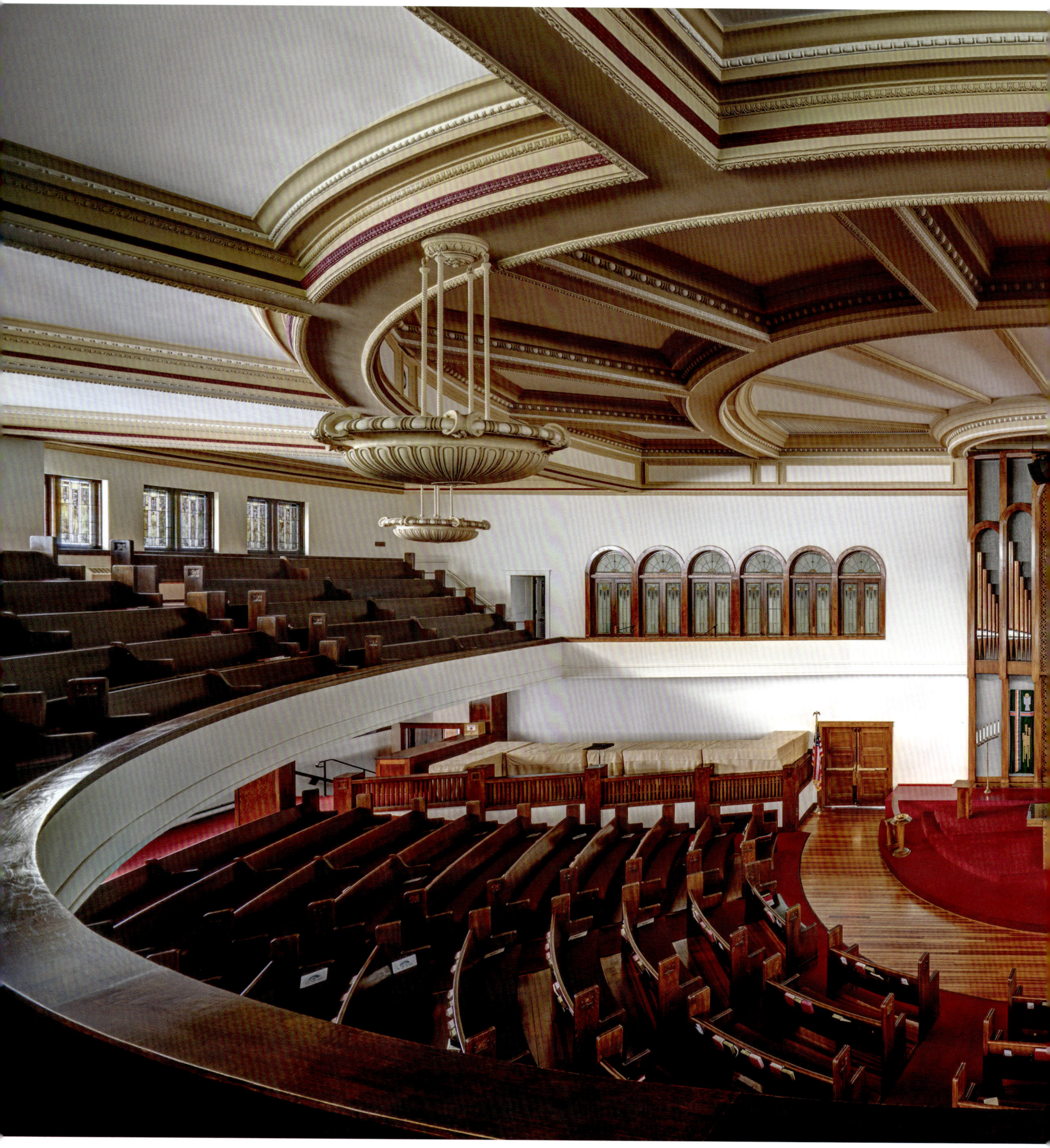

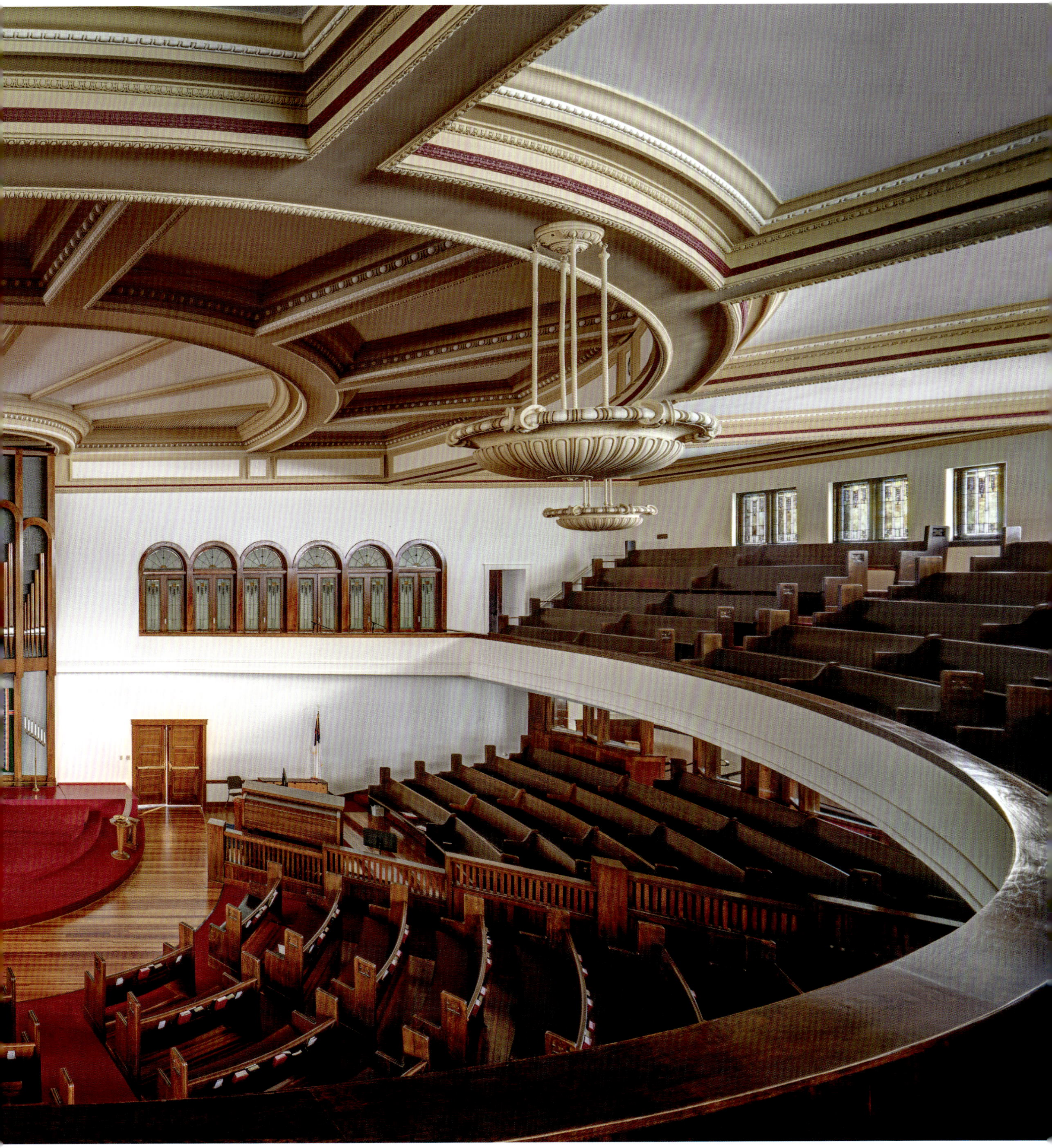

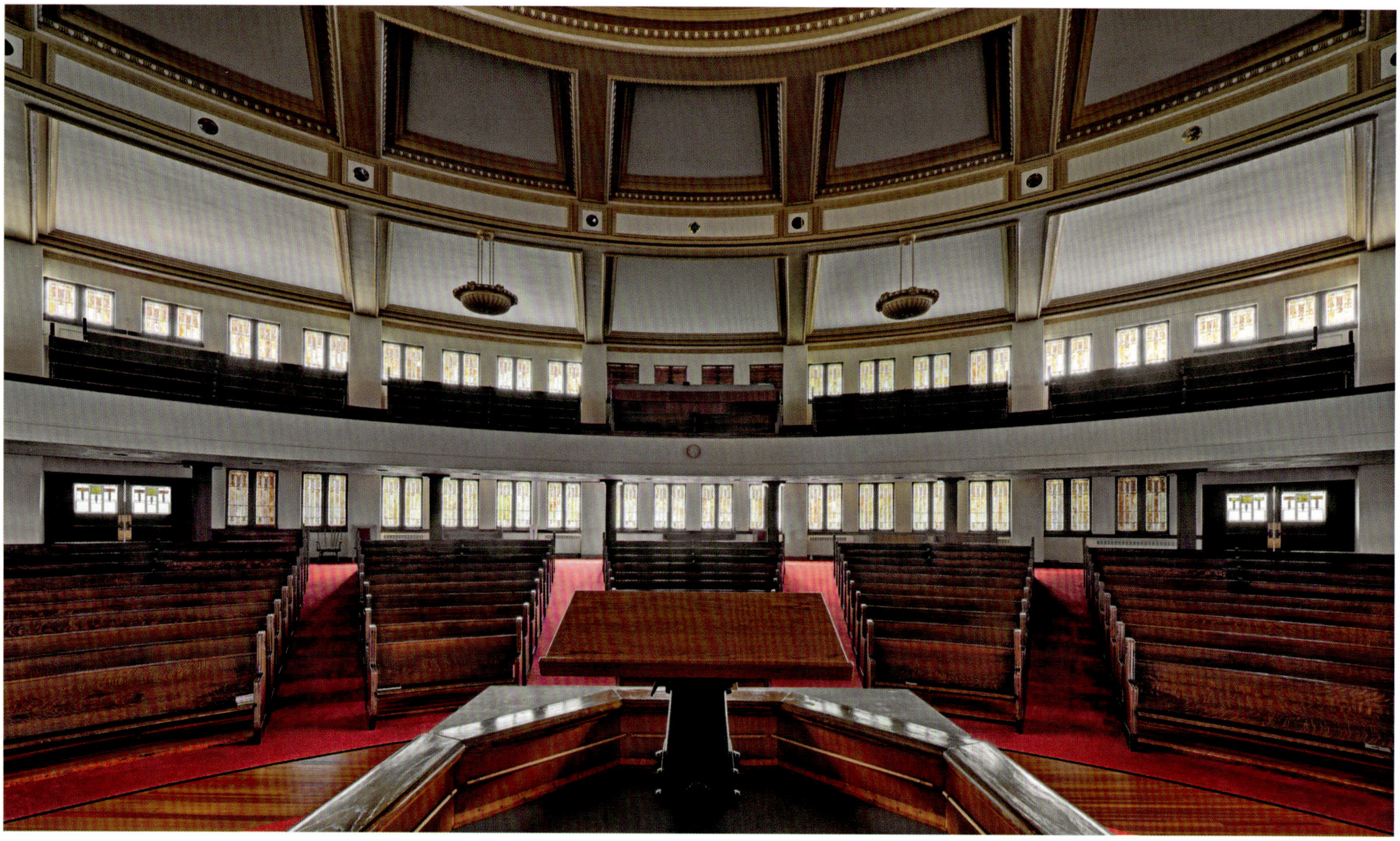

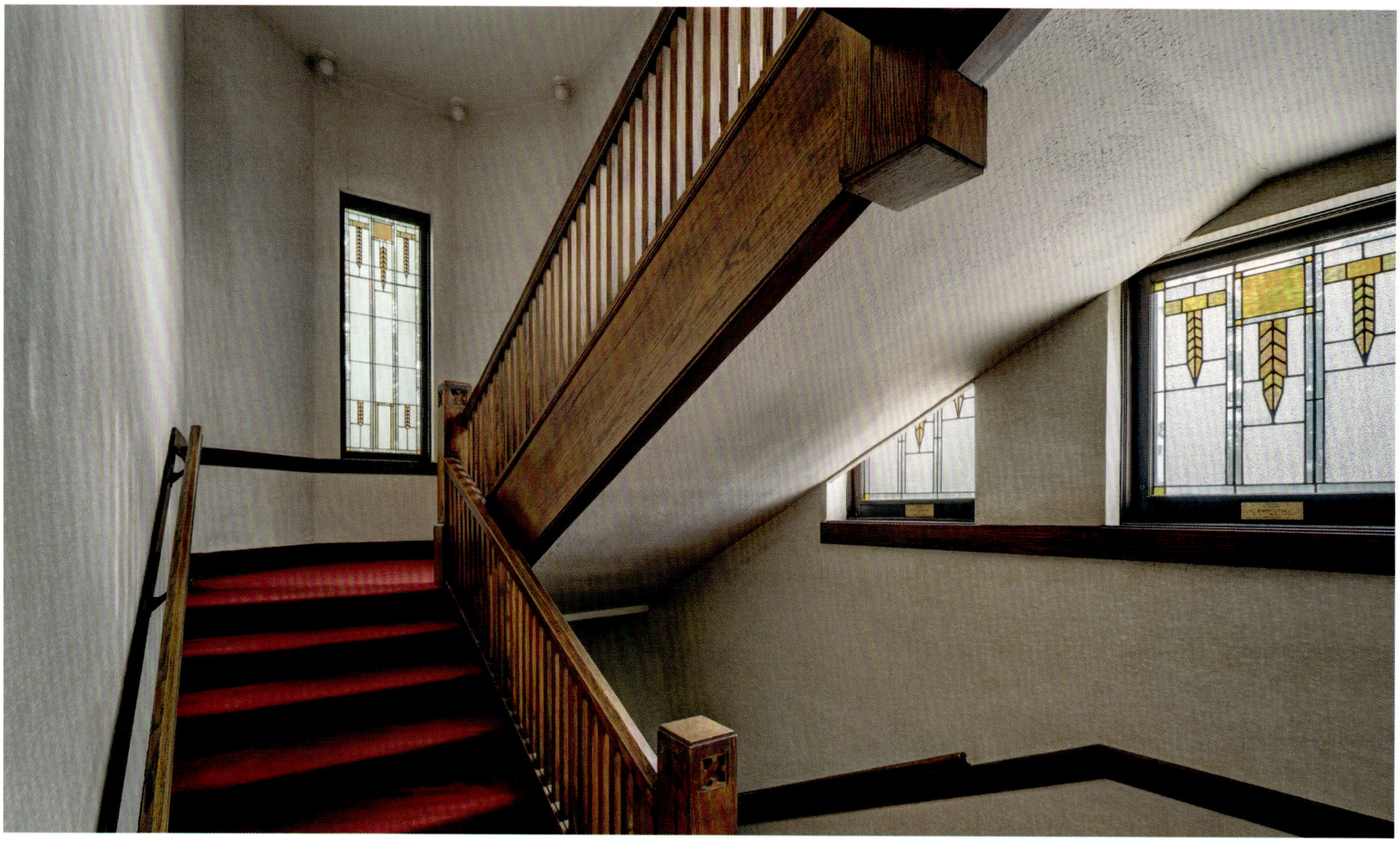

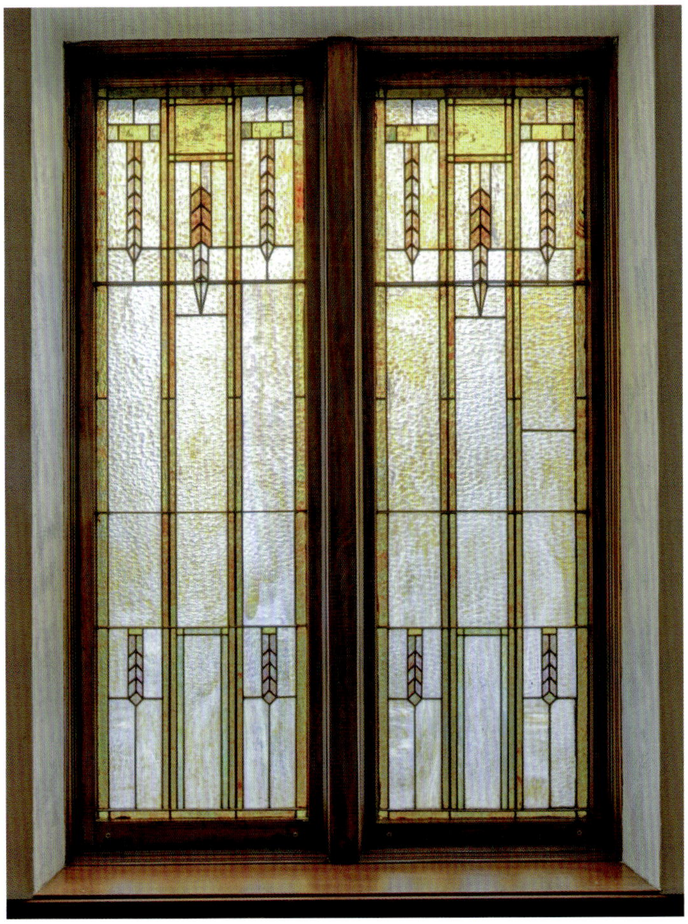

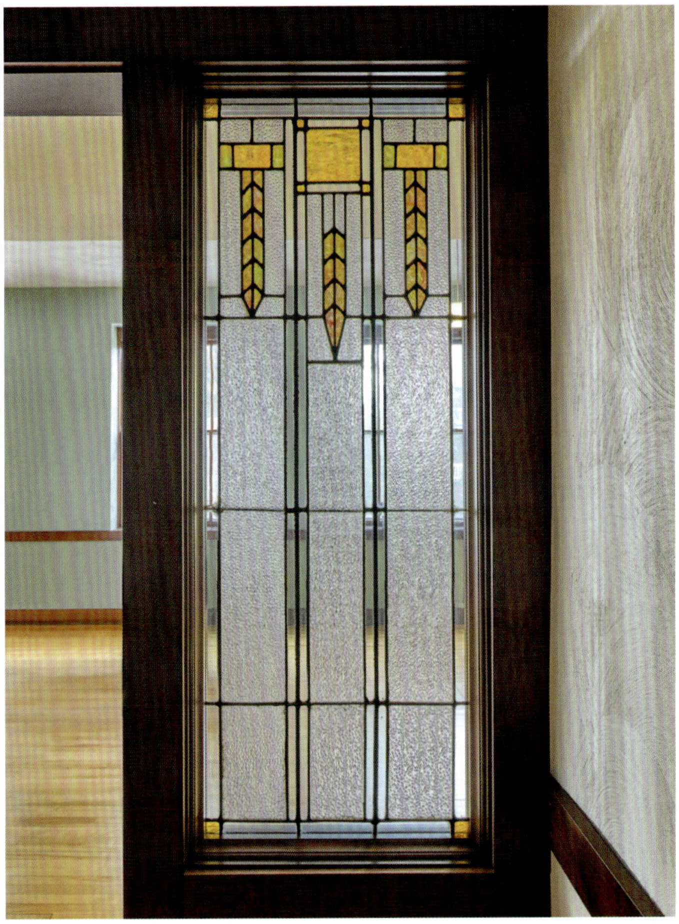

The art glass may have been designed by W. C. Jones but is similar to designs by Elmslie during his partnership with William Gray Purcell.

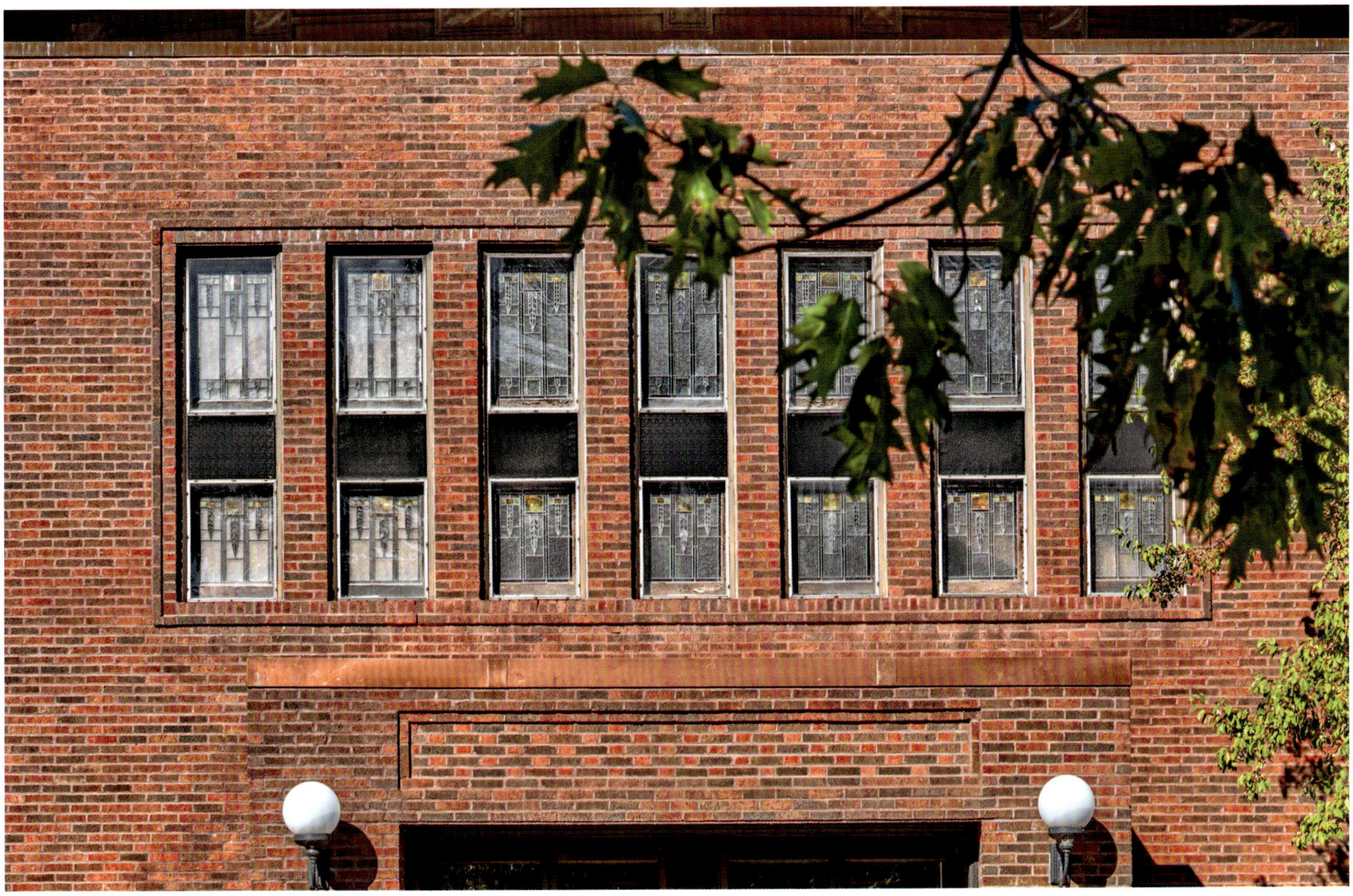

STANDARD ELEVATOR COMPANY FACTORY

1891, CHICAGO

Originally a strongly horizontal two-story building, with the second story a mezzanine that overlooked an interior manufacturing well, it underwent significant changes over time. To provide sufficient light and air, the façade was pierced with the maximum possible number of windows. By 1898, the Otis Elevator Company had taken over Standard and its building. In 1900, Otis commissioned Adler to design an expansion. Following the death of Otis that same year, his son Abraham worked with Samuel A. Treat to extend the building and add the four-story addition. The building is now used as a warehouse by the University of Illinois at Chicago. Unfortunately, many of the windows have been bricked over.

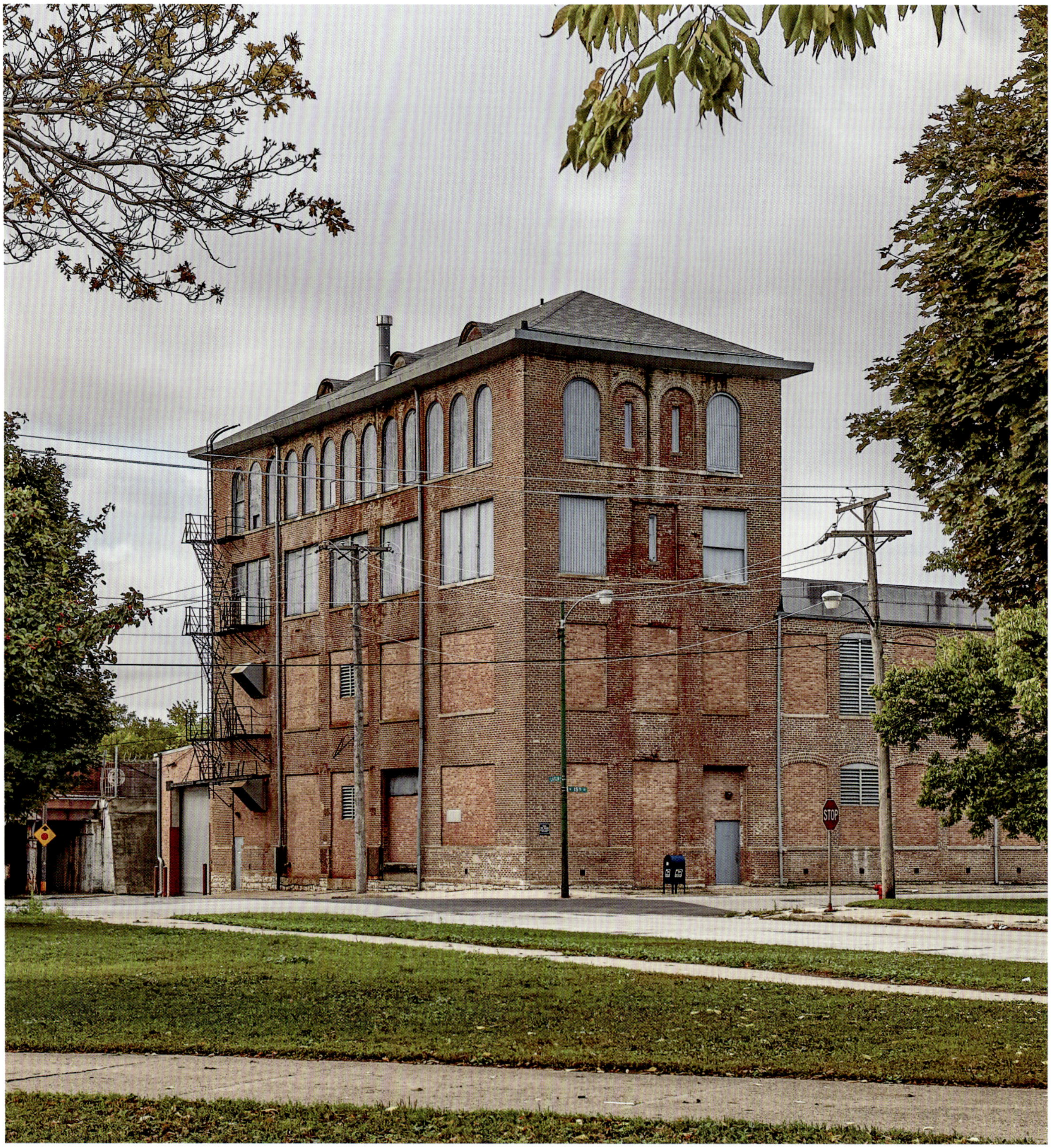

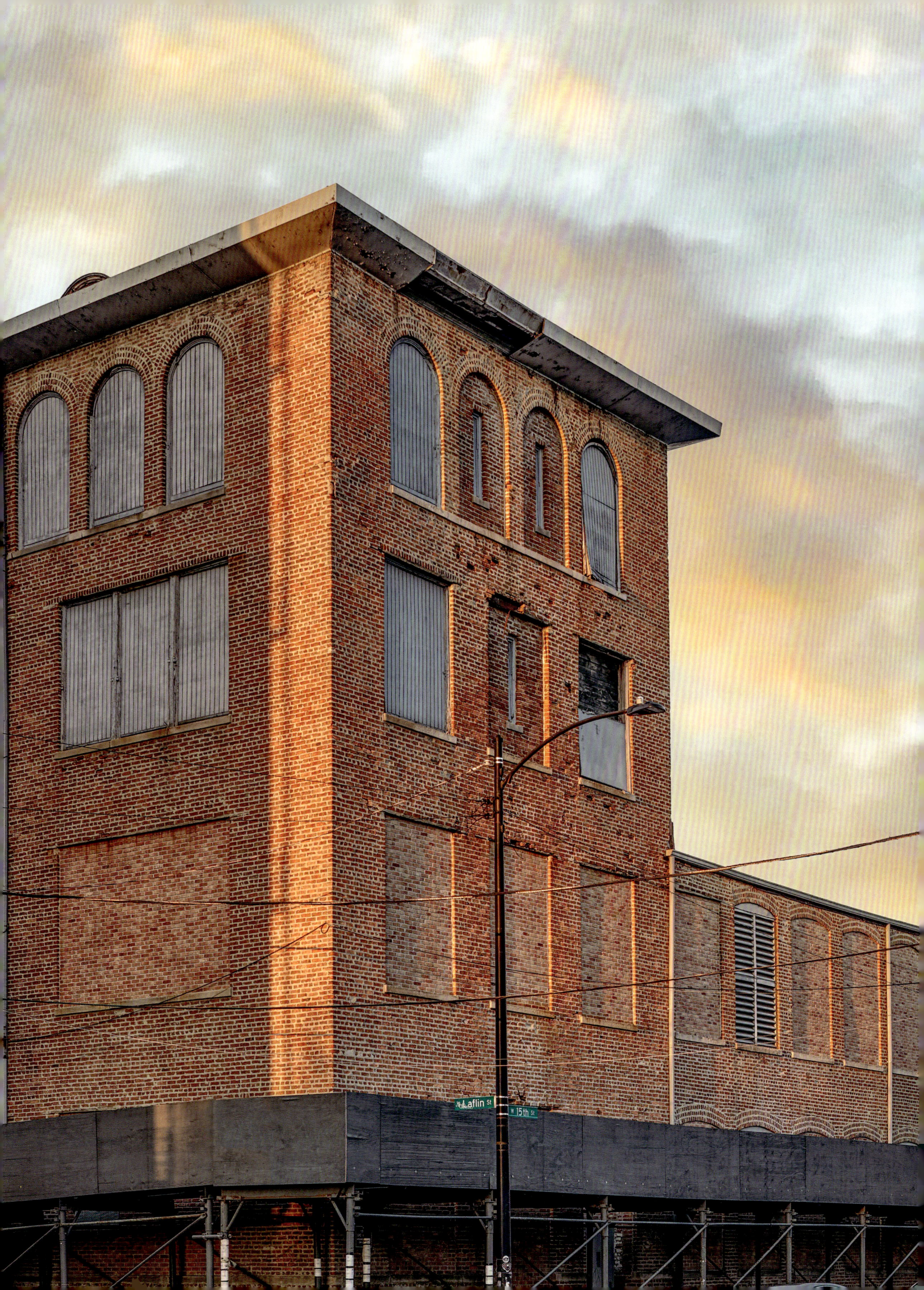
Laflin St
W 15th St

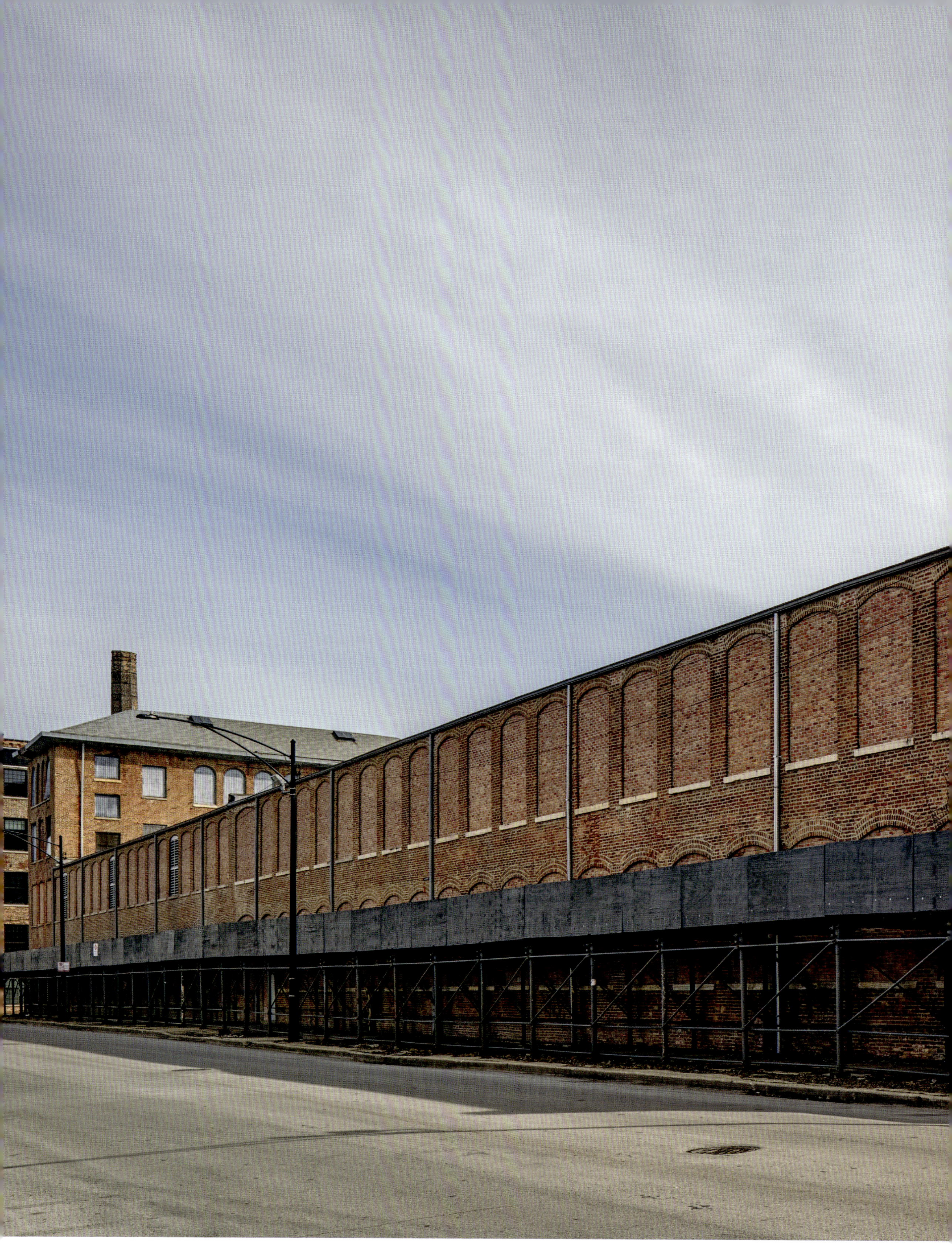

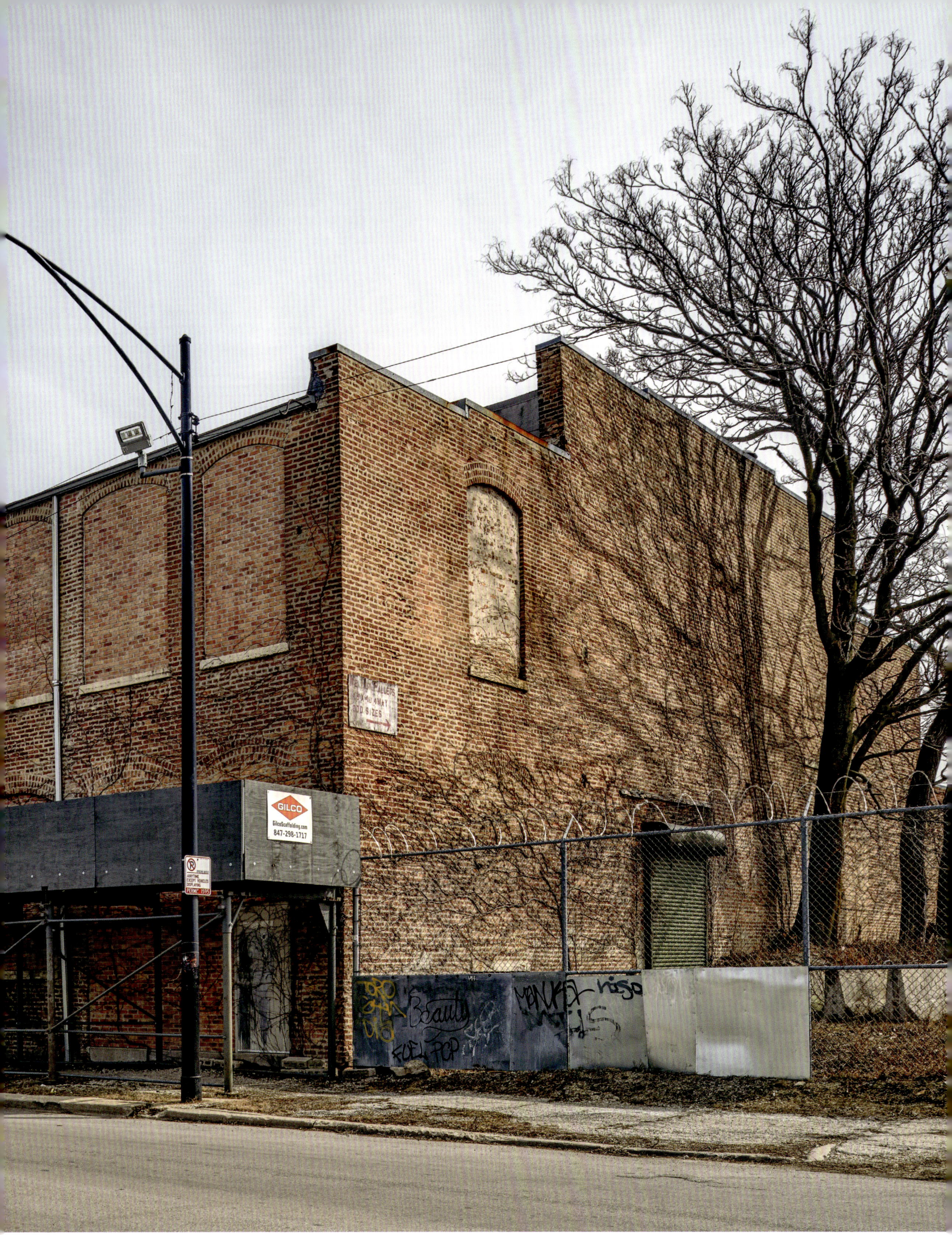
GILCO
847-298-1717

WOLF, SAYER & HELLER WAREHOUSE

1893–94, CHICAGO

Adler & Sullivan were commissioned in 1893 to design this warehouse addition to the meat packing plant of Wolf, Sayer & Heller. Until recently, the area just west of Chicago's downtown, known as the Fulton Market, was occupied by meat packing plants, produce markets, and light manufacturing facilities. As these facilities closed or moved to the suburbs, the area deteriorated until many of the vacant buildings were converted to loft apartment buildings, encouraged by the neighborhood's close proximity to the Loop. Wolf, Sayer & Heller is one of the buildings that was converted. Now, new buildings—including the headquarters of McDonald's—dot the area.

When the commission was received, Frank Lloyd Wright was still with Adler & Sullivan and may have been involved in the design, since he received a commission in 1896 to design a house for one of packing company's partners, Isadore Heller. This three-story house still stands in Chicago's Hyde Park neighborhood.

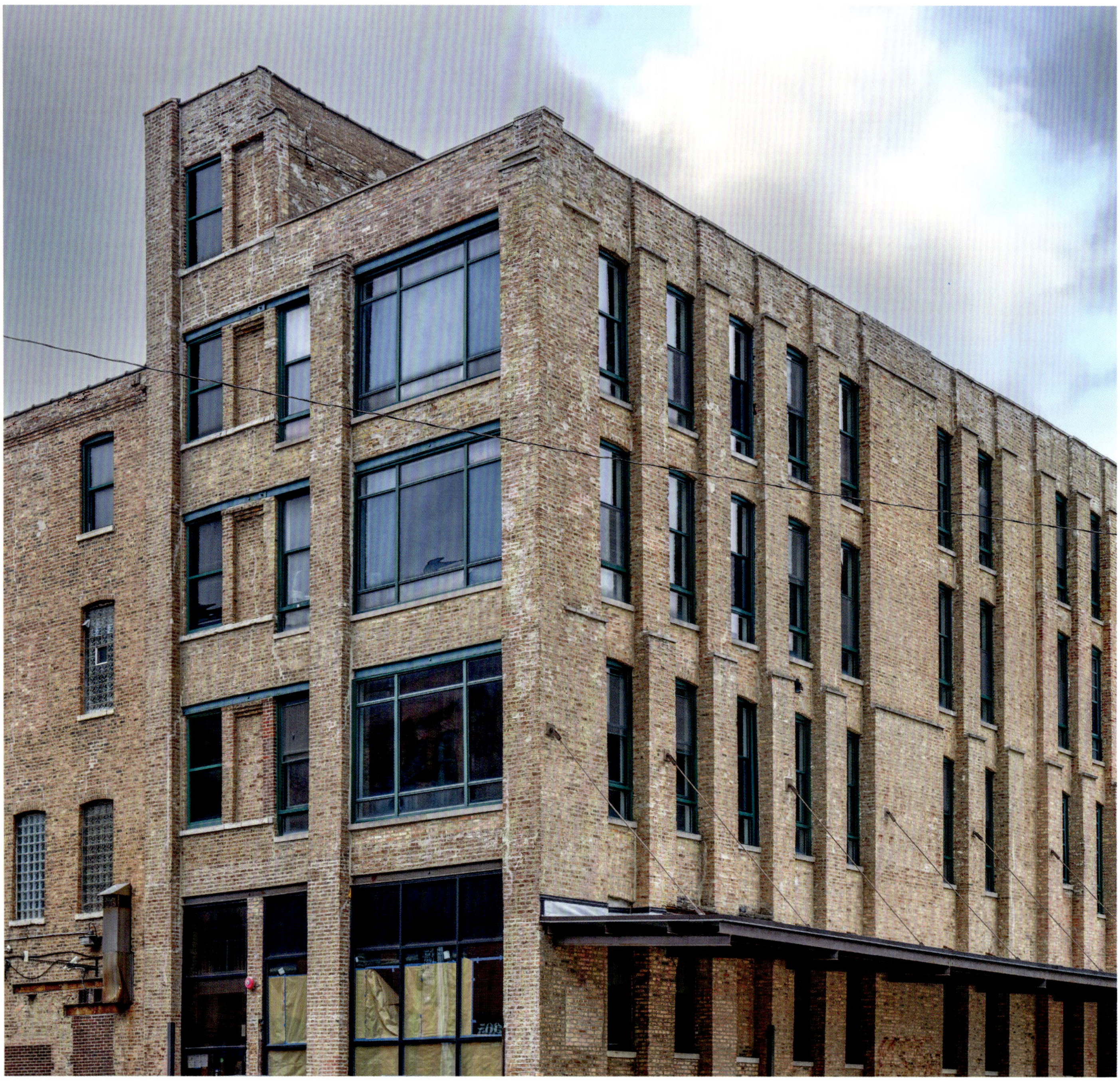

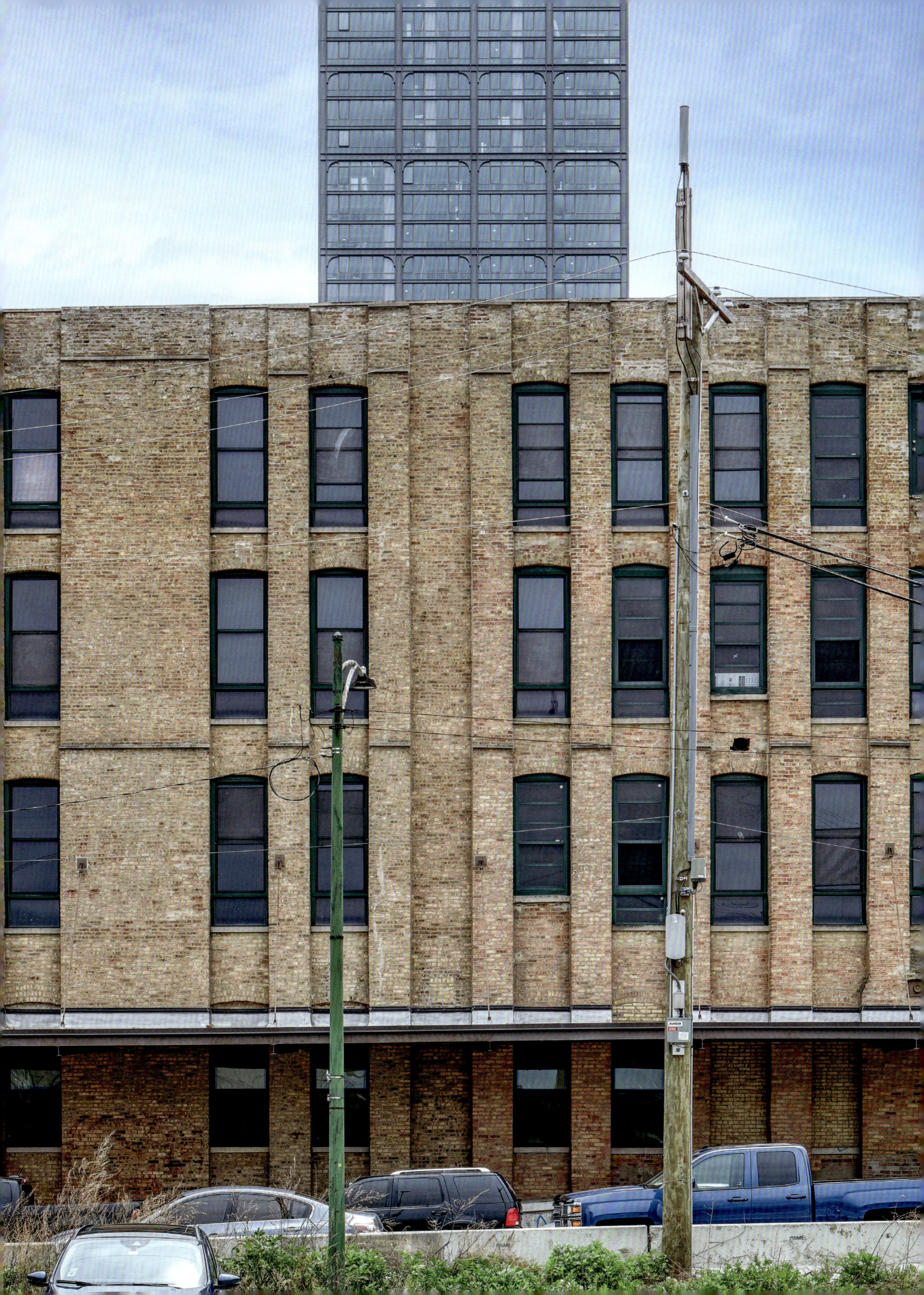

EUSTON & COMPANY LINSEED OIL PLANT

1899–1900, CHICAGO

Although the Chicago River teems with pleasure and tour boats and, increasingly, with kayaks, most people would be surprised to learn that Chicago was once America's busiest port, and the river was its main artery. Its banks once were lined with factories, lumber yards, and grain elevators, whose raw materials mostly arrived by water, whether from inland rivers or the Great Lakes. Eventually, larger and larger ships made the river so congested that a conscious decision was made to move major port facilities south on Lake Michigan to the mouth of the Calumet River.

It was only logical for a linseed oil plant to be constructed on the North Branch of the river, since the raw materials for linseed oil, in this case, flax seeds, would arrive by water. Linseed oil has many uses, but it is mainly used as a source for oil-based paints. The plant was built in two phases: a seed-crushing plant in 1899 and a linoleum plant completed in 1902 (since demolished). Some of the smaller structures still stand, including the corner office building, with its distinctive hipped roof. The original second-story casement windows have been replaced by double-hung windows.

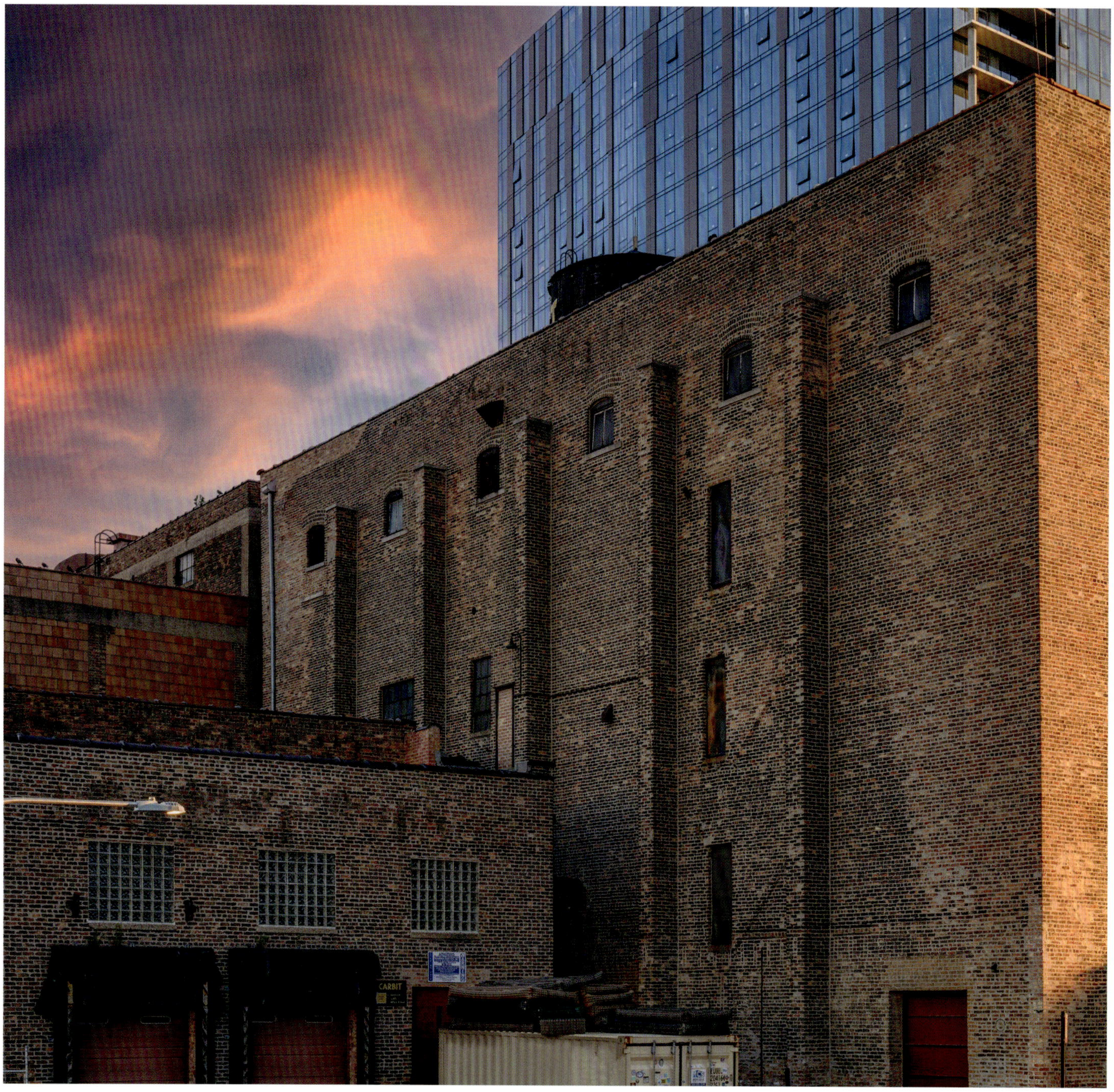

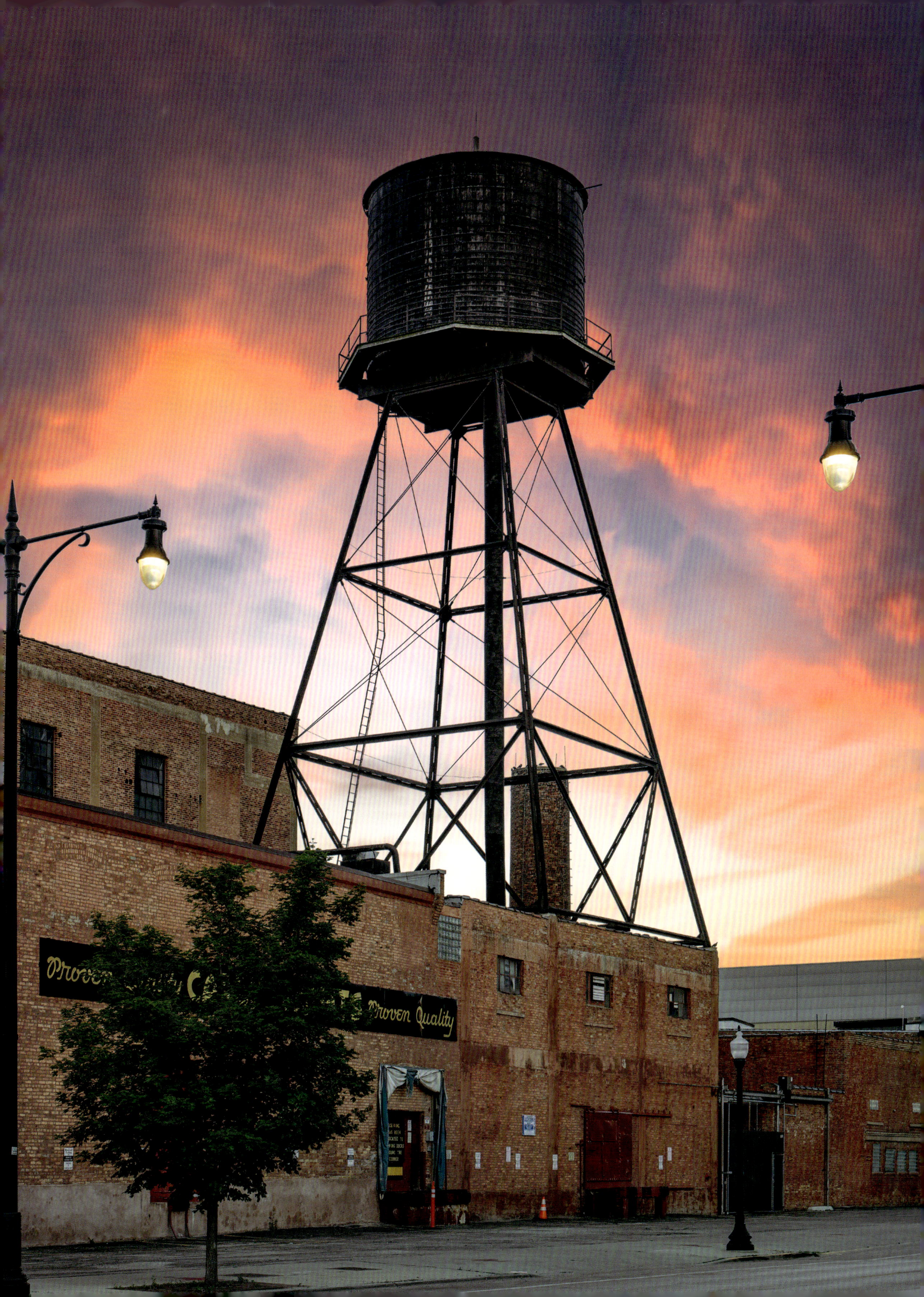
Proven Quality

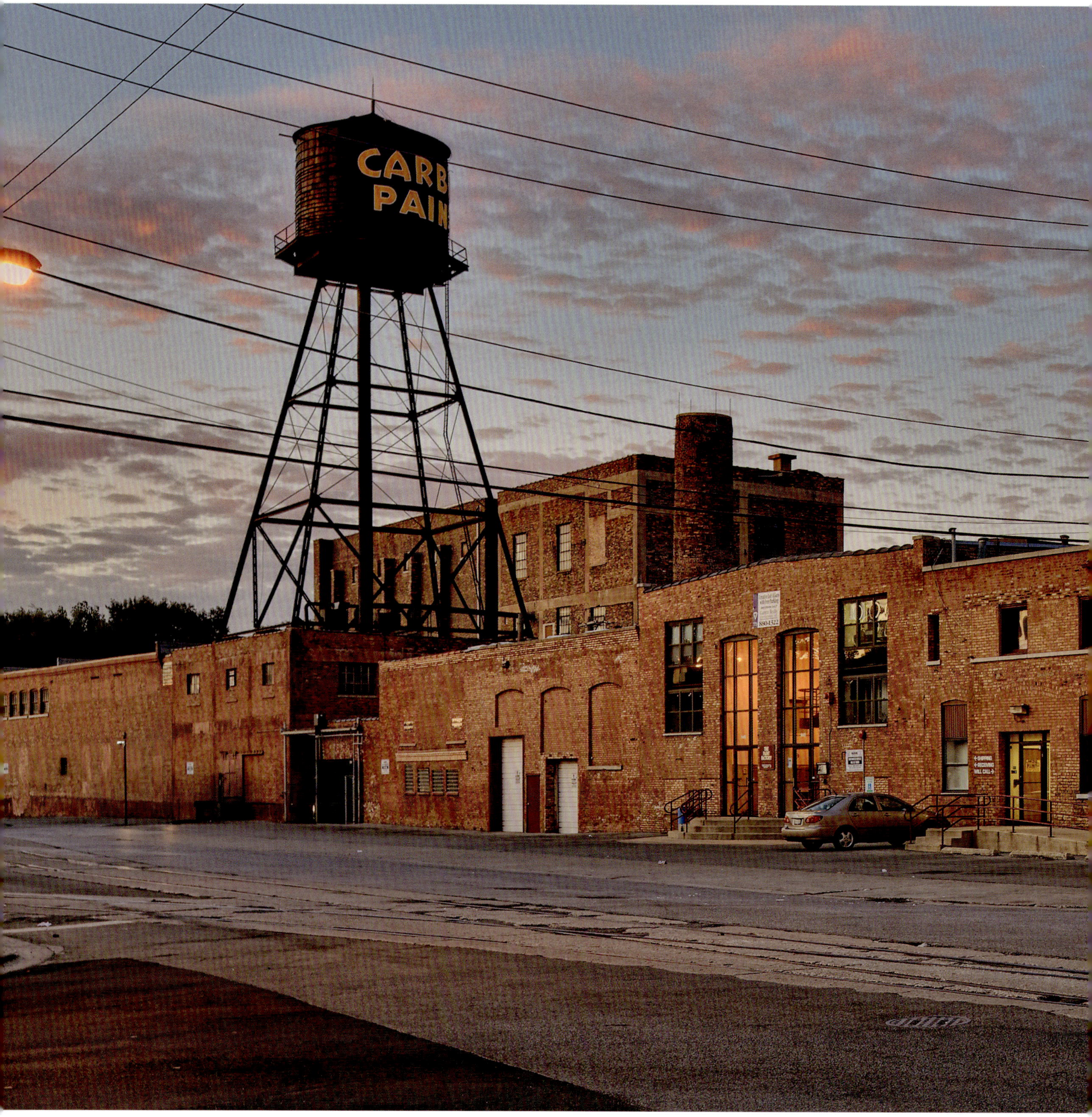

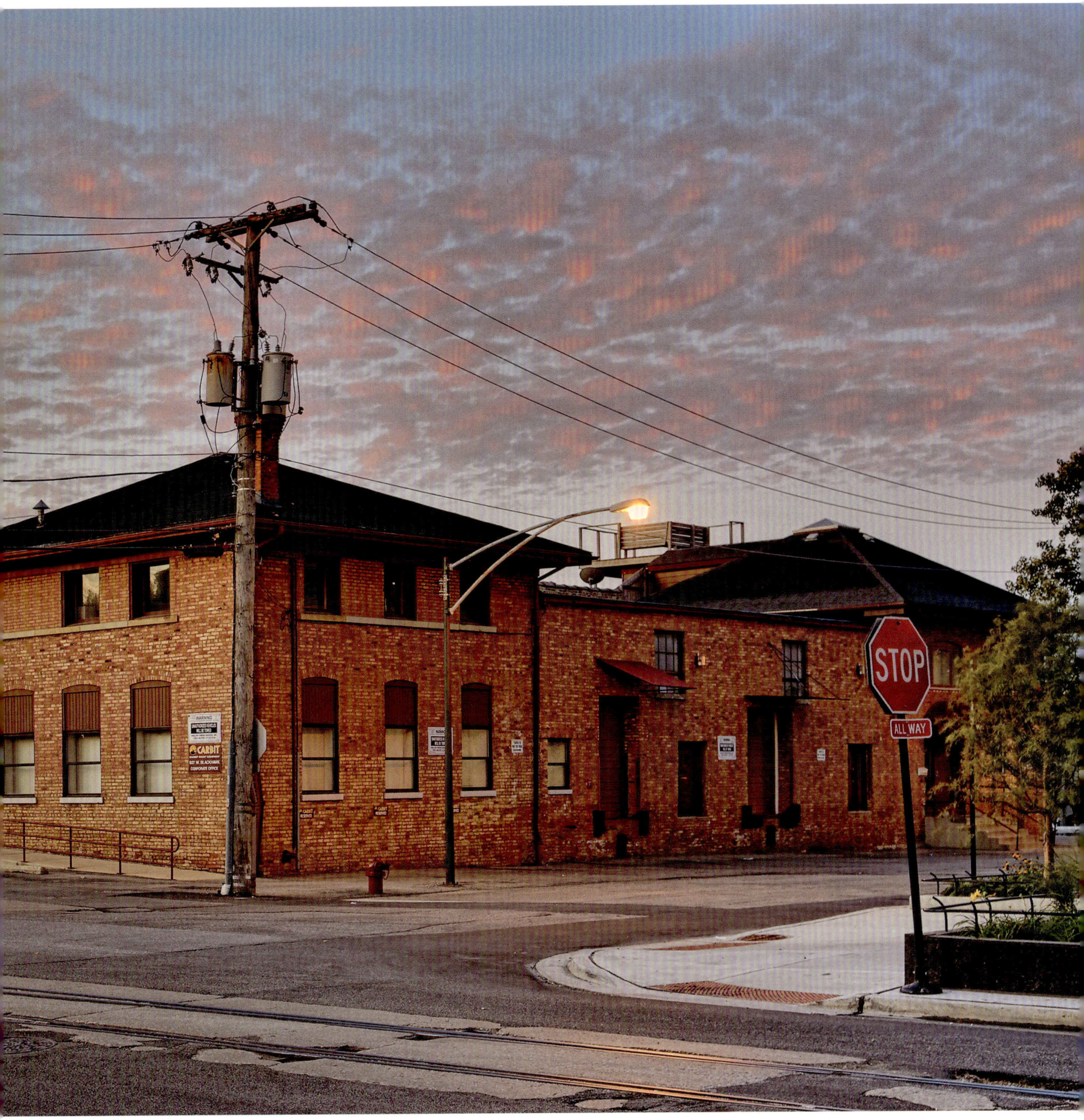
STOP
ALL WAY

DECLINE AND TRIUMPH

Sullivan was a faithful worker, a tireless thinker, an extraordinary talker … He could be arrogant and unnecessarily decisive … he lost many jobs because he would not compromise his ideals or play fast and loose with vital conceptions … He liked to be alone to think and write … He lived alone most of his life, and when he drank, he drank alone. Yet he was the most interesting, fascinating, inspiring and encouraging companion anyone could have."

George Grant Elmslie, *quoted by Hugh Morrison in* Louis Sullivan: Prophet of Modern Architecture

George Grant Elmslie was Sullivan's most faithful friend and was clearly distressed when he was finally forced to leave the firm in 1909 due to Sullivan's lack of commissions, after twenty years of collaboration and employment. For some time, Elmslie had been on half pay, with the understanding that he would inherit the firm upon Sullivan's retirement or death. But half of what became essentially nothing was not enough, so Elmslie left to begin what became a successful partnership with another former Sullivan employee, William Gray Purcell.

In the five years since the last of the Schlesinger & Mayer commissions had been completed in 1903, Sullivan had averaged but one completed building per year. Perhaps the most significant for his future career was the National Farmers Bank in Owatonna, Minnesota, the first of the small-town banks that would be the highlight of Sullivan's last years. Although the actual design was partially Elmslie's, Sullivan would eventually build seven more on his own.

Elmslie also did much of the design for the now demolished Babson House in Riverside, Illinois, but he made it clear in a 1936 letter to Frank Lloyd Wright that the surviving Bradley House in Madison, Wisconsin, was largely Sullivan's own design. Although he wouldn't have Elmslie's help after the Bradley, Sullivan would sometimes have the assistance of young architect Parker Berry.

In the same letter, Elmslie mentioned Sullivan's design for St. Paul's Methodist Episcopal Church in Cedar Rapids, Iowa. His disputes with the client led to Sullivan's replacement with another architect, who "made a mess of the original design …" Elmslie was asked to step in "and bring back some of the original idea," which he did while refusing any payment. It was another example of how, according to Elmslie, "I had to defend him, time and again, and pacify his clients." It was this ability, as much as Elmslie's talent, that Sullivan would miss in the years to come.

In addition to the banks, Sullivan did a small office building and a department store, both in Iowa. But it is the banks that are best known. Despite variations in detail, the banks share simple cube-like forms and elaborate decoration. Although smaller in scale than their big city counterparts, the interiors of the banks provide the same sense of dignity and solidity that banks were then thought to require.

Ironically, influential critics continued to praise the work of Sullivan, though it seemed to have little effect on his business. As quoted in Twombly's biography, Montgomery Schuyler wrote that "a new work by Louis Sullivan is the most interesting event which can happen in the American architectural world today. There is nothing like the professional interest which his works inspire since Richardson ceased to produce a quarter of a century ago."

In a sense, the banks and Sullivan's last commission—the façade for the Krause Music Store in Chicago—were a last hurrah for the kind of decorative designs that Sullivan had championed throughout his career. Instead, architecture was moving toward a stripped-down classicism and then to a functionalism that eschewed decoration altogether. That, indeed, may be the reason Sullivan's remaining buildings are so admired and even revered.

Sadly demolished in 1960 to make way for a subdivision of ordinary homes, the commission for the Henry B. Babson Estate in Riverside, Illinois was a major achievement for Sullivan. Built for an entrepreneur in early phonographs in 1908-09 with a construction cost equivalent to nearly $2 million today, the design was the architect's personal statement in the maturing Prairie style begun by Sullivan's former student, Frank Lloyd Wright. It was located in the planned community of Riverside, Illinois, laid out in 1869 by famed landscape architects Frederick Law Olmsted and Calvert Vaux, designers of New York's Central Park. In Chicago, Olmstead would later design the site for the 1893 Columbian Exposition and both Washington and Jackson Parks.

Period black-and-white photographs never do justice to Sullivan's color choices, in this case, according to a contemporary publication, "partaking of the colors of the landscape." The first floor was expressed in "oriental brick," with the second covered in "polychromatic" rough-finished wood. Each end had covered porches, and the second floor featured an arched and cantilevered balcony. The extensive landscaping was designed by Jens Jensen, creator of many of Chicago's parks. At the time, the house was compared favorably to Wright's nearby Coonley House and estate, which survives. The Village of Riverside was added to the National Register of Historic Places in 1969 and declared a National Historic Landmark the following year.

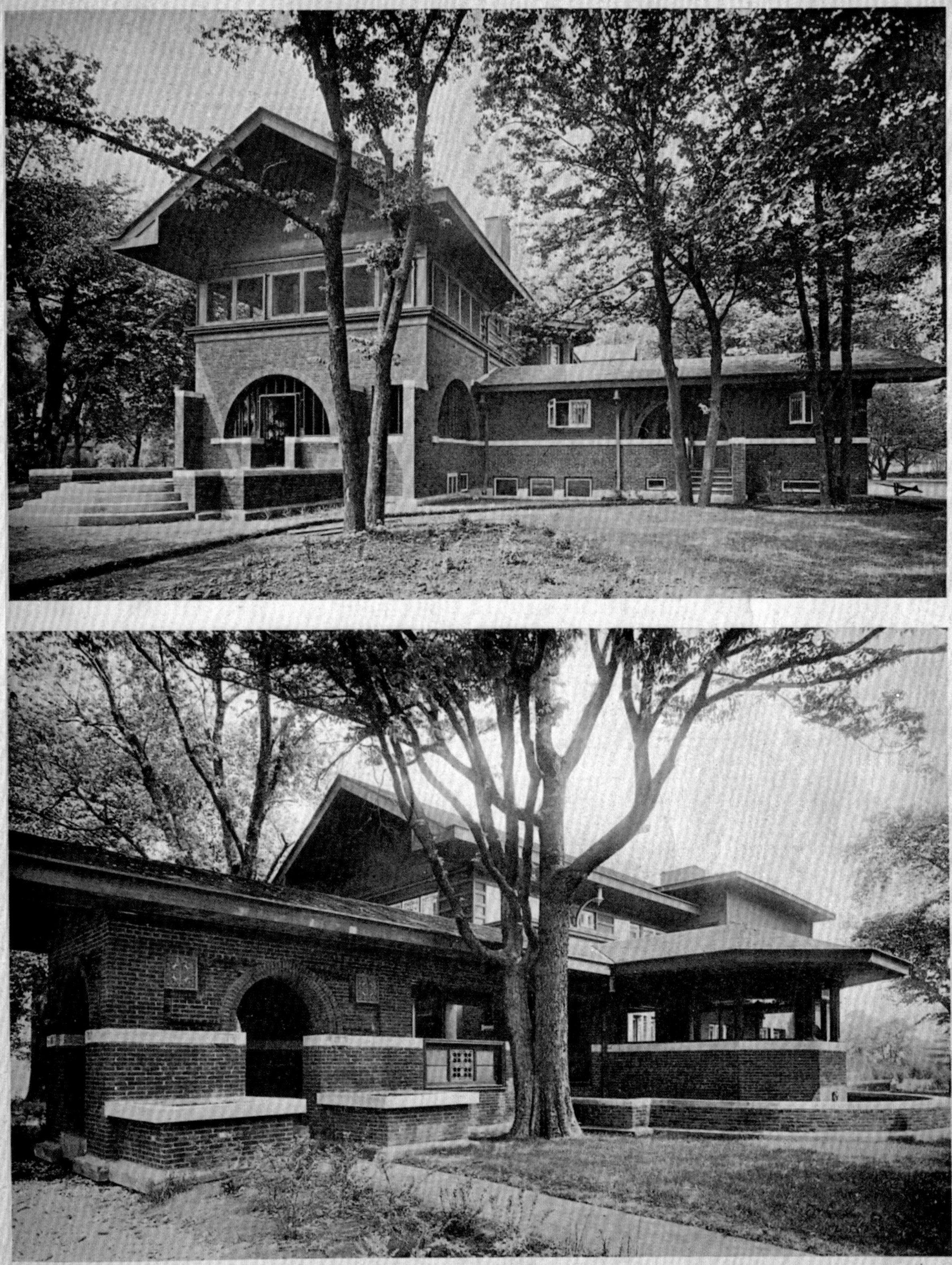

HOUSE AT RIVERSIDE, ILL.
LOUIS H. SULLIVAN, ARCHITECT.

Photo from The Brickbuilder (1910), courtesy of the Ryerson and Burnham Libraries, the Art Institute of Chicago.

HAROLD AND JOSEPHINE BRADLEY HOUSE

1909–13, MADISON, WISCONSIN

The commission for the Bradley House came from Sullivan's former client and friend, Charles R. Crane, who had also been responsible for the earlier commission to design the Holy Trinity Russian Orthodox Cathedral in Chicago. Josephine was Crane's daughter, and the house was meant to be a gift for her and her husband, University of Wisconsin biochemistry professor Harold Bradley. Sullivan prepared a plan after meeting with the couple, which they rejected as too grandiose. Revised plans were submitted in December 1909 and formed the basis for what we see today. As with the Babson House, the lower story of the Bradley House was brick, and the upper story was wood board and battens.

Sullivan, who told the Bradleys he was building the house for Crane and was answerable only to him, eventually withdrew. The house was then completed by local Madison architects Claude & Starck, with the assistance of—once again—George Grant Elmslie. Understandably, because they never felt their actual wishes were honored, the Bradleys were never happy with the house, and in 1917, it was sold to the Sigma Phi fraternity, who still occupies it. After a 1972 fire badly damaged the second floor, the fraternity restored it to its original condition. As for the Bradleys, in 1914, they had a more modest house, which still stands, designed for them by Elmslie and his partner William Gray Purcell. The Bradleys' original house was added to the National Register of Historic Places in 1972 and was declared a National Historic Landmark in 1976.

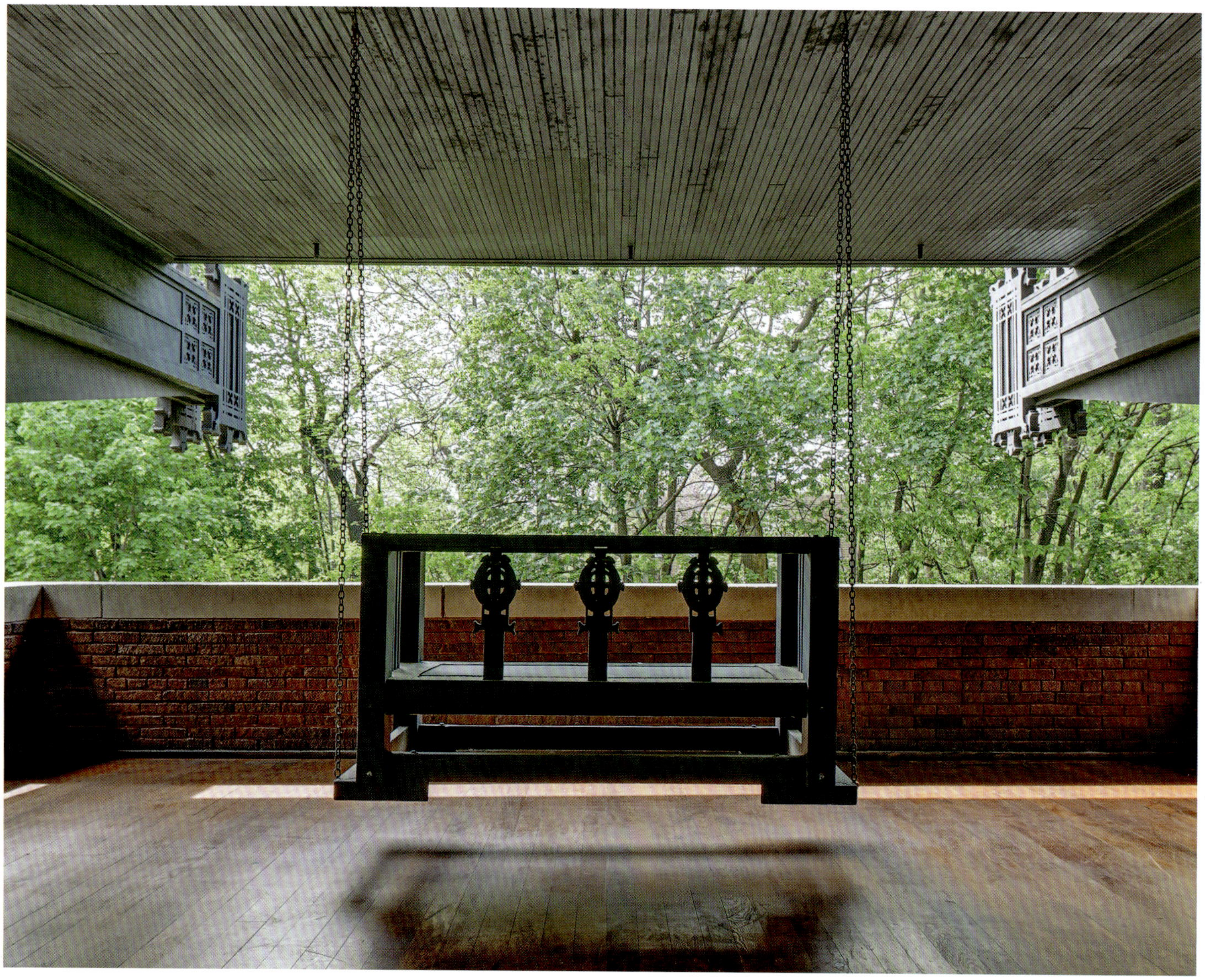

While the basic design is Sullivan's, including the interior layout, many of the details (lighting, art glass, etc.) were likely done by Elmslie.

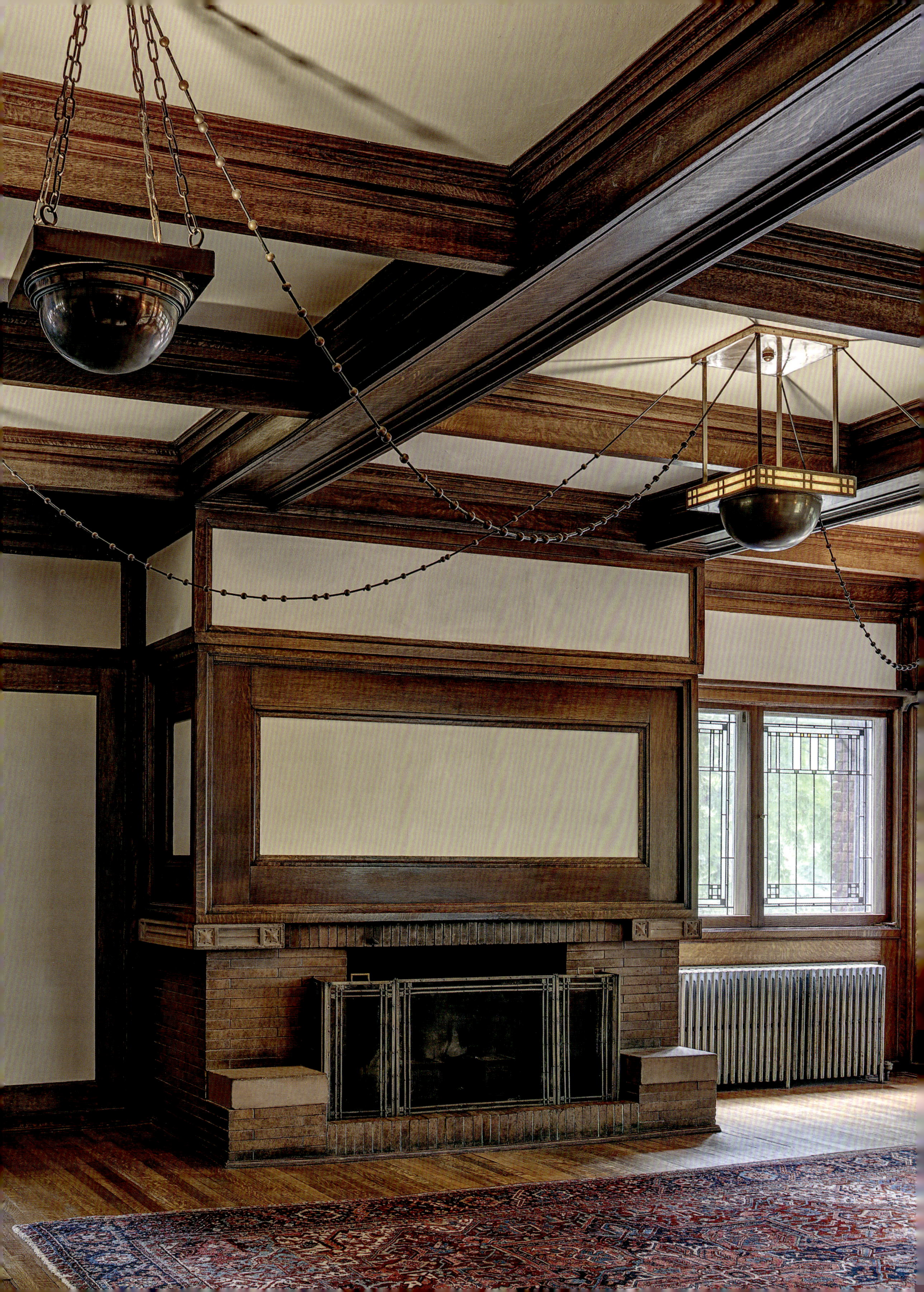

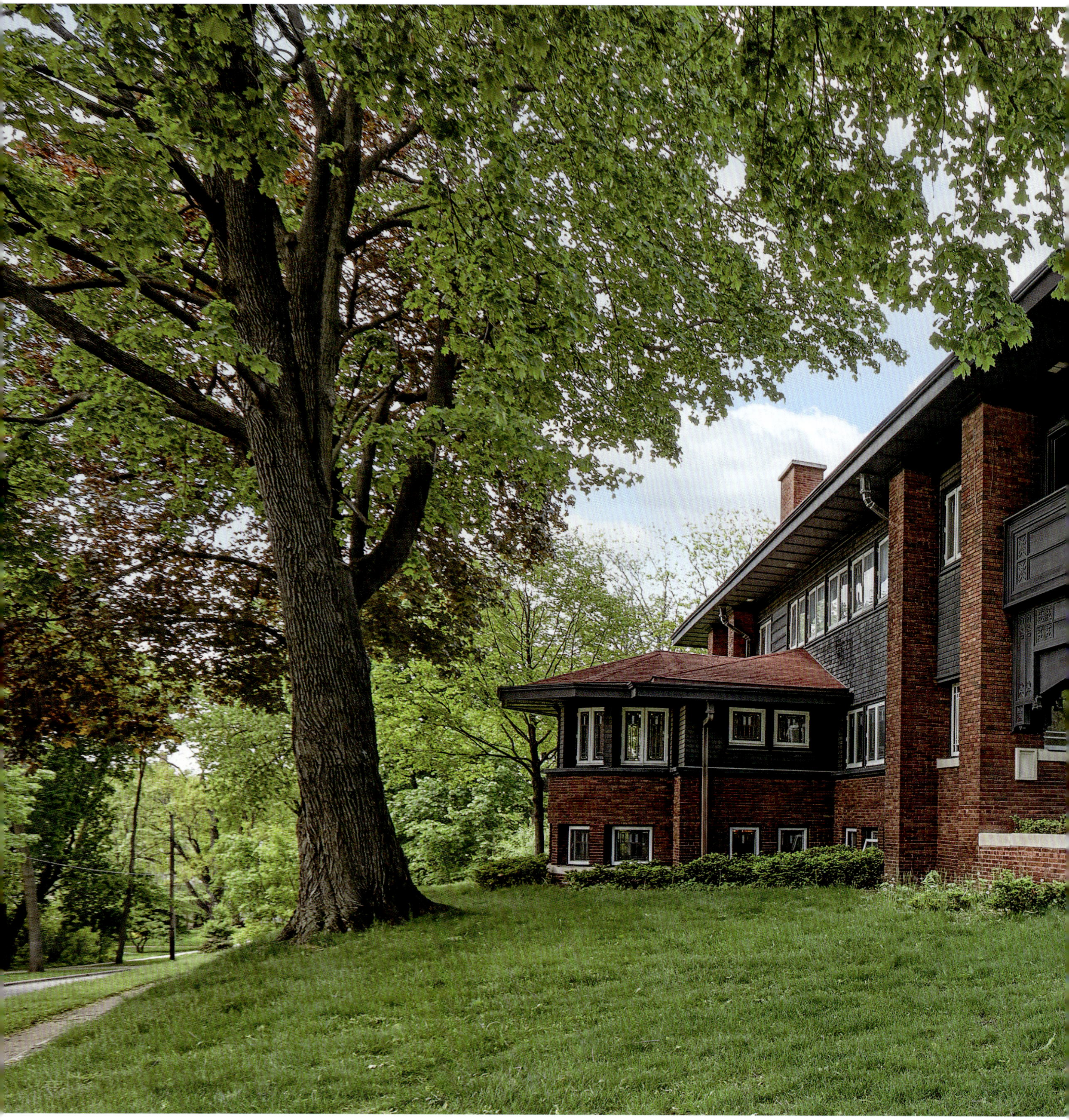

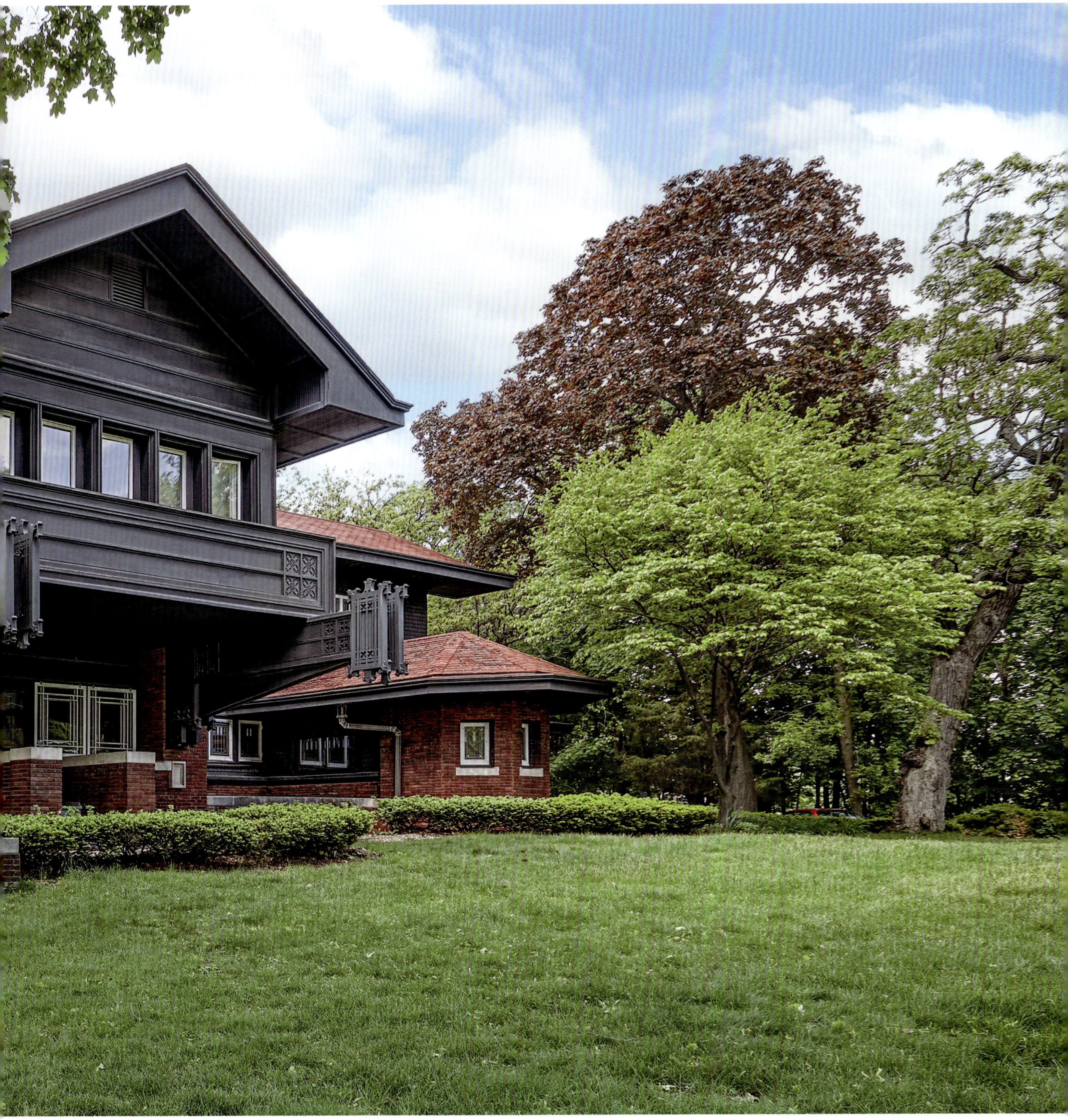

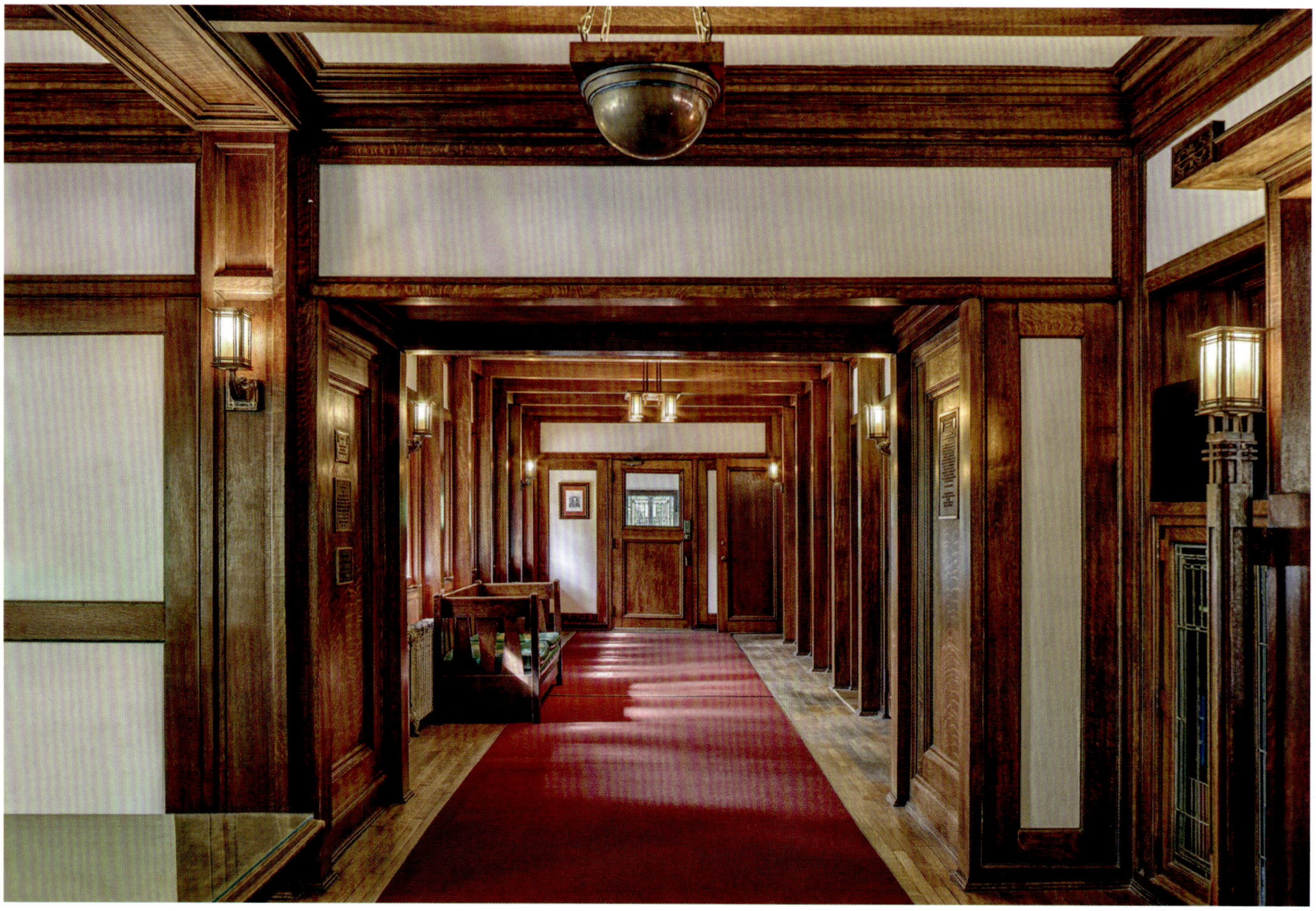

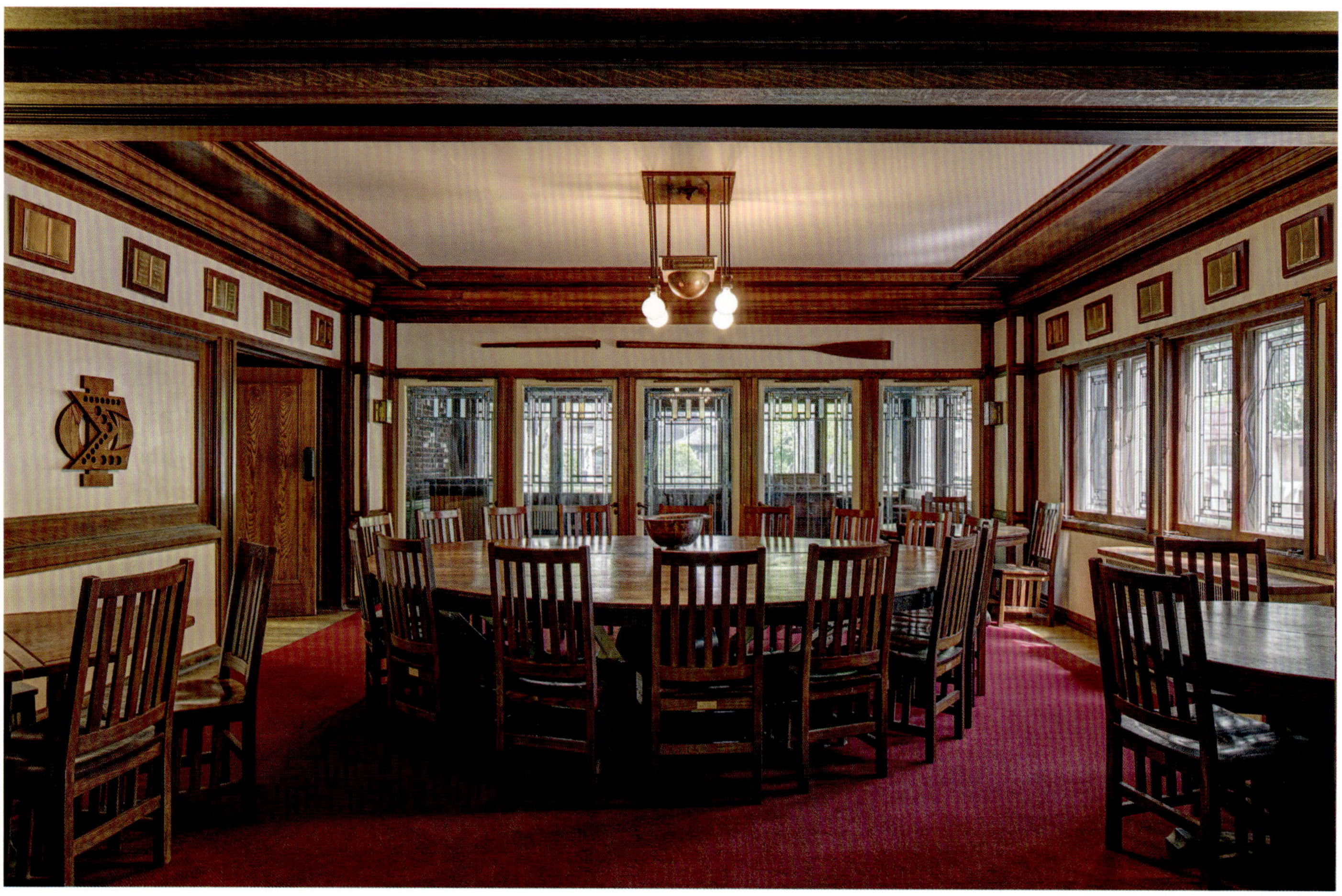

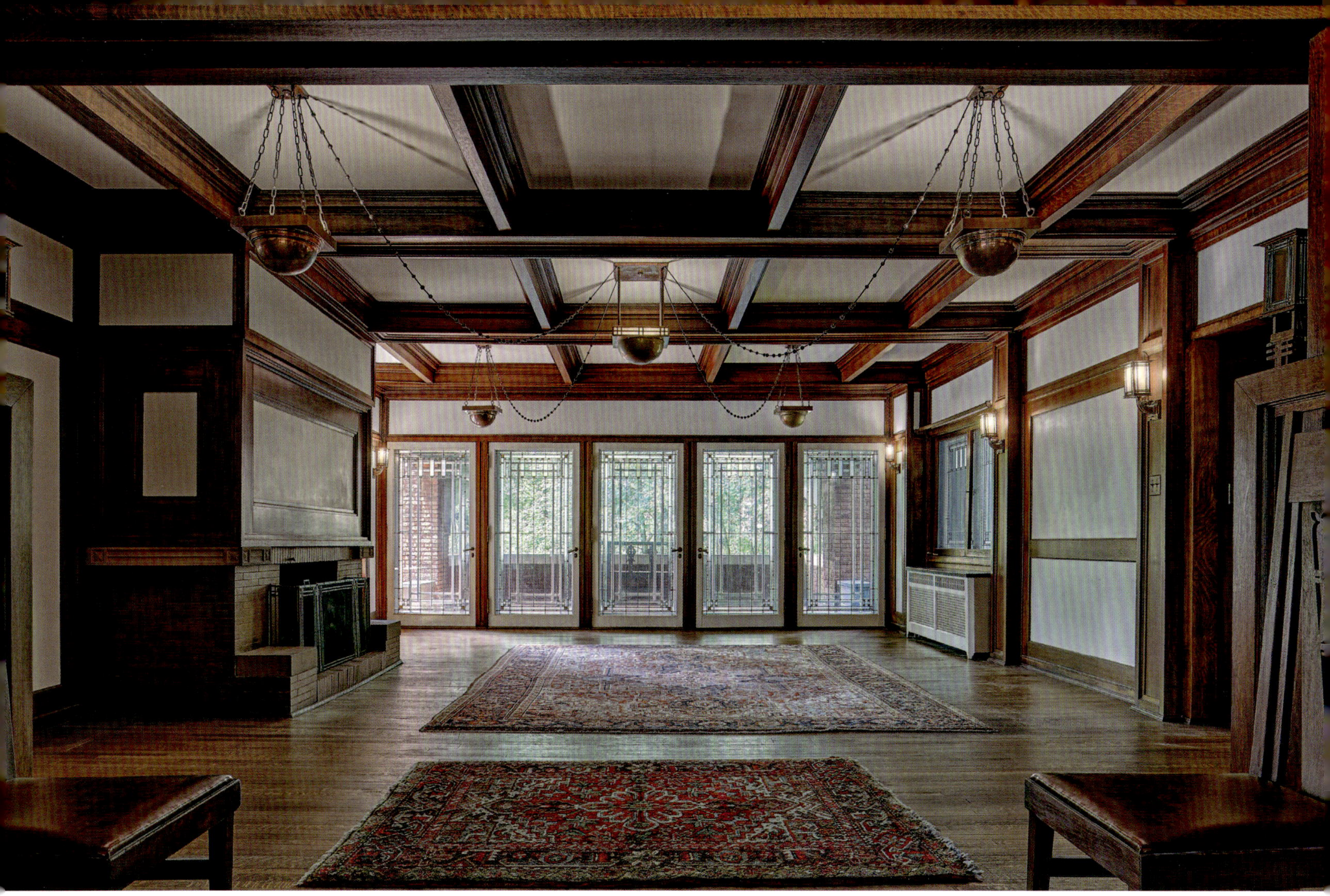

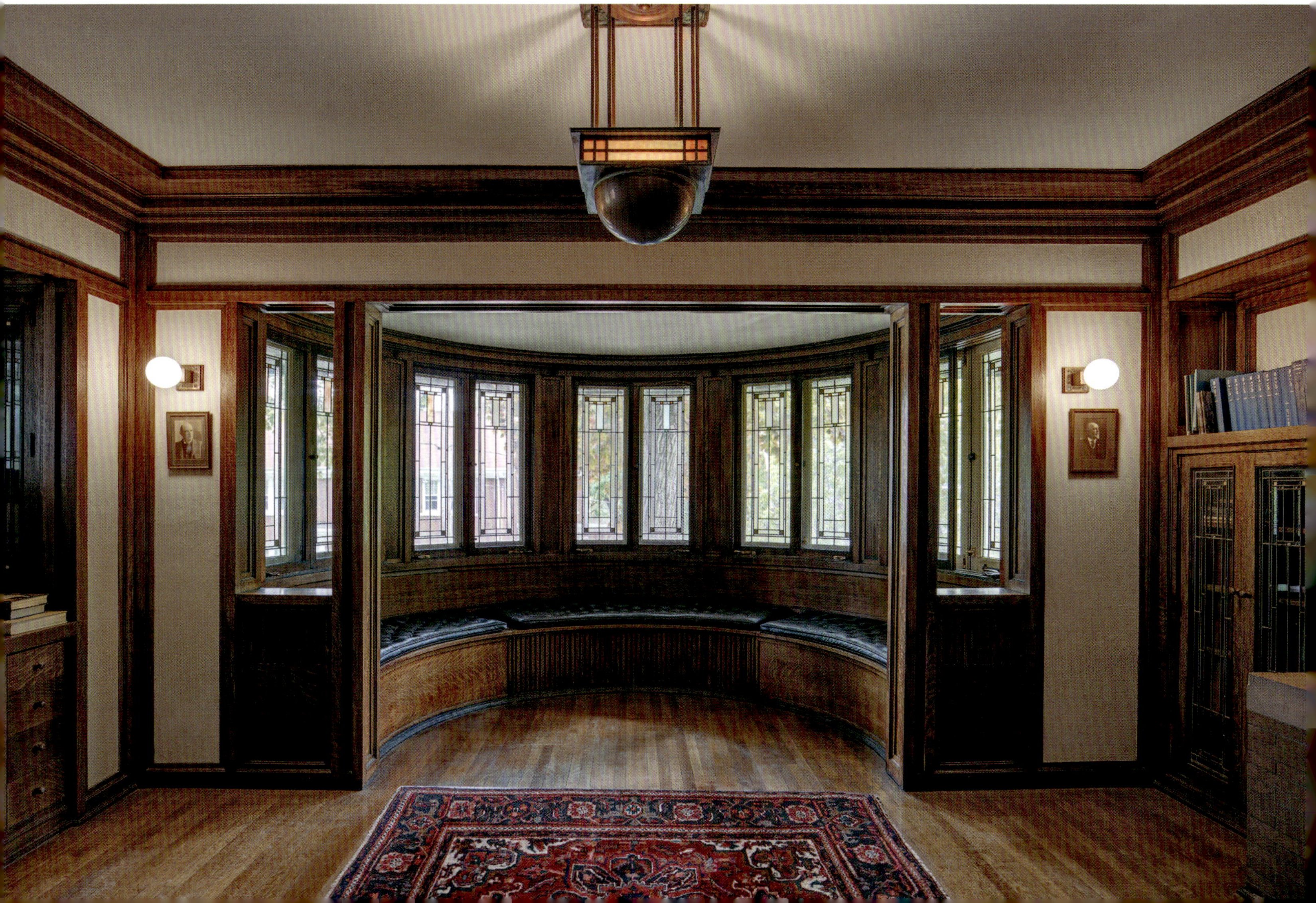

NATIONAL FARMERS BANK

1908, OWATONNA, MINNESOTA

Sullivan's first bank, considered by many to be the best of the group of eight, was, according to George Grant Elmslie, largely designed by himself. In a 1936 letter to Frank Lloyd Wright correcting Wright's errors in a review of a Sullivan biography, Elmslie stated that "not only were all the working drawings and every last detail of decoration, inside and out, mine, but the main motif of the design as well." While it's always wise to question Wright's version of events, there's not as much reason to doubt Elmslie, who faithfully served Sullivan until he could no longer afford to do so.

In his biography of Sullivan, Robert Twombly suggests that while Elmslie must be considered a full partner in the bank's design, the overall conception, including the choice of materials and mechanical systems, was Sullivan's. In any event, both Wright and Elmslie were writing long after Sullivan's death and thus Sullivan's ability to set the record straight.

The commission came Sullivan's way through the bank's president, Carl K. Bennett, who had read and been impressed by an essay that Sullivan had written on architecture that had appeared in *The Craftsman* magazine. As a result, there was not only a sympathetic meeting of minds but also a budget that permitted almost free rein to the architect.

Unlike the Classic-Revival style that typified even small-town banks at the time, the National Farmers Bank derives its dignity and strength from its solid cube shape, pierced by typical Sullivan arches on the main elevations. The main banking room is a sixty-eight-foot square and is fully forty feet high. Prominently sited on a corner, this cube is flanked by two-story extensions.

The exterior is clad in red brick, with a green terra cotta band infilled with colorful mosaics. Corner cartouches are executed in the same brown terra cotta used for the cornice. Green and yellow leaded glass fills the exterior arches. Restorations in 1958 and from 1976–81 returned the bank to a more original condition after earlier ill-advised remodelings.

On a sad note, Bennett's bank was a victim of the collapse of agricultural prices in the early 1920s and was forced to declare bankruptcy. Bennett tried to restore his finances in New York to no avail and ended up managing properties that the nearby Carlton College owned in Minneapolis. The architectural masterpiece that Sullivan brought into being was added to the National Register of Historic Places in 1971 and was designated a National Historic Landmark in 1976.

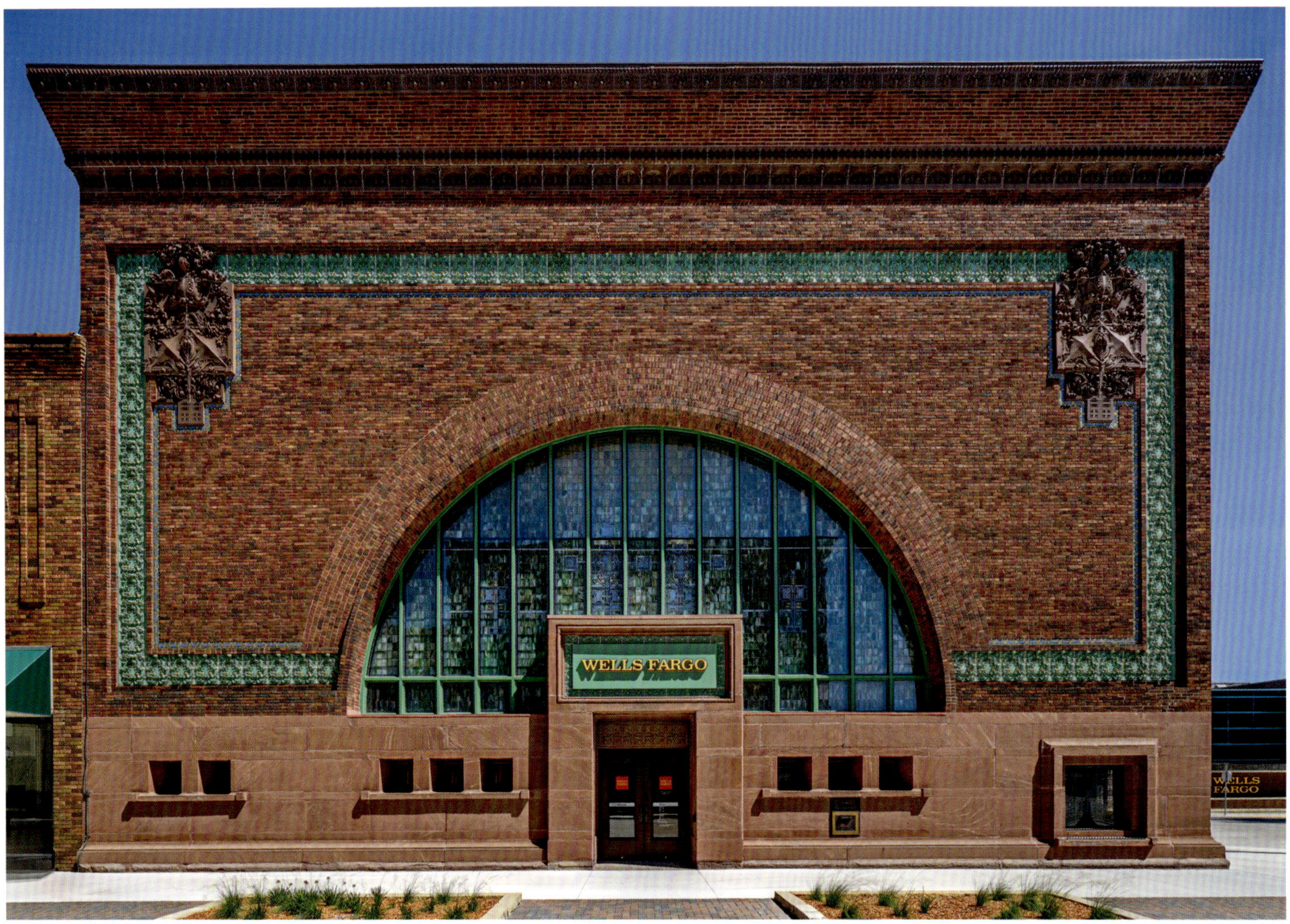

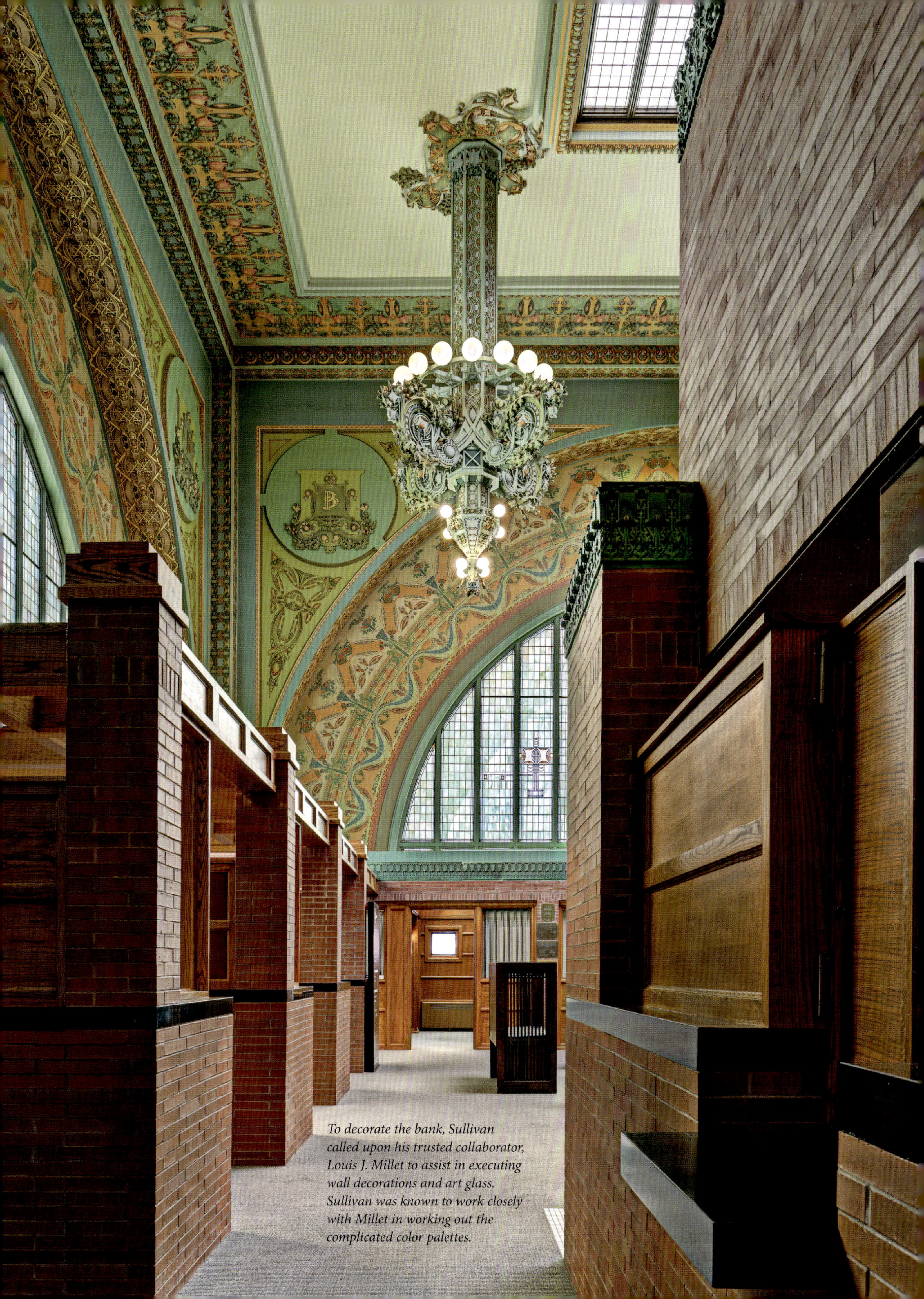

To decorate the bank, Sullivan called upon his trusted collaborator, Louis J. Millet to assist in executing wall decorations and art glass. Sullivan was known to work closely with Millet in working out the complicated color palettes.

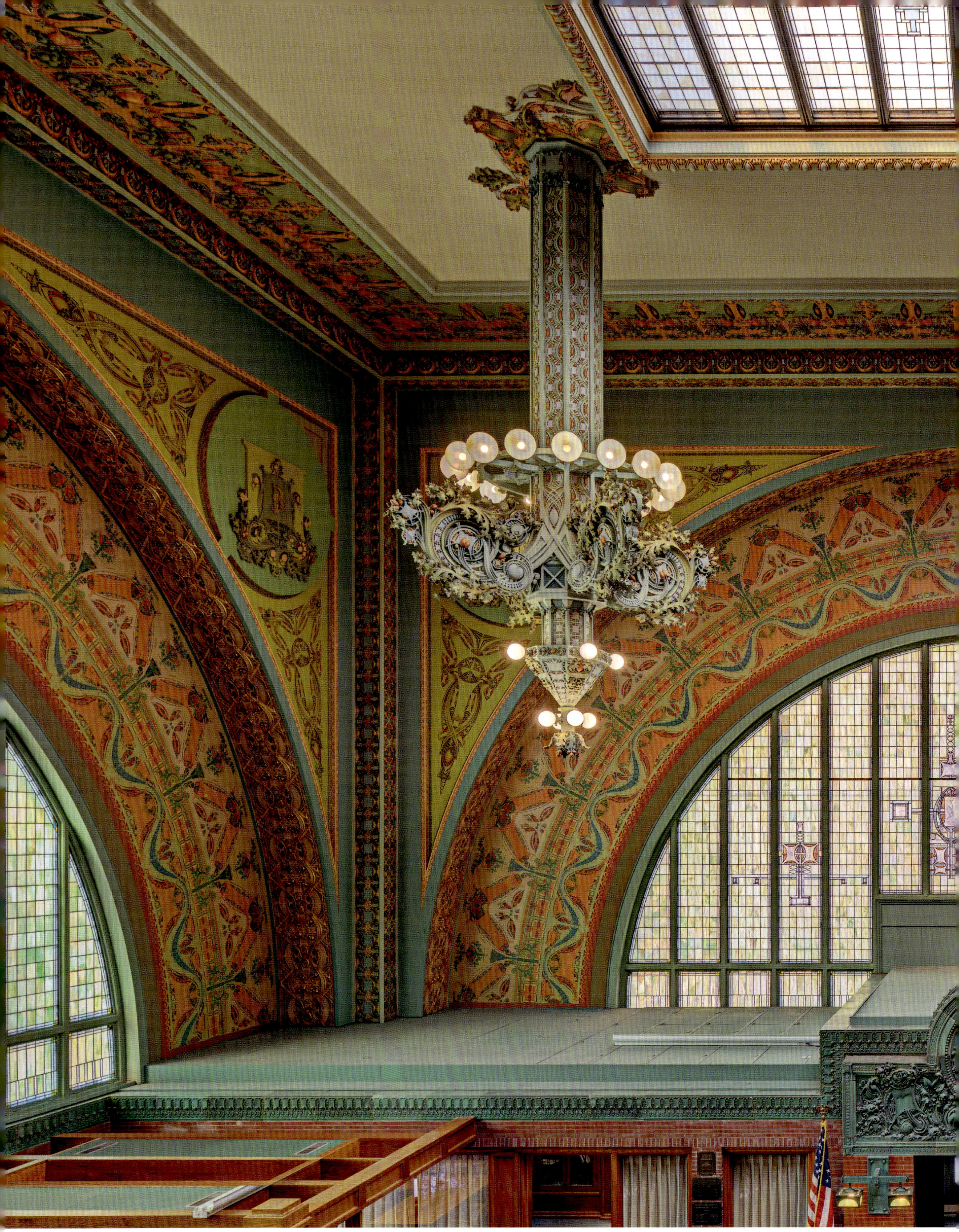

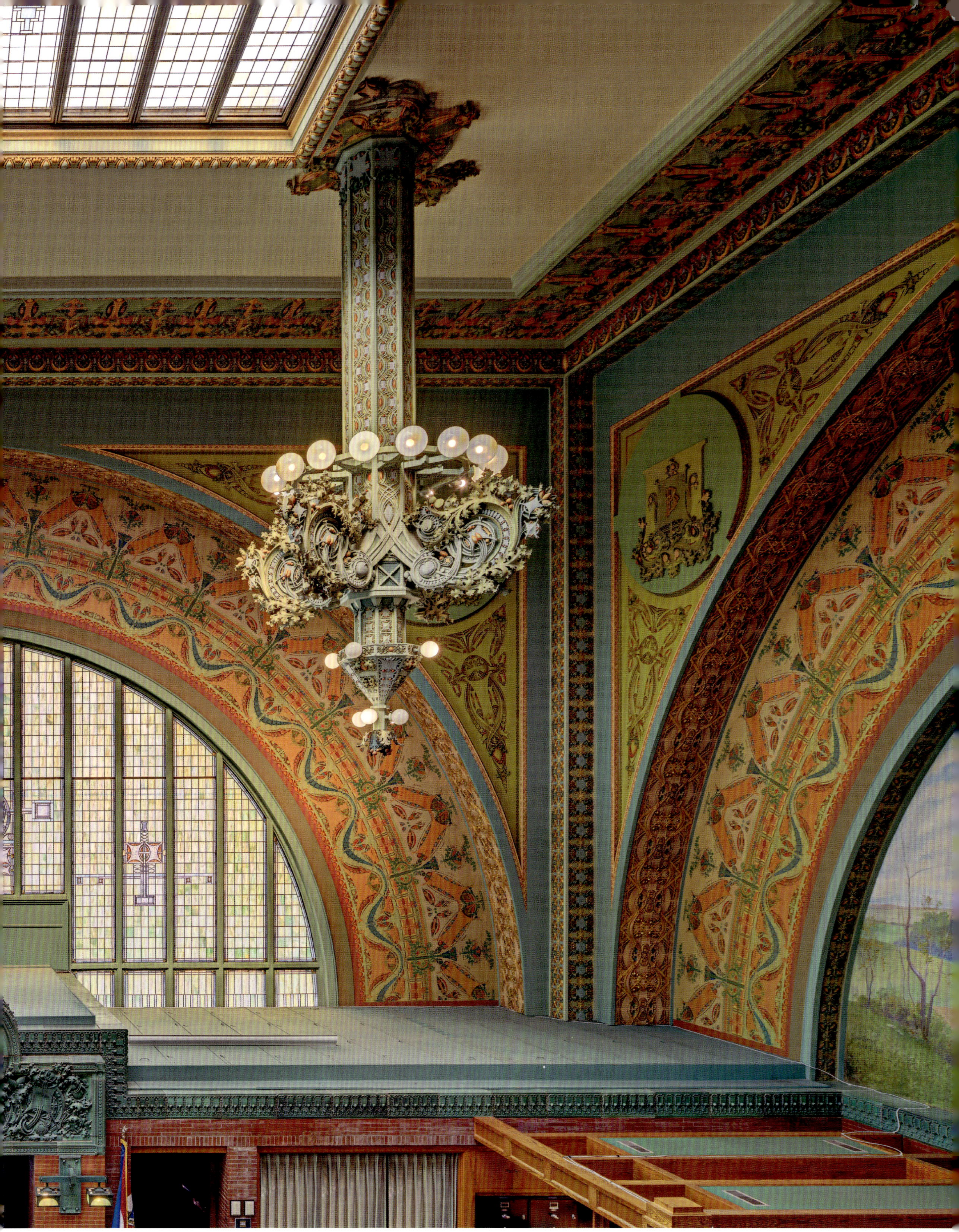

The intricate electroliers were cast by the Winslow Brothers, and the extensive terra cotta ornament was produced by the American Terra Cotta Company, whose modeler Kristian Schneider had worked on many of Sullivan's major buildings.

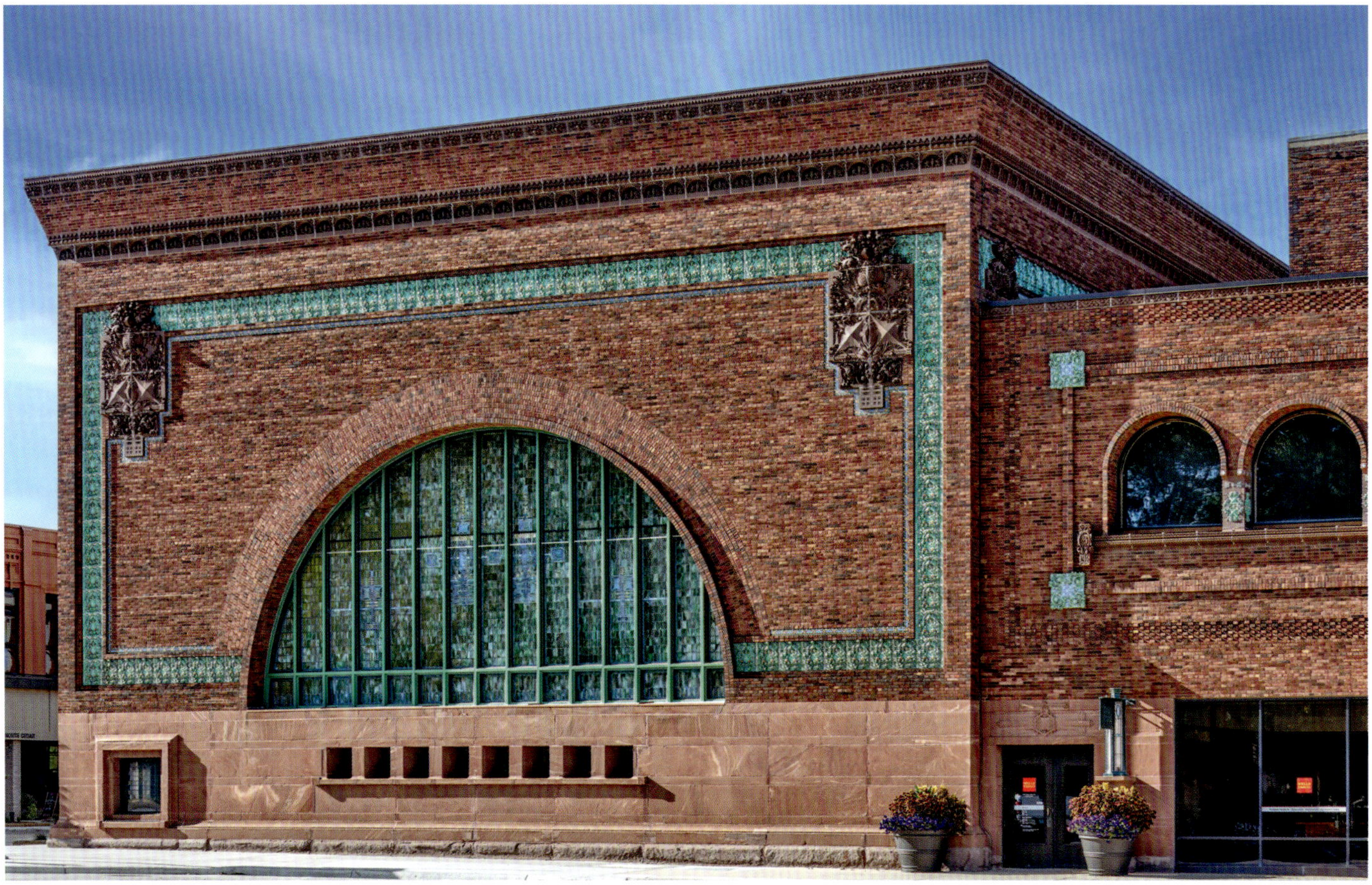

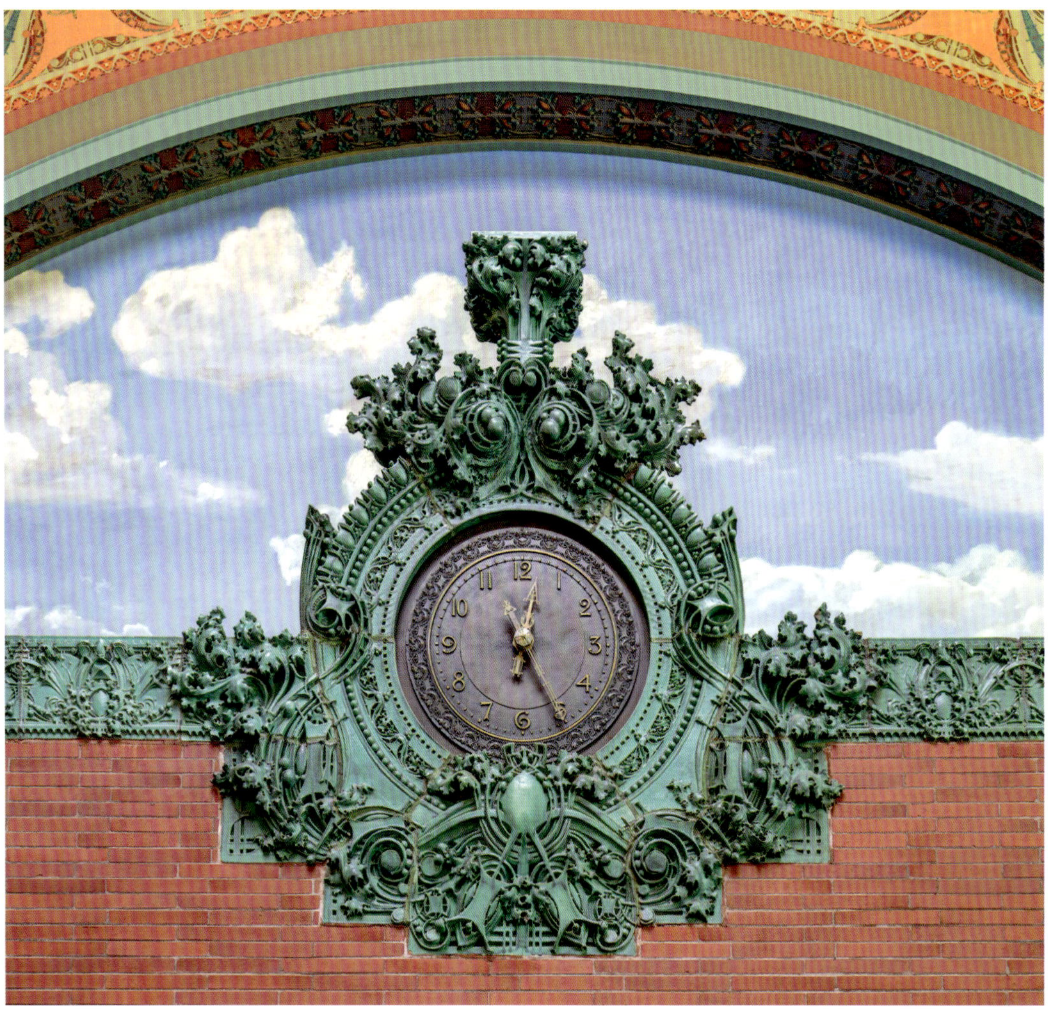

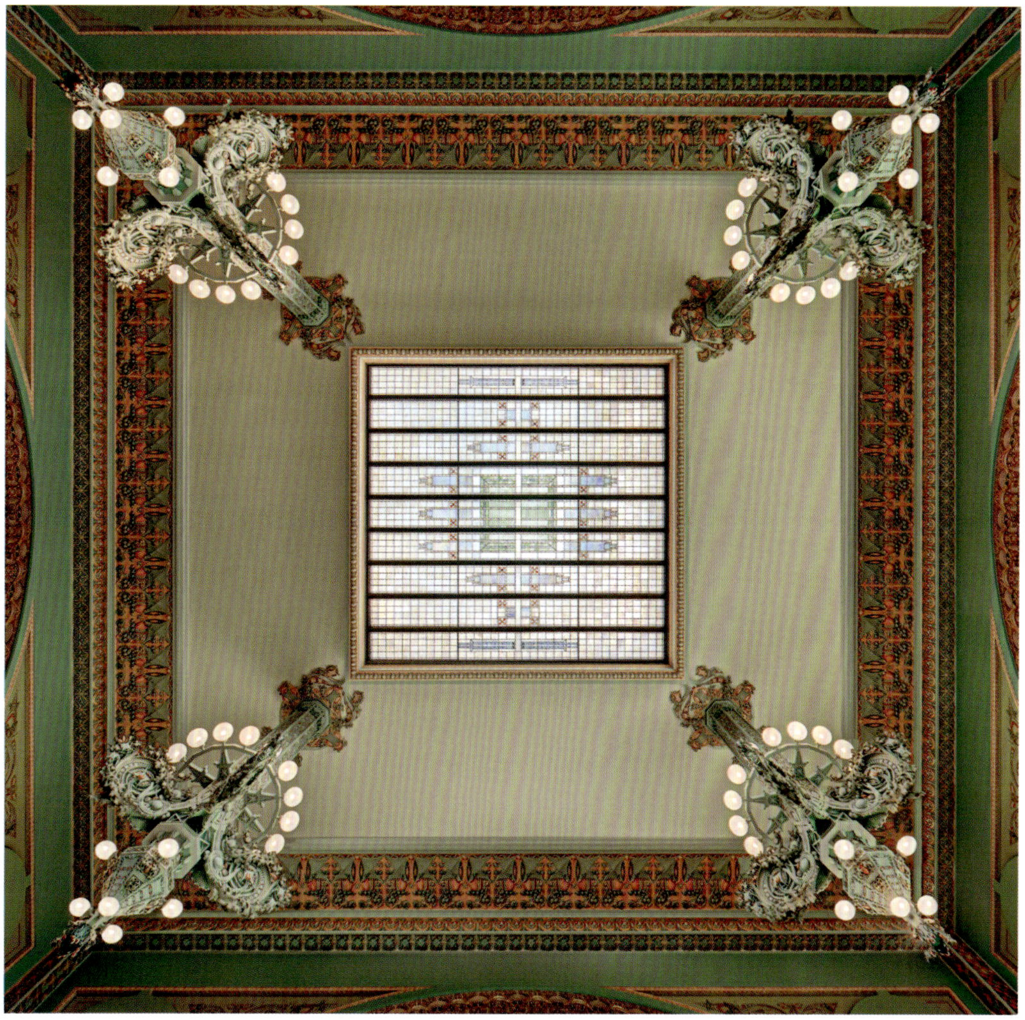

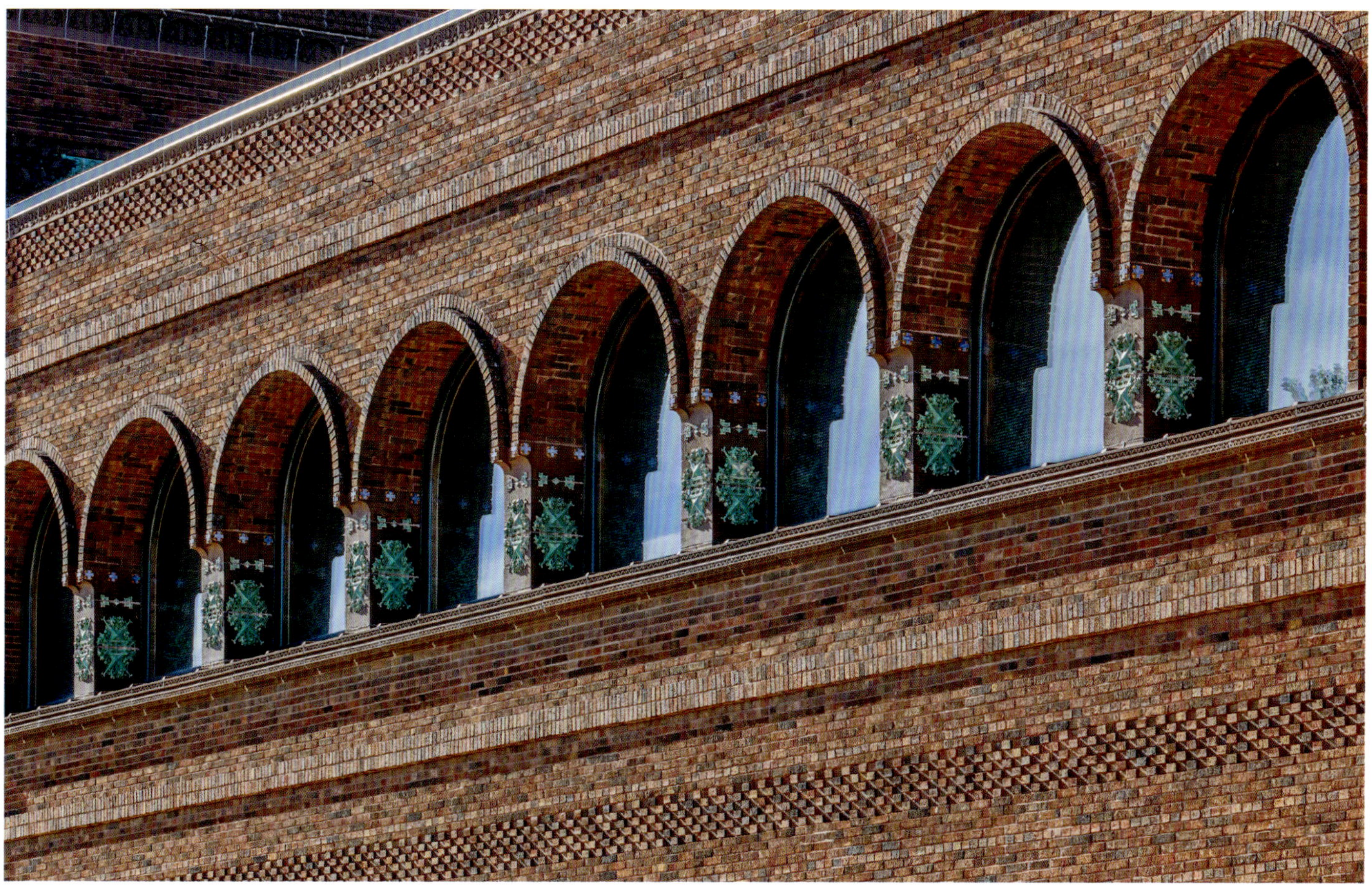

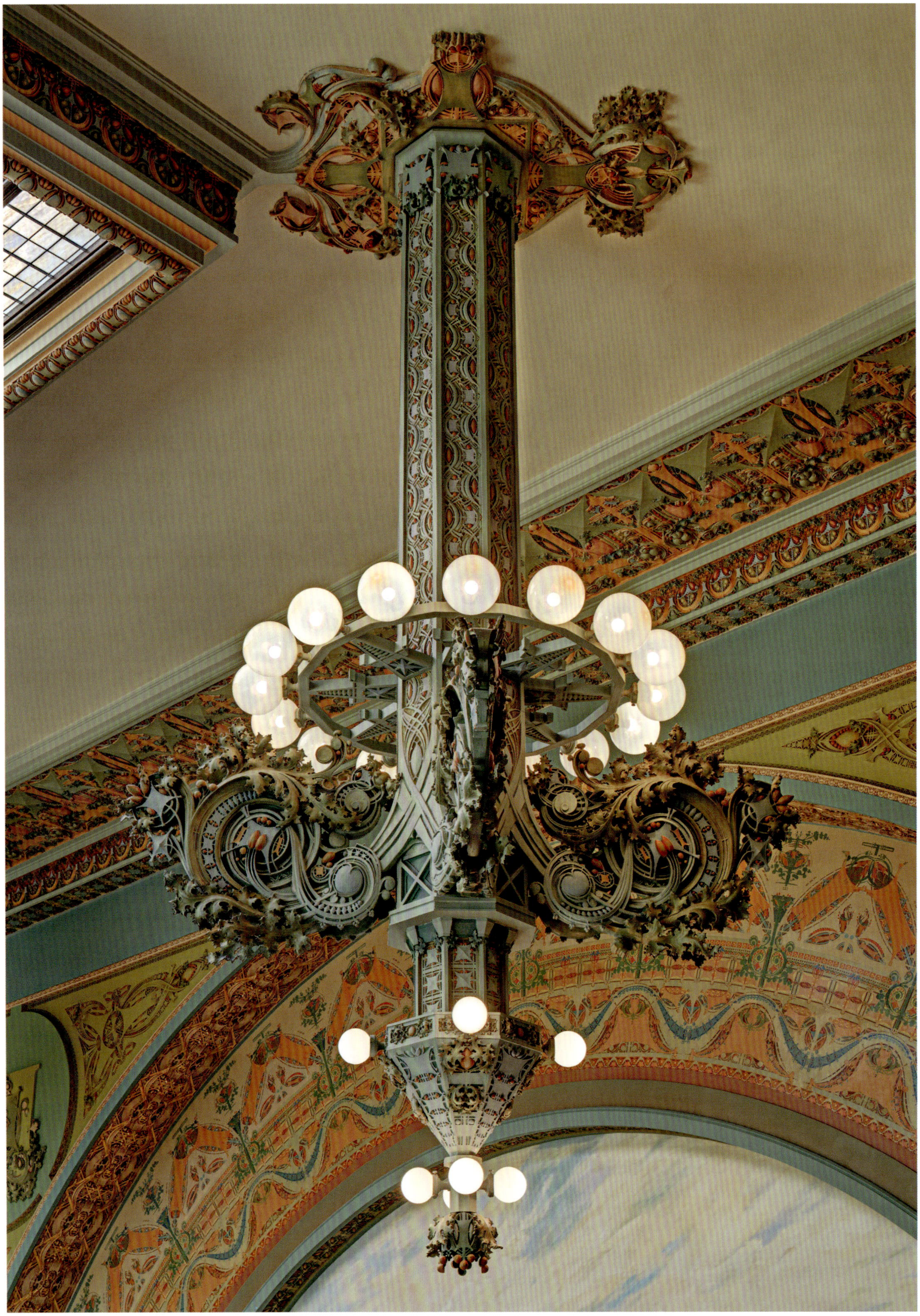

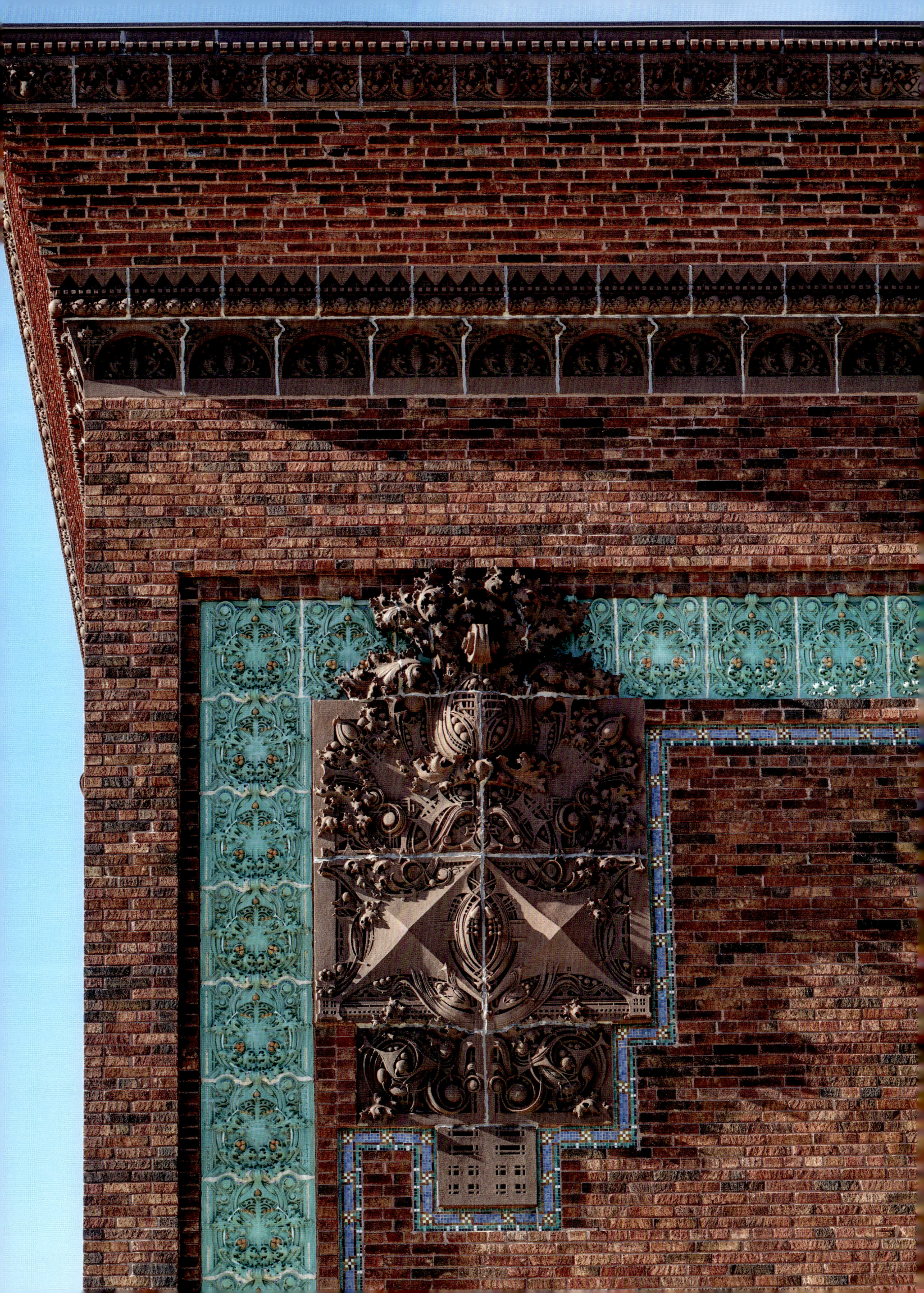

PEOPLES SAVINGS BANK

1911, CEDAR RAPIDS, IOWA

Commissioned by its first vice president and head of the building committee, F.H. Shaver, the Peoples Savings Bank is a rectangular building that features a central space with clerestory windows, its shape reflected on the exterior as a prominent belvedere or tower with corner spires. Sullivan chose variously-shaded brown bricks for cladding, resulting in what he said created "the effect of an antique oriental rug."

Chicago restoration architect Wilbert Hasbrouck's firm undertook a major restoration in 1991 to restore features lost over time. Unfortunately, a major flood of the nearby Cedar River in 2008 filled the bank with over twelve feet of water, requiring additional repairs and restoration. It was added to the National Register of Historic Places in 1978.

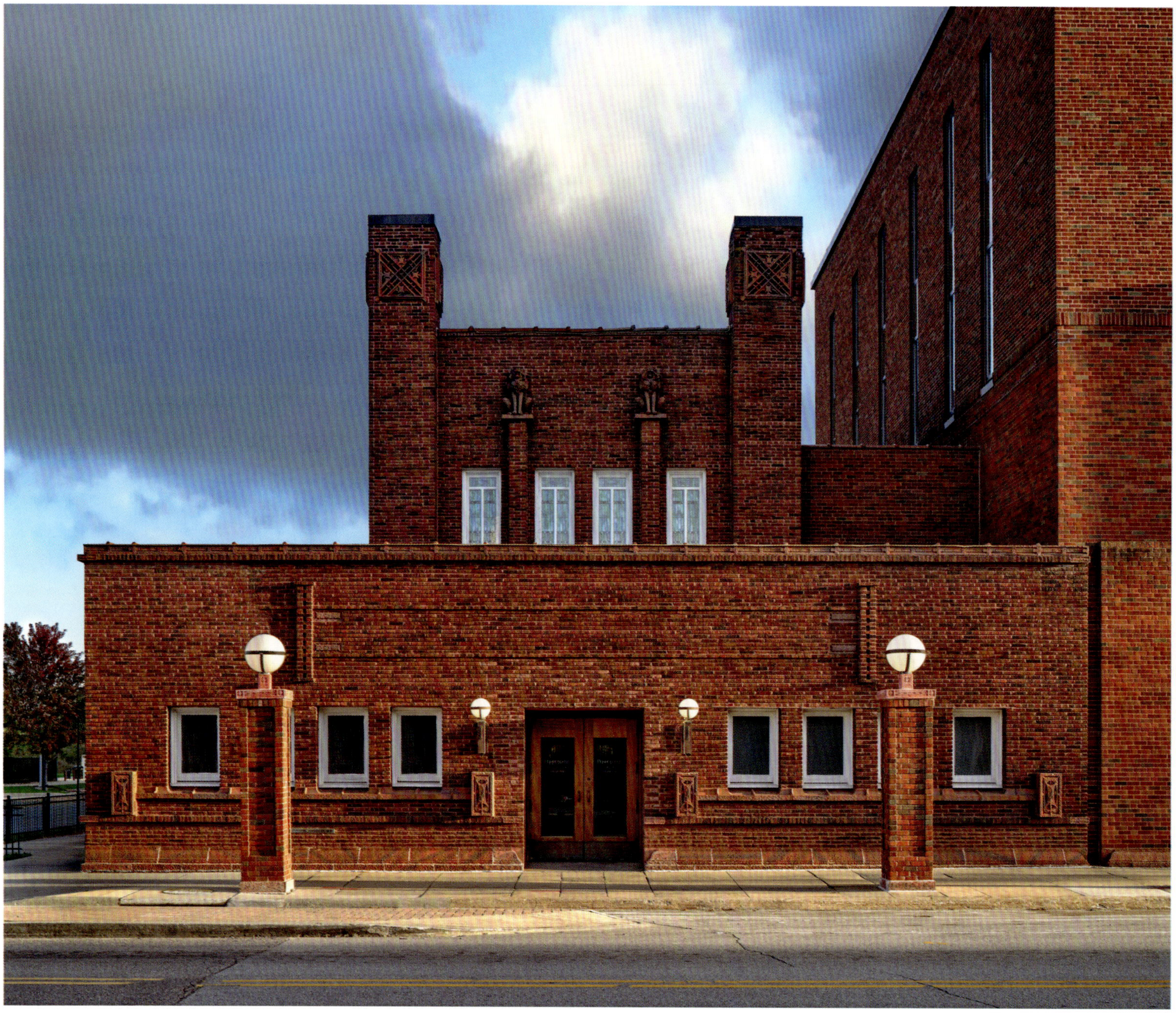

(Opposite) The interior includes four murals by Chicago artist Allen Philbrick (1879–1964), a long-serving faculty member at the School of The Art Institute of Chicago. They represent the agriculture, commerce, and industry of the area.

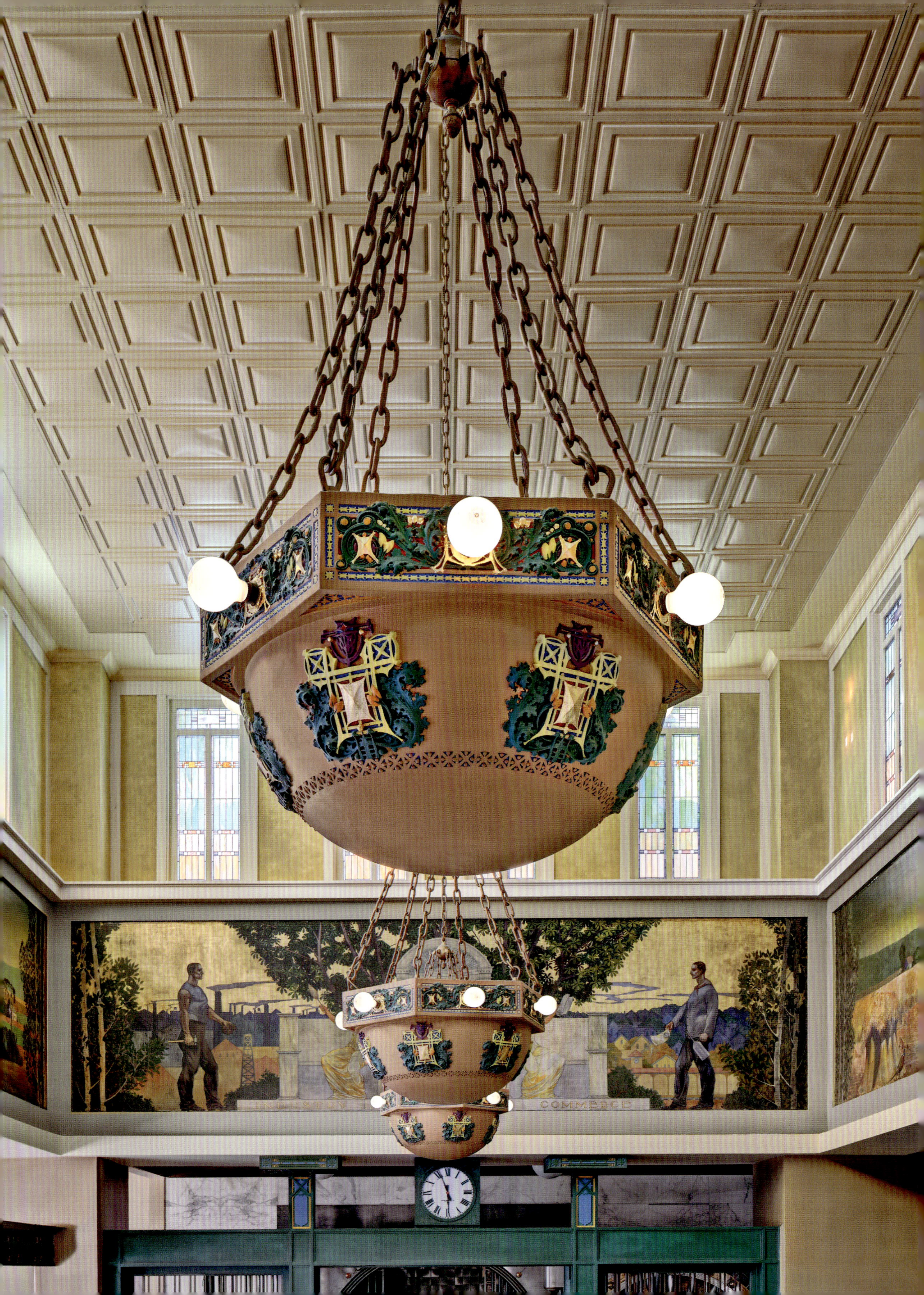
COMMERCE

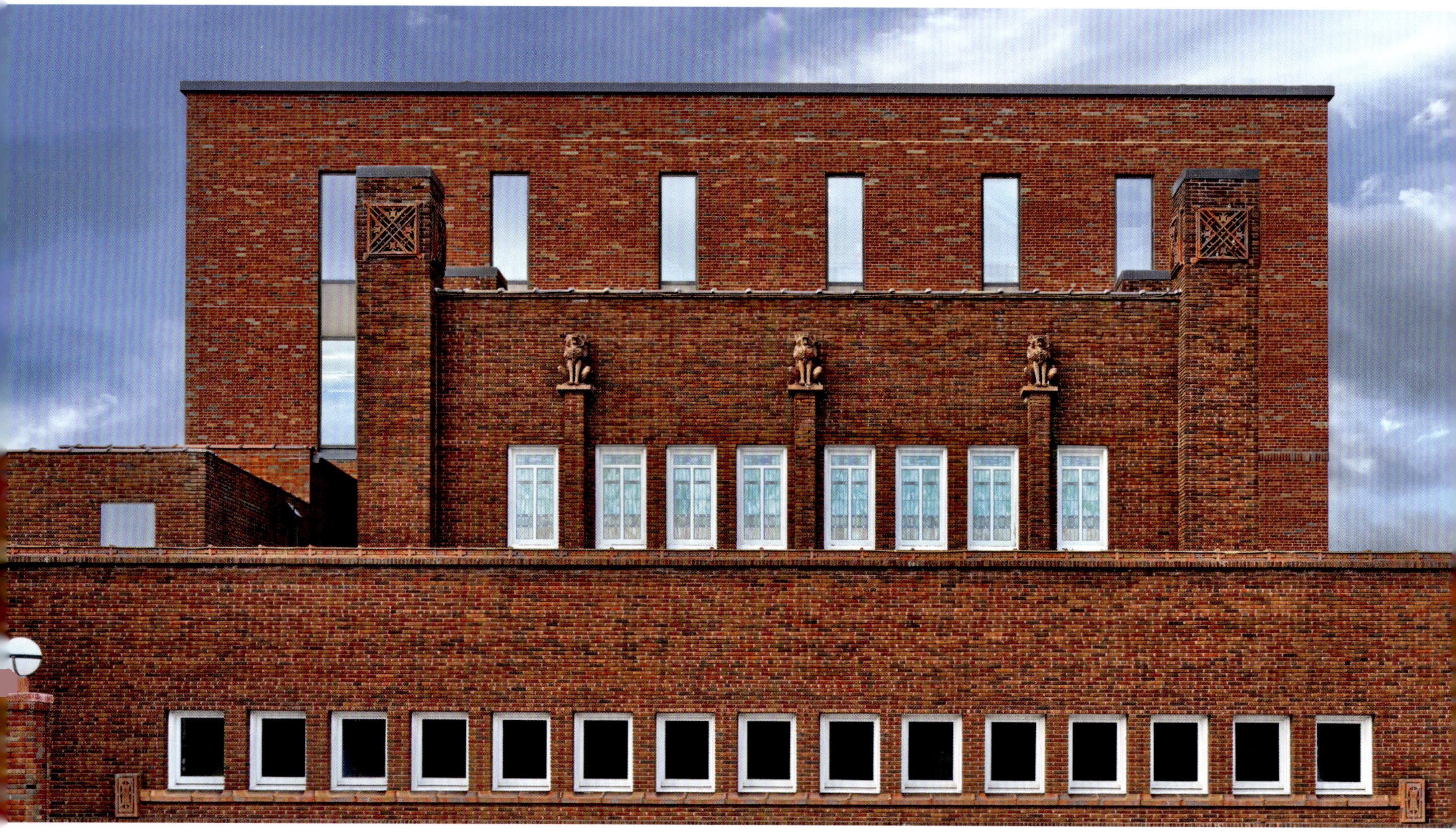

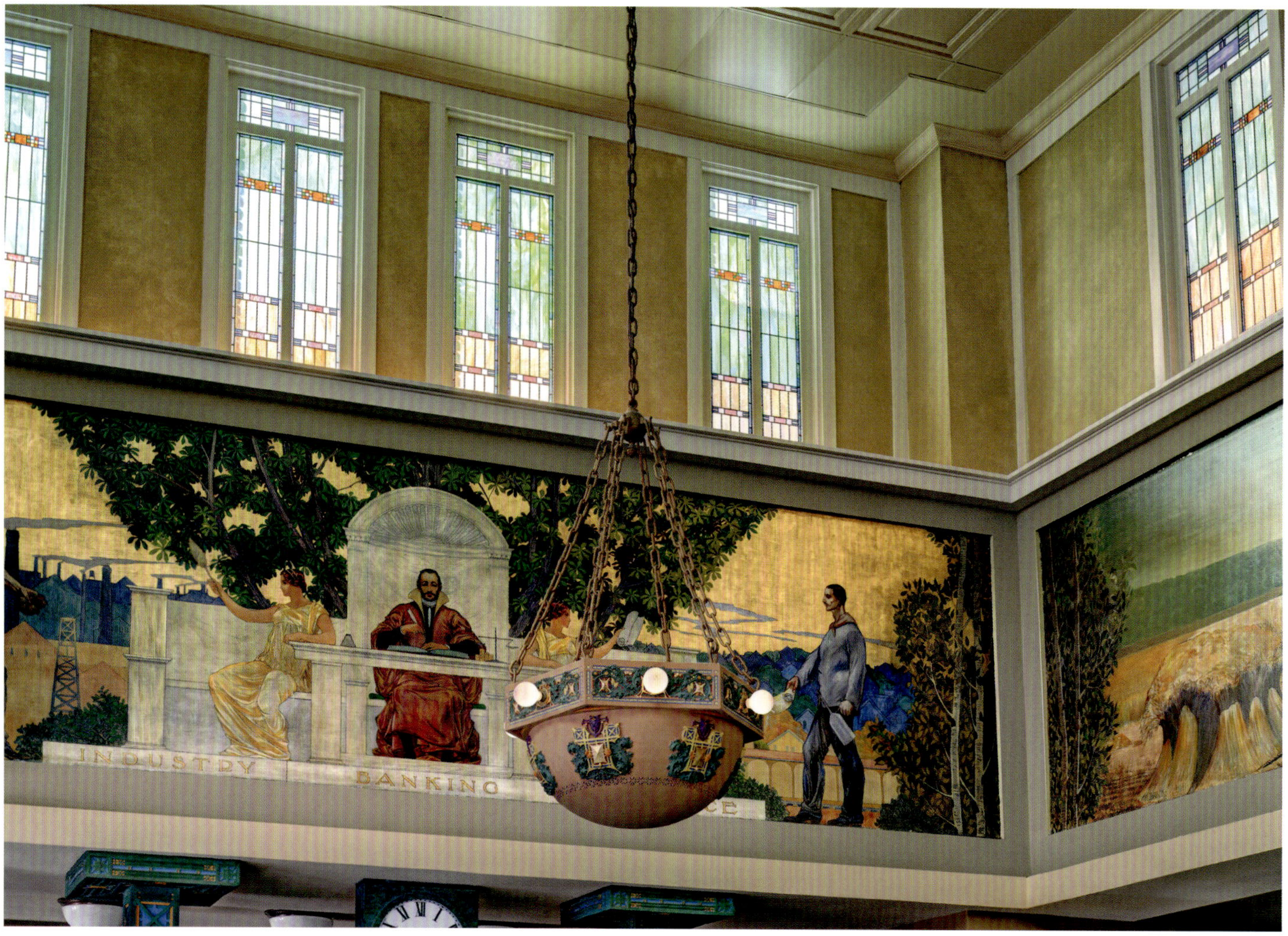

One of three suspended indirect fixtures which consist of copper colored plaster globes with multi-colored terra cotta plaques.

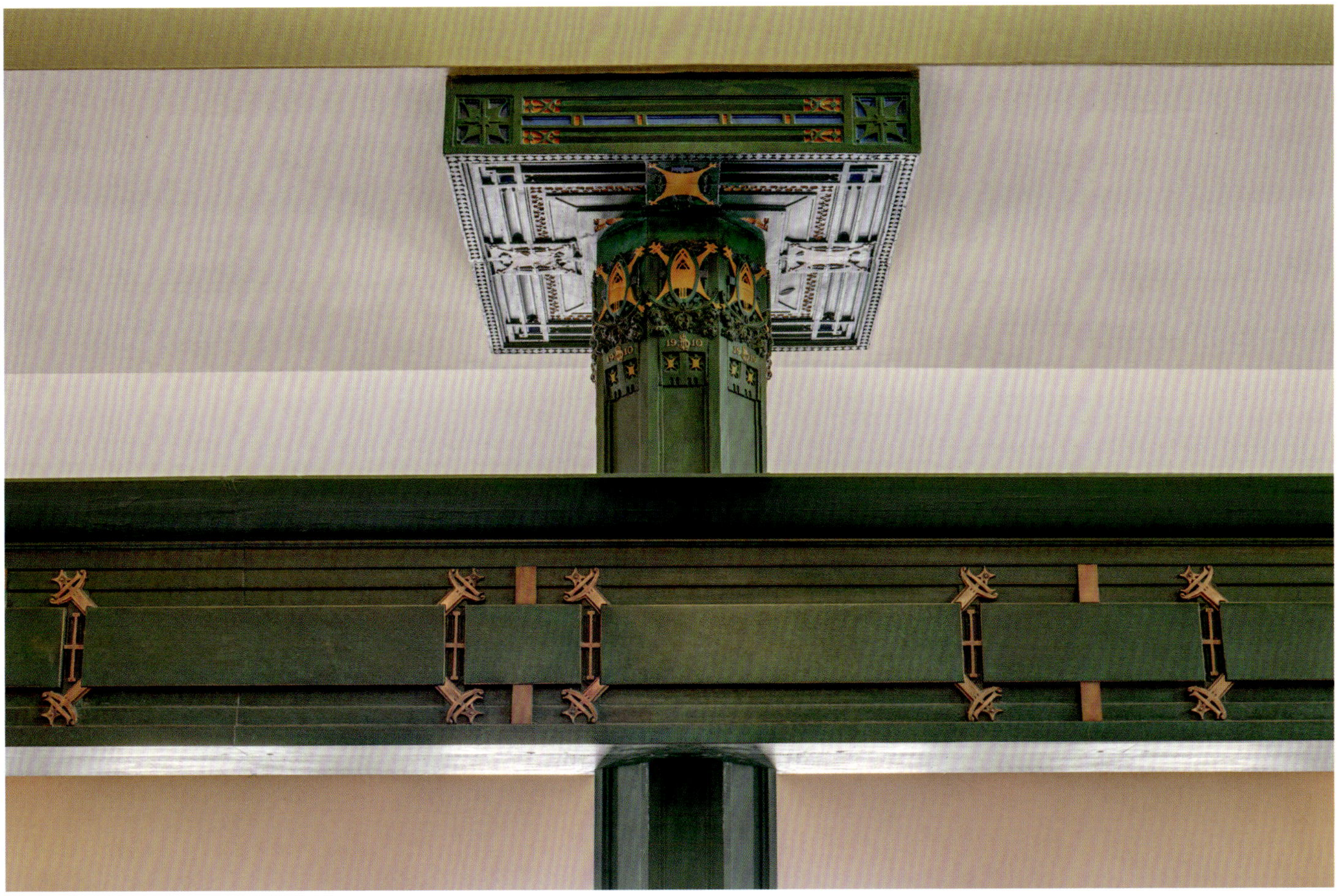

One of the ten column capitals and a portion of the ornamental connecting beam that spanned the six teller cages.

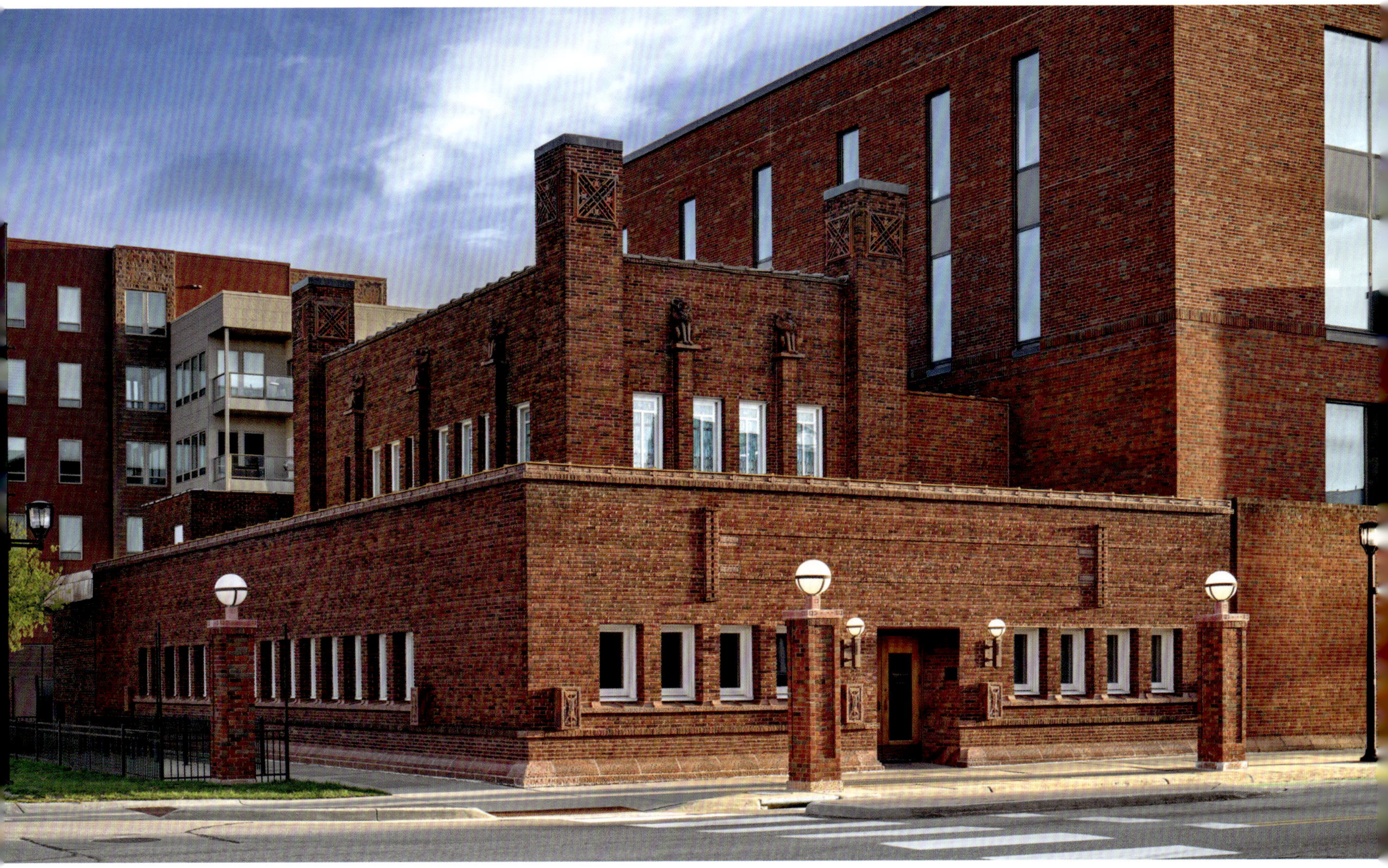

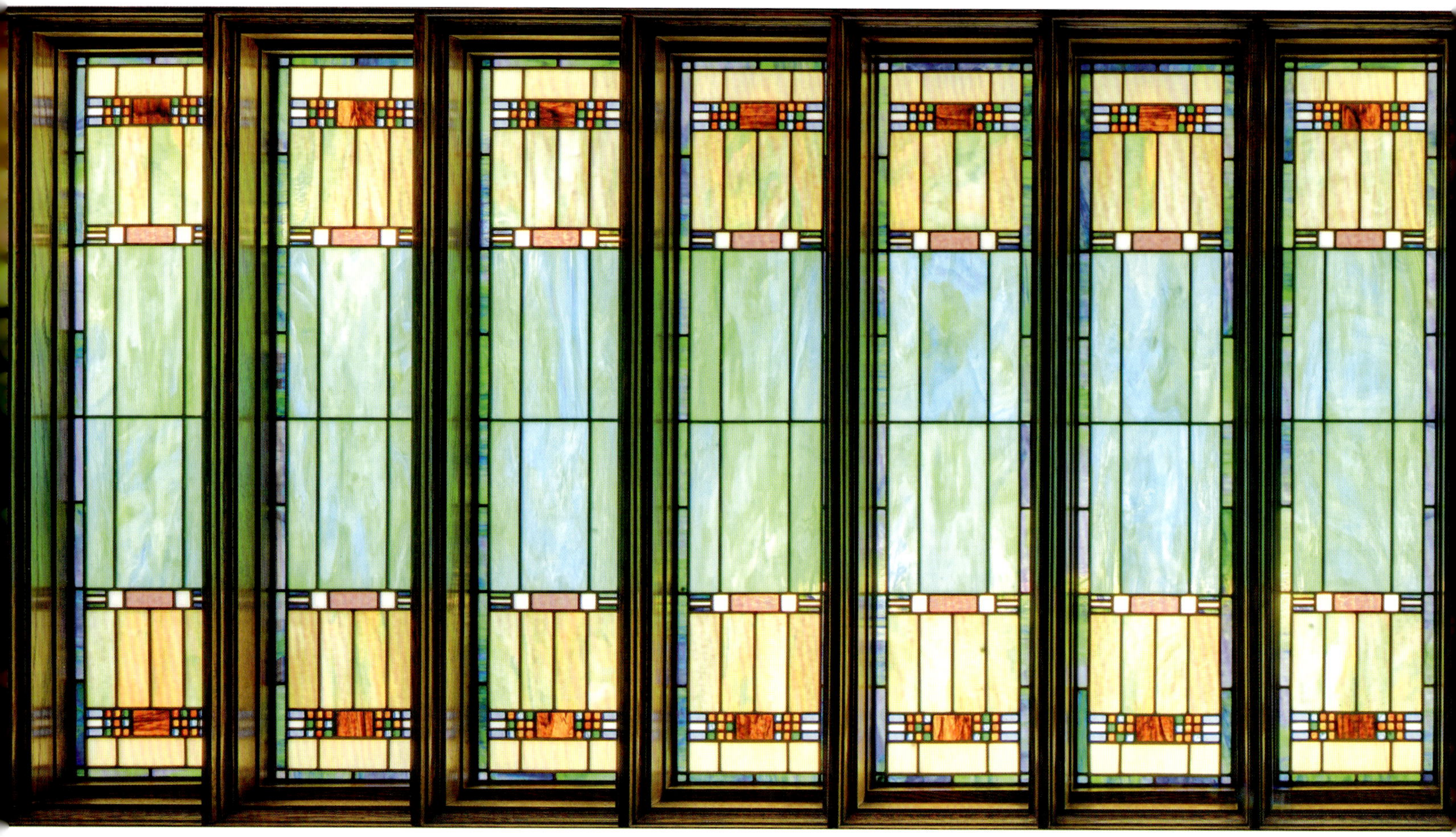

This was the last commission Elmslie worked on, and the glass designs are likely his, including the laylight above.

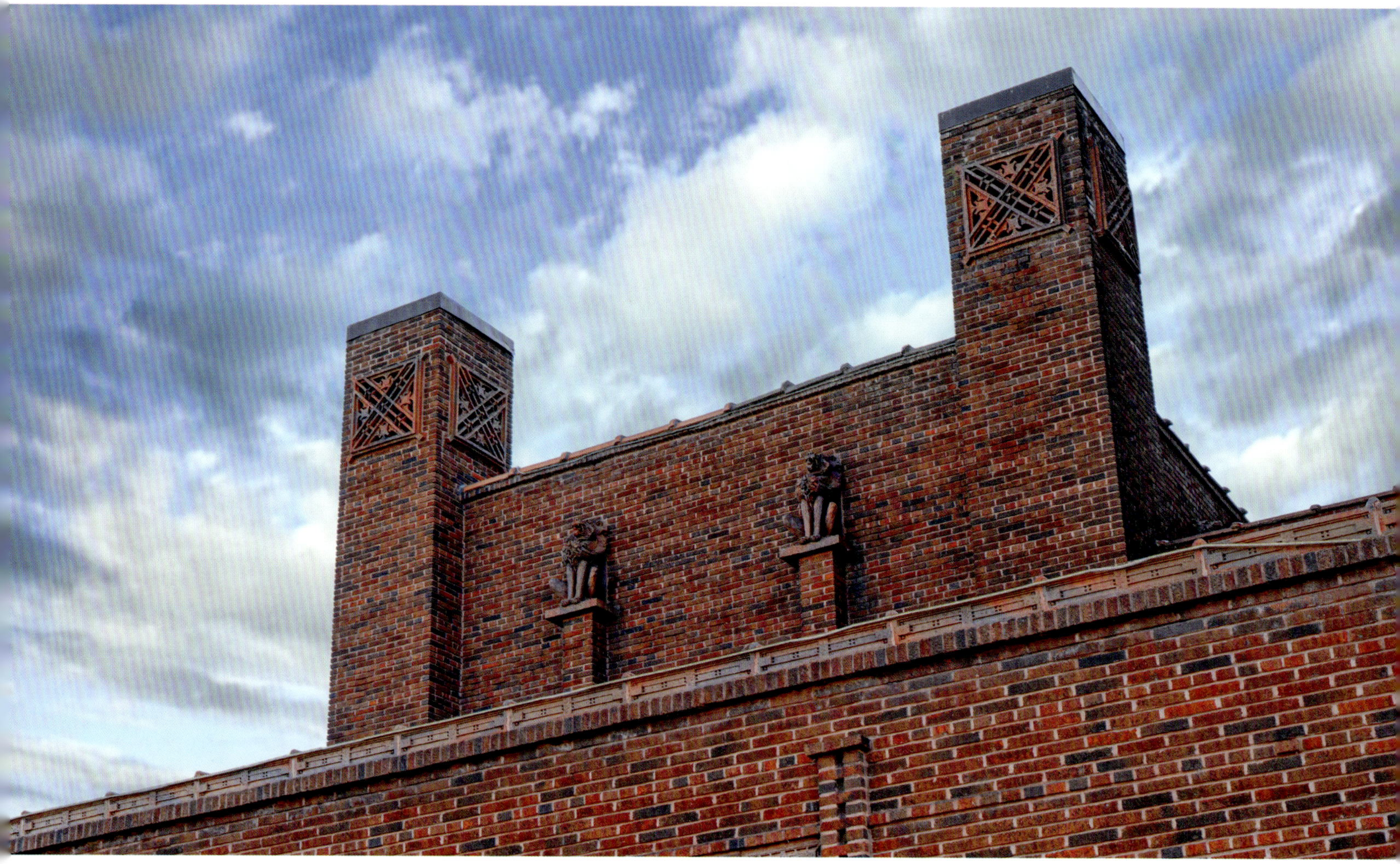

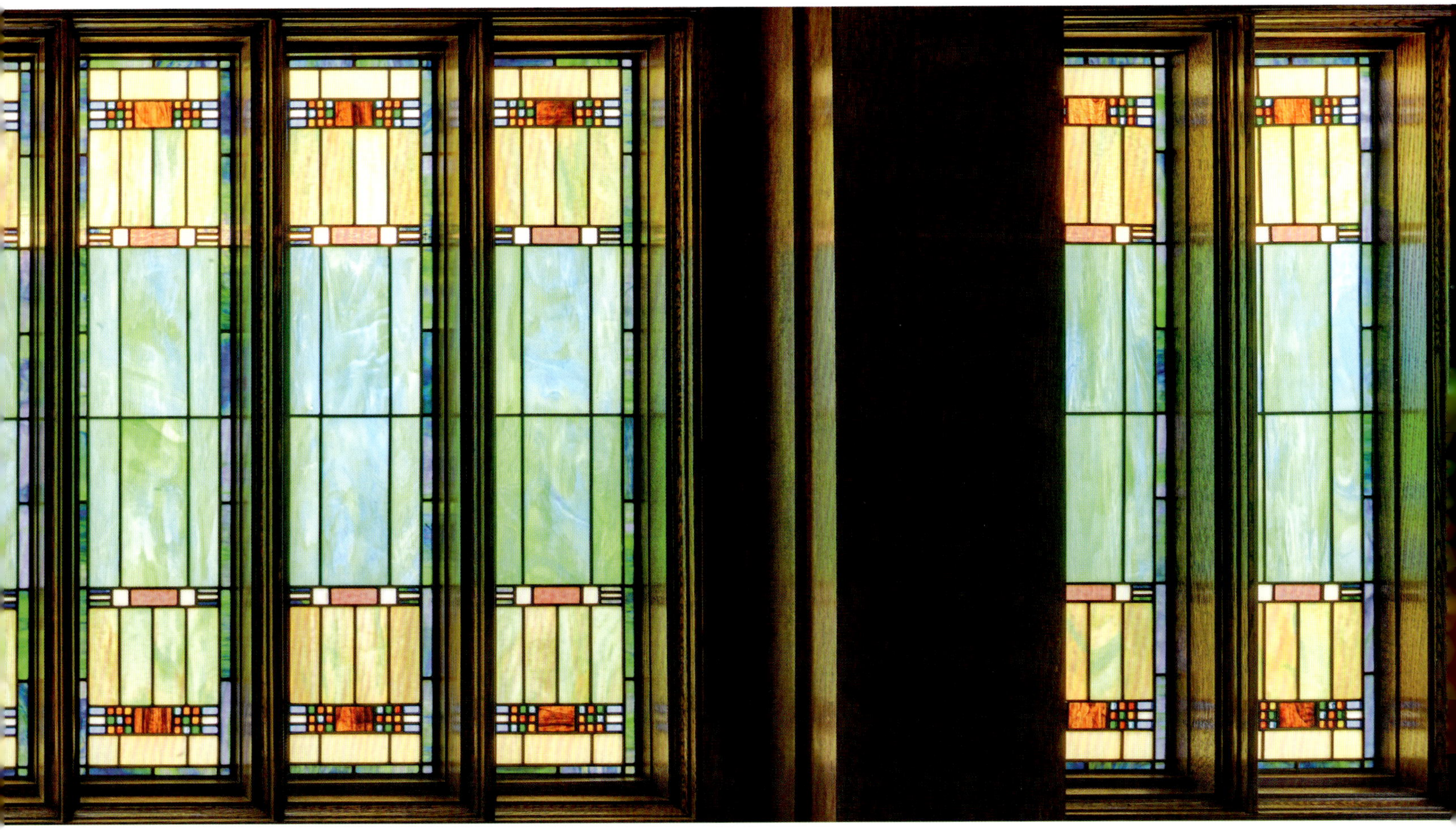

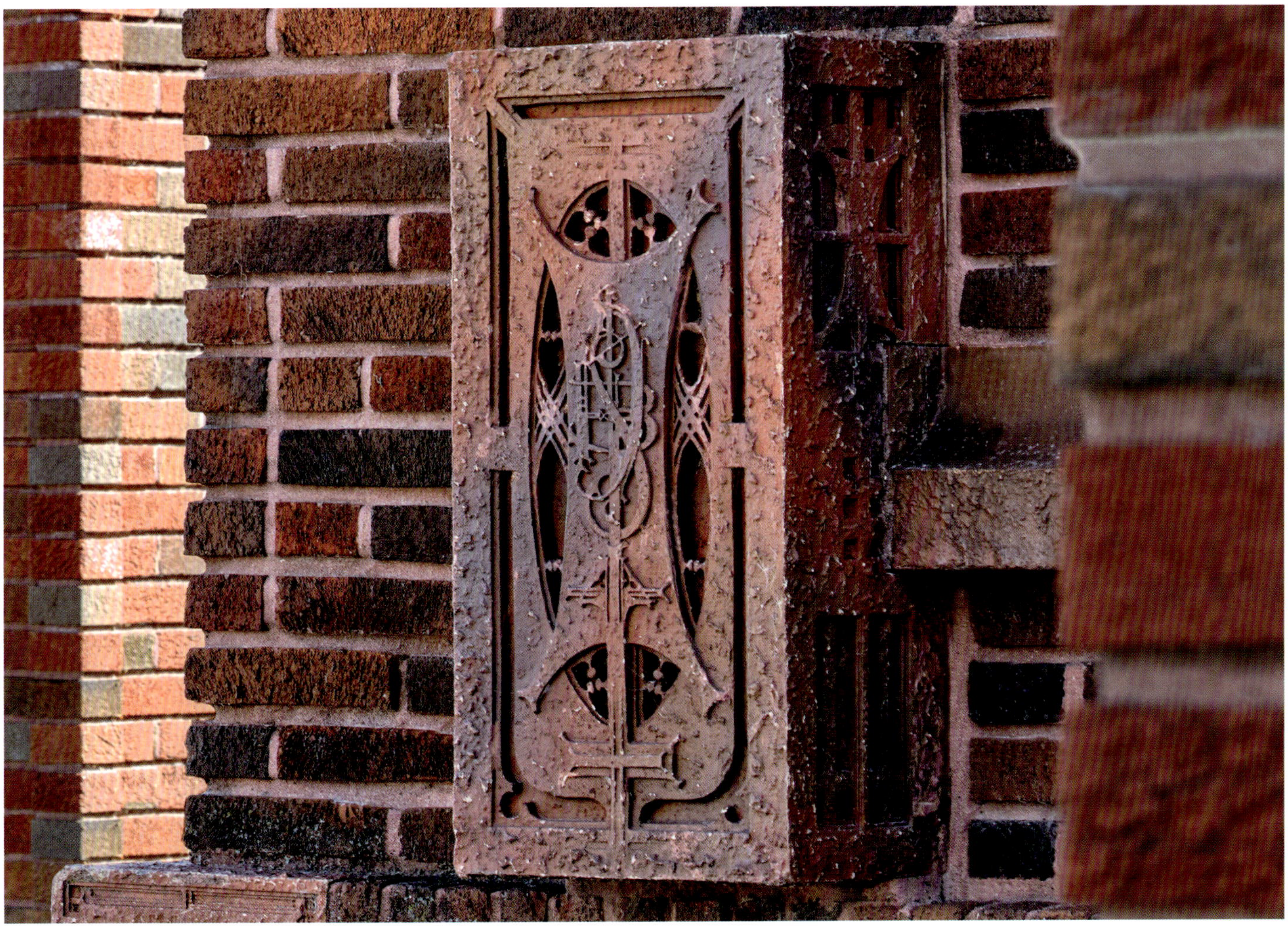

HENRY C. ADAMS LAND AND LOAN OFFICE

1913, ALGONA, IOWA

Henry Adams originally commissioned the building as a bank; however, since he failed to acquire the necessary charter, the building was initially used as a real estate and farm loan business. In 1917, Adams finally gave up hope of getting the charter. Sited on a corner, the exterior of the building is clad in mottled tapestry brick, with detailing in burnt orange and polychrome terra cotta. The main entrance is recessed, flanked by urns, and highlighted by art-glass windows. The side façade has a row of art-glass windows flanked by mullions topped with terra cotta capitals.

Over its history, the building has served as a headquarters for an insurance company and as a men's clothing store. It is now occupied by the Algona Area Chamber of Commerce. Its ongoing restoration is being conducted by the local Sullivan Building Foundation. The building was added to the National Register of Historic Places in 1998.

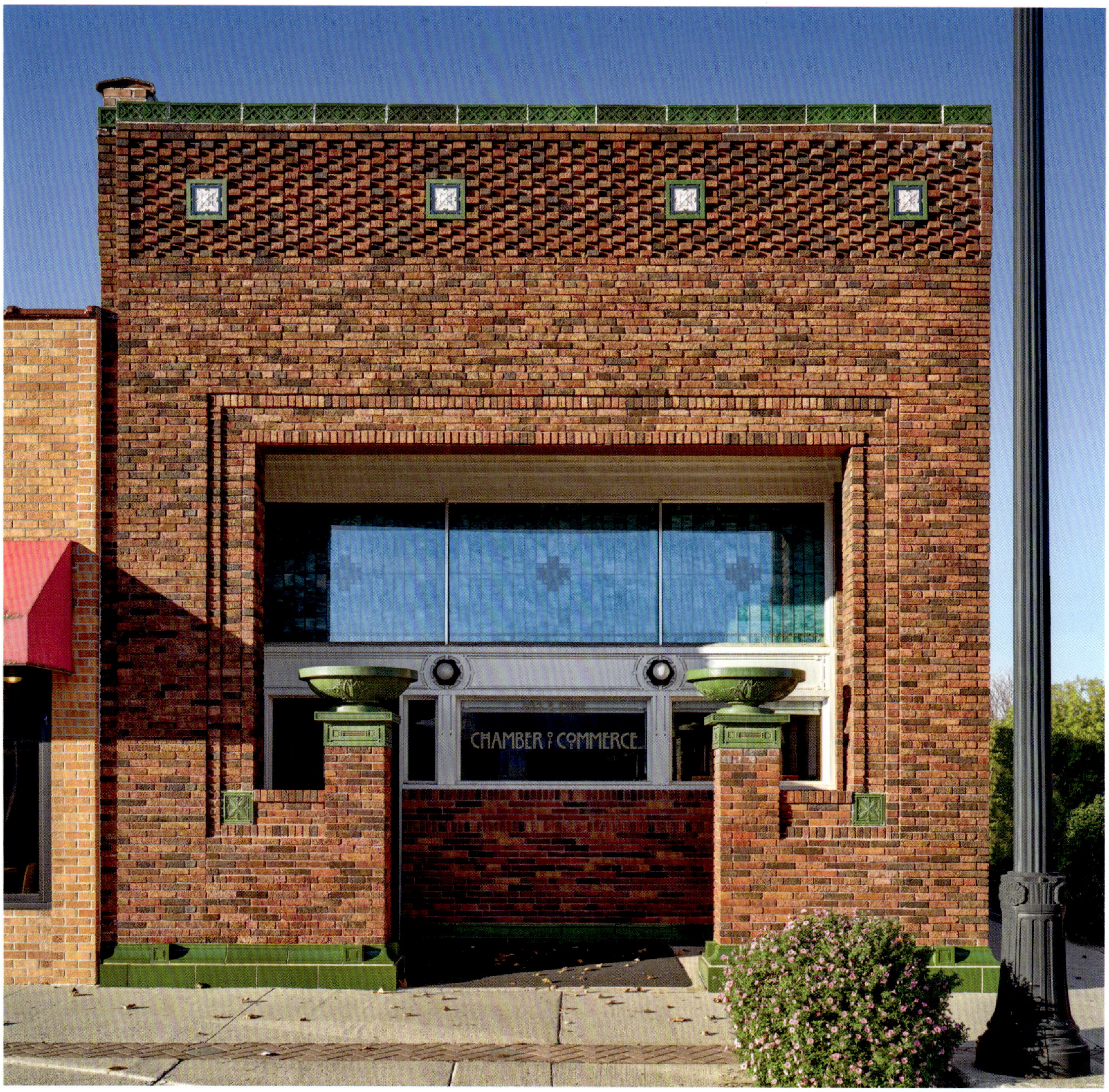

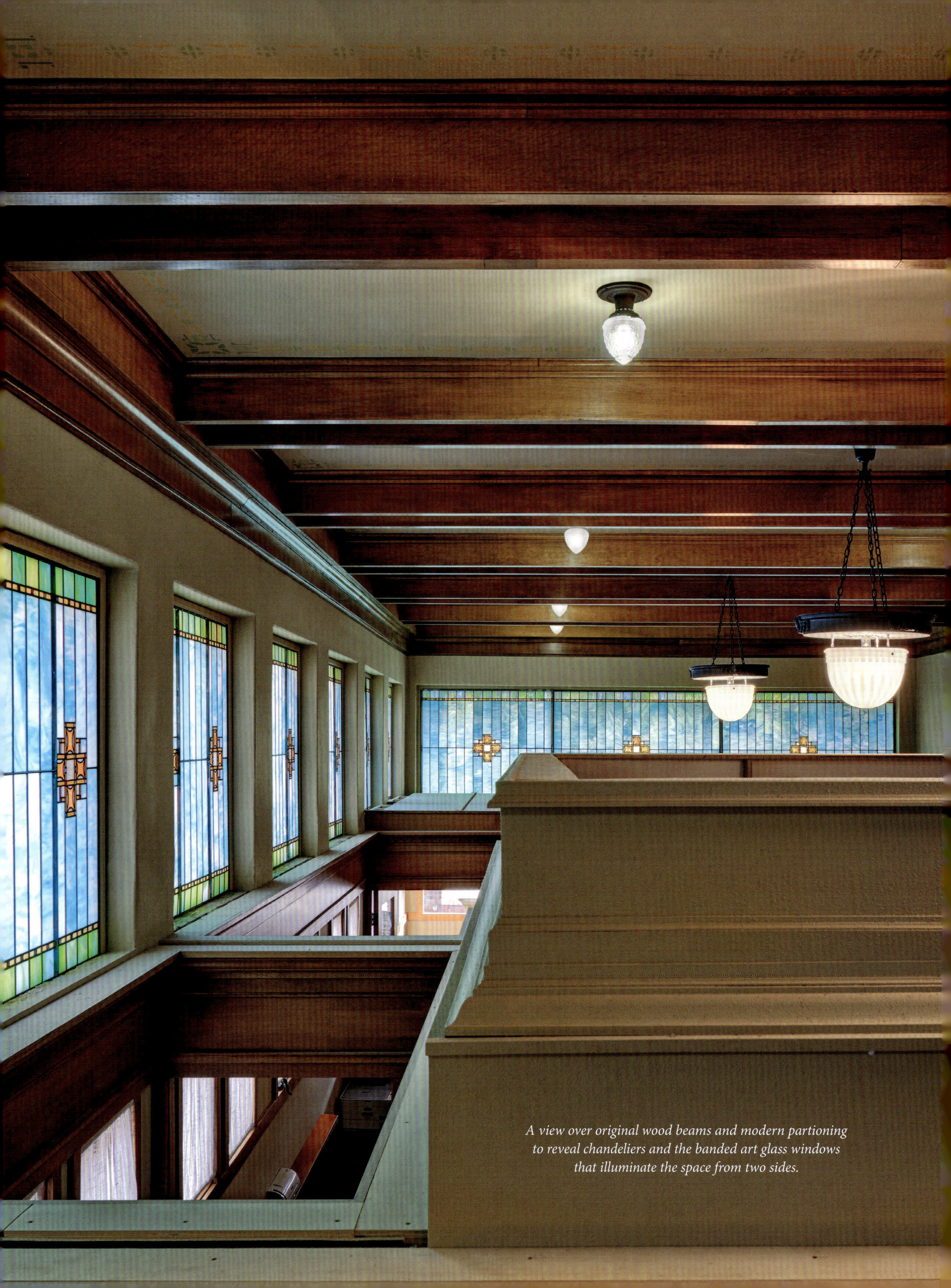

A view over original wood beams and modern partioning to reveal chandeliers and the banded art glass windows that illuminate the space from two sides.

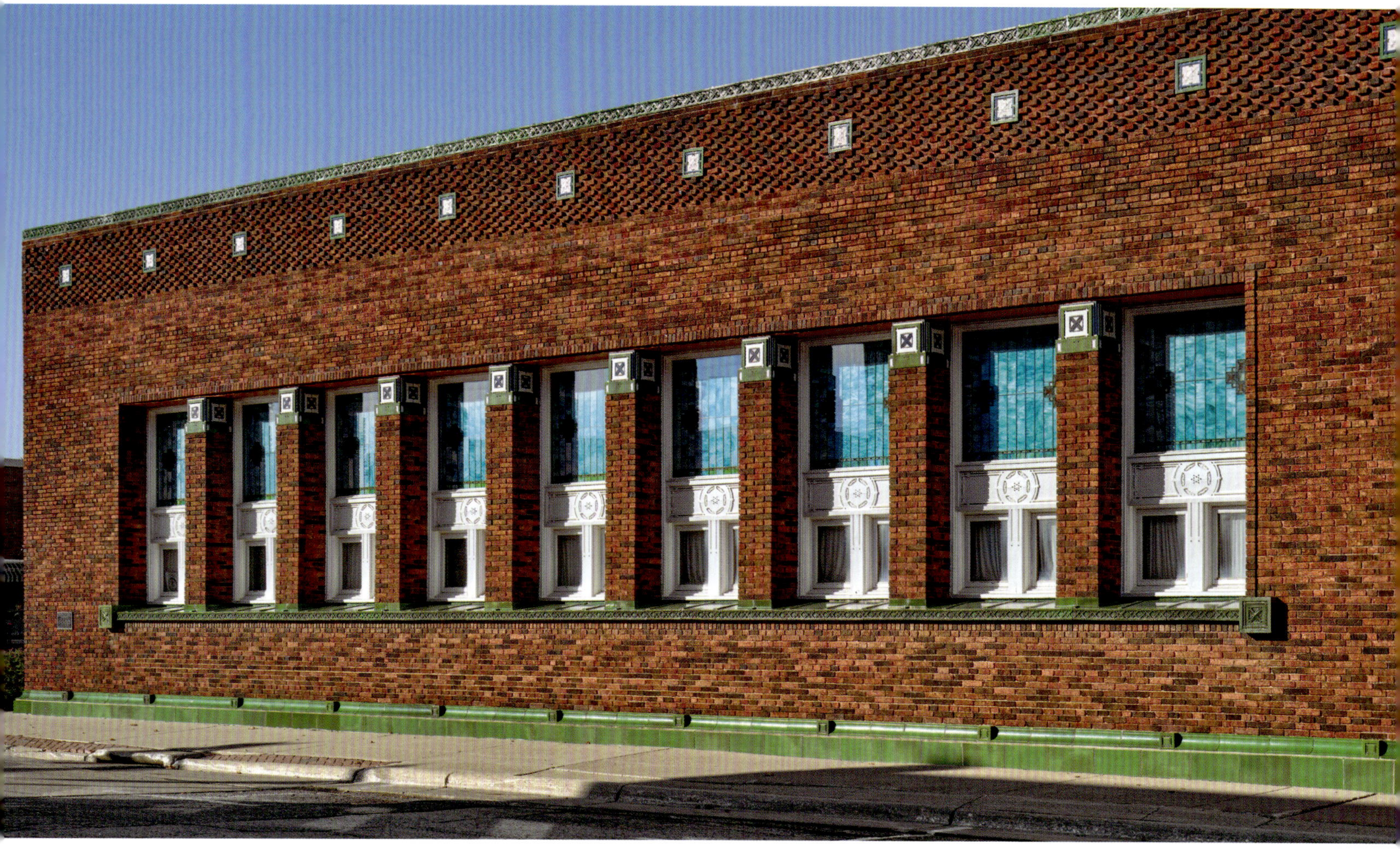

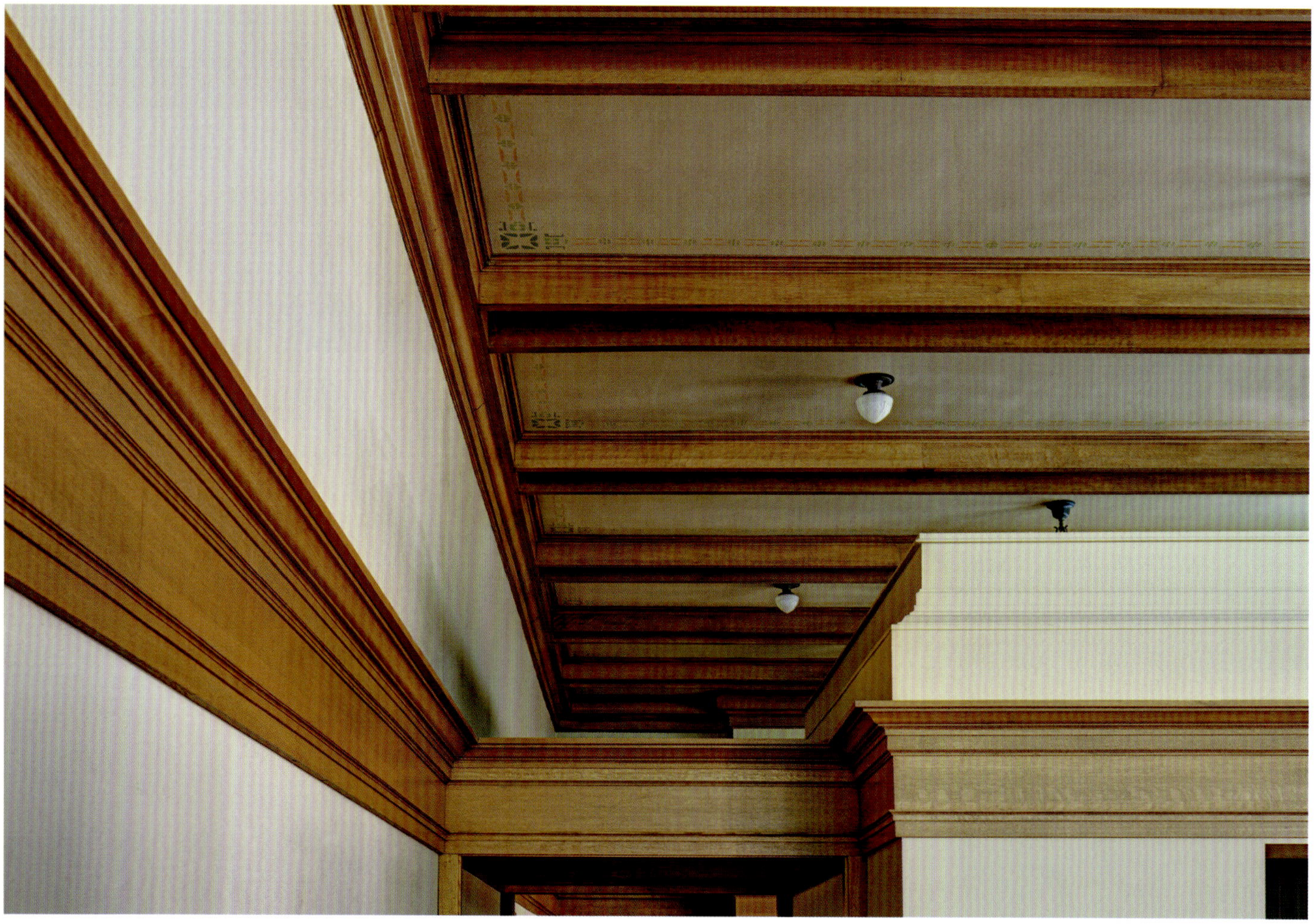

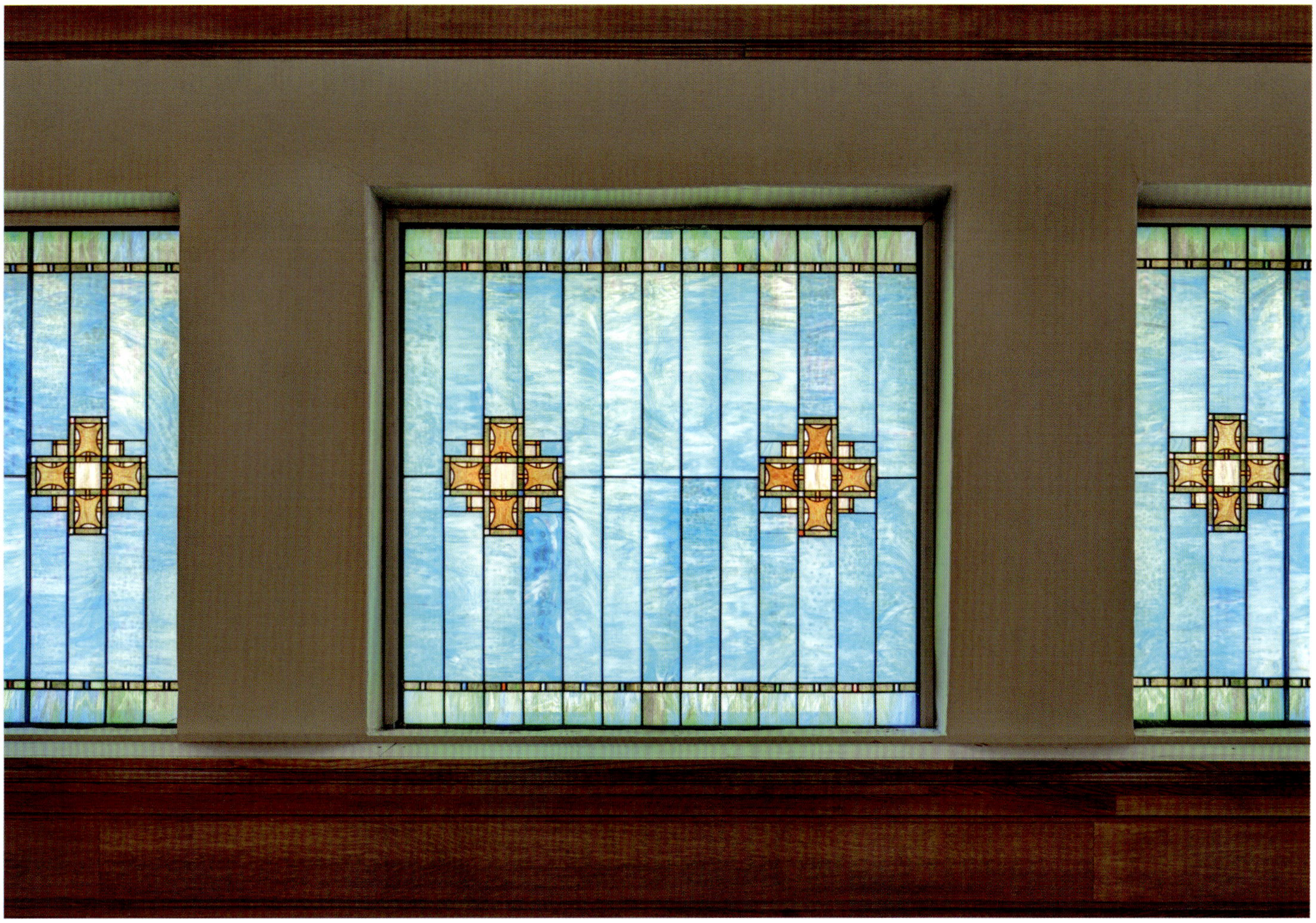

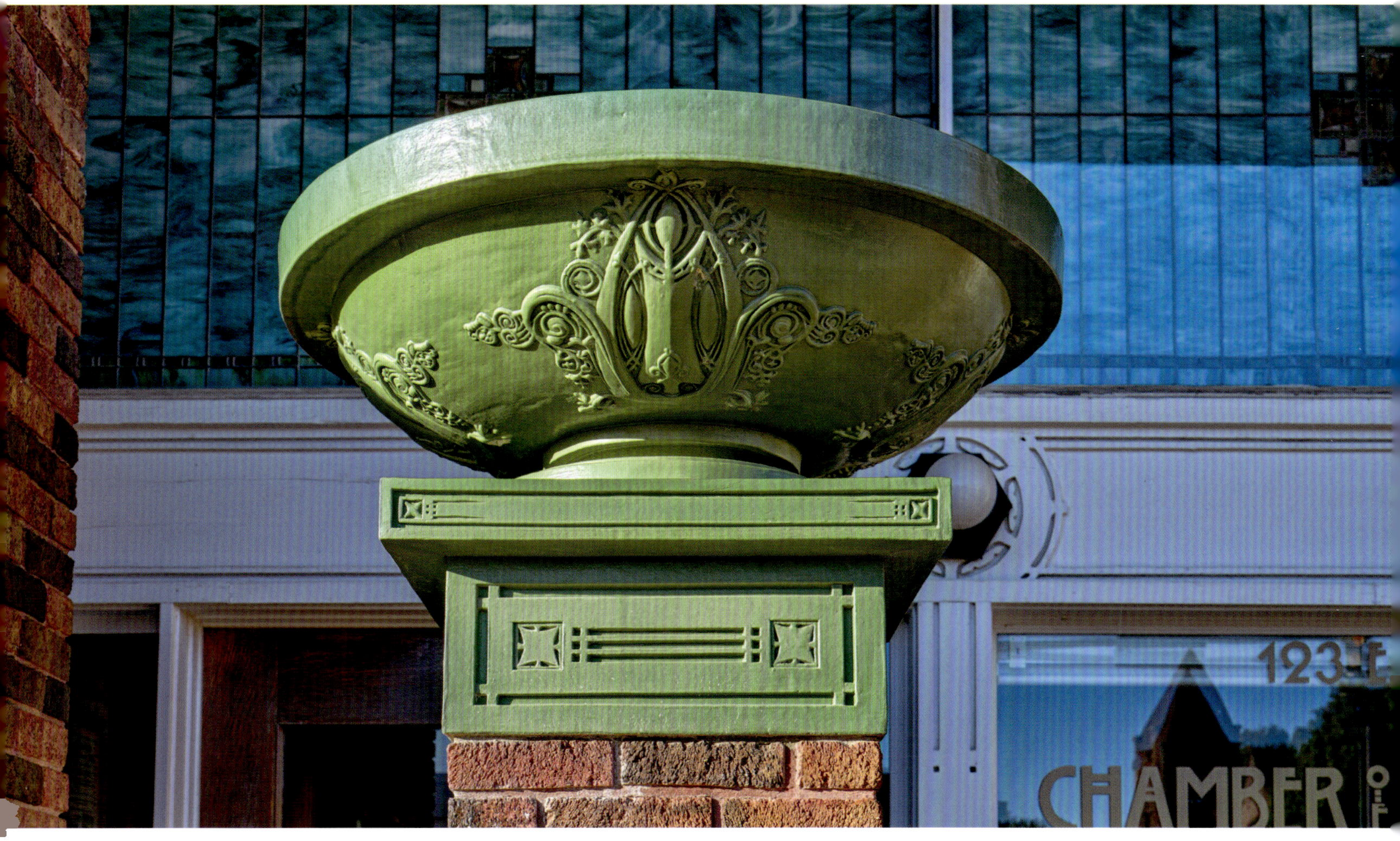
123 E
CHAMBER

PURDUE STATE BANK

1915, WEST LAFAYETTE, INDIANA

Located near the campus of Purdue University, the Purdue State Bank, the smallest of Sullivan's banks, now houses a Chase Bank branch. Its trapezoidal shape was dictated by its triangle-shaped lot. Despite its shape, the bank is similar in detail to the Henry C. Adams Land and Loan Office, with walls of reddish-brown brick with patterned coursing but with more restrained use of terra cotta ornament, perhaps to keep costs down. The main entrance was framed in terra cotta and featured a bronze name plaque above the door, since removed. Unfortunately, the door has been removed, the space now devoted to an ATM machine. The interior has been much changed over the years and has little or no original features.

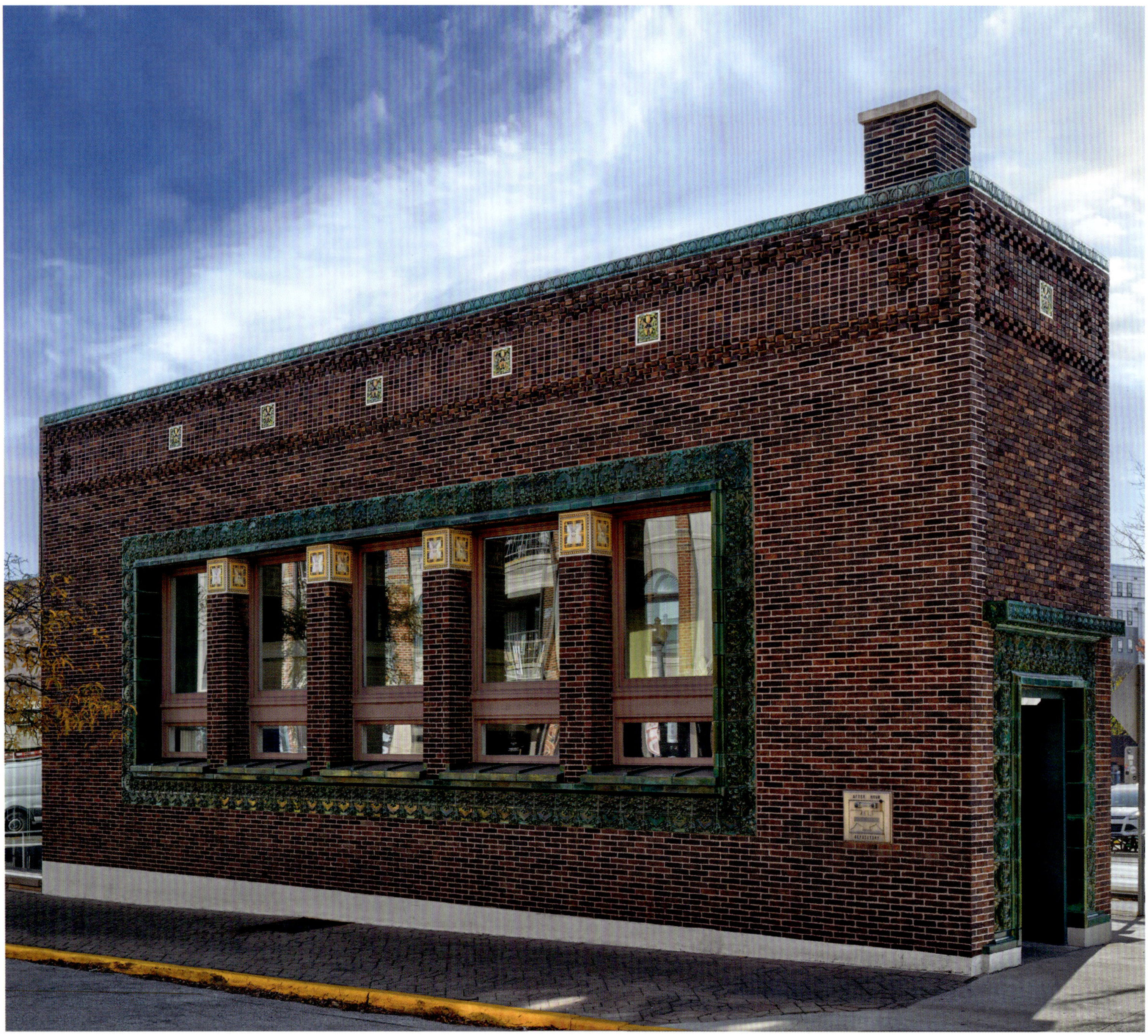

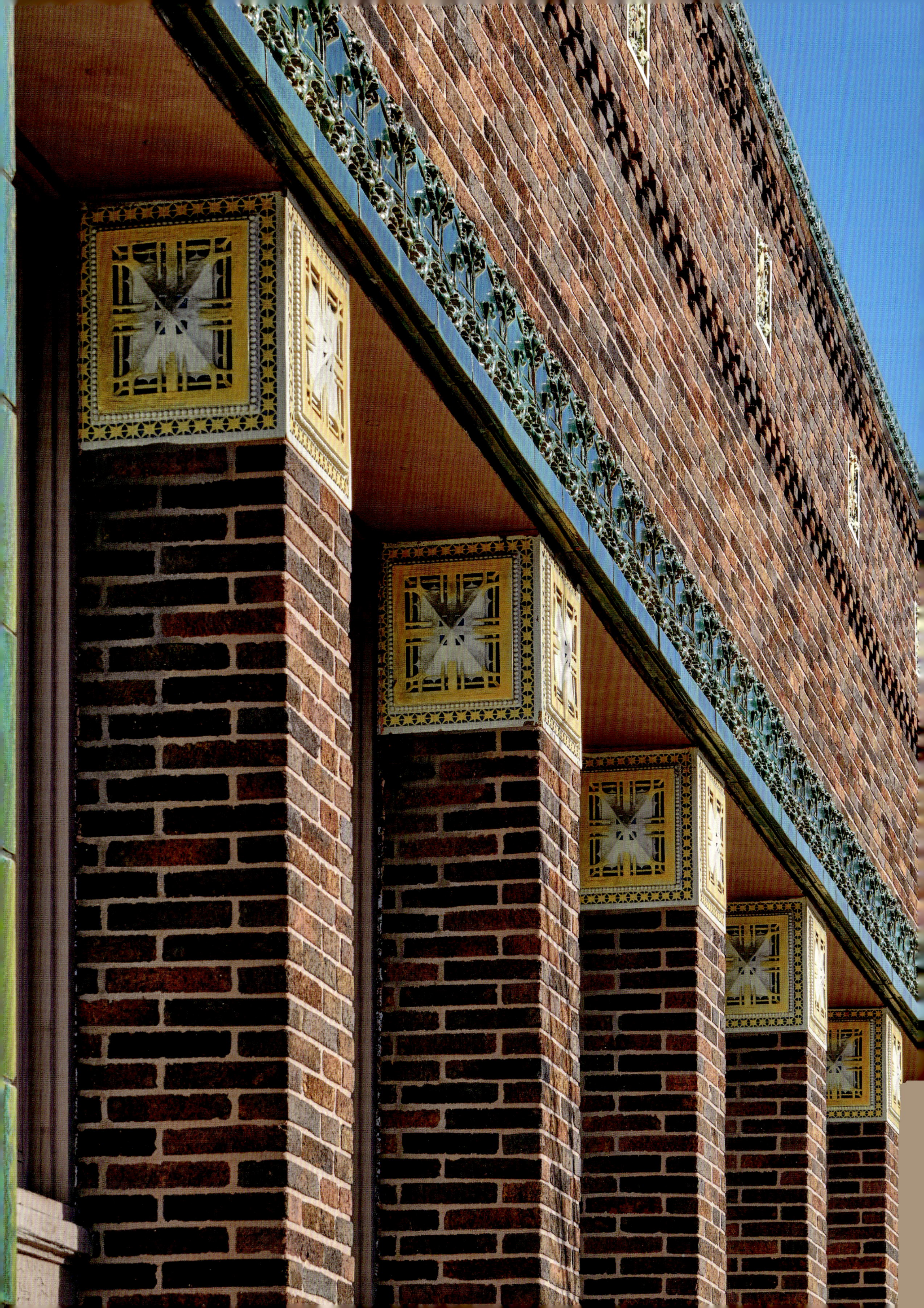

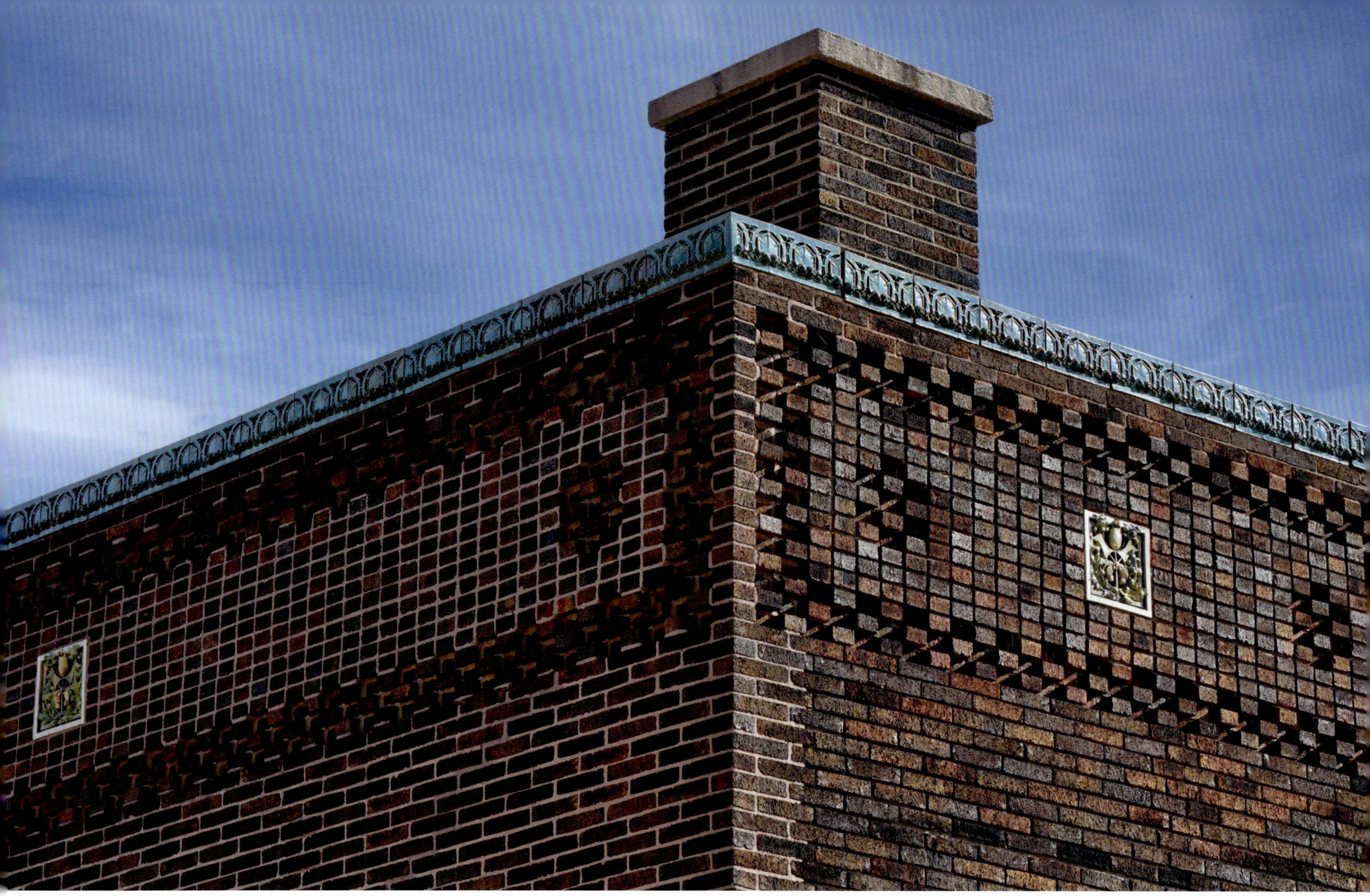

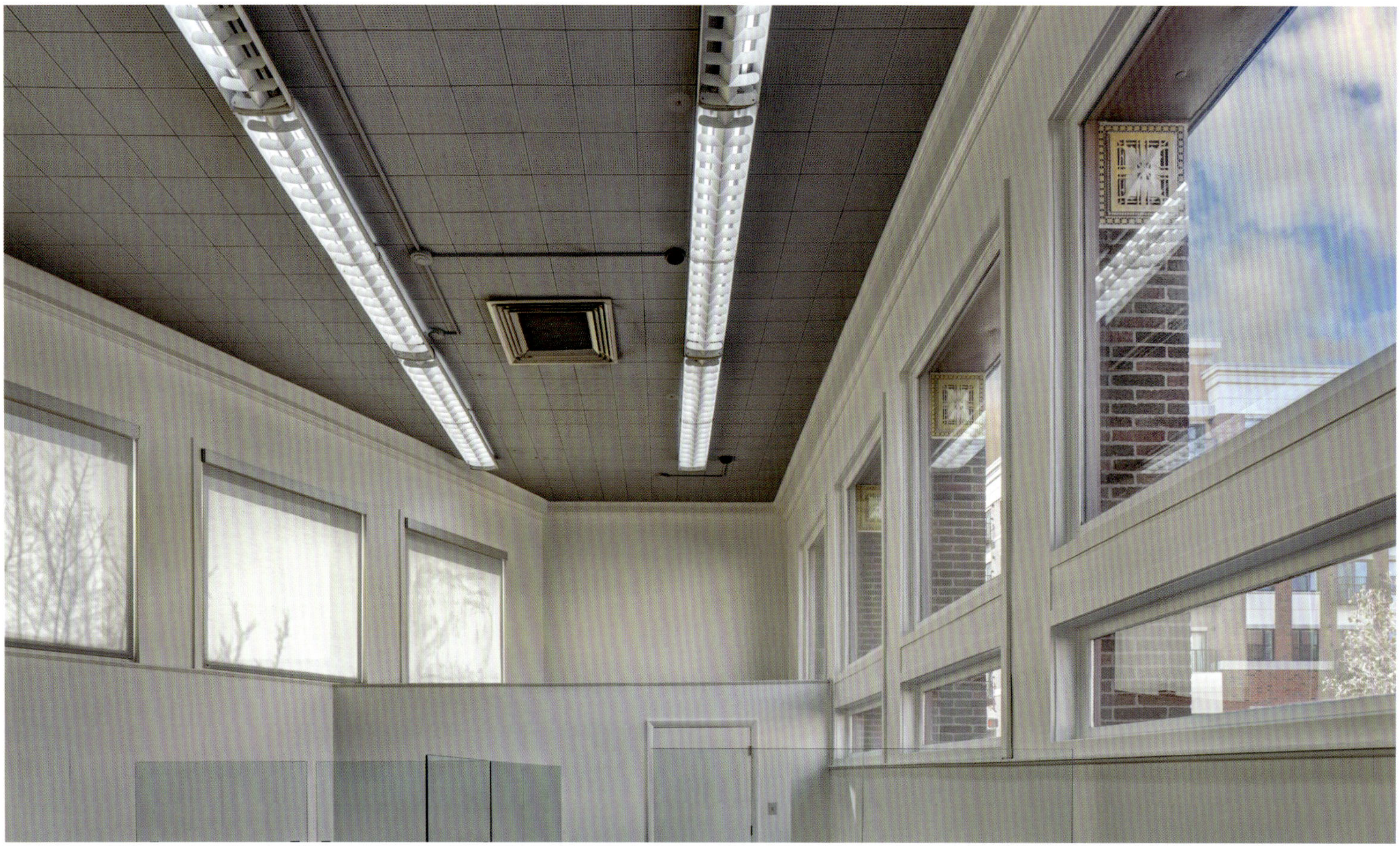

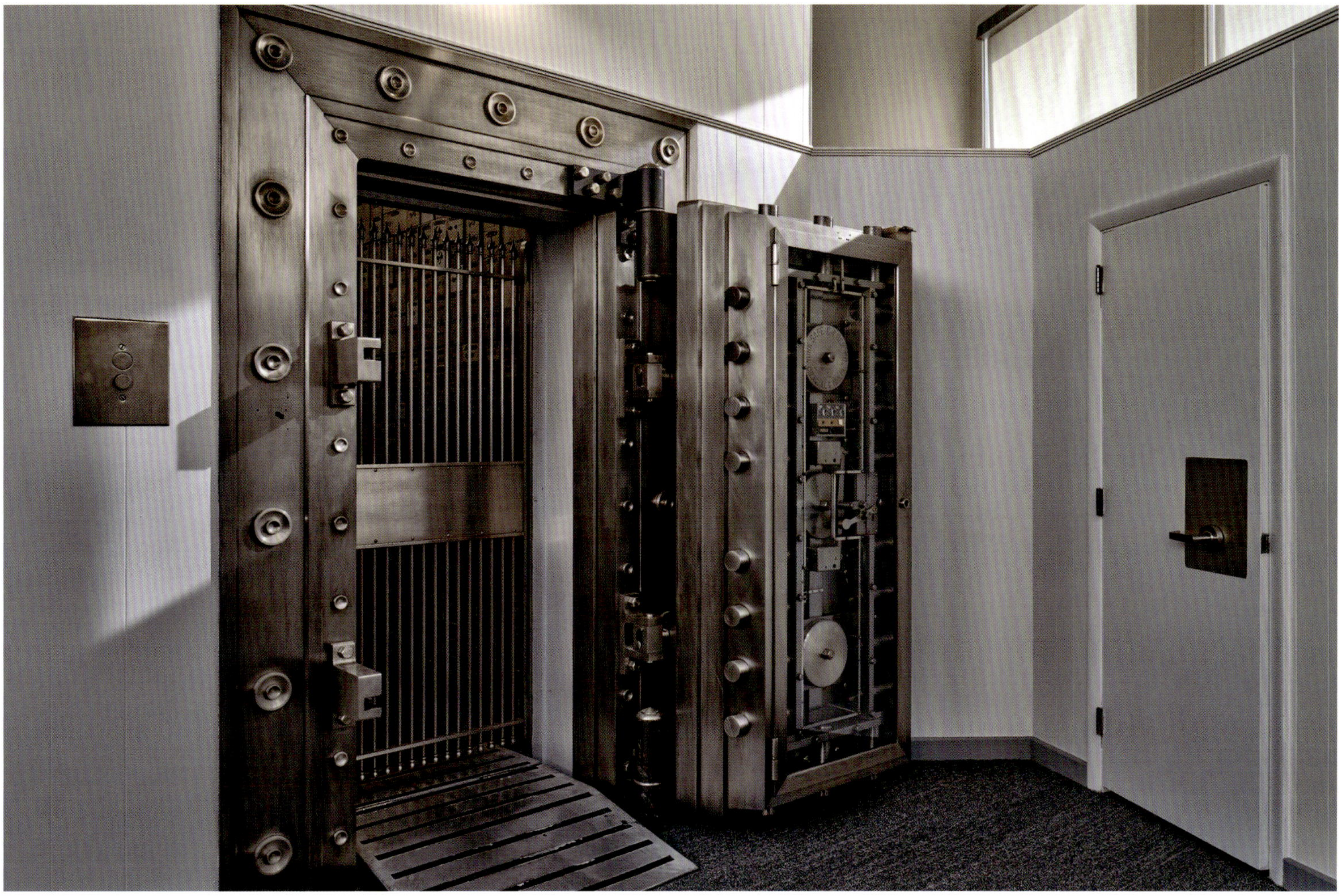

The vault is essentially all that remains of the original interior.

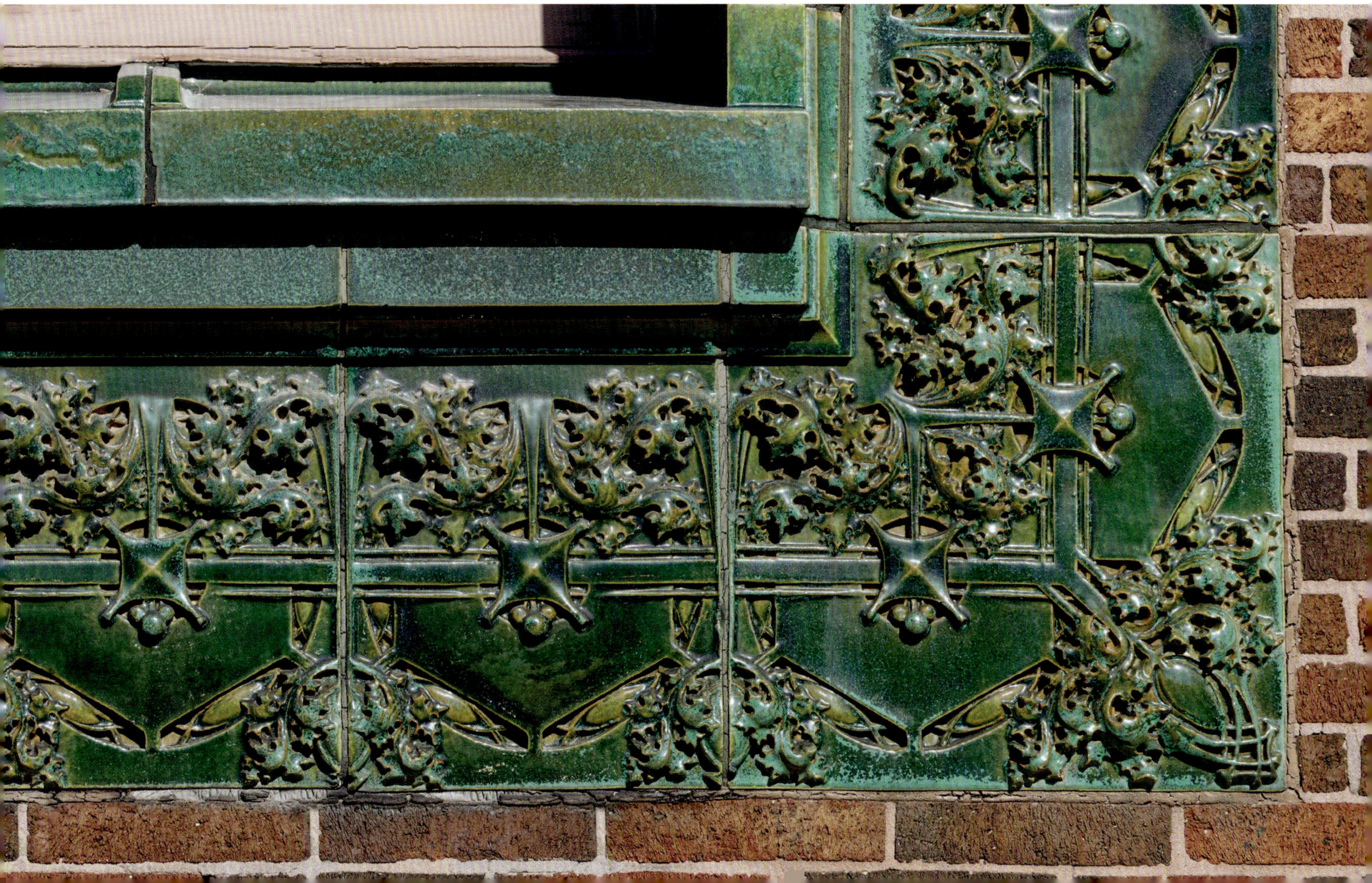

MERCHANTS NATIONAL BANK

1915, GRINNELL, IOWA

Lovingly maintained, the bank is a simple rectangular box, faced with patterned brick in hues that vary between light brown to blue-black, the overall effect being a warm reddish-brown. Its entrance is truly spectacular, flanked by golden lions and topped with an intricate terra cotta cartouche pierced with a circular art glass window. Lions were a typical decorative motif for bank buildings and were used by Sullivan for most of his banks, as well as for the much larger Union Trust Bank in St. Louis.

The side elevation includes ten recessed art-glass windows, separated visually by gold-finished load-bearing columns with foliate capitals. The only other decorative element is the elaborate terra cotta cornice. Trees planted in front of the bank, which partially obscured the façade, were removed in 2013. It was added to the National Register of Historic Places in 1976 and is now occupied by the Grinnell Area Chamber of Commerce. Tours are available.

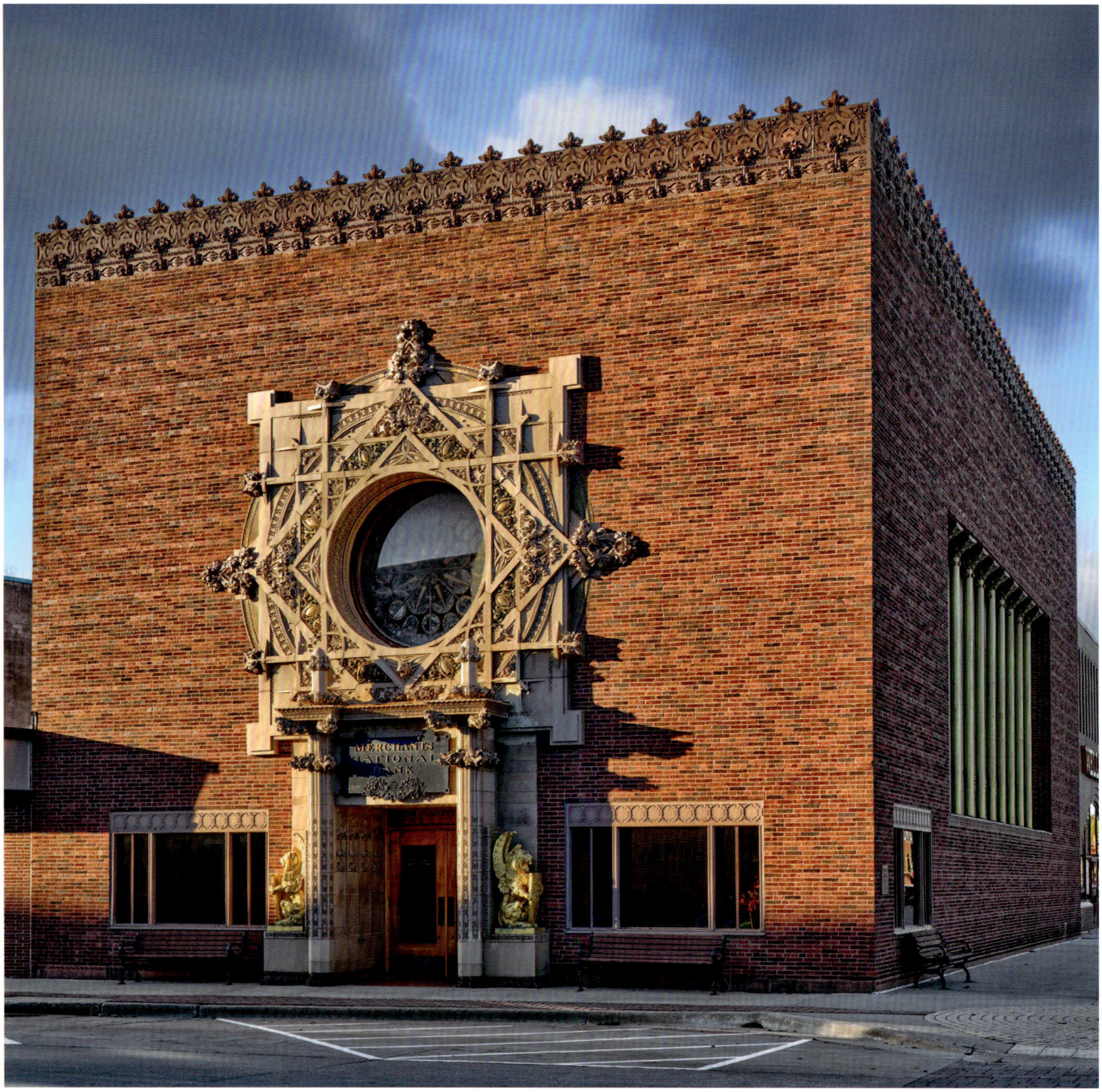

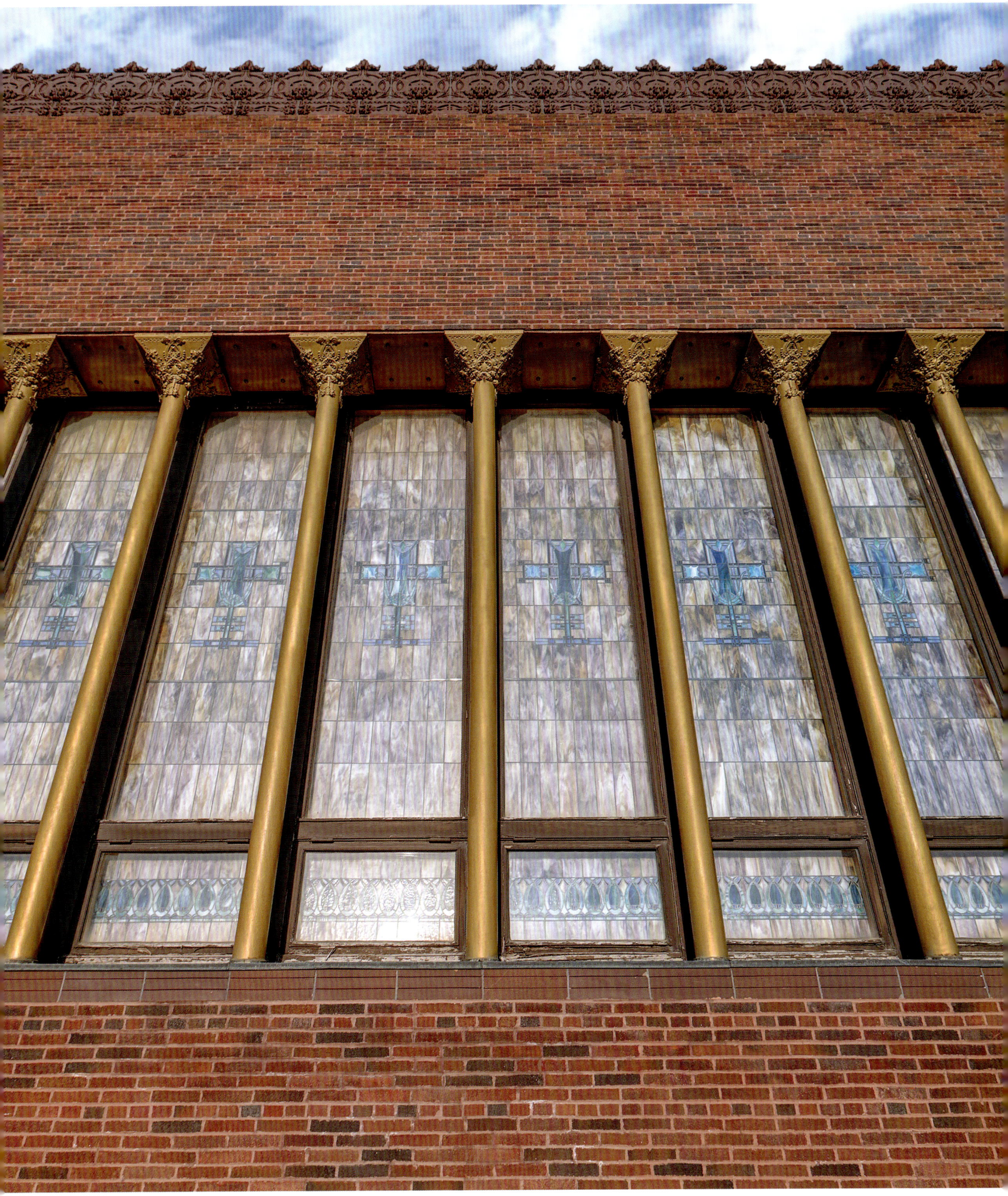

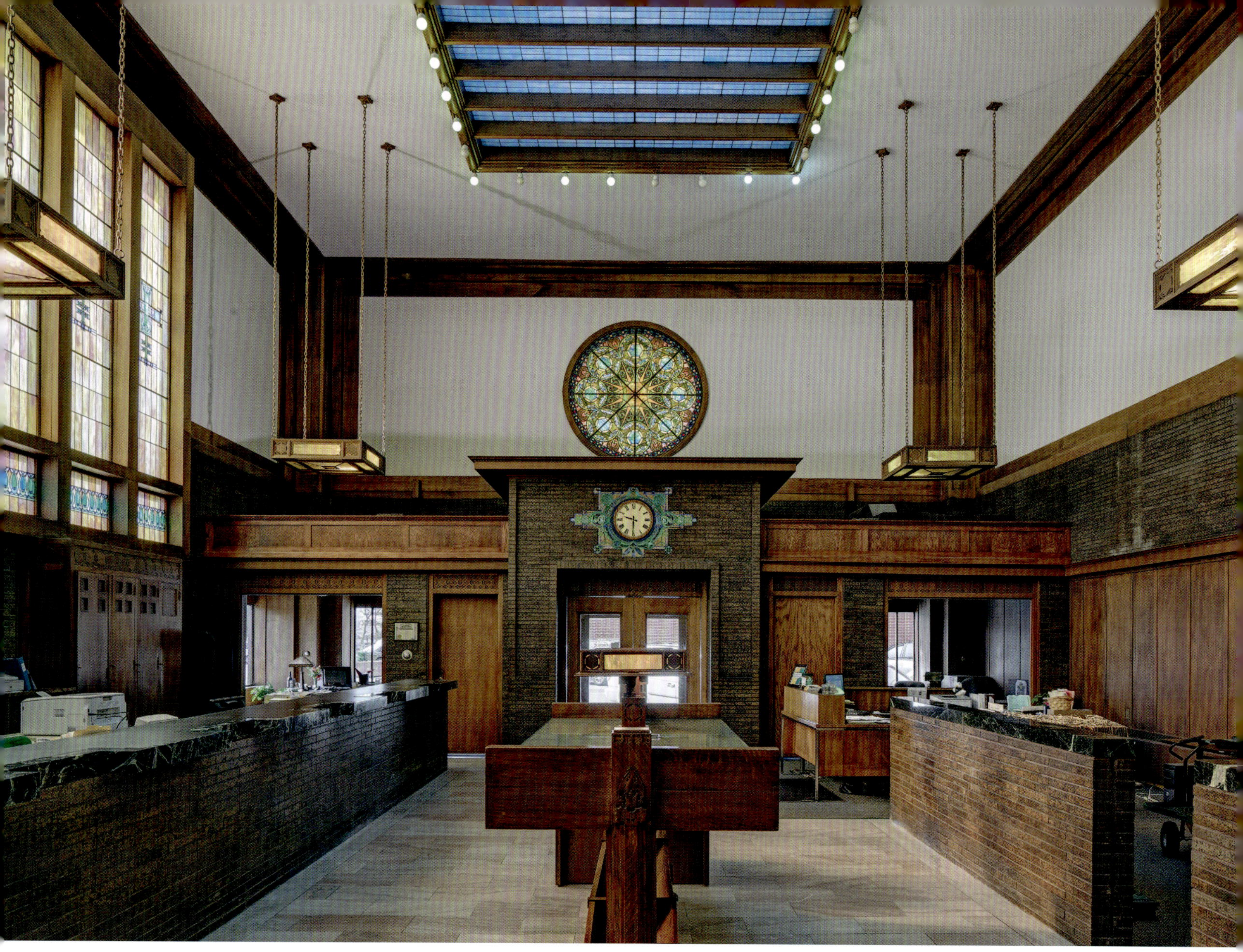

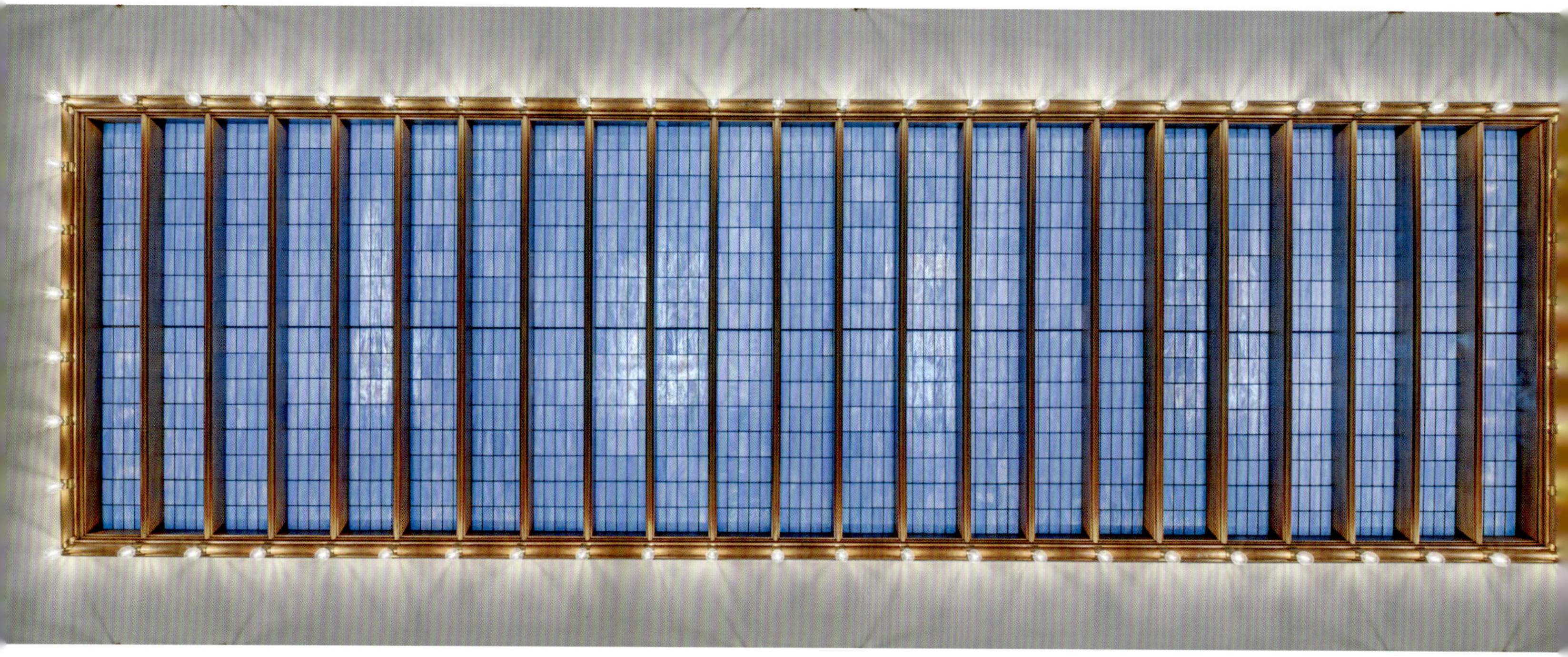

The interior is restrained, with art glass providing most of the color. Textured Roman brick is used for counters and part of the walls.

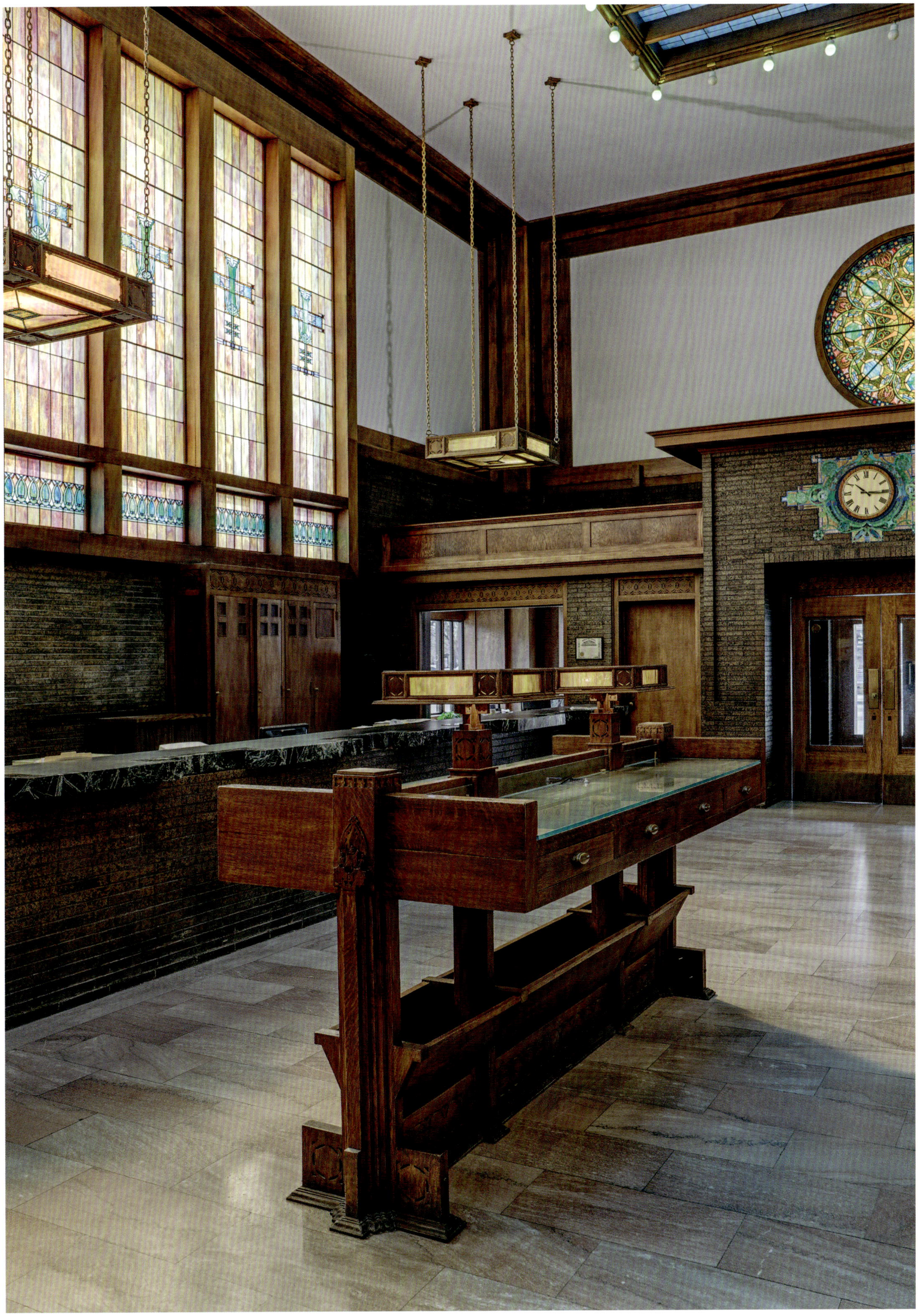

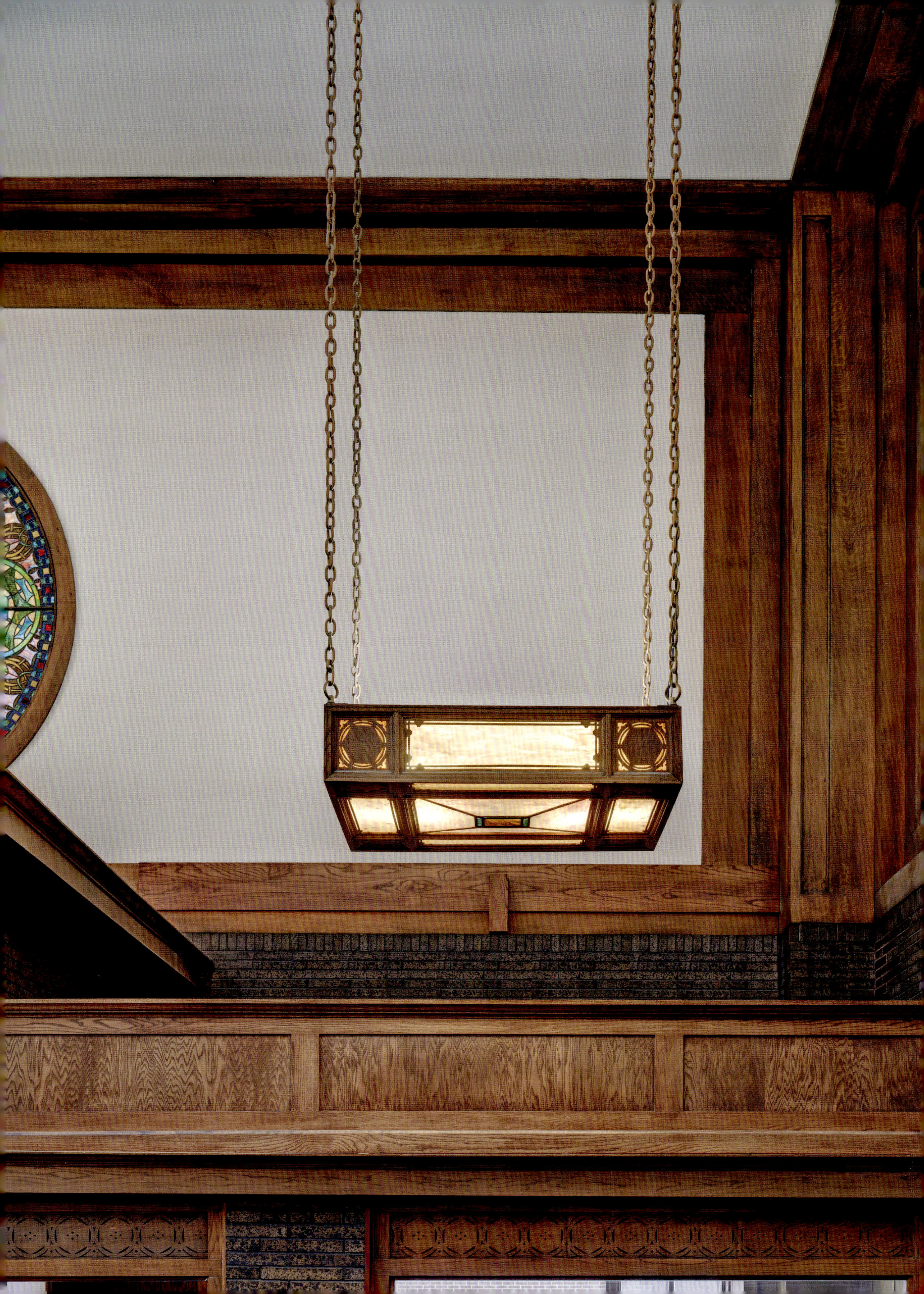

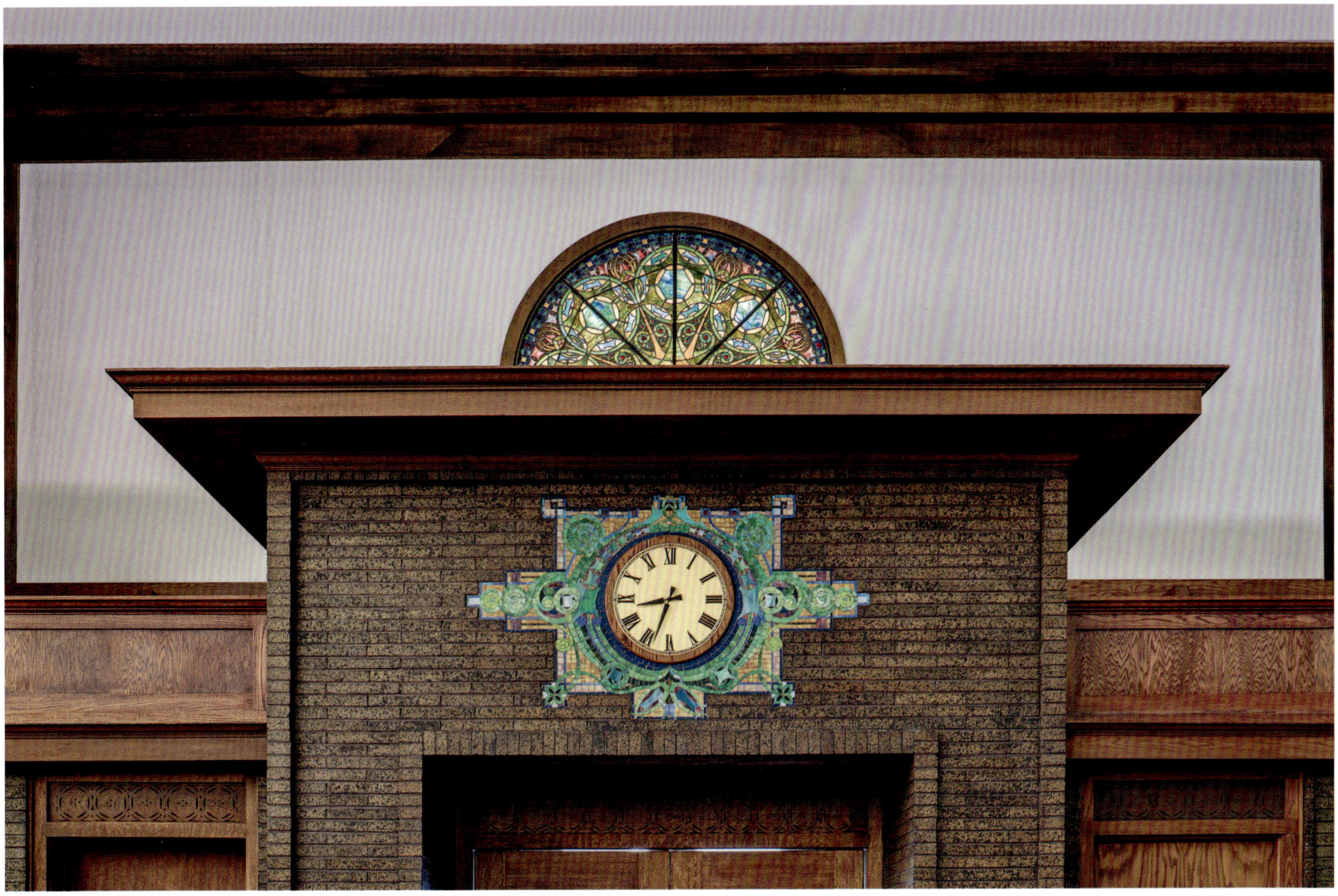

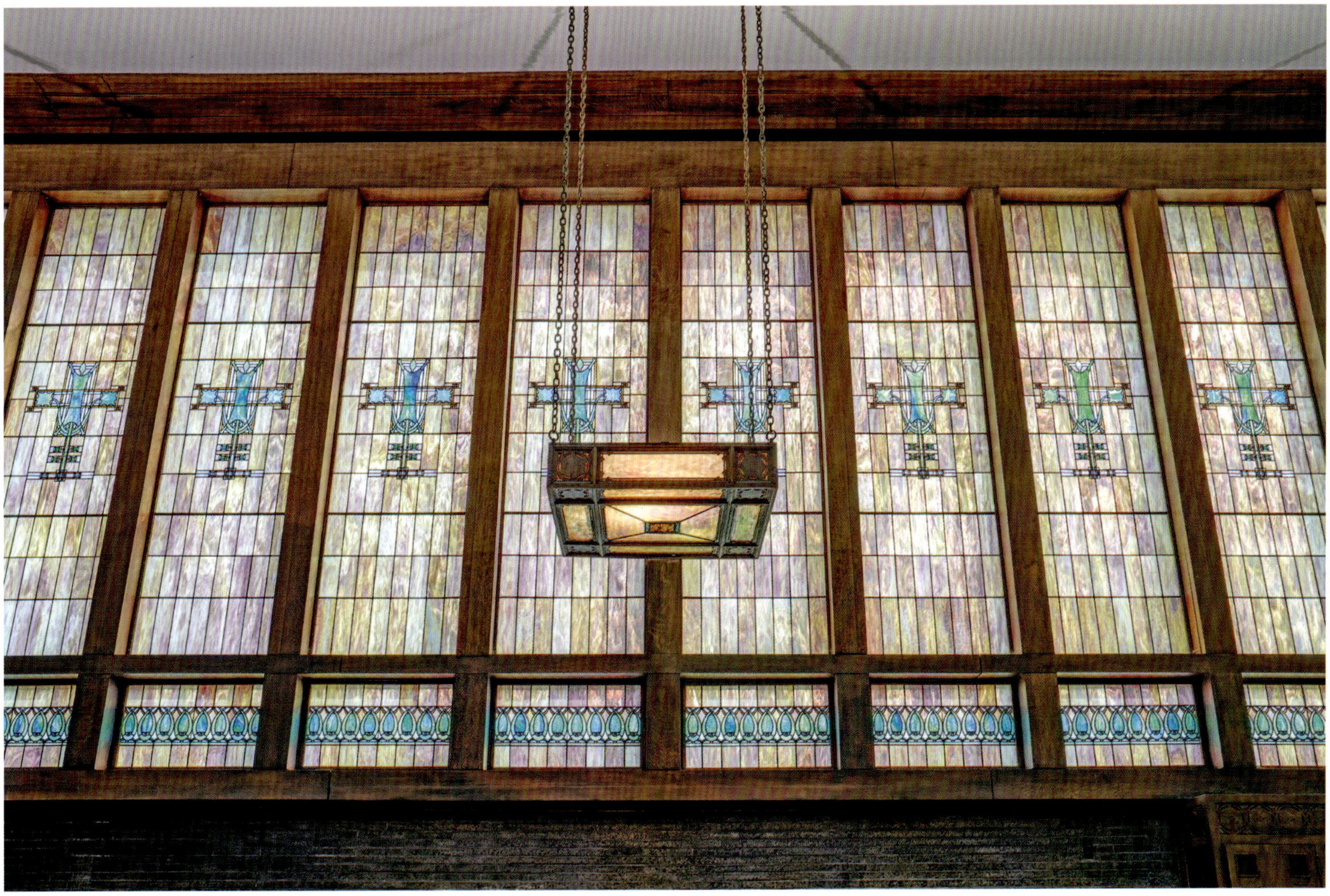

HOME BUILDING ASSOCIATION

1915, NEWARK, OHIO

Alone among Sullivan's banks, the Home Building Association—known as "The Old Home"—is clad not in brick but in gray-green terra cotta panels. The two-story building (offices on the second floor) is located on a prominent corner of the town square across from the Licking County Courthouse. It has only two facades, since it has neighbors on both sides. The main entrance is on the smaller of the two facades, notable for a mosaic with the "Old Home" slogan at its center, said to be executed by frequent Sullivan collaborator Louis Millet. The other, larger side also includes mosaics and art glass windows, all of it framed by Sullivan's typical geometric borders.

The building has a star-crossed history. After serving as the home of the original and a later bank, the building became a butcher shop; a jewelry store; and, finally, an ice cream shop. It is now owned by the Licking County Foundation, which acquired the building as a gift from Steven Jones in 2013, who purchased it in 2007 to ensure its preservation. Exterior restoration began in 2019 and was completed in 2021. Interior restoration began in November of 2023 and is scheduled for completion by June 2025, when it will become the home of Explore Licking County, the area's convention and visitor's bureau. It was added to the National Register of Historic Places in 1973.

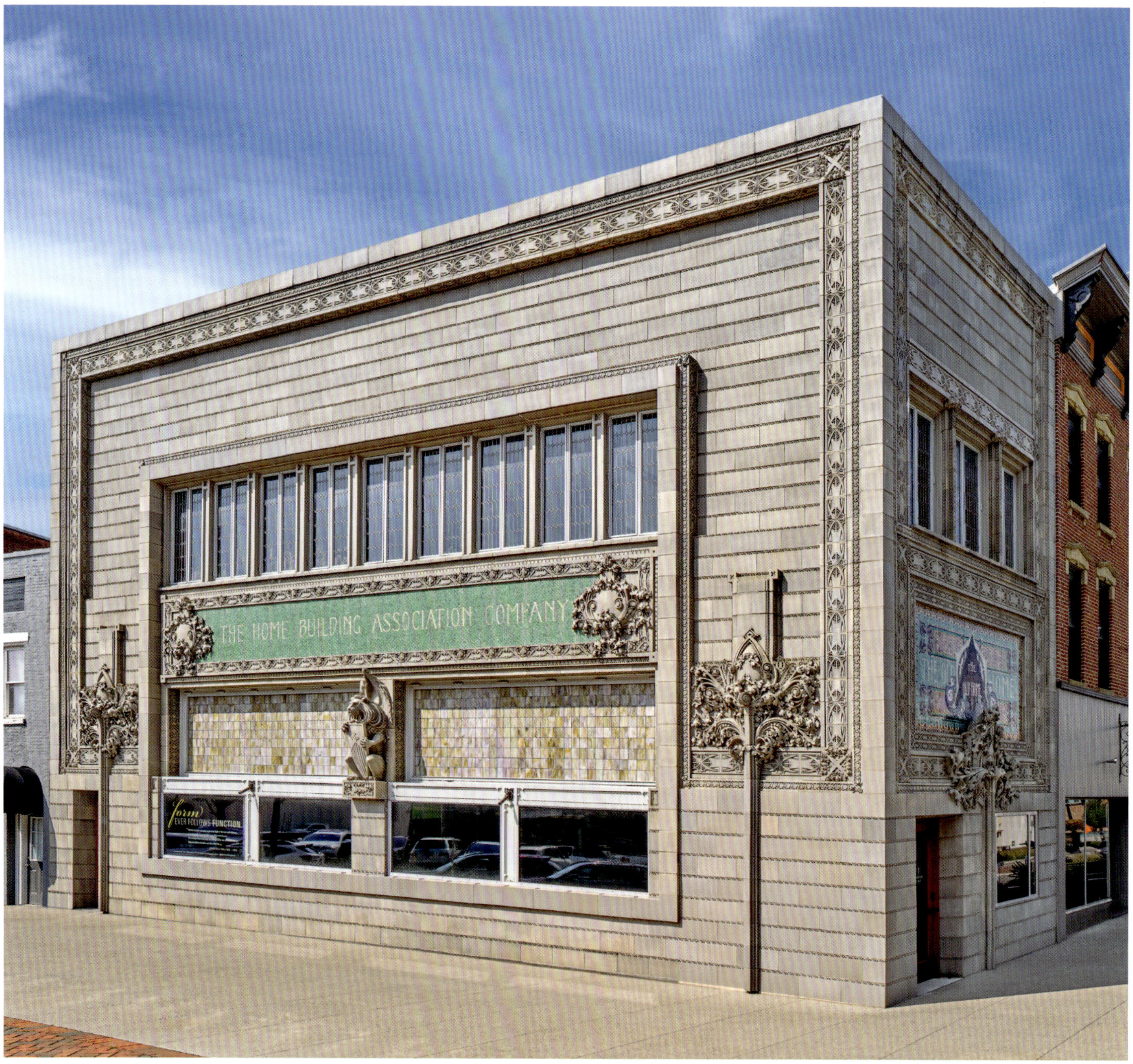

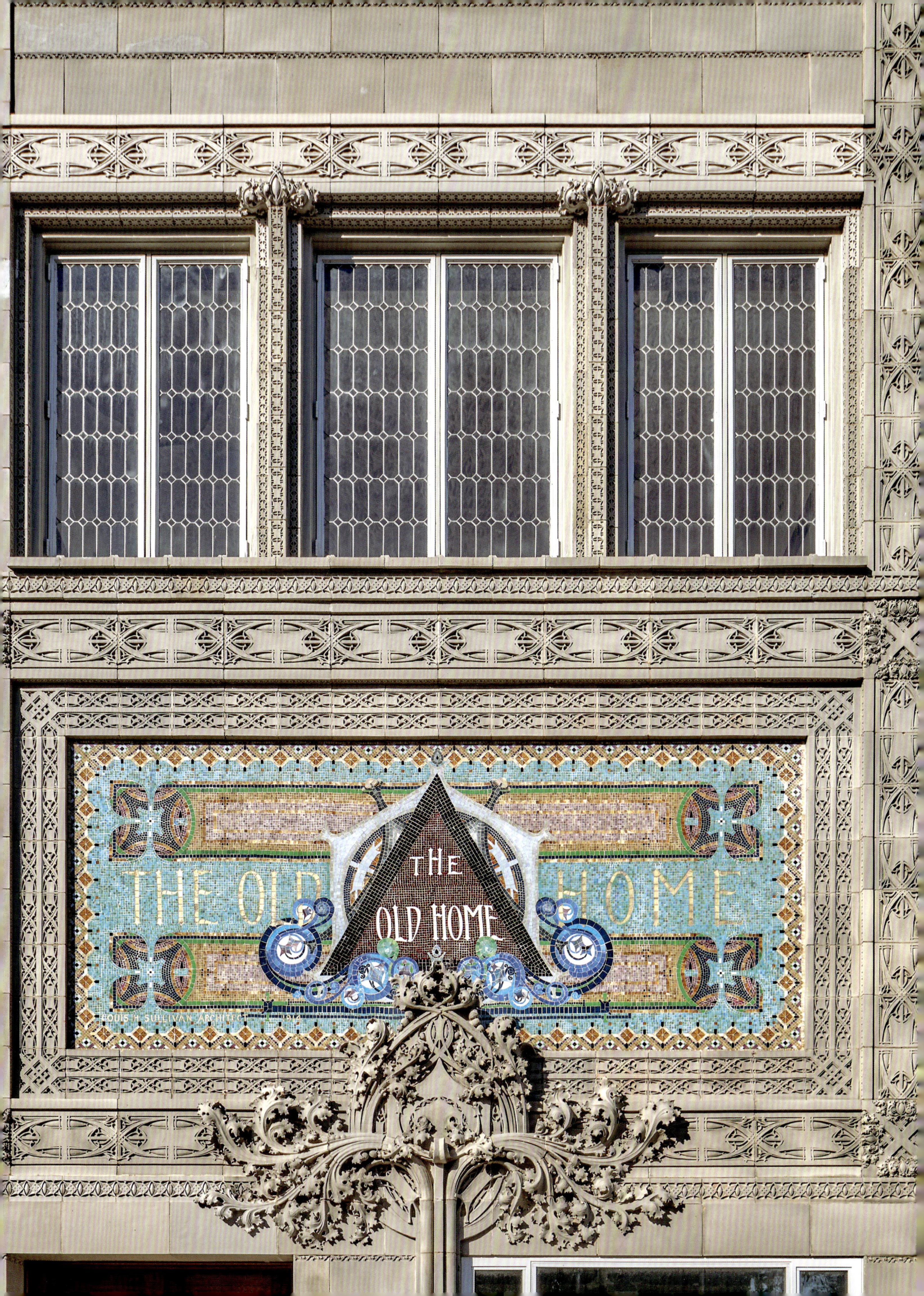
THE OLD
HOME
THE
OLD HOME
LOUIS H. SULLIVAN ARCHITECT

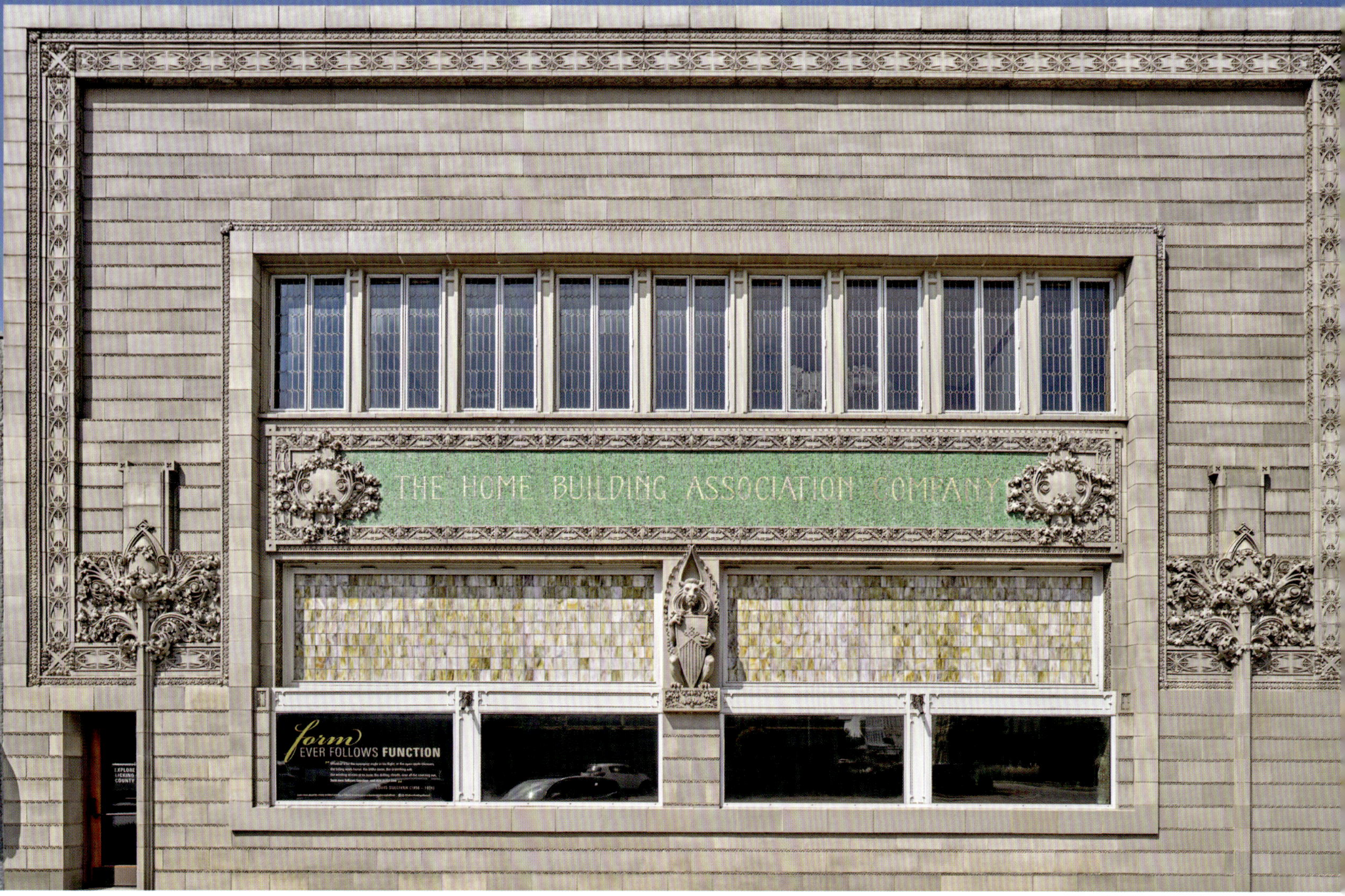

On the second floor, pre-restoration, the original leaded glass banded windows.

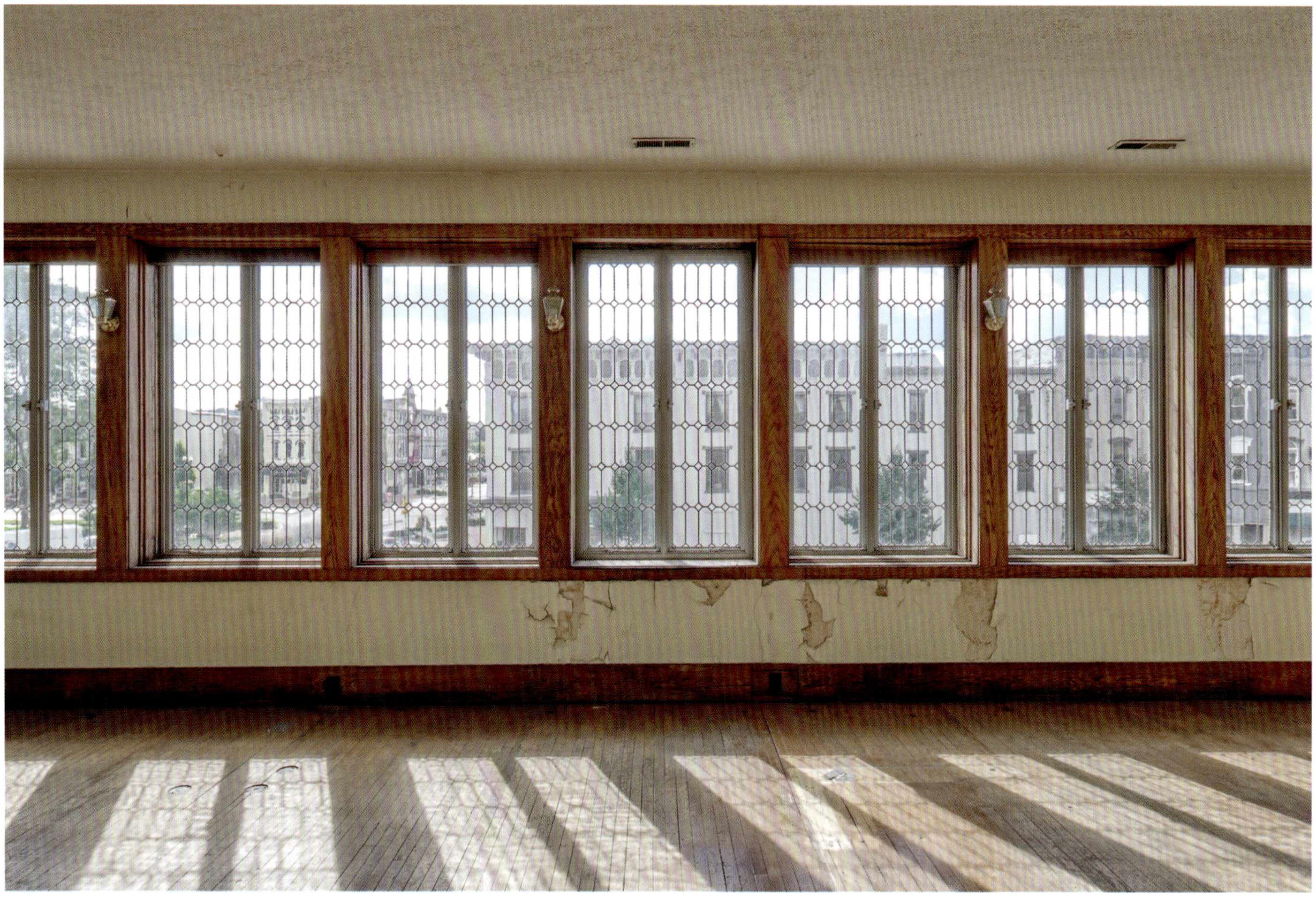

Restoration of the banking floor has begun, for completion in 2025.

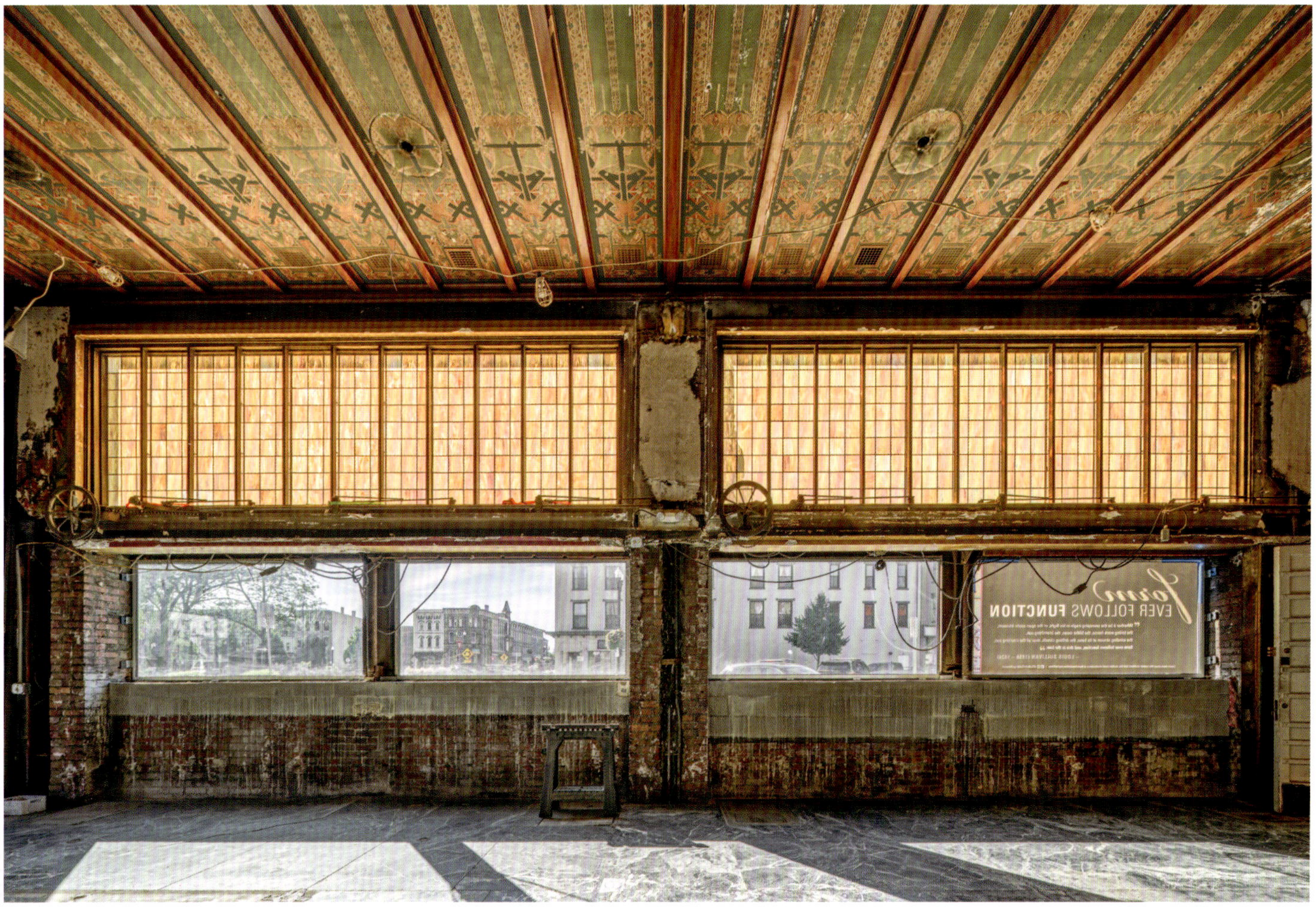

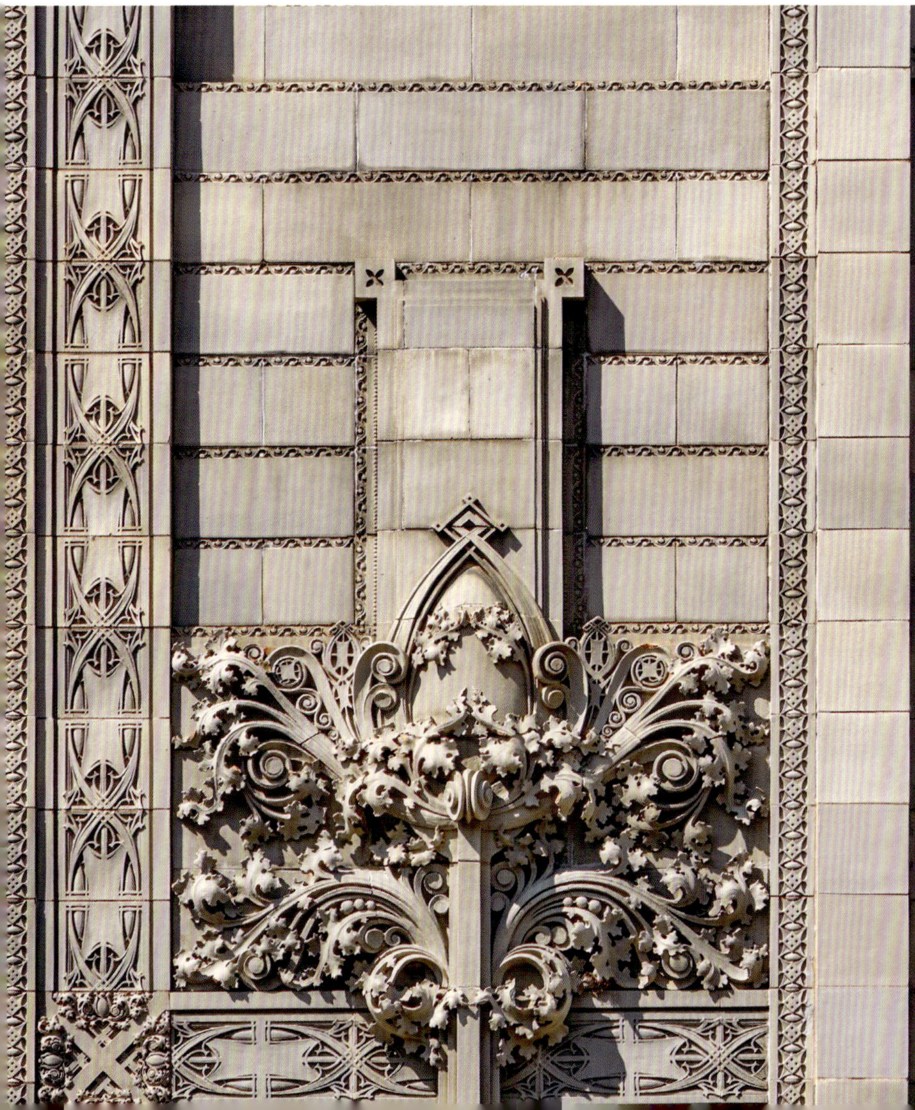

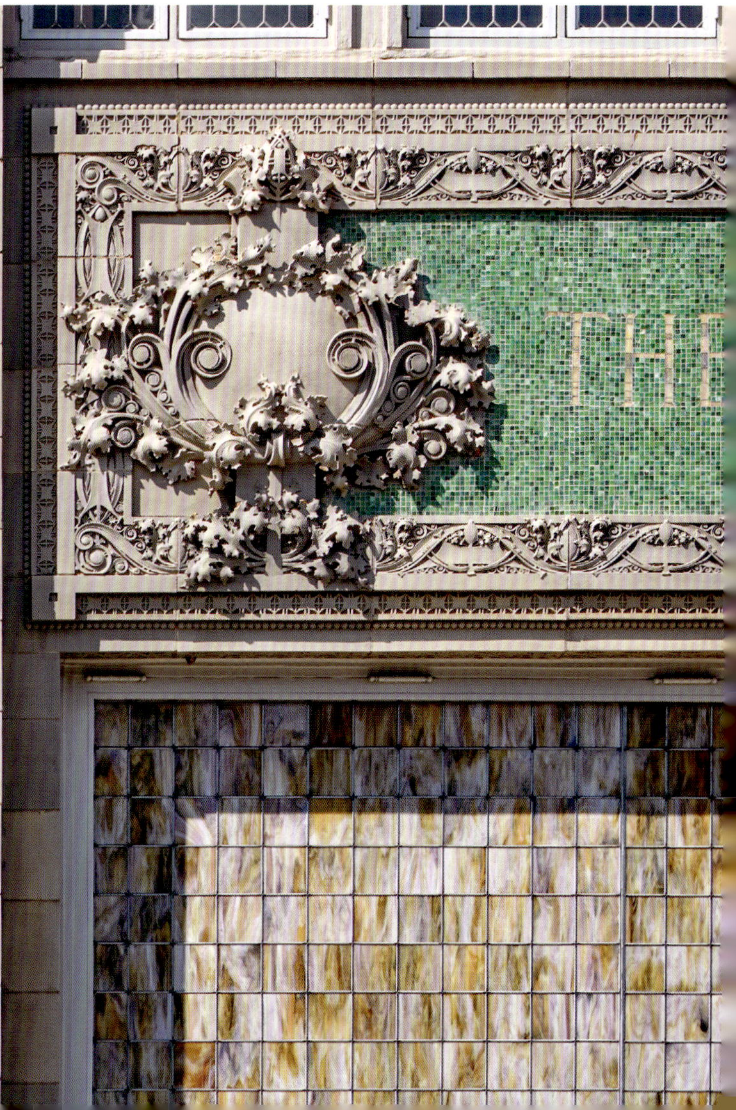

PEOPLES SAVINGS AND LOAN ASSOCIATION

1918, SIDNEY, OHIO

In his biography of Sullivan (see Bibliography), Hugh Morrison quotes a story about the building's genesis, told by the bank's later president, C.E. Studevant. It seems he had been told by a banker from Cedar Rapids, Iowa, of the satisfaction that the clients expressed with Sullivan's design for their Peoples Savings Bank. When Sullivan came to Sidney at the request of his clients, he listened to their requirements and then spent two days sitting across from the proposed site. He then produced a sketch for approval. According to Morrison, "One of the directors said he rather fancied some classic columns and pilasters for the façade, whereas Sullivan started to roll up his sketch and depart, saying only that they could get a thousand architects to design them a classic bank, but only one to design a Sullivan bank, and it was either one or the other."

The story certainly rings true. This time, the architect got his way and, apparently, was proud and happy with the result. The building is very similar in form to the Merchants National Bank in Grinnell, Iowa. Above the main entrance is an elaborate mosaic, executed by Louis Millet, with the simple word "Thrift" in the center. The usual lions stand guard. The side façade includes nine art-glass windows, framed in terra cotta, and above them is the bank's full name in mosaic, also executed by Millet. The name of the bank has been changed slightly to "Peoples *Federal* Savings and Loan Association," and the bank remains largely as originally designed. It was added to the National Register of Historic Places in 1972 and has also been designated a National Historic Landmark.

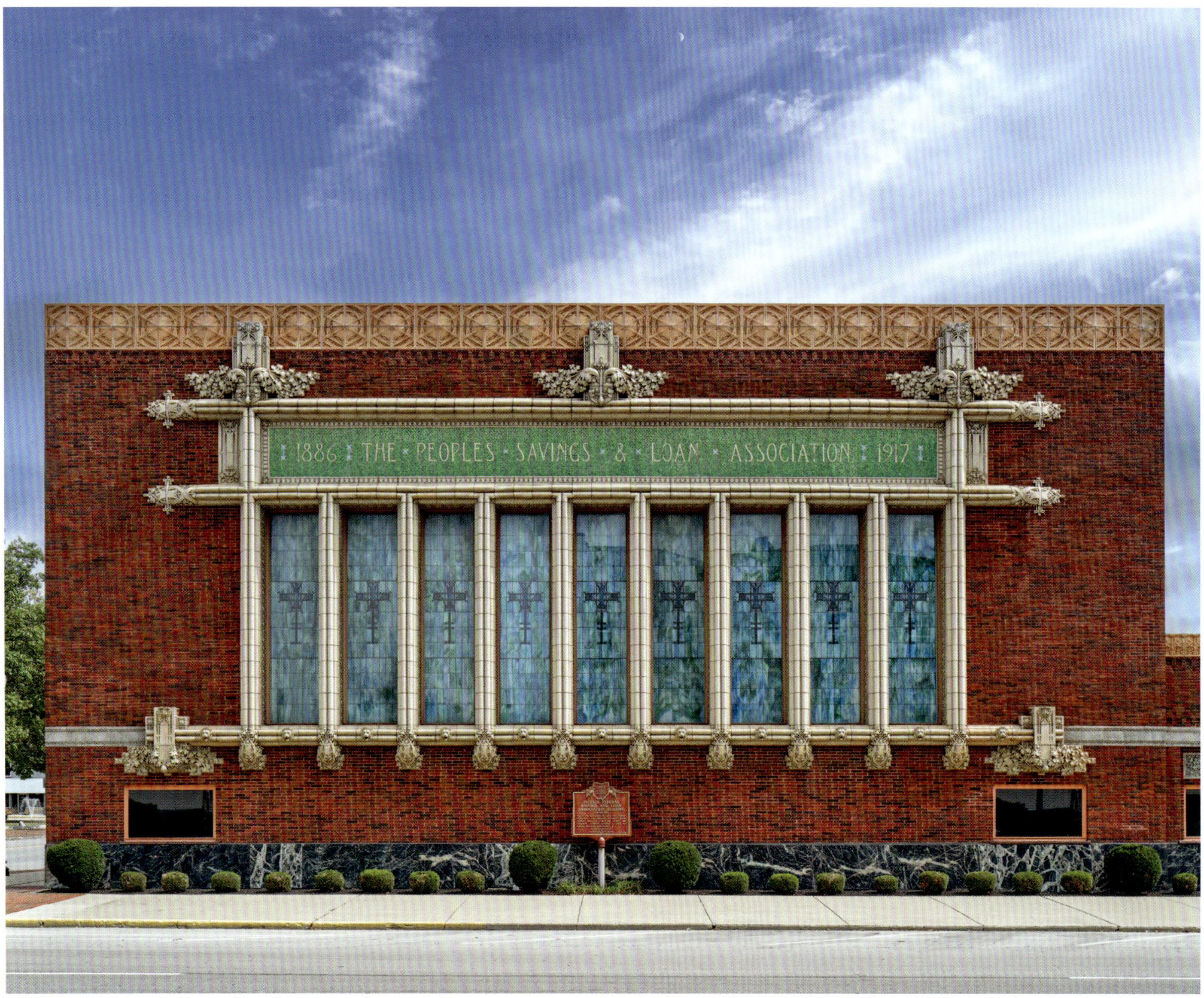

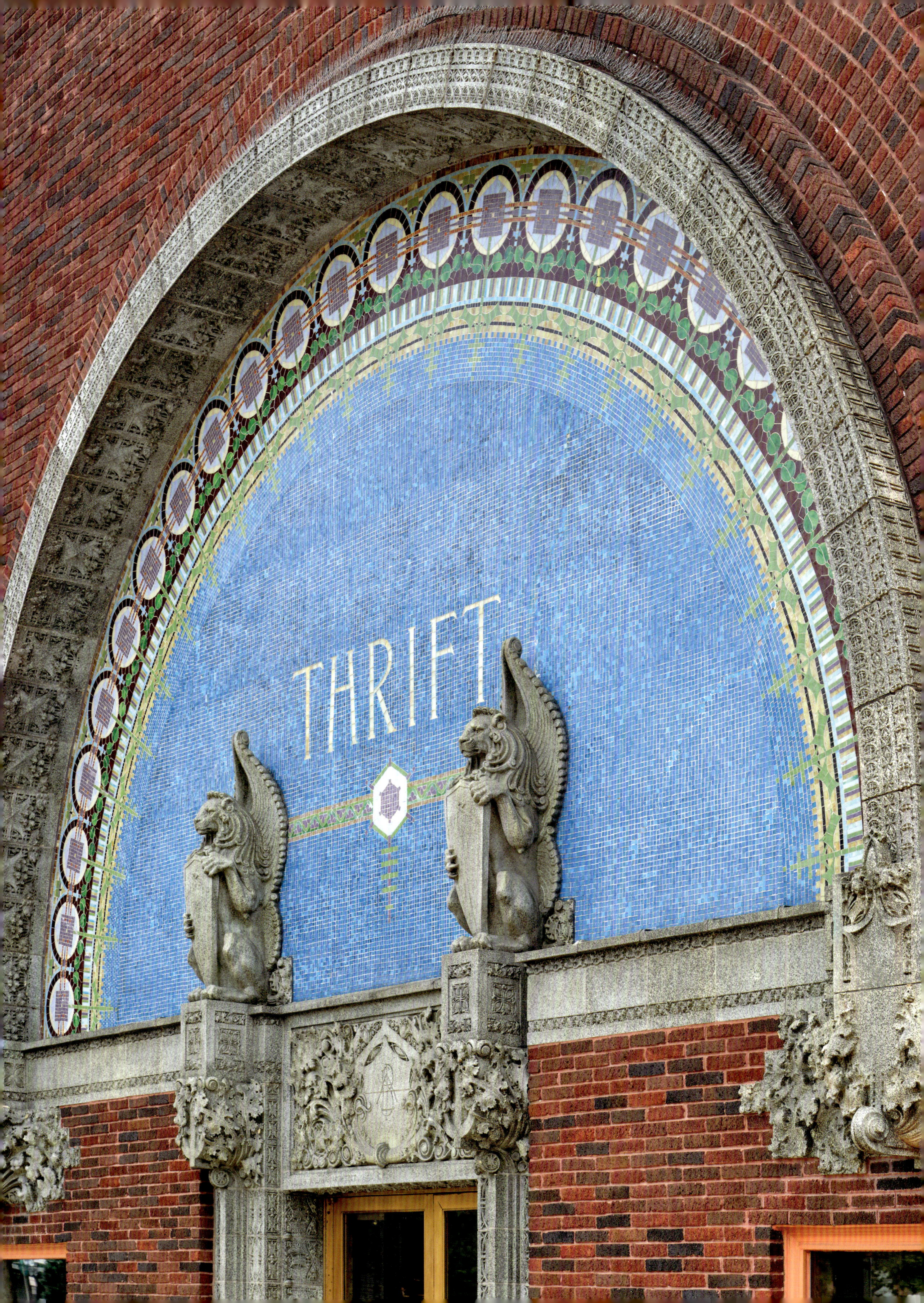
THRIFT

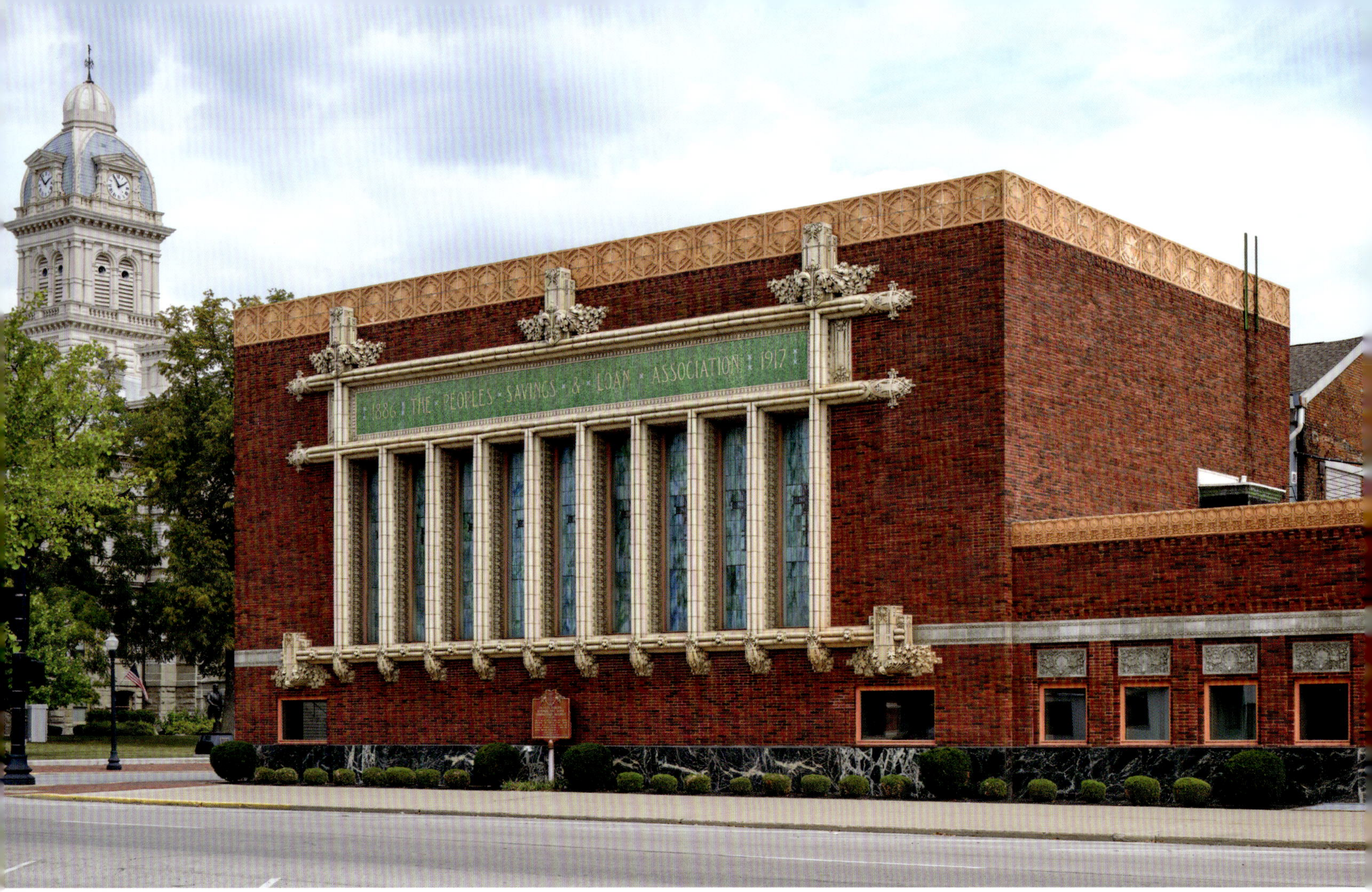
1886 · THE · PEOPLES · SAVINGS · & · LOAN · ASSOCIATION · 1917

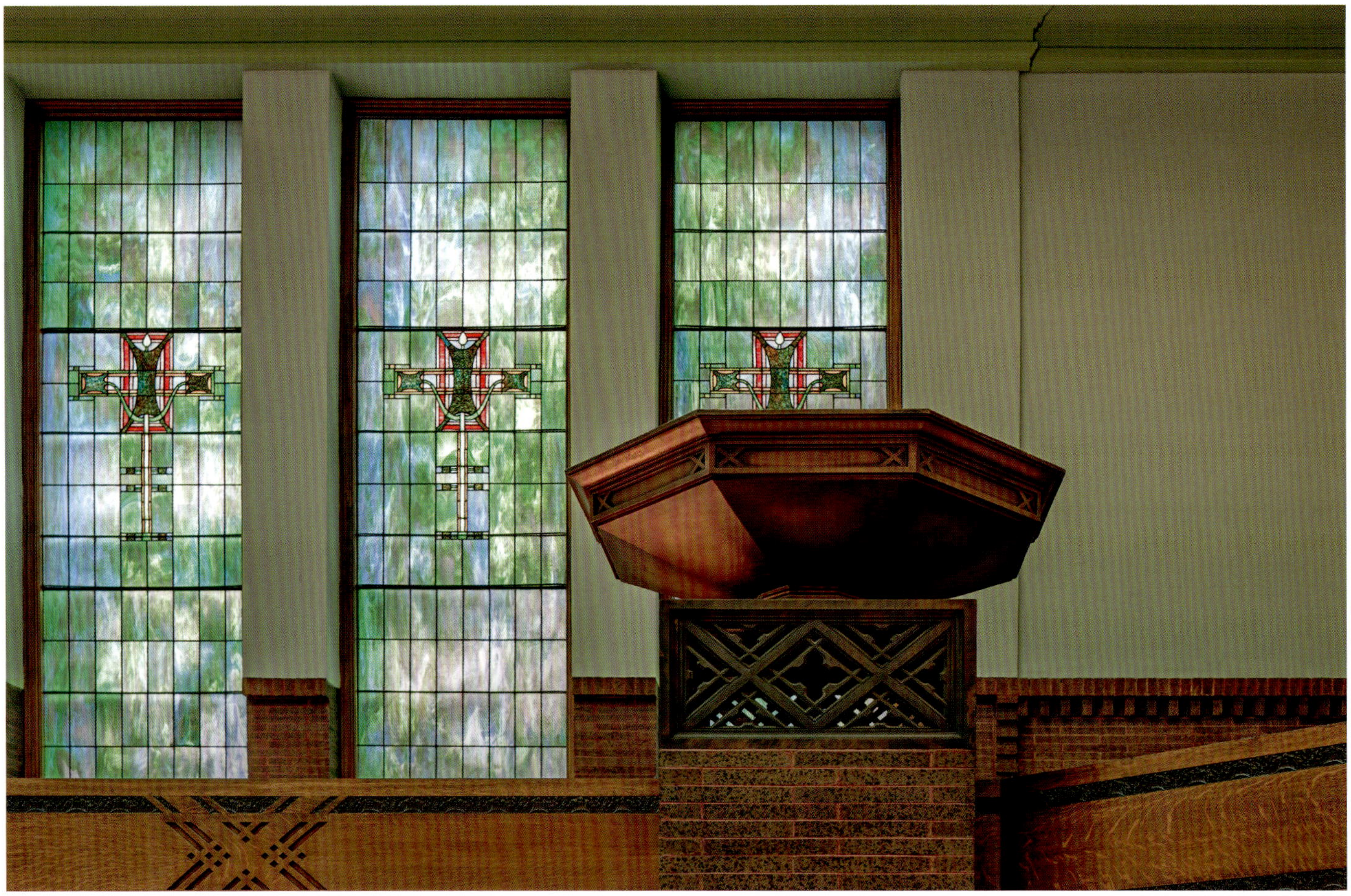

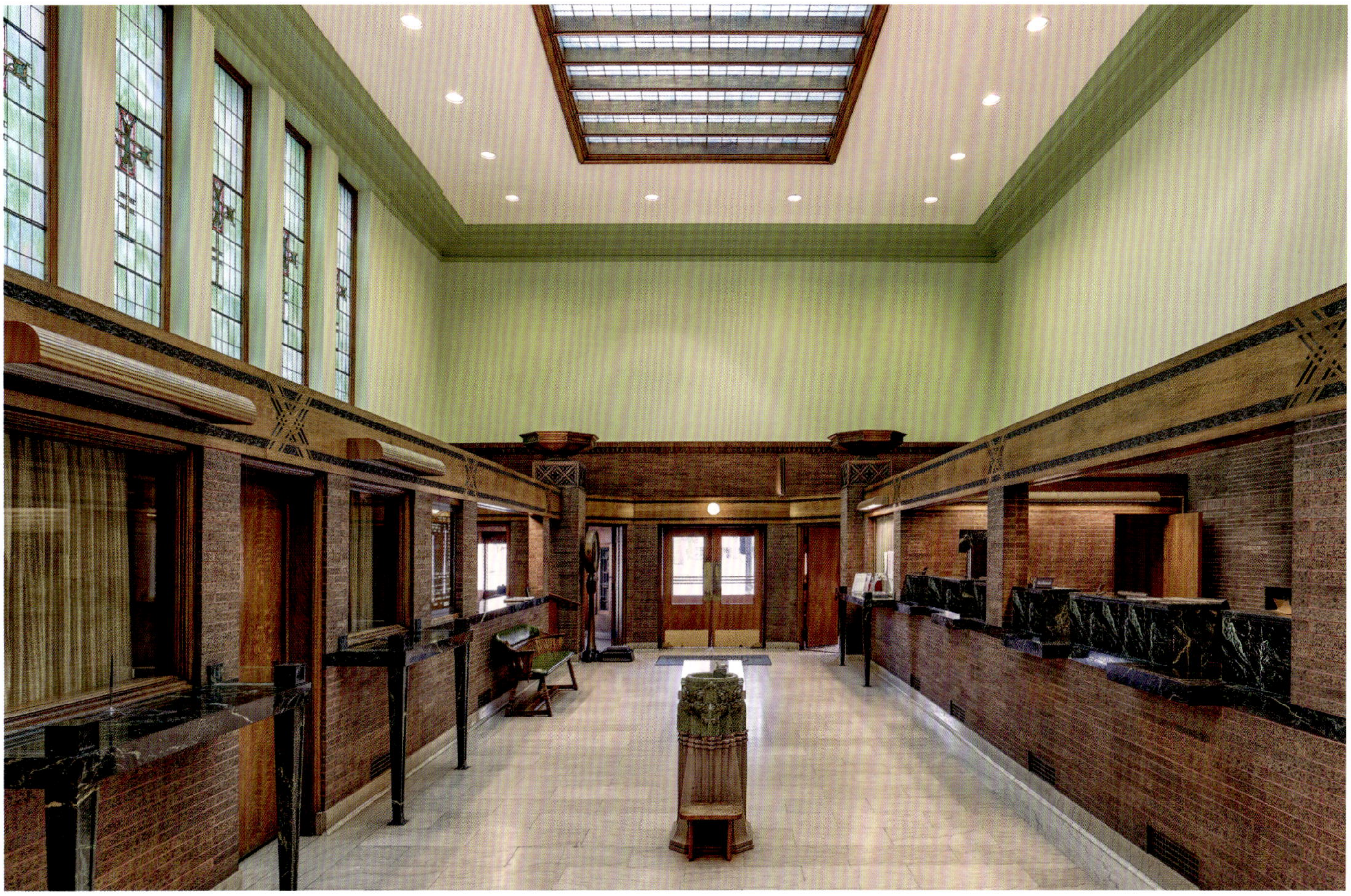

Like the Merchants National Bank in Grinnell, Iowa, Roman brick is a feature of interior surfaces, with color, and natural light, coming from the art-glass windows and a skylight.

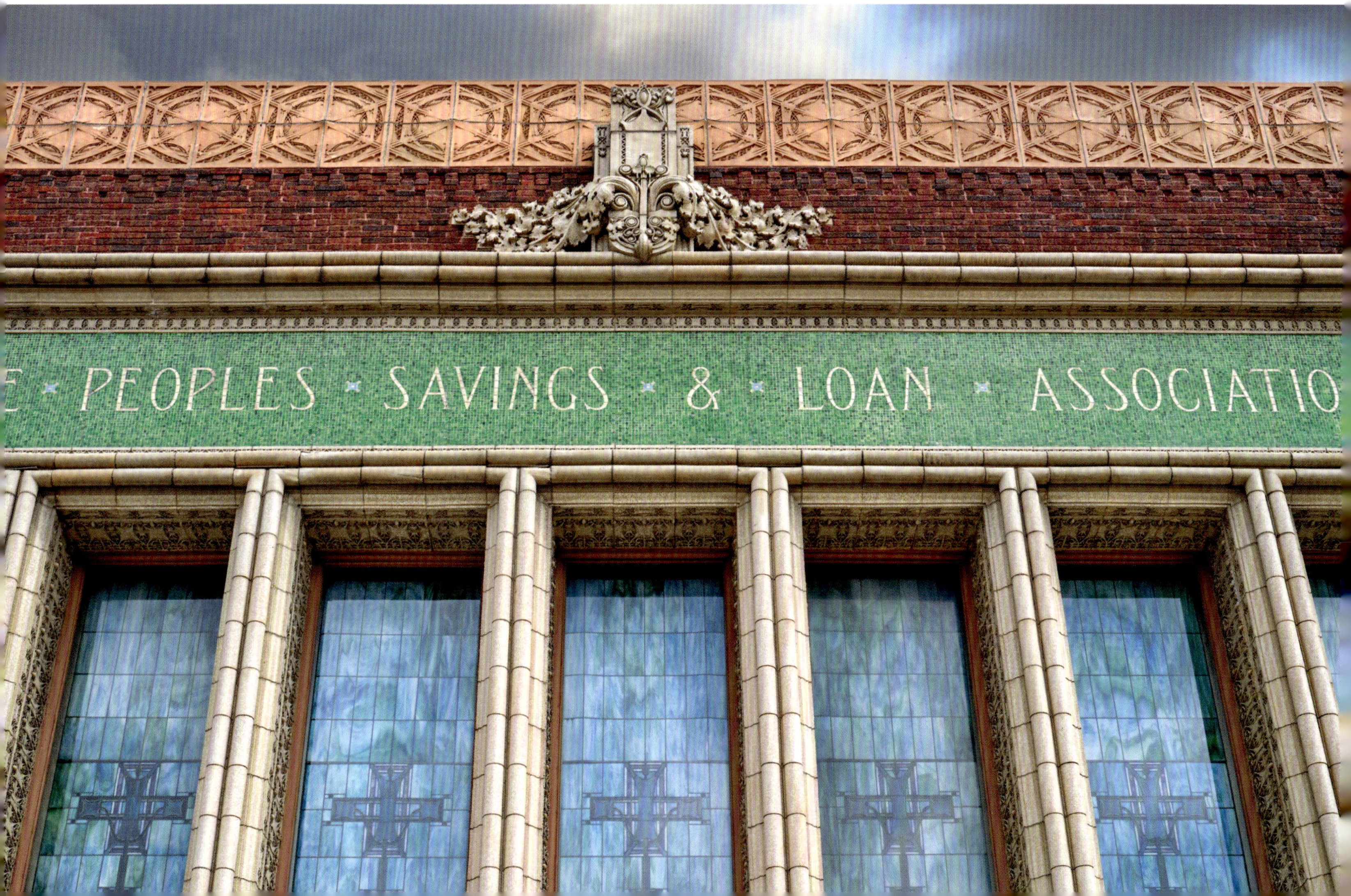

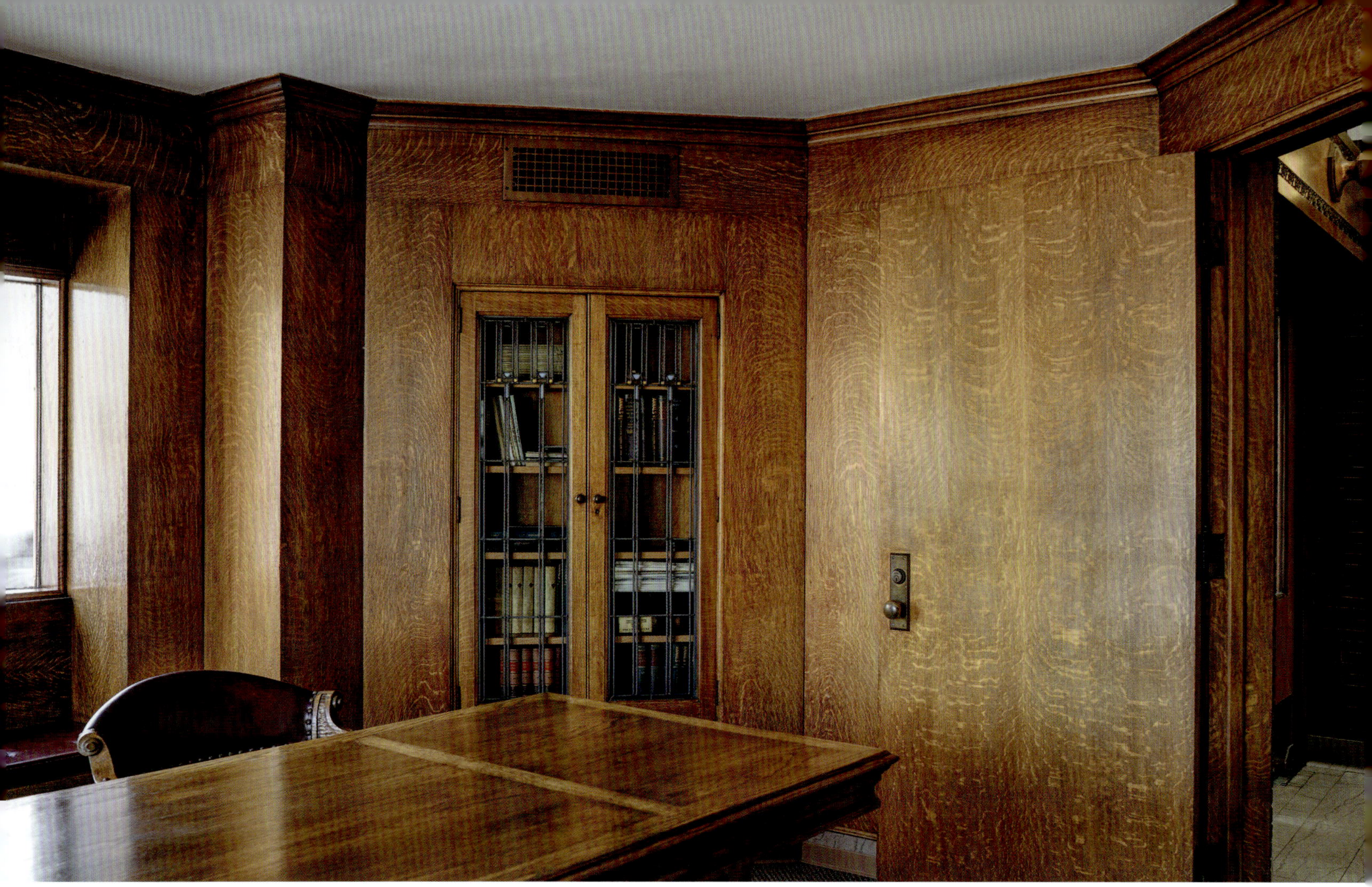

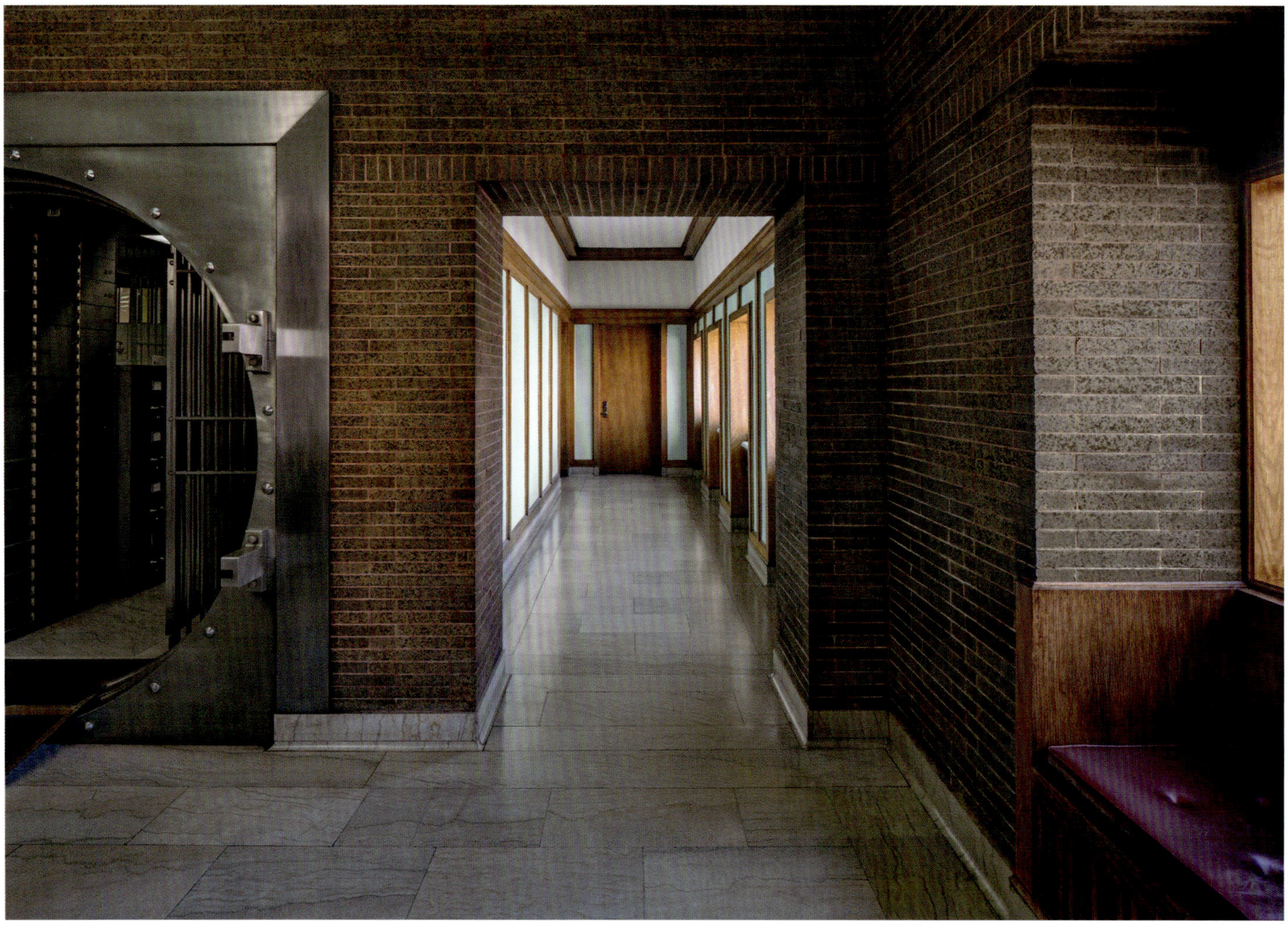

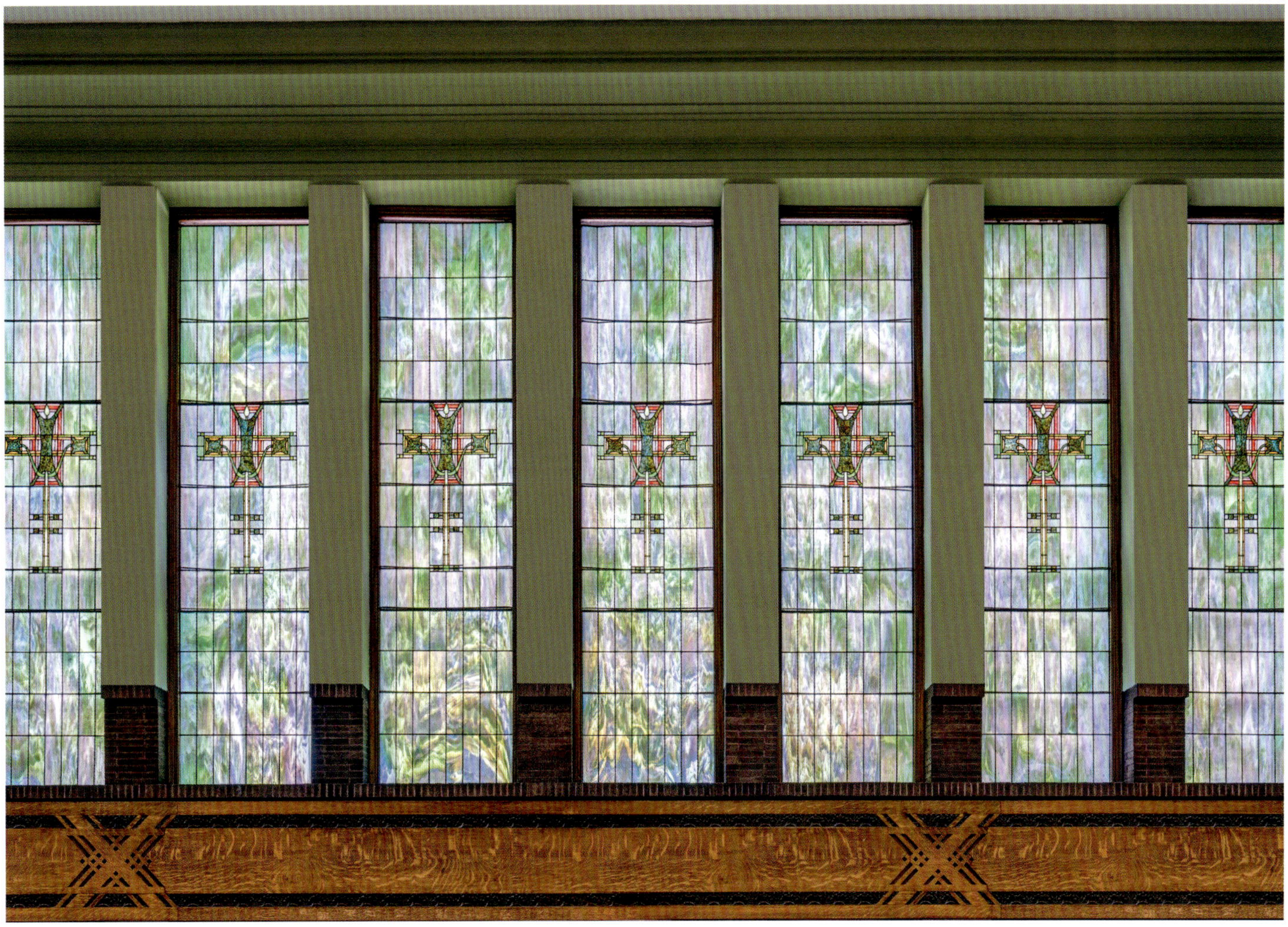

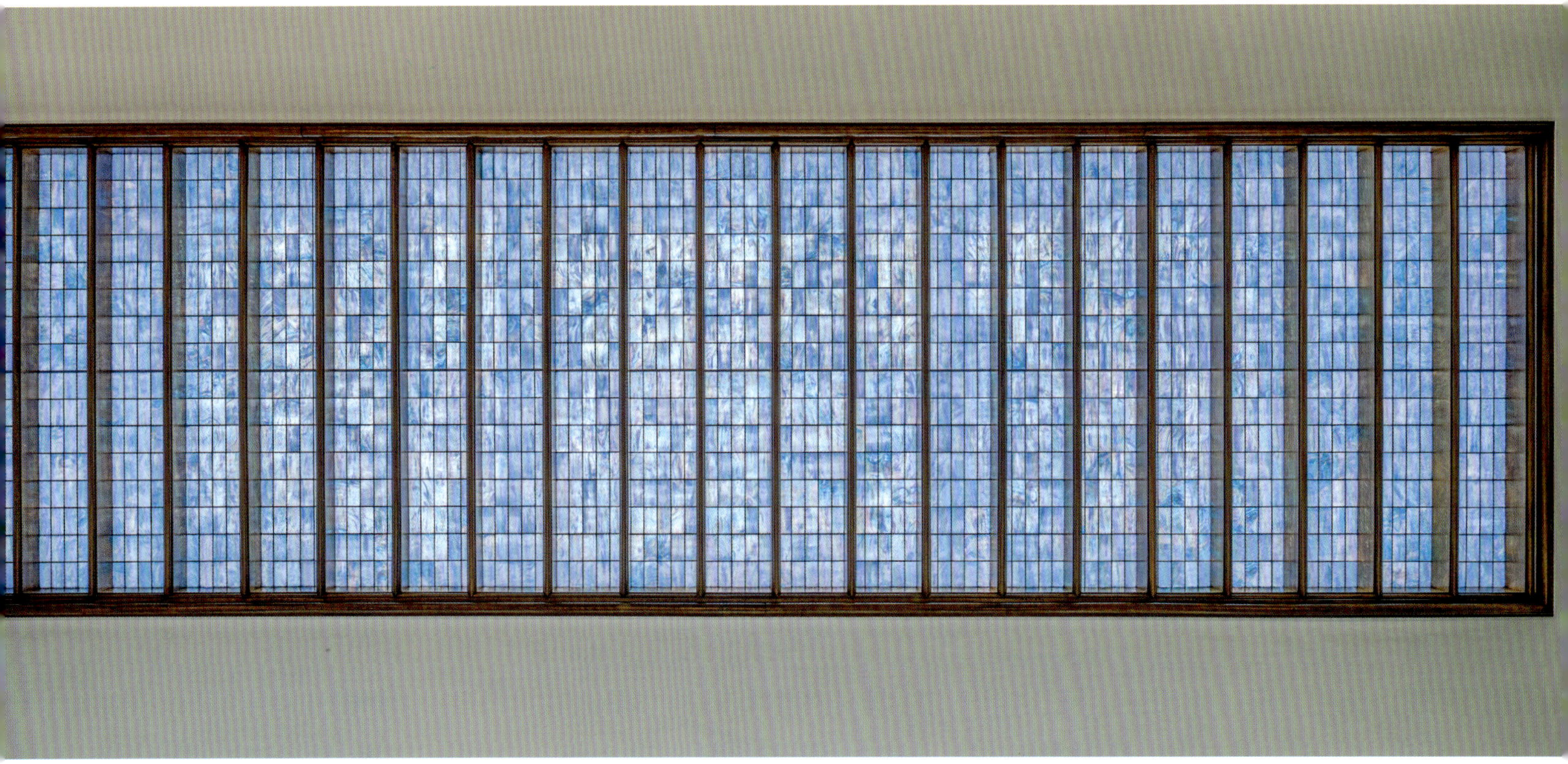

FARMERS AND MERCHANTS UNION BANK

1919, COLUMBUS, WISCONSIN

For the Farmers and Merchants Union Bank, the last "Jewel Box" bank that Sullivan designed, he received the commission from the bank's president, J. Russell Wheeler, apparently through his wife's influence. Although not always the case with Sullivan's designs, as Wheeler later wrote, "I remember that the building cost far more than I had planned … I feared to mar the beauty by cutting much …"

The Farmers and Merchants Union Bank is similar in form to most of the other banks, with its terra cotta decorations being perhaps the most elaborate. The front façade is symmetrical, although the main door is offset. The name of the bank is etched into the marble in gold. The panels on either side have the bank's founding date, 1861, and the date of the new building, 1919. The eagle at the top of the façade honored Wheeler's father. It symbolizes "Old Abe," the mascot of the 6th Wisconsin Infantry Regiment, with whom Wheeler's father had served during the Civil War.

The lunette art-glass window is matched by a similar one at the other end of the main banking floor. The five arched art-glass windows on the side are surrounded by elaborate terra cotta moldings. Flanking them are buttresses topped by elaborate capitals with globe finials. The bank was added to the National Register of Historic Places in 1972 and named a National Historic Landmark in 1976. It retains its original name.

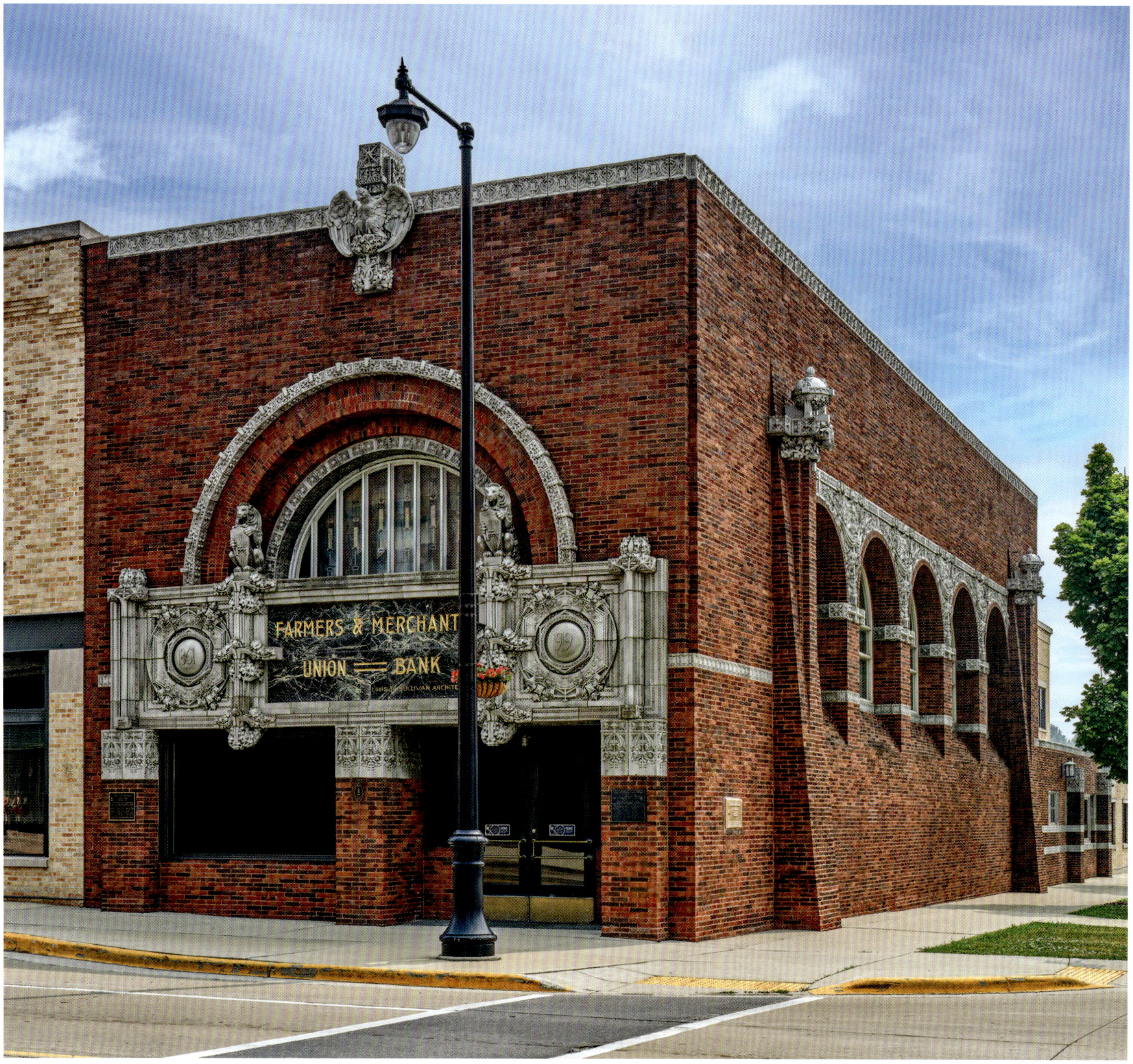

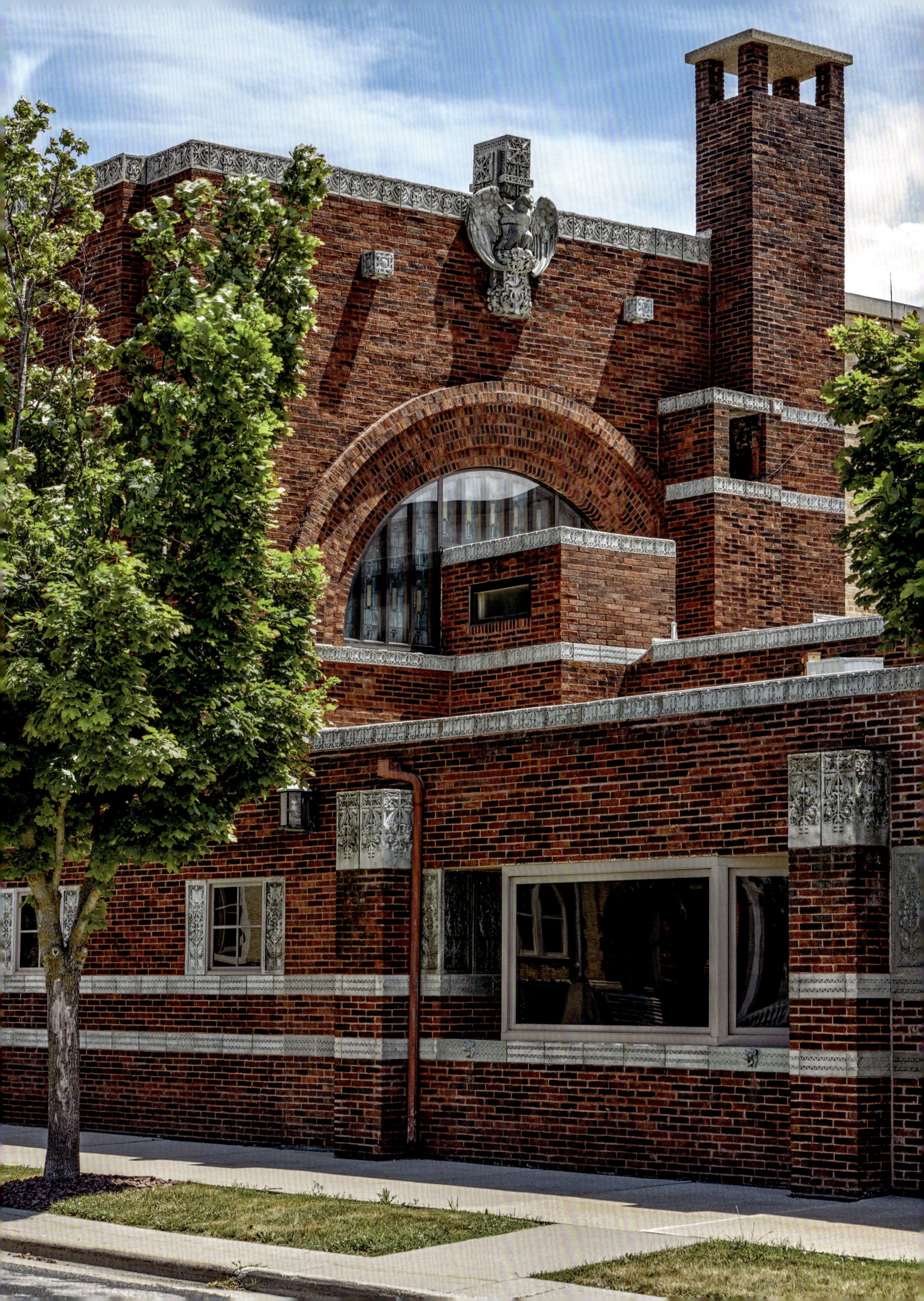

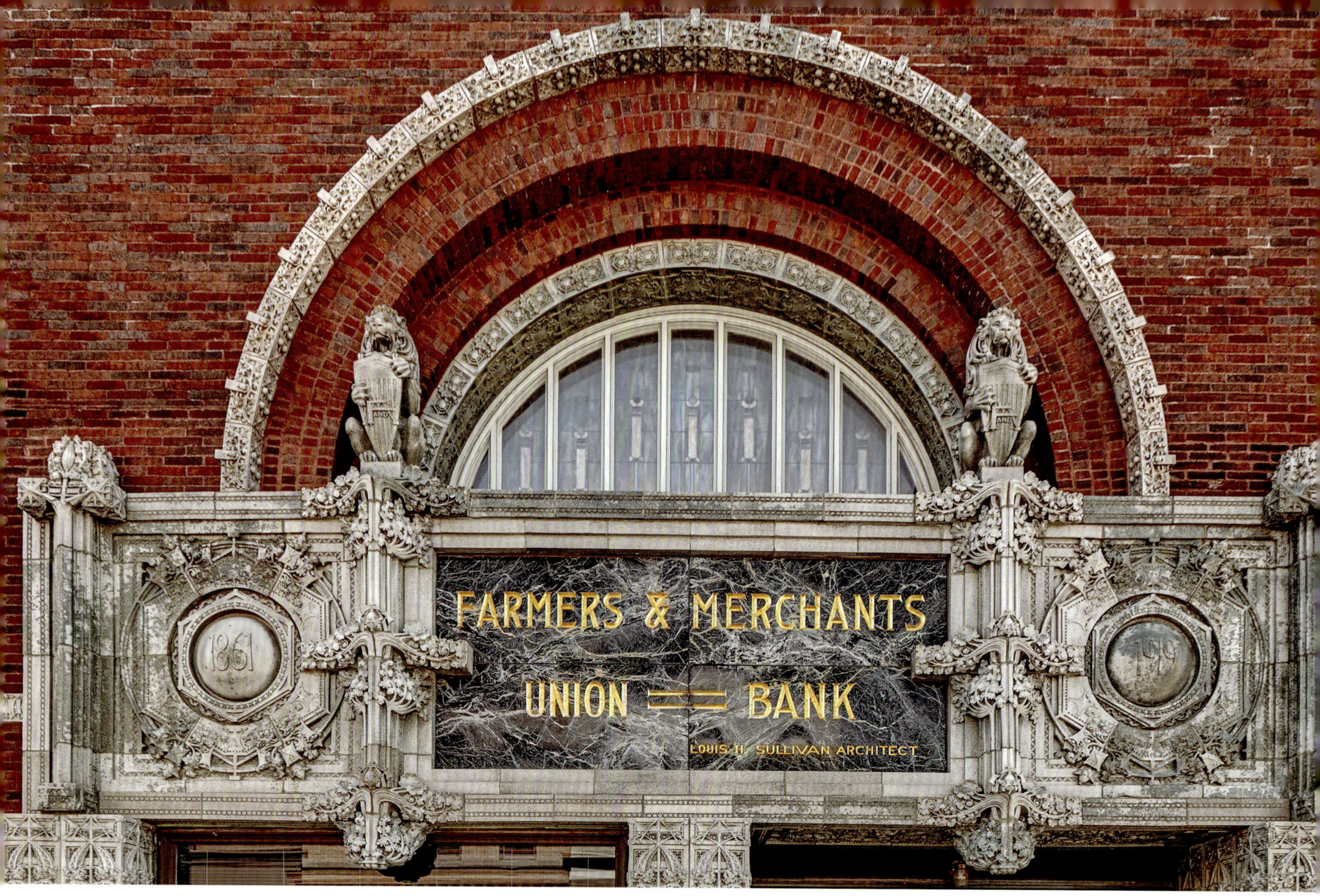
1861
FARMERS & MERCHANTS
UNION BANK
LOUIS H. SULLIVAN ARCHITECT

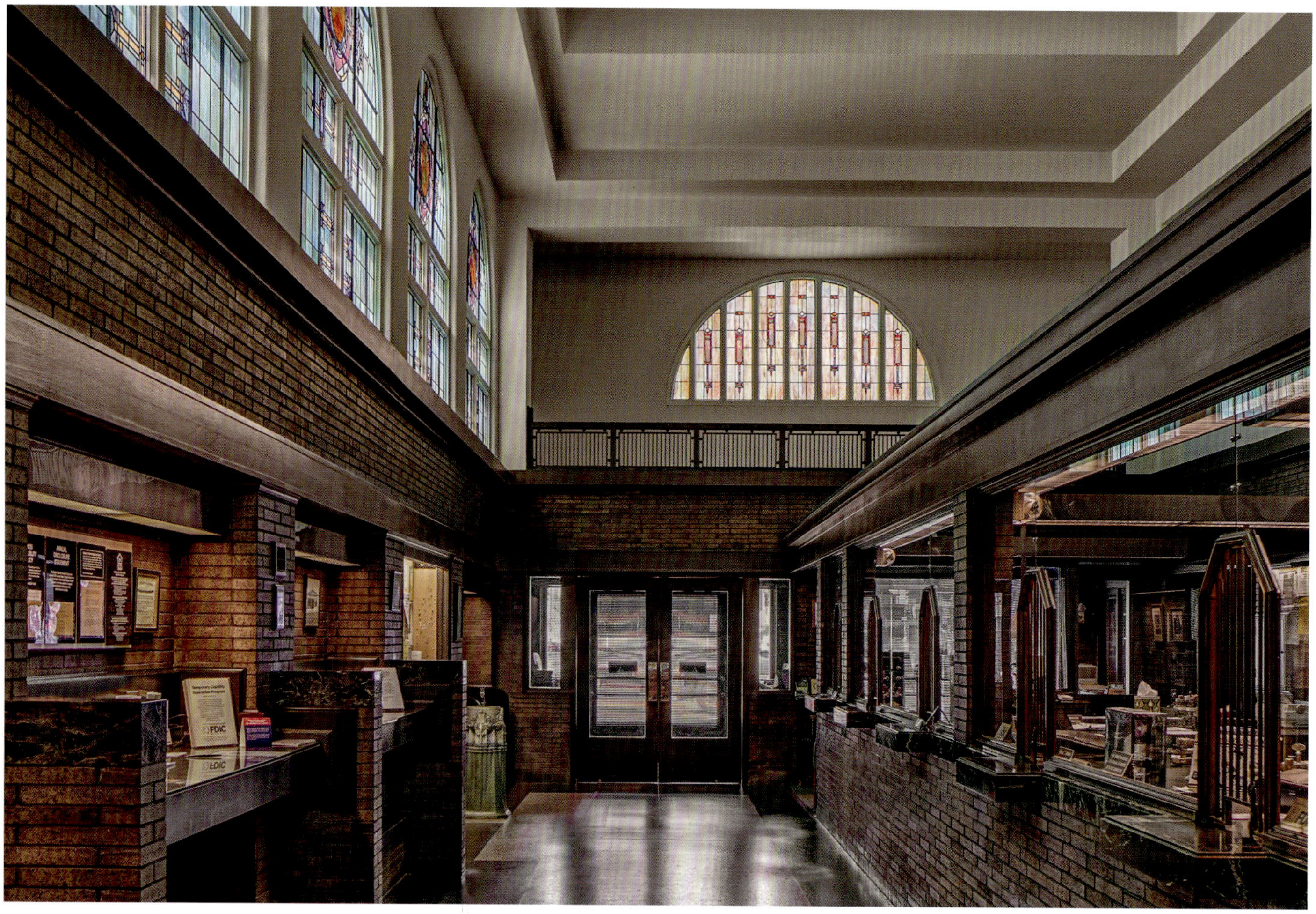

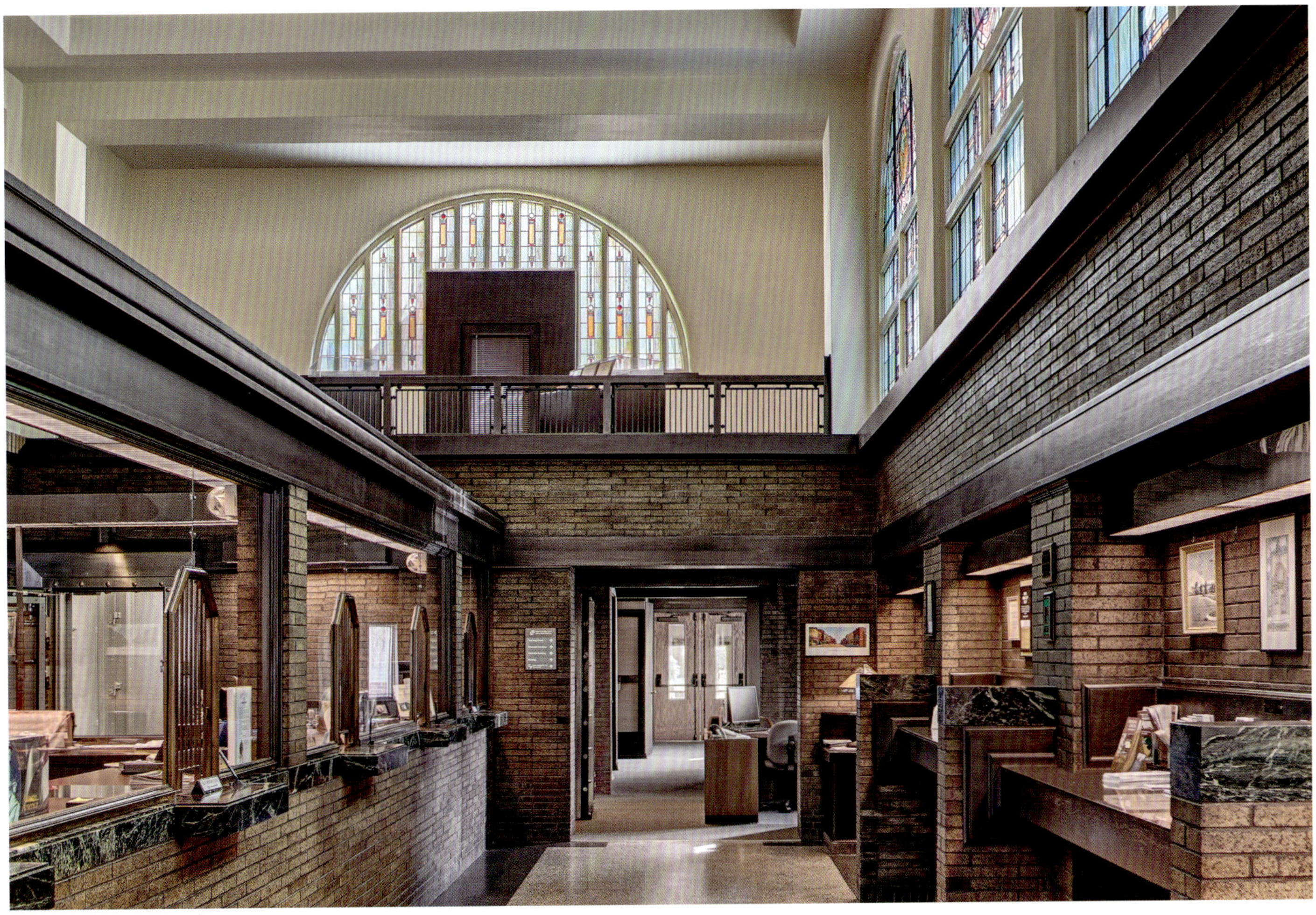

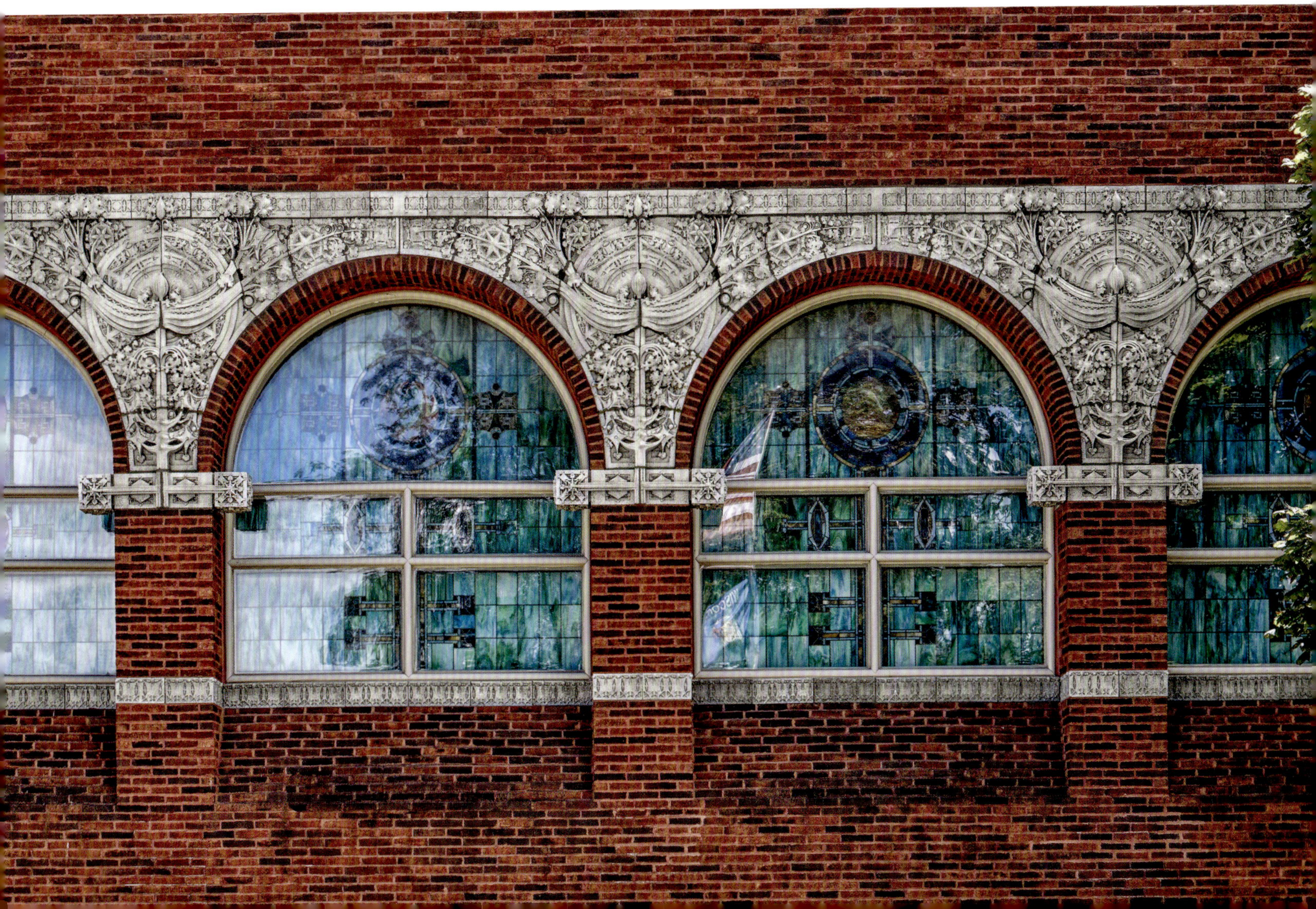

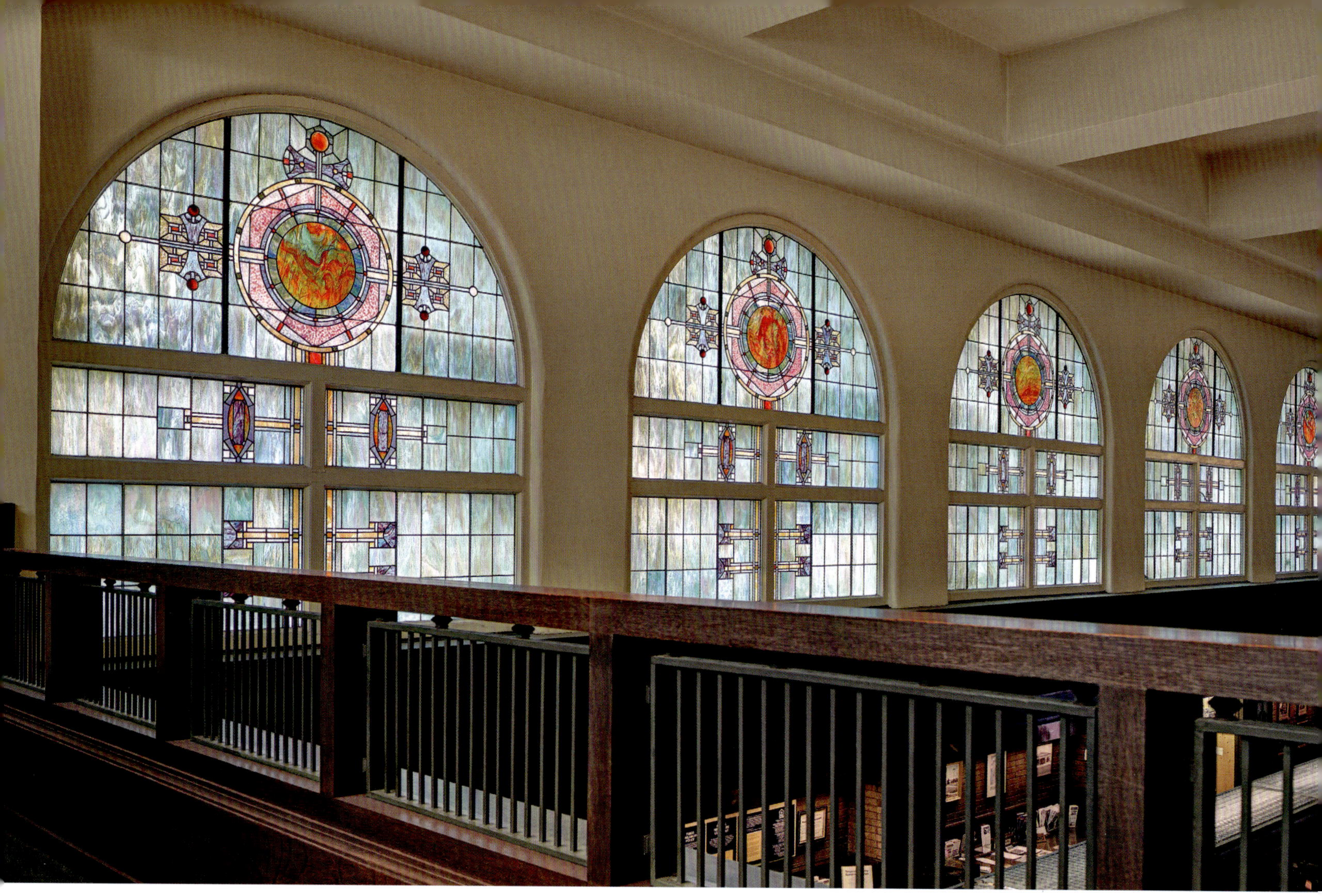

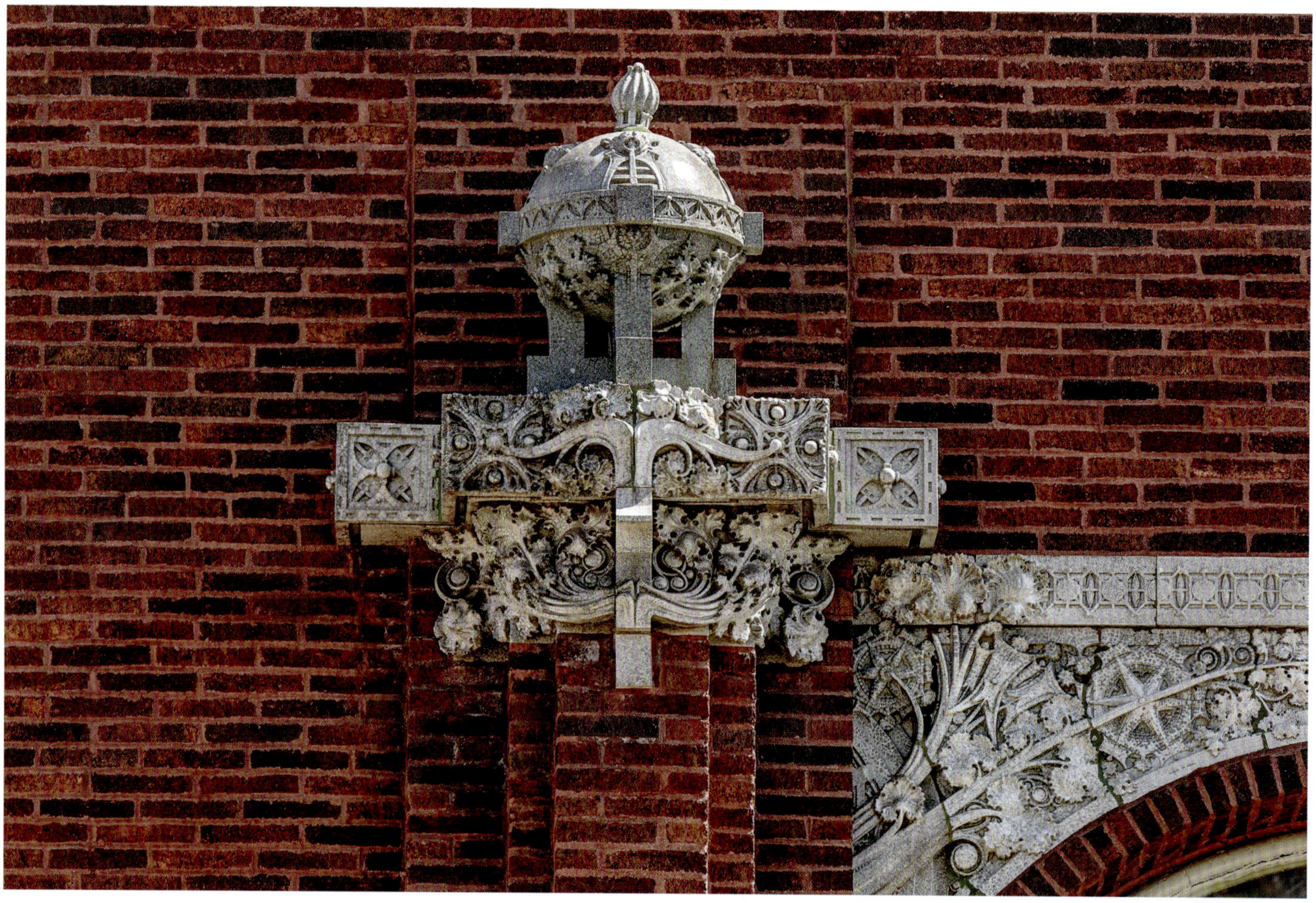

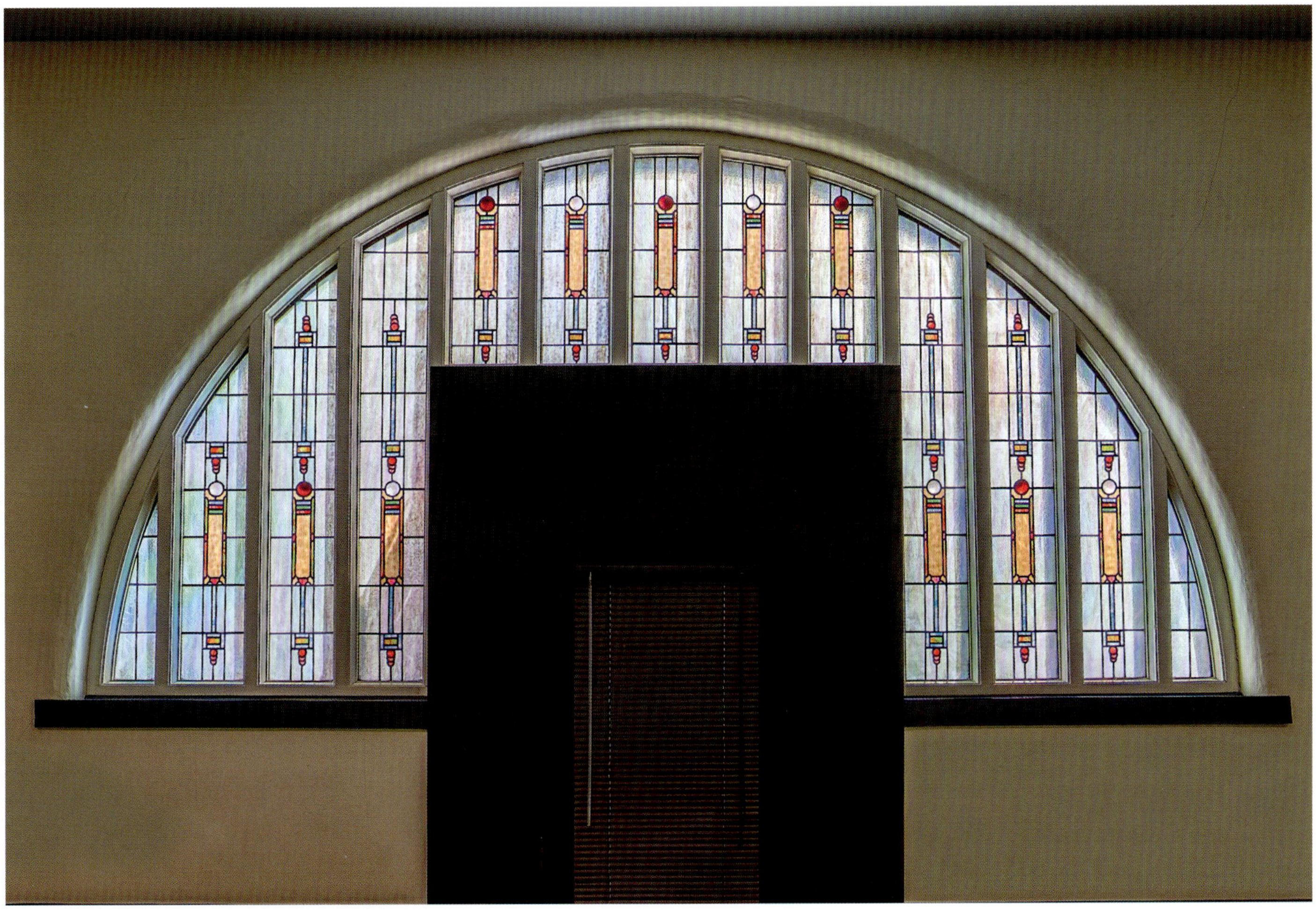

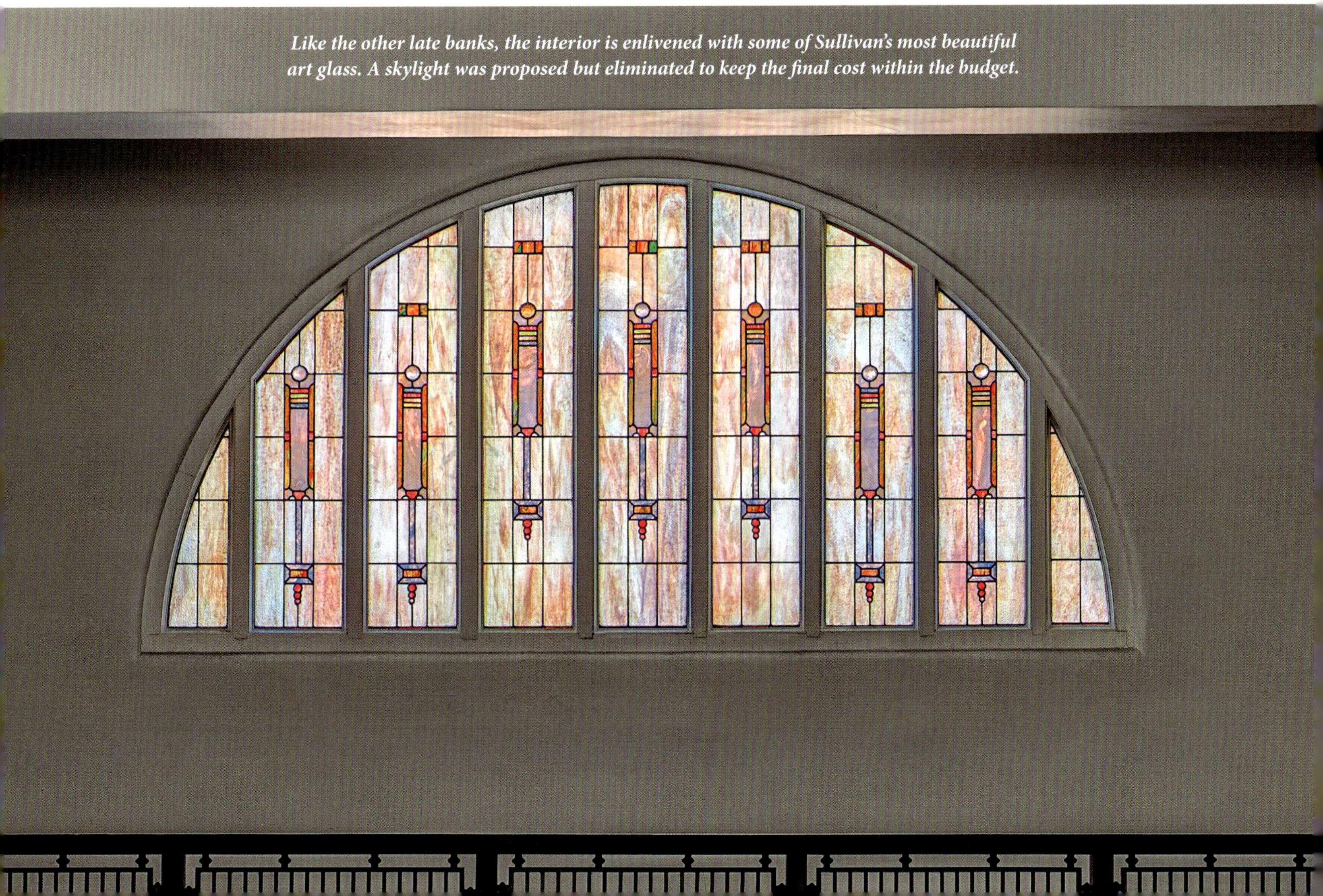

Like the other late banks, the interior is enlivened with some of Sullivan's most beautiful art glass. A skylight was proposed but eliminated to keep the final cost within the budget.

KRAUSE MUSIC STORE

1922, CHICAGO

Sullivan's last design was the facade only for a small music store standing next to similar storefronts on Chicago's North Lincoln Avenue. Nevertheless, Sullivan provided as much care and attention as he would have lavished on a much larger project. The building itself was designed by young architect William Presto, who had assisted Sullivan with the drawings for the Farmers and Merchants Union Bank in Columbus, Wisconsin. According to the report prepared for Chicago's Commission on Historical and Architectural Landmarks, "... the two architects enjoyed working together ... and spent many hours over lunches and dinners discussing architecture."

After Presto established his own practice, he received the commission to design a music store for William P. Krause, with a second-floor apartment for his family. He thought Sullivan would be a perfect choice to design the facade. At the time, Sullivan was at his lowest ebb, living in a rented room, and existing primarily on the generosity of his friends. As usual, he chose terra cotta for his design and, for the last time, traveled to the American Terra Cotta factory in Crystal Lake, Illinois, to work personally with modeler Kristian Schneider (they had first worked together on the Auditorium Building).

When the Depression ruined his business, Krause committed suicide, and his widow rented to and eventually sold the building to a funeral home. It has since served as a gift shop, a design studio and is currently home to a medical technology company. The owners, Pooja and Peter Vukosavich, restored the facade and remodeled the interior spaces in 2005 and received Driehaus Foundation and A.I.A. Awards for their efforts. The building was declared a Chicago landmark in 1977 and added to the National Register of Historic Places in 2006.

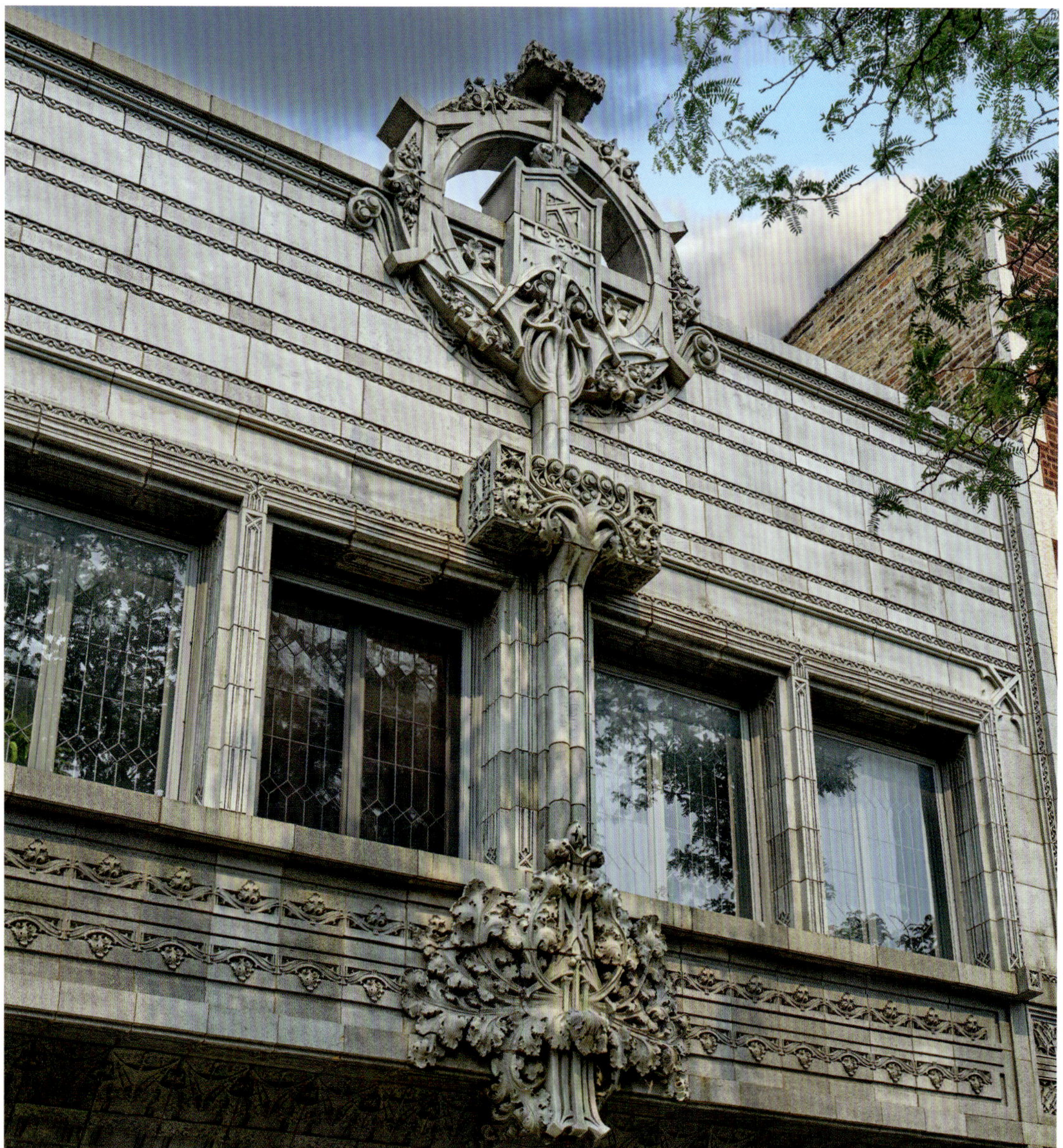

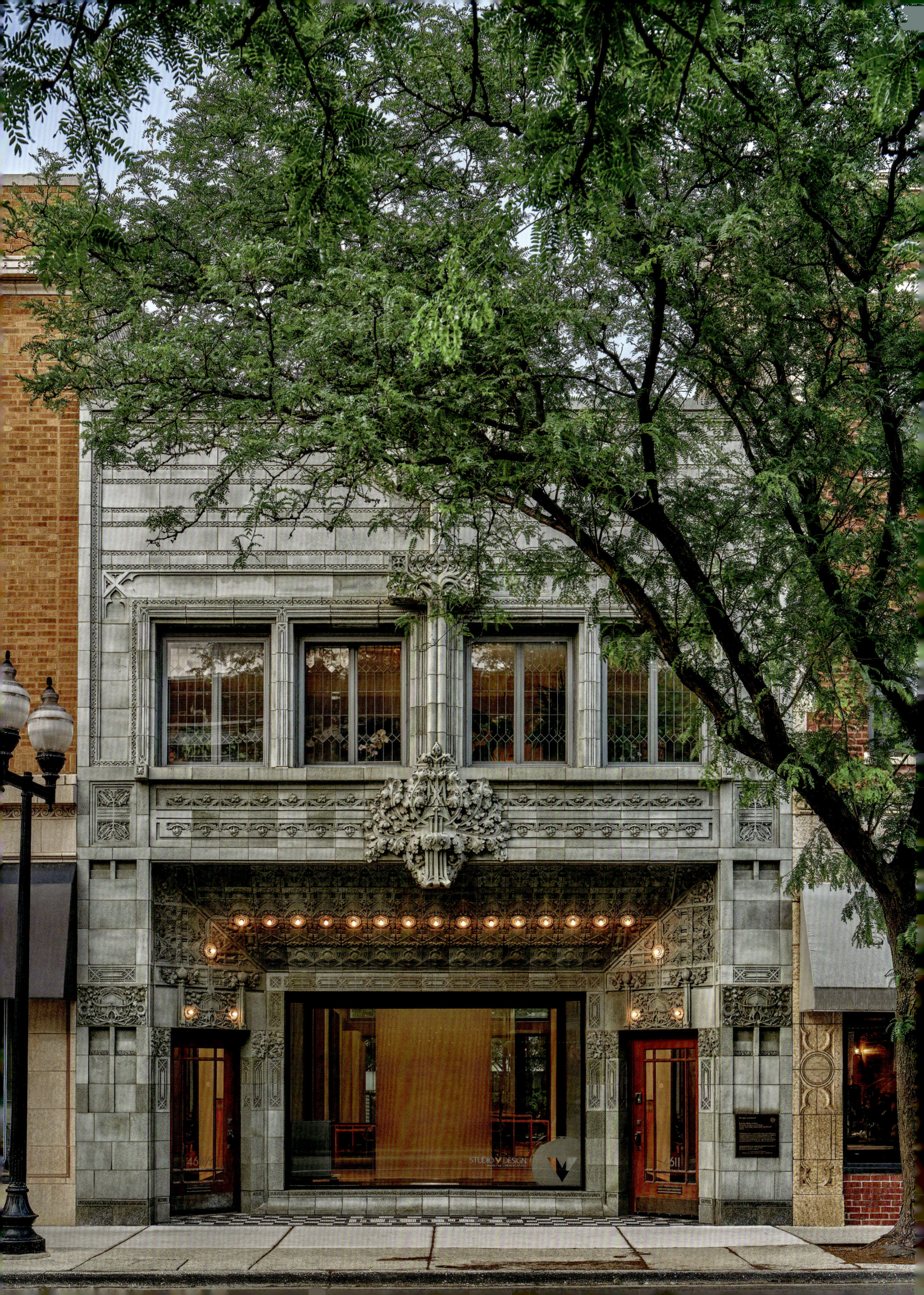
STUDIO V DESIGN

FRAGMENTS

Sadly, far more buildings designed by Louis Sullivan have been demolished than have survived. All the survivors are included in these pages. Thanks to Tim Samuelson, we were alerted to two fragments of lost buildings that survive as elements of later, non-Sullivan-designed buildings. In the interests of completeness, we add to these a pedestal for a statue of an Illinois political figure.

This staircase was once part of an 1892 Adler & Sullivan apartment building for Adler's friends, Adolph and William Loeb. Part of the building was demolished in 1924 when Randolph Street was widened; the balance in 1974. A slice of the building, including the staircase, was retained to provide roof access for the building next door. It's likely that Frank Lloyd Wright had a role in designing the original building, since the partners were busy with more important commissions. When Wright was shown a photo of the staircase by Richard Nickel, he was reported to have said: "Oh! So you found that one, did you?" In fact, it has elements of other Arts & Crafts influenced designs that Wright did during this period.

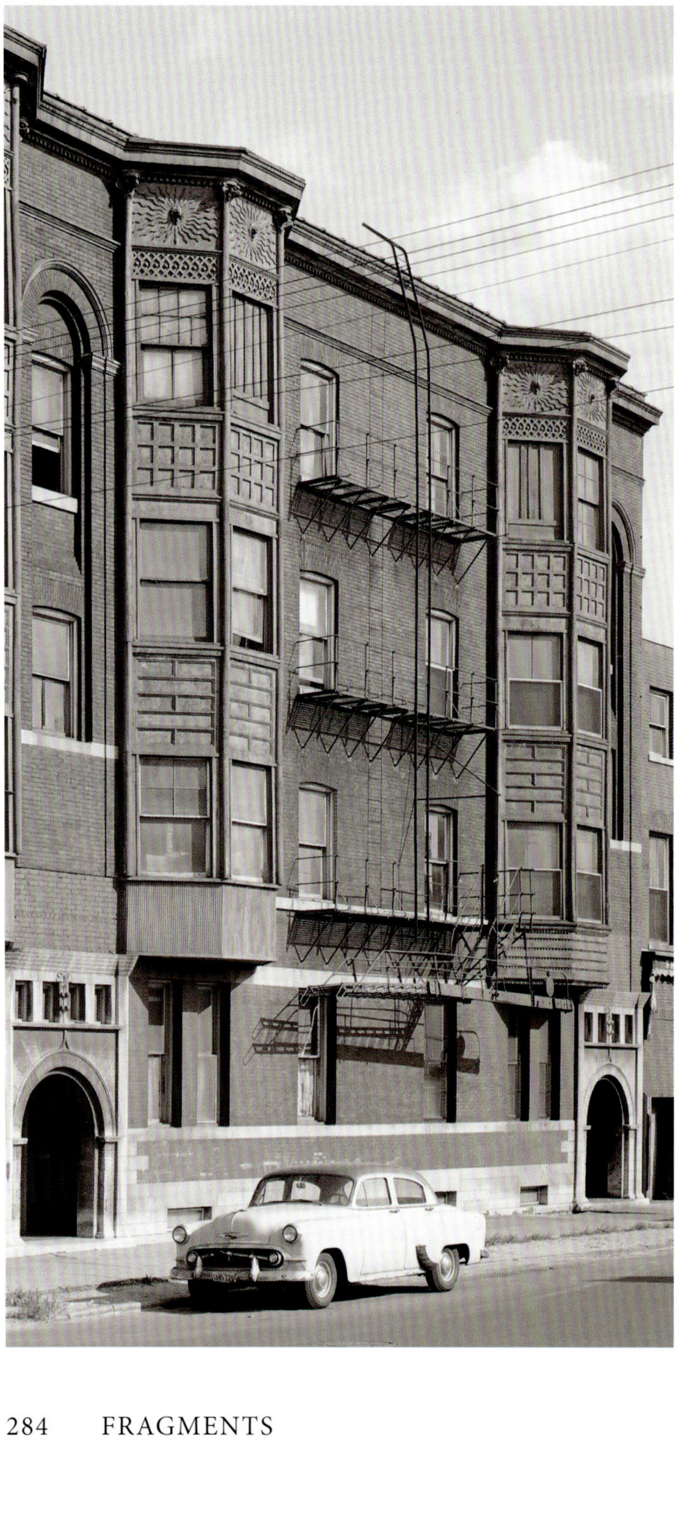

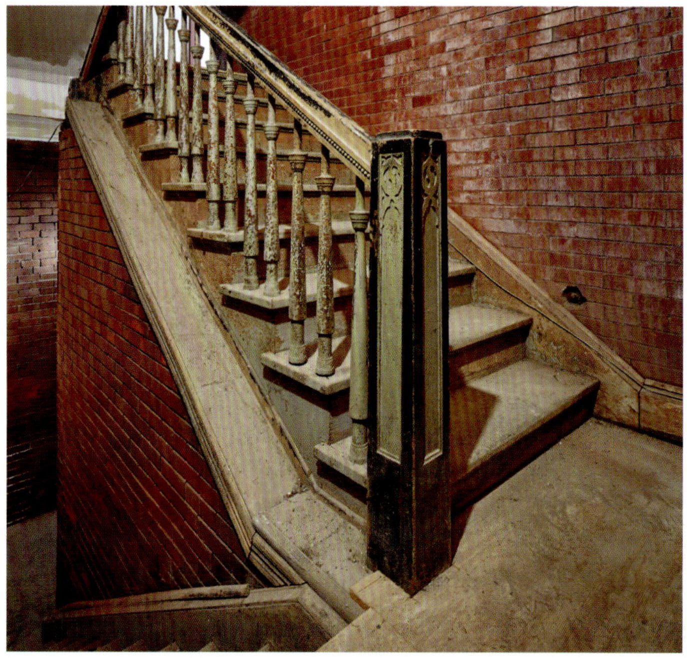

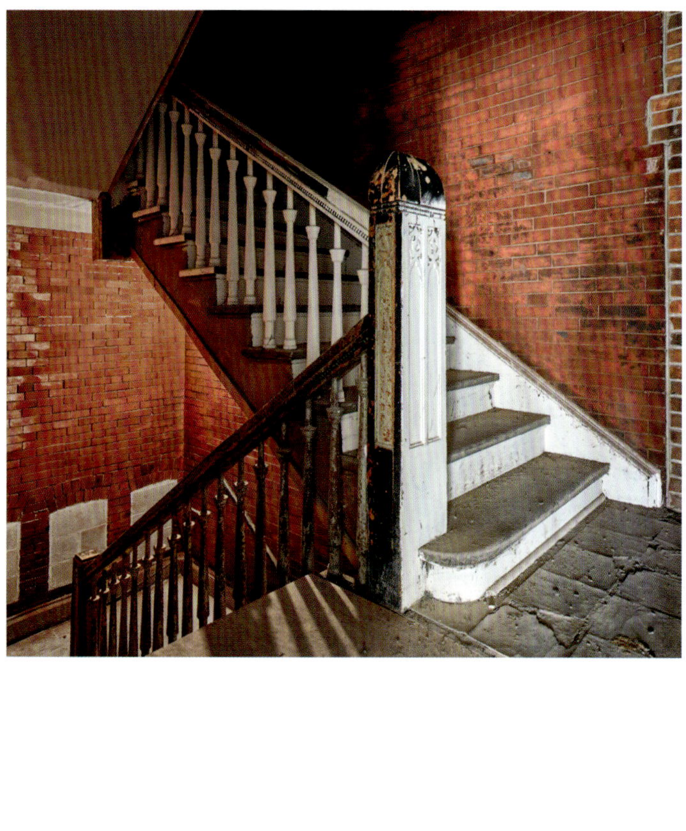

This chimney was once part of Hammond Library of the Chicago Theological Seminary, once located on Ashland Avenue, across from Union Park. The library stood next to the Seminary's Philo Carpenter Chapel, to which one of the library's chimneys was later—and it must be said, strangely—attached. The Seminary later moved to Hyde Park, but the chimney and chapel survive as part of the First Baptist Congregational Church.

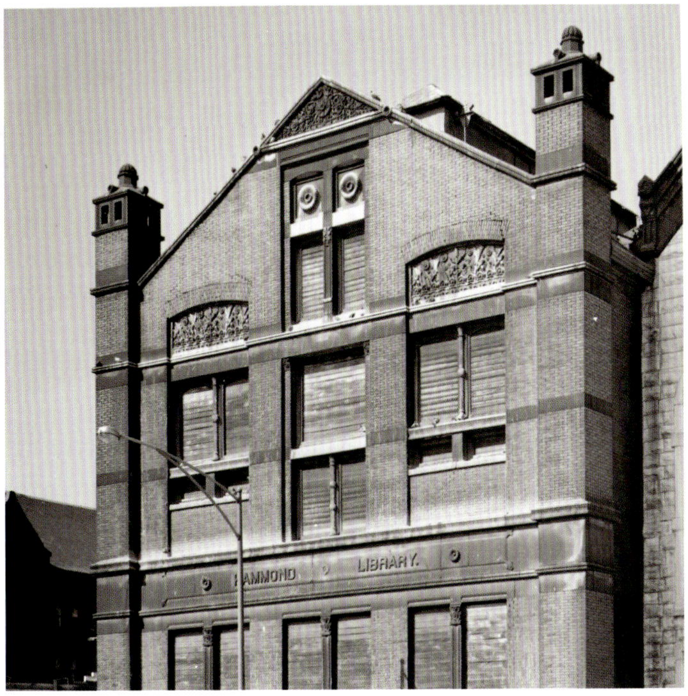

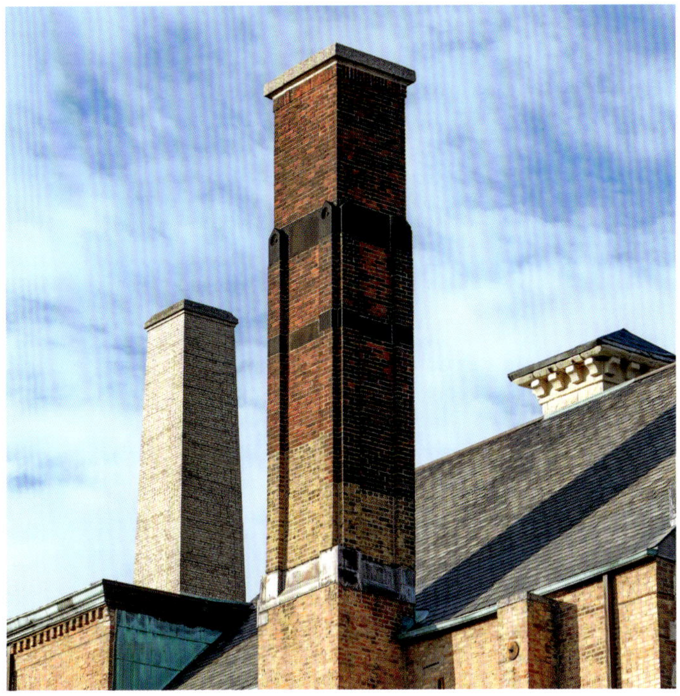

Sullivan was commissioned in 1922 to design the pedestal, including the back wall, for a statue by Leonard Crunelle of John M. Palmer, who served as governor of Illinois from 1869–1873. He was a consequential figure in the state, having also served as a United States Senator and a Civil War Major General. The statue is located on the grounds of the Illinois State Capital in Springfield.

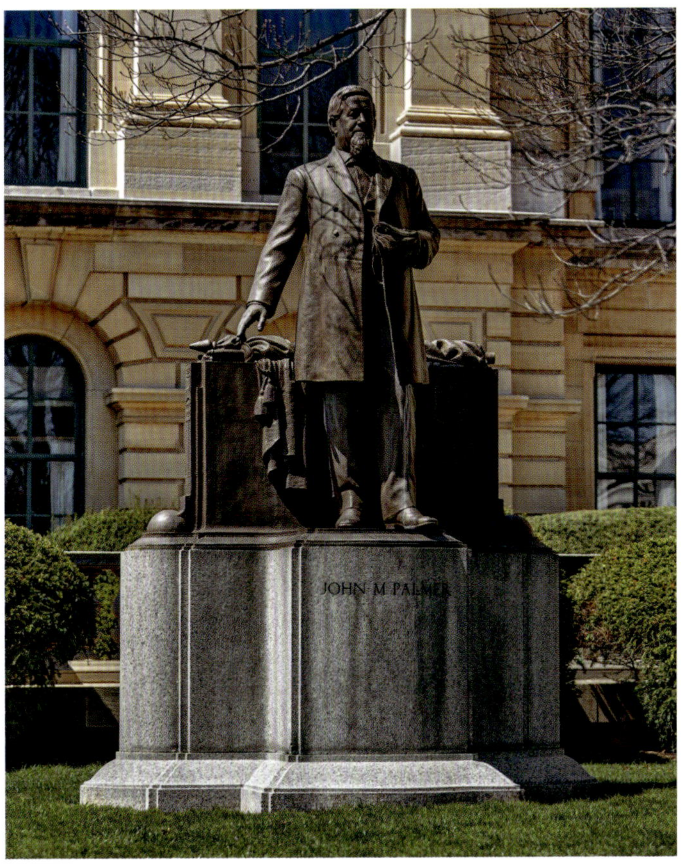

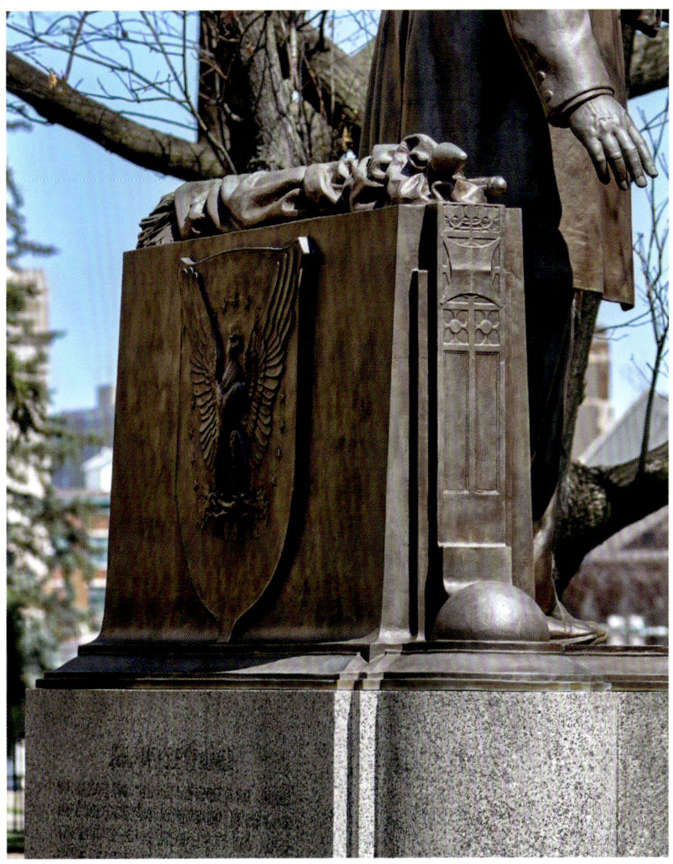

SELECTED BIBLIOGRAPHY

There have been several biographies and many studies of Louis Sullivan and his work. I have listed below those that were most helpful in preparing this book. Of the biographies, the most recent, reliable, and readable is Professor Robert Twombly's *Louis Sullivan: His Life and Work*. And I would again like to express my admiration for Professor Joseph Siry, whose writing on Sullivan's Auditorium, Guaranty, and Carson Pirie Scott buildings were so helpful. Our book on Frank Lloyd Wright's Unity Temple also owed much to the scholarship of Professor Siry. Finally, special praise must be given to the late Richard Nickel and Aaron Siskind and to authors John Vinci and Ward Miller for *The Complete Architecture of Adler & Sullivan*, a labor of many years that is an indispensable catalog of their work.

Books

Condit, Carl. *The Chicago School of Architecture: A History of Commercial and Public Building in the Chicago Area, 1875–1925*. Chicago: The University of Chicago Press, 1964.

Connelly, Willard. *Louis Sullivan: The Shaping of American Architecture*. New York: Horizon Press, 1960.

Elia, Mario Manieri. *Louis Henry Sullivan*. New York: The Princeton Architectural Press, 1996.

Frazier, Nancy. *Louis Sullivan and the Chicago School*. New Jersey: Crescent Books, 1991.

Millett, Larry. *The Curve of the Arch: The Story of Louis Sullivan's Owatonna Bank*. St. Paul: Minnesota Historical Society Press, 1985.

Morrison, Hugh. *Louis Sullivan: Prophet of Modern Architecture*. New York: W.W. Norton, 1935.

Nickel, Richard, Aaron Siskind, John Vinci, and Ward Miller. *The Complete Architecture of Adler & Sullivan*. Chicago: Richard Nickel Committee, 2010.

O'Gorman, James F. *Three American Architects: Richardson, Sullivan and Wright, 1865–1915*. Chicago: University of Chicago Press, 1992.

Samuelson, Tim. *Louis Sullivan's Idea*. Edited by Chris Ware. Chicago: Alphawood Foundation, 2021.

Sullivan, Louis. *The Autobiography of an Idea*. New York: The Press of the American Institute of Architects, 1924.

_______*Kindergarten Chats and Other Writings*. New York: Dover Publications, 1979.

Twombly, Robert. *Louis Sullivan: His Life and Work*. Chicago: The University of Chicago Press, 1987.

_______(Editor). *Louis Sullivan: The Public Papers*. Chicago: The University of Chicago Press, 1988.

_______(With Narcisco G. Menocal). *Louis Sullivan: The Poetry of Architecture*. New York. W.W. Norton and Company, 2000.

Siry, Joseph M. *The Chicago Auditorium Building: Adler and Sullivan's Architecture and the City*. Chicago: The University of Chicago Press, 2002.

_______*Carson, Pirie, Scott: Louis Sullivan and the Chicago Department Store*. Chicago: The University of Chicago Press, 1988.

Schmitt, Ronald E. *Sullivanesque: Urban Architecture and Ornamentation*. Urbana and Chicago: University of Illinois Press, 2002.

Szarkowski, John. *The Idea of Louis Sullivan*. Boston: Bullfinch Press, Little Brown and Company, 2000.

de Wit, Wim. *Louis Sullivan: The Function of Ornament*. New York and London: W.W. Norton & Company, 1986.

Wright, Frank Lloyd. *Genius and the Mobocracy*. New York: Horizon Press, 1949.

_______*An Autobiography*. Petaluma, CA: Pomegranate Communications, 2005.

Articles

Gebhard, David. "Louis Sullivan and George Grant Elmslie." *The Journal of the Society of Architectural Historians* 19, no. 2 (May 1960): 62–68.

Neumann, Dietrich. "The Centuries Triumph in Lighting: The Luxfer Prism Company and their Contribution to Early Modern Architecture." *The Journal of Architectural Historians* 54, no. 1 (March 1995): 24–53.

Peisch, Mark L. Letter to the editor, with letter from George G. Elmslie to Frank Lloyd Wright dated June 12, 1936, attached. *The Journal of the Society of Architectural Historians* 20, no. 3 (October 1961): 140–41.

Siry, Joseph M. "Adler and Sullivan's Guaranty Building in Buffalo." *The Journal of the Society of Architectural Historians* 55, no. 1 (March 1996): 6–37.

Sprague, Paul. "A New Chapter in the Life of Louis Sullivan: Margaret Hattabough Sullivan and Lester Sullivan." *Arris* (Published by the University of North Carolina Press) 13, (2002): 39–53.

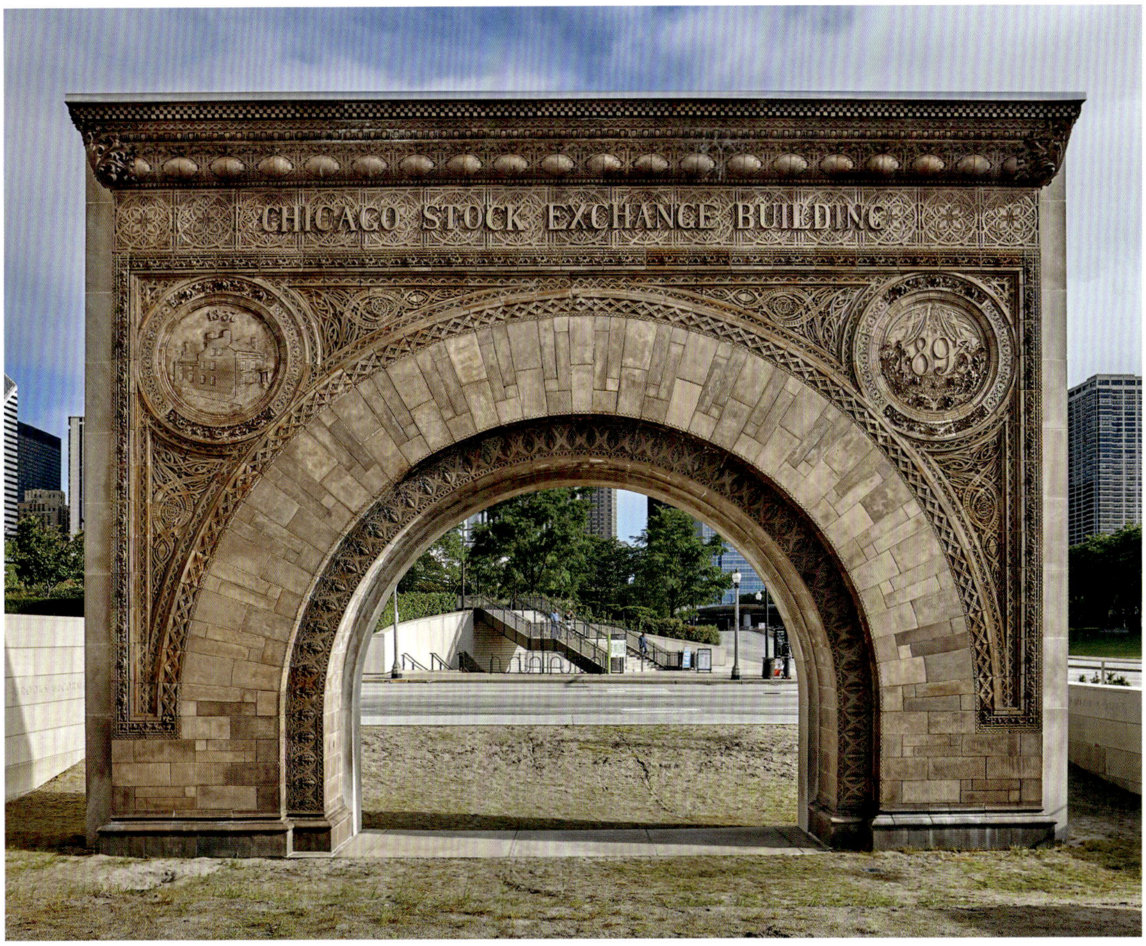

The LaSalle Street main entrance of the Chicago Stock Exchange Building was saved and reconstructed on the grounds of the Art Institute of Chicago.

INDEX OF SULLIVAN DESIGNED BUILDINGS

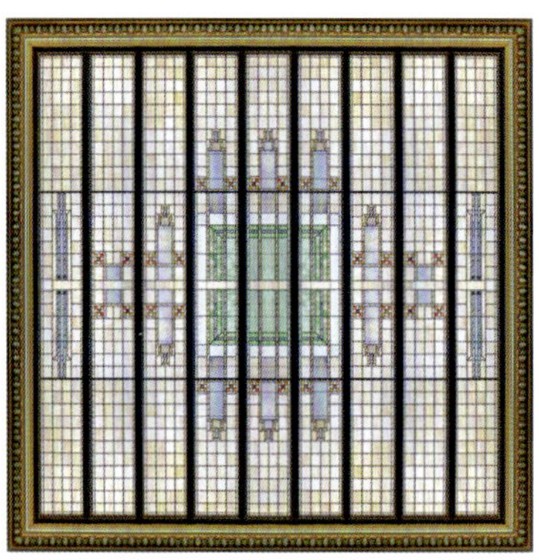

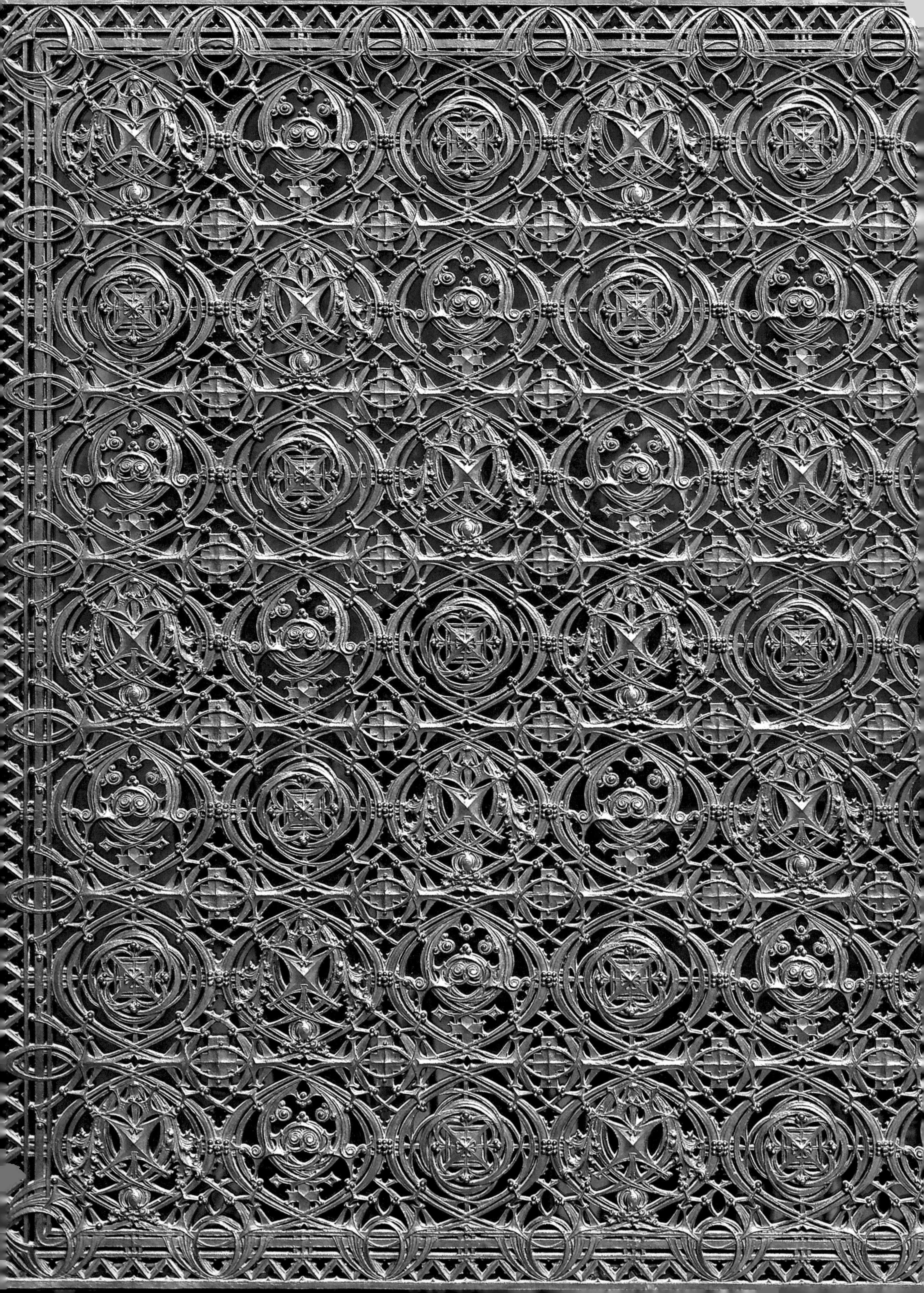